EISENHOWER, KENNEDY, AND THE UNITED STATES OF EUROPE

The Franklin and Eleanor Roosevelt Institute Series on Diplomatic and Economic History

General Editors: Arthur M. Schlesinger, Jr., William J. vanden Heuvel, and Douglas Brinkley

1. **FDR AND HIS CONTEMPORARIES:**
    Foreign Perceptions of an American President
    Edited by Cornelis A. van Minnen and John F. Sears

2. **NATO: THE CREATION OF THE ATLANTIC ALLIANCE AND THE INTEGRATION OF EUROPE**
    Edited by Francis H. Heller and John R. Gillingham

3. **AMERICA UNBOUND**
    World War II and the Making of a Superpower
    Edited by Warren F. Kimball

4. **THE ORIGINS OF U.S. NUCLEAR STRATEGY, 1945-53**
    Samuel R. Williamson, Jr., and Steven L. Rearden

5. **AMERICAN DIPLOMATS IN THE NETHERLANDS, 1815-50**
    Cornelis A. van Minnen

6. **EISENHOWER, KENNEDY, AND THE UNITED STATES OF EUROPE**
    Pascaline Winand

7. **THE ATLANTIC CHARTER**
    Edited by Douglas Brinkley and David Facey-Crowther

EISENHOWER, KENNEDY, AND THE UNITED STATES OF EUROPE

Pascaline Winand

St. Martin's Press
New York

First published in the United States of America 1993

Printed in the United States of America

ISBN 0-312-09096-X

Library of Congress Cataloging-in-Publication Data

Winand, Pascaline.
Eisenhower, Kennedy, and the united states of Europe / Pascaline
  Winand.
          p. cm. — (Franklin and Eleanor Roosevelt Institute series on
      diplomatic and economic history)
      Includes bibliographical references and index.
      ISBN 0-312-09096-X
      1. Europe—Foreign relations—United States. 2. United States-
  -Foreign relations—Europe. 3. European federation. 4. European
  Economic Community. 5. Eisenhower, Dwight D. (Dwight David),
  1890-1969. 6. Kennedy, John F. (John Fitzgerald), 1917-1963.
  I. Title. II. Series.
  D1065.U5W56 1993
  327.7304—dc20   92-38981
                                                          CIP

CONTENTS

ACKNOWLEDGMENTS

In the course of this project I have received generous assistance from many sources. Professor William Parker of Yale University took the time to read the whole manuscript and provided both encouragement and pressure when it was needed. Some years ago, I was fortunate enough to work with professors Harold D. Woodman, Myron Q. Hale, and especially Patrick Hearden of Purdue University and Ambassador Alfred Cahen of the Université Libre de Bruxelles, who provided the impetus for embarking on this project. Grants from the Belgian National Fund for Scientific Research, the Mellon-West European Program at Yale University, and the European University Institute's Research Project on the History of European Integration under the direction of Professor Richard T. Griffiths in Florence, helped to make it a reality. I am particularly thankful to the Commission of the European Communities for giving me a grant to help publish this book. I would also like to thank the staffs of the Franklin Roosevelt Library, the National Archives, the Eisenhower Library, the Kennedy Library, the Johnson Library, the Yale University Library, the Princeton Library, and the Monnet Archives in Lausanne for their valuable assistance. I am also indebted to many policymakers for their time and openness during interviews, and for their comments on earlier drafts. A special thank you to Professor Robert R. Bowie, Max Kohnstamm, and Ambassador John W. Tuthill for their detailed and valuable suggestions on the manuscript. Thank you also to professors and graduate students at Yale, Purdue, the Université Libre de Bruxelles, the European University Institute and Carnegie Mellon University for their invaluable help in editing the manuscript and offering critiques; they know who they are.

Finally my warmest thanks go to my colleagues, my family, and close friends whose support and understanding literally made this study possible. A special thanks to my friend Kathy Stuart for her insightful and witty comments on the manuscript.

ACRONYMS AND ABBREVIATIONS

ACUE   (American Committee on United Europe)
AEC   (Atomic Energy Commission)
ANF   (Atlantic Nuclear Force)
BAC   (Business Advisory Council)
Benelux countries   (Belgium, the Netherlands, and Luxembourg)
CAP   (Common Agricultural Policy)
CEA   (Council of Economic Advisers)
CED   (Committee for Economic Development)
CEEC   (Committee for European Economic Cooperation)
CFEP   (Council on Foreign Economic Policy)
COFR   (Council on Foreign Relations)
CSC   (Coal and Steel Community, same as ECSC)
ECA   (Economic Cooperation Administration)
ECE   (Economic Commission for Europe)
ECSC   (European Coal and Steel Community)
ECU   (European Currency Unit)
EDC   (European Defense Community)
EEC   (European Economic Community)
EFTA   (European Free Trade Association)
EPC   (European Political Community)
ERP   (European Recovery Program)
(EUR)   (European Bureau in the State Department)
Euratom   (European Atomic Energy Community)
FTA   (Free Trade Area)
GATT   (General Agreement on Tariffs and Trade)
HA   (High Authority, European Coal and Steel Community)
IAEA   (International Atomic Energy Agency)

IRBMs	(intermediate-range ballistic missiles)
ISA	(Division of International Security Affairs)
JCAE	(Joint Committee on Atomic Energy)
JCS	(Joint Chiefs of Staff)
MFN	(most-favored-nation)
MLF	(Multilateral Force)
NAC	(North Atlantic Council)
NPA	(National Planning Association)
NSC	(National Security Council)
OECD	(Organization for Economic Cooperation and Development)
OEEC	(Organization for European Economic Cooperation)
PPC	(Policy Planning Council)
PPS	(Policy Planning Staff)
SACEUR	(Supreme Allied Commander, Europe)
Seven, the; (or, the Outer Seven)	(the United Kingdom, Norway, Sweden, Denmark, Switzerland, Austria, and Portugal)
SHAPE	(Supreme Headquarters, Allied Powers, Europe)
Schuman Plan	(Plan announced by Robert Schuman for the creation of the first European Community, the European Coal and Steel Community, Schuman Declaration, 9 May 1950)
Six, the	(Belgium, the Netherlands, Luxembourg, France, Italy, West Germany)
SPD	(Social Democratic Party)
TAA	(Trade Agreements Act)
TCC	(Temporary Council Committee)
TEA	(Trade Expansion Act)
WEU	(Western European Union)

INTRODUCTION

President Kennedy once said, "It is the men, not merely the stated policies that determine the effectiveness of American foreign policy."[1] The Frenchman Jean Monnet, a leading advocate of European integration, and a man who had many influential friends in the United States, partly echoed him: "Nothing is possible without men: nothing is lasting without institutions."[2] In this age of profound change in Europe, a study of the American administration's attitudes towards the unification of Europe, and the continuous dialogue between American supporters and opponents of European integration, and their European counterparts, will help contribute to a better understanding of how patient and determined individuals bring about such changes.

Some Americans still fondly remember the first steps of the fledgling European Communities in the 1950s as opening the prospect of the creation of a "United States of Europe," somewhat akin to the United States of America. They remember Jean Monnet's visits to the United States. "Mr. Europe" liked to speak of the establishment of a "sort of second America" and named his action group for European integration the "Action Committee for the United States of Europe."[3] While some Americans hoped the American federal system could be transplanted in Europe, Europeans were generally more skeptical. Despite its obvious limitations, the concept of a United States of Europe nevertheless served as a rallying point for some American and European supporters of European integration during the post World War II years, hence its inclusion in the title of this book.

The idea of establishing some kind of union or federal system in Europe was not new, of course. Plans for European unions had been proposed much before the 1940s or 1950s, having been authored by William Penn, Victor Hugo, Immanuel Kant, Aristide Briand, Richard N. Coudenhove-Kalergi, to name only a few. Yet the great dislocations of World War II did more than any of these proposals to dramatize the need for European unification. Plans for a "United States of Europe" flourished in the European resistance and among Europeans in exile, and were given a close reading in the United States.[4] This book accordingly starts with World War II, as planners in

Washington, in and out of government, were actively searching for solutions to establish a peace compatible with American interests, a peace that would guarantee the United States a "spacious living area for freedom."[5] As we shall see, a united Europe came to be seen by top-echelon members of the American administration as a key element in the American blueprint for a peace settlement that would result in economic prosperity, political stability, and the dedication of western nations to common values and principles, such as democracy and the expansion of international trade. During the Cold War, European integration became one of the main elements of American strategy for strengthening the Atlantic Alliance. By providing stability and prosperity for the West, European integration also held the prospect of one day opening the door to negotiations with the Soviet Union from a position of strength, which in turn might mean the end of the artificial division of Europe into East and West.

Today, the Iron Curtain has vanished. Eastern and Central European countries are fighting to define their political and economic futures, while the members of the European Community look forward to the realization of the objectives of the Single European Act, with the prospects of a truly integrated internal market of 345 million consumers. The Maastricht Treaty, with its ambitious goals of economic and monetary, as well as political, union awaits ratification by the twelve member countries of the European Community. Now, as in the past, the United States considers European developments both as an opportunity and a challenge, if not a threat. What does the future hold for Europe? Will there be instability, civil war, fragmentation, and uneven economic fortunes, or peaceful revolution backed by solid economic and political commitments? Should there be a Marshall Plan for Eastern and Central Europe? Is such a plan viable? Should there be a Europe at several speeds? How fast should one go from one speed to the next without breaking the transmission? As we prepare to step into the twenty-first century, we might do well to pause for a moment and reflect on the experiences of our predecessors in dealing with European challenges; they might help us to invent the future with a sense of what we have and have not accomplished in the past.

It is my sincere hope that this book will be read not only by students, teachers, and researchers, but also by a larger public outside of academe. While the former may find the notes useful for their own research, nonacademics can very well dispense with them. Hence their location at the end of this book.

This book is organized both chronologically and thematically in an effort to maintain narrative momentum, while at the same time providing some conceptual guidance. The first chapter is meant as an introduction only, and therefore does not go into details about particular developments such as, say, the creation of the European Payments Union. The focus is on those European unification initiatives that commanded the attention of the Eisenhower and Kennedy administrations, with some discussion of the Johnson years. The rise and fall of the European Defense Community (EDC), American reactions to the birth of Euratom and the European Economic Community, the Free Trade Area negotiations, the birth of the Organization for Economic Cooperation and Development (OECD), the idea of an "Atlantic partnership between equals" and the story of the ill-fated Multilateral Force, are some of the topics addressed here.

The analysis of the period is based mostly on primary sources, including privileged access to the papers of various participants in the events. It also draws on a large number of personal interviews with participants of various American administrations, either conducted by the author herself,[6] by the staffs of presidential libraries and universities, or by journalists and politicians. There are obvious pitfalls in using interviews. For example, participants will tend to remember events selectively and to reinterpret them. Consciously or not, some will deny that they advocated a given line of policy, especially if it was unpopular or failed. Yet I believe interviews can help to place in perspective the significance of a specific document, and identify the social and organizational setting from which it emerged.[7] They are also useful in uncovering informal connections among individuals that cut across various bureaus, agencies, or departments—connections that would remain invisible in a simple look at the organizational charts of a given administration. Through interviews, it becomes possible to determine the influence of a given individual within an administration relative to other individuals, to see whether his official rank did in fact correspond to his "unofficial" rank in dealing with specific issues in which he possessed particular expertise, say, on European affairs. Interviews also throw light on how certain appointments were made, whether for political reasons, because of friendship ties, or on the express advice of outside advisers to the administration, both in the United States and abroad. In other words, interviews help make history come to life.

I have also tried as much as possible to avoid generalizations and to refrain from identifying the "United States" as a monolithic government with calculated intentions, or as a conglomerate of large organizations functioning as a unit.[8] My main concern was to "ask questions about the humans who worked in . . . large organizations,"[9] their contribution to new policies, their continuing support for policies evolved under previous administrations, and their relations with the president, their colleagues, friends, or acquaintances outside the government, including unofficial actors—such as Jean Monnet—and some journalists. One might object that by doing so, I have perhaps complicated the narrative with an unnecessary wealth of detail, yet I believe such detail is needed to provide a more lively and accurate account of events.

In an attempt to assess both continuity and change in American attitudes towards European integration, I have tried to show how certain individuals or groups within, or closely linked with, the American administration,[10] helped define the rationale for the policy of American support for European integration and to what extent they succeeded in implementing this policy. I have also emphasized how American policy,[11] and particularly American rhetoric,[12] were periodically refined and adapted to changing economic, political, technological, and strategic circumstances, and how the specific policy of American support for European integration, and the rhetoric employed in justifying it, changed accordingly and related to the overall policy.

A key assumption of this book is that members of a given administration, including the president and his advisers,[13] all have a specific vision, image, or perception of the external world, which significantly influences the way they evolve, implement, and redefine foreign policy. A related assumption is that in the early stages of an American administration, or in the interregnum between two administrations, these government officials, through "bargaining games" among themselves, define a set of assumptions about American interests in the world, threats to these interests, and how best to protect them.[14] During this process, specific players, or groups of players, what we might call "coalitions" of players, emerge, who each have or share a more or less coherent set of assumptions about the world, a "grand strategy" or a "grand design." As we shall see, de Gaulle's grand strategy for Europe did not match that of Kennedy. During the Kennedy administration, the views of American "Europeanists", who were devoted to the advancement of European integration, conflicted with those of the "Atlanticists," and "Internationalists," who preferred to dilute European integration within an Atlantic or international framework. The cohesion of European supporters relative to other groups partly explains the remarkable consistency of American support for European integration during the Eisenhower and Kennedy administrations. This support, tempered with a dose of healthy criticism, continued during these years despite declining economic fortunes in the United States and major disagreements with European allies, notably over the Suez Canal. Cohesion and consistency did not mean that "Europeanists" were always successful in supporting or proposing certain policies. American support for the European Defense

Community, the Multilateral Force, and British entry in the Common Market are clear examples of unfortunate tactics, wishful thinking, and disappointed hopes. The factors contributing to negative outcomes, or to the misperception of the possibility of a favorable outcome, were not only economic, technological and political. Other considerations include the attitudes of Europeans themselves towards a given "European" or "Atlantic" venture, as well as certain dynamics within the American government itself, and within the group of American "Europeanists."

Decisionmakers typically have limits on how much information they can process, and how much money, time, and physical energy they can afford to spend on a given problem. These constraints circumscribe their margin of maneuver. For instance, the assessment of how much an American president will have to draw on his political "capital" to support a given line of policy in Congress might well determine whether the president will continue to pursue such a line of policy, or whether he would prefer to "spend" his political capital on other issues that rank higher on his list of priorities. It might be argued that the Multilateral Force was *partly* sacrificed to Johnson's "Great Society." The president's attention span and that of his advisers are also important in gathering support for a given policy, and seeing it through. The Vietnam War drew considerably on the reserve of attention of the Johnson team, to the point of leaving very little attention for European affairs. Thus the alleged decline of American support for European integration and American interest in Europe under Johnson was more apparent than real and originated in part in the reduced reserve of attention of the Johnson team. Under Kennedy, the Cuban Missile Crisis similarly preoccupied the administration, which helps explain the lack of preparation for the Nassau meeting in December 1962, which greatly contributed to the demise of the Multilateral Force (MLF) and furnished de Gaulle a handy, if only an additional, reason for vetoing British entry into the Common Market.

An examination of the dynamics within the group of Europeanists also helps explain why the policies they pursued met with defeat, and why they persistently pursued these policies in the face of clear indications that they would fail. Small groups have the advantage of working in more informal ways than complex organizational units, thereby freeing time to focus on specific problems. Their values also tend to be more consistent than those within a larger decision-making structure. The result is often a more "efficient" defense of those particular values. Yet small groups also have their drawbacks, and the Europeanists were no exception. Consistency of values can translate into too much conformity, to the point of excluding or ignoring dissenting views of a particular member of the group, or else preventing such an individual from expressing these views. Despite Walt Rostow's warnings, for example, most American Europeanists failed to assess the importance of the nuclear question for British entry into the Common Market. They made no contingency plans in case the negotiations should fail, and some of them indulged in blind optimism or wishful thinking and overlooked information that challenged their faith in the eventual success of the negotiations.[15] To be fair to the Europeanists, Kennedy's own loose, informal, and open organizational style also helps to explain why some Europeanists vehemently pushed for the Multilateral Force in Europe in the absence of a clear policy signal from Kennedy or his secretary of state.

Notwithstanding these remarks, American Europeanists did contribute substantially to gathering support in the United States for European integration, which in turn played no small role in lending legitimacy to supporters of European unity in some European countries. Europeanists were part of a unique network of friends, close acquaintances, and colleagues, in which both Americans and Europeans contributed to a common cause: the advancement of European integration as an essential element in pursuing the larger goal of an acceptable peace settlement. Americans and Europeans did, of course, pursue separate and distinct interests, but as a key American supporter of European integration has noted, at the time "they were somehow secondary."[16] On the European side, Walter Hallstein, the first president of the European Economic Community, later bore testimony to this unique period of cooperation, in which people shared common goals and often built close bonds of friendship in the process of "co-conspiring" in a common enterprise: "It was real cooperation—free of all the overtones which are now hampering our relations. There was no question about making choices. It was a natural feeling of people working for the same goals. Defense against Communism was a common cause. Building Europe was a common cause—unreservedly—taken as such by both partners. And this influenced the way they cooperated. There was an exchange of documents without any special care of secrecy."[17]

Some of the bonds and connections had been developed during or shortly after World War II, as these people focused their energies on laying the foundation for an acceptable international order; some dated back to an even earlier period, as in the case of the Dulles/Monnet association. This cooperation allowed for an informal exchange of views between American Europeanists and Europeans devoted to the cause of European integration, an exchange that often bypassed established governmental channels. On the American side, the informality of these contacts succeeded in reaching the highest levels of the American administration, including the president. A simple lunch between, say, Jean Monnet, who then headed the Action Committee for the United States of Europe, Kennedy, and Under Secretary George Ball or White House Adviser McGeorge Bundy, probably did more to promote the views of Jean Monnet and his fellow European "conspirators" than any *official* visit by European statesmen. Kennedy's informal organizational style facilitated such contacts.

The most favorable period for influencing any given American policy is during its formative stages, that is, just before or after an administration takes office. By making the most of his contacts with Americans close to the president (among them Secretary of State John Foster Dulles and Under Secretary George Ball), as well as those in the lower echelons of the American administration, Jean Monnet and his collaborators were able to circumvent the heavy organizational machinery of the American government and to influence American policy in its formative stages, lobbying for their idea of a united Europe. This was so even during the Eisenhower administration, which has been singled out as a military type of organization. Friends in high places and their dedication to the common goal of European integration made it possible for Monnet and other supporters of European integration to maintain a continuous exchange of views with their friends and colleagues across the Atlantic. I am not arguing, of course, that Monnet and other European advocates of European integration determined American policy towards European integration, neither am I suggesting that American leaders dictated European initiatives for European integration. What I am describing, rather, is a cross-fertilization process among the views held by the members of a group that we might call, for lack of a better term, the Euro-American intelligentsia for the uniting of Europe.

For two main reasons this informal cooperation began to show signs of fatigue and to decline in influence, particularly during the last years of the Johnson administration and under the Nixon administration: first there was the lack of progress of Europeans themselves towards the twin goals of economic and political integration, which translated into a lack of interest on the part of Americans for European integration; and, second, the disappearance from governmental circles of the generation of American Europeanists and hence of contact points for expressing the views of European supporters of European integration. Increased economic competition between the United States and the European Economic Community, as well as a European tendency to criticize or oppose certain American political or military initiatives, did much to usher in an eclipse of the support by the United States for European integration. In recent years, however, the Single European Act, the Maastricht Treaty, and other significant developments in

Europe have revived the interest of the American administration and American academic and business circles in European integration. Signs of this interest include the burgeoning budgets of certain academic institutions and the occasional reliance on the advice of the old guard of American Europeanists by some members of recent American administrations. Faced with the challenge of a highly volatile European situation, Washington has dusted off the idea of a partnership between the United States and a tightly integrated European Community, which Kennedy advocated some thirty years ago. No longer reduced to the expression of "Fortress Europe," the EC is now seen once again by the American government as a key element of stability on the European continent.

1

Setting the Stage:
American Policy Towards European
Integration from Roosevelt to Truman

POSTWAR PLANNING

" Like the little girl in the nursery rhyme, a European union, from the point of view of our long-run economic interests, can be either very, very good, or horrid,"[1] so ended a State Department report prepared in the fall of 1943. As American policymakers gradually became committed first to a policy of all possible aid to the Allies short of war in April-June 1940 and then to entering the war in order to win an acceptable peace, so too did they begin to make plans for a viable world order in accordance with their concerns for economic prosperity at home and international security. While some administration officials viewed a united Europe as one of the essential pieces in the jigsaw puzzle of an acceptable world order, others did not. By the end of the Roosevelt administration, the supporters of European integration had been overruled by their opponents, who much preferred worldwide arrangements to a European union, which, both for security and economic reasons, they viewed as a potentially dangerous regional organization. It was only a matter of a few years, however, before American support for a united Europe became official policy under the Truman administration. Although by then circumstances had markedly changed in Europe, many of the arguments both for and against American support for European integration had already been articulated under Roosevelt.

American postwar planning displayed a unique pattern of collaboration between the administration and private institutions. One of these institutions was the Federal Council of Churches of Christ in America, presided over by a future secretary of state and a staunch supporter of European integration, John Foster Dulles. Another was the Council on Foreign Relations (COFR). Founded in 1921, this influential foreign-policy planning organization drew its limited membership mostly from the elite of the American business, academic, law, media, and government communities.[2] During World War II, the council contributed most to American postwar planning by working closely with the State Department. At the end of the war, some of its members were then asked to participate in various U.S. delegations to organize the peace.[3] Two important figures of the future Eisenhower administration participated in the council's work: John Foster Dulles took part in some its meetings, while his brother Allen held a prominent position in it and later became its president. They were both friends of the Frenchman Jean Monnet, who already thought at the time of encouraging the creation of a European Federation or some type of European "entity" that would transform European states into "a common economic unity."[4]

The Dulles brothers belonged to "The Best and the Brightest," most of whom were upper-class Ivy League graduates with law degrees and came from white, Anglo-Saxon, Protestant backgrounds. They and some of their colleagues and close friends frequently moved from one position to another in education, private enterprise, and government, thereby weaving an intricate network of connections between the American government, the private sector, and academia. Most were members of private institutions such as the COFR that functioned as consensus-building organizations in foreign affairs, situated as they were between business, academia and the government. By disseminating policy recommendations to the appropriate circles before the formulation of policy, the COFR, along with similar institutions such as the Business Advisory Council (BAC), the Committee for Economic Development (CED), and the National Planning Association (NPA), ensured that their views would be heeded at the highest levels of the American government.[5]

This special relationship between private institutions and the government had profound implications for the orientation of American policy towards European reconstruction and integration after the war. The top-level administrators of the Marshall Plan were also prominent businessmen, who were affiliated with brain trusts such as the COFR.[6] During the war, the council, working in tandem with the Roosevelt administration, laid some of the groundwork for the attempts these people and their collaborators later made to direct European reconstruction towards the creation of a peaceful and unified Europe.

As early as September 1939, the COFR, upon the initiative of Walter H. Mallory, its executive director, and Hamilton Fish Armstrong, editor of *Foreign Affairs,* proposed to investigate and report on the impact of the war upon the policies of the United States for the State Department. Secretary of State Cordell Hull and Under Secretary of State Sumner Welles, who later became chairman and vice-chairman of the administration's newly created Advisory Committee on Post-War Foreign Policy, readily accepted the free help. From early 1940 to the end of the war, 682 memoranda were transmitted to the Department of State by the council; these were underwritten by grants from the Rockefeller Foundation totaling approximately $300,000.[7] Council members were brought into direct contact with the State Department and other participating government agencies. Some of its research secretaries worked part-time in the Division of Special Research in the Department of State, while prominent members such as Hamilton Fish Armstrong were brought in as members of the Advisory Committee on Post-War Foreign Policy. And so it was that members of the COFR worked side by side with future initiators of the Marshall Plan, such as Assistant Secretary of State Dean Acheson, William L. Clayton, and Charles Bohlen, all of whom took part in the Advisory Committee on Post-War Foreign Policy.[8]

Of the junior members of the American Eastern Establishment who later became influential in American foreign policy after the war, many had joined the American government as junior officers in the course of World War II, or had been assigned specific duties at the peace conferences. Among them were Dean Acheson, John McCloy, John Foster Dulles, and McGeorge Bundy. These men later played key roles in European affairs under the Truman, Eisenhower, and Kennedy administrations. Some were friends of Jean Monnet, who had spent much time in the United States in the 1920s and 1930s, and had established lasting connections with leading American lawyers, businessmen, and bankers, with whom he shared a commitment to multilateralism and a Eurocentric view of world affairs. The rising foreign-policy leaders believed that the United States possessed a vital interest in the future of Europe, and were determined to ensure a leading position for the United States in shaping the postwar world. In this they followed in the footsteps of their illustrious elders, not the least of whom were lawyer and Secretary of War Henry L. Stimson and investment banker Thomas Lamont, who held the view that American democratic values could not survive without similar values being maintained in Europe and in the United Kingdom. A corollary of that basic assumption was that American economic well-being greatly depended upon the economic "viability" of Europe, and on its adherence to the sacred principles of multilateralism, which pre-supposed the abandonment of nationalism and protectionism in Europe.

During World War II, American support for the idea of a unified Europe reflected these basic concerns. More than anything the United States wanted a congenial world to live in. Some American businessmen, the "realists," had at first anticipated considerable advantages in doing business with the Axis and with a United Europe ruled by an efficient Germany, and others felt that the United States could compete very well with a German-dominated economic area. Yet, after detailed study of the overall impact of a possible German victory, the COFR, the State Department, and several business groups soon reached the conclusion that the United States would in fact be hemmed in, economically as well as militarily, by a unified totalitarian world. All concurred: the independence of Britain and the British Empire, as well as of Continental Europe and its dependencies, was vital for the economic well-being of the United States.[9]

Britain was "the most important market for the agricultural surplus of the temperate climate countries of the Western Hemisphere and the Far East."[10] While the prosperity of the United States and other temperate countries was contingent upon that of the United Kingdom, the economic wealth of the United Kingdom was largely dependent on its trade with continental Europe, since the European Continent "supplied about one-third of the United Kingdom's exports."[11] Continental Europe was also of direct economic interest to the United States. In 1937, United States export trade with the Continent still amounted to $1,360 million, i.e., 41 percent of U.S. total export trade and 27 percent of U.S. imports were with the Continent. This meant that despite several decades of hostile and discriminatory tariff policies between the United States and the Continent, which had occasioned a gradual decrease in the relative importance of the European market for the United States, this market remained one of the most important to the United States. Therefore, if the European economy became totally dominated by a powerful Germany, United States export trade with the Continent would suffer greatly.

There could thus be no acceptable peace settlement for the United States with a victorious Germany. In December 1941 the United States entered the war, not only to win the war but also to win the peace. But what sort of peace did the Roosevelt administration, and the intelligentsia advising it, want? High up on the list of priorities were "Full employment at home with a rising standard of living" and "the maintenance of ample opportunities at home for free competitive enterprise." A COFR study explained that these two objectives could best be attained through the "expansion of mutually beneficial trade with foreign countries" and "national security in the framework of an international organization."[12]

There was no doubt that the United States would emerge from the war with an agricultural and industrial production well beyond the needs of domestic consumption. If the American economy could not find outlets for its products in foreign markets a "sense of frustration" was "certain to develop." To avoid this, and achieve full employment and a rising standard of living at home, the best solution was to guarantee that other countries would have access to the American market in order to reinvigorate their own economies and earn sufficient dollar exchange to pay for American goods. American prosperity would then spread purchasing power throughout the world. For those who believed in the virtues of multilateralism, "the community of interest in expanding world trade" was indivisible.[13] Secretary of State Cordell Hull was a particularly strong advocate of multilateralism and dreamed of eliminating "all forms of discriminatory treatment in international commerce" and reducing "tariff and other trade barriers."[14] His primary objective was the elimination of British imperial preferences. American leaders also made plans for controlling international cartels, stabilizing monetary policy and reorganizing international finances, all of which they viewed as prerequisites to a liberal foreign trade policy.

Could the economic unification of Europe contribute to liberalized trade? Many in the Roosevelt administration dreaded the resurgence of European economic nationalism. In 1941 Assistant Secretary of State Dean Acheson insisted that one of the contributions European countries could make to the peace settlement was "to avoid the excessive economic nationalism which before the war caused them to erect preposterous trade barriers and otherwise facilitate domestic production of such products as wheat and sugar, to the detriment not only of the more efficient overseas suppliers who depend so largely on disposing of their surpluses by export but to the detriment of consumers in the European countries as well." Acheson calculated that the best time to extract concessions from European nations was right after the war, when their needs would be most acute and American bargaining power at its strongest.[15]

Some American policymakers thought that European economic integration in the form of a customs union would help remove intra-European and financial barriers, thereby achieving a greater degree of complementarity among European countries. A European customs union meant first that an area defined as Europe, exclusive of the Soviet Union and the United Kingdom, would be controlled by a single regional authority instead of a multitude of national governments engaged in cutthroat competition with one another. The obvious advantage of having a single authority to direct European economies, they thought, would be a greater trade coordination among European countries as a well as a simplification of trade policy with the rest of the world. For one thing, a central authority, if endowed with sufficient economic and political power, would be in a position to resist the demands of national pressure groups for protection against imports from other European countries. For another, foreign countries, instead of having to deal with numerous economic and political entities, each possessing its own set of tariffs, would only have to make agreements with a single authority for all of Europe.[16] Planners also envisaged ambitious schemes for European monetary unification, considered the creation of a regional transport authority for Europe, and foresaw far-reaching reforms in European agriculture. European collaboration in agriculture, they hoped, would discourage Europeans from producing crops which were cultivated artificially and help American farmers to recapture "over one-fourth of the world-market,"[17] which, in their minds, European countries had robbed them of in the past. Never mind that this would entail considerable shifts of population from European farms into cities.

Taking the long view, American planners concluded that a greater degree of economic efficiency in Europe would be conducive to a higher level of real income, which in turn would foster an increased European demand "for imports of raw materials, food, and manufactured articles, of which the United States would be the principal beneficiaries."[18] They also anticipated that economic prosperity would foster political stability on the Continent and thus contribute to international security. Integrating Germany within an economically and politically unified Europe was the key ingredient in the planners' recipe for an economically "viable" and politically stable Europe.

Germany was like a double-edged sword. On the one hand, German military potential threatened European and international security. On the other hand, a prosperous Germany was a major determinant of European economic recovery and viability—which in turn benefited the United States. How could one best control Germany? Besides military disarmament and denazification, Treasury Secretary Morgenthau thought of depriving the aggressor nation of all its heavy industries and of transforming the Ruhr and the Saar into an industrial desert, i.e., an agricultural land. This was the so-called Morgenthau Plan, which both Roosevelt and Churchill briefly endorsed at the Octagon Conference in Quebec in September 1944. The American Press and Congress were highly critical of the president for endorsing the plan, however, and the impending elections forced him to dissociate himself from Morgenthau and his plan. This signaled a victory for those members of the administration who opposed punishment economics, which they thought would create German resentment and jeopardize any peace settlement in Europe.

Germany accounted for about three-fourths of European coal production and half of its steel output. The partisans of a softer peace for Germany insisted that German steel and coal would be badly needed for European reconstruction. They also emphasized that German-manufactured products would help Europe gain foreign exchange from the proceeds of sales to overseas countries. A COFR study noted that one could not regard "as really effective any post-war economic control" that would "so weaken German production as to retard the restoration of a vigorous economic life in the European countries" that ultimately depended "on German markets and German supplies."[19] Among the top-level officials, Secretary of War Henry L. Stimson, a friend of Jean Monnet, strongly opposed Morgenthau for wanting to transform the Ruhr and the Saar into a "ghost territory," thereby depriving Europe of one of its most important sources of raw materials. By 1943 most planners counseled instead a controlled demobilization of Germany's current self-sufficiency by encouraging a return to its former dependence upon European and world markets and resources for its prosperity.

In September 1941, similarly preoccupied with the German problem, John Foster Dulles claimed that the solution to the war-breeding political divisions of the Continent lay in "the political reorganization of continental Europe as a federated commonwealth." One year later, Dulles wrote that "Germany ought to be integrated into a unified Europe."[20] Around the same time, George Kennan, a young foreign service officer, advised the State Department to integrate Germany in some form of European federation after the war, rather than partitioning it.[21] Dulles, Kennan, and other planners thought this would have the advantage of checking German military power, while also channeling German economic resources and skilled labor towards European recovery. In a nutshell, the supporters of European political and economic unification hoped that a united Europe would help diminish European economic nationalism, contribute to European prosperity, and increase Europe's political stability and security, most of all by integrating Germany within a European framework. Yet European unification carried potentialities both for peace and for war.

One nightmare scenario envisaged the possibility that a European union might become dominated by a single power or group of powers with belligerent intentions. Among the candidates for hegemony on the Continent were Germany and the Soviet Union. Yet planners calculated that disaster might be avoided by establishing an effective international security system after the war. Another scenario foresaw the development of a protectionist Europe surrounded by high tariff walls. As a sense of "European nationhood" developed, the government of a European union might then consider using "the economic weapon as a means of furthering continental policy."[22] A strong European entity and the creation of similar entities as a reaction to it might then result in "the break-up of the world organization in favor of a series of power blocs acting in unstable equilibrium without the ballast provided by the smaller nations."[23] This was Secretary of State Cordell Hull's recurring nightmare. While his immediate collaborator, Sumner Welles, supported the idea of a European union, Cordell Hull thought such a union might lead to the formation of other economic power blocs and undermine prospects for a liberal trade policy and the formation of an international organization after the war. Worse still, United States support for a European union might undermine immediate prospects for peace, since Soviet Russia would most likely fear German domination of the union, which would pose a direct threat to its security.

While President Roosevelt himself had some sympathy for the creation of regional arrangements and mistrusted on the whole the potential effectiveness of an international organization, the strong reservations of his secretary of state ultimately succeeded in convincing him against giving too much support to regional proposals. Whereas State Department documents had earlier studied the impact of "a political unification" of Europe and had considered the implications of a "European Customs Union" for the United States, by January 1944 planners spoke only of "closer economic and political collaboration" in Europe.[24]

The possibility of alienating Soviet Russia probably is what convinced Roosevelt to put the creation of some sort of European federation on the back burner. The president perceived the Russians as a friendly people, whose hostility sprang from a sense of insecurity vis-à-vis Japan and Germany, and the West's aversion to bolshevism. He accordingly envisioned a postwar world order designed by wartime allies, in which the Soviet Union would be granted a prominent place. In order to enlist the cooperation of the Russians to help to rebuild the Continent in a way acceptable to all Allies, Roosevelt hoped to make them partners in the peace, side by side with the United States. Yet just before his death, in April 1945, Roosevelt appeared to waver between an attitude of conciliation towards the Soviet Union and a more forceful affirmation of United States interests.

WITH OR WITHOUT THE RUSSIANS?
FROM PAN-EUROPE TO WESTERN EUROPEAN INTEGRATION

When he took office, President Truman still planned to build a stable peace by cooperating with the Russians. The president initially proposed a pan-European peace settlement that would foster the economic integration of the Continent. During the war, planners in Washington had hoped to return prosperity and stability to the strategically important region of Eastern Europe by encouraging it to function as the agricultural part of a larger union, including the more industrialized region of Western Europe. The new President now proposed to "help unify Europe by linking up the breadbasket with the industrial centers through a free flow of trade." To achieve this goal, he contemplated the creation of a vast network of "free waterways for trade" in Europe that would be part of a wider network of waterways the world over, including the Suez, Kiel, and Panama canals.[25] Unfortunately, Stalin refused to have Truman's proposal for the internationalization of inland waterways mentioned in the final communiqué of the Potsdam Conference on 1 August 1945.

The Truman administration soon became divided over whether to rebuild Europe in cooperation with the Russians or not. Convinced that a drifting apart of Western and Eastern Europe would breed instability in Europe, some junior officers in U.S. missions and embassies abroad and in the State Department made plans for an all-European economic and political settlement with supranational institutions. They hoped that a regional approach, if accompanied by measures for intra-European trade liberalization and currency convertibility, would help unleash Germany's productive power and, beyond that, revive European economies. Once Europe's economic health was reestablished, the old nations would then be able to dispense with American economic help, and would gladly follow the lead of the United States in adopting a liberal multilateral trade policy. Senior officers in the State Department, including Under Secretary Dean Acheson, Assistant Secretary for Economic Affairs William Clayton, and Secretary James F. Byrnes backed their young colleagues.[26] By the end of 1946, their efforts, with Jean Monnet's prompting, resulted in the creation of the Economic Commission for Europe (ECE).

Prospects for a pan-European settlement dimmed as the possibility of organizing the peace in cooperation with the Russians looked more and more remote. In April 1946, Secretary of State Byrnes formally proposed a twenty-five year four-power disarmament treaty on Germany to the Soviet Union. Moscow answered in the negative. By 1947, there was a consensus in Washington that pacifying the Soviet Union might well carry with it a heavy price: the unification of Germany, and perhaps that of Central Europe, under Soviet domination. Planners began to talk in terms of a division of Europe and Germany into western and eastern regions. George Kennan, who headed the Policy Planning Staff, advocated the mutual and realistic recognition of spheres of influence in Europe, which would identify and define limits to Soviet expansion, while allowing the United States and its European allies to later negotiate a postwar European peace settlement with the Soviet Union from a position of strength.

Strength first meant the development of sound economic conditions in Western Europe. There was growing uneasiness in Washington as Americans watched European economic conditions deteriorate further despite American aid programs to Europe and American efforts to promote a multilateral currency and trade system. The terrible winter of 1946-47 served to emphasize the failure of current American initiatives to revive European economies. Britain's announcement that it could no longer support the financial burden of helping Greece and Turkey further contributed to a sense of urgency. The administration responded with the Truman Doctrine.

On 12 March 1947 Truman addressed Congress and promised help to nations threatened by totalitarianism. Truman's Special Message to Congress linked aid to foreign nations with defense against communism, yet planners in Washington, including George Kennan, Secretary of State George C. Marshall and Secretary of Commerce W. Averell Harriman, did not fear a direct Soviet attack. Rather, Kennan and his colleagues anticipated the possibility of European economic disintegration and political turmoil.[27] The help Truman offered was to be "primarily through economic and financial aid" which was "essential to economic stability and orderly political processes." In this phrasing was encapsulated one of the most basic tenets of the future European Recovery Program (ERP). Direct help to Europe, primarily economic and financial, would restore economic viability on the Continent and thereby foster political stability and security. American economic strength would thus prime the pumps of democracy. Abundance and prosperity, not war, would hold the forces of revolution and totalitarianism in check. To quote George Kennan, America was learning "to utilize with wisdom and discretion that formidable margin of surplus energy and material values which [it had] shown itself capable of producing, and one might also say, incapable of not producing."[28]

The failure of the Moscow Council of Foreign Ministers in April confirmed top-echelon American policymakers in their expectation that German reunification organized in cooperation with the Soviet Union would mean

Soviet domination over Germany and the extraction of huge reparations payments from current German production, which would further retard European recovery. By the same token European integration looked increasingly appealing to them as a strategy for channeling German resources towards the reconstruction of Europe, even if this meant partitioning Germany. Addressing the National Publishers Association on 17 January 1947, Republican John Foster Dulles proposed the concept of Western Europe as a single economic unit of which the "basin of the Rhine, with its coal and industrious man power" constituted "the natural economic heart." "From that area," said Dulles, "ought to flow vitality not merely for Germans but for Germany's western neighbors. If that happens Western Europe, at least, with its 200 million people, could develop into a more prosperous and stable land." He concluded that the German problem called "for some application of the federal solution" to Europe much after the pattern of the United States.[29] George Marshall joined Dulles at Moscow in advocating—unsuccessfully—the creation of a supranational agency to supervise the Ruhr. This crucial region was to remain part of Germany, but Germany's neighbors were to have equal access to its resources. Disputes were to be resolved at the European level by the supranational authority. Marshall insisted that a viable European settlement called for "a European solution in a Europe which includes Germany."[30] In the spring of 1947, key officials in the State Department echoed Dulles's creed for European economic integration as a way of channeling German energies towards the reconstruction of Europe, while making German rehabilitation acceptable to the French. George Kennan also calculated that a prosperous Europe, with Germany's industrial potential anchored firmly to the West, would give the United States and its allies a much more secure economic and political base from which to negotiate an overall European peace settlement with the Soviet Union in the future. An early advocate of the integration of Germany into some sort of European federation, Kennan now joined Harold Van B. Cleveland, Charles P. Kindleberger, Colonel Charles Bonesteel, Ben T. Moore, and other junior officers in their advocacy of European economic integration, and possibly political association or federation, as a way of maximizing American and European efforts towards European recovery.

In May 1947 Kennan and his Policy Planning Staff advised Acheson, then under secretary of state for economic affairs, to encourage Europeans to work collectively in elaborating and carrying through a European recovery program with the help of American dollars. "The program for American aid should be," wrote Kennan, "if possible, supplementary to a program of intramural economic collaboration among the western European countries."

The United States would provide a massive influx of aid for a limited period of four to five years. Western Europe might then be able to stand on its own feet without American dollars and become a stable partner for the United States. Communists were to be barred from participating in the program. Finally, the program was to be "designed to encourage and contribute to some form of regional political association [enabling] the western zones of [Germany and Austria] to make the maximum contributions to economic restoration in Western Europe."[31] When Acheson addressed the Delta Council in Cleveland, Mississippi, on 8 May 1947, he underscored the fundamental importance of achieving "a coordinated European economy." A few weeks later, Under Secretary Clayton wrote a foreboding memorandum for Acheson and Marshall in which he diagnosed acute economic distress in Europe and impending social and political chaos. Acheson, Clayton, Kennan, and Marshall took immediate action.

On 5 June 1947 Marshall delivered his famous speech at Harvard University, based mainly on Clayton's and Kennan's recommendations, and drafted by Charles E. Bohlen, Marshall's special assistant. The speech called for a European-wide recovery plan and encouraged European nations to cooperate in establishing and programming it jointly. The United States would provide both advice and financial aid. There was no specific mention of a blueprint for European economic integration even though a prior draft of Marshall's speech had foreseen a role for the United States in fostering "the growth of European unity."[32] For the time being, Marshall preferred to leave it to Europeans to think up schemes for European economic integration, while tilling the ground for integration by encouraging regional collaboration as a first step.

One of the side effects of American insistence on a coordinated approach, based on pooled resources and shared information, was to make the Marshall Plan unacceptable to the Soviet Union. On the surface, Marshall's invitation to assist in the return of normal economic conditions to the Continent was not limited to Western Europe. Yet the plan was specifically presented in such a way as to make Soviet participation unlikely. The decision to invite the Soviet Union and its satellites to join the venture had not been an easy one. On the one hand, the plan would have had very little chance of being accepted throughout the world and would have made the United States responsible for the division of Europe had it excluded the Soviet Union a priori. On the other hand, Soviet participation could have killed the plan in Congress, whose members would not have looked with favor upon communist participation, let alone upon appropriating the funds for what might be a ruinous endeavor costing countless American dollars for Soviet recovery.

The masterminds behind the recovery plan settled for a gamble: by couching the speech in general terms, by stating that the policy of the United States was "directed not against any country or doctrine but against hunger, poverty, desperation, and chaos," by avoiding any references to communism, they in fact ensured that, should the Soviet Union refuse to participate, the onus for the division of Europe would come to rest on its shoulders. Not only that, but by opposing the plan, the Soviets would also place themselves "in the position of partisans of hunger, poverty, desperation, and chaos," which could only undermine their hold on countries with large communist parties. Kennan and others were almost certain that the Soviet Union would decline to participate. "We did not feel," said Bohlen, "that the Soviet Union would accept American verification of the use of the goods and funds. Furthermore, we did not think the Soviet Union would be able to maintain its control over Eastern Europe if those countries were able to participate in the cooperative venture."[33] The offer was open-ended, but American leaders hoped that Eastern European satellites would "either exclude themselves by unwillingness to accept the proposed conditions or agree to abandon the exclusive orientation of their economies."[34]

The gamble paid off. Fearing that participation in the plan would draw Eastern European countries within the orbit of the United States and eventually encircle the Soviet Union with capitalist countries, and strongly opposed to the reconstruction of Germany's economy, Moscow ended up assuming the responsibility for the division of Europe. At the Paris Conference, Molotov did present a Soviet plan, but this plan amounted to a denial of the spirit of "joint approach" upon which the American offer was predicated. Indeed, Molotov recommended that each country submit what amounted to individual shopping lists to be filled by the United States. On 2 July Molotov rejected the Marshall Plan. Shortly afterwards, Albania, Hungary, Romania and Yugoslavia, Finland, then Poland and Czechoslovakia declined participation. To Averell Harriman, now secretary of commerce, this was a tactical blunder on Molotov's part: "he could have killed the Marshall Plan by joining it."[35]

After the collapse of the Paris Conference, American leaders began to turn away from Roosevelt's globalism and his policy of conciliating the Soviet Union. The two main obstacles to making American support for European integration official policy under Roosevelt and immediately after the war thereby disappeared. As the Truman years unfolded, hopes for building the peace in cooperation with the Soviet Union and for establishing an overall international free trade system appeared more and more distant. While Cordell Hull's maneuvers had earlier succeeded in convincing

Roosevelt to turn away from European integration, the Truman administration would soon endorse it as one the best ways of buttressing the "free world" against the menace of totalitarianism, or more precisely, communism.

The administration abandoned hopes for pan-European unification schemes based on East-West cooperation, at least for the short-term, and concentrated their efforts on Western Europe. In preparation for Marshall's speech, Kennan had insisted that Western Europe must be given priority over all trouble spots.[36] He and his colleagues now focused on reviving the western zones of Germany while integrating them within an economically prosperous Western Europe. Without German recovery, there would be no European recovery and vice versa. "We cannot revive a self-supporting Western European economy without a healthy Germany playing its part as a producing and consuming unit," wrote Harriman two months after Marshall's speech. One year later a State Department Policy Statement read: "Germany is potentially one of the most important European suppliers of such acutely needed commodities as coal, mining machinery, and industrial equipment. At the same time she is potentially an important market for European goods. German economic recovery is therefore vital to general European economic recovery. On the other hand, German economic recovery is largely dependent on the economic recovery of other European countries since they are the chief markets for her goods. It is U.S. policy that the fullest possible recognition be given this interdependence in order to achieve the greatest over-all benefits for the European Recovery Program."[37]

If Germany failed to achieve an economic revival within the context of Western Europe, U.S. leaders, including Marshall, Secretary of Defense James V. Forrestal, Army Chief of Staff Dwight D. Eisenhower and others feared that the whole of Germany might combine its industrial resources and technological advancement with enormous Soviet manpower. About three months before Marshall's speech, Kennan had insisted "that either a central German authority be established along lines that will make it impossible for the Soviet Union to dominate Germany and tap its resources, or that we retain complete control over the western zones of Germany."[38] The Truman administration now clearly opted for the second choice in order to prevent Soviet encroachment in West Germany and to buttress Western Europe against communism. Aid would be suspended to governments that included communists, warned Marshall in the spring of 1948, thereby stating publicly what some of his peers had long been saying behind the scenes.[39]

The stakes were high, for beyond the restoration of Western Europe and West Germany the very way of life of the United States was at stake. Without Europe, concluded Kennan in the summer of 1949, "we would be a lonely nation in the world in the sense that we would be on the minority side not only in the sense of world resources but also in the sense of philosophy and outlook on the world."[40] Kennan expected that the development of an independent center of power in Europe would relieve the United States of "some of the burden of 'bipolarity.'" John D. Hickerson, director of the State Department's Office of European Affairs, went one step further and spoke of the creation of "a third force which was not merely the extension of U.S. influence but a real European organization strong enough to say 'no' both to the Soviet Union and to the United States, if our actions should so require."[41] For the time being, the presumption was that as that third force, Europe would most often side with the United States.

Over the long haul, the American administration hoped that a revitalized Western Europe would in fact do much more than contain the Soviet Union and communism. "Communist revolution finds fertile seed in capitalist economic breakdown," Stalin had once told Harriman.[42] The Secretary of Commerce and his American colleagues were quick to conjure up the western counterpart to that statement: Western European economic prosperity breeds fertile ground for detaching Eastern European satellites from the Soviet Union. The United States administration had originally intended to encourage commercial exchange between Eastern and Western Europe, with Eastern Europe shipping raw materials and foodstuffs to Western Europe; this they calculated, would have reduced the need for American dollars. Notwithstanding the growing rift between East and West, Kennan, Clayton, and their peers now hoped Western European integration and prosperity would exert an irresistible pull on Russian satellites, and made plans for a long-term reunification of Europe. In a letter to Averell Harriman in December 1948, Under Secretary of State Lovett wrote that the objective of the United States should "continue to be the progressively closer integration, both economic and political, of presently free Europe and eventually as much of Europe as becomes free."[43] Short-term plans for containing the Soviet Union did not mean that the Truman administration had abandoned all hopes of building an international community based on the principles of democracy and free trade in the long term. Western European integration, a form of the regionalism Cordell Hull had opposed, appeared to some members of the Truman administration not so much an impediment to internationalism, as a possible step towards it.

On 15 July 1947, sixteen European countries agreed to create a Committee for European Economic Cooperation. By 22 September, the CEEC delivered its report, which detailed European joint needs for recovery. The next year, on 16 April 1948, the sixteen nations finally agreed on the creation of the Organization for European Economic Cooperation (OEEC). Both the report Europeans handed in to Americans in September and the scope of the

OEEC were a disappointment to Americans. To reach the twin goals of increasing European production and integrating European economies, the American administration touted the merits of relying both on market incentives and supranational planning. Yet Europeans seemed to have a strong aversion to joint programming. They were equally unconvinced by Under Secretary of State William Clayton's plea for clearing unions and currency clearing schemes. The British objected most strongly to any supranational schemes. The OEEC fell victim to their aversion.

By the spring of 1948 European participants in the CEEC discussions faced the challenge of transforming the CEEC into a permanent organization: the European companion organization to the Economic Cooperation Administration (ECA), administered by those Americans responsible for the European Recovery Program. Mainly to increase chances for their own national recovery and to hold German recovery in check, the French advocated the creation of a strong European organization. Not so with the British, who pointed out repeatedly that real authority should ultimately be vested in national governments and not in some sort of supranational body. Foreign Secretary Ernest Bevin and his colleagues conveniently explained their aversion to a strong OEEC in terms of their special links with the Commonwealth, thereby hiding another reason for opposing it, i.e., their hope to continue dealing bilaterally with the United States as a world power. Great Britain, Bevin would later emphasize to the American ambassador to the United Kingdom, was "a world Power as opposed to a purely European Power." Status as a world power required staying away from entangling commitments with the European continent from which the United Kingdom could not "extricate" itself should Europe embark on policies that were prejudicial to British interests or British "position as a world Power."[44]

The Americans, on the other hand, wanted the British to take the lead in fostering European integration and to encourage the creation of an organization that would become a major vehicle for it. The ultimate goal of the European Recovery Program, thought Marshall, must go beyond economic cooperation to the "closer integration of western Europe." What the State Department wanted to avoid was the creation of an organization that would amount to "a review and discussion group" engaged in eternal and fruitless discussions of plans for customs unions and other schemes that it would never see through to completion. Instead the State Department summoned forth a blueprint for a dynamic European organization with a "strong secretariat with clearly defined powers" under the leadership of an outstanding European personality.[45] The organization would act independently of national governments in initiating and carrying through its own projects.

The United Kingdom blocked all efforts to give the organization independent authority, and when the OEEC emerged from the April Convention for European Economic Cooperation, it was little more than a vehicle for intergovernmental cooperation, and not, as the Americans had hoped, a supranational organization. Subsequent American moves to place a prominent European personality at the post of director general of the OEEC to energize the organization with new supranational vigor and international prestige were also resisted.[46]

The OEEC controversy brought home one reality to the Americans, something Dean Acheson had been saying since October of 1949: the United Kingdom would never merge its sovereignty with that of a continental European grouping and should therefore be exempt from American plans for an integrated Western Europe. All that could reasonably be hoped for from the British was their benevolent support for European integration and their collaboration with a continental grouping that would be truly integrated; these hopes were dashed as well. Tired of waiting for British cooperation, the United States hoped that the initiative would now come from the French.

Some American policymakers, including Ambassador to France David K. E. Bruce, had objected to severing the United Kingdom from the European integration process on the grounds that the interdependence of the British and European economies made it impossible for European integration to succeed without the British. An additional ground for not letting the British isolate themselves from the Continent was a strong French aversion to facing the Germans alone on the Continent, without British participation. Yet activity in the security/military sphere, as well as the French initiative of the Schuman Plan, ended up replacing the initial blueprint for Western European integration under British leadership, with European integration based on Franco-German reconciliation under French leadership and American protection. American commitment to Europe via the Atlantic Alliance insured that European integration would occur under the protection of the United States and within an Atlantic framework, which both encouraged and impeded progress towards European integration.

THE SCHUMAN PLAN AND THE AMERICAN MILITARY GUARANTEE

As the situation further deteriorated with the Soviet Union, American leaders began to wonder whether economic recovery would be sufficient to bring Europe back to its feet. In January 1948 Foreign Secretary Ernest Bevin warned the State Department against "the further encroachment of the Soviet tide" and insisted it was time to "reinforce the physical barriers which still guard our Western civilization."[47] Washington received similar warnings from French Foreign Minister Georges Bidault in early March. Meanwhile the Soviet Union staged a coup d'état in Prague in February. James Reston of the *New York Times* was quick to see the implications: Europe could not withstand the Communist menace on its own and needed an American military guarantee.[48] An alarming 5 March telegram from General Lucius Clay, the military governor to Germany, reported that "within the last few weeks" there had been "a subtle change in Soviet attitude," which gave him "the feeling that [war] may come with dramatic suddenness." The telegram was widely publicized and contributed to fueling what the Alsop brothers called a "prewar atmosphere."[49] Presumptions that Italian democracy and perhaps Norway might fall prey to the communist tide further contributed to a sense of urgency. This played into the hands of the French and the British who were intent on securing American participation in the defense of Europe.

On 22 January 1948, Ernest Bevin had delivered a speech to the House of Commons that displayed an uncharacteristic British enthusiasm for the creation of a political community of European states with initial French, Dutch, Belgian, Luxemburger, and British participation. The Bevin initiative resulted in the signing of the Brussels Defense Pact on 17 March 1948. The signatories of the treaty promised each other mutual assistance in the event of armed attack. Noteworthy also was their commitment to foster European economic recovery through the coordination of their economic activities, and "the elimination of conflict in their economic policies, the coordination of production and the development of commercial exchanges."[50] This phrasing was designed to strike a responsive chord with the originators of the Marshall Plan and encourage otherwise ardent supporters of European unification in the United States into bringing the Americans into a military alliance with Western Europe. More than French or British maneuvers, however, the fear of the spread of communism to Western Europe ultimately caused the United States to renege on the sacrosanct principle not to enter into any peacetime alliances outside of its control. More specifically, it was the realization that the Marshall Plan and economic recovery alone were not enough to restore European self-confidence.

Until now the beneficiaries of Marshall Plan aid had been asked to walk a tightrope on the road to recovery while overlooking the abyss of their own military impotence. Although Kennan publicly brandished the threat of Soviet domination over the rest of Europe, the architect of containment believed that the Soviet threat was mainly political rather than military. Yet Europeans feared a Soviet armed attack just as much as political subversion, and their anxiety is what really mattered. John Hickerson, chief of the Office of European Affairs in the State Department, ended up convincing his colleagues that a military alliance with Europe was a necessity not so much because there was a real danger of Soviet military offensive, but because Europeans were convinced that it existed. Since Europeans lacked sufficient confidence in themselves to bring about a full recovery, the Truman administration would lend a helpful hand in bolstering this self-confidence by making an explicit commitment to defend Europe. Hickerson and his friends assured Congress that they had no intention of stationing American troops on the Continent; Europeans would provide the manpower themselves, and, if need be, the United States would furnish the armaments to Europeans. In other words it was "a question of committing, not forces now, but the potential of Pittsburgh or Detroit."[51] The adoption of the Vandenberg Resolution on 11 June, and the subsequent signature and ratification of the North Atlantic Treaty on 4 April and 25 July 1949 sanctioned American commitment to European security.

While some American leaders hoped European recovery and European economic integration would pick up momentum under the military guarantee of the United States, some were not so sure. John Foster Dulles remarked at the time that "the Economic Recovery Act and the Atlantic Pact were the two things which prevented a unity in Europe which in the long run may be more valuable than either of them."[52] The Marshall Plan encouraged the recognition of both an American and a Soviet economic and political sphere of influence in Europe, and the North Atlantic Pact created, according to Kennan, the "irrevocable congealment of the division of Europe into two military zones: a Soviet zone and a U.S. zone." Western European economies could conceivably prosper and mature under this arrangement, yet it would also preclude "the development of a real federal structure in Europe which would aim to embrace all free European countries, which would be a political force in its own right." The United States, whose original intentions had been to make Europe self-sufficient and to divest itself "gradually of the basic responsibility for the security of western Europe," would now become entangled in "a legal perpetuation of that responsibility." Kennan prophesied: "In the long-run, such a legalistic structure must crack up on the rocks of reality; for a divided Europe is not permanently viable, and the political will of the U.S. people is not sufficient to enable us to support western Europe indefinitely as a military appendage."[53]

Notwithstanding Kennan's illuminations and Dulles's insights, both Congress and the administration continued to encourage European unification. Yet not all argued for the same type of unification, or at the same time. In 1947, members of Congress, along with influential journalists such as Walter

Lippmann, had begun to openly advocate the unification of Europe. On 21 March, Senators J. William Fulbright and Elbert D. Thomas, together with Representative Hale Boggs, had introduced concurrent resolutions in the Senate and in the House stating that the "Congress favor[ed] the creation of a United States of Europe within the framework of the United Nations." The resolutions passed with a large majority in Congress and were widely publicized in the American Press. Yet when the time came to consider legislation to implement the Marshall Plan, Congress and the State Department seemed more hesitant to advocate European unity publicly. While some congressmen sought to link American aid to progress towards European integration, others, led by Senator Arthur Vandenberg, insisted that the initiative must come from Europeans. Linking the provision of aid to progress towards integration, they pointed out, would only serve to antagonize Europeans who would see the Marshall Plan as a vehicle of American interference in their domestic affairs. The State Department held an essentially similar view. The preamble of Title I of the Foreign Assistance Act of 1948 heeded these concerns and simply read: "The policy of the people of the United States is to encourage those countries through a joint organization to exert sustained common efforts . . . which will speedily achieve that economic co-operation in Europe which is essential for a lasting peace and prosperity." This was a far cry from attempts by Senator Fulbright, Senator Henry Cabot Lodge, and Representative Boggs to amend the bill with calls for European "political unification," "economic integration," and "cooperation and unity."[54]

Senator Fulbright, along with other key personalities in business, academic, and government circles, sought to galvanize public and governmental enthusiasm for a united Europe in the United States and in Europe through the activities of the American Committee for a Free and United Europe, which sponsored speeches and articles by leading policymakers and journalists. The Economic Cooperation Administration, which ran the European Recovery Program, needed no such prompting, and wrestled with the State Department in an attempt to publicly press on Europeans the need for European unification and supranational institutions. While the State Department was deeply sympathetic to any efforts that might transcend national sovereignties in Europe, it was equally concerned that public advocacy of detailed American blueprints for European unification might be construed in Europe as an attempt to snatch the initiative away from Europeans. The result was, once again, a compromise, best exemplified in Paul Hoffman's speech to the OEEC's council on 31 October 1949. The head of the ECA urged Europeans to form "a single large market within which quantitative restrictions on the movement of goods, monetary barriers to the flow of payments, and eventually, all tariffs are permanently swept away." In order to build "an expanding economy in Western Europe through economic integration," he suggested adapting existing organizations or creating "new central institutions."[55] This, he said, would greatly improve Europe's competitive position in the world. Heeding the State Department's concerns, Hoffman refrained from mentioning ECA's plans for a European central bank and a trade commission.

Hoffman's public emphasis on the need for European economic integration came against the backdrop of the surrender of China to the communists, the explosion of the first Soviet nuclear bomb, and recession in the United States. Coupled with growing nationalism in Western Europe, particularly in West Germany, these events emphasized the need for tightening the West and for using American dollars in a more efficient way. European integration looked increasingly appealing both as a way of maximizing each U.S. dollar spent in Europe and as a means of integrating Germany within Western Europe without having it play a dictatorial role. More unity in Western Europe, calculated Washington planners, would also lead to greater productivity on the Continent, which in turn would sustain renewed American efforts for rearmament, without, however, impairing the chances of European recovery. In early 1950, the House of Representatives voted the phrase "economic unification and federation" as one of the objectives of the Foreign Economic Assistance Act, after having been tempted to write "political federation." The State Department was more cautious and continued to refrain from advocating plans for political unification, which it felt were largely premature. The State Department also shied away from any attempts to link the provision of Marshall Plan aid to progress towards integration. The Schuman Plan served to show the administration that Europeans could indeed seize the initiative. The following year, Eisenhower would publicly press for the political unification of Western Europe.

On 9 May 1950, French Foreign Minister Robert Schuman made an historic declaration at the Quai d'Orsay that led to the creation of the European Coal and Steel Community (ECSC) and marked the beginning of a Franco-German rapprochement. Jean Monnet, who then served as general commissary for the French Plan of Modernization and Equipment, was the real initiator of the plan and had persuaded Schuman to endorse it. The Schuman declaration proposed to pool coal and steel at the European level "as a first step in the federation of Europe." Since coal and steel production were two essential ingredients for building the machines of war and were located mostly in Germany and France, the new "solidarity in production thus established [would] make it plain that war between France and Germany [had become] not merely unthinkable but materially impossible."[56]

When Schuman told Acheson of his planned declaration, the secretary of state first saw the Schuman Plan as a proposal to establish an international cartel. Aided in his efforts by his friends John McCloy, the U.S. high commissioner to Germany, and David Bruce, the American ambassador to France, Monnet quickly moved to reassure Acheson that the Schuman Plan was anything but a cartel, and tried to convince him that it was essential that the United States react positively to it. Acheson in turn convinced Truman to announce official support for the Schuman Plan.

Despite this official endorsement of the Schuman Plan, American reactions were mixed. The plan offered a chance to put an end to the age-old Franco-German conflict, integrate Germany within the West, and use the ECSC as a stepping stone towards more far-reaching progress on the road to European federation. John Foster Dulles wrote Monnet that its political implications were "even more important than the economic" since it would bring about "a genuine union of interest"[57] between Germany and France. Averell Harriman, the U.S. special representative in Europe, wrote Acheson that the "proposal may well prove the most important step towards economic progress and peace of Europe since [the] original Marshall speech on ERP. It is [the] first indication of [a] bold, imaginative, concrete initiative on [the] part of [a] European country in attacking two basic problems . . . integration of European economy and conclusive alignment of Germany on [the] side of [the] West with minimum political and military complications."[58] Yet fears were expressed in various quarters in the United States that the plan would encourage the recrudescence of national and international cartels and impede free trade. Some American leaders were also preoccupied by the possible emergence of a "third force" in Europe. The Schuman Plan was theoretically open to "all countries that wanted to participate in it."[59] But did this mean that a united Europe would choose to adopt an attitude of aloofness, or disengagement and neutrality, in world politics? William Diebold, a member of the Council on Foreign Relations, was most explicit in voicing his fear of a neutral Europe: "There is often no sharp distinction between steps toward the desirable end of strengthening Europe, materially, politically and spiritually, and measures which increase the possibility that Western Europeans may try, however futilely, to disengage themselves from the main currents of world politics."[60]

Despite these misgivings key Americans lent their support to the Schuman Plan. Two close friends of Monnet, Ambassador to France David Bruce and a Treasury official named William M. Tomlinson, headed a group at the American Embassy in France that helped Monnet and his staff draft several sections of the treaty. At Monnet's request, Robert Bowie, general counsel to John J. McCloy, prepared the drafts dealing with antitrust. George Ball, a lawyer whom Monnet had first met in Washington during the war, served as a consultant to the French government on the drafting of the treaty.[61] Behind the scenes, John J. McCloy and Robert Bowie, both friends of Monnet, were active in strengthening the resolve of the Adenauer government to join the ECSC in view of the mounting pressures of powerful industrial groups in Germany. Backing Monnet's efforts, they advocated the reorganization and deconcentration of the coal and steel industries of the Ruhr so as to prevent the Ruhr from dominating German policy and from putting French industry at a disadvantage.[62] On 18 April 1951 Belgium, France, Italy, Luxembourg, the Netherlands, and the Federal Republic of Germany signed the Paris treaty. The High Authority of the Coal and Steel Community, headed by Monnet, started meeting one year later in August 1952. That same month, Acheson declared: "It is the intention of the United States to give the Coal and Steel Community the strong support that its importance to the political and economic unification of Europe warrants."[63]

Right from the beginning of the Schuman initiative, the British refused to participate in the discussions for the establishment of the Coal and Steel Community. Their refusal was poorly received in Congress, where some members sought to cut all Marshall Plan aid to the British if they did not join the Community. The administration succeeded in fending off this menace and drew a long-overdue conclusion: with a little help from American friends, the French would now have to take the lead in federating Europe.

2

The European Defense Community, the European Political Community, and the ECSC Loan

THE TRUMAN ADMINISTRATION AND THE EUROPEAN DEFENSE COMMUNITY

On 25 June 1950, North Korea invaded South Korea. The outbreak of the Korean War prompted the administration and Congress to dramatically increase the defense budget. It also intensified the shift away from the initial policy of primary reliance on economic tools to rebuild a "viable" Western Europe. By the fall of 1951, the administration gave priority to rearmament rather than economic recovery to meet the possibility of a Soviet threat. To Acheson, Adenauer, and to many Europeans, the aggression in Korea appeared as a prelude to a Communist onslaught on Western Europe via Germany. Monnet, recalled George Ball, "was quick to see the implications. . . ." The Americans would intervene and "American intervention would not only jeopardize the Schuman Plan, it would create serious problems for European unity. It might well stir up an atmosphere of panic in Europe while increasing American insistence on a larger role for Germany in the defense of the West."[1] Monnet was right on all counts. On 30 June, Truman authorized military intervention in Korea. The next month, John McCloy declared German rearmament necessary so the country could defend itself in case of attack. Acheson was equally convinced that Germany's participation in the defense of Europe must no longer be "secondary but primary. . . . Korea had speeded up evolution." European defense must now be based on a forward strategy; Germany's contribution must not only be military but emotional and political as well. [2] By July of the next year, President Truman approved an interdepartmental memorandum which insisted that "substantial German sovereignty" be restored. The authors concurred that "in general the Germans should be given full power to run themselves and that our mission there should be changed from one of 'occupation' of the territory of a defeated enemy to one of military assistance to a partner who is freely contributing to our mutual defense."[3]

The question was not whether Germany should be rearmed but how this should be done. On 12 September 1950 at the New York Foreign Ministers' Conference, Dean Acheson announced a decision that, according to him, was "a complete revolution in the attitude of the American people."[4] Four to six divisions of United States troops would be sent to Europe and included in a NATO defense force to be commanded by an American, most likely Eisenhower. German divisions were to be integrated within the new united command structure and put under the command of the NATO commander-in-chief; they would not be a constituted army. The Americans also envisaged lifting economic controls over Germany to enable it to fully contribute to the rearmament effort. Previous American plans to avoid discrimination against the Germans after the war now came full swing: Germany would be rearmed, its sovereignty restored.

Schuman and Monnet could hardly have been less enthusiastic. Not only did Acheson's proposal threaten European efforts towards economic recovery with the specter of growing inflation and deficits, but rearming Germany might ruin the chances for success of the Schuman Plan as well. If, they reasoned, the Germans were allowed to rearm at the national level, and reestablish their sovereignty, the attractiveness of the Schuman Plan to Germany would be considerably diminished. Would not the Germans, asked Monnet, demote the plan to a purely technical exercise? Wouldn't they be tempted to play the East against the West? At any rate, the French would deem German rearmament a threat to their security and would be reluctant to sign on the dotted line of the Coal and Steel Community Treaty with the Germans. Monnet countered with the Pleven Plan, named after French Prime Minister René Pleven, who had worked closely with him during World War II. On 24 October 1950, about one month after Acheson's announcement at the New York conference, Pleven proposed the creation of a European army of mixed nationalities with a single executive and a European defense minister; the army would be answerable to a Common Assembly to be shared with the ECSC. West Germany would contribute units to the European army, but these units would not be allowed to form divisions. There would be no independent German general staff or defense ministry.

Initially, Washington policymakers, including both the president and Acheson, reacted with "consternation and dismay." They deemed the Pleven Plan "hastily conceived without serious military advice and . . . unrealistic and undesirable." The proposal seemed "designed for infinite delay on German participation." The European framework for this participation would have to be established first, and there was no telling how long it would take for a European military and political structure to be established. Also, "the second-class status accorded Germany was all too plain."[5] Were the French in fact maneuvering once more to keep the Germans in a subordinate position? Acheson was not averse to a European army as such; he had in fact himself earlier envisaged the formation of either a "North Atlantic Army" or a "European army" in which Germans would be enlisted, thus avoiding the recreation of a German General Staff.[6] Yet by the spring and summer of 1951 the secretary of state had reached the conclusion that a European Defense Community would be acceptable only if it did not detract from NATO's strength and did not delay Germany's contribution to the defense forces of Western Europe. He viewed the European Defense Community solution as "a long term approach" to the problem of European defense "as long as it is clearly a part of and under [the] NATO umbrella." In the long run, if tensions between East and West abated and the presence of U.S. troops was deemed undesirable, the existence of a European defense force could then ensure that European national forces would not be reconstituted "solely under national control." In the short run, however, the creation of a European army was not to "unduly interfere" with NATO's forces or "complicate [its] command structure." The European army and its command structure had to be strictly integrated within NATO. To fulfill the immediate objective of the participation of German troops in the defense of the West, Acheson emphasized the need to quickly return a substantial degree of political equality to Germany. He also advocated the formation of German contingents within NATO as an interim measure, so that there would not be "undue delay in [the] buildup of an effective defense of [the] Continent," while plans for a European army were developed.[7]

In military circles, the proposal for a European army did not arouse great enthusiasm either. General Eisenhower initially rejected association with the project, which seemed to him "almost inherently, to include every kind of obstacle, difficulty, and fantastic notion that misguided humans could put together in one package." He thought the plan would most likely foster division rather than unity in Western Europe, and was militarily unsound and ineffective. Above all, Eisenhower strongly suspected the French to have put forward the proposal for a European army on the assumption that the plan would never be adopted and that German rearmament, if contingent upon the realization of a European army, would topple down with it, or at the very least be considerably delayed.[8] A lunch appointment with Jean Monnet on 21 June 1951 at SHAPE (Supreme Headquarters Allied Powers, Europe) apparently convinced Eisenhower to change his position to that of an ardent supporter of the European army.[9] Monnet pointed out to him that the crux of the matter was not so much military effectiveness as political soundness. The critical issue was not the size of the divisions or other technicalities, but the creation of a common European outlook, a "solidarity of destiny." Eisenhower saw the light: what Monnet proposed to him was "that the French and the Germans should wear the same uniform"; the real issue was to organize relations between men, thus the problem was "more a human problem than a military one."[10] Eisenhower decided to support the European army scheme as an essential contribution to European integration, without which no viable solution could be found to the German problem. Following up on his discussion with Monnet, General Eisenhower, recently appointed Supreme Allied Commander, Europe (SACEUR), made a strong plea for European economic and political integration before the English Speaking Union in the great ballroom of Grosvenor Place, Park Lane, on 3 July 1951. He described the benefits to NATO as incalculable: a united Europe would have the political and psychological self-confidence, the economic health, and hence the resources to assist the United States in furthering the objectives of the Atlantic Pact, no longer as a recipient of American aid, but as a partner.[11]

Yet he and Acheson continued to insist that the European army must be strictly integrated within NATO, so that there would in fact be no autonomous European command. Meanwhile, Ambassador Bruce made vehement attempts to convince Acheson that a European army should be supported not only "for reasons of long-range security and other interests" but also as the best way of quickly setting up a solid European defense in the short run. A European army, he pointed out, would allow Europe to rearm not through the separate efforts of national governments but through an integrated European defense structure, which would "produce effective defense more quickly, and strengthen NATO, by reducing [the] number of its major elements to three: United States, Brit[ain], and Europe." Confident that a European army would hasten rather than delay a German contribution, Bruce recommended waiting to rearm the Germans until the completion and ratification of the EDC treaty.[12] Acheson disagreed. He was worried by the tendency "to treat Eur[opean] integration and a Eur[opean] Army as final solutions for all problems."[13] Many Europeans, he insisted, did not favor the

European Army scheme. The Dutch, for example, objected to it because, in the absence of British participation, it might expose them to French leadership or to German domination. By July the Americans had reached a compromise position, which largely heeded Acheson's concerns for an immediate defense effort while underwriting the creation of a European defense force.

On 30 July 1951, Acheson and Acting Secretary of Defense Lovett submitted to the president a joint policy paper on the problems of the defense of Europe and the German contribution, which Truman approved that same day. In essence the paper recommended simultaneous progress on three fronts: the establishment of a European Defense Force that would serve under NATO, "raising German troops at the earliest possible date" and restoring German sovereignty. The European defense force and NATO would work together, each reinforcing the other. "Continental European arrangements" would mainly serve to "offset" French and German fears, while the NATO framework would deflect the objections of those who feared European integration, particularly the British. In other words, the United States would support the creation of a European army and, in general, European integration, only if it were organized within the safe compounds of an Atlantic Community controlled by the United States. The EDC was not to "constitute a separate European field army but would be based on the idea of European contingents which could be disposed of by the Supreme Allied Commander in Europe in accordance with military necessity." There would thus be no autonomous European command. To put it bluntly, the European army would be only an appendage to NATO. Furthermore, the creation of the EDC was "not to be a condition precedent to the actual beginning of the German contribution to the defense effort."[14] Although too watered down for the taste of some Europeans, support for the European army concept had now become official American policy. Despite Acheson's and Lovett's insistence that negotiations on the EDC should not delay German rearmament, they did just that.

Spurred on by Monnet, Eisenhower repeatedly affirmed his support for the European Army and European economic, political, and military unification. After a meeting with Monnet in November 1951, the general agreed to stress "the need for European amalgamation—political as well as the earlier steps involved in the Schuman Plan and the European Army" at the eighth session of the North Atlantic Council in Rome. Eisenhower was all the more willing to do so since he believed "implicitly in the idea." Unless "Denmark, Holland, Belgium, Luxembourg, France, Italy and western Germany form[ed] *one* Federated State," he wrote in his diary, the millions the United States had spent on the Economic Cooperation Administration would go to waste. But the United States could "*afford* to spend a lot" to encourage the development of a unified Europe because they would "*get* something successful, strong, sturdy."[15] On 26 November, the general addressed members of the NAC in terms that showed him to be a faithful supporter of European integration. Not only did he emphasize the advantages of Western European unification—economic, military, and political—but he also unequivocally voiced his support for the creation of a European defense force. Such a force, he said, would incorporate German strength without having it pose a threat to the alliance. "German help," insisted Eisenhower, "will be tremendously important as is freely given; and it can be so given, I believe, through a European Defense Force. It could stand alongside the Schuman Plan—which must be successful—and the two would constitute great steps toward the goal of complete European unity!"[16]

By 1952 the administration publicly advocated both the economic integration of Western Europe and its military and political unification. In the context of the Korean War, American support for European unification in its various guises became a convenient tool in an ideological, strategic, and economic war against the Soviet Union. In a letter addressed to President Truman on 4 January 1952, Eisenhower directed the president's attention towards three areas where "significant accomplishment" was "possible in Europe without great expenditure of money." These would be, first, the "rapid implementation of the Schuman Plan," second, reaching an agreement on the European Defense Force, and, third, taking "concrete and practical steps" towards "the political and economic union of Western Continental Europe." The political and economic unification of Western Europe, he felt, was "a *sine qua non* of permanent security" because, without it, there could not be any "long-term economic health in this region; and, without economic strength, adequate military force [could not] be maintained."[17] To Eisenhower and much of the American administration, European unification had now become a *sine qua non f*or the defense of the West. A supranational Europe with a greater degree of economic, political, and military unity defined a framework that would not only strengthen Europe economically and politically, but would also ensure a greater European contribution to common defense, thereby strengthening the Atlantic Alliance. The European Defense Community was seen as a first step towards this process of European integration.[18] During the Eisenhower administration, Secretary of State John Foster Dulles supported it as the "panacea for Europe's difficulties, a symbol of its regeneration and a touchstone of its future."[19]

On 26 May 1952, the United Kingdom, France, West Germany, and the United States signed the Bonn Convention, which was to restore West

Germany's sovereignty. One major qualification was attached to the convention, mainly because of European fears of the resurgence of German nationalism: German sovereignty would be restored only upon the ratification of the EDC by all signatories. The EDC thus became the touchstone of the end of occupation in Germany. The EDC treaty was signed the day after the signing of the Bonn Convention on 27 May. Dean Acheson hailed the signing as "one of the most important and far-reaching events of our time . . . the beginning of the realization of an ancient dream—the unity of the free peoples of Western Europe." "However vital defense may be at this time," Acheson concluded, "the true meaning of the EDC extends far beyond the field of defense."[20] Congress added concrete commitments to the administration's pronouncements. The Mutual Security Act of 1952 provided that part of the funds would go to the "organization which may evolve from current international discussions concerning a European Defense Community." Congress specifically recommended that "the act should be so administered as to support concrete measures for political federation, military integration, and economic unification in Europe."[21]

Both the State Department and the Mutual Security Agency anticipated great gains from the EDC. They hoped to centralize military aid to Europe through a strong EDC Commissariat, which would make American aid more effective. Yet a strong Commissariat was not acceptable unless under the control of a democratically elected European parliament. In March, British Foreign Minister Anthony Eden had put forward a proposal for integrating the institutions of the Schuman Plan and the European Army, and all future European organizations based on the principle of supranationalism, within the existing organs of the Council of Europe.[22] To Monnet, Eden's proposal epitomized the intergovernmental approach to European unification, as opposed to the supranational approach he favored. He countered with a proposal to hold European elections within the six member countries of the ECSC (Belgium, the Netherlands, Luxembourg, France, Italy, West Germany) by 1953 to elect a new assembly for the Schuman Plan and the future EDC. Through the American Embassy in France, and notably Finance and Economic Adviser William Tomlinson and Consul Stanley Cleveland, Monnet and his co-worker Max Kohnstamm made their views known to the State Department. Monnet insisted that the Council of Europe could not help in the preparation of common institutions for the Coal and Steel Community and other projected communities. The Coal and Steel Assembly had "effective powers," while the Assembly of the Council of Europe was "entirely consultative." The council, of which the United Kingdom was a member, could "not be part of the community anymore than the Pan-Amer[ican]

Union [was] represented in the US Government."[23] Put bluntly: the British would be informed of what had been decided and Monnet would welcome their association with the communities, but they could not become part of the communities unless they accepted some sacrifice of British sovereignty. The new assembly Monnet proposed would have responsibility for drafting a treaty creating a European political community.

A draft treaty was prepared by a "Constitutional Committee" of an enlarged ECSC Assembly. It provided for a directly elected People's Chamber, a Senate elected by national parliaments, a European Executive Council, a Council of National Ministers, and a European Court common to the three communities. The "European Community" would take over the functions of the EDC and ECSC about two years after the election of the People's Chamber, while also having powers in foreign affairs and economic policy. The draft treaty made provision for the establishment of a common market for the Six in which goods, capital, and persons would circulate freely.[24]

Meanwhile American professors Carl Friedrich and Robert Bowie were busy developing preparatory studies for a European federal constitution at the request of a special committee in which Paul-Henri Spaak played a prominent role and whose members no doubt influenced the work of the Constitutional Committee. Friedrich and Bowie asked the American Committee on United Europe to fund their work.[25] Enthusiastic backers of Monnet, such as Tomlinson, endorsed the European Political Community (EPC) proposal because of its potential for consolidating federal power in Europe and contributing to the creation of a common market. Some quarters were more cautious. When national delegations of the Six met to consider the draft treaty in late 1953, John Foster Dulles and other State Department officials in the Eisenhower administration warned against solutions that might weaken the supranationality of the ECSC and the EDC through a mishmash "of national and supranational elements," which seemed "to make these two components equal."[26] Another concern was that debates over the EPC might prejudice the ratification of the EDC and German rearmament.[27] Dulles explained to American missions in Europe that the primary objective of the United States was "sufficient agreement on EPC to permit the ratification of the EDC."[28]

During the later months of 1952, the EDC was plagued by ratification difficulties in European parliaments. In Germany, the treaty faced the hostility of the S.P.D. (Social Democratic Party) and was criticized as giving too many privileges to the French. Both the Dutch and the French were fearful of a possible domination of the EDC by Germany, especially since prospects for the accession of the United Kingdom to the EDC looked quite remote in view of its admission to the nuclear club in October. In addition, French involvement in Indochina began to weigh heavily against a "European policy" that entailed tying up French troops in Europe and losing a fair amount of French national sovereignty. Facing the Germans alone on the Continent with a limited number of troops was not an appealing prospect to the French. Meanwhile, in the United States, the McCarthyite "primitives" attacked the Truman administration and especially Dean Acheson. Eisenhower's request to be relieved from his duties as Supreme Commander of the Allied Powers in Europe, and his subsequent victory over the Democrat Adlai Stevenson, further weakened the influence of the current administration and its weight in European affairs.

Throughout the last months of 1952, Acheson consistently refused to press publicly for the ratification of the EDC for fear that the United States might appear to force the EDC down French throats, primarily to serve American interests.[29] On 14 December 1952 Monnet met with the secretary of state in Paris. A disappointed Acheson lamented that he and most of the American public had "no current knowledge of any activity" as far as the Schuman Plan and the European political union were concerned. He felt momentum had been lost since June, that "retrogression had set in, and that we might now be on the verge of complete disaster." If "the European effort fell apart," he dramatically threatened, "all basis for American policy would begin to disintegrate." Perhaps the United States would even withdraw its military forces from Europe. Monnet tried to breathe optimism into Acheson's pessimistic ruminations and to convince him to make a declaration supporting the unification of Europe, including the EDC, to help the cause of European integration. Acheson refused to make such a declaration since a new administration was about to take over.[30] Yet he did advise John Foster Dulles, the secretary of state-to-be, to recommend to Eisenhower "the dispatch of a New Year's message to General Ridgway at Paris that might include a statement strongly endorsing the E.D.C."[31] Adenauer had also written to John McCloy in December to ask him to convince Eisenhower to "make a strong appeal to European governments" for the European idea at the very start of the new administration. President Eisenhower obliged. On 6 January 1953, Eisenhower released a public message to Chancellor Adenauer which read in part: "You will probably know about my New Year's message to General Ridgway in Paris in which I stressed the importance of a growing European unity and the establishment of a European Defense Community. I believe such a development would contribute much to promote peace and the security of the free world.[32]

THE EISENHOWER TEAM AND EUROPEAN INTEGRATION

The close and enduring friendship between Dulles and Monnet, as well as the sympathies of President Eisenhower and his own acquaintance with Monnet, no doubt played a role in shaping American policy towards the EDC. Yet Dulles and the president supported the EDC for reasons of their own, and in their own way. John Foster Dulles believed that increased European unity ultimately was up to Europeans themselves, yet he also thought that the United States possessed in Europe "both moral rights and political power." It had acquired those rights and this power by becoming involved in European wars. "Now American blood, shed in two European wars [gave the United States] the moral right to speak,"[33] Dulles said in 1947. The new secretary of state was deeply convinced that United States foreign policy must support and defend certain moral standards at home and abroad. Moral bankruptcy was the most ominous threat to Dulles's version of a "free world" congenial to United States interests. He believed that a United States that merely stood by "while the barbarians overran and desecrated the cradle of our Christian civilization . . . would not be a United States which could defend itself."[34] Moral strength, the sharing of common principles, and a sense of mission would thus provide the cement needed to seal the unity of the Atlantic Alliance. As the EDC episode would show, moral rectitude was the position from which Americans addressed their European allies with a clear and sometimes loud voice.

While his secretary of state brandished the menace of the moral decrepitude of the West, Eisenhower did not so much emphasize moral strength as he stressed the importance of economic power for the survival of the "free world." The president perceived a crucial link between American security on the one hand and fiscal responsibility on the other. He accordingly defined the Soviet threat not so much in terms of direct confrontation with the West as in terms of economic danger. In a 1953 radio address, Eisenhower noted that "by their military strength [the Soviets] have hoped to force upon America and the free world an unbearable security burden leading to economic disaster. They have plainly said that free people cannot preserve their way of life and at the same time provide enormous military establishments." This observation led to an inevitable conclusion:"the relationship . . . between military and economic strength is intimate and indivisible."[35] The implications helped circumscribe a "New Look" for American strategy, in which alliances were given a special recognition and importance. While the president emphasized that "the United States on its own initiative would never start a major war,"[36] the administration hoped to regain the initiative in selecting the means to deter and respond to an aggression. "The way to deter aggression," Dulles told the Council on Foreign Relations in January 1954, is "for the free community to be willing and able to respond vigorously at places and with means of its own choosing."[37] The United States no longer intended to match an external attack with an equal level of response, as had been the case under the Truman administration. Rather, according to historian John Lewis Gaddis, "the central idea was that of asymmetrical response—of reacting to adversary challenges in ways calculated to apply one's own strengths against the other side's weaknesses, even if this meant shifting the nature and location of the confrontation."[38] The president gave an example: "An invasion of Europe in overwhelming strength by conventional forces did not mean that our reaction had to be limited to force of the same kind."[39] "Massive retaliatory power" offered a possible alternative. In order to make the threat of the use of nuclear weapons credible, the administration purposely blurred the difference between conventional and nuclear weapons. The top-secret statement of the "New Look," NSC 162/2, approved by the president in October 1953, specified that in case of an aggression "the United States [would] consider nuclear weapons to be as available for use as other munitions."[40]

By being able to select the means of response to aggressions, rather than multiplying them, the United States would reach another desirable goal: reducing costs. From the inception of his term in the White House, the president stressed the need for fiscal responsibility and a balanced budget. The new presidential team had partly been selected with this concern in mind. In his memoirs, Eisenhower recalled that when his administration took office, "there was no one among my immediate associates not dedicated, in principle, to the proposition that both federal expenditures and the public debt must be reduced." In basic agreement with Dulles's blunt statement that "if economic stability goes down the drain, everything goes down the drain," Eisenhower set out to achieve a balanced budget, partly by streamlining its own defense by relying less on conventional forces, partly by counting on a little help from friends.[41]

NSC 162/2 acknowledged that the United States could not "meet its defense needs, even at exorbitant cost, without the support of allies."[42] In exchange for the protective nuclear umbrella of the United States, Eisenhower anticipated American allies would provide most of the ground troops to counter local aggression, and, inevitably, financial support, notably by buying American weapons. "Centrally located and strong in productive power," the United States would provide "mobile reserve forces of all arms, with emphasis on sea and air contingents."[43] Uniting Europe militarily through the EDC offered the prospect of cutting down American troops on the Continent, and, by the same token, American military expenditures. A united Europe had two main features to commend itself to the administration: it had the resources and the manpower to contribute substantially to the security of the West, while it also opened the prospect of a desirable market for United States products, which, in turn, would help sustain prosperity at home and enhance military strength. Secretary of State Dulles insisted it was essential that "Europe itself furnish the preponderant strength to insure its own security." And this was only possible "if the resources of the individual nations of Western Europe [were] joined together."[44]

Eisenhower relished the prospect of a united Europe that would, after an initial period of help from the United States, largely be able to finance its own destiny. The sooner Europe united, he thought, the sooner United States assistance to Europe could be decreased, to the greatest benefit of American taxpayers, Europeans, and the West as a whole. For only an independent, self-respecting Europe could play a role commensurate with the aspirations of its people and act as an adequate partner of the United States. Time and time again while SACEUR (Supreme Allied Commander, Europe), then as president of the United States, Eisenhower insisted that American "psychological, intellectual, and material leadership" could help Europe "build her initial forces" and regain her confidence, but that some day Europe would have to provide for its own defense. "In the long run," wrote Eisenhower, "it is not possible—and most certainly not desirable—that Europe should be an occupied territory defended by legions brought in from abroad, somewhat in the fashion that Rome's territories vainly sought security many hundred years ago."[45] Dutch Foreign Minister Dirk Stikker wrote in his memoirs that his talks with Eisenhower convinced him that the president's support for the European Defense Community was motivated by his desire to send American boys back to the United States. Towards the end of his administration, when the American balance of payments showed increasing deficits, Eisenhower's calls for reducing American troops in Europe became more pressing.

Yet, despite very strong views on the matter, the president did not take substantial action because of the opposition of Secretary of State Dulles, much of the State Department, and part of the military to a withdrawal of United States troops from Europe. In the context of the EDC, Dulles urged Eisenhower to dispel the impression that the United States planned to pull out of Europe. He insisted that the French had been encouraged by the United States to maintain and build up their forces in Indochina, and dreaded the prospect of facing a rearmed Germany under the EDC unless the United States and the United Kingdom kept "troops in Europe substantially as at present."[46]

Eisenhower's interest in the potentialities of a united Europe for the West had arisen while he was still chief of staff of the army under Truman.[47] In June 1951, as supreme allied commander, Eisenhower jotted down in his diary that he could see no satisfactory solution to the European security problem unless there existed "a U.S. of Europe—to include all countries now in Nato; West Germany and . . . Sweden, Spain and Jugoslavia, with Greece definitely in if Jugoslavia [were]." Significantly, he added: "If *necessary,* [the] U.K. could be omitted."[48] Eisenhower later reduced his original list to Belgium, Luxembourg, the Netherlands, France, Denmark, Italy, and West Germany. By December 1951, Eisenhower had given up on British direct participation in the EDC and in a European political union and wrote Foreign Secretary Anthony Eden that he preferred Great Britain to continue "to carry out her world-wide responsibilities."[49] At the same time he hoped that the British would at the very least lend their strong backing for the establishment of the EDC and the European Political Community, while also exerting leadership in fostering European integration. Eisenhower tried to impress on his old friend Churchill that the EDC would fail if it were not for "the active, enthusiastic, and incessant moral support of Great Britain."[50] In order to dispel the false impression of many Europeans that the British were in fact antagonistic to the whole idea of a European army and a European continental union, Eisenhower recommended that both the United States and Britain make public pronouncements in support of the European army. Consequently, in early 1952, Truman and Churchill announced their intention to give emphatic support to the EDC while refraining from participation. In an address to a joint session of Congress on 14 January 1952, the British prime minister also noted the "real and rapid progress" Europe had made toward unity, and affirmed that the United States and Britain ought "to help and speed it."[51] Yet President Eisenhower later bemoaned Churchill's obvious preference for the prospect of an Anglo-American partnership and became frustrated with his lack of enthusiasm for the concept of European unity. Both he and Dulles tried to convince Churchill that Europe's future would be considerably jeopardized unless the European army and the Schuman Plan were a success. There would be no such success, however, unless the British exerted "*leadership* in bringing about this development" and showed they were willing to help "politically, economically and otherwise."[52] Failing strong British support and leadership, Eisenhower and Dulles opted for shock tactics to elicit European support for the ratification of the EDC.

The new administration had just taken office in 1953 when John Foster Dulles made a television speech to the nation. The United States, he said, had made a substantial investment in Western Europe, and it was now time for the Europeans to show they could provide returns on that investment in the form of effective unity. The secretary of state backed this encouragement with a threat: "if, however, there were no chance, and that I just refuse to believe, but if it appeared, there were no chance of getting effective unity, and if in particular France, Germany, and England should go their separate ways, then certainly it would be necessary to give a little rethinking to America's own foreign policy, in relation to Western Europe."[53] This was nothing less than threatening a return to American isolationism. Dulles's appearance before American television cameras was the prelude to his visit, accompanied by Mutual Security Agency Director Harold Stassen, to several European countries in late January and early February. The president intended to "dramatize the government's continuing interest in the region,"[54] and to push for the EDC.

Hearing that Dulles and Stassen would pass through Luxembourg, Jean Monnet immediately wrote to Dulles, underscoring the special significance of their visit, since it would more or less coincide with the opening of the European Common Market for Coal on 10 February, "a great date in European history." Dulles replied that it "would be a pleasure to pay our respects to this functioning community which in so important an area replaces the costly rivalries of the past."[55] Monnet's welcoming address to his guests on a very cold winter day, forty-eight hours before the opening of the first Common Market, echoed Dulles's words. "The European Coal and Steel Community," said Monnet, "is the beginning of this union of the peoples of Europe who, renouncing at last their age-old divisions, will soon unite in a strong, prosperous and peaceful community to the benefit of their populations, free peoples and civilization as a whole."[56]

Even though Dulles returned to the United States on the same day, Monnet had enough time to suggest the appointment of an ambassador at large or a special United States representative, whose main task would be to push for European unification. He was deeply convinced that the European venture would not succeed without the strong backing of the United States. Hence, he insisted on the importance of appointing an American representative ranking above other American representatives in Europe to underscore the importance to the United States of European integration. Earlier that winter in Bonn, Monnet had discussed a similar proposal with Adenauer, who had been thinking along the same lines.[57] Alfred Gruenther, Eisenhower's former chief of staff at SHAPE, and a close friend of Monnet, had also been toying with the idea and had written his former boss in early January suggesting the name of David Bruce. Eisenhower had shown himself favorable to the idea of a roving ambassador who would "visit with all the appointed ambassadors in their own region and attempt to promote common understanding and viewpoint," yet he did not see how he could call on a prominent Democrat such as David Bruce at the very start of a Republican administration.[58]

During his conversations with Monnet in Luxembourg, Dulles voiced his own objections to Monnet's proposal. To begin with there were already too many ambassadors, and he felt that adding another ambassador at large would be a great mistake. He did, however, sound more positive about the possibility of appointing a special representative. Would Lewis Douglas be all right? Monnet was noncommittal and boldly suggested that David Bruce might be more acceptable.[59] Dulles hesitated at first. David Bruce was close to Acheson. Appointing a liberal Democrat like Bruce would be anathema to some at a time when McCarthyism reigned supreme.[60] Yet Bruce was a close friend of Foster's brother Allen and had been associated with John Foster Dulles during the negotiations for the Japanese Peace Treaty in 1951. He was also a friend of Monnet's from the Marshall Plan days, and one whom Monnet held in great esteem. Monnet's advice eventually prevailed, and Dulles decided to go along with his scheme. Yet Jean Monnet did not put all of his eggs in one basket. Unsure at first whether Dulles would accept his proposal, Monnet telephoned his old friend Alfred Gruenther the day after Dulles had boarded his Flying Fortress to return to the United States. Would Gruenther please telephone Douglas MacArthur II so that he could try to expedite Bruce's appointment? In doing this Monnet hoped to directly secure the agreement of the president, and put pressure on Dulles. Douglas MacArthur II had enjoyed the confidence of Eisenhower as his former chief adviser in international affairs, while the general was SACEUR. He was now serving as counselor in the Department of State,[61] being one of the select few whom Dulles really trusted and relied upon for advice in foreign affairs. Gruenther agreed to write to MacArthur, emphasizing that Eisenhower thought highly of Bruce's qualifications, although he would most likely object to his being a Democrat. There was no need for MacArthur's good offices, though. Once on the plane, Dulles and his assistants had had a thorough discussion on the matter.[62] Two days later, on 10 February, after clearing it with Eisenhower, the State Department got in touch with Bruce, who was shooting turkeys in the South. Bruce agreed to take on the job; he did not ask for any specific title. Dulles eventually recommended to the president that Bruce be designated not only as United States Observer to the European Defense Community Interim Committee but also as United States Representative to the ECSC. Thus, he felt, the United States would send a clear signal that it was interested in the EDC "as part of a broader six-country development and not solely as a necessary arrangement for our mutual defense."[63] Both the spirit and the letter of Monnet's proposal had thus been respected. Ten days after Monnet had shared his plans with Dulles, President Eisenhower announced that David Bruce would soon leave for Europe to serve in the two capacities Dulles had suggested, with the additional responsibility of observing the progress made towards the creation of a European Political Community.[64] The next day Dulles telegraphed Monnet, telling him the good news. "This appointment," he emphasized, "is of course indicative of the great importance which the President and the US Government attach to the movements in Europe to develop a unified six nations Community."[65]

Soon Bruce presented his credentials to Jean Monnet and rejoined his young co-worker from the Marshall Plan days, William ("Tommy") Tomlinson, who headed the Paris United States Embassy group charged with supervising activity relating to the six members of the Common Market prior to Bruce's arrival. Tommy was a very close friend of Jean Monnet, whom he met with frequently during the Eisenhower years, until Tommy's death in 1955.[66] Monnet's lobbying efforts were thus successful in establishing privileged American conduits in Europe through which he could communicate his views to Washington, where they had a good chance of reaching top-level decisionmakers, not the least of whom were the secretary of state and the president. First of all, there was a direct link with both the president and his secretary of state. There were also privileged lines of communication through Bruce and Tomlinson in Europe, with Alfred Gruenther and others playing on the sidelines. In private circles, McCloy, the former high commissioner for Germany, now chairman of the Chase National Bank in New York, and particularly George Ball, to name only a few, frequently helped Monnet. In addition, Monnet adroitly used appointees in Dulles and Eisenhower's inner circle, such as Douglas MacArthur II, to lobby for his views.

In an administration that counted many Europeanists, Monnet could rely on quite a few of his friends and sympathizers, who had a privileged hearing in the King's Court and that of his secretary of state. Familiars of the president and secretary of state included Robert Murphy, who had met Monnet in 1937-38 in Paris and then again in 1943 in Algiers. Murphy had served as chief civil affairs officer under Eisenhower during World War II, and was now given the job of assistant under secretary of state for United Nations affairs.[67] Eisenhower used him as a trouble-shooter who often mediated between allies and the administration in handling sensitive questions such as the territorial division of Trieste between Italy and Yugoslavia, or the control of the Suez Canal. Livingston Merchant, who had been Dulles's deputy during the negotiations for the Japanese treaty, and recently held the position of deputy to William Draper, the Special Representative in Europe, was now appointed assistant secretary for European Affairs.[68]

Robert Bowie, the new head of the Policy Planning Staff in the State Department, had first met Monnet in Paris shortly after the declaration of the Schuman Plan. Bowie was then managing on behalf of McCloy the implementation of Law 27, which had been adopted by the Allied High Commission to deconcentrate the coal and steel industry in Germany. He was later asked to coordinate that law with the negotiations for the Schuman Plan. He soon became closely involved with Monnet in the preparation of the articles of the Schuman Plan Treaty itself.[69] Another old friend of Monnet's, Walter Bedell Smith, who had close ties to his former boss, Eisenhower, with whom he had served as chief of staff during World War II, was appointed to the prize post of under secretary of state. An ex-director of the CIA and a former director of the American Committee on United Europe, Smith now held the major responsibility for administering the State Department while Dulles busied himself with traveling and formulating American foreign policy. For "purely personal reasons," Smith resigned from his post in August 1954 but continued to do temporary work for the government as an unofficial adviser.[70]

As for the secretary of state himself, he had met Jean Monnet at the Versailles Peace Conference of 1919, where he was acting as legal counsel to Bernard Baruch, the United States representative on the Reparations Commission. John Maynard Keynes and Jean Monnet were serving on the British and French delegations, respectively. Foster Dulles and Jean Monnet were both born in the vintage year of 1888 and soon became close friends. During the 1920s and 1930s Monnet and Dulles were frequently associated in common endeavors such as the saving of the zloty (the Polish currency) and the dissolution of Kreuger and Toll in the wake of the chaos that followed the suicide of Ivar Kreuger, the Swedish "Match King," in March 1932. When Eisenhower appointed Dulles as his secretary of state, an elated Monnet telegraphed him: "My dear Foster the news of your nomination has moved me deeply . . . The burden is heavy but the task ahead is great and the reward full of promise if peace can be not only kept but developed." Monnet did not lose this opportunity to reaffirm his faith in the credo of European integration: "To attain this goal," he continued, "I believe that the prompt creation of a United States of Europe is essential and I know how much you share these convictions. Good luck and God bless you. Jean." Dulles promptly cabled back: "Greatly appreciate your cable and look forward to our continuing association. I share your conviction that it is of the utmost importance promptly to create greater unity politically, economically and militarily in Europe. This, as you know, has been my conviction for many years."[71]

Dulles's brother Allen shared this conviction. Allen, who was also a close friend of Monnet, had shown an early interest in European integration, notably as a member of the Council on Foreign Relations, and later became vice-chairman of the American Committee on United Europe.[72] In 1953, President Eisenhower appointed him as director of the Central Intelligence Agency. Allen Dulles thus succeeded Walter Bedell Smith as head of the CIA.[73] The closeness of Allen and his brother John translated in part into a smooth relation between the CIA and the State Department, while their common dedication to European unity and their interest in European affairs made them particularly prone to listen to Jean Monnet and his friends, whether for better or for worse.

President Eisenhower had known Monnet from the war years, yet the two men only became closely associated in 1951. That year Monnet met with Eisenhower to convince him to support the European army and was asked to be one of the "Three Wise Men" charged with carrying out most of the responsibilities of the newly created Temporary Council Committee (TCC), a task that consisted of matching NATO military needs with the economic capabilities of the member nations. Shortly after Christmas 1951, Eisenhower sent Monnet a letter in which he thanked him for his New Year's present, most likely some bottles of the delectable Monnet Cognac which Jean used to send to his best friends and associates once a year. The letter showed Eisenhower's esteem and friendship for Jean Monnet. "Touched by [his] kindly thoughtfulness," Eisenhower wrote: "Although the assignment to this post brought to my wife and to me many disappointments due to the severance of ties that seem to grow more valuable as the years pass, yet we have been compensated by the opportunity of forming new friendships among people that we admire and esteem. Among these we are bold enough, and most certainly exceedingly proud, to number you."[74] When Eisenhower was elected president of the United States one year later, Monnet sent him a note echoing the message he had sent to his friend Dulles, offering "most sincere congratulations" for his election while once again reaffirming the importance of European unity for the attainment of peace.[75] Eisenhower's answer was short and to the point: "Thank you for your message and look forward to continuing coop[eration] for the great goals ahead."[76]

Although the administration had many ties with Monnet, the European connections of the Eisenhower team extended beyond Monnet. René Mayer, who succeeded Monnet as president of the High Authority of the ECSC in June 1955, had known Dulles since 1949. On the German side, Dulles was an intimate friend of Adenauer, whom he admired for his strength of character and his constructive achievements in Germany. One of the strongest bonds between the two men was their deep commitment to religion, which was one of their favorite topics of discussion. To give another example, Walter Hallstein, Adenauer's deputy when he was chancellor and foreign minister, was friends with Robert Bowie and David Bruce, which helped him establish a comfortable working relationship with John Foster Dulles, whom he admired as "one of the shrewdest politicians" and as "a lawyer statesman with great drafting abilities, an artist."[77] Dulles's artistic talents were unfortunately less evident on the diplomatic side, as his unskillful advocacy of the EDC would show. Yet Dulles's influence and that of his Europeanist colleagues were decisive in another negotiation that ran parallel with American efforts for EDC ratification: an American loan to the ECSC.

Foreboding signs for the ratification of the EDC treaty appeared during 1953. Détente was one of them. Stalin's death in March, the uprising in East Berlin—the first attempt at revolt within the Soviet bloc—and the end of the Korean War on 27 July, all signaled a lessening of the threat to be countered, and thus a reduced need for German rearmament and the EDC. The ECSC was not faring much better. By mid-June 1952, all of the signatories of the ECSC Treaty had ratified it, yet concrete manifestations of its alleged advantages were not forthcoming. Having initially prompted Dulles, Eisenhower, and other key members of the Eisenhower administration to strongly support the EDC, Monnet, aware of growing opposition to the EDC in France, not least from de Gaulle, encouraged the American administration to support European integration by showing American confidence in the chances of the ECSC through a loan from the American government to the ECSC.

THE ECSC LOAN AND THE EDC

The common market for steel opened on 1 May 1953, following shortly after the opening of the common market for coal in February. Impressed by these concrete achievements, American public opinion was largely favorable to Monnet, whom eulogistic profiles in influential American newspapers featured as "Mr. Europe."[78] All the ECSC needed now was the official reaffirmation of the administration's support, which Monnet thought essential for the ultimate success of the ECSC and the advancement of European unity. The Bruce/Dulles connection played a key role here. In late April David Bruce informed Dulles that Jean Monnet would be coming to New York in the first week of June to receive an honorary degree from Columbia University. Why not invite Monnet to Washington as an official guest, suggested Bruce. Dulles readily acquiesced and wrote Eisenhower that he found

Bruce's idea excellent. On 12 May, the White House issued a press release announcing the official visit of Monnet and explaining his role as one of the outstanding leaders of the movement for European unification.[79] On Dulles's suggestion a meeting with the President was arranged on 3 June, while Dulles himself met with Monnet several times during his visit to the United States.

Shortly after their arrival in the United States in late May, Monnet and ECSC Vice President Franz Etzel set out to enlighten American steel industrialists on the merits of the ECSC. Through a masterful presentation of their version of the facts, they succeeded in neutralizing the skepticism, if not the outright opposition, of some key industrialists like Clarence Randall, the Chairman of the Board of the Inland Steel Corporation, who had previously written a series of articles criticizing the ECSC as a giant cartel and an encouragement to *dirigisme*. This was no small achievement, given the great influence those industrialists could exert on the Republican Party and hence on the current government. Progressively zeroing in on his objective, Monnet also met with General Donovan, the Chairman of the American Committee on United Europe, and had dinner on 28 May with Thomas Dewey, governor of the state of New York and a central figure in the Republican Party with close ties to Dulles, whom he had appointed to fill an unexpired Senate term in 1949. Also present at the Brooks Club that night were important figures from American financial circles, some of whom were Monnet's friends. George Ball and Robert Bowie had been invited, along with Monnet's intimate friend Justice Felix Frankfurter. Having thus secured his rear guard both in the political and economic spheres, Monnet marched off to the State Department and the White House.

Ten thousand guests were present to watch Monnet receive his honorary degree from Columbia University on 2 June. The next day Monnet met with President Eisenhower at nine o'clock in the morning. Their meeting lasted for about half an hour. Faithful to his own thinking, Eisenhower reaffirmed his support for European unity and was quite sympathetic to the efforts of Monnet and his peers to implement the Schuman Plan Treaty. The publication of a communiqué right after the meeting, a rare occurrence, gave some indication of the president's sympathy. Later that day Monnet and the two vice-presidents of the ECSC met with Dulles and a group of high ranking policymakers from the administration. Monnet then proceeded to convince Capitol Hill that the European movement was making great strides. In doing so Monnet painted a relatively optimistic picture of the situation.

On 5 June, "Mr. Europe" told the Senate Foreign Relations Committee of his faith in the "inexorable development" of a United States of Europe. The draft treaty for a European political authority and a common parliament had just been published and now underwent the close scrutiny of the governments of the Six. If the governments approved it and ratification ensued in their respective parliaments, Monnet insisted, this would mean nothing less than the creation of a European federation. Steady progress on the political treaty was all the more necessary to legitimize the creation of a European army. The European people would not accept the creation of a European army if it were not controlled by a civilian authority: there would be no European army if there were no Europe.[80] Seeking to strengthen the chances of the EDC, Monnet proposed to move away from public explanations that presented the European army as "an entity in itself."[81] As part of this strategy, Monnet now focused the bulk of his energy on making the ECSC a success. This was perhaps not so much a choice as a necessity: the new president of the ECSC had enough on his hands with the infant ECSC, and little time to devote to anything else. While in Washington, Jean Monnet and the two vice-presidents that accompanied him also made "vigorous efforts"[82] to convince their American interlocutors that the ratification of the EDC treaty was not the only decisive factor for the advancement of European unification, even though it remained an important factor.

The Monnet visit to the United States in May and June was vastly successful in gathering support for the Schuman Plan both on Capitol Hill and in the administration. After testifying on the Hill on the 4 and 5 June, and meeting with Senator Fulbright, Monnet wrote a "personal and confidential" letter to Dulles in which he recommended that he and the president write to Senator Wiley, chairman of the Committee on Foreign Relations, to obtain support for a loan to the ECSC. The moment was "exceptionally favorable" for a public announcement of the decision of the United States government to make a loan to the ECSC, wrote Monnet. President Eisenhower was ready to support it, so too was the Senate Committee on Foreign Relations. Better still, the ECSC Assembly met on 15 June in its annual session. "It would make a profound impression on the Assembly, and indeed in Europe generally" if Monnet, Etzel, and Spierenburg could show that the United States intended to participate in the development program of the ECSC. The fact that the American participation would be on a loan rather than a grant basis would "mark a break with the form in which most American aid to Europe ha[d] been furnished in the past few years." This would show the American people that US-European relations had entered a new era, and bolster the self-respect of Europeans "by showing that the United States ha[d] confidence in them." A consummate salesman, Monnet enclosed a short memorandum outlining "points that may be useful in any communication that might be decided upon."[83] A draft letter, mainly the work of Robert Bowie and Thruston B. Morton, the assistant secretary of state for congressional relations, then circulated in various bureaus in the State Department for revisions. The final output incorporated some of Monnet's suggestions. On 15 June, Eisenhower sent letters to both Senator Wiley and Representative Robert B. Chiperfield, chairman of the House Committee on Foreign Affairs, in which he confirmed his commitment to European integration and strongly recommended that the United States government or one of its agencies provide part of the financing for the development program of the ECSC as a "tangible and useful way" of fostering European unity. Heeding Monnet's advice, Eisenhower suggested that 15 June might be an appropriate occasion to express the approval of both the House and the Senate committees for the progress made so far and their "keen interest in the success of this and future steps towards European integration." The next day the president received very favorable replies from Wiley and Chiperfield. Eisenhower then made the exchange of letters public in a White House press release the following day.[84]

After much lobbying, Monnet had obtained part of what he wanted: official expressions of support by the president and Congress for the ECSC. As planned, Monnet proudly reported on the exchange of letters to the Common Assembly on 19 June and thanked Dulles, Eisenhower, and the Congress for their support.[85] Yet, despite auspicious beginnings, still more lobbying was needed to secure a definite commitment to the loan from the American government and an agreement on its terms. If made in a timely fashion, this commitment, calculated Monnet, would indirectly enhance the chances of the EDC by emphasizing American support to European unity.[86]

In part due to Monnet's efforts, the Eisenhower administration went on record as strongly favoring the EDC. At the very beginning of his presidency, Eisenhower had reiterated not only his support for European unity but also for the EDC.[87] Dulles's exhortations further amplified the administration's commitment. Where he and Monnet differed was in how to express that commitment. Monnet advocated encouragement of the EDC along with other manifestations of European unity and thought of indirect ways of showing American support to the EDC, such as a loan to the ECSC. By contrast, Dulles exhorted and threatened, perhaps endangering rather than helping the chances of the EDC.[88] Upon his return from his mission to various European capitals in February, Dulles publicly deplored the slowness of the ratification of the EDC treaty.[89] Yet in reporting to the president during his trip, Dulles appeared confident that "ultimate success" was "possible and even probable."[90] A significant development in March seemed to augur well for the EDC: on 14 March 1953, the West German Bundestag gave final approval to the EDC treaty. The next month, Dulles added another element to his support of the EDC by affirming that the objectives of NATO could not be realized without the success of the EDC.[91] Increasingly, the EDC became part of a package deal: without the EDC, American policy towards the containment of communism in Europe, concretely embodied in NATO, would be considerably jeopardized; without the EDC, the United States might reappraise its commitments to European defense. During the debates on the Mutual Security Act of 1953, Dulles indicated that there were no really good substitutes for the EDC. The Richards Amendment to the Mutual Security Program appropriation for 1953–54 showed that a majority of members of Congress was ready to support that conclusion. In its final form the amendment specified that half the funds provided for European military assistance would be made available only to the EDC or its member countries. Should the EDC fail to become a reality, the funds would not be released unless Congress agreed to reconsider the provision upon recommendation of the president. This last provision was a concession to the State Department and to Eisenhower, who tried to convince Congress that heavy dollar-diplomacy pressure tactics would only hamper the efforts of Western European governments to ratify the EDC by showing the EDC as an American scheme. The United States "cannot compel unity," insisted the State Department in a letter to Representative Chiperfield, chairman of the House Committee on Foreign Affairs.[92] Yet the State Department evidently suffered a lapse in memory and its tactics decidedly tilted towards pressure diplomacy, both behind the scenes and in public statements by the Secretary of State.

From 10 to 14 July, the foreign ministers of the United States, the United Kingdom, and France met in Washington. Secretary Dulles and Lord Salisbury of the United Kingdom seized this opportunity to remind French Foreign Minister Georges Bidault of the great efforts made by the United States and the United Kingdom in favor of European unity and to express their wish to see an early ratification of the EDC.[93] In September 1953, Ambassador to France Douglas Dillon informed the State Department that prospects for French ratification were promising, particularly in light of Adenauer's sweeping electoral success and thus his ability to make concessions to the French, notably on the Saar question, without jeopardizing the position of his government. The State Department could not agree more: an airgram to the Embassy on October 5 concurred with the Embassy that it was now "time for an all-out push with a view to ratification and implementation by early 1954." In September, hoping for French ratification of the EDC, the United States practically doubled its aid to the French in Indochina, but to no avail. Adenauer's victory might now have heartened the pro-European

French and signaled a possible chance for the EDC to be approved by the French National Assembly. Yet one would have to move quickly. In mid-October, David Bruce, now holding the additional title of United States observer to the Interim Committee of the European Defense Community, recommended energetic action since the Laniel government in France now seemed to want to "evade taking positive steps to bring about EDC ratification in France," even though Prime Minister Joseph Laniel and Foreign Minister Bidault would most likely have obtained a majority if they had asked for a vote on the EDC.[94]

The "all-out push" recommended by the State Department took the form of private and public pronouncements by the secretary that amounted to thinly veiled threats. On 16 October, Dulles met privately with Bidault at the French Embassy, with Bowie present. The secretary revealed his anxiety and disappointment about the slowness in the ratification of the EDC. The United States, he said, had spent about $30 billion on Europe through the Marshall Plan and military aid. American "strategic planning ha[d] been based on [the] development [of] real strength in Europe through unification." It was now time to see results, or else the United States would "be forced against [their] will to explore new alternatives which [would] be presented to [them] by the changed situation in Europe resulting from failure of [the] EDC."[95] Shortly before his trip to Europe in February, Dulles had expressed interest in discussing possible alternatives to the EDC. The result was a meeting at the Pentagon on 28 January with officials from the State Department, the Mutual Security Agency, and the Joint Chiefs of Staff. Dulles's intention was to find an alternative to the EDC credible enough to convince the French and the Germans that the United States did not need to defend the whole of Western Europe to ensure its own security. If the alternative seemed sufficiently unpalatable, it would force the French and the Germans to go along with the EDC. As early as September 1952, various bureaus and offices in the Department of State had attempted to find alternatives to the EDC in case the treaty was not ratified. Among the possibilities being considered were direct German membership in NATO, the rearmament of Germany outside NATO, German association with NATO, some kind of German nonmilitary contribution to NATO, and "a retreat to a peripheral defense of Europe based on an arc from Norway through the British Isles to Spain, Italy, Greece and Turkey." Paul Nitze, who then headed the Policy Planning Staff and would soon be replaced by Bob Bowie, now recalled that "even the best alternatives we could come up with did not look very good." Even the option of peripheral defense did not preclude the need to "maintain considerable forces in Europe to avoid losing Europe in the cold war." Moreover, the troops would be "in a militarily unfavorable position." General Omar N. Bradley, Chairman of the Joint Chiefs of Staff, concluded that German troops in sufficient concentration were necessary to hold the center of Europe. The United States did not possess "enough atomic weapons to plaster all of Europe. Twelve German divisions would put a completely different picture on the situation. It would force [the Russians] to a considerable build-up before they could attack" and serve as a guarantee that the United States would be given appropriate warning.[96] About a year later, the January 1953 meeting adjourned without definite proposals for plausible alternatives.

By August Eisenhower approved a statement adopted by the National Security Council, NSC 160/1, for implementation. The statement reaffirmed the importance of the EDC as a way of securing a German contribution to the defense of Europe, preventing the resurgence of German militarism, and tying Germany firmly to Europe. It also noted: "The United States should support with all available means the creation of the European Community and the ratification of the EDC Treaty. No satisfactory substitute for this solution has yet been found." This apparent lack of alternatives did not prevent Dulles from brandishing the threat of examining new alternatives to the EDC by the time of his October meeting with Bidault. This was so even though key officials in the State Department and Dulles himself kept insisting that alternatives should not be considered at this time, especially in European embassies, for this might give Europeans the false impression that the United States had given up on the EDC.[97]

Ten days after his meeting with Bidault, Dulles reiterated his threat in slightly different words before the National War College: if the EDC did not succeed, the United States would have to adopt a totally different vision of their foreign policy. Meanwhile, Ambassador to France Douglas Dillon and Douglas MacArthur, who was in Europe as head of the U.S. Delegation at the Paris tripartite working group, also made threats to Prime Minister Laniel.[98] Throughout the weeks leading to the Bermuda Conference in December, Dulles expressed his concern and his disappointment in the delay of ratification of the EDC treaty. His disappointment was all the more acute because of his expectation that Adenauer's overwhelming electoral success and his willingness to resolve the Saar matter would help carry the EDC through the French Assembly. In late November Dulles sent a letter to the German chancellor in which he repeated the litany of reasons for United States support for the EDC: Franco-German unity as the "only foundation for the development of any real strength in Europe" and "the resources which the United States in its own enlightened self-interest ha[d] been pouring into Europe." These resources would "be wasted and [would] not serve the long-term purpose for which they were appropriated" unless the EDC were ratified. The chancellor could play a vital role in helping the French if only he would remove one obstacle by reaching an agreement with them on the Saar. [99]

At the Bermuda Conference of the heads of the governments of the United States, the United Kingdom, and France in early December 1953, Foreign Minister Bidault insisted that there would be no ratification of the EDC unless Germany agreed to let the Saar territory remain autonomous. Prime Minister Laniel was ill with pneumonia but set the tone of the conference with the pronouncement of his emissaries and with private conversations with Eisenhower and Churchill, who came to visit him while he was officially sick. The day the conference opened, Germain Vidal, Joseph Laniel's cabinet director, told Tyler, first secretary of the embassy in France, that there was "no chance [the] EDC Treaty [could] be ratified for several months and then only if greatly increased assurances and commitments [were] given by [the] British and [the] US." At the conference, Bidault urged both Churchill and Eisenhower to agree to give a twenty-year guarantee that British and American forces would remain on the Continent at their current strength. France, he said, "alone among the great Western powers, was making the humiliating sacrifice of integrating its forces with those of another nation which had long been its enemy." The sacrifice necessitated some guarantees and concessions on the part of its allies. Bidault stressed the considerable difficulties his government was facing in obtaining parliamentary approval for the EDC. Churchill and Eisenhower concurred in chastising the foreign minister for his defeatism and showed a marked reluctance to guarantee that their forces would remain at their current strength on the Continent for twenty years. The American president sounded a note that would be repeated and amplified by his secretary of state a few days later: "without the EDC the whole NATO concept would have to be overhauled."[100]

The secretary of state's campaign reached a crescendo in his only too well-known "agonizing reappraisal" speech at the North Atlantic Council on 14 December 1953. The speech was the product of the joint efforts of Livingston Merchant, Robert Bowie, and John Foster Dulles, and received the complete approval of the president. When Dulles met with his main advisers in Paris just two days prior to his speech, most of them, including David Bruce, recommended being tough with the French to shock them into bringing the EDC to a vote in the French Assembly. Ambassador Douglas Dillon, who was more skeptical of the chances of the EDC, was just recovering from surgery and did not participate in the meeting. In his absence, his assistant Theodore Achilles most likely joined his colleagues in advocating a "hard-boiled" line with the French. The French, reasoned the hard-liners, would ultimately comply and ratify the EDC for fear of being isolated from their allies. The day before his "agonizing reappraisal" speech, Dulles met with Adenauer in the afternoon, then with Monnet. Adenauer, who had long pressed David Bruce on the virtues of adopting a hard line towards the French, now saw "less difficulty [in] bringing the EDC to a vote," and was confident that the Saar problem would be solved. He calculated that the chances of the EDC were about 310 votes in favor and 300 against and felt that after the presidential elections in France the "new government would initiate parliamentary process leading to definitive vote." Dulles concluded that the time was indeed ripe to provoke a salutary shock in France and spur the election of a government that would favor the EDC. The secretary of state addressed the North Atlantic Council in the following terms: "If however, the E.D.C. should not become effective; if France and Germany remain apart, so that they would again be potential enemies, then indeed there would be grave doubt whether continental Europe could be made a place of safety. That would compel an agonizing reappraisal of United States policy."[101] The next day, at a press conference, he not only reiterated his threat of a possible "agonizing reappraisal," but also made it clear that the United States "was not at the moment making any plans on the supposition that EDC would fail." The United States "was interested in trying to create a situation so that the Western countries will not commit suicide. If they decide to commit suicide, they may have to commit it alone. If events compelled the United States to an agonizing reappraisal, one of the elements of that reappraisal would be the disposition of United States forces." Theodore Achilles approved of the "measure of shock treatment" that Dulles's "press conference administered." Unfortunately, Dulles's shock treatment may have helped finish off the patient.

On the whole, the results of the hardliners' tactics were disappointing. Dulles's statement succeeded only in irritating the French president and his foreign minister and in branding the EDC as an American diktat in France, even though it was a French initiative. Moreover, the results of the French elections did not augur well for the EDC's adoption. On 6 January, a new French president, René Coty, was elected, and the Laniel-Bidault government was reinstated. The President's sickness had prevented him from participating in the debate on the EDC, which probably helped his electoral success.

Meanwhile, in mid-December, Monnet had several conversations in Paris with Dulles, Secretary of the Treasury Humphrey, Foreign Operations Administrator Stassen, and their advisers on the proposed loan to the ECSC. Monnet suggested a public announcement by the United States government asking Congress to approve a loan to the ECSC "of a certain amount, with terms and conditions to be determined by subsequent negotiations"; this would help the EDC by reaffirming U.S. support of the European Community. United States support would in turn incite the British to make quick progress in their plans for association with the European Community, which could mean a difference of at least twenty votes in favor of the EDC in the French Parliament. Chancellor Adenauer fully supported Monnet's plan. The Frenchman intended to announce American approval of the loan to the ECSC before the Common Assembly meeting convened on 14 January 1954.[102] In the meantime, Dulles reaffirmed his support for the EDC, this time also underscoring the achievements of the ECSC. About a week after his "agonizing reappraisal" speech, Dulles made another statement, dealing primarily with NATO and the EDC, before the National Press Club, and he had two copies of it forwarded to Monnet through Bruce.[103] While the address to the NATO ministers had made no mention of the ECSC, Dulles now spoke of it, thus heeding Monnet's advice, and emphasized that "much progress" had already been made towards economic and political unity. A press release from the White House on 23 December similarly underscored the achievements of the ECSC and reaffirmed Eisenhower's hope that a loan might soon be negotiated with the ECSC. The White House did not, however, officially ask Congress to approve the $500 million loan that Monnet had requested. By 13 January 1954, after numerous memoranda and telephone conversations in Washington, the administration submitted a proposal to Monnet. Yet Monnet found it unacceptable and thus had little to show the Common Assembly of the ECSC in mid-January.[104]

Even though Dulles pleaded Monnet's case with his colleagues, and particularly with the Secretary of the Treasury and the Director of the Foreign Operations Administration, they persisted in their conviction that a $100 million loan to the ECSC would be sufficient to demonstrate American support for European unification. Dulles insisted that such a small amount could hardly "capture European imagination" or provide the political impetus needed to get the EDC through, yet he eventually had to concede to his colleagues. Commenting on the American proposal, Monnet objected not only to the amount of the loan but also to the suggestion that the United States government might conduct a project-by-project review of the loan funds. Such a proposal, argued Monnet, would jeopardize the independence of the High Authority and "might be the cause of considerable misunderstanding and thus be detrimental to relations between the United States and the Community."[105]

During the next few months Monnet again and again pressed Dulles to begin negotiations on a loan. When Dulles attended the meetings of the Berlin Conference in early February, Monnet arranged to meet with him three times. Personal diplomacy proved effective once again. While Dulles tried to impress on his colleagues the urgency of starting negotiations on the loan, he and Monnet worked on a communiqué in which the U.S. government would announce its agreement to open negotiations in Washington; the communiqué was subsequently released on February 20. About one month later David Bruce sent a formal letter to Monnet inviting him to send a delegation to Washington to start negotiations for the loan. Monnet promptly wrote Dulles emphasizing the importance of his forthcoming visit to the United States at a time when European integration needed money, but even more so the "evidence of support of European integration by the United States." [106] The ratification process of the EDC was indeed entering a crucial stage in France, and the ECSC itself was having a hard time weathering the attacks of the EDC's critics.

Monnet arrived in the United States on 6 April 1954 and met with Dulles and Ben Moore, the director of the Office of European Regional Affairs, that same afternoon. The next day Monnet called on Bowie in the State Department and had a cocktail with Merchant at Blair House. The stage was set for another series of Monnet's brilliantly persuasive performances. The first meeting on the Coal and Steel loan negotiations took place at the State Department on Thursday 8 April. Dulles tried to shape the tone of the meeting by reminding his colleagues from the Treasury, the Foreign Operations Administration, and the State Department of its "historical significance since it was the first time the United States. . . had the opportunity to deal with a sovereign Community representing more than national states." Using his usual positive approach, Monnet pointed out that the ECSC was only the beginning of a united Europe and proceeded to outline its main achievements while at the same time defusing potential criticism, particularly regarding the insufficient efforts of the ECSC to eliminate cartels. Yet his was not an easy task. Secretary of the Treasury Humphrey was adamant that the loan should not exceed $100 million. The United States, he told Monnet, had not succeeded in balancing its budget, and the American coal and steel industries were facing grave problems, which in turn made them reluctant to condone a loan to the ECSC. Monnet encountered many other obstacles during subsequent meetings with representatives of State, the Treasury, the Foreign Operations Administration, and the Export-Import Bank. Personal diplomacy came in handy to overcome them. With Dulles, Monnet discussed the necessity for low interest rates. Dulles then arranged a meeting between Monnet and the president, who gave him his blessing for the loan. Monnet's old friend Walter Bedell Smith similarly assured Monnet that he would help him get the loan no matter what obstacles his colleagues threw in his path. During the last stage of the negotiations, Monnet had dinner with his lawyer, Donald Swatland, and Samuel Waugh, who agreed to launch a joint attack on Humphrey so he would stop insisting on a "closed mortgage" that prevented the Community from getting further loans in Europe. Three days later they did exactly that and thus removed one of the main stumbling blocks to the loan. One of Monnet's youngest collaborators, Jean Guyot, also played an important role in the negotiations. After more battles over the interest rate, the terms of payment, and the wording of the communiqué, an agreement was finally reached on a $100 million loan to the ECSC for twenty five years, to be disbursed by the Treasury and USAID. The agreement was signed on 23 April 1954.[107] This was too late to change the declining fortunes of the EDC.

THE DEATH OF THE EDC

The year 1954 witnessed a combination of circumstances that inexorably led to the defeat of the EDC. By April, the Benelux countries (Belgium, the Netherlands, and Luxembourg) as well as Germany had all completed ratification. Even though the Italian government refused to support the ratification of the EDC until its Western allies helped Italy protect its rights in Trieste against the Yugoslavians, Italy was expected to cause no major problems. Yet the Laniel government was divided over the issue of the EDC. The same day that Luxembourg completed ratification action, 7 April, General de Gaulle launched an attack against the EDC. Dien Bien Phu fell on 7 May. By 12 June, the Laniel government was defeated on a vote of no-confidence. Two days later President Coty chose Pierre Mendès-France to form a new government; the new prime minister was not an enthusiastic supporter of the EDC. In March, Under Secretary Walter Bedell Smith had told the National Security Council (NSC) that "there was a very slight prospect that any successor government to Laniel's would ratify the EDC."[108] History proved him right when the French Assembly rejected the EDC by a vote of 319 to 264, with 43 abstentions, on 30 August 1954.

Meanwhile the Eisenhower administration alternately used threats and encouragement to strengthen the resolve of the French government to ask for a vote on EDC. As encouragement, the United States released a text of "Assurances Concerning EDC" on 16 April,[109] thereby reaffirming its intention to maintain in Europe its fair share of the forces needed for the joint defense of the North Atlantic area so long as a threat to that area existed. In late February Eisenhower had directed the State and Defense departments to consider assurances that might be given the French in accordance with Bidault's request at Bermuda.[110] A 5 March meeting of the NSC pitted State against Defense. Defense Secretary Charles E. Wilson did not believe further assurances to the French would help the chances of the EDC, while his deputy, Roger M. Kyes, plainly advocated warning the French to proceed with the ratification of the EDC or else the United States would pull its forces from Western Europe. Acting Secretary Walter Bedell Smith took the opposite position and counseled the president to release a statement with reassurances to the French that would basically be nothing more than "a rehash of older reassurances." Eisenhower balked at first and "inquired, somewhat irascibly" whether such assurances were really needed. "Must we go on forever coddling the French?" he asked. "We have stationed forces in Western Europe, we have constructed bases, and lots of other things. How much more must we do?" Referring to an earlier statement by David Bruce, Smith told the president that all that was needed was an effort "to get timid men to overcome their own uncertainties," and convinced him to side with the State Department. Even though he was very worried about giving the impression that the United States would forever allocate dollars to support American troops around the world, the president insisted that American national security interests now required a front line running east of the Rhine and told the NSC he "had no slight idea of reducing the number of troops in the next two years. The European nations [were] not yet ready to take up the slack." [111]

On the morning of 13 April, three days prior to the release of the American assurances, the British signed an association agreement with the heads of delegations of the EDC Interim Committee and made a pledge similar to that of Americans, thereby meeting another French demand for ratification of the EDC. [112] The State Department had originally planned to use the assurances to pressure the French into holding the EDC ratification debate prior to the Easter holidays on 16 April. [113] Yet David Bruce soon realized that this deadline was unrealistic in light of Laniel's reluctance to push for an early vote on EDC. The United States and the British, he wrote the State Department, "should ask the French Government to fix prior to Easter recess a date for an uninterrupted debate in which a vote of confidence may be used." Bruce further recommended playing the card of the U.S.-U.K. special relationship to alarm the French. Could Secretary Dulles perhaps stop in London to talk to Churchill and Eden, he asked? The French might then think that the British and the Americans were concocting a "review of European affairs to possible French disadvantage"; this would make them "see the specter of a revived and exclusive Anglo-American alliance." "We have tried reason, persuasion, generosity, understanding, sympathy, patience," he added. "All have failed and I see no alternative but to deal with [the] French as cold-bloodedly as they deal with us." [114]

The secretary of state heeded Bruce's advice. He visited London and talked to Eden on 12 April. The next day MacArthur II called on Prime Minister Laniel in the evening at his private residence. Mrs. Laniel "sat quietly in another corner of the room" while the two men, who had worked together in the Resistance, discussed the EDC. If the French government did not fix a date for the debate on EDC by 15 April, warned MacArthur, the United States "would be obliged to go quietly ahead and work out alternative courses of action." He then metaphorically compared "the countries that were joined together in the collective enterprise of making Europe" to "a group of mountain climbers who were roped together." They now "had left the last resting camp and were attacking the peak," which was their very survival. "Halfway between the last camp and the peak one member of the group, France, suddenly refused to go forward or backward. It simply wished to camp on a ledge and remain there until it perished." Not only that, but it wished the other members of the group to perish with it. Neither the United States nor the other members of the group had any desire to perish with France, however, and MacArthur concluded that "the time had come when, if France would not budge, the rest of us must cut the rope and leave her on the ledge."[115] Dulles used less colorful language but reiterated essentially the same threat in his meeting with Bidault and Laniel, which MacArthur and Dillon also attended, on 14 April. "There could be no more unfortunate position for a free nation today than to stand alone and apart from the others," Dulles told his French interlocutors. If France did not bring the EDC to a vote soon, it would not only have deplorable consequences for France itself, but would also produce a chain reaction and provoke a return to American isolationism, which would in turn threaten the security of "the free world." Dulles struck a deal with Laniel: the United States would issue a declaration of assurances 36 hours after the French government had fixed the date of the debate.[116]

In accordance with their pledge, the Americans released a public text of their assurances on EDC on 16 April, after the French Cabinet decided to ask the National Assembly on 18 May to "take all action necessary so that the debate will take place immediately thereafter." A personal message from the president to the prime ministers of the six countries that had signed the EDC treaty preceded the public release on 15 April; the message was addressed to all of the signatories of the EDC to avoid giving the impression that it was aimed solely at the French and also to indirectly bolster the chances of ratification in Italy.[117] The State Department directed American officials in Europe to convince their European colleagues that the assurances were not just a restatement of old American policy but also contained new commitments, including an "explicit commitment" to the forward strategy and a "formal commitment" by the United States if the EDC were ratified to maintain its fair share of forces in Europe as long as a threat to Europe existed.[118] The pledge was not finite in time; it thus answered French concerns that NATO might lapse before the EDC but did not meet Bidault's demand for the retention of American forces in Europe at their current level for the next twenty years.

Assurances notwithstanding, what Laniel and Bidault needed most was American diplomatic and military support in Indochina. The Four-Power Conference on Korea and Indochina opened in Geneva on 26 April.[119] Four days earlier Dulles and Dillon had had a conversation with Bidault and French General Paul Ely on the EDC and Indochina. The French made a desperate plea for an American intervention to "save Dien Bien Phu." Yet the Americans were noncommittal and stood by their original position of refusing to intervene as long as the United Kingdom declined to participate as well. On the following day, Dulles informed Eisenhower that the chances of the EDC looked somewhat better, but he added that if Dien Bien Phu fell, the French government would "be taken over by defeatists."[120]

Dien Bien Phu fell on 7 May. Dillon realized that any efforts to force the EDC to a vote before the Indochina crisis was resolved would be fruitless. Indochina and the EDC were inextricably intertwined. "If we fail to reach agreement with [the] French for joint, effective and hopeful action in Indochina," telegraphed Dillon, "the Laniel government which is living on borrowed time granted by National Assembly in the hope that, thanks to United States support, an honorable solution can be reached at Geneva, will probably fall. A government pledged to peace in Indochina at any price is then likely and such a government is also likely to bury EDC for good."[121] Dillon proved right on most counts. On 12 June the Laniel government fell on a vote of confidence, 304–292, for its handling of the Indochina situation, and, ironically, for its alleged maneuvers to get an American intervention in Indochina.[122] The new prime minister, Pierre Mendès-France, continued linking Indochina and the EDC. If the Indochina crisis were settled and the Expeditionary Corps returned to France, he told the Americans, the French people would be more likely to vote positively on the EDC. He plainly indicated that he wished "the EDC vote to follow an Indochina settlement because of the enlarged prestige such a settlement would give him in the Assembly."[123] Despite his previous recommendation to avoid any attempts to force a vote on the EDC before the Indochina crisis was resolved, Dillon now became quite concerned over Mendès-France's tendency to put the EDC and Europe completely on the back burner until he reached a settlement on Indochina. The American ambassador to France felt some "shock" was needed to spur the French to consider the EDC problem, and sided with his colleague David Bruce in recommending not an exclusively American initiative, which would have been ill received in France, but rather a joint U.S.-U.K. initiative.

The Churchill-Eden visit to Washington in late June provided the opportunity to heed Dillon's advice. On 25 June, Eisenhower, Dulles, Merchant, and the American ambassador to the United Kingdom, Winthrop Aldrich, met their British colleagues at the White House. The president asked at what point action should be taken to preserve Germany in case the French continued their delaying tactics. Dulles answered that such point would come if the French Assembly failed to ratify the EDC before the summer holidays, which would further delay the entry into force of the Bonn Conventions and the restoration of German sovereignty, which were contingent on the ratification of the EDC. The Americans concurred with Eden: if sovereignty were not restored to Germany soon, Adenauer's policy of European cooperation would be jeopardized and his political position seriously undermined in Germany. The Soviet Union might then be able to "pull the Germans across the line."[124] An Anglo-American study group met in London from 5 July to 12 July to consider various options for improving West Germany's status if the EDC was not ratified in the very near future.

By mid-July the British and American ambassadors to France were instructed to approach the French Government and explain British and American motives in seeking to obtain authorizations for de-coupling the Bonn Conventions from the EDC treaty before Congress and the British Parliaments adjourned at the end of July. This would then enable the Americans and the British to immediately open formal negotiations with the French for separating the EDC from the Bonn Conventions in the fall should the EDC still not be ratified. A "short and simple agreement" to be concluded between the Four Powers who signed the Bonn Conventions would do the trick. With Adenauer's support, German rearmament would be deferred until ratification of the EDC. In approaching French Government officials to inform them of Anglo-French policy, the British and American Ambassadors were "to leave no doubt" that their countries continued supporting the EDC "in full force."[125] Yet supporting the EDC with "full force" did not mean being naive. Both Washington and London were actively considering alternatives to the EDC behind the scenes, although they agreed not to discuss them publicly. They similarly instructed their ambassadors not to reveal to the French the existence of tentative Four Power protocols drafted by the Anglo-American study group. Public knowledge of their existence, they calculated, might risk strengthening the position of French opponents to the EDC.[126]

A fervent believer in "personal contacts," Secretary Dulles then flew to Paris on 13 July to "talk things over on a basis of complete frankness and intimacy" with Mendès-France. Dulles proceeded to warn Mendès-France that any delay in French ratification of the EDC would play into the hands of the Soviet Union. The Soviet scheme was not only to "drive a wedge" between France and Germany but "also between the NATO powers." He emphasized that the EDC must be ratified and German sovereignty restored soon, or else the Soviet Union would continue to harass France in hopes of defeating the EDC and of achieving control over Germany. The United States, Dulles told Mendès-France, might also abandon the forward strategy in favor of a peripheral defense, if Congress were not satisfied soon that Germany would participate in West European defense. Admitting to being a "complete neophyte" in foreign affairs, and thanking Dulles for his "very frank statement," Mendès-France nevertheless set out to outline his strategy for ratification of the EDC. To him, the worst thing that could happen was "to put the EDC to a vote and have it turned down," this "would represent a Soviet victory of the first magnitude and would be a disaster for France, NATO and Western unity." Mendès-France wanted a substantial majority for the EDC in the Assembly, even if this meant postponing the vote further. As Dulles pointed out that key American states had ratified the Constitution by only one vote, Mendès countered that a slender majority would not do since the treaty would then have to face the Council of the Republic "where there was a tremendous majority against it." The only hope for overriding the council would then be to obtain an absolute majority of 314 votes in the Assembly, and such votes were clearly not at hand for the time being.[127]

During the ensuing weeks, Mendès-France's tactics increasingly worried Dulles. In early August Bruce and Dillon reported that Mendès-France envisaged "substantial changes"[128] in the treaty to make it more palatable to the assembly. In fact, the changes he contemplated were indeed substantial. From 19 August to 22 August, the six EDC foreign ministers met in Brussels to consider the new *protocole d'application* Mendès-France had presented to them just prior to the conference. The *protocole* essentially aimed at eliminating the supranational character of the EDC by giving each member country a veto right for a period of eight years, which would have effectively paralyzed the EDC.[129] Dillon wrote the State Department that the French proposals were "unacceptable beyond our worst expectations." The State Department was in complete agreement, especially since the proposals also contained severe discriminations against Germany.[130] The Brussels Conference adjourned in failure when Mendès-France rejected the counterproposals that Belgian Foreign Minister Spaak presented on behalf of France's partners. This did not inspire hope for the chances of the ratification debate which finally opened on 28 August in the French Assembly.

The day the Brussels Conference ended, Churchill wrote Dulles that he planned to urge Mendès-France to "stake his political fame on getting EDC through." "Code name" was " 'Bite' like old times." Dulles answered, "Am greatly cheered by your message. Let us 'bite' hard and I think we should get something not only digestible but invigorating."[131] Dulles's hopes soon collapsed. Mendès-France, despite previous affirmations to Dulles that he was a fervent advocate of European unity, made clear that, at the very least, he was not a staunch advocate of the EDC when he refrained from taking sides in favor of the EDC treaty that he presented to the assembly on 29 August. Even though he had written Dulles that he planned to "make plain" to Mendès-France "the awful consequences which might follow a flop,"[132] Churchill showed that he was only too eager to give up on the EDC and short-circuit Dulles in favor of a NATO solution. Towards the end of the Brussels Conference the British prime minister prepared a top-secret note for the Foreign Office and the Ministry of Defense in which he recommended study of a plan for bringing West Germany into NATO. Should France veto the plan, there would be "a new N.A.T.O., if necessary without the French." As for the Americans, "they ought to have seen that EDC was hopeless a year ago."[133] Shortly afterwards the Joint Chiefs of Staff confirmed that the only acceptable alternative to EDC was to bring West Germany into NATO. They also insisted that French participation was vital to the plan. France had to remain part of NATO, for a neutral France would deny the use of her territory to the new NATO powers and deprive them of ports, airfields, transportation facilities, communication facilities, and, above all, French forces, which the British were not prepared to replace by stationing additional forces on the Continent.

On 23 August, Churchill met with Mendès-France in London. Mendès-France told him that "he was absolutely sure that the Chamber would not agree to EDC." Churchill felt "very sorry for him" and told him somewhat unconvincingly that "France would never get so good a bargain with Germany as they had got in E.D.C." Churchill seemed much heartened, however, when discovering to his great surprise that "Mendès-France himself was much keener about NATO." Writing to Dulles, Churchill implied that Mendès-France was riding on the heels of "the deep feeling in France that in E.D.C. they will be bound up in civil and military affairs with the much more active and powerful West Germany, whereas in the N.A.T.O system the United Kingdom and the United States of America counter-balance Germany to her proper proportions."[134] Churchill thought nothing should be done before the debate in the French Assembly took place.

Bruce made a last ditch attempt to continue applying pressure on France through joint U.K.-U.S. action to save the EDC, but his initiative met with strong British resistance. Bruce strongly recommended convening a new meeting of the six EDC foreign ministers at British and American initiative and with U.S. and U.K. participation. The main objective of the meeting would be to demonstrate once again France's isolation from its partners on EDC after Brussels, thereby forcing anti-EDC elements in France to reassess their positions. The British retorted that there was no need to repeat the Brussels Conference, where French isolation had already come in full view. A new conference with U.K.-U.S. participation could in fact run the risk of strengthening the opponents of the EDC instead of weakening them. If France was being bullied by its partners even prior to the signing of the EDC, they argued at the time of the Brussels Conference, why sign the treaty at all? A new conference would only comfort them in this line of thought. Dillon backed Bruce's proposal, and Eisenhower and Acting Secretary Smith were tempted to approve it, yet the Americans ultimately bowed to the British and decided to wait until the ratification debate took place.[135]

Predictably, the EDC died on 30 August. Shortly afterwards Eden suggested that Dulles convene a nine-power meeting in London with British and American participation. Having long busied themselves with finding alternatives to the EDC, the British now wished to move swiftly to put forward their own proposal for admitting the Federal Republic to NATO before the Americans took the initiative. In any event, the Americans preferred to defer to the British. Not only did they not have much of an alternative of their own to propose, but American leadership was so resented in Europe that Dulles finally concluded that a European-sponsored plan might have a better chance of succeeding than a plan sponsored by the Americans. The United States, he told Eden, would be at the conference as "a friend and counselor and was deeply interested in the results but looked to the Europeans to put forward proposals."[136]

The result was the revival of the Brussels Treaty and the revamping of the Western Union into the Western European Union (WEU), enlarged to include Italy and Germany. Notwithstanding its new European label, the WEU was entirely devoted to NATO both in structure and strategy, which enabled Germany's allies to control its air and naval production and to put a cap on its manufacture of nuclear and chemical weapons. In exchange for accepting such controls, West Germany regained sovereignty and became a member of NATO. By the end of December 1954, the French had ratified all of the treaties and protocols of the new accords. About four months later, on 5 May 1955, the Western allies recognized the Federal Republic of Germany. Four days after that, Germany was accepted as a member of NATO.

Dulles's first reaction to the rejection of the EDC was anger and despair. In a press release following the defeat of the EDC, the secretary of state called the French rejection of the EDC "a saddening event." The first draft of his statement read "grave event." Believing such a tone of bitterness would further endanger American leadership in Europe, Walt Butterworth, then America's deputy chief of mission in London, persuaded Dulles to tone down his "lament on the death of EDC." The final product blamed French nationalism and communism while summoning, once again, the specter of American isolationism: "The French rejection of the European Defense Community is a saddening event . . . The French negative action, without the provision of any alternative, obviously imposes on the United States the obligation to reappraise its foreign policies, particularly those in relation to Europe . . . It is a tragedy that in one country nationalism, abetted by communism, has asserted itself so as to endanger the whole of Europe."[137]

Dulles's next reaction was to criticize the Eden Plan for not being sufficiently supranational and to evoke not only French responsibility in the fall of EDC but also that of the British. He even asked Adenauer whether he thought that Eden was perhaps a neutralist. Monnet did nothing to contradict him. About two weeks after the defeat of the EDC, he informed Dulles through David Bruce that he viewed the British suggestion of transforming the Brussels Treaty "as a camouflage and dangerous decoy because it would give [the] impression that European unity can be achieved without transferring powers of decision to common institutions." What was needed was a European solution and a European initiative. Paul-Henri Spaak of Belgium thought likewise. He entertained Dulles in his illusion that a supranational solution was still possible after all and that the EDC was not really dead and could perhaps be resurrected by banking on the salutary effect that the fear of imminent German rearmament would have on France. Monnet concurred: the EDC was not dead, only "sorely wounded," and all that was needed now was to leave the way open to reexamine an EDC arrangement in the future. Under no circumstances would he accept the re-creation of a German national army and the return of nationalism and dissensions to Europe. If need be, Monnet told Adenauer, Dulles, and Bruce, he would announce his intention not to seek a renewal of his mandate as president of the High Authority "in order to be able to act freely" and "fight any understanding productive of a German national army."[138]

Meanwhile, Dulles rushed to Bonn on 16 September to strengthen the faltering prestige of his old friend Adenauer in his own country and to reassure him that the United States had not given up on restoring sovereignty to West Germany. He then bypassed Paris on his way to London, thereby snubbing the French for failing to ratify the EDC. The trip to Bonn greatly heartened the chancellor, and sealed a deep friendship between the two men.[139] Not so with Eden: Dulles's initiative did nothing but disrupt Eden's carefully orchestrated tour of European capitals that promoted his ready-made substitute for the EDC. The chancellor, who had shown earlier every inclination to accept Eden's plan, now sided with Dulles. A 17 September communiqué by Adenauer and Dulles did not even mention Eden's proposal for a nine-power conference. It did however amply pay tribute to European integration, a great objective that "should not be abandoned because of a single defeat." Dulles did, perhaps, not do much to back Eden's initiative, but his visit to Adenauer had at least the merit that it succeeded in introducing Washington's new rhetoric into the communiqué.

Just after the fall of EDC, Butterworth had written Assistant Secretary of State for European Affairs Merchant insisting that Dulles's bitterness might hinder "the cause of European integration—which we must not think of as dead because EDC has been defeated." Eisenhower concurred: "We cannot sit down in black despair and admit defeat,"[140] he wrote his close friend and colleague, Walter Bedell Smith. Heeding Eisenhower's opinion, Dulles now turned away from bitterness and approached Congress with a positive attitude. After attempting to infuse a dose of supranationalism in Eden's plan, the secretary of state shifted to a strategy of attempting to diminish the impact of the defeat of the EDC by pointing to the supranational elements of the treaty that had been salvaged through the Western European Union agreements, no doubt with the intention of appeasing Congress.[141]

The EDC debacle had indeed prompted senators and representatives alike to reassess the efficiency and legitimacy of the tactics of American diplomacy. During the spring, Congress had strongly favored reenacting the Richards amendment, and it finally settled in mid-June on a compromise that prevented delivery of arms to Italy and France, which had not yet ratified the treaties, while permitting delivery to those countries that had already ratified.[142] Deeply disappointed with the failure of their tactics for helping EDC ratification, Congress now criticized the administration, and particularly American diplomats, for failing to anticipate the defeat of the EDC. Dulles's frequent trips to Europe and the blatant failure of the administration to provide a viable alternative to the EDC, when the odds against its success were high, were severely criticized. Writing a report for American senators after the EDC débacle, Brigadier General Julius Klein blamed Dulles's expeditions for lulling Europeans into a false sense that the United States would step in and solve what were essentially European problems.[143]

3

After the EDC:
New Hopes and New Tactics

EUROPEAN INTEGRATION UNDER SCRUTINY

After the EDC débacle, the State Department engaged in a reexamination of its policy towards Europe and decided to keep supporting European integration while adopting more discreet tactics than in the past. Though the rejection of the EDC was "a setback and not a defeat for the idea of European integration," it now remained to ensure that the setback indeed did not turn into outright defeat. Supporters of European integration in the administration quickly moved to show American support for "the unifying forces and institutions within Europe" and concentrated their efforts on the ECSC as the most "advanced action towards integration" and "a rallying point for those upholding the idea of a united Europe."[1] Intent on using every opportunity to bolster the ECSC, the State Department welcomed the renewed interest of the British to become associated with the ECSC as a token of their intention to associate more closely with the Continent and to help European federation gain political acceptance in Europe.[2]

Despite the support of top officials in the State Department and the White House for the ECSC as the best avenue towards European integration, its activities were being scrutinized by those members of the administration that entertained some doubts regarding its compatibility with American interests. In the fall of 1954 a depressed American coal industry did not look with favor on European restrictions on imports of American coal.[3] If restrictive practices were being pursued within the framework of the ECSC, some pointed out, then the United States, by its recent loan of $100 million to the Community, would in effect have indirectly sanctioned these practices. In

February 1955, Joseph M. Dodge, Chairman of the Council on Foreign Economic Policy (CFEP), which coordinated foreign economic policy matters among the various executive agencies, sent a memorandum to the State Department describing cartel developments in the ECSC and asking whether the United States should not revise its policy towards the Community in light of those developments. State proceeded to find a convincing line of defense for the ECSC and handed in its response to Dodge's memo by mid-March.

There was no denying it: there did exist restrictive arrangements both in the steel and coal industries of the ECSC. Its steel producers had indeed established a cartel to set minimum prices for exports from the ECSC. Yet, insisted the State Department, producers had done so without the approval of the Community, and the agreement did not involve an allocation of markets. Also, if the Community had so far felt unable to take action against the cartel, it was not because it sanctioned its existence, but because of the limitation of the ECSC Treaty's anticartel provisions, which could take effect only if the export cartel had a detrimental impact on intra-ECSC competition. Could the agreement between the ECSC and the United Kingdom be instrumental in establishing restrictive agreements on prices? The State Department answered with a pirouette: yes the agreement could possibly be used for such a purpose, but this was neither the spirit nor the letter of the ECSC Treaty or, for that matter, of the agreement itself, which "was entered into primarily to strengthen the political significance of the ECSC and to give impetus to the movement towards European unity."

Another point raised by the CFEP memorandum concerned exclusive scrap importing arrangements between the OCCF (Office Commun des Consommateurs de Ferraille), a private scrap organization primarily responsible for ECSC scrap imports, and certain privileged American scrap dealers. The very existence of the OCCF within the Community seemed to go against antitrust law, while its exclusive purchasing arrangements with only two or three large American producers placed small American producers at a disadvantage. The State Department countered with another pirouette: the scrap import purchasing arrangements were temporary; they were a response to the specific problems encountered within the ECSC because of the removal of trade barriers. The State Department ended its memo on an optimistic note. The ECSC Treaty contained provisions against restrictive practices that "while quite analogous to U.S. antitrust legislation, [were] completely unprecedented in Europe." They pointed "the way for other efforts in Europe to encourage more competitive and dynamic economics."[4] What was needed was a little more time, patience, and encouragement on the part of the United States to help Europe develop a competitive market.

With this the ECSC's case rested; it would be constantly reopened. By the end of the year, though, there seemed to be a consensus within the administration that the ECSC was doing the best it could given the circumstances. Its efforts in breaking up the "GEORG" coal cartel, which controlled the sale and allocation of all Ruhr coal, as well as its success in eliminating other obstacles to trade, were listed in its favor. Yet the administration kept consulting privately with the High Authority on ways to take more efficient action against restrictive practices. In the last analysis, the crux of the matter was the willingness of the administration, particularly the State Department, to tolerate some restrictive practices in the short term, while expecting further trade liberalization of European markets and awaiting further progress in Europe towards supranationality in the long term.

The same spirit presided over the conclusion of another issue: the potential imposition of restrictions on the export of American steel scrap to the ECSC. By March 1955 steel production from the Community had almost doubled. In August the Commerce Department noted that the Community now provided 60 to 65 percent of world steel exports. This production boom did not worry American producers much, since they exported less than 4 percent of their production and were not so much interested in direct steel exports as in indirect exports of manufactured products, such as cars. Only over the Latin-American market did any real conflicts of interest occur, but they were not substantial enough to provoke outright hostility on the part of the steel producers. Yet expanded output in the Community also had the side effect of increasing ECSC's demand for American scrap for steel production in considerable proportions, thereby provoking price increases that directly affected American steel producers. Facing growing complaints, the administration was forced to address the issue. In this specific instance, the State Department was pitted against all of the other agencies of the interdepartmental Advisory Committee on Export Policy, which favored imposing quantitative export controls on scrap. In June 1955 the State Department and the American mission to the ECSC enjoyed a temporary victory when the secretary of commerce agreed to leave export controls on steel scrap at their current levels. An official letter from President of the High Authority Monnet to Secretary Dulles played no small role in this victory.

On 17 March Monnet wrote Dulles an unequivocal letter in which he drew attention to the dire consequences that might follow the imposition of quotas on scrap exports to the ECSC. Faced with a serious shortage, the Community would then have no other option but to establish "a system of allocation and quotas which would restore national markets for scrap." This might jeopardize "the free operation of the common market for steel," and set back European economic integration. Monnet emphasized the key link "between steel production within the Community and the defense efforts of the member states of the Community." Slowing down steel production within the Six would impair "the high level of general economic activity" that underlay "increased standards of investment and consumption in Western Europe" and contributed to stable economic conditions in the West.[5] Thus, not only were European integration and the prospects for a free market in Europe at risk (and implicitly, outlets for American producers) but also the military contribution of key American allies to the defense of the West and the very foundation of western stability—economic viability. The point was well taken; Monnet's letter seemed to rehash the very rhetoric that the administration had developed in favor of European integration and served his specific goal of preventing the imposition of quantitative restrictions on the export of American scrap.

Monnet then sent an emissary to Washington to make his point even clearer. The choice fell on Albert Coppé, second vice-president of the High Authority, who expanded on the arguments contained in Monnet's letter and conscientiously answered the queries of officials from the State, Commerce, and Treasury departments, the Foreign Operations Administration, and the Export-Import Bank. Coppé agreed that the steel industry of the ECSC was currently overly dependent on the use of scrap. This, he said, might be remedied in the future by increasing the use of pig iron instead of scrap in the steel making process, but it would take time to make the conversion. Hence, he could only emphasize that the ECSC badly needed a continued flow of American scrap to maintain its steel production at a high level.[6] Assistant Secretary of State for Economic Affairs Samuel Waugh and his staff, as well as the Office of European Regional Affairs and Acting U.S. Representative to the ECSC Robert Eisenberg, then acted to support Monnet's conclusions, which found a receptive ear with the president himself. The Commerce Department, as well as other agencies, ultimately had to yield to both the State Department and the White House. In August the Commerce Department attempted to reopen discussions on the imposition of an export quota on ferrous scrap and semifinished steel products. Dulles quickly briefed Eisenhower, who declined to give his approval to an export quota on steel scrap. The issue was settled that same month at a CFEP meeting, where it was agreed that the current situation did not warrant the imposition of export controls. To calm the apprehension of the Commerce Department, the CFEP added that "steps to protect the availability of the domestic scrap supply" would be taken in case "a more serious situation" developed.[7] Once again, to the detriment of immediate American economic interests, the administration ended up siding with the proponents of European integration. Yet the EDC débacle signaled a setback for the cause of European integration in the administration, and a much deeper disappointment outside government circles.

For a while Dulles himself appeared somewhat hesitant to heed Monnet's suggestions, the more so since his friend seemed to have moved out of the public eye. On 9 November Monnet told a special meeting of the members of the High Authority of his decision not to seek the renewal of his mandate as their president. The next day he sent a letter to each foreign minister of the six ECSC member states. On 30 November, in a speech before the Parliamentary Assembly of the ECSC, Monnet recognized that "the decision to transfer new powers to European institutions depended on parliaments and governments. The stimulus would thus have to come from outside." Hence his decision to work with forces on the outside, mainly political parties and unions, to further the cause of European integration. Monnet's unexpected announcement caused some turmoil in Europe. On 1 December, the ECSC Assembly unanimously adopted a resolution that encouraged Monnet to reconsider his decision, but Monnet persisted.[8] Dulles was equally dumbfounded by Monnet's move and expressed "deepest regret" at his action for he believed that "the Community in this formative stage" would have benefited from Monnet's wise leadership.[9] The Frenchman was in turn pained by David Bruce's decision in the fall to terminate his current assignment, and he pleaded with Dulles to keep Tomlinson in his post as deputy United States representative to the ECSC. Monnet also urged Dulles to keep the American representation to the High Authority separate from European intergovernmental organizations, such as NATO or the OEEC, as a confirmation of the American commitment to the supranational, as opposed to the intergovernmental, approach. Unfortunately, in this specific instance, Dulles did not oblige his friend: the administration, he wrote Monnet in December, had not yet reached a decision on whether to keep the American representation to the Community separate from that to other intergovernmental organizations.[10] David Bruce resigned in January 1955, and was not replaced until 1956, when Walton Butterworth succeeded him as United States representative to the ECSC, with the rank of ambassador. By then what was popularly known as the "Relaunching of Europe" was well on its way.

RENEWED COMMITMENTS: THE RELAUNCHING OF EUROPE

In mid-April 1955 the acting representative to the ECSC reported on a conversation he had just had with Jean Monnet, who was still president of the High Authority. Mendès-France's Cabinet had fallen on 6 February 1955, which made it impossible to have a meeting of foreign ministers to designate a successor to Monnet until a new cabinet was constituted. The

ECSC Treaty specified that the president of the High Authority could not leave his post until a successor had been designated. Monnet accordingly had to stay on longer than he had anticipated. But by April Monnet seemed to have second thoughts on leaving the presidency. Progress towards a united Europe could be expected from the Six in the near future, he told an American. Plans were currently being discussed for extending "the scope of the CSC by bringing fuel oil and electric power under the jurisdiction of the High Authority, and by working out a separate organizational framework for the integration of transportation and atomic energy within the six countries. A single legislative Assembly and Court of Justice would continue to serve the enlarged Community." A decision on whether or not to proceed with further integration was to be reached at the next meeting of the ECSC Council of Ministers around 18 April, he continued. Both Chancellor Adenauer and French Foreign Minister Antoine Pinay had asked him "to remain as President of the High Authority to take charge of the extension of the Community." Monnet had agreed to do so if the six governments were truly willing to proceed with further integration and gave him "the necessary mandate." He did not wish the United States to become involved at this stage or to contact the foreign offices of the Six; this, he said, "might have unfavorable effects."[11] Little did Monnet's American listener know that he was speaking of nothing less than the preparation of the Messina Conference in June, which was to lead to the signing of the Rome Treaties and the creation of the European Economic Community and Euratom within about two years.

After the defeat of the EDC, Monnet and other protagonists of European integration sought to bring new life to their cause. Most agreed that European integration, to have the best chance of succeeding, now needed to be pursued in the economic field, thus paving the way for later political and military integration. Both Jean Monnet and Belgian Minister of Foreign Affairs Paul-Henri Spaak initially came out in favor of extending the authority of the ECSC to pursue integration in "limited but decisive fields."[12] In September 1954 the Belgian and Dutch administrations set out to study how this might be done. By December the Common Assembly of the ECSC proposed enlarging the ECSC to transportation as well as to other energy sources such as gas, electricity, and the atom.[13] Atomic energy seemed by far to be the most promising area for integration, so much so that Monnet thought it might need a separate organization.[14] Louis Armand, then president of the SNCF, and a gifted engineer, was largely responsible for arousing Monnet's enthusiasm for the creation of what later came to be known as Euratom. Armand expected to obtain substantial help for the project from the United States within the framework of the "Atoms for Peace" program recently launched by Eisenhower.

By 1953 the McMahon Act, which established the American policy of unilaterally denying nuclear technology even to wartime allies of the United States, looked increasingly obsolete. The Soviet Union had detonated its first nuclear weapon in 1949, and the United Kingdom had followed on its heels in 1952. To meet the challenge, the Eisenhower administration set out to maintain the lead in the nuclear field by developing the peaceful applications of nuclear technology. On 8 December 1953 President Eisenhower addressed the delegates of the United Nations General Assembly. He proposed that the Soviet Union and the United States contribute normal uranium and fissionable materials to an International Atomic Energy Agency (IAEA) under the surveillance of the United Nations. The fissionable material "would be allocated to serve the peaceful pursuits of mankind. Experts would be mobilized to apply atomic energy to the needs of agriculture, medicine, and other peaceful activities. A special purpose would be to provide abundant electrical energy to the power-starved areas of the world."[15] By July 1957 Eisenhower's proposal came into being with the creation of the IAEA in Vienna. The debate over the modification of the McMahon Act that followed Eisenhower's speech was contemporaneous with discussions of the ratification of the EDC. The 1954 Atomic Energy Act allowed the private sector in the United States to engage in the construction of nuclear plants both at home and abroad and permitted the sale of patents and fissile materials to other countries.[16] The United States proceeded to sell enriched uranium for nuclear plants abroad via bilateral agreements. Included, notably, were some of the six members of the ECSC.

Louis Armand, who had earlier written a report for the OEEC on Europe's future energy needs, understood the advantages that Europe and European integration could reap from the recent shift in American policy in the nuclear field. An atomic EDC, which would benefit from American technology and British cooperation, he told Monnet, would launch Europe on the road to independence both in the energy and in the military fields.[17] Western European nations were becoming more and more wary of their excessive dependence on energy imports. Expanded coal production was not likely to meet growing energy needs in Europe, with the result that Europeans would have to foot an increasingly expensive bill in oil imports. Mastering nuclear technology and channeling the power of the atom to meet energy needs in Europe through a European Atomic Energy Community would prevent this from happening. Experts hoped that nuclear energy would be competitive with classic thermic and water plants by 1965. After talking to Monnet, Armand tried to sell his project to Edgar Faure, whose Cabinet had replaced that of Mendès-France on 23 February.

Seduced by Armand's idea, Monnet decided to make the atom the engine for the relaunching of Europe. To him, nuclear energy offered great prospects for helping the cause of European integration. Except for France, nuclear industry virtually did not exist on the Continent. Contrary to other sectors in Europe, there were as yet no vested interests in the field of the peaceful uses of atomic energy: one could thus start with a clean slate. In April, acting as Monnet's emissary, Albert Coppé told Americans that a European Community for atomic energy would "identify the Community with the power of the future and capture the public imagination."[18] Monnet anticipated yet other gains from this atomic community. Such a community, he felt, would also prevent the Germans from developing an independent nuclear industry. They had perhaps renounced the manufacture of nuclear weapons, yet one could not guarantee that the Federal Republic of Germany would not one day decide to go from peaceful uses of nuclear energy to military uses. The best way of avoiding this, thought Monnet, would be to control German nuclear industry through Euratom and its member states. Intent on having the Germans participate in Euratom on an equal basis with the other members, however, Monnet insisted that the new community must be exclusively limited to the peaceful uses of nuclear energy. This was also the demand of the German socialists, who later made German participation in Euratom contingent on preventing the creation of a bomb in Europe. Monnet's stubborn opposition to using Euratom for military applications, and, indirectly, to helping build a French bomb, did not please the advocates of the French nuclear program, who threatened to have Monnet's new child suffer a fate similar to that of the EDC.

Satisfied with his plan for relaunching European integration both through a separate organization for atomic energy and the extension of the scope of the ECSC to new energy fields, Monnet set out to sell it to the Six. After the defeat of the EDC in France the initiative would have to come from any country but France. As always looking for a spokesman, Monnet chose Belgian Foreign Minister Paul-Henri Spaak to present his plan to the Six. A fervent Europeanist, Spaak cautiously awaited the propitious moment to present the proposal, so as not to run into French opposition. In March 1955, once France had ratified the Paris agreements, Spaak wrote a letter to Adenauer, French Foreign Minister Antoine Pinay, and Italian Foreign Minister Gaetano Martino in which he presented Monnet's proposal. Should they accept it, he explained, Monnet would agree to stay on as president of the High Authority. The proposal did not meet with the enthusiasm Spaak hoped for. The French were especially reticent. Edgar Faure, whose government included Gaullist ministers, did not look with favor on a new European initiative with supranational overtones, nor, for that matter, on maintaining "Mr. Europe" as the head of the High Authority. Both Faure and his foreign minister agreed that some new action was needed in the energy and transportation fields, but not necessarily by extending the authority of the ECSC, which to Gaullists was the epitome of supranationalism.

Fortunately, the Monnet/Spaak proposal met with more sympathy from Prime Minister Joseph Bech of Luxembourg and Johan William Beyen, who was minister of foreign affairs of the Netherlands with Joseph Luns. Yet Beyen preferred overall economic integration to the sectoral or functional approach advocated by Jean Monnet. The defunct European Political Community had included a proposal for a General Common Market, which largely originated from Beyen. The Dutchman now sought to bring it back to life. Writing to Spaak in early April, he criticized the sectoral approach for having "the tendency to solve problems in one sector to the detriment of other sectors or the interests of consumers" and "to lead to the exclusion of foreign competition." To him, the best avenue of integration was "to create a supranational community with the task of bringing about the economic integration of Europe in the general sense, reaching economic union by going through a customs union as a first stage."[19] Pierre Uri, one of Monnet's closest collaborators, assented, but for different reasons. The Germans, he argued, would prefer to negotiate with the Americans or the British to obtain nuclear technology rather than with their partners within the Six who did not yet have much to offer. It was an entirely different matter to build a Common Market on a six-country basis, which would then encompass a community for atomic energy: this the Germans would understand.[20]

On 21 April Beyen made his plan public before the council of the European movement. Spaak, who was originally somewhat fearful of such an ambitious scheme, was then forced to follow suit. The Benelux memorandum that Spaak, Beyen, and Bech subsequently presented to Monnet on 5 May was a careful blend of Monnet and Beyen's approaches towards European integration. There would be both a general Common Market and a series of sectoral initiatives in the fields of transportation and energy, with a special emphasis on the creation of an atomic community. By 9 May, Monnet had told the ECSC Assembly that he viewed the sectoral and the overall approaches as equally valid and mutually non-exclusive. Five days later the Assembly unanimously adopted a resolution asking the foreign ministers of the Six to appoint an intergovernmental committee to draft new treaties for further European integration. The stage was set for the Messina Conference.[21]

From 1 June to 3 June 1955, the foreign ministers of the Six met at Messina, Italy, under the leadership of Joseph Bech. The atmosphere was one of gloom. Heeding French demands, the Six first proceeded to replace Monnet as the head of the High Authority with René Mayer, a former *Président du Conseil*. The Benelux memorandum then served as a starting point for discussing options for relaunching European integration. The final communiqué of the conference espoused the memorandum in its essentials and called for further European economic integration through common institutions. An intergovernmental committee was appointed to translate intentions into specific agreements and treaties. Both the sectoral- and the common-market approaches were to be studied. Shortly after Messina, Spaak was chosen to head the intergovernmental committee. Committees and subcommittees were then set up to explore possible avenues of economic integration. Unsatisfied with the work of the committees, which emphasized technical difficulties rather than formulating a single plan, Spaak gathered a small group of experts in which Hans von der Groeben and Pierre Uri, with his extraordinary writing skills, both played leading roles. In the spring of 1956, after a short stay on the French Riviera, the team produced a report that Spaak approved, and which was then used as a basis for negotiating the Rome Treaty. In its essentials, the Spaak report advocated the focus of functional integration on atomic energy. Other sectors such as oil, electricity, gas, and transportation were found less promising. As for overall integration, the report favored the creation of a customs union with a common external tariff as opposed to the realization of a free trade area, which was deemed less conducive to real economic integration.[22]

The report was a compromise among divergent perspectives. The French held a clear preference for Euratom, in which they hoped to play a prominent role while also controlling the Germans. They were not so keen about the creation of a general common market, in which they feared competition from their neighbors, the more so since their price levels were much higher than some of their partners. Not so with the Germans, who favored overall economic integration and would have preferred to deal bilaterally with the United States or the United Kingdom instead of Euratom in obtaining nuclear technology for the creation of their own nuclear industry. Because of their export-oriented economies, the Benelux countries also supported the idea of a common market. On the other hand, the Belgians were not so favorable to Euratom: they preferred to continue selling Congolese uranium to the United States rather than supplying it to Euratom.

The Messina Conference received a lukewarm reception in the United States. At that point, European integration seemed to much of the American public and also to a substantial part of Congress to have an uncertain future: Jean Monnet, the "father of Europe," the symbol of European unity in the United States, had recently lost the presidency of the High Authority to René Mayer. Despite Mayer's close personal links with Bruce, Dulles, and Walter Bedell Smith, his election at Messina to replace Monnet was perceived in the United States as a setback for European unity and a personal blow to Monnet.[23] In the months following Messina other developments seemed to portend further setbacks for the "Europeanists." In October 1955 the people of the Saar rejected its Europeanization, favoring instead the region's return to Germany. The next month Great Britain withdrew its representative from the Brussels deliberations on European integration.

Notwithstanding these developments, the Eisenhower administration showed considerably more interest in the future of European unity than it publicly displayed. Despite the apparent disenchantment with European integration, best symbolized by Bruce's resignation in January 1955 and Dulles's initial noncommittal reaction to Monnet's plea for a separate mission to the ECSC, the State Department, and particularly the Office of European Regional Affairs, continued to support European integration, although they refrained from expressing such support publicly. They did this for two main reasons. There was a lack of agreement within the State Department and among U.S. representatives abroad on what was meant by "European integration." Should the ECSC approach be favored over looser cooperative arrangements, such as the OEEC, some asked? Also, the defeat of the EDC had taught American "Europeanists" that it was best for the United States to speak with a soft voice. As a matter of strategy the United States therefore tried to refrain from making too many public comments on European integration, except when asked to do so by Europeans. This attitude continued to be encouraged by prominent European figures like Spaak and Monnet until well after Messina. In November 1955, Bruce, who had left the State Department in February and now served as consultant, reported that he had asked both Spaak and Monnet whether the United States "should become more active." Their reaction was "most emphatic that we should continue to stay entirely in the background."[24] Meanwhile, the State Department exploited every opportunity to demonstrate its support for the CSC.

Upon René Mayer's accession to the presidency of the High Authority, Dulles sent him a letter wishing him success in his new job and hailing the ECSC for "its pioneering achievements" in encouraging the cause of European integration.[25] Dulles then flew Assistant Secretary Waugh to Luxembourg to meet with Mayer, who seized on the opportunity to tout the merits of keeping American representation to the ECSC separate from that to an organization with military applications such as NATO. The Community, he said, should not be "associated with any organization with a military color," for this would preclude neutral countries such as Switzerland or Austria from being associated with it at a later stage of its development. While in Luxembourg, Samuel Waugh also stopped by to see his good friend Jean Monnet, whom he was surprised to find "downright happy over the opportunity he now ha[d] to work for better government in France, and to speak more freely on his favorite subject—United States of Europe." Commenting on the visit to his friend and colleague Walter Bedell Smith, Waugh added: "Undoubtedly you are right, though, underneath it all he cannot help but be unhappy over the action of his own government. I still think he is a big man." Dulles also thought Monnet was a big man but deplored his being sidetracked by the French government. In talking to Adenauer in the United States shortly after Messina, the secretary "expressed regret that his friend Monnet was no longer in a position to help" in the area of European integration.[26]

Despite efforts from the State Department to show American support for the ECSC, it took about ten months after Bruce's resignation in January 1955 for the United States to offer tangible proof of its renewed commitment to European integration. The official manifestation of that commitment came on 10 October 1955. On that day the State Department announced Eisenhower's decision to establish a separate American mission to the ECSC as a token of the importance the United States attached to the Community. Walton Butterworth was later appointed to the position with the special rank of ambassador, which further demonstrated American interest in the Community.[27] In this particular instance, Monnet and Mayer's pleas for a separate American representation to the ECSC were critical in convincing Dulles and his advisers to support the idea. Yet it was Eisenhower's influence that ultimately prompted Dulles to go along with Monnet's proposal for the creation of a European atomic energy pool after the pattern of the ECSC. Monnet also showed his American friends that he was not inactive, even though he no longer held an official position.

When returning to the United States after meeting with Monnet and Mayer, Waugh carried in his suitcase a few copies of a collection of Monnet's speeches, *Les Etats-Unis d'Europe ont commencé*. Monnet had asked him to deliver them to his close friends in the United States government, including the president. Eisenhower later thanked Monnet both for the book and for his expressions of friendship, which Waugh had transmitted to him on Monnet's behalf, and assured him that they were "fully reciprocated."[28] Monnet's negotiating skills and persuasive power then succeeded in convincing Ambassador Dillon, Dulles, and the president of the importance of his Action Committee for a United States of Europe, whose creation he proudly announced on 13 October 1955. Dulles decided to resume his association with Monnet, even though his friend no longer occupied an official position.

Yet the secretary remained cool towards the idea of a European atomic pool, for he did not know what form it would take: would it be an atomic CSC? Would it be a private enterprise? Dulles was not sure and refrained from committing the United States to support it until he had more information. Talking to German Foreign Minister von Brentano in late September, Dulles told him the United States was "sympathetic" towards the idea of a European atomic pool but "until European plans were made more precise" they did not wish to commit themselves "to something which was unknown and which might not be possible under present legislation."[29] The next month, shortly after the Action Committee became a reality, Dulles met with Monnet in Paris at his request. They met again in December. During the first meeting, Monnet explained his efforts and those of his associates to establish a European pool for the peaceful use of atomic energy and informed Dulles of his committee's intention to adopt a resolution on a European Atomic Commission after the pattern of the ECSC in January 1956. Monnet asked for the Eisenhower administration's backing of his initiative, notably for dealing with the British but also with the Germans. He was indeed much preoccupied with the possibility that the Germans might never sign or ratify the Euratom Treaty if the United States agreed to sign bilateral treaties with Germany. Would Dulles please try to delay the bilaterals? Dulles assured him that the United States intended to work with a European atomic agency "to the maximum extent possible," but he added that this would depend on what form it would take. By December, Dulles was much more committed to Euratom and promised "he would do what he could with [the] Germans and [the] British."[30] Although Monnet was instrumental in securing Dulles's backing for what later became Euratom, it was Eisenhower's steadfast support for European integration that ultimately forced him to take a closer look at Monnet and Armand's initiative.

At the 267th National Security meeting at Camp David, Maryland, the president referred to his speech before the English Speaking Union in London four years earlier and renewed his vows for a united Europe. He strongly encouraged members of the NSC to publicly stress "the great advantages of a more nearly united Europe—cultural, economic, moral, and otherwise." The next day, on 22 November 1955, Dulles sought to remedy his relative ignorance about the prospects for the peaceful use of atomic energy in Europe and asked Under Secretary Hoover to try to give him a clearer picture of the situation. The result was a 6 December memorandum, prepared in the Office of European Regional Affairs, on European integration and the peaceful uses of atomic energy. Assistant Secretary of State Merchant lost no time in sending it to Gerard Smith, the secretary of state's special assistant for atomic affairs, commenting that he now considered the issue "as primarily your pigeon." The next day Dulles publicly reaffirmed his support for European integration in a speech in Chicago.[31] Three days later he sent a letter to Foreign Secretary Harold Macmillan that gave the full measure of American support for the six-nations approach and its ramifications, including those in the nuclear area.

DEFINING "EUROPEAN INTEGRATION"

By the end of May 1955, just prior to Messina, the State Department and American representatives abroad had finally reached a consensus on a definition of European integration: "supranational authority and responsibility . . . arrangements less binding were merely cooperative." The ECSC approach "pav[ed] the way for the truly integrated association, politically, economically and otherwise, of member countries, and especially Germany and France, upon which [the] long term welfare, strength, and security of [the] Atlantic Community may well depend." On the other hand, the Western European Union did not "appear to [the] Department to offer promise of accelerating integration in this sense." As for the OEEC, it was an "institution designed [to] maximize effective cooperative arrangements, and only over [a] very extended period of time, if ever, [was] it apt to become [the] framework for arrangements involving waivers of sovereignty in favor of [an] authority such as now existed for [the] CSC."[32] While there then existed an agreement on how to define European integration, there remained significant differences of opinion within the administration as to whether it was actually justified in assigning greater importance to the ECSC. Some pointed out that the political prospects of the ECSC and its possible offshoots did not necessarily warrant giving it that much attention. Was it not better to support looser associations such as the OEEC, which had a better chance of actually achieving something? By the end of the year, the administration clearly favored the six-nations approach. The reasons for this tendency to side with the Six were mostly anchored in old fears and old hopes.

As always, Germany occupied a central position in the mosaic of American strategy towards Europe. Creating an atomic authority for Europe offered the possibility not only of furthering European integration along the lines of true integration *á la Monnet* but also of forging "a new link between Germany and the West."[33] If the West failed to channel German energies and loyalties towards European integration, the ghost of German nationalism would reawaken, and the tendency to exploit East-West tensions would be great. In turn, German nationalism would then "breed predatory and competitive nationalism elsewhere in Western Europe, from which only the Soviet bloc could benefit."[34] The American government had long viewed European nationalism as the very antithesis of economic efficiency, and a threat to American security. This fear was now rendered more acute by apparent economic progress in the Soviet Union. Specifically, the State Department projected that "despite present surface evidence of recovery, boom, prosperity and growth in Western Europe, the USSR will, by 1975, have overtaken Western Europe's aggregate GNP, unless political and economic decisions are made to increase its power and accelerate its growth."[35] If Germany looked East, German economic power would fail to accrue to the West, and Soviet power would benefit. If Germany looked East, lacking the strong pull of a common European endeavor, the West would be weakened by competitive economic nationalism in Europe. A lack of unity and strength in the West would diminish its prestige in the eyes of developing nations, which would then cast their eyes towards the Communist bloc for leadership. Another scenario, in which all was well that ended well, corresponded to this rather dismal chain reaction.

Supporting new initiatives for European integration, and notably for the creation of a common atomic authority for Europe, offered the advantages of reviving the European movement and then anchoring Germany, the engine of European recovery, more closely to the West. It would also allow Europeans "to make the best use possible of their inadequate resources in this field."[36] The project would thus satisfy one of the most important requirements for the cohesion of the West, namely economic viability; more so, since progress in one field could then "set in motion ancillary and concomitant developments which would lead, over time, towards a real United States of Europe."[37] President Eisenhower himself concurred. It was of paramount importance to demonstrate to "all countries in Western Europe individually that each and every one would profit by the union of them all and that none would lose." The ultimate and desirable goal was to develop in Western Europe "a third power bloc, after which development the United States would be permitted to sit back and relax somewhat."[38] Instead of the disaggregation of the West, instead of having some European countries as well as developing countries look East, European unity would guarantee the cohesiveness of the "free world." For "a solid power mass in Western Europe would ultimately attract to it all the Soviet satellites, and the threat to peace would disappear."[39] The two scenarios, the bad one and the good one, were essentially symmetrical: economic power and political cohesion, be it in the West or in the East, would exert an irresistible pull and attract "protégés," or satellites, from the opposite sphere in the manner of dominoes. It now remained to ensure that the good scenario would take place; this involved supporting European integration while at the same time safeguarding American self-interest.

The British could potentially play a substantial role in European integration. However, as early as July 1955, officials in the State Department had mostly written them off as participants in a future European atomic energy authority, since they seemed "to be more interested in cooperative efforts within the OEEC framework than a six-nations approach."[40] In November the British declined to join the Six in building either Euratom or a Common Market. In justifying their decision to their American allies, they invoked their ties with the Commonwealth and the incompatibility of their policy of free trade with the protectionist aspects of a common market. Would it not be better, they asked, to develop the idea of cooperation in the field of atomic energy within the framework of the OEEC?[41] The answer came from the secretary of state the following month, clear almost to the point of bluntness. In his letter to Macmillan, Dulles gave a full lecture in American strategy towards the Soviet Union, Germany, and European integration and strongly defended the six-nations approach. Dulles wrote to Macmillan that he did not expect the Soviet Union to resort to direct military confrontation to extend its sphere of influence over the rest of Europe. The main danger would come from political subversion, from the "battle for men's minds." It was therefore essential to preserve the West's "unity and strength" to counter subversion from the East. Not surprisingly, Germany held a prominent place in maintaining this strength. Dulles had full confidence in his friend Adenauer, who had shown himself ready to cooperate with the West. But what if, in the long run, once Adenauer passed away, Germany were to be tempted to further its own interests on terms detrimental to the security of its allies? Dulles did not look with favor upon the creation of a neutral Germany, or worse still, an East-oriented Germany. In order to prevent these ominous developments, it was crucial "to so tie Germany into the whole complex of Western institutions—military, political and economic—and to so command her loyalties that neutrality or orientation to the East [would] be commonly accepted as unthinkable."

This was then Dulles's response to the "battle for men's minds": a close-knit European Community in which Germany would find its place.

The EDC experience had clearly shown him, however, that the United States "should not prescribe" to Europeans their course of action. The will to unite had to come from the Europeans themselves: "Anything other than objective advice and cooperation could well be self-defeating." Dulles thus gave Macmillan friendly advice: the United States did not see any inherent conflicts between the cooperative and the supranational approaches toward European integration, but—and here came more advice—he, Dulles, as well as the president had decided to give their full support to the six-nations approach. The "closer unity" inherent in this approach offered the best hope of realizing European potential for security, prosperity, and influence in world affairs and of strengthening the "cohesion of the wider European grouping." In keeping with the administration's policy of fostering European unity for its potential political gains while temporarily disregarding its short-term economic disadvantages, Dulles continued: "It may well be that a 'six-nations' community will evolve protectionist tendencies. It may be that it will show a trend toward greater independence. In the long-run, however, I cannot but feel that the resultant increased unity would bring in its wake greater responsibility and devotion to the common welfare of Western Europe."[42]

European independence was thus acceptable inasmuch as Europeans assumed greater responsibilities for their own destiny. Burden-sharing would become a recurrent topic as the 1950s drew to a close (and even more so during the 1960s), as American economic muscle increasingly showed signs of strain and American political and military might seemed overextended. Under the Nixon administration, doubts would surface about the wisdom of giving undue encouragement to the development of a united Europe. Indeed, Europeans—seemingly reluctant to shoulder American responsibilities and, worse still, not content to merely follow the lead of their former tutor—would often sound voices of dissent from that of the United States. Once speaking in unison, these voices, instead of allowing the happy and weary tutor to "sit back and relax," could conceivably be a divisive force within the alliance. Key officials in the Truman and Eisenhower administrations had foreseen, even encouraged, the development of a third-force Europe. But they had assumed Europe would unite and enter into a mutually beneficial partnership with the United States, with which it would share similar interests. As economic competition between the United States and the European Economic Community intensified, the image of partnership between tutor and full-grown protégé appeared blurred to some in the United States. Interests did not always coincide, and dissenting European voices were too often heard at times when the United States was most in need of its allies' support. It was a thin line that separated partnership from independent venture. But a united Europe could not go it alone without first reaching political and military maturity, and this would not occur for some time. In 1955, the European Common Market was still entirely under discussion. The dangers were perceived, but accepted, as a necessary evil on the road to the West's increased economic well-being, political unity, and strength.

4

Euratom and the U.S.-Euratom Agreement

EURATOM FIRST

With European integration on the move again after the unfortunate EDC saga, Monnet demonstrated his preference for Euratom over the more ambitious proposal of a Common Market. Whereas Euratom could "identify the Community with the power of the future and capture public imagination," he and his emissaries told American officials that the Common Market seemed to be "a pretty nebulous project"[1] for the Six, and especially for the French, with a slim chance of being ratified. Priorities within the Eisenhower administration paralleled this tendency. During the months leading to the Treaties of Rome, the American leadership devoted much more attention to the creation of Euratom than to the realization of a Common Market. Both the lack of in-depth discussions of the potential effects of a European Common Market on the United States, prior to the signing of the Rome Treaties, and repeated statements by John Foster Dulles, who insisted that the approval of Euratom should not be delayed by Common Market negotiations, clearly substantiated the priority of Euratom in high-echelon American policymaking.[2]

To the Americans, as well as to many European officials, the relaunching of Europe through integration in the field of atomic energy appeared more manageable than the creation of a Common Market in which specific progress could not, so it seemed, realistically be expected for some time. In a dispatch to the Department of State, the American ambassador to the United Kingdom made an interesting plea for concentrating on the field of atomic energy. All European institutions created to enhance European cooperation or integration, he remarked, had come into existence and found their "vitality from some major and immediate political need or because of some important outside catalyst." In the case of the ECSC, the necessity of finding a rapprochement between France and Germany had provided the main impetus. Both the OEEC and the European Payments Union, although they were "truly European institutions," had come into being largely because of American "parentage." In the case of the European Payments Union, the Americans had provided the capital. The Western European Union "was made possible by the British promise to maintain troops in Europe." Unfortunately, the European scene now appeared devoid of such catalysts. Atomic energy seemed to be the only place where an "outside stimulus" could be applied successfully. The patient would be reinvigorated by a well-administered dose of an American contribution to a new European agency for atomic energy. To put it another way, the United States would "in effect provide the capital for an atomic EPU." By doing so, the United States could then exert its influence "on the form of the European institution to be developed."[3]

Using the atomic energy issue to extract political benefits from European nations presupposed an agreement within the American administration on what exactly was meant by a European agency for atomic energy. If the Common Market appeared to some as a "pretty nebulous project," the idea of a European atomic pool also needed further clarification. What should the United States support? A European initiative within the OEEC or an atomic pool based on the ECSC approach? Dulles concluded that the six-nations approach offered the best chance of fostering European integration. On 9 January 1956, the secretary of state suggested to Eisenhower that he order the Atomic Energy Commission (AEC) and the Department of State to "study on an urgent basis" steps the United States could take to foster integration within the Six in the field of atomic energy, while assuring that bilateral agreements between the Six and the United States did not impede such integration. Eisenhower approved the secretary's memo.[4] In his State of the Union address a few days earlier the president had put the United States on record as not only favoring further European integration but also as being willing to give assistance to Western European countries "in the field of peaceful uses of atomic energy."[5]

By late January, the State Department and the AEC were hard at work discussing concrete ways in which the United States could further the idea of European integration à la Monnet in the field of atomic energy. During a meeting of top officials from both agencies on 25 January, Dulles panegyrized the movement towards European integration, which he pictured as having recently risen from its ashes under the great guidance of Paul-Henri Spaak and, above all, Jean Monnet. Five days before that meeting, Monnet had met with Dulles, as well as with Gerard Smith, the special assistant to the secretary of state for atomic energy affairs, and Admiral Lewis Strauss himself. He hoped to convince them of the importance of concluding an agreement between the United States and the European atomic community. Monnet possessed a powerful argument in favor of helping Euratom. Two days earlier his Action Committee had unanimously adopted a resolution favoring the creation of a supranational community for atomic energy to be patterned after the ECSC. The projected community would own fissionable materials and control their utilization for pacific use. Monnet forwarded a copy of the resolution to Dulles, emphasizing that it had every chance of being adopted by each of the parliaments of the Six during the next few days or weeks. Having secured the support of most political leaders of noncommunist parties and labor leaders in the six countries, Monnet felt certain that the resolution represented "the will of the parliamentary Western Europe."[6] Yet obstacles remained before Euratom could become a reality.

While the State Department and the president appeared sold on the six-nations approach, some European countries were more hesitant, above all, the British. The United Kingdom was strongly averse to the creation of Euratom[7] and to a Common Market with a potentially high tariff. Having refused to join the Six, the British, instead of gaining access from within to an important market for their nuclear reactors and enjoying protection from outside competition by a common external tariff, now faced the prospect of having to compete as outsiders against the Six. British atomic superiority could not be denied, but, over the long haul, there was every likelihood that the Six would catch up with the United Kingdom; cooperation and the common external tariff wall would bring this about. The British had yet another fear: that the knowledge acquired through Euratom would allow the Six to build atomic bombs. For, as the Six grew in economic power, political unity (and its corollary, a common military policy) would become more likely. More generally, the British government disliked the prospect of "the creation of a central *bloc*—inward- rather than outward-looking—whose development might well encourage all the fissiparous tendencies of the old but fragmented continent."[8] On the whole they feared being isolated, economically and politically. The increasingly precarious situation of the British trade balance, and the weakening of the so-called special relationship between the United States and Britain, did much to intensify this fear.

By early 1956 two plans for a European nuclear development competed with each other: an OEEC plan conceived as a cooperative enterprise; and the Spaak committee's study for a European atomic organization with supranational characteristics. No longer participating in the Spaak discussions, the British now applied determined energy to promoting the OEEC plans to the detriment of the Spaak proposals.[9] The United States was hardly supportive of such tactics. When talking to Macmillan in Paris on 15 December 1955 Dulles made it quite clear that the United States favored creating an atomic agency in Europe that would appeal to the Germans while also reconciling French and German interests. When Macmillan pointed out to him that the United Kingdom and other OEEC nations dreaded the prospect of a supranational community surrounded with high tariff walls, Dulles answered that he felt the community and the OEEC approaches were mutually compatible and could develop side by side.[10] A State Department memo said essentially the same thing and also established a clear distinction between the two approaches. While the OEEC was just a loose group of countries which did not have the capacity to act as a single state, a supranational Euratom could be dealt with as a single unit. This had a major implication for any OEEC venture in atomic energy: the United States could conceivably provide classified information to a group of countries acting as a single state, but, for security reasons, could not do so for a loose association of countries.[11]

The advocates of the six-nations approach within the American administration pointed out that the community approach and a Euratom safeguards system would not necessarily compete with the universal control system to be established through the creation of the International Atomic Energy Agency (IAEA). Despite the merits of the IAEA, certain limitations were apparent: the agency could not be expected to have access to classified material. In addition, since it included the Russians, it would "undoubtedly be in for a good deal of rough sailing." Whatever the opinion of the IAEA, American interests came first. If U.S. agreements with specific countries or groups of countries proved to "yield the greatest benefits" to the United States, this was the avenue to be followed.[12] Since progress towards the IAEA would be relatively slow, some analysts reasoned, why not rely on a regional control system such as Euratom to serve as a stepping stone to the IAEA? Once the IAEA was completely operative, Euratom might then be treated as one nation by the International Agency. Critics of Euratom took the opposite side of this argument. Giving a preferential treatment to Euratom by allowing it to escape the safeguards requirements imposed on other members by the IAEA, they insisted, would undermine the chances of establishing a universal safeguard system.[13] But there were other obstacles to Euratom besides the British-sponsored plan for organizing European atomic cooperation within the OEEC and the criticism that it would undermine the international approach of the IAEA and Eisenhower's whole "Atoms for Peace" initiative.

One such obstacle was the existence of British and American bilateral agreements with Belgium. A supplier of uranium through the Congo, Belgium had been given access to restricted atomic data that were not available to the rest of the Six: by emphasizing inequality among the Six, this special status could prove a stumbling block to the creation of Euratom. Another obstacle was thrown up by the Germans. When Monnet met with Dulles and Bowie in Paris in late December 1955, he asked them not only to pressure Eden during his forthcoming visit to convince the British to be more supportive of European integration schemes but also warned them of serious difficulties within Germany. While Adenauer, the unions, and German socialists supported Euratom, German industrialists hoped to obtain a more favorable treatment by dealing bilaterally and directly with the United States. German Minister of Defense Franz-Joseph Strauss was sympathetic to their demands. His viewpoint was also crucial in determining the German position. In discussions with members of the Six and the United States, he advocated "the freedom for German private industry to own and freely dispose of fissionable materials, subject only to control by the German government through the Länder and a general review by Euratom." This ran directly counter to one of Euratom's central features: the common ownership of all fissionable materials by the Community. Monnet's view was that the material should be sold to Euratom by the United States and subsequently leased to individual and public users, not to countries.[14] He also advocated that Euratom itself exercise control. On December 17, Monnet and Spaak insisted that the United States must make it clear to the Germans that they could expect more cooperation from the United States by dealing on a multilateral rather than a bilateral basis. When Dulles met with West German Minister for Foreign Affairs von Brentano that same day, he emphasized strong American support for the six-nations approach and added that only this approach would provide adequate controls over "materials of weapon quality produced in the process of making energy." During the next few months, American officials kept repeating this very point to their German counterparts, including Franz-Joseph Strauss and Adenauer himself. By stating their preference for the six-nations approach they hoped to strengthen the hand of those within the German government who were favorable to ownership and control by Euratom, especially since the German socialists had insisted that Euratom confine itself to the peaceful uses of atomic energy as a precondition of their joining Monnet's Action Committee.[15]

THE ATOMIC ENERGY COIN AND THE SIX DONKEYS

The United States harbored fears of its own concerning Euratom. One worry, which it shared with the German socialists and the British, was Euratom's potential use by the French, the Germans, or any other European nationality to acquire atomic weapons manufacturing capability. Those whom Monnet called the French "technicians," and who included the military and many socialists, indeed intended to use the technology acquired through Euratom for military as well as peaceful applications. Because of the German socialists, Monnet found himself compelled to repeatedly reaffirm the peaceful orientation of Euratom. The January resolution of his Action Committee implied that Euratom members as a unit would renounce the right to manufacture atomic weapons. Monnet's plan was also to bring all French plutonium into Euratom. The United States largely agreed with such views. The French, warned one American analyst, would, by 1957, possess enough plutonium to manufacture weapons.[16] It was imperative to reach an agreement with them that would confine this plutonium to peaceful uses. For one thing, if the French controlled their own atomic development, the Germans might be prompted to compete with them nationally. For another, other European countries could be tempted to produce material for atomic weapons clandestinely. James Conant, the American ambassador to Germany, dreaded the prospect of a multitude of national chemical plants because reprocessing fuel elements for such plants would put the production of plutonium on a national scale. This "would not in itself constitute manufacture of atomic weapons but would be a long and dangerous step in this direction." He concluded that control of the Six required at the very least "a supranationally controlled chemical reprocessing plant." As far as the production of enriched uranium was concerned, a similar control needed to be exerted "where U-235 was produced which could be used in a weapon."[17] Conant conceded that "if Germany [were] to support a real supranational European authority, a very large carrot in the form of what [the] United States [was] offering would have to be put in front of the mouths of the six donkeys."[18]

In attempting to contribute to the development of a supranational European community, while at the same time preventing it from gaining access to atomic weapons, the United States paved the way for the not-so-equal partnership that President Kennedy would propose a few years later: a European economic and political contribution to the alliance, without military maturity. In the meantime, the Eisenhower administration debated internally on the best way of utilizing the "atomic energy coin," which was currently at its peak value, to extract "non-atomic political benefits"[19] from its partners. These benefits were a mixed blessing: supranational integration on the one hand, with the by now familiar political advantages for the United States and the West, and the challenge of preventing, or at least delaying, the acquisition of nuclear weapons by European nations.

Upper-echelon American policymakers such as Dulles and Eisenhower clearly hoped to use Euratom to discourage the production of atomic weapons in Europe.[20] The carrot to be put in front of the mouths of the six donkeys was nothing less than the promise to provide substantial quantities of uranium 235 at a very advantageous price. The State Department and the AEC agreed that it was contrary to American interests to help the Six build an isotopic separation plant for the enrichment of uranium. Special Assistant for Atomic Energy Affairs Gerard Smith outlined key objections to this potential American contribution to Euratom and European atomic independence. First, the technology for the enrichment plant was directly related to the know-how for atomic weapons production. Second, for this very reason, the proposal would be hard to sell to Congress. Third, there was "the specter of possible Communist take-over of the plant." Finally, from an economic standpoint, the United States "would be making the Europeans independent of us and giving up our monopoly on marketable enriched uranium." At issue, then, was the reluctance of the United States to grant independence to Europeans in the atomic field for political, strategic, and economic reasons. Self-interest dictated that the United States prevent Europeans from acquiring the technology for gaseous diffusion that could allow them to build their own uranium enrichment plants and thus feed their own nuclear power plants. But enlightened self-interest also required that alternative ways of contributing to the six-nations approach be proposed to Europeans, while simultaneously discouraging them from building enrichment plants.

It would be easy enough, reasoned some analysts, to point out to Europeans that such plants were tremendous consumers of electric power, would take a long time to be amortized, and thus made little sense from an economic standpoint.[21] But political gains could, in the eyes of Europeans, outweigh economic costs. They needed a bigger carrot—especially the French, who counted on the construction of an enrichment plant, within the framework of Euratom, to defray the costs they would incur by constructing a plant themselves and to fulfill their ambitions for nuclear independence. In the course of 1956, the strategy unfolded. On 22 February 1956 Eisenhower made it known that the United States would make 20,000 kilograms of uranium 235 available for sale or lease to foreign powers and research reactor programs.[22] Then, on 17 November 1956, the President announced that the price of enriched uranium sold abroad would be considerably reduced.[23] In addition, the United States would also guarantee an almost unlimited supply of uranium to feed foreign nuclear power plants. Both these announcements were tactical moves to dissuade Europeans from spending money to build their own enrichment plants. With the new low price for American enriched uranium, the price of European-produced uranium 235 would be double or triple that offered by the United States. American tactics worked: during the early months of 1957, the Six gradually abandoned the idea of building their own enrichment plants. On 12 December 1956, the United States also declassified data from the first American enriched uranium power plant in Shippingport, Pennsylvania, which was to go into operation only nine months later. This was done to ensure that the European pool would prefer American technology to British technology, thereby preserving an important export market for American industry.[24]

Meanwhile, in the spring, the issue of the control and ownership of fissionable material occasioned much debate throughout Europe and within the American administration. Lewis Strauss, the chairman of the AEC, expressed three main concerns:

1. Would Euratom possess enough authority to exert the necessary controls over the material and to safeguard classified information?
2. Would the creation of Euratom mean the socialization of atomic energy in Europe, thereby running counter to the cherished principle of free enterprise?
3. The United States was already committed to a number of bilateral agreements with various European countries—what would become of these?

Monnet and the State Department, whose views converged on most issues, argued the case for Euratom as best as they could. First, they pointed out that Euratom would possess a high degree of supranationality, which in itself guaranteed integration of control and thus more effective control than would be possible if atomic energy programs were administered by several national authorities.[25] In a conversation with Lewis Strauss in Paris, Monnet then insisted that Euratom's primary goals were "far removed from ideas of socialization." Euratom could not "in any sense affect either the property rights or laws existing in several countries," nor could it "influence the relations between public and private enterprises in the States." In fact, Euratom's main purposes were: "(1) to stimulate and ensure European atomic development on a sufficiently broad base to allow furnishing such needs of the area as could not be done nationally and, (2) to furnish a satisfactory mechanism whereby fissionable material would be subjected to the necessary security controls."[26]

The final concern of Admiral Strauss was the existence of the bilateral agreements. In this specific instance the State Department and the AEC were mostly at odds. Strauss opposed suspending or delaying the bilateral negotiations, while Dulles, urged on by Jean Monnet and others, sought to delay bilateral agreements with prospective Euratom members, especially with Germany. In January 1957, Monnet told Dulles that if the United States agreed "to give bilateral aid of a substantial character to Germany before EURATOM was signed up, it would almost surely mean the end of EURA-TOM."[27] Concluding a bilateral agreement with the Germans, indicated René Mayer, would considerably weaken their interest in the supranational approach. Conversations between the State Department and Franz-Joseph Strauss, the German minister for atomic affairs, made it clear that this was indeed the case.[28] In one such conversation, the secretary of state, responding to Franz-Joseph Strauss, who had just voiced once again his concern that Euratom would destroy free enterprise (thus being in tune with Lewis Strauss, the chairman of the AEC), came to the defense of Euratom. Euratom would not be socialistic, he said. But one needed adequate controls to guarantee that atomic energy would be used for peaceful purposes, all the more so because of the by-product plutonium. "The larger and more responsible the safeguard organization the more control [would] be facilitated. This would be better than multiple controls of many individual countries involving complicated policing." Dulles then called forth the specter of nuclear proliferation: "It is appalling to contemplate a multiplicity of uncontrolled national atomic developments leading to multiplying atomic weapons programs. If you set up a pattern allowing the thing to spread on national lines there will be the danger of irresponsible action." [29] Here, in a nutshell, were the fears of the State Department and an indication of how it hoped Euratom could help counter these fears.

The State Department also had concerns about signing a bilateral agreement with Germany, for the French might considerably resent it. More generally, it insisted that bilateral agreements with future Euratom members be delayed in order to convince the Six that they would be better off dealing with the United States on a multilateral rather than a bilateral basis, thereby strengthening the Euratom concept. By contrast, Admiral Strauss, doubting that Euratom would soon come into existence, was reluctant to delay negotiations and anxious to show Congress progress in the peaceful uses of atomic power abroad. The question was finally resolved in January 1957 upon consultation with the Six, who agreed to transfer benefits and obligations from their bilateral agreements with the United States to Euratom. By so doing, any German, Italian, French, or other bilateral atomic energy agreement with the United States lost its potential adverse effect on the Euratom negotiations. Yet the issue of the potential use of Euratom for military applications was what worried the Americans the most.

Early in February 1956, Douglas Dillon, United States ambassador to France, had urged his government not to insist that France give up her right to manufacture nuclear weapons, even though Monnet was pushing for all members of Euratom to renounce this right. He pointed out that one of the main attractions of Euratom to much of the French government was the chance to acquire new technology that could be used to advance the French atomic program. Should the United States, by unfortunate statements, lead the French to believe that the United States "favored their renouncing [the] right to manufacture atomic weapons, such a feeling would arouse [a] storm of anti-American protest."[30] It would also doom Euratom in France, especially in the French Assembly where the majority seemed in favor of maintaining the French right to manufacture nuclear weapons (although they did not all agree on the immediate need for manufacturing such weapons). The end product would be nothing less than a repeat of the EDC saga. Three days later, René Mayer, who then was in Washington, told Admiral Strauss and Dulles that Euratom would never be accepted in the French parliament if it asked the French to give up atomic weapons. French Minister of Foreign Affairs Antoine Pinay had told Spaak exactly the same thing right from the beginning of the consideration of Euratom. Dulles proposed a compromise solution: so as not to impede the development of the IAEA agency "there might be an agreement that 'fourth countries' would not make atomic weapons for a period of time—say five years—during which an effort would be made to eliminate these weapons by agreement between the United States, the Soviet Union and the United Kingdom."[31]

The president of the French Council of Ministers, Guy Mollet, accepted the idea of a moratorium and recommended that the French agree to test their atomic bomb only after 1 January 1961. In early July 1956, Louis Armand delivered a brilliant speech before the French Assembly in favor of Euratom and European unity. His matter-of-fact presentation was greeted with enthusiasm.[32] Mollet's announcement that Euratom would not prevent the development of a French bomb removed the last obstacle to the ratification of Euratom in France. Although he was initially opposed to France's developing its own nuclear weapons, Mollet had to bow to his opponents, mostly Gaullists, who actively campaigned against Euratom and insisted that it would prevent France from becoming the fourth atomic power.[33] By 6 November 1956, Adenauer, overruling the opposition of Erhard and Strauss, reached an agreement with Mollet that the Euratom Treaty would allow the French to develop their own nuclear weapons. This agreement removed a further obstacle to ratification of the Euratom Treaty. The final Euratom Treaty implicitly left the door open for French manufacture of nuclear weapons. Although the United States ended up reluctantly accepting that Euratom might leave the door open for members to pursue their own nuclear military programs, they also dealt a fatal blow to Euratom in France by forestalling the construction of an enrichment plant under Euratom's guidance. Euratom would see the light of the day, but it already contained the seeds of its own destruction, mostly because the stakes in its creation had been considerably lowered for the French.

THE U.S./EURATOM AGREEMENT

On 26 July 1956, Egyptian President Nasser nationalized the Suez Canal. This patent demonstration of Europe's vulnerability in the energy field and of its dependence on the United States for major foreign policy initiatives had important consequences for Euratom. Ironically, it was not so much friendly American advice as anti-Americanism in some European countries after Suez that helped the fortunes of the Euratom and EEC treaties.[34] Dulles probably contributed more to European unification by refusing to back the French and the British at Suez than by vigorously pushing for the EDC. In September, Monnet's Action Committee seized upon the momentum of the Suez mishap to draft a resolution that emphasized Europe's increasing dependence upon imported energy sources and the deplorable consequences for world peace of this weakness in the energy field. The resolution recommended appointing a committee of three "Wise Men" to draw up within two months a program for the production of atomic energy in Europe.[35] The committee, consisting of Louis Armand, Franz Etzel, and Francesco Giordani, was effectively established during a meeting of the foreign ministers of the Six at Brussels on 16 November 1956. The next day Monnet told Ambassador Dillon that "a broad scale and generous program of U.S. support for Euratom, both in the supply of materials and in technical cooperation," might do much to repair Atlantic solidarity, which was in need of some patching up. Eisenhower's announcement on November 18 that he had approved the recommendations of Lewis Strauss to make available 20,000 kilograms of U 235 to foreign countries to be used solely for peaceful purposes lent some credence to the possibility of an American contribution to Euratom. Here, clever tactics in presenting such an American contribution to Europeans were essential. Monnet recommended showing strong American support for Euratom as soon as the treaty had been signed.[36]

In the meantime, Monnet's American connections did not remain inactive. Robert Schaetzel, who served as assistant to Gerard Smith, also happened to know Max Kohnstamm, the vice-president of Monnet's Action Committee, with whom he frequently exchanged letters. During one conversation with Kohnstamm, just a few days before Monnet mentioned to Dillon the idea of launching a generous program of support for Euratom, Schaetzel discussed ways of making Euratom attractive in the United States. One such way was for the United States and Euratom to cooperate in the creation of reactors that would use plutonium to produce energy. Europe was to serve as a testing ground for the reactors, instead of constructing them in the United States. The idea of testing reactors on the European market rather than in the United States, where energy was less costly than in Europe, later found its way into the Agreement of Cooperation between Euratom and the United States Government, signed on 8 November 1958 after much congressional debate. So, too, did the idea of jointly developing new reactor types.

When the three Wise Men handed in their report, "A Target for Euratom," to the Six in May 1957, it already contained the seeds of the U.S.–Euratom agreement. Pointing out that the average cost of electricity in the United States amounted to about two-thirds of what it was in Europe, the three experts spoke of the benefits to be derived by the United States from "the large-scale industrial application of atomic power" in Europe. Europeans, on the other hand, would gain from American technical expertise in the field of atomic energy, while the United States would also provide fissile materials to get the power plants going. U.S. and European industries, as well as the American and the European atomic energy commissions, would undertake joint projects to develop new reactors and adapt old ones. "Target" spoke of a "two-way traffic, a close partnership as equals" that could be built "between the United States and Euratom and their respective industries," thereby prefiguring Kennedy's famous "partnership between equals" speech.[37]

The three Wise Men planned to come to the United States in January. During his conversation with Kohnstamm, Schaetzel declared himself favorable to the idea. He emphasized, however, that the initiative should come from the Europeans, and suggested that they contact the State Department in order to show that they had not come on a strictly technical visit. Yet the State Department did not follow Schaetzel on this point. Tempted once again to display American leadership, Dulles agreed with Ambassador Dillon that the United States should "take the initiative in issuing the invitation." The American ambassador to Belgium, Frederick Alger, then approached Spaak, who "warmly welcomed the idea" of a visit to the United States and also thought that the initiative should come from the United States. Just a few days before Christmas 1956, Strauss and Dulles issued a press release inviting the three Wise Men to the United States for conversations with government officials and the private sector.[38]

In late November, Monnet had written to Dulles, who had gone to Florida to recover from an abdominal cancer revealed earlier in the month, wishing him a speedy recovery. Feeling anxious about the general situation, Monnet intended "to go to the United States soon on a strictly private basis" and felt "the need of breathing some other air than 'European,' and talking to some of [his] old friends." Monnet also planned to make the most of his old friendships. It was indeed one of Monnet's greatest skills to make his friends and colleagues feel useful, making them all the more eager to be used—not so much to serve Monnet but to serve the cause of European integration that he defended. When Monnet came to the United States in mid-January 1957 it was to prepare the ground for a speedy ratification of the Euratom Treaty.

In conversations with Dulles and Admiral Strauss, Monnet kept emphasizing the importance of slowing down the bilateral agreement with Germany, which, if completed, would surely sound the death knell of Euratom. One such conversation with Strauss, during a prolonged dinner, lasted no less than five hours and ended at midnight. Monnet later reported to Dulles that Strauss now seemed to agree that he should not press for bilateral agreements with the Six as long as a speedy signing of the Euratom Treaty was in sight, although he had not yet committed himself. At the end of the visit, Monnet also touched base with Eisenhower. Having failed to meet with him during his stay, Monnet wrote to Eisenhower to tell him about his conversations with Dulles and Strauss on Euratom and the Common Market and to send him his "respectful compliments and best wishes."[39]

Upon returning to Europe, Monnet emphasized to the members of his Action Committee the importance of establishing an association between Euratom and the United States that, through Euratom, would lead to a partnership between equals in mutual interest,[40] again foreshadowing Kennedy's "partnership between equals." Using arguments similar to those he had put forward for the American loan to the ECSC, Monnet maintained that such a mutually profitable agreement would be a first for the old Europe, which since World War II had been receiving all too many "aids and grants." The Wise Men would help define the contents of the agreement.[41] Further tilling the ground for a profitable visit of the Wise Men, Monnet then sent numerous letters to his friends in the United States, making sure that they understood the true significance of the visit. The letters were addressed to

André Meyer of Lazard Frères on Wall Street; John McCloy of the Chase Manhattan Bank; Donald Swatland of Cravath, Swaine and Moore; Gerard Smith; Robert Bowie; and John Foster Dulles. Monnet took special care to introduce Max Kohnstamm, who was officially to accompany the three Wise Men, as "a very intimate friend of his." He asked his American friends to treat him as his alter ego and accord him the same favors that they granted Monnet when he was in the United States. In mid-January, Monnet's old friend Donald ("Swat") Swatland had arranged for a private meeting between Monnet and Strauss. Monnet now asked him to organize a similar meeting with Kohnstamm, the three Wise Men, and Lewis Strauss. Writing to Dulles's secretary, Monnet asked that Kohnstamm's phone calls be treated as his own had been in the past and go directly through to Dulles. Reaching the top level of the State Department, Monnet then wrote to Dulles that he should fully trust Kohnstamm. He also asked for a favor: could Dulles please arrange for Monnet's two "very good friends," the Wise Men Louis Armand and Franz Etzel, to be received by the president?[42] Monnet further prepared the ground for the visit of the three Wise Men by sending Kohnstamm ahead as their emissary.

"The Wise Men are not coming to Washington with hat in hand and palm extended," Kohnstamm told journalists in Washington. They were coming to see how Europe could use atomic energy to become less dependent on Middle East oil supplies for its survival. Thus introduced, the three Wise Men and their entourage arrived in the United States on 4 February. Upon their arrival, Dulles met with them and Kohnstamm and arranged for the group to see the president.[43] During the meeting with Dulles and other officials, including Bowie, Butterworth, Smith, Schaetzel, and Cleveland, all of them friends of Monnet, Armand made a dramatic presentation on the need for Euratom. Europe, he told them, had been "born rich" in energy, but this strength had been built on the predominance of coal. With the gradual replacement of coal by oil as a source of energy, Europe now had become an importer of energy, and depended more and more on the Middle East for its survival. If new energy sources were not made available in Europe, the standard of living of Europeans would soon reach a ceiling, since "the standard of living of any industrial country tend[ed] to be proportional to its energy consumption." Atomic energy was thus necessary both to meet the energy gap and to shield European countries from economic underdevelopment, which could only result in political unrest. America could take its choice: either Europe would become its real partner within ten years or it would become an "underdeveloped territory." In the first case, Europe might well enter into competition with the United States, but healthy competition was far better than dealing with a desperate and increasingly aloof Europe.

Two days later, Franz Etzel, one of the Wise Men and the vice-president of the High Authority of the ECSC, made a similar, although less inspired, presentation to the president and Strauss. Eisenhower spoke warmly of the need for European unity. He welcomed the day when economic unification would lead to political unification and thus transform Europe into a "third world power" that would help the world withstand Communist domination. The most telling words in Etzel's speech, he commented, were "mutual partnership." Eisenhower concluded the interview with assurances that Euratom would have his own, and his administration's, full backing. On 8 February, a joint communiqué echoed Etzel's words by welcoming "a fruitful two-way exchange of experience and technical development, opening a new area of mutually beneficial action on both the governmental and the industrial level and reinforcing solidarity within Europe and across the Atlantic." The communiqué further indicated that "the availability of nuclear fuels" was "not a limiting factor," thereby showing that the United States would be willing to contribute fuels to the nuclear power plants that the Wise Men planned to have installed in Europe within ten years. Somewhat unrealistically, the Wise Men spoke of a "total generating capacity of 15,000,000 kW."[44] In order to help the Wise Men solve technical problems and meet their objectives, the communiqué recommended appointing a joint group of American and European experts. The State Department and the AEC having thus publicly given their blessing to Euratom, the three Wise Men proceeded to try to gain the support of American industry.

During a visit to the power plant of Shippingport, near Pittsburgh, Louis Armand, the railway man, made a good impression on Admiral Hyman Rickover, who had directed the construction of the first American atomic submarine. Armand, Etzel, and Giordani, president of the Italian National Research Council, also met with a distinguished group of American industry representatives in New York in the presence of officials of the State Department and the AEC. The meeting was an attempt to assess realistic ways of launching Euratom. More help was forthcoming in March, when Washington confirmed that American experts[45] would go to Luxembourg by the middle of the month. That visit was the result of the common initiative of Kohnstamm, Bowie, and Smith, who thought that the American experts could help the Wise Men draft their report by pointing out what to say "on matters such as production and investment costs."[46] On 25 March 1957, representatives of the six ECSC countries signed the Euratom and EEC treaties in Rome. By 7 May, Lewis Strauss of the AEC had issued a communiqué acknowledging the three Wise Men's report and pledging American technical and material help.

The Euratom Treaty gave Euratom the right to own and control fissionable materials, whether imported or produced by Euratom. Although Euratom was to be devoted exclusively to the peaceful uses of atomic energy, loopholes in the treaty made it possible for members to pursue national nuclear military programs. This was, quite obviously, a concession to vested interests in France. In February, in a conversation at the Department of State, at which Admiral Strauss was present, Foreign Minister Spaak had sought to make this particular aspect of the treaty more palatable to the American leadership. He indicated that it was "unfortunate but politically indispensable" to maintain "at least a theoretical possibility to engage in the weapons program" to gain the support of the moderate Right in France for Euratom and the Common Market. Mollet, who had initially been opposed to a military program, had changed his mind for this very reason. As for technicalities, "Under the Treaty military uses would be subject to the same strict control and inspection as civil uses, up to the point of the actual fabrication of a bomb." Spaak hoped that, "provided the treaty did not formally prevent the French from engaging in military production, they would not in fact carry out a military program, in particular because of the very high cost involved." This was a pious vow in light of recent developments that gave every indication that France would manufacture a bomb in the not-too-distant future.[47] On the condition that the fissionable materials furnished by the United States and their derivatives would not be used for military purposes by Euratom, Strauss approved the preliminary draft of the Euratom Treaty presented by Spaak in early March. The AEC hoped to discourage Euratom members from engaging in nuclear military ventures by convincing other suppliers of uranium, such as Canada and South Africa, to insist that the uranium they sold to Euratom be restricted to peaceful purposes. Three days before the Six signed the Rome Treaties, Dulles sent a letter to Spaak stating that the Department of State and the AEC saw "nothing which would appear to preclude the subsequent negotiation of a fruitful cooperative arrangement between the United States and EURATOM."[48] While retaining the sole control and ownership of materials, Euratom only later conceded to the United States the right to inspect its control system, and took it upon itself to guarantee that fissionable materials sold to Euratom by the United States would under no circumstances be used for military purposes.

With the signing of the Euratom and EEC treaties, the road was now open to an American joint program with Euratom. The Soviet Union's launching of Sputnik on October 1957 further played into the hands of the supporters of Euratom. Sputnik directly challenged the credibility of the American nuclear guarantee to Western Europe. Calculating that the United States might not want to risk its cities to protect its allies, some Europeans aspired to develop nuclear weapons of their own to counter Soviet nuclear blackmail. Intent on nonproliferation, and especially on preventing the construction of a French bomb or Franco-German cooperation, the United States and the British attempted to sidetrack these aspirations by proposing some second-best solutions to Western European nuclear impotence. One such solution was the deployment of intermediate-range ballistic missiles, controlled in part by Europeans, in some NATO countries. It pleased no one. The missiles were reluctantly accepted only by Italy, Turkey, and Britain. Failing to satisfy their allies in granting them full access to the military applications of the atom, the United States fell back on the peaceful uses of atomic energy. Although it was initially reluctant to grant Euratom full control of its own safeguard system, the United States eventually gave in, in part to silence dissatisfied voices in Europe.[49]

Sputnik played into the hands of Euratom for yet another reason: it was a patent demonstration that the Soviet Union had surpassed the United States in rocket technology. What could the United States do to meet the challenge? asked American industrialists and government officials. One option was to try to catch up with the Soviet Union by emphasizing research in rocket development. Another was to concentrate on developing civilian atomic power, an area in which the Soviet Union apparently lagged behind. To some, Euratom offered the perfect opportunity to test American nuclear power plants on a large scale. Two faithful Europeanists from the State Department, Bob Schaetzel and Stanley Cleveland, made a special trip to Luxembourg to discuss the odds of a joint U.S.–Euratom program with Max Kohnstamm, prior to his departure for the United States in October.[50]

Interest in the development of a civilian atomic energy program showed in the organization of numerous meetings and conferences shortly after the Sputnik shock. In mid-October, Columbia University, of which Eisenhower had formerly been the president, hosted a conference on American atomic power policy as part of its semiannual "American Assembly" series. The Atomic Industrial Forum held its fourth annual conference about one week later. Kohnstamm, whom Monnet trusted to negotiate the U.S.–Euratom joint agreement, attended both meetings. Addressing 64 leaders drawn from the private and public sectors, at Columbia on 19 October, Kohnstamm praised European integration, Euratom, and Euratom/American cooperation. Four days later he took part in a COFR study group on Western European integration. Monnet's friend George Ball, who also happened to have been present at the Columbia conference, chaired the meeting. The main subject tackled by the study group was again Euratom, investigating how it could cooperate with the United States in building power stations in Europe. The participants gave much less attention to the Common Market. Shortly afterwards Kohnstamm attended the Atomic Industrial Forum, where he delivered a speech on 29 October.

While in the United States, Kohnstamm also touched base with government officials. Gerard Smith, who had just been appointed as assistant secretary of state for policy planning, gave him his full blessing, while suggesting that the initiative in the United States should come from Admiral Strauss. Subsequent conversations, notably with Philipp Farley, who had recently replaced Smith as special assistant for atomic energy affairs, confirmed that the way to obtain the joint agreement was not by exerting political pressure via the Joint Committee on Atomic Energy (JCAE) in Congress, but by going through Admiral Strauss of the AEC and through the president.[51] The problem with the AEC was that it leaned towards favoring a program of subsidies to prop up the American atomic industry by making it more competitive in foreign markets. The alternative to subsidies, a joint demonstration program with Euratom and the concomitant development of U.S.-type reactors in Europe on a large scale, had not yet won the favor of the AEC. In an effort to court the top man at the AEC, Kohnstamm met with Admiral Strauss twice during his stay—once at Strauss's office and once during a banquet in the Grand Ballroom of the Waldorf-Astoria hotel, where Strauss and Sir Edwin Plowden, the chairman of the United Kingdom Atomic Energy Authority, were the guest speakers.

Kohnstamm then decided to lobby the Export-Import Bank. What better person to contact than Monnet's old friend Samuel Waugh, who was now the president and the chairman of its board of directors? With Waugh, Kohnstamm discussed the feasibility of a loan to Euratom, thereby setting the stage for a new "political" loan much after the pattern of the previous loan to the ECSC. After Kohnstamm's departure for Europe, Schaetzel, who had previously worked for Samuel Waugh, continued to press his former boss to bring in the Export-Import Bank to support Euratom. Monnet himself, he assumed, would do the rest of the work during Waugh's imminent visit to the ECSC in Luxembourg.[52] During the following months, Kohnstamm and some of his American friends continuously networked and lobbied for a joint U.S.–Euratom agreement.

At the end of November, Kohnstamm called a meeting in Paris to evaluate the feasibility of a joint program of cooperation between the United States and Euratom. The results were inconclusive. Kohnstamm insisted that the "baby"

Euratom needed an outside stimulus from the United States right from the moment of its official birth in January 1958. Failing that, he told the Americans, there would be few U.S.-type reactors constructed in Europe, and Europe would be left mostly with voluminous graphite-gas reactors, with which the French and the British had the most experience. In order not to bank Europe's atomic future on just one type of reactor, he argued, the United States and Euratom might share the cost of experimenting with at least four demonstration power reactors of different types in the European market. The graphite-gas reactor, which was much favored by the French military because its by-product of plutonium could be used in bombs, would thus be just one of the four demonstration reactors. It was essential also to experiment with a heavy-water natural-uranium reactor, with which Canada had the most expertise, and, of course, with those reactors preferred by the United States—General Electric's Boiling Water Reactor (BWR) and Westinghouse's Pressurized Water Reactor (PWR). Ambassador Butterworth responded that the United States should not provide Euratom with much outside help, particularly financial: Europe must be the main engine of Euratom, not the United States. The United States could provide some assistance to Euratom, but could not be "one of its two legs." How could Kohnstamm dream that the United States would ever contribute dollars to the construction of a new British-type reactor, especially if the British were not willing to disburse pounds for it themselves? When the meeting ended, Butterworth's position had won the day: the participants agreed that Euratom's proposal for a joint program with the United States should only speak of the "extensive development of U.S.-type reactors in Europe." The avowed preference of Butterworth and his colleagues had far-reaching implications for Europe's future.[53]

While the graphite-gas and heavy-water natural-uranium reactors both used natural uranium, American reactors required enriched uranium. Developing American reactors in Europe had the disadvantage of making European power plants dependent on a steady flow of enriched uranium from the United States, since Euratom ultimately decided not to build its own enrichment plant. This did not seem to bother Max Kohnstamm much, or for that matter, Armand, one of the masterminds behind the joint U.S.-Euratom agreement. The natural-uranium plants, he anticipated, were too large and could probably not economically be developed on a large industrial scale. Armand believed that the enriched uranium power plants, which utilized light (natural) water and took up relatively little space, were those of the future. It was not important that Europe depended on the United States for enriched uranium. What was important was to gain access to American technology by constructing and developing light-water reactors with the United States. This strategy had the advantage of associating Euratom with the nuclear power plants of the future, in which the United States was far ahead of Europe, while at the same time allowing Europe to plan for the distant future. In the long run, France and Great Britain seemed to have enough technological advancement to compete with the United States in the construction of breeder reactors, which utilized very enriched uranium. Armand's gamble proved him right on one count: the PWR and the BWR light-water reactor types currently provide more than 90 percent of all the electricity generated by nuclear power plants. Yet light-water reactors also turned out to be far more costly to develop than experts had originally estimated. Armand's assumptions that a world market of nuclear fuels would develop and that Europe would have easy access to uranium in the future were proven wrong. In the context of the American advocacy of nonproliferation, there could hardly be any talk of a world market for nuclear fuels.[54]

Yet Kohnstamm and Armand did not foresee this development at the time. In late 1957, they were solely intent on convincing the Americans to back their project of U.S.-Euratom cooperation, which, they hoped, would go a long way towards making Europe more of an equal partner of the United States. Their task was by no means easy. Shortly after the unsuccessful conclusion of the Kohnstamm-Butterworth meeting, Schaetzel sent Kohnstamm two letters in which he strongly emphasized the need to "establish a high-level position in the U.S. favorable to the project." Only then could one quiet the voices that criticized a program of building reactors in Europe rather than at home. Schaetzel thought that Monnet was the man for the job. He was the only person who could provide the necessary catalyst to persuade Eisenhower and the "other big bosses" to support the project. A forthcoming NATO meeting in Paris would be the perfect occasion for Monnet and Armand to meet with Eisenhower, Dulles, and Strauss. The initiative, insisted Schaetzel, should come from Euratom and be presented as an "important political move." On another level, it was perhaps equally important to "insure a sympathetic and effective staff follow-through" of the project in the United States, especially since Euratom would probably lack experienced staff during its first months of operation. In order to speed up the agreement, Monnet's Action Committee might also hire experts to draft a detailed plan addressing the technical and organizational aspects of the proposal. Euratom and the United States would then "be working towards modifications of a plan" rather than each developing widely diverging projects. Schaetzel then presented the final part of his triptych for making the project a success. It was not enough to win the support of the administration, he maintained; the program also had to be palatable to Congress. Douglas Dillon, who had recently been appointed deputy under secretary of state for economic affairs, was responsible for supervising the entire American foreign aid program. He would most likely be charged with defending the project in Congress. Dillon was very well informed about the project, but, since he was also coming to Paris, a little more work on him could not hurt. "His active support is indispensable," wrote Schaetzel. Schaetzel was right: Dillon's role proved decisive. His testimony in favor of a Euratom-controlled safeguard system helped calm the strong reservations about Euratom held by the "redoubtable" Joint Committee on Atomic Energy (JCAE) in Congress.[55]

Kohnstamm followed Schaetzel's advice and promptly set to work on a detailed draft of the proposed agreement, which he subsequently sent for comments to Allen Vander Weyden, Schaetzel, Butterworth, Stanley Cleveland, Armand, and some of his colleagues. Schaetzel counseled him to highlight the "sense of urgency" in the paper, while Butterworth advised him to make clear that the program was something that Euratom needed and really intended to do. The United States could only ally itself with a truly committed partner. Philip Farley of AEC contributed a further comment. Kohnstamm's paper did not sufficiently bring out the "strong technical" reasons for supporting the enriched uranium approach. As planned, Monnet met with Dulles, Eisenhower, and Strauss on 15 December. Although Monnet mainly spoke about the French financial situation, he also reiterated his attachment to "a vigorous Euratom program." Farley and Kohnstamm met twice in mid-December to devise a strategy for playing Monnet for his full value. Monnet was expected to come to Washington in January. By that time Armand would have taken up his functions as president of Euratom and could "get agreement in principle from the Euratom Commission that Euratom ought to undertake a power demonstration program for the construction of a million kw by a given date, *mainly in enriched uranium power reactors.*"[56] Once in Washington, Monnet could then easily point out that a detailed "prospectus" was necessary to work out the terms of the agreement and ask the United States to agree to provide technical, political, and economic experts in order to help Euratom draft a preliminary prospectus. Kohnstamm was hesitant to ask the advice of experts from the national atomic energy programs of the Six, who might lack enthusiasm for the project in view of their own national interests, and thus turned to American experts.[57]

NO FLYING START

On 1 January 1958, the Euratom and EEC treaties officially went into effect. But Euratom did not get off to a flying start. Armand, its new president, fell sick at the very beginning of his mandate. For internal political reasons in the Netherlands, Kohnstamm was denied a seat on the Euratom Commission. In addition, the Six failed to decide on a location for the new institutions. To top it all off, Armand seemed to have rather strange ideas about how Euratom should operate administratively. In light of these unpromising beginnings, the American connection and the proposed agreement with Euratom acquired added importance as possible galvanizers for the success of Euratom. One needed to act fast, however, or else Europe could soon divide into rival national atomic energy programs with Euratom serving only as a coordinating agency, lacking any program of its own. The State Department did not lag behind. On 25 January, Eisenhower approved Dulles's recommendation to appoint Butterworth, at that time representative to the ECSC with personal rank of ambassador, to the additional post of United States representative to Euratom and the EEC, also with ambassadorial rank. Butterworth was to head a single mission, thereby emphasizing that the United States saw "all three Communities as part of a single movement towards the political and economic union of Western Europe."[58]

Monnet arrived in the United States at the end of January. After long conversations with him, Schaetzel and his staff secretly prepared detailed memoranda outlining points to be raised with Strauss in a forthcoming meeting. Strauss was to be told that the program with Euratom should truly be a joint program and that speed was of the essence in supporting it, the more so since congressional hearings were imminent and Euratom member countries were tending to develop their own programs along national lines. As a matter of tactics, Monnet and the Americans agreed that the United States must take the initiative "to achieve the indispensable rapid action" but that "this must not be done openly." To this end, there were to be "informal and confidential discussions with Armand" and other Euratom Commission members to prepare both for a visit by Armand to the United States and for the "release of a statement indicating U.S.-Euratom agreement in principle to a joint program." Finally, American experts were to fly to Europe to assist the Euratom Commission in drafting the details of a joint program. The day after the memos were drafted, Strauss and Acting Secretary Christian Herter sent a short memo to Eisenhower recommending that he approve in principle a cooperative U.S.-Euratom agreement. The memo spoke of the construction of "several U.S.-type reactors, to be completed by 1962 or 1963 and designed to produce 1 million kilowatts of electrical energy." Europeans were to bear most of the cost, with the United States providing about half the financing for reactors in the form of a loan. It also provided for U.S.-European research cooperation in developing U.S.-type reactors to be constructed by Euratom. For the more distant future, the United States was to share with Euratom the results of its research on more advanced reactor types. This was all very much in tune with Schaetzel and Monnet's advice. The memo recommended that the program be made public only after talks were held with the Euratom Commission. This would preserve the political impact of the program and, as Monnet and Schaetzel had suggested, demonstrate that the initiative had come from the Europeans. Eisenhower signed the memo. A few days later Monnet met with Dillon, Waugh, and the president. While he spent much time discussing France's financial problems, Monnet probably also mentioned the joint program to Eisenhower.[59]

During the next few months, the strategy worked out by Schaetzel, Monnet, and Kohnstamm unfolded. In mid-February, Schaetzel, Vander Weyden, and some of their colleagues joined Butterworth and members of the Euratom Commission in Luxembourg to signify American interest in the program. On 28 February, Butterworth transmitted to Armand an invitation from Dulles and Strauss to come to Washington in April to discuss the U.S.-Euratom program. Unfortunately, illness prevented Armand from accepting, and Kohnstamm had to go in his place. Meanwhile, a joint working party with European and American experts was set up to prepare for Armand's visit. In early March 1958 Kohnstamm flew to the United States. He wanted to develop both a schedule and a procedure for the working party to follow in order to best achieve congressional ratification of the joint program.[60] The study group met in Luxembourg from 20 March to 3 April. American experts reported to Butterworth, while representatives of Euratom reported to Kohnstamm. Among the American delegates were such top-level officials of the AEC as Mr. Richard W. Cook, deputy general manager of the AEC, and Vander Weyden, while Stanley Cleveland and Robert Schaetzel represented the State Department. The result was a detailed first draft of a "Memorandum of Understanding" signed by Kohnstamm, Butterworth, and Cook, which contained the essence of a future joint agreement.[61] Despite this auspicious beginning, talks soon bogged down.

The reason for the delay was the protracted debate on the control by Euratom of its own safeguard arrangements. While State largely sided with Euratom, the AEC insisted on unilateral inspection rights by the United States to prevent Euratom from using American nuclear materials for military use. This point remained a bone of contention even though the chairman of the AEC had previously given his approval to the preliminary draft of the Euratom Treaty in March 1957. Failing to achieve a common position on this issue, State and the AEC were ill-equipped to face Congress and request a joint agreement with Euratom. By the beginning of May, the joint working group, who had come to Washington to put the last touches on the Memorandum of Understanding, had completed their work. In order to speed up negotiations, Monnet met with Dulles on 10 May. By the end of the month, the Euratom Council of Ministers had signed the Memorandum of Understanding and initialed an Agreement of Cooperation. Yet the AEC continued to voice objections, leading the *New York Times* to write of "a disturbing lack of coordination among different government agencies."[62] In this case, as in many others, Eisenhower ended the debate by siding with his secretary of state. By 17 June, the president had approved the Memorandum of Understanding, which was then signed by Strauss, Dulles, and Eisenhower himself. On 23 June, Eisenhower finally sent an agreement to Congress for approval. This was by no means the end of the checkered career of the U.S.-Euratom agreement. The JCAE seemed in no hurry to initiate hearings on the subject. Monnet, Armand, Kohnstamm, and their American friends decided to take action and persistently lobbied the JCAE and the administration for rapid approval of the agreement.

For Monnet and Armand, a speedy approval for the agreement took on added significance in view of the rather slow beginnings of both Euratom and the Common Market. The French economic situation did not augur well for the quick implementation of the EEC Treaty, while Euratom had become mired in organizational difficulties. Somewhat unwisely, Monnet and Armand came to identify the success of Euratom with the success of the joint program. During a lunch with Monnet, Armand suggested that it might be well for Kohnstamm to make a special trip to the United States. Butterworth and Schaetzel disagreed and told Kohnstamm it would be a mistake to come at this stage of the negotiations. It would be wiser for Armand himself to travel to Washington after the agreement had been negotiated to establish personal links with those AEC and State Department officials who would be responsible for its implementation. In order to substitute for his presence in Washington, Kohnstamm devised other ways of stimulating the negotiations. In early July he suggested that Monnet should write to Dulles and McCloy. McCloy could prove useful because he was a good friend of McCone, who had just been appointed the new chairman of the AEC. On 13 July, Monnet wrote Dulles asking him to use his "influence and energy to make sure that the agreement pass[ed] Congress before the holidays." As a postscript, he added: "I understand that Sen[ator] Clinton Anderson is the difficulty and might be extremely susceptible to some attention!"[63] Senator Clinton Anderson (D-New Mexico), the influential vice chairman of the JCAE, was indeed the problem. So, too, was a rather undiplomatic move on the part of Eisenhower.

Although hearings on the U.S.-Euratom program were scheduled to start before the JCAE on 16 July the committee decided to delay the hearings for another week. A few days earlier Eisenhower had written a letter to the ranking Republican member of the Appropriations Committee on Public Works. In it, he voiced his strong disapproval of the additions the JCAE had appended to the program of domestic reactor construction that the administration had just sent to Congress. Admiral Strauss, who had consistently resisted building domestic reactors with government money in the hope that the private sector would shoulder the responsibility of atomic power production, was seen as the main culprit. There was a strong presumption that it was he who had advised the president to write the letter, especially because he had just quit his job as chairman of the AEC to become Eisenhower's adviser for nuclear affairs. The letter angered the Joint Committee, including its Republican members. It especially angered Senator Anderson, whose personal dislike for Strauss was well known in Washington. The senator convinced his colleagues on the JCAE to cancel the 16 July hearing on the Euratom agreements. Why discuss a program of more than $100 million for Euratom, if the administration refused to finance a domestic program for atomic development? When the hearings eventually opened on 22 July, Congress, and most of all Senator Anderson, repeatedly pointed to the advantages granted to Euratom that were denied the domestic program. Anderson was particularly opposed to selling the first nine tons of uranium 235 to Euratom on a deferred payment basis. How could one trust an international agency that did not have any real financial responsibility! he exclaimed. Also, the Euratom program gave priority to the PWR and the BWR light-water reactor types, commercialized by Westinghouse and General Electric, to the detriment of other more recent prototypes. Would it not be better, he asked, to bank on the development of new prototypes rather than to seek to perfect old ones?[64]

Despite Senator Anderson's antagonism, all was not lost for the Euratom agreement. Most of the other members of the JCAE were generally favorable to a joint program, especially since American industry favored the agreement as a way of gaining export markets in Europe and of experimenting with American reactors on a large scale. The Middle East crisis in Jordan and Iraq further played into the hands of Euratom supporters by demonstrating once again Europe's need to develop alternative energy sources. Finally, as Dillon adroitly pointed out during the hearings, if the United States refused to go along with the agreement, Europe might well look elsewhere for its supply of fissionable materials. The constant lobbying efforts of Monnet's friends also helped to bring the JCAE along. Kohnstamm wrote long and informative letters to Senator John Pastore (D-Rhode Island), an influential member of the JCAE. George Ball, who still continued to advise Monnet from his law firm (Cleary, Gottlieb, Friendly and Ball), made efforts to approach Senator

Anderson privately. Dean Acheson's intercession on behalf of the program also proved particularly helpful. Finally, Samuel Waugh's support for Monnet and European integration helped Euratom obtain a long-term loan of $135 million from the Export-Import Bank.[65] By the end of August, Congress had granted its full approval to an international agreement with Euratom pursuant to Section 124 of the Atomic Energy Act of 1954. This special international agreement was needed to establish the legal basis for allowing the United States to enter into an agreement with a group of countries such as Euratom, as opposed to a single country. After the summer recess, Congress approved an Agreement of Cooperation between Euratom and the United States, which was nothing less than a legislative version of the Memorandum of Understanding. The official signing of the U.S.-Euratom agreement took place in Brussels on 8 November 1958.[66]

It now remained to execute the agreement, and this was no easy task. Organizational changes within the AEC made it difficult to develop clearly defined guidelines for implementing the program.[67] On the European side, Armand suffered from a nervous breakdown. He had not taken part in the official signing of the U.S.-Euratom agreement in November and eventually resigned in February 1959. De Gaulle's coming to power did not help the cause of Euratom, which he considered as the epitome of supranationalism. The U.S.-Euratom agreement gave him and the French Commissariat à l'Energie Atomique ready-made arguments for criticizing Euratom as an extension of American technology. In 1961, Etienne Hirsch, who had re-placed Armand as the head of Euratom, was not reappointed to his position. This was de Gaulle's way of indicating his disapproval of Hirsch's all-too-"European" initiatives. By contrast, Hirsch's successor faithfully followed the directives of the French government, which made Euratom's suprana-tional character less and less credible. More than any single factor, however, it was the decline in oil and gas prices that plagued Euratom. Beginning in 1959, oil prices started going down, in part because of the discovery of new fields in the Middle East, the North Sea, and the Netherlands. Only in 1973 did they rise sufficiently to make nuclear power competitive. Results of the joint U.S.-Euratom agreement were disappointing. Only three light water reactors were built under the program. Their total capacity did not exceed 750 MWe, which looked insignificant when compared with the 15000 MWe the three Wise Men had predicted in their report. Although additional agreements were negotiated with the United States in 1960 and then later during Kennedy's presidency, the new administration soon denounced co-operation with Euratom as a drain of American technology that did not provide much benefit to the United States.[68]

5

Europe at Sixes and Sevens and the OECD

THE COMMON MARKET: WAIT AND SEE

When Harold Macmillan met with Dulles in Paris in December 1955, he told his American counterpart that there were growing fears among OEEC countries that a "tight" integration of the Six would result in "high tariffs and other protective measures." Should this be the case, the community of the Six would "create a source of division rather than of strength." Dulles answered that the United States supported "European unity, not high tariffs," and proceeded to list American motives for favoring the Community. A few days later, the counselor of the Canadian Embassy approached the State Department and voiced concerns that echoed those of Macmillan. He was told in convoluted diplomatic language that since the Six did not yet have any concrete economic agenda, the attitude in Washington was to wait and see. As for Eisenhower he anticipated great gains for peace from a "third force" Europe "with about 250 million people," which he hoped would create "an industrial complex comparable to the United States, having, in fact, more skilled laborers than the U.S."[1] At that time, the president and most of the administration were not so much concerned with the potential discriminatory features of a "third force" Europe as with maintaining momentum to ensure that Euratom and the EEC would come to life, in that order.

Dulles insisted that approval of Euratom should not be delayed by Common Market negotiations and fretted at the prospect of linking the two treaties—a position advocated mainly by the German, Belgian, and Dutch governments. Euratom was of "immediate importance,"[2] while Common Market negotiations would be lengthy. Whereas the French showed every indication that they would ratify the Euratom Treaty, the chances that they would also ratify the Common Market Treaty were far less certain. By putting all their eggs in the same basket, the Six could well end up with nothing. Shortly after the defeat of the EDC another setback might well deal European integration a fatal blow. Yet interest for the Common Market proposals grew during the months following the Venice Conference of 29-30 May 1956, at which the foreign affairs ministers of the Six had approved the Spaak report on European integration. At the conference, Spaak was asked to chair a new intergovernmental committee with a view towards drafting two separate treaties: the Euratom Treaty and the Common Market Treaty.[3] As a successful conclusion to the negotiations for both Euratom and the Common Market appeared increasingly probable, the Eisenhower administration began to actively consider the consequences of European economic integration for the United States.

In mid-August, in the aftermath of the Venice Conference, the newly created Council on Foreign Economic Policy (CFEP), in which top-level officials took part, established a subcommittee to study the effects of European economic integration on American trade and other economic interests.[4] Earlier that year a member of the administration had written to Joseph Dodge, the council's chairman, suggesting that the CFEP "explore the implications for the U.S. of genuine progress toward economic integration in Europe," for he felt that many in the government "plugg[ed] this line actively" without being aware of potential discrimination against American trade. Concrete results were not forthcoming until November, however. Meanwhile, in July, the Department of State attempted to provide some guidance to American diplomatic missions by defining under what conditions preferential arrangements would be acceptable to the United States.

The discrimination against outside countries inherent in customs unions and free-trade areas was deemed admissible because the elimination of trade barriers among participants could foster a more efficient allocation of resources. This, in turn, could contribute to expand world trade. However, the United States was willing to accept preferential arrangements that did not "involve the elimination of restrictions on substantially all of the trade of the participating countries" only if such arrangements also contributed to American political objectives: the ECSC was a case in point, since it encouraged the closer political integration of Western Europe.

Although the State Department generally favored the Common Market, it nevertheless voiced concern about certain features of the Spaak report. The State Department did not feel that the proposed European Commission and the Council of Ministers would provide "effective institutions capable of acting independently of national government in coordination of domestic economic policies."

The Spaak report also remained disturbingly obscure on provisions for preventing private business from organizing export ententes to trade with non-EEC countries, including the United States, of course. What good would the Common Market be if private arrangements replaced governmental barriers? Finally, the State Department was most interested in observing how agriculture would function within the Common Market.[5] By the end of the year, these concerns were more clearly articulated. A British initiative, taken up for the first time by the OEEC in July 1956, provided cause for greater concern.

The British proposal for an industrial free-trade area, including the Six as a single unit and those OEEC countries that agreed to join, increasingly became a topic of discussion in the fall. What in fact were the intentions of the United Kingdom? pondered United States officials. Was the British plan (Plan G) an attempt to torpedo the Common Market or was it a genuine effort to bridge the gap between the Six and other European countries? In his visit to Washington in January, Prime Minister Eden had revealed the British hostility towards the Common Market. What now? As both the Euratom and Common Market Treaties seemed on their way to completion, the British government appeared to have channeled its energies away from hostility and towards efforts to find a workable solution to coexistence with the Six. René Sergent, the secretary-general of the OEEC, believed that the British were sincere and made this known to Dulles.[6] Other sources indicated that many officials in the British government now believed it in their best interest to join a Free Trade Area (FTA) that would allow them to keep their ties with the Commonwealth, gain equal access to the markets of Germany and the other Six, and also make it possible for the United Kingdom to resume its interrupted leadership in the movement toward European unity.[7]

Although the Americans initially appeared to support both the Free Trade Area and the Common Market approaches, it soon became clear that it was inclined to favor the latter. In early October, steel industrialist Clarence C. Randall, who had just replaced Dodge as chairman of the CFEP, wrote an enthusiastic letter to Dulles in which he praised the Common Market as "the most significant economic event in my generation." Having recently returned from his trip to Europe in September, Randall, a former opponent of the ECSC, now recommended that the United States "promptly make a public statement in support of the project." On 29 October in Miami, Florida, President Eisenhower endorsed both the Common Market and the Free Trade Area proposals as important contributions to European economic integration. Yet this approval came on the condition that the Common Market would be created first and the Free Trade Area "thereafter," "gradually, over a period of years," and "around the common market."[8]

By 15 November, Joseph Davis, chairman of the Subcommittee on Regional Integration, delivered his report on the "Effects of Regional Economic Integration on U.S. Trade and Other Economic Interests" to the CFEP. It was a compromise between the attitude of the State Department and the president, who supported both the Common Market and the Free Trade Area, and the more critical position adopted by the Treasury and the Federal Reserve, whose reservations surfaced in some of the phrasing. Specifically, the report recommended that "European arrangements promote rather than retard the achievement of currency convertibility and a multilateral system of trade in the free world." Special arrangements for protecting agriculture in the Community figured prominently on the list of American worries, as did concern for restrictive trade practices by European private business. Fearing the prospect of "an inward-looking regional bloc" surrounded by high trade barriers, the subcommittee recommended using the GATT (General Agreement on Tariffs and Trade) as a controlling device. With these qualifications, the report recommended a renewed American commitment to European integration through both the Common Market and the Free Trade Area because of their contributions to the cohesion of the free world and to the overall level of international trade. The British proposal was endorsed in light of its potential for linking "the United Kingdom more closely to the Continent" and for providing "a stimulus for closer European political association, a long sought United States objective."[9]

Political considerations were thus uppermost in the acceptance of the Free Trade Area proposal. These would gradually lose precedence in the late fifties as the U.S. economic outlook started to deteriorate. The report was forwarded abroad to all missions concerned with the request that they report regularly on economic integration developments and the recommendation that they avoid public statements on European integration that could give the impression that the United States was "prodding the Western European Countries into these projects." The lesson of the EDC had been a hard one, but by now it was also well assimilated.[10]

On 15 January 1957 the State Department issued a press release that echoed the CFEP report: the United States would support both the Free Trade Area and the Common Market if they contributed to the expansion of multilateral trade and convertibility of currencies on the one hand, and the "cohesion of Western Europe within an expanding Atlantic Community" on the other. The document stressed certain developments in Common Market proposals that would continue to attract the attention of the United States, thus revealing latent concerns of the administration. Of these, policies relating to agriculture took precedence. Recognizing the importance of the

European market for American agricultural exports, the press release acknowledged the wish of the United States "to study carefully the possible impact of common-market arrangements" on the United States.[11] This was hardly surprising in light of the significance of sales of American agricultural products to the EEC. The numbers spoke for themselves. By 1957, agricultural exports to the EEC totaled almost $1.1 billion. By 1960, they reached over $1.15 billion. And, two years later, the EEC had become the most important market for American farm exports. This development was extremely significant both in terms of domestic politics in the United States and in terms of international policy, given the influence of powerful American farm lobbies and, more importantly, the growing share of United States farm production being exported, which by 1962 was almost one-sixth of the total agricultural production in terms of dollar value.[12]

In 1957, the concerns over the consequences of the Common Market were not yet well articulated; the Common Agricultural Policy was not a reality at the time. But American policymakers already anticipated some of its possible consequences. As the negotiations for the Common Market neared their conclusion, the administration used diplomatic channels with the Six to convey American concerns over certain aspects of the Common Market Treaty. In January, a State Department telegram to the American embassy in Belgium inquired whether a common agricultural policy would not intensify preferential trade among the Six at the expense of other countries, particularly the United States. Such a development would be hard to reconcile in GATT, and the United States would in all likelihood object. The State Department recommended arranging a meeting as soon as possible with Robert Marjolin, the economic adviser to French Foreign Minister Pineau, to discuss these pressing issues. John Tuthill, counselor for economic affairs at the embassy in France and a devoted Europeanist, was to participate in the discussions.[13]

About a month after the signing of the Rome Treaties, the deputy under secretary of state for economic affairs, Douglas Dillon, transmitted a State Department report on the EEC Treaty to the CFEP that reaffirmed American commitment to the Common Market, while recommending further negotiations in GATT to protect the interests of other countries, especially in agriculture.[14] Dillon requested urgent consideration of the report by the CFEP in light of the impending meeting of the Intersessional Committee of the Contracting Parties to the GATT in Geneva on 24 April. By 16 April the CFEP had approved the conclusions of the State Department report almost verbatim. Noteworthy in the report were, once again, a concern for the provisions of the Common Market Treaty relating to agriculture that encouraged the conclusion of long-term contracts among the Six "to promote trade among them in agricultural products and those with respect to minimum prices for such products." The report also expressed concern for the potential size of the external tariff of the Community, and the imposition of restrictions on American imports for balance-of-payments reasons. A final concern cited "the establishment of new tariff preferences favoring the Community members as a result of the arrangements affecting the overseas territories."

In conversations with German officials, Dulles had earlier hailed the association of Africa with Europe. Africa, he insisted, was the "big hinterland of Europe." If only Europeans could bring about a peaceful transition to self-government in the region, they would be able to tap the great resources of that continent, and Europe, in association with America, would become "one of the greatest forces in the world." Some members of the administration did not agree with Dulles's enthusiastic vision, but saw the concrete consequences of an association of overseas territories with the Community as a threat to the exports of third countries, and particularly those of Latin American states. Much more would be heard on this topic under Kennedy. For the time being, Dillon recommended not pushing for changes in the Common Market Treaty during the GATT meeting, as this might jeopardize the chances of its ratification by the various European parliaments. It was much better to wait until the treaties had been ratified, as then and only then would the United States and its partners in GATT be able to give a "definite consideration to the treaty."[15] Determined to make the Rome Treaties a success, Dulles could not refrain from applying some pressure behind the scenes and warned French officials that a failure on their part to ratify the Rome Treaties, following the EDC disaster, would have "a catastrophic effect on United States attitudes toward Europe."[16] So the case of the Common Market rested temporarily, awaiting the ratification of the treaties by the Six. Meanwhile, the British proposal for the Free Trade Area for all goods other than agricultural products underwent close scrutiny by the American administration.

THE FREE TRADE AREA NEGOTIATIONS
AND THE SIX FAVORITES

Harold Macmillan became prime minister in January 1957 and pressed vigorously for the adoption of "Plan G" by European negotiators. When the council of the OEEC met in February, its members agreed to initiate formal negotiations for the Free Trade Area. Suspicions about the motives of the United Kingdom were aroused, however, by a set of proposals from the

British Foreign Office, which called for the grouping of European regional organizations into one single assembly assisted by specialized commissions, notably in the military, cultural, and economic fields. The prospect of this simplification of European regional organizations, especially since it included economics, appeared to threaten the very institutions of the European Coal and Steel Community, Euratom, and the Common Market. The Eisenhower administration reacted with a mixture of puzzlement and suspicion towards the "Grand Design." Had not Macmillan and other British officials affirmed earlier that the Common Market formed the "necessary base" for the Free Trade Area they proposed? The State Department readily agreed with the contention of the British Foreign Office paper that the OEEC was the "most appropriate instrument for overall economic cooperation." Where their views differed was on the "tendency [to] blur [the] vital distinction between merely cooperative arrangements (OEEC) and genuine integration (CSC)." A telegram sent to certain American embassies in Europe noted that the State Department was "seriously concerned over [the] implication that six-country developments CSC, EURATOM, Common Market should in some way be subordinated to [the] OEEC." Very much in a now familiar line of thought, the telegram stressed that American support for the Six was "based not only on expected economic and technical advantages, but even more on [the] hope that these developments represent[ed] steps towards [an] increasing political union, which would further contribute greatly to [the] strength and cohesion of [the] Atlantic area as a whole." The main concern was that the British proposal would dilute the movement of the Messina countries towards "genuine integration," thereby preventing them from acting as "a unit within Atlantic organizations."[17] Timing was also crucial: only when the Euratom and Common Market Treaties had been signed and put into effect could the United States conceive of an association between the Six and other OEEC countries (such as the Free Trade Area). Most important, then, was to safeguard the capacity of the Six to act as a cohesive unit within a larger organizational framework; this presupposed both the success of negotiations then going on among the Six and the creation of institutions at the six-countries level.

The British had a quite different set of priorities. Throughout the month of April, Macmillan worried about the prospects for the Free Trade Area. To one of his friends, he wrote : "The official negotiations in Paris for a marriage between the Common Market and the Free Trade Area may have reached an impasse by the end of May." To another: "What I chiefly fear, and what we must at all costs avoid, is the Common Market coming into being and the Free Trade Area never following."[18] Macmillan resolved to reverse that order, if at all possible. His tactics included putting pressure on the French and the Germans to reach an agreement on the Free Trade Area prior to the ratification of the Common Market Treaty, and advocating the "Grand Design."

Christian Pineau, the French foreign minister, and his German counterpart, Von Brentano, agreed not to go along with the British proposal of placing the Free Trade Area first on the agenda. They also concurred in their assessment that the most objectionable feature of the Grand Design was the proposal to include all the NATO countries in a single great assembly. In a conversation with Dulles, Ambassador to Germany David Bruce, and other American officials in early May, Chancellor Adenauer unambiguously indicated that Germany had no intention of joining such a scheme. Dulles retorted that the United States had no intention of joining either: "superimposing rather vague, more generalized plans" could indeed endanger "the prospects for practical European projects." The secretary took the opportunity to reiterate his strong support for the Common Market, sounding an alarmist note in case the treaty was not ratified in the near future. Should the Common Market Treaty fail after the EDC, he insisted, American public opinion would no longer support Europe: "complete sovereignty for the many nations of Europe [was] a luxury which European countries [could] no longer afford at U.S. expense."[19]

Meanwhile, Macmillan wrote to Peter Thorneycroft, the chancellor of the exchequer: "We must not be bullied by the activities of the Six. We could, if we were driven to it, fight their movement if it were to take the form of anything that was prejudicial to our interests. Economically, with the Commonwealth and other friends, including the Scandinavians, we could stand aside from a narrow Common Market. We also have some politico-military weapons." Macmillan concluded that the United Kingdom must take the lead either in widening the narrower Common Market into the Free Trade Area or, if the Six would not cooperate with the British, "in opposing it."[20]

Positive action was taken in the fall of 1957 by appointing Reginald Maudling as the minister in charge of negotiating with the Common Market countries and other OEEC countries. In October, the OEEC Council set up the Inter-Governmental Committee to conduct the negotiations and elected Maudling as chairman.[21] That same month a State Department telegram provided guidance to its European embassies on American policy towards the FTA for the OEEC ministerial meeting in mid-October. The telegram underlined the importance of the success of the FTA negotiations for the United States, with this qualification: that the Free Trade Area would include the Common Market *as a unit*. If this were the case, the FTA could in fact reinforce European unity and extend the economic benefits to be derived from the establishment of the Common Market to an even larger area. Conversely, a breakdown of the negotiations "could adversely affect European cohesiveness to [the] detriment [of] US political and possibly (through NATO) to US strategic objectives." A failure of the negotiations could also be detrimental to the American objective of expanding the multilateral trading system "by forcing recourse to bilateral deals." For the moment, however, the number-one priority was the success of the Common Market, and the United States wished to "avoid any delay in its implementation because of possible divergences re[garding] FTA." Accordingly, the U.S. delegation at the OEEC meeting was to participate in the negotiations only in a "limited manner," without making "detailed comments on various specific issues." In other words, the United States would not support the FTA as enthusiastically as it supported the Common Market, but would nevertheless "try to prevent the negotiations from breaking on key issues."[22] This policy hardly satisfied the United Kingdom, but neither did it satisfy agencies outside the Department of State, which lacked clear guidance on the matter.

On 1 January 1958, the Common Market and Euratom treaties officially took effect. The administration now started taking an even closer look at what they perceived as the discriminatory aspects of the Common Market, adopting a distinctly passive approach towards the Free Trade Area. The deterioration of American economic fortunes in 1958 help to explain the more cautious attitude towards the Common Market and the "hands-off" attitude towards the FTA. Following an unusual trade surplus in 1957, American exports declined in 1958 by 14 percent to $17.9 billion, while imports decreased by 3 percent to $12.6 billion. The trade surplus of 1957 totaled $6.5 billion, but the 1959 trade surplus was down to $5.5 billion. Paralleling this trend were growing balance-of-payments deficits—about twice of what they had been in the early 1950s. The dollar's flight abroad reached disturbing proportions in 1958, while the gold outflow totaled $2.3 billion. More and more the American economy seemed to be getting out of step with a much healthier European economic situation. While the United States reduced its interest rates to "prime the pump" of its faltering domestic economy, major European currencies returned to limited convertibility at the end of 1958. This had the side effect of increasing the volatility of interest rates, as short-term capital markets became internationalized. Low interest rates adopted by the United States to stimulate growth at home were mirrored by European policies, particularly in Germany, that attempted to control an overexpanding economy and curb inflation by contracting the money supply; hence the higher interest rates in Europe, which attracted American funds. Increasingly, concerns about the dollar shortage transformed into concerns about a dollar glut, and confidence in the dollar declined.[23] The United States quickly drew appropriate conclusions from the move to convertibility of the principal European nations, and the establishment of the European Monetary Agreement. In January 1959, a joint United States-Canadian Communiqué stated: "Convertibility has removed the financial justification for discriminating against dollar suppliers, and should be followed by further moves. . . . The United States and Canadian Governments will be watching with close and sympathetic interest the way in which the logic of the new situation is translated into action."[24] The new set of circumstances also contributed to the American administration's growing reluctance to condone just any kind of European integration, and the FTA took the brunt of the criticism.

On 8 April 1958, Clarence Randall, having just returned from a trip to Paris where he had spoken to Embassy officials and the economic staff of USRO,[25] wrote Dillon that he was somewhat puzzled with America's lukewarm support for the Free Trade Area, which paled in comparison with United States' ardent support for the Common Market. To him, the FTA offered a way of associating the British with the Continent, and, as such, was a key element in the integration of Europe. Unless the British were tied to Europe, the new Common Market would "so dominate the picture that the OEEC [would] gradually disintegrate. This would be a move towards fragmentation rather than unity." Randall accordingly counseled supporting the concept of the FTA "clearly and unequivocally."[26] But by April the United States, while still being on record as favoring the aims of the FTA negotiations, made it known to the participants that it would lend its support to the FTA only if it were consistent with the GATT objective of expanding multilateral trade and did not endanger the political and economic unity of the Six. This was still the American position by mid-June, when Macmillan was scheduled to visit the United States.[27] From that point the American government remained disturbingly silent in public on the FTA.

Meanwhile, John Foster Dulles was active in trying to convince German Minister of Economic Affairs Erhard to shift his preference from the Free Trade Area to the Common Market.[28] Jean Monnet was also active. In October, his Action Committee, while insisting that the community of the Six was open to those European countries that were ready to delegate part of their sovereignty to common institutions, noted that the reality of the Community "must be respected in the ongoing negotiations for a Free Trade Area."[29] In mid-November he told John Tuthill (who swiftly transmitted

Monnet's views to the Department of State) that it would be best to cease the activities of the Maudling Committee and initiate "bilateral negotiations between the EEC and each of the 11 countries starting with the British." To Monnet the "OEEC type negotiation was hopeless."[30] In December 1958, the United States observer at the Maudling negotiations refused to act as a mediator in attempting to rescue the talks, although strongly urged to do so. By that time all hope was indeed lost for a successful conclusion of the Maudling negotiations.

The failure of the talks was extremely ill received by the business community. Hoping that British influence within FTA would help mitigate the protectionist and "dirigiste" tendencies of the Common Market, American industrial and banking circles had on the whole been favorable to the FTA. Alarmist statements were now being made in the specialized press about the potential economic war that might ensue between the discriminatory grouping of the Messina countries and the rest of the OEEC. This outburst of indignation soon calmed down, however, with the announcement of the return of Europe to convertibility and the first lowering of trade barriers among the Six in January 1959.[31] The British, who had been urging speedy progress in the Maudling negotiations in order to have something tangible to present at the Commonwealth Conference in September and to preempt the Six's lowering of tariffs among themselves, were now left in the lurch. They countered with a new bridge-building initiative: the EFTA, a European Free Trade Association among the "Outer Seven," namely, the United Kingdom, Norway, Sweden, Denmark, Switzerland, Austria, and Portugal. The new negotiations were to lead to the creation of the EFTA in January 1960. Despite the potential of the Common Market for discriminating against American exports and despite declining economic fortunes in the United States, the State Department continued to champion the cause of the Six for mainly political reasons. In Europe "at sixes and sevens," the Six clearly came out of the gate as favorites.

The United States adopted a Janus-like posture towards "regional discrimination." The EEC was tolerated, even encouraged, because of its political implications; the EFTA was not, precisely because it lacked these political implications, although it could not be explicitly discouraged. To the outside world the United States administration presented a confusing picture. On the one hand, the United States indicated its willingness to support a free trade area among the Outer Seven, while, on the other hand, it appeared decidedly cool towards the idea. Periodically, scandals flared up in the press, with revelations that the United States in fact opposed the EFTA, followed by the usual reassurances to the contrary by United States officials. Some quarters of the administration were decidedly cool towards the idea. In a conversation with Monnet, John Tuthill told him that the American "refusal to intercede in the Free Trade Area discussions was in fact a position." To him "the British proposal was so unfortunate and so badly presented that there was nothing to do but let it run its course and result in dismal and public failure." The fact that the United States "kept out of the debate indicated," according to him, "a recognition that the situation had to become worse before constructive suggestions could be made." He was deeply convinced that the Stockholm negotiations would end in dismal failure, but "must be allowed to run their dreary course" anyway.[32] A lack of coordination between the State Department, other departments, and United States embassies and missions abroad helped blur in the public eye the unsympathetic attitude of American Europeanists in Washington and in Europe towards EFTA.

During a trip to Europe in the fall of 1959, Clarence Randall wrote to Edward Galbreath, one of his assistants on the CFEP, asking what was in fact the policy of the State Department towards EFTA. Galbreath answered that "political considerations [were] considered of overriding importance,"[33] and included some position papers for Randall's guidance. One document, made in preparation for the president's trip to Europe, termed a free trade area among the Outer Seven "a difficult issue." EFTA was acceptable as long as it conformed to GATT without threatening the Six or hurting the economic interests of other countries, including the United States.[34] Not surprisingly, the State Department could give no clear-cut guidance on how American diplomats were supposed to half-heartedly support EFTA, so as to conform to American objectives, without offending the Outer Seven. When he returned from his trip to Europe, Clarence Randall recommended that the CFEP undertake a thorough study of the problems of the Six and the Outer Seven. But State decided to go it alone, bypassing the council. In April of the following year, Galbreath wrote a memorandum to Randall evaluating the policy pursued by the State Department: "The policy adopted by State was to give open support and encouragement to the Common Market while expressing some doubts and uncertainty about the Outer Seven. This policy proved disturbing to the U.K. and other members of the Outer Seven. I believe that had this subject been laid before the CFEP, a policy might have been suggested that would have helped to avoid such a serious split between the Six and the Seven."[35]

One month earlier, Eisenhower and Adenauer had issued a joint communiqué that praised the Common Market proposal for an acceleration in tariff reductions as a "major contribution to a general lowering of world trade barriers"[36] while criticizing the organization of the Outer Seven for its contribution to trade divisions on the Continent. When Macmillan and Eisenhower met later that month, the president had to listen to the recriminations of the prime minister against American lack of tact, while Foreign Secretary Selwyn Lloyd went so far as to suggest that American support for the Common Market proposal might trigger a trade war between the United Kingdom and Germany, which in turn might require the United Kingdom to withdraw its troops, thereby leading to the breakup of NATO.[37]

The absence of American support for the EFTA had the combined effects of arousing British resentment against the United States and setting in motion a reappraisal of British policy towards the Common Market that would lead to the British application to join the Common Market in 1961. In September 1959, President Eisenhower had told de Gaulle he felt that "the British were not hostile per se to the Common Market and that the Outer Seven which they were setting up might perhaps provide a bridge for coming in at a later date with the Common Market."[38] De Gaulle dissented, and Eisenhower ultimately proved to be right. In the meantime, British proposals to join only two of the European Communities, namely the ECSC and Euratom, did not trigger any great demonstration of enthusiasm within the State Department. The proposal of the minister of state for foreign affairs, John Profumo, presented to the Western European Union in June, was considered "largely meaningless" by the State Department, because the ECSC and Euratom were now regarded by the Six "as steps towards the common market" and were "likely to be merged with the common market at a future date." Accordingly, the "Six would regard British membership in the two subsidiary organizations as undesirable unless the U.K. joined the Common Market."[39]

THE EUROPEAN COMMUNITIES UNDER SCRUTINY

American policy towards the Common Market was less ambiguous than its policy towards EFTA. The United States "support for European economic and political integration along the lines of the Messina countries" approach continued mainly for political reasons. The relative indifference of the administration towards the failure of the Free Trade Area negotiations blatantly contrasted with the outburst of enthusiasm that followed the ratification of the Common Market and Euratom treaties. In January 1958, the United States mission to the ECSC qualified the progress that had been made recently in the unification of Europe as "almost a political miracle."[40] That same month, the appointment of Butterworth as representative to the EEC and Euratom, in addition to the ECSC, was intended as a demonstration of

American support to European supranational integration.[41] The United States then gave further support to the Communities by becoming the first nation to invite the presidents of the three European Communities to make an official visit.

Secretary of State Christian A. Herter issued the invitation; John Foster Dulles died of cancer on 24 May. On 9 June, Walter Hallstein, president of the Common Market, Etienne Hirsch, president of Euratom, and Paul Finet, president of the ECSC, arrived at Washington National Airport. Herter, who was attending the East-West conference in Geneva, could not meet them personally. Instead Douglas Dillon, now under secretary of state for economic affairs, and other State Department officials and ambassadors greeted them at the airport. The presidents and their aides were then driven in individual cars to Blair House, the president's guest house, which was normally reserved for heads of state or governments making official visits to the United States. Americans were somewhat surprised to see three presidents for Europe instead of one. From June 9 to June 12, the three presidents visited top-level officials from the State, Treasury, and Commerce departments. They also met with leading members of Congress, including Senator Fulbright, as well as with representatives of the AEC and the Export-Import Bank. Although always an ardent supporter of European integration, Eisenhower nevertheless expressed the hope that "material progress" in Europe might now be matched by the equal progress towards a "European concept" through "the strengthening of spiritual values," i.e., "common dedication to common values." Determined to strengthen the prosperity of the "free world," as compared to that of the Communist world, the president was curious to see how the growth of the European Community compared with the growth of the Soviet Union. Having called jointly on Eisenhower, Dillon, Secretary of Commerce Lewis Strauss, and Secretary of the Treasury Robert Anderson, the three presidents then met individually with representatives in their own areas of expertise. Etienne Hirsch of Euratom established close contacts with the congressional JCAE and the AEC and discussed concrete means for cooperation between Euratom and the United States in advanced research. Meanwhile, Paul Finet called on the secretary of the interior and the secretary of labor and spoke of the pressing coal crises in the United States and in Europe. Walter Hallstein and his aides met with Secretary of Agriculture Ezra Benson, who no doubt inquired about agricultural arrangements among the Six and their potential for discriminating against the United States.[42]

On the recommendation of the State Department, the three presidents then spoke with Dillon about the possibility of establishing a permanent representation of the European Communities in the United States, as the counterpart to the United States Mission to the European Communities. Dillon promised to see how this might be arranged both legally and administratively. A common representation in Washington was all the more important in view of the anti-Communities mood prevalent in the national embassies of certain members of the Six. (Max Kohnstamm, who accompanied the three presidents, later pointed out that the Belgian Minister, Mr. Bassompierre, had often spoken against the Six to the Department of State and was quite displeased at the prospect that the three presidents would be housed at Blair House.) An added reason for a representation of the Communities in Washington was the necessity to have competent staff on the ground to launch U.S.-Euratom cooperation.

While in the United States, the three heads of the Communities also touched upon the burning question of where to establish the capital of Europe. The Americans selected Luxembourg as the obvious equivalent of the District of Columbia in the United States.

Finally, Kohnstamm and Hirsch paid a visit to Princeton's Institute for Advanced Studies and exchanged views with the director of the Institute, Robert Oppenheimer, and other fellows about the creation of a European University. The Americans advised their European visitors to start with a small but top-level university, with an emphasis on those fields that were directly relevant to the development of Europe: social sciences, economics, and law. Professors from the exact sciences would also be brought in to educate the "leaders of tomorrow" about the problems of the future.[43]

The joint communiqué resulting from the visit referred to Eisenhower's continued support of the European Communities "because of the significant promise they hold for enhancing the strength and well-being not only of Europe but of the entire Free World." Just prior to the visit, Eisenhower had told the German minister of economics, Ludwig Erhard, of his hope to see a closer political coalition among the Six. "The resultant prosperity," he predicted, "will culminate in a community of such great strength that added to ours it will do much to nullify Communism." Intent on economizing American dollars, the president looked forward to a rosy future in which the neutralization of communism would save the money now being channeled into defense and allow Europe and the United States to provide much needed help to developing countries.

Despite presidential enthusiasm, points of contention surfaced in some of the phrasing of the joint communiqué in June. Among these were references to American interest in further progress towards the removal of trade restrictions in Europe and to American concerns for "the restrictive import measures adversely affecting the United States coal exports," which certain members of the Six had adopted. Upon his return to Europe, Finet reported that the Americans, while hoping that Europe would unite both in the economic and political levels, also feared that lower wage levels in Europe (compared to those in the United States) might give European industrial products a leading edge over American products on world markets and in the United States.[44] In his conversation with Ludwig Erhard in early June, Eisenhower touched upon that very same topic. Now that the Common Market had come to stay, American support for European integration became more cautious. While Eisenhower told Erhard that he felt confident that "as the member nations of the common market develop[ed] in prosperity, they [would] tend to lower their trade barriers in order to increase their trade around the world,"[45] the United States consistently, both publicly and behind the scenes, encouraged the Common Market to adopt "liberal, low-tariff policies" in the industrial and agricultural field.[46] Despite continued support for European integration, the United States would under no circumstances endorse "restrictive trade arrangements under the cover of European integration."[47] This warning was destined both for EFTA and the European Communities.

The ECSC was of particular concern to the United States. Throughout 1955 and much of 1956, the State Department had steadily defended the ECSC against criticism from other agencies relating to the Community's export cartel for steel exports. It had also resisted recurrent attempts by the Commerce Department to impose limitations on scrap imports from the United States by the Community.[48] Yet by June 1956, the State Department itself was beginning to lose patience with the ECSC's lack of progress in dealing with the national steel cartels and the "Brussels export cartel." The State Department warned René Mayer that as a result of lack of action on the part of the ECSC Americans now saw the ECSC as "a reincarnation of the prewar international steel cartel."[49] This had the undesirable side effect of undermining American confidence that further attempts to unify Europe would expand international trade rather than restrict it. In early February of 1957, Clarence Randall warned ECSC representatives that the Community should review its scrap import policy or suffer the consequences.[50] About three weeks later the Department of Commerce temporarily suspended the licensing of ferrous scrap. René Mayer learned about it in the newspapers.[51] Shortly after the signing of the Rome Treaties, Mayer visited Washington to conclude negotiations with major American banks on arrangements for the High Authority's first loan in the United States market, which temporarily dispelled American disenchantment with the activities of the ECSC. Mayer suggested holding urgent discussions on scrap import.[52] Yet scrap imports did not remain the sole issue of concern for the United States.

The Wise Men report had predicted that Europe would suffer from a lack of fuel. Yet in 1958, a slowdown in economic expansion, together with a rapid increase in the consumption of oil as a substitute for coal, created an overproduction of coal in Europe. While consumption of coal in the Community dropped by 33 million tons, productivity in the coal mines increased by a high 7 percent, which created far-reaching unemployment problems. A drop in transatlantic freight charges added to the crisis situation by making American coal more competitive with European coal. Of the three main coal-producing countries—Belgium, France, and Germany—Belgium was the most affected by the crisis. Anxious to maintain its export markets for coal in the Community, the United States closely monitored the situation. When signs of excessive coal production appeared in Belgium in 1957 and 1958, the State Department and American exporters got together with the Belgian authorities to determine how best to adapt delivery schedules of American coal to the Belgian situation. As a result of the negotiations, American coal exports declined from their former record levels. American coal exporters seemed more or less satisfied with the agreement. Yet in 1959 pressures for drastic import restrictions on coal continued in Belgium. The decision of the Belgian government to close certain unprofitable mines, notably in the region of the Borinage, caused severe unrest in the country.[53]

The German coal situation also warranted close attention from the Americans. In September 1958, when the Germans placed coal imports under licensing control the United States protested vehemently. In December, a top-level German official flew to Washington to warn the administration that a virtual embargo on German coal imports would be imposed in the near future. Again the United States reacted strongly. After further deliberations, the German government imposed only a customs duty with a duty-free quota. Even though this action was less restrictive than the one that had previously been considered, the Americans still applied pressure on the High Authority and the German government to increase the duty-free quota from 4.2 to 5 million metric tons. As a result, the American share of the duty-free quota rose from 3.6 to 4.4 million metric tons. Meanwhile, the German coal industry attempted to cancel contracts with American exporters.[54]

By February 1958, the coal crisis had reached such proportions that the High Authority of the ECSC decided to consider community-wide measures to deal with the coal surplus. The High Authority proposed to take emergency measures—production cuts, import quotas, and relief payments to the unemployed—under the "manifest crisis" procedures of the ECSC Treaty. The

State Department was not pleased at the prospect, to say the least. In a telegram to American embassies and missions in Europe, the Department asked its representatives to inform key people at the High Authority that the United States government and its coal industry would react very unfavorably to additional restrictions on American coal imports. Although the State Department had insisted that the ECSC curtail its production, it did not consider the coal crisis in the Community "to be critical on a Community-wide basis," it was, rather, a "special problem affecting Belgium and Germany." It would be bad politics, continued the telegram, to invoke a "manifest crisis" at this time, for such a move might have a "bad psychological effect reflecting on [the] economic equilibrium of [the] Six and could be capitalized on by those countries unsympathetic [to] European integration and by [the] Soviet bloc."[55] The problem was eventually brought to the attention of Herter and Dillon, who met personally with representatives from the American coal industry. On 13 March, high officials from the State, Interior, and Labor Departments organized a meeting with industry representatives to discuss the ECSC proposal to declare a "manifest crisis." The industry's representatives insisted that it would be a "disaster for the United States coal industry" if the ECSC imposed further restrictions on imports of American coal, especially since the districts that depended the most on exports were already suffering from high unemployment. "Further restrictions on imports of coal from the United States," said one representative, "would be unfair, and amount to hostile action."[56] American embassies and missions lost no time in informing the High Authority and its member states of these strongly voiced opinions. By 14 May, the State Department could utter a sigh of relief. On that day, the Council of Ministers of the European Coal and Steel Community rejected the High Authority's proposals for invoking a "manifest crisis." Although Germany had consistently taken the lead in opposing production cuts and the declaration of a "manifest crisis," it was French Prime Minister Debré and Industry Minister Jeanneney who ultimately torpedoed the proposals of the High Authority. In doing so, they patently displayed not only the reluctance of de Gaulle's government to recognize the supranational character of the High Authority but also the French insistence on the primacy of the nation-state even in times of crisis. Somewhat hypocritically, in light of America's continuous resistance to the proposals of the High Authority, the American representative to Luxembourg deplored "the lack of political leadership" demonstrated by the High Authority in dealing with the coal crisis, as evidenced by "its willingness continuously to modify and weaken its proposals without assurance of obtaining agreement of council."[57]

Meanwhile, the State Department recorded both the pluses and minuses of de Gaulle's return to power in June 1958. On the negative side was the general's dream of restoring France to Great Power status, able once again to play an independent role in foreign affairs. Moreover, de Gaulle had consistently opposed European integration. By contrast, the State Department thought that France's proper role, which would be a factor of strength for the whole alliance, was in leading a unified Europe, and not "in spending her limited resources in an attempt to maintain a worldwide 'Great Power' position." In addition, France's nationalism posed the threat of a possible reversal of alliances. There were, however, a number of positive factors. Despite de Gaulle's aversion to supranational arrangements, the Americans calculated that he would probably have neither the political backing nor the time to damage the Communities. After all, he required the support of farmers, labor, industry, and party leaders in France, many of whom were committed to the Common Market. He also needed the financial and diplomatic support of his European partners as well as that of the United States and the United Kingdom to solve the Algerian crisis and the French economic mess. The best strategy to ensure that France would not take a position contrary to the course of European integration and American interests, American policymakers reasoned, was to avoid exerting pressure directly on the French government and to "work as much as possible through France's five partners and through the institutions of the European Communities."[58] By doing so, the United States would protect their interests and avoid becoming the easy target of French nationalists.

While June 1958 signaled de Gaulle's return to power, it was equally crucial for American trade, as it was the month in which existing American trade legislation was due to expire. Another key date was 1 January 1959, when the Six were scheduled to reduce their internal tariffs by 10 percent. In an address to the Senate Committee on Finance in June 1958, Dulles pointed out that tariffs among the Six would be completely eliminated by 1972. Accordingly, the United States needed to take urgent action to negotiate reductions "advantageous to our export trade" in the common external tariff of the Six before it became "firmly established." Dulles asked that the Trade Agreements Act be renewed for a period of five years so as to be better able to influence the commercial policies of the new community.[59] Similarly, a CFEP document made it clear that in proposing a new round of negotiations, the United States was motivated by the need to lower the common external tariff to assure easy access for American goods and, more generally, by the desire to foster liberal policies in Europe in the interest of outside countries.[60]

Ensuring the renewal of the trade agreements was not an easy task, given the mounting protectionist calls for restrictions on imports and the tendency for Congress to lend a sympathetic ear to complaints from its constituents in an election year. Members of Congress seemed more inclined to grant the executive branch special powers to raise tariffs than to lower them. They also were quite prepared to authorize the president and other governmental agencies to oppose any tariff reductions that posed a threat to national security by impairing American capacity to produce certain "strategic goods," the definition of which was left fairly open.[61] The Eisenhower administration nevertheless succeeded, after a vigorous domestic campaign, in obtaining a rather liberal new trade legislation package. On 20 August 1958, Eisenhower signed the new Trade Agreements Act, which empowered him to cut existing tariffs by 20 percent during GATT negotiations over the next four years, provided that no tariffs were reduced by more than 10 percent in one year. Article A of Section 350 authorized the president to negotiate not only with foreign governments but also with their agents, a provision that was specifically aimed at the Community.[62] Armed with this new authority, the administration proposed a new round of multilateral tariff negotiations in October 1958. Six months later the contracting parties to the GATT approved the United States' proposal. This set in motion the so-called Dillon Round of trade negotiations, which was completed in 1962. Worried about declining trade surpluses and otherwise unfavorable economic indicators, the United States decided to go on the offensive on other fronts as well. Dillon's vigorous appeals within the GATT for a reduction of European quotas on dollar goods largely succeeded: most quotas were removed by the early 1960s.[63] Meanwhile, Secretary of the Treasury Robert Anderson encouraged America's allies to share the economic burden of the United States by contributing more to foreign aid[64] and by participating more fully in the costs of Western defense. Finally, United States efforts were brought to bear on yet another front: the transformation of the OEEC into the OECD.

THE BIRTH OF THE OECD

In late March 1956, Henry Owen and Leon Fuller completed a report on "The Future of NATO" for the Policy Planning Staff. The report referred to a recent NATO study that projected a faster long-term economic growth rate in the European Soviet bloc than for the western industrialized countries. The study predicted that the bloc countries would "have outstripped Western

Europe in total output, and probably by a wider margin in industrial output" by 1975. Fuller and Owen concluded that Western Europe would be left behind unless it benefited from a more effective economic integration, both on the Continent and within the North Atlantic area. They anticipated that a better coordination of economic policies would foster "rapid and sustained economic growth" through a "freer flow of goods, and services" and "of capital and people." In turn, a freer flow of resources would promote political cohesion in the area and increase "Western solidarity in the face of Soviet economic maneuvers." In addition, faster growth in the West would also allow the industrialized countries to agree on a joint development program for developing countries. While countering Soviet penetration in developing countries, such a program would also serve as an "effective political guarantee" and attract funding from both the private and the public sectors. How might closer economic integration be encouraged? No new institutions were needed, wrote Fuller and Owen, all one needed to do was to transform the Organization for European Economic Cooperation. Although this organization had originally been conceived as an exclusively European organization to deal with European recovery problems, its main objective—"the liberalization of European trade and payments"—was nearing completion, and the OEEC now increasingly devoted its energies to economic relations between North America and Western Europe. The authors drew the appropriate conclusion: perhaps the United States and Canada should join the OEEC as full members, thereby showing the Atlantic character of the organization. To avoid an exclusively "North Atlantic" label, however, the revamped OEEC would adopt a "neutral designation," such as "Organization for Economic Cooperation," and it would be "open to other countries outside of Europe and North America (e.g., Japan)." Owen and Fuller did not believe that the new organization would interfere in any major way with efforts towards European union. At the same time, they viewed further economic and political integration within the Atlantic Community as a possible antidote to another European integration fiasco. Efforts towards European integration were under way for a Common Market and a European atomic energy organization, but after the failure of the EDC, how could one be sure that they would succeed? As a result, it was better to place one's hopes in a tighter Atlantic Community than in a lagging movement toward European integration. The new OEEC would provide some of the cement needed to bind the West together. Yet within that organization, the United States would have to "participate as an equal partner in the process of bargaining and mutual policy review and coordination," while also being prepared to "provide leadership and to contribute resources commensurate with its economic capacity."[65]

The idea of an equal partnership, this time with a united Europe, would later be taken up by the Kennedy administration, which counted Henry Owen among its *éminences grises*. The new administration would also emphasize growth and trade liberalization to counter the Soviet threat. But by that time the Common Market and Euratom would be going concerns, and the threat to be countered would be not only Soviet growth but also the challenge of the new European Common Market. In the late 1950s the idea of a new OEEC was revived by those who worried about the split between the Six and the Seven. The new, or revamped organization, also came to be seen as an antidote to the exclusionist orientation of the new Communities.

In April 1959, Clarence C. Randall, the chairman of the CFEP, had a conversation with an old friend of his, Clarence Hunter, the "Treasury's man in Paris." Hunter told him that the newly appointed officers of the European Economic Community, including President Walter Hallstein and Vice-President Robert Marjolin, were "getting a little stuffy" and had "fallen into the habit of referring to each other as 'Your Excellency,' " Randall later wrote in his diary: "All this bores me terrifically. The president of the United States is such a simple down-to-earth person that I am not willing to admit that there is any responsibility in the world so great as to justify the individual in getting stuffy. They are old hat as far as I am concerned, and when I encounter that attitude, I am always tempted to say in a loud voice, 'Nuts!' " Hunter also spoke somewhat nostalgically of the days when the OEEC served as an "informal forum" where the seventeen member states "settled a great many questions without heat by sitting around a table." The "new Economic Community," he deplored, "has changed all this. 'The Six' now come to the Organization for European Economic Cooperation as a bloc, and the old friendliness is giving way to tensions, which is unfortunate."[66] This analysis of the situation struck a receptive chord in Clarence Randall,[67] a free trader who had been present at the creation of the OEEC. About a month later, Randall penned a memorandum to Malcolm Moos, the speech writer, suggesting that Eisenhower publicly endorse the OEEC. As "an informal Parliament of Europe," the OEEC could serve as a bridge between the Six and the Outer Seven.[68] In late August, Randall went one step further and suggested that the position of Secretary General within the OEEC be strengthened and that he be "clearly given the task of speaking for Europe as a whole." This was an old American dream, which had successfully been thwarted by the British; in any event, Randall's proposal was designed not only to mend the rift between the Six and the Seven, but also to put an alternative proposal to the British plan for a European Free Trade Association on the table.[69]

About the same time Randall was pondering ways to reinforce the OEEC, Monnet took a similar, if bolder, reading of the situation. The old OEEC, he thought, had fulfilled its objectives by distributing American aid at the start of the Marshall Plan and by eliminating quantitative restrictions. On 27 December 1958, a number of European countries, including the United Kingdom, had returned to convertibility, thereby signing the death warrant of the European Payments Union, which had been created by the OEEC. The old organization increasingly appeared as an empty shell, left open to British maneuvers to sink the Common Market.[70] On 9 June 1959, John Tuthill had a conversation with Jean Monnet prior to his departure for Princeton in the United States. Monnet diagnosed four types of problems that needed to be addressed within the free world: the speedy removal of quantitative barriers; the reduction of tariffs; the "coordination of economic and financial policies in order to fight inflation, depressions, etc."; and aid to developing countries through "price stability for primary products" and "economic development and technical assistance." All of these issues, said Monnet, could be tackled "via a new organization in which the United States would participate actively rather than as an observer as in the OEEC." The organization would consist of "(1) the Common Market acting as a unit, (2) the United Kingdom, (3) the United States, (4) and—if the United States insisted—Canada, and (5) one of the other OEEC countries selected by the OEEC itself." The OEEC would not be abolished, but would be left as a sort of base from which the new organization would operate. More than just providing a bridge between the Six and the Seven as in Randall's proposal, the organization was also to act as a bridge between the developing countries and the democratic nations of the West. To this effect, members of developing countries were to be allowed to participate in discussions that pertained to their specific problems. Monnet also had something else in mind: he wished to rehabilitate the Common Market vis-à-vis the United States. By enlisting the United States, the United Kingdom, and perhaps Canada as full-fledged members of the new organization, Monnet hoped to show that an integrated Europe would not be a third force surrounded by high tariffs but rather a force oriented toward "the entire free world," and most of all toward the United States and the United Kingdom. In turn, a united Europe, with American and British support, would help anchor Germany even more closely to the Six.[71]

About two weeks after his conversation with Tuthill, Monnet sent a memorandum to Under Secretary of State Douglas Dillon entitled "A New Era of Atlantic Relations," in which he further elaborated his proposals. Western European nations, he insisted, had achieved full economic recovery and no longer needed American aid; they were now ready for "the full responsibilities of partnership." As for the Common Market, it meant nothing less than the emergence of a "Second America of the West" with a "common political objective." By contrast, the Free Trade Area would have been a "purely commercial arrangement." In his view, the new preferential arrangements contemplated by the Seven would be a "defensive arrangement with only a token commitment to European unity." As such it would "threaten to complicate, rather than to solve, the problems of cooperation." European and Atlantic cooperation problems would be best addressed by launching a new initiative that went beyond American proposals for tariff reductions. The economic institutions of the United Nations would not do the job for the obvious reason that the Soviet Union and its satellites were members of that organization. NATO was not adequate to the task of solving the common trading and economic problems of Atlantic nations because it was "primarily an alliance for defense against hot war." Also, NATO did not include Sweden and Switzerland, which were important industrialized countries. Monnet recommended a new institutional approach to the problem of transatlantic cooperation, proposing to create a "consultative council" within the OEEC in which the United Kingdom, the United States, Canada, and the Common Market, "acting as one," would each be permanently represented by a delegate. One or two delegates would represent the other member nations. Monnet emphasized the consultative nature of the new organization to differentiate it clearly from Common Market institutions: there were to be no votes in the proceedings of the council, which would simply be a "systematic mechanism for discussion among the leading industrialized areas." Similarly, Dillon's proposal in December for the new OECD stressed its consultative nature and insisted that its powers be limited to making recommendations. Monnet's hope that the Six would act as one within the OEEC Council later turned into a disappointment. Precisely because the Six proved unable to act as one, Monnet later lost interest in the new OECD, although he had been one of its main architects.[72]

While in the United States in early July, Monnet discussed his memorandum with Dillon and other State Department officials. About a month later, Tuthill, who had had frequent conversations with Monnet since his return from Washington, wrote Dillon that what Monnet had in mind was not so much the establishment of a subcommittee within the OEEC but an "Action Committee" that would be related to the OEEC in somewhat the same way that the Security Council was related to the General Assembly of the United Nations. In conversations with Monnet, Tuthill had tried to convince him that it might be best not to reorganize the OEEC. He now pointed out to Dillon that Monnet felt less inclined to use the OEEC at all. Tuthill declared himself "sympathetic" with Monnet's objective of forging a wider association, which would include the United States and the United Kingdom, for two main reasons. One, it was time to drop all pretense of adopting a "sympathetic" attitude towards the "British-inspired Outer Seven." Without explicitly saying so, Tuthill implied that it might be better to dilute their initiative in a wider Atlantic initiative. Second, Monnet's initiative might be helpful in ensuring that the British and the Common Market did not make an agreement "(via a Free Trade Area for Europe) which, in effect, cover[ed] British, French, Belgian and Portuguese possessions, present and past, but [did] not take adequately into account the needs of other underdeveloped countries." Tuthill most certainly had in mind certain Latin American countries that actively traded with the United States and depended on European markets for their exports.[73]

During Monnet's visit to Washington, Eisenhower had requested that Monnet write to him directly to explain his views on European integration more fully. He did so in mid-August, seizing the opportunity to stress the need for a "partnership between the United States and a United Europe" in order to negotiate from a position of strength with the Soviet Union so as to "build up a long term understanding between Russia and the West that might one day become an association." Anticipating Eisenhower's proposed meeting with Khrushchev, Monnet cautioned the Americans against making a separate peace with the Russians over the heads of Europeans, for then European nations might also seek to make their own peace, "separately, nationally, and with disastrous results." The United States and Europe, Monnet maintained, had to deal with common problems jointly. One such problem was the American balance-of-payments deficit. Only when Europe and the United States had solved their balance-of-payments problems would it be possible to achieve high growth rates in the West, which in turn would make it possible to assist developing countries.[74] In early June, Dillon had spoken along the same lines at Harvard University, where he emphasized that the West needed to achieve high growth rates to catch up with the Soviet economy, which now appeared to be growing faster than that of the United States. Soviet economic progress, said Dillon, threatened to detach developing countries from the free world by "projecting an image of the Soviet system as the magic blueprint for achieving rapid progress." In order to counter this threat, the United States, aided by its allies, would have to accelerate its domestic growth so as to show developing countries that a "free society" would best correspond to their aspirations. To complete this offensive for democracy in the developing world, Dillon added two other elements to the package for freedom and progress—lowering trade barriers in the West to ensure outlets for goods produced in developing countries, and granting developing countries financial and technical aid. Finally, Dillon stressed the need for a better coordination of the economic policies of the industrialized nations.[75] Although neither Monnet nor Dillon made mention of a newly organized OEEC, it soon became clear that the new organization was to serve exactly the objectives they had outlined.

In late 1959, Dillon went to Europe and conferred with various officials in London, Brussels, Bonn, and Paris. In Bonn he met with Adenauer alone, and in Brussels he met with the commissioners of the European Economic Community. In Paris he met with French officials and representatives of the EFTA countries. In his talks with top British cabinet officials in London, Douglas Dillon was quite straightforward about American preference for the EEC as compared with the EFTA agreement, which had just been initialed in Stockholm. In reporting to the president, the under secretary of state summarized his conversation with the British as follows: "I told them that while we would not oppose the EFTA arrangement we could not view it with any great enthusiasm because it did not have the same political content as the EEC and would mean discrimination against our exports."[76] The British understood the point well. In his memoirs, Macmillan remembers that it was during the last months of 1959 that the British government understood "the increasing anxiety" of the American government towards the existence of two economic blocs in Europe, especially at a time when "the Cold War was at its height" and the United States was experiencing balance-of-payments difficulties.[77] A revitalized OEEC, with the participation of the United States and Canada, thought Dillon, would offer the appropriate forum for dealing with the current rift in Western Europe, and above all, it would prevent a merger of the EFTA and the EEC, which would probably destroy the EEC. On this point Monnet, Dillon, and Adenauer saw eye to eye. One of the worst fears of the president of the Action Committee was to see the OEEC in its current form, without the tempering influence of the United States and Canada, being utilized as a tool by the British to criticize and weaken the EEC.[78]

On 16 December 1959, Dillon sent a telegram to President Eisenhower in which he proposed that the United States initiate negotiations both to mend trade rifts in Western Europe and to galvanize industrialized countries into helping developing countries. The Western Summit Meeting later that month, he felt, would be the right place to make a proposal. Time was of the essence, for unless the United States took the lead, European trade dissensions might turn "into a bitter political split," and "the opportunity for capitalizing on the present willingness of the Europeans to step up their development may have been lost."[79] The proposal met with the president's approval. On 19 December, Monnet wrote Eisenhower asking him to allow the executive organ of the EEC—the Common Market Commission—to represent the Six during the negotiations.[80] Two days later, at the close of the Western Summit Meeting, a communiqué proposed the establishment of a trade committee to iron out some of the political differences between the Six and the Seven. In his address to the informal meeting of the Special Economic Committee in Paris on 12 January, Dillon gave three by now familiar reasons for the American initiative: to deal with the economic and political dangers posed by the trade problems created by the EFTA and EEC split, to allow for greater European participation in development assistance, and to revitalize the OEEC in order to strengthen the relationship between the United States and its partners.[81] As would later become obvious in the negotiations leading to the signing of the OECD Convention on 14 December 1960, the United States did not favor granting the new organization any real decision-making powers in the area of trade. The reluctance stemmed from two issues: the United States wished the GATT to "remain master in its own house"[82] by refraining from duplicating its work, and the United States saw that "there [was] no longer the need or justification for the regional discrimination which was permitted during the early days of the Marshall Plan."[83] Although the EEC Commission was not permitted to act as the spokesman of the Six in the negotiations, the Commission was nevertheless allowed to contribute to the development of new statutes for the revamped OEEC.[84]

In December 1959, at a meeting in Paris of Adenauer, de Gaulle, Eisenhower and Macmillan, Tuthill had succeeded in getting the Big Four to authorize the creation of a "new organization with objectives quite different from that of the OEEC." In order to bypass the "stagnant" OEEC Secretariat, the Americans, spurred on by Tuthill, insisted that the negotiations take place outside of the OEEC buildings in Paris. The French government, which saw eye to eye with the Americans on the need to water down EFTA, was only too glad to provide facilities at Avenue Kleber. A drafting committee composed of French, British, and American representatives and the governor of the Bank of Greece prepared draft bylaws for the new organization, which were then submitted to all OEEC members and Canada. After rather lengthy negotiations the new bylaws were agreed upon, "completely eliminating the old OEEC bylaws"; the secretary general and his deputy were also to be replaced. Hoping for even more drastic changes, Tuthill "favored firing the entire OEEC Secretariat" and giving the new secretary general a free hand to hire new personnel. But Tuthill "made a tactical error" in listening to the legal advisor to the American delegation, who counseled to "forget the legal aspects" and "just authorize the new Secretary General to fire anyone, having in mind the new objectives."[85] To Tuthill's dismay, the new Secretary General did not fire anybody. When the OECD was finally ready to set up shop, the new organization took over the old OEEC headquarters. In a way, then, Monnet's first proposal to Dillon, to use the OEEC as a base, carried the day, rather than Tuthill's proposal for a completely new organization. Reborn from its own ashes, the OEEC metamorphosed into the OECD, with an emphasis on economic cooperation and development. It lost its exclusively European character in the process. The OECD Convention went into effect under the Kennedy administration on 30 September 1961.

Throughout 1960, the United States remained on the whole favorable to the Six, while also insisting that "the Common Market follow liberal, low-tariff policies in the industrial and agricultural field."[86] The State Department welcomed a proposal by the European Economic Community to accelerate the Rome Treaty tariff provisions and to reduce the Common Market's external tariff by 20 percent. The British protested and interpreted American support for the EEC's initiative as a further proof of American hostility towards EFTA. But here again the Six started out as favorites. Proof of the special treatment accorded to the Six came in February, when Ambassador Butterworth received an official note from the European Communities requesting the establishment of a mission in Washington. The State Department immediately set out to draft a law that would authorize the president of the United States to grant diplomatic privileges to the staff of the mission. The law was later submitted to Congress and led to the creation of the current Delegation of the Commission of the EC in Washington.[87] Yet support did not mean blind optimism.

In November 1959, the secretary of commerce had appointed a top-level task force, which included Dillon, Waugh, and Randall among its members, "to advise the Government on what it should do to increase exports." Throughout the end of the Eisenhower administration, the State, Treasury and Commerce Departments were busy studying specific ways to expand exports.[88] At a meeting of the Bilderberg group in Bürgenstock in May, an American participant, probably George Ball, noted "extreme vigilance" in the United States "with regard to the trade policies of the Seven and the present or future steps taken by the Six over their common external tariff." "It was not therefore impossible," he pointed out, "that a certain amount of 'agonizing reappraisal' would take place in America after the presidential elections." The United States would probably not adopt an outright negative attitude towards the Common Market, "but American pressure might be exerted within GATT and the International Monetary Fund in order to bring about a general lowering of world tariffs."[89]

American pressure within GATT started in September 1960. On 1 September, Clarence Randall went over to Geneva to serve as the U.S. representative to the new tariff conferences. He took such a hard line on agriculture, chastising the Six for their protectionist agricultural policy, that it threatened to doom the conference to failure. Upon returning to the United States, Randall asked Karl Brandt of the Council of Economic Advisers in the White House to write a report on the EEC for him. Karl Brandt obliged and produced a memorandum in which he blamed Europeans, on whom the United States had lavishly spent "some $80 billion" to get them on the road to recovery, for not realizing that the United States was "in a tough spot" and needed "their cooperation for their own sake and security at least as much as our own." Brandt recommended a potent medicine to remedy the American balance-of-payments problem and expected the Europeans to provide the main ingredients. The Germans, he said, must spend more on NATO defense and aid programs for developing countries. Second, the United States must promote its exports and negotiate trade liberalization in GATT. Third, and most importantly, the EEC "must refrain from agricultural autarchy" and stop subsidizing its agriculture. This was perhaps a hard thing to do given Adenauer's and de Gaulle's "agricultural fundamentalism," but it was in the interest of Europeans and Americans alike. If the EEC erected high barriers against American agricultural exports, he warned, the United States would retreat into protectionism and shut its doors to EEC industrial goods. The situation appeared "extremely dangerous" to him because agricultural interest groups were hard to dislodge from their protectionist positions, once established. Accordingly, he recommended that the United States use "maximum moral suasion and sternest warning" "for averting the drift into new belligerent agricultural protectionism in the EEC countries."[90]

Would the new administration follow agonizing reappraisal tactics to protect American economic interests? How did Kennedy plan to deal with the European challenge? Europeanists in Europe and in the United States made sure that they would have a say in shaping the new policies, many of which had been initiated under Eisenhower.

6

The Kennedy Team and European Integration

In the area of European affairs and European unity, John F. Kennedy is often remembered for his support and advocacy of the "Grand Design," best epitomized in the climax of his Atlantic partnership speech in Philadelphia on American Independence Day, 4 July 1962. He is remembered as sympathetic to European integration and its advocates. Yet the young president did not come to the presidency with well-defined views of the role that European unity was to play in the somewhat larger scheme of European, Atlantic, and international settlements or of the desirability of strong American support for it. Kennedy no doubt had a deep interest in European affairs, particularly the United Kingdom, where he had spent many summers during his college years while his father served as the United States ambassador to Britain. His immersion, since childhood, in public affairs, which pervaded discussions at the family dinner table, as well as his interest in historical processes in general, left him well informed about the European scene. However, he was not particularly dedicated to the idea of European integration as such. Many of his closest and most influential advisers on European affairs, whether in the State Department, in the Defense Department, or in the White House, perceived that although the president was not opposed to European integration it was not a topic or an issue that preoccupied him greatly.[1] At best the president-elect was a skeptic. Special Assistant to the President Arthur Schlesinger remembers that "Both his collection of pre-1960 campaign addresses, *The Strategy of Peace,* and his 1960 campaign speeches were notable for the absence of particular theories beyond general affirmations of the desirability of 'a stable, creative partnership of equals.' "[2]

Thanks to the good offices of George Ball, whom Kennedy had commissioned shortly after his election to head an interregnum task force on foreign economic policy, Kennedy soon moved from a position of strong skepticism to cautious and pragmatic support, though still tempered with a certain measure of skepticism. This meant that he generally backed European unity as a desirable objective for the unity of the West, without, however, being tied to any specific form of unity, or any specific means of achieving it. Unity, he felt, was a matter for Europeans themselves to decide. Schlesinger remembers: "As for the character of that unity, he did not think nationalism altogether a bad thing. He knew that the United States would not lightly renounce its own sovereignty; this made him a bit skeptical of rigid supranational institutions in Europe. Though he had the greatest affection and respect for Jean Monnet, he was not tied to Monnet's formulas—or those of anyone else."[3]

EUROPEANISTS IN HIGH PLACES

Notwithstanding the rather temperate degree of support for European integration à la Monnet that the president and some of his advisers in the White House initially displayed, forceful backing for Monnet's proposals were to be found both among top-ranking officials and at lower levels of the United States administration, most of all in the State Department and in American missions in Europe. So strong were the cohesion and devotion of Monnet sympathizers that the policies they advocated insinuated themselves into the fabric of the administration and acquired a momentum of their own. Not all were successful, and some met with substantial opposition, but most received a fair hearing from the president.

The Europeanists' number-one man in the Kennedy administration was, without a doubt, George Ball. In January 1960, Ball addressed the National Industrial Conference Board in New York. Advocating further progress towards political integration in Europe, he adjured his fellow citizens to adopt a posture of more than benign neutrality towards the EEC. His speech aroused the interest of Massachusetts Senator John F. Kennedy, who won the Democratic nomination in July.[4] During the presidential campaign, Ball had strongly lent his support to Adlai Stevenson, a former law colleague of his in Chicago and a close friend. But Kennedy did not hold this against him. In January 1961, Kennedy offered Ball the position of under secretary for economic affairs, the number-three position in the State Department under the existing administrative structure. Kennedy had been impressed and largely satisfied with the task force report on economic and commercial policy that Ball had written during the interregnum. William C. Foster, a Republican, was originally the preferred choice. But Senator Fulbright, at the urging of Stevenson, succeeded in convincing the president that another Republican appointee after "giving Republicans so many top posts in State, Treasury and Defense was manifestly unfair to Democrats who had worked hard for his election."[5] The offer to Foster was withdrawn, and thus Ball moved into a high position on the seventh floor at Foggy Bottom. A few months later, Ball's standing in the State Department was upgraded during what came to be known as the "Thanksgiving day massacre," a comprehensive reorganization and reshuffling of Kennedy appointees in November of 1961 on the weekend of the Harvard-Yale game.[6]

The misfortunes of Under Secretary Chester Bowles benefited George Ball. During the Kennedy campaign, Bowles had served as Kennedy's chief adviser on foreign affairs, giving up his house seat to work full time for Kennedy. Congressman Bowles stood "as a major figure in the liberal, Stevensonian wing of the Democratic party, whose doubts the Massachusetts senator badly needed to overcome if he were to gain his party's nomination,"[7] hence Kennedy's efforts to ensure his participation in the presidential campaign. By surrendering his house seat, Bowles hoped to secure the post of secretary of state from the future president, whom, he anticipated, would feel a sense of obligation towards him. His expectations were disappointed. Dean Rusk was named number-one man in the State Department, while Chester Bowles was appointed as senior under secretary of state, the number-two position. He did not hold this position very long, however.

There was no love lost between the president's brother, Robert Kennedy, and Bowles. Also, the Rusk/Bowles team by no means functioned optimally: responsibilities were ill-defined[8] and Rusk's more cautious approach towards the reorganization of the State Department, which Kennedy had directed upon assuming office, contrasted starkly with Bowles's bold attempts to bring new blood into the apathetic State Department that Kennedy felt he had inherited from the Eisenhower era. By bringing young, energetic people into the State Department at ambassadorial positions, a largely positive undertaking, Bowles unfortunately also succeeded in alienating a large portion of the old guard of the foreign service, many of whom were forced into early retirement. Worse still, Bowles became a political liability to the Kennedy administration by symbolizing the administration's commitment to the left. He was increasingly the target of conservative attacks. For example, Senator Barry Goldwater, a Republican from Arizona, urged Bowles's dismissal because he encouraged "a soft policy toward communism."[9] By November, Kennedy succeeded in moving Bowles from the position of under secretary to a new post as special representative and adviser on Asian, African, and Latin American affairs, with the rank of ambassador. The position seemed to be better suited to his interests in the developing world, but did not allow Bowles easy access to the chain of command in Washington and was thus largely frustrating.

Meanwhile, George Ball became the preferred choice for the number-two job in the State Department. Late in July, in a letter to Adlai Stevenson, Bowles had indicated his willingness "to do some reshuffling with George Ball, leaving us both in our Under Secretary positions." Implicitly, this reallocation of responsibilities would have left Ball largely responsible for European policy and Bowles free to devote himself to the long view of foreign policy while he dealt with, essentially, extra-European issues in the Middle East, Southeast Asia, and other areas.[10]

Chester Bowles had a high opinion of George Ball. In a letter to Eugene Rostow, dean of the Yale University Law School, Bowles expressed his admiration for a memorandum Ball had recently prepared on the question of Europe and the United Kingdom, deeming it "one of the ablest presentations" he had seen.[11] This was a high compliment, especially in light of Bowles's view that in foreign policy the young president listened too much to advisers who had "a European-oriented view." This applied "to McGeorge Bundy . . . and to Dean Acheson more than Dean Rusk." Bowles disavowed the narrow European perspective, which he felt no longer applied to the current international situation. The policy had been "developed in the old days when the British ran Europe, balanced the forces of Europe . . . and a peaceful Europe, it assured you a peaceful world, because the world was run by Europe. The affairs of India were not handled in Bombay or Calcutta, they were handled in London. The affairs of Indonesia were handled not in Djakarta but in the Hague, and so with France."[12] Two months before his being reshuffled along with some other members of the administration, the under secretary alluded in rather strong terms to the lack of sensitivity European allies showed to their global responsibilities. In August 1961, President Kennedy asked for Bowles's opinion on the difficulties America was having in obtaining support in the United Nations for its position on Berlin. Bowles responded that the United States could not convincingly advocate self-determination in Europe if it allowed allies such as France or Portugal to veto American support for that very principle in Africa or in Asia. To him it was high time for the United States "to find the courage to lead our alliance rather than to follow it and to raise the vision of some of our NATO allies to the requirements of a world rather than a European power balance."[13]

The under secretary also criticized the operation of the Bureau of European Affairs as one of the three geographic bureaus in the Department of State where there was "a tendency to cling to outworn assumptions, to resist new approaches, and to gloss over setbacks."[14] The culprit was the Eisenhower inheritance, embodied in the presence of old hands such as Foy Kohler,[15] the assistant secretary for European affairs. Clearly, Bowles would have preferred an outsider to head the European bureau. His first choice for the job was Averell Harriman. Instead, Kohler was appointed: "a very fine person, a very able Foreign Officer." But you could not "expect a man of that training to take many great risks."[16] Repeatedly, Bowles voiced his frustration in having to deal with geographic bureaus "largely dominated by men who carried similar responsibilities under the Eisenhower Administration, who [were] emotionally involved in past mistakes, and committed in varying degrees to old assumptions, old concepts and old policies."[17] The under secretary particularly resented the foot-dragging by the European Bureau in cooperating with the Policy Planning Council on the much needed preparation of alternatives in dealing with the Berlin crisis. Foot-dragging by the State Department equally exasperated Kennedy. But the victim of the reorganization that Bowles advocated for the Department of State turned out to be the hapless Bowles himself. George McGhee, whom Bowles had praised highly for his work and for his administration of the Policy Planning Council, replaced Ball as the junior under secretary, while George Ball, whom Bowles also admired, became under secretary and the number-two man in the State Department.

Despite his resentment of the excessive influence of European-oriented thinking in the Kennedy administration, Bowles was interested in European affairs. Recognizing the importance of the Common Market, he also understood the desirability of bringing England into the concert of a unified Europe, a policy that the American "Europeanists," after an initial period of hesitation (particularly under Eisenhower), now strongly endorsed. Anticipating the post-de Gaulle and post-Adenauer era on the old continent, Bowles looked forward to a time when the British would seize the leadership in building a united Europe, to which they would contribute their "extraordinary competence in the art of persuasion and compromise and of democratic government."[18] Going even further, Bowles also hoped that the United States would snatch the initiative from the Soviet Union in pressing for closer integration through the institutionalization of American and European economic and political interests.[19] Noting that Great Britain seemed well on its way to joining the EEC, Bowles wondered whether other countries might not become associate members in "a Common Market which might eventually include North America?" Such "trading partnership" might then "gradually be transformed into a loose political confederation."20

In some ways, Bowles's pronouncements echoed Monnet's preoccupations with the need to work towards an Atlantic Community in which both the United States and a united Europe would function as equal partners, possibly delegating "real powers to common institutions, even at the political level."21 But timing was of the essence here. For Monnet and the Europeanists, the establishment of a strong European Community had to be first, and only after that could Atlantic unity be considered. There would be no Community so long as the partnership advocated by Monnet contained a junior and a senior partner. Only two equal senior partners could build a community. Also, Monnet, and for that matter Kennedy, did not envisage including North America in the Common Market. Merging North America and the EEC into some sort of Atlantic economic community was, rather, the view of the Atlanticists such as Herter.22

Once Bowles had been conveniently weeded out of the high councils of foreign policymaking, George Ball, a true Europeanist, became the number-two man in the State Department, although the ranking is somewhat misleading. In European affairs, Ball was the number-one man, a dominant influence on issues that particularly related to European integration and economic matters. Dean Rusk, the Secretary of State, was indeed inclined to delegate most issues pertaining to Europe, and more specifically European integration, to Ball.23 True, Rusk was interested in European relations, the Atlantic Alliance, Germany, the United Kingdom—after all, he had been a Rhodes Scholar, which accounted for the "soft spot" he felt for the British—but his interest in European affairs was more general. While Rusk was not opposed to European integration, he preferred to have Ball take the lead in this particular area.24 President Kennedy mostly listened to Ball and to his own special assistant, McGeorge Bundy, for advice on what Monnet was trying to accomplish in Europe.

One can claim that on matters concerning European unity, Kennedy was in some ways "educated" by George Ball. Like Bundy in the White House, Ball exerted one of the strongest influences on the president in European affairs. Yet Ball had some misgivings about Kennedy before entering the president's service. Some were quickly dispelled, some lingered on. Would the young Kennedy act very much like his father's offspring? Ball wondered. The old Kennedy represented everything Ball abhorred, most of all American isolationism. As ambassador to London under Roosevelt, Joseph P. Kennedy had, according to Ball, "been a rabid isolationist, who . . . had inexcusably undercut President Roosevelt in 1940 by testifying before the Senate Foreign

Relations Committee against the Lend-Lease legislation for which his president was valiantly fighting." Ball reproached the older Kennedy for having been "a capitulationist when the Soviets threatened to sweep the earth," a man who had "thought it likely that Europe would, at least for a period of time, be wholly taken by the Communists." He was a man "who had been against Americans trying to stay in Berlin," criticized the British loan, and "opposed aid to Greece and Turkey, American participation in Korea, and the Marshall Plan."[25] Would President Kennedy also be an isolationist? Ball carefully checked Kennedy's record before giving him his wholehearted support. Somewhat reassuring to Ball were the writings and speeches of Kennedy prior to his election. His voting record was encouraging as well: Kennedy had supported both the Truman Doctrine and the Marshall Plan. In 1949, he had also voted to renew the Trade Agreements Extension Act, significant because Ball was to devote considerable time and energy to evolving and then defending the new Trade Expansion Act. As a senator, Kennedy had taken rather daring positions in foreign policy. In 1953 he had attacked French policy in Indochina, then criticized French policies in Algeria. What worried Ball most, however, was Kennedy's advocacy of a policy of leadership by the United States "in the UN, in NATO, in the administration of our aid programs and in the exercise of our diplomacy [to shape] a course toward political independence for Algeria."[26] This sounded suspiciously like meddling by the United States in a matter the French could best settle themselves. Despite these reservations, Ball decided that the pluses outweighed the minuses, and cast his lot with Kennedy, in the expectation that the president, whom he thought "equipped with a bright and alert mind," would soon also arm himself with a more sophisticated view of foreign affairs. In this regard, the "exceptionally able people"[27] Kennedy gathered about him would play a crucial role.

In matters pertaining to European unity, George Ball was helped in his coaching of the president by a very efficient *éminence grise*—Monnet—who enjoyed access to many levels of official Washington. Monnet had first met Ball during the Roosevelt administration, in the context of administering Lend-Lease.[28] Monnet soon came to value the young lawyer highly, and the two of them became friends. In 1945 Ball served Monnet as his general counsel when the Frenchman came to Washington as president of the French Supply Council, an organization whose purpose was to replenish France's badly needed raw material supplies and equipment destroyed in the war.[29] Monnet hired Ball not to serve as a legal technician but rather, according to Ball, "to help him reduce his ideas to coherent exposition and, in the process, help him think." The Monnet method consisted of "circl[ing] a problem like an airplane approaching an undersized field in a cup of the mountains, volplaning down in ever tightening spirals until he finally reached the runway he was seeking. Yet . . . while zeroing in on a problem, he would frequently dart off to explore a new target made visible by a sudden opening in the fog." Ball's role, during what he called their "collective spiral cogitation," was to help Monnet draft documents, for "Monnet himself was no writer; he evolved letters, papers, plans, proposals, memoranda of all kinds by bouncing ideas against another individual—a combined amanuensis and collaborator."[30] In his memoirs, Monnet remembered his friend and collaborator as a brilliant and courageous man with "a high moral authority," who was dedicated to a united Europe and, beyond that, to fostering the general interest of the Atlantic Alliance.[31]

Largely satisfied with Ball's earlier performance, Monnet later called him in August 1947 to serve incognito in helping to draft the report of the Committee for European Economic Cooperation. Sir Oliver Franks chaired the committee and Jean Monnet functioned as vice-chairman. Ball worked with Monnet and his immediate staff only because Monnet "did not wish the other European representatives to know he was consulting anyone from [Ball's] side of the ocean." So Ball worked "in an office under the stairs at 18 Rue de Martignac, the headquarters of the French Planning Commission. It was a tiny room (probably not larger than nine by ten feet), but it became [Ball's] intermittent hideout for several years."[32] During this period Ball also became the very close friend of Robert Marjolin, Monnet's deputy. Marjolin later asked his friend to help him draft the plans for the OEEC. During 1949, George Ball continued working with Monnet in the context of the French Plan of Reconstruction. Ball then became involved in the preparation of the European Coal and Steel Community Treaty after the announcement of the Schuman Plan in May 1950, resuming his position under the stairs at Rue de Martignac, visiting Monnet only when Monnet wished to see him. He thus had the peculiar privilege of being "a private American actively working for a participating government."[33] At the time, Ball maintained close contact with official representatives of the United States government, such as the ambassador to France, David Bruce, and William Tomlinson,[34] Bruce's financial attaché. Working very closely with Tomlinson, Ball sometimes transferred his "operations" to a small office in the embassy right next to Tomlinson's office. Ball needed to dictate in English, and the embassy's secretaries came in handy to overcome the limitations of Monnet's staff on that score. Ball and Tomlinson co-conspired with Monnet "in full mutual confidence, sensitive to the problems he was encountering," while Monnet acknowledged Tomlinson's own problems in communicating with Washington. The two Americans thus functioned as effective conduits for communicating Monnet's views to Washington and vice versa. The "complete sharing of information and insights" between Monnet and his American co-conspirators was possible only because they all "believed fervently" in Monnet's goal of a united Europe, which, they felt, "was quite as important to Americans as to Europeans."[35]

Walter Hallstein, then head of the German delegation for the negotiation of the Schuman Plan, who later became the first president of the EEC Commission, likewise testified to a period of intense and unreserved cooperation between people who shared common goals, worked hard toward their achievement, and built close friendship bonds in the process of working together in a common enterprise: "It was real cooperation—free of all overtones which are now hampering our relations. There was no question about making choices. It was a natural feeling of people working for the same goals. Defense against the Communists was a common cause. Building Europe was a common cause—unreservedly—taken as such by both partners. And this influenced the way they cooperated. There was an exchange of documents without any special care of secrecy."[36]

When Monnet became the first head of the European Coal and Steel Community, he asked Ball to be his American adviser. Even after Monnet declined to continue as president of the High Authority in 1954, Ball served as an adviser to the European Coal and Steel Community, and later to Euratom and the EEC. Monnet consulted him on a nonprofessional basis whenever the two men met on either side of the Atlantic. And during the Kennedy administration, Jean Monnet kept in constant touch with George Ball. The Frenchman was a dedicated user of the telephone, and the two men frequently called one another.

President Kennedy's appointment of George Ball as the third- and then second-ranking officer in the State Department is of crucial importance for understanding American policy towards European integration during his administration. Ball brought to his new job—this time officially—the same method and spirit that had characterized his work in Paris with Monnet. Around him he organized a group of people whom he trusted implicitly. Few in number, they shared his views on European integration. A common experience of all was that they had somehow been connected as private citizens or as United States officials to the European integration movement and had lived through World War II. Some were longtime friends or acquaintances of Jean Monnet.[37] George Ball's close connections under Kennedy included such key figures as David Bruce, Robert Schaetzel, Henry Owen, John Leddy of the Treasury, Admiral Lee of the Defense Department, and Ambassador John Tuthill.[38]

Already in August 1960, Kennedy had asked Adlai Stevenson to help him develop a program of action for the first few months of the new administration somewhat "reminiscent of the celebrated Hundred Days of the first term of Franklin Roosevelt." Stevenson then commissioned Ball to write the report for him. Ball immediately set to work and lost no time in asking Monnet to contribute to the project by helping him define American policy towards Europe as well as "measures for the strengthening of ties between Europe and the United States." He insisted that Monnet keep the project strictly confidential since the program was "known to only four or five people in the United States."[39] This small group included Robert Schaetzel, who became Ball's deputy under Kennedy. Schaetzel, in turn, asked his close friend Max Kohnstamm, Monnet's assistant, to contribute his thoughts to the project, and also conducted extensive talks with René Foch on U.S.-European relations in the nuclear field. The final product, the so-called Stevenson Report, heeded the suggestions of Monnet and his colleagues and included a twenty-page paper outlining a plan for a "Policy for Partnership Between a United Europe and America within a Strong Atlantic Community."[40]

In January 1961, just before the new administration took office, Ball, Bowie, Tuthill, and Butterworth met with Monnet in Europe. Monnet, who preferred to do business over simple, even frugal, but high-quality meals, repeatedly invited his American friends to discuss U.S.-European relations over lunch or dinner. On 1 January, Bowie was invited to lunch at Monnet's residence at Houjarray. About a week later, Monnet had dinner with the Butterworths; and on Friday the thirteenth, a fortnight before Kennedy was inaugurated as president of the United States, Monnet arranged for Ball to meet with his collaborators, Max Kohnstamm and François Duchêne, at the headquarters of the Action Committee in Paris on Avenue Foch.[41] The succession of dinners and lunches continued when Monnet came to Washington in March. On the first day of the month, Ball invited Monnet for an informal dinner at home. Also present at the dinner were top members and advisers of the Kennedy administration who were involved in European affairs, including David Bruce, Walt Rostow, McGeorge Bundy, Robert Schaetzel, and last but not least, Dean Acheson. After several more lunches and dinners with Monnet, Ball took him to see the president, with whom Monnet discussed his plans for an Atlantic partnership over lunch and during other long conversations.[42] Monnet, who already knew of Kennedy's "intelligence and charm," was struck by his "dynamism" and his thirst for knowledge. He found that the young president possessed good political sense and was much respected in the administration, where Monnet sensed an atmosphere somewhat reminiscent of the Roosevelt years: constant discussion and "very open consultations," with the final decision belonging to the president. The president, Monnet wrote to Adenauer, was a "very simple, careful and direct man," a "man of action."[43]

Kennedy, very much attracted by his personality, was quite impressed by Monnet, too, and came to have great respect for him. George Ball can take most of the credit for providing Monnet with a good introduction to the president by explaining to Kennedy what Monnet was trying to accomplish in Europe. When Monnet came to Washington in March 1961, he found many members of the administration ready to espouse his views on the importance of European integration for the stability of the Western world. The selection of many Europeanists as part of the new Kennedy team seemed reassuring; it showed the president's commitment to putting Europe first on his policy agenda. While George Ball and his assistant Robert Schaetzel ended up in the State Department, McGeorge Bundy served in the White House. Members of previous administrations were counted among the supporters or sympathizers of European integration in the Kennedy administration. Douglas Dillon in the Treasury, David Bruce as ambassador to Great Britain, Schaetzel, and Tuthill all helped ensure continuing support for European integration between the Eisenhower and the Kennedy administrations, a support which, as in the past, was largely bipartisan. A member of the Truman administration and one of the instigators of the Marshall Plan, Averell Harriman—a Democrat and Bowles's preferred choice as assistant secretary for European affairs—gradually gained influence under Kennedy, rising from roving ambassador to assistant secretary of state for Far Eastern affairs in November 1961 and to under secretary of state for political affairs in 1963. Republican John McCloy, an acquaintance of Monnet's from the Roosevelt years[44] and a close friend, served as Kennedy's principal disarmament adviser. McCloy was instrumental in drafting legislation that led to the establishment of the United States Arms Control and Disarmament Agency. Meanwhile, Democrat Acheson was commissioned to write a report on NATO, and Bowie came in as a consultant.

The core of the American Europeanists closely connected to George Ball, and key European figures such as Monnet, Hallstein, Marjolin, Hirsch, Mansholt, and Jean Rey, formed a network not only of colleagues, but also of friends devoted to a common cause. These bonds of friendship increased the cohesiveness of the group and made it possible for a relatively small number of men to exert a strong influence within the Kennedy administration. Within the State Department, the dominant influence in European affairs was exercised by George Ball. Next in importance came the Bureau of European Affairs, which enlisted the energies of Europeanists such as Robert Schaetzel, an influential figure in the Kennedy administration and a friend of Monnet, whom he met often. In 1959, Schaetzel, as a recipient of a Rockefeller Public Service Award, had spent a year in Europe on sabbatical leave from the State Department. His task was to study the origins of the European Communities. During the transitional period between the Eisenhower and Kennedy administrations, Secretary Herter delegated Schaetzel to assist the new team in drafting several reports covering balance-of-payments, foreign economic policy, and disarmament issues. Schaetzel then served as senior assistant to Ball when Ball was under secretary for economic affairs and was his special assistant until he became deputy assistant for Atlantic affairs in the spring of 1962. The two men worked very closely together and saw eye to eye on the issue of European integration. Schaetzel had known Monnet and Max Kohnstamm since the negotiations for the U.S.-Euratom agreement. When Monnet came to Washington during the Kennedy years, he frequently used Schaetzel's office, to the point where Schaetzel's secretary became very much his own.[45]

The third major influence came from the Policy Planning Council (PPC), which was particularly active in such issues as the Multilateral Force (MLF), an American proposal for giving Europeans a role in nuclear defense through a mixed-manned nuclear force that would be Atlantic, or perhaps European. As chairman of the PPC, Walt Rostow, and his assistant Henry Owen, played a key role in European affairs. Rostow, an early proponent of European unity, had served as assistant to the executive secretary of the Economic Commission for Europe and had known Monnet since the war. Henry Owen met Monnet for the first time at the beginning of the Kennedy administration at a party given by McGeorge Bundy and developed a great admiration for him. During Monnet's frequent visits to Washington, Owen came to appreciate his shrewdness and his aptitude for obtaining advice on how to lobby for his views most effectively in the American government. Yet Owen's interest and enthusiasm for European integration were first aroused by Max Kohnstamm, whom he esteemed greatly.[46]

On the ambassadorial side, David Bruce,[47] a close friend of Monnet's from the days of the Marshall Plan who had enjoyed the privilege of being appointed successively to the positions of ambassador to France, U.S. representative to the ECSC, and ambassador to Germany, now became ambassador to Great Britain upon the recommendation of Dean Acheson.[48] This was a key position for the negotiations surrounding British entry into the Common Market—a policy strongly advocated by the Kennedy administration. John Tuthill became the American representative to the OECD and was subsequently appointed as United States representative to the European

Communities in Brussels, succeeding Walton Butterworth. Considering the important mandate that Kennedy gave his ambassadors, namely to "oversee and coordinate all the activities of the United States Government"[49] in their countries or fields of expertise, these appointments were extremely significant. John Tuthill negotiated the OECD and subsequently became closely involved in the negotiations searching for a solution to the so-called "chicken war."[50] He was on friendly terms with Marjolin, whom he had known in Paris where he had served as economic minister. While in Brussels, Marjolin and Tuthill would have lunch once a month at *Comme chez soi.* Hallstein and Etienne Hirsch were also his friends. Tuthill had met Monnet in Paris in 1956, when he was economic minister. When he negotiated the OECD and opened the first United States delegation to the organization, Tuthill's office was at the corner of Avenue Foch and Rue de la Faisanderie. Monnet's office was right next door, at 83 Avenue Foch. While in Paris, Tuthill saw Monnet two or three times a week, and each time Monnet traveled to Brussels, he went to see Tuthill.[51] George Ball, who had the highest opinion of John Tuthill, kept in close touch with him and with Jean Monnet throughout the Kennedy administration. When Tuthill went over to Brussels as special representative to the European Communities, John Leddy,[52] also a member of the "Cabal," succeeded him as the American ambassador to the OECD.

In the Treasury Department, Douglas Dillon, who had been ambassador to France during the EDC negotiations, now became secretary. During the last years of the Eisenhower administration, he had been appointed deputy under secretary of state for economic affairs. He had then been promoted to under secretary of state for economic affairs in July 1958 and to under secretary of state in April 1959.[53] In these capacities Dillon not only took on the responsibility for revamping the American foreign aid program but also devoted much energy to transforming the OEEC into the OECD. During that time, John Leddy was the under secretary's special assistant. His association with Dillon continued during the first years of the Kennedy administration, when he served as assistant secretary of the treasury for international affairs. A faithful Europeanist, Leddy made his views known to Dillon, who, although a sympathizer of European integration, was less enthusiastic than the hard core of Europeanists around George Ball. During the discussions that led to the creation of the OECD, Leddy, Tuthill, and Dillon frequently met with Monnet in Paris. Tuthill and Leddy tried to impress upon Dillon that the West needed both a new organization and the end of the OEEC. Yet Dillon did not initially pay much attention to the details of the proposal. Tuthill was somewhat disappointed when Dillon told Leddy that he approved of the United States joining the *OEEC.* Dillon had missed the point, Tuthill later recalled, yet Leddy noted that his general agreement with the proposal was good enough: one could now go ahead with the creation of the OECD.[54]

Although he did not formally belong to the administration, Dean Acheson became a foreign policy adviser to President Kennedy, notably on NATO, Berlin, and the Cuban Missile Crisis. He was convinced of the importance of European unity for the stability of the West, and was particularly interested in tying Germany closely to the West. But he also had a tendency to take a broader view of the whole matter, always seeing European integration within the wider framework of the Atlantic Alliance. He probably looked upon the dedicated Europeanists in the State Department and elsewhere in the administration with a tinge of amusement and considered their enthusiasm for set lines of policy, especially for the MLF, somewhat excessive. Acheson markedly preferred a policy of cold-blooded calculation in international affairs. He did, however, lend his support to the idea of an integrated European Community. His report on NATO, a study commissioned by the president, unequivocally stressed the importance of European integration for the United States and the Western world, emphasizing the crucial variable of Franco-German solidarity, which de Gaulle and Adenauer both endorsed. In his view, there could be no viable coalition between Western Europe and North America without West Germany. It was for this reason that "Schuman and Adenauer set about binding France and Germany together, in order to offset the Soviet Union's potential power to detach Germany by its control over the unification issue, over the eastern boundary, and over the fate of Berlin." European integration promised a strengthened Europe, with which the United States could work better than with a host of "separate weaker nations." Against the Soviet threat, "the essentially national and loosely coordinated efforts of the past [would] no longer suffice."[55] Taking the long view, Acheson also looked beyond European integration toward the development of an "Atlantic commonwealth, in which common institutions are increasingly developed to address common problems." The United Kingdom was to become associated with the European Community, casting away any hopes for a special relationship with the United States.[56] Yet the "special relationship" remained very much alive under Kennedy, as the 1962 Nassau meeting would amply demonstrate. In any event, the Acheson Report was approved by the president in April 1961 in its essentials and was disseminated throughout the government for implementation that same month. Henry Owen of the Policy Planning Staff, Secretary of Defense Robert McNamara, and his advisers Paul Nitze and William Bundy (assistant secretary of defense and deputy assistant secretary of defense, respectively) helped Acheson develop the report.

Both Nitze and Bundy worked at the Division of International Security Affairs (ISA), which functioned as a mini-State Department within the Defense Department. Nitze, who had participated in the long hearings for legislation authorizing, and appropriating for, the Marshall Plan, had several connections with Europeanists serving in the Kennedy administration, and these helped smooth relations between ISA and the agencies or embassies in which the Europeanists worked or advised. Back in the early 1940s, while working in the Office of the Coordinator of Inter-American Affairs, Nitze had been Schaetzel's first boss. Nitze had met Bowie when he took over the Policy Planning Staff. Douglas Dillon was also a close acquaintance of Nitze's, but the connection was professional rather than personal. Dillon was five years younger than Nitze, who had been his father's personal assistant when he worked for Dillon, Read & Company. Also through Dillon, Read & Company, Nitze became a close friend of Howard Bruce, David Bruce's older brother. During the Marshall Plan days, when David occupied the Paris office of the Marshall Plan, and again when David served as ambassador to Great Britain under Kennedy, Nitze would stay at his home. He was one of the very few people Nitze turned to for help.[57] After his nomination, Kennedy asked Paul Nitze[58] to chair a group to "consult . . . on national security problems with the ablest and most experienced authorities in the nation, without regard to party." Nitze called on David Bruce, as well as on Roswell Gilpatric and James Perkins. When Kennedy appointed him as assistant secretary of defense for international security affairs, Nitze, who had hoped to obtain the higher position of deputy secretary of defense, was at first "much chagrined." Yet as time went by, he found that his job allowed him to "assure the president and Dean Rusk Pentagon support for the type of policy they and [he] believed to be necessary," and was rather satisfied with his role. Notwithstanding Nitze's personal connections with many Europeanists, he and his staff occasionally took positions that differed from those of the staunch Europeanists in the State Department. For example, Nitze vigorously opposed the idea of an MLF, advocating instead increased participation of NATO allies in American nuclear planning. In any event, Secretary of State Dean Rusk tended to agree with Nitze and McNamara that the "Cabal" for the MLF was being carried away by misguided enthusiasm for a line of policy doomed to failure.[59] Robert McNamara, although initially quite skeptical of the military value of the MLF, later became, with George Ball, one of its supporters; yet his support derived from political reasons following de Gaulle's saying no to the British application for entry into the Common Market.[60]

THE PRAGMATISTS

Meanwhile, McGeorge Bundy, William's brother, established his quarters in the White House. Shortly after his election, Kennedy considered making him his secretary of state. Walter Lippmann and others strongly approved of such a move. But the prospect of working under an ex-Republican who had backed Eisenhower in 1952 and 1956 proved too much for Adlai Stevenson and he let Kennedy know he would refuse to serve under Bundy.[61] The president then offered Bundy various other positions in the State and Defense departments. Bundy finally opted for the post of special assistant to the president for national security affairs in the White House, where his staff gradually organized itself into a foreign affairs agency.

In 1961, Kennedy abolished the heavy machinery of Eisenhower's Operation Coordinating Board so that the State Department could take the lead in foreign policy planning and coordination.[62] But, although he originally wanted to rely more heavily on the Department of State in foreign policy, in practice the White House itself became the locus of a strong foreign policy staff. This was so partly because of Kennedy's style in dealing with foreign affairs and partly because of his impatience with the slowness of operations in the State Department. Kennedy further assigned a great share of the blame for the Bay of Pigs fiasco to the State Department and its poor advice. Increasingly, he began depending more on the White House Staff in matters of foreign policy. This signified a division of labor between the pragmatists of the White House Staff, generally more concerned with giving punctual answers to immediate problems, and the State Department, whose people generally took a longer view. The Kennedy style tended to lean towards the former. Indeed, Kennedy's pragmatism was the basis for many of Ball's complaints about the president, who called him "the pragmatist *par excellence*," concerned as he was with "action and day-to-day results." Ball lamented that "when one tried to point out the long-range implications of a current problem or how it meshed or collided with other major national interests, Kennedy would often say, politely but impatiently, 'Let's not worry about five years from now, what do we do tomorrow?" George Ball was "frequently disappointed by his reluctance to face the longer-range implications of either acting or not acting." He found Kennedy "intellectually alert and quick to understand a given problem" but he was not, Ball thought, "profound in either his analyses or his judgment."[63]

McGeorge Bundy, too, was a pragmatist. A member of the Kennedy administration commented on his fascination with "operational problems, how to do it, how to plan it . . . instead of the reflective questions like 'Where is that leading us?'" According to the same source, McGeorge Bundy "was above all the pragmatic operational man. He hated to do anything conceptually."[64] The Bundy style differed markedly from that of planners in the State Department—especially Walt Rostow—who tended to approach policy in a more conceptual manner, considering historical forces.

Under Kennedy, McGeorge Bundy quickly became the major figure in foreign policy among the White House Staff. His job was to assemble information from the State and Defense departments and the intelligence community and present a choice of alternatives to the president. Bundy also controlled access to the president, who spent more time with him than with State Department officials.[65] The State Department, it is true, was located a few blocks away from the White House, which made physical access to the president less convenient. Bundy's frequent meetings with the president and his control over the flow of information to the White House gave him a major influence in the formulation of foreign policy. The specific organization and role of the National Security Council (NSC) under Kennedy helped Bundy gain such influence. In contrast to the Eisenhower days, the NSC met much less frequently. Kennedy disliked large and formal meetings in which it was more difficult to decide high national security matters effectively.[66] He preferred to empower task forces to deal with specific policy issues. Bundy bore the major responsibility for organizing these task forces, which, by drawing officials from several departments, took some of the authority in foreign affairs away from the State Department. While the NSC itself became "little more than a shell,"[67] its staff grew in importance. Despite the importance of the NSC staff, however, Kennedy took great care that it would not block access to the other departments. The president "kept in close communication with his key Cabinet officers and other agency heads, and dealt periodically with officials at the Assistant Secretary level."[68] The NSC staff in no way substituted for the State Department or for other agencies in the government. It was, according to Schlesinger, "helpless without allies throughout the permanent government." But it did take the lead in bringing together all the right people on specific issues, especially whenever "the Department of State's response did not measure up to the president's expectations."[69] The staff thus functioned as an "honest broker" and an "agent of coordination"[70] in foreign affairs, roles Kennedy had originally intended for the State Department.

McGeorge Bundy enlisted the energies of brilliant and able intellectuals and scholars. Walt Rostow became Bundy's first deputy. An officer in the Office of Strategic Services during World War II, he had then served as assistant to the executive secretary of the Economic Commission for Europe, which he had himself been instrumental in creating.[71] He knew Monnet well and was a firm supporter of European integration. Kennedy had first intended to appoint him head of the Policy Planning Council, but Dean Rusk preferred to have his old friend George McGhee in this post,[72] and so Rostow was named deputy to McGeorge Bundy. The two men divided up the work: Bundy "was clearly in charge of the shop" and handled "the urgent business, except for Laos and Vietnam," while Rostow focused on long-range problems and the developing world. In European affairs, the primary responsibility rested with McGeorge Bundy, although Rostow would come in "when things were hot." For example, he drafted Lyndon Johnson's Berlin speech and came to the Acheson meetings on European policy.[73] In November 1961, Rostow was "reshuffled" along with Bowles and other officials. He moved from the White House to the State Department, where he took the position of counselor and chairman of the Policy Planning Council, which Kennedy had originally intended for him. The job was better suited to his inclination to ponder over the long-range implications of policymaking. McGeorge Bundy did not work well with him: their personalities clashed. Bundy the pragmatist had a hard time finding common ground with Rostow the conceptualizer. Thus Rostow took up the State Department's top planning position, where he played a crucial role in shaping American policy towards Europe, working closely with such "theologians" as Henry Owen, Rostow's deputy for basic national security policy, on the seventh floor of the State Department.

The Europeanists around George Ball disagreed with Rostow on the relative priorities to be assigned to the economic, political, and nuclear factors in the European integration process. Rostow deplored the obsession of the "whole Atlantic Establishment," which he felt included people such as Ball, Monnet, McGeorge Bundy, and the European Bureau in the State Department, all of whom were in favor of the "Monnet sequence." The Monnet sequence entailed giving priority to the tariff negotiations and the entry of Great Britain into the Common Market; then gradually moving on toward political union; and finally, dealing with the nuclear question in Europe. As an economist, Rostow harbored strong reservations about the assumption that tariff negotiations alone would yield political results for the unity of Europe, unless the nuclear question was dealt with simultaneously. How could there be "a Common Market settlement while the UK remained a national nuclear power, specially linked to the United States?" Very early on, Rostow urged putting forward the Multilateral Force as a genuine, firm proposal on the part of the United States, and not merely as a trial balloon. It was "a major regret" of his "that Monnet came so late to understand the critical power and influence of the nuclear question." But within the "Atlantic Establishment," he was isolated in his dissidence. Only after the Nassau Conference did Monnet and Kohnstamm take the nuclear issue seriously, while the administration decided to carry the MLF at a higher pitch. Until that time, the general reaction among Rostow's friends whenever he insisted on the nuclear dimension was, in his own words, "down, Buster."[74]

Carl Kaysen succeeded Rostow as McGeorge Bundy's deputy. To Bundy, Kaysen was not only an old friend from his days at Harvard, but he became *the* deputy,[75] supplanting both his predecessor, Rostow, and his successor, Francis Bator, in terms of personal and professional affinity with McGeorge Bundy. Carl Kaysen was not well known by the public, was not a "celebrity," yet, in the words of Joseph Kraft, he was "one of the really influential figures inside the Administration" and maintained good relations with both the White House and the State Department.[76] If McGeorge Bundy was an old friend, so too was George Ball, whom Kaysen had first met in 1945.[77] Although Kaysen sympathized with, and expressed some interest in, European integration, his attitude was, again, more pragmatic. He played a key role in trade policy. He also exerted a major influence on security issues. In this respect, he regarded the MLF, with amusement, as a slightly absurd proposal that the Europeans did not really want.[78] David Klein, a very able foreign service officer and an expert on both Germany and the Soviet Union who had served as the staff officer for European affairs on the NSC staff after working on the Soviet Desk in the Department of State, also belonged to the group of the pragmatists.

In general, the White House Staff, especially those on the NSC, thus tended to adopt a more tempered, less dogmatic attitude towards the whole issue of European integration. McGeorge Bundy was not only amused by the enthusiasm displayed by some of his friends and colleagues for such ideas as the MLF, but also disturbed by the degree of their enthusiasm.[79] Yet this did not signal a lack of interest in European affairs, or in European integration, on Bundy's part. In 1948, Bundy had worked in Washington for the agency responsible for implementing the Marshall Plan. In the 1950s he taught a course in modern foreign policy at Harvard, which dealt mainly with European foreign policy. During the Kennedy administration Monnet became a friend, and many of Bundy's friends had been friends of Monnet during the war.[80] Bundy supported the movement for a more European Europe, but much like President Kennedy, he was not tied by rigid formulas. Although he espoused the "Monnet sequence" in its essentials, he basically felt the shape and timing of European integration was something for Europeans to decide. Pragmatism and cool calculation were the order of the day in this matter, as in any other matter pertaining to foreign policy.

INTERNATIONALISTS AND ATLANTICISTS

Other forces within the administration worked to temper the enthusiasm of the "Cabal." The internationalists, who favored an international order with strong international institutions, did not view the establishment and consolidation of a regional entity like the EEC favorably. Free traders saw the EEC as an impediment to the free flow of trade. There were also lingering Atlanticists, mostly of the moderate faction and mainly represented by Christian Herter, the former secretary of state, whom Kennedy appointed as special representative for trade negotiations. Herter, who had been one of the artisans of the Marshall Plan, favored American support for the admission of Great Britain into the Common Market as a way of fostering a closer relationship between the United States and the Common Market. He felt that the creation of the EEC was a "revolutionary thing," which would help constitute a free-trade area that "would allow the development of mass-production, healthy competition, modern marketing techniques and other practices . . . in turn leading to a vastly increased productivity on the continent."[81] However, developments, or the lack of developments on the political side, were more worrisome. Noting that "substantial divergences" existed "in the matter of closer political ties"[82] within the EEC, ranging from those favoring supranational institutions to those preferring a loose confederation, Herter pointed out that British membership in the Common Market would add "still another viewpoint, probably one which is leery of supranational institutions and real political unity." Assuming that the chances for European political unification improved, Herter also worried about the possible encouragement of "a school of thought, at times quite vocal, which is interested in the political unification of Europe in order that Europe may become a third force, holding place with the United States and Russia in the determination of world policy." The prospect of a Gaullist-type Europe, less dependent on the United States and leaning towards a "middle-ground or neutralist attitude between the more belligerent positions of the Soviet bloc and the United States,"[83] in no way enchanted Herter, who evoked the terrifying prospect of the breakup of the Atlantic Alliance as a result of such neutralism.[84] In spite of this gruesome prospect, Herter did not advocate Atlantic political unity as an immediate solution. He felt that toying with thoughts of Atlantic political unity was an exercise in futility so long as European nations had not yet determined the degree of their commitment to a European federation. In this, Herter differed from Clarence Streit, the original advocate of an Atlantic union, and some of his followers, who placed Atlantic unity first on the agenda and contended that "European unity should be achieved within the framework of Atlantic institutions."[85] While Herter deemed Atlantic political unity "vaguely remote," the question of American relations with the Common Market was a more pressing issue. Crucial here was the economic policy of the United States: if restrictive practices, notably in the agricultural field, continued to be adopted by the Common Market, they would greatly hamper efforts toward building an "Atlantic partnership." On the military side, Herter had been one of the initiators of the MLF under Eisenhower. Its objectives, according to him, were to discourage nuclear proliferation by creating a fourth effective nuclear power and discouraging the French and other European nations from becoming separate nuclear powers. The new NATO nuclear force would not "avoid the need for increased non-nuclear forces," and "was not intended to be a total answer to the problem of Europe's defense."[86] In addition, the force would have to be clearly subordinated to NATO command and control.

On the whole, Herter's attitude towards European unity did not differ markedly from that of the Europeanists. Where it did diverge, however, was on the issue of timing: whereas the Europeanists put the effective organization of Europe first on their list and Atlantic unity as a rather remote objective, Herter thought that "the integration of Europe and discussions for the formulation of a true Atlantic Community [could] proceed along almost parallel lines."[87] Building on existing institutions, consolidating the trade partnership with Europe (perhaps joining the Common Market), and agreeing on a defense for Europe acceptable to both the United States and Europe were prerequisites to building common Atlantic political institutions. In other words "Sound Atlantic unity . . . must be built on a firm economic and military basis; and while we must also push for political ties, such ties must mark not the beginning but the crowning achievement of union."[88] No matter "how nebulous" the development of a true Atlantic Community appeared, the ultimate objective was to be "kept constantly in mind."[89] Herter thought it could reasonably be attained within ten years. His views were shared by a number of well-known statesmen in the United States, some of whom belonged to the Kennedy administration, although priorities often differed within that group. The first and/or second Declarations of Atlantic Unity were signed by such prominent figures as Chester Bowles, Christian Herter, Thomas Finletter, William Clayton, Averell Harriman, Hubert Humphrey, Henry Kissinger, and John McCloy. The second Declaration of Atlantic Unity, endorsed by the NATO Parliamentarians' Conference on 12 November 1962, recommended, among other things, "form[ing] a trade partnership between the European Economic Community and North America as a basis for an Atlantic Economic Community, but open to all other qualified nations of the free world," and "establish[ing] a governmental commission on Atlantic Unity to draw up a Charter for an Atlantic Community suitably organized to meet the challenges of this era."[90]

Atlanticists, internationalists, pragmatists, and Europeanists exerted some degree of influence on the formulation of policy towards Europe. Yet, on many crucial issues, such as the Trade Expansion Act, the Europeanists succeeded in achieving a remarkable consistency of policy throughout the Kennedy administration and beyond, extending well into the Johnson administration. The cohesiveness of the group, the clarity of their goals, and the consistency of their values go a long way toward explaining the efficient way in which they defended certain lines of policy, despite many conflicting forces. It also explains why they remained blind to certain clues that indicated that the means they had chosen to support their goals would fail, as in the case of the MLF and British entry into the Common Market.[91] In their efforts they were sometimes helped, sometimes hindered, by the pragmatists, whose avowed function was to "keep them honest." The pragmatists learned from the hard-core Europeanists, the Europeanists learned from the pragmatists, and friendships were built. In the process of working in the same administration and on similar issues, their views collided or ultimately converged. In December 1959, about one year before being elected president of the United States, a young senator observed that "it is the men, not merely the stated policies, that determine the effectiveness of American foreign policy."[92] As we shall see, Europeanists played an influential role in the formulation of Kennedy's agenda in European affairs. Implementing this agenda was another matter.

7

Kennedy's Inheritance

THE BOWIE, BALL, AND ACHESON REPORTS:
CONTINUITY AND NEW INITIATIVES

When Kennedy took office, he inherited some key Europeanists from the previous administration as well as some of their planning for the post-Eisenhower era. The Bowie Report, "The North Atlantic Nations: Tasks for the 1960's," is a case in point. The report is known especially for its proposal of a Multilateral Force under NATO control. But the report dealt with a considerably larger framework than that of NATO. It addressed the wide range of issues that would confront the Atlantic nations in the 1960s in the economic, political, and military fields, and it sought to propose solutions that would deal with common problems through NATO as well as other institutions.

The Bowie Report was prepared for Secretary Herter. Livingston Merchant and Gerard Smith, the assistant secretary for policy planning who had succeeded Bowie after he returned to Harvard in 1957, helped Bowie gather a small staff drawn from various institutions both inside and outside of government. Among these institutions were the Rand Corporation, the Princeton Center for International Studies, the American Mission to the European Communities in Brussels, the American Embassy in Bonn, and the Department of Defense.[1] In addition to the original group, Robert Bowie also called upon several individuals for papers on specific topics. Robert Komer of the CIA and Henry Owen were particularly good recruits.

Bowie, Owen, and some of their friends later became key *éminences grises* under the Kennedy administration. Henry Owen continued on the Policy Planning Staff and became one of the linchpins of the MLF undertaking, while

Robert Bowie was called in as a consultant by Kennedy. The report that Bowie had drawn up during the Eisenhower administration found an attentive audience in the councils of Europeanists in the new administration. Some of its conclusions were strikingly similar to those of a task force report on foreign economic policy that George Ball had prepared for Kennedy in December 1960. Ball had suggested the creation of this task force in the Stevenson Report, recommending that it be directed by the under secretary designate for economic affairs, which he much expected to be himself.[2] Ball drew on the help of consultants from the academic community, from organizations such as the Council on Foreign Relations, and from law firms such as Robert R. Nathan Associates. Specifically, he consulted Robert Bowie and Walt Rostow on foreign economic aid. The Acheson Report, commissioned by Kennedy in early 1961, incorporated some aspects of both the Ball and Bowie reports, including Bowie's MLF proposal, although with considerably less enthusiasm than Bowie had evidenced. Henry Owen, who had served on Bowie's study team, helped Acheson develop his report, together with Paul Nitze and, once again, Bowie himself. The interconnections among the three reports demonstrate the level of continuity between the Eisenhower and Kennedy administrations. The appointment—during the decisive periods of the interregnum and at the very beginning of the new administration—of Europeanists from the Eisenhower administration and other circles had a crucial impact on American policy towards Europe during the Kennedy years.

The Bowie Report successively addressed the military, economic, and political dimensions of Atlantic relations. We shall change the order somewhat and discuss the economic dimension of the report first. Bowie recommended three main areas of action for the Atlantic nations: economic growth, coordination of economic policies, and economic integration. Economic growth was needed to meet the demands of growing populations in both the United States and Western Europe, to cover the increasing cost of defense equipment, and to sustain economic development programs in the Third World. Growth was also needed to ensure the "pursuit of liberal trade policies." Bowie pointed out that an environment of sustained growth would facilitate adjustments between the Six and the Seven, while it would also help developed countries absorb more imports of raw materials and manufactured goods from developing countries. Last but not least, continued growth was essential to counter the Soviet economic challenge.

Bowie's exaggerated assessment of the Soviet economic threat determined how he appraised the position of the Atlantic nations relative to that threat and the means he suggested to counter it. A comparison of the economies of the "Communist bloc" and the Atlantic nations showed the superiority of the latter. Bowie warned, however, that the bloc would eventually catch up with the Atlantic nations. Bowie predicted that bloc investment would "about equal that of the NATO countries in absolute amounts" by 1970, with a larger proportion of that investment being "devoted to direct industrial investment which may considerably exceed similar investments by NATO countries in absolute terms."[3] This would, in turn, stimulate a more accelerated rate of growth in the bloc than in the NATO grouping. Bowie saw 1970 as a potential turning point for the fortunes of the West. Echoing the Bowie Report, Acheson later adopted the year 1970 in his own report as the very last date by which "a more tightly knit Atlantic commonwealth" must be achieved.[4] The Bowie Report recognized the growing interdependence of the Atlantic nations and recommended a number of ways to pool their resources in order to offset Soviet growth and to ensure "vigorous economic growth with high employment" in the West.[5] These included the coordination of economic policies, the removal of restrictions to trade, and cooperation in research.[6] Steady growth would allow the Atlantic nations to "clearly carry significantly greater burdens from present resources with little sacrifice in material well-being."[7] Without such growth, they would face an increasingly hostile world. The Kennedy administration likewise emphasized the need to accelerate economic expansion, increase trade, and maintain a solid substratum of economic security for the well-being of the Atlantic nations.

The coordination of economic policies among the nations involved was essential to the success of the entire strategy. Bowie deplored the reluctance of the United States to discuss American "budgetary and monetary policies with its allies as a matter of common concern," an attitude that had the deplorable effect of contributing "to European skepticism about the proposed OECD."[8] The Kennedy administration would later heed his advice on that point. American domestic economic policies and the balance-of-payments deficit would increasingly be discussed and presented to allies not just as the problems and responsibilities of the United States, but as those of a community of free nations. Yet, within this community, some nations were more important than others. Together, the United States, the European Community, and the United Kingdom accounted for "70% of Free World GNP."[9] Accordingly, it was especially important for these nations "to work together more intimately." The OECD offered the perfect framework for them to coordinate their economic policies.

To complete the blueprint for an economically secure West, Bowie added two key components besides growth and cooperation: trade and economic integration. The core group of the NATO countries accounted for "60% of

Free World Trade," while the EEC and EFTA countries accounted for 24 percent and 18 percent of that trade, respectively. Moreover, "50% of the total external trade of all NATO countries [was] carried out among themselves."[10] Hence the importance of removing most obstacles to trade among the Atlantic nations. Within the Atlantic trading area, the Common Market occupied a key position. There was no denying that the EEC would cause adjustment problems for outsiders. More intra-European trading could displace the exports of third countries. By increasing competition among its members, the Common Market would also render them more competitive on world markets. Finally, "it would tend to hold domestic and attract outside capital," not necessarily a plus for the United States because of its unfavorable balance of payments.[11] Bowie was nevertheless generally optimistic about the overall effect of the Common Market, which he hoped would develop into a more prosperous area, offering more outlets for American goods. There was, however, an important caveat: the Six would have to enter into negotiations with the United States to "reduce the common external tariff on a multilateral non-discriminatory basis."[12] This was a way of saying that the European Communities needed to maintain an outward orientation, not only toward the United States, but toward other nations as well. The ultimate goal was to "move toward free trade at least among the advanced countries."[13] The United States would be the champion of free trade and carry along in its wake both the EFTA and Common Market countries. By initiating wide-ranging trade negotiations in GATT, Americans would possess enough leverage to prevent the Six-Seven quarrel from festering and to inoculate those countries against the temptation to adopt discriminatory trade policies. The Bowie Report, in effect, contained Kennedy's new Trade Expansion Act (TEA) in embryo. In order to meet the needs of both Atlantic and developing countries, Bowie proposed an ambitious revision of U.S. trade agreement legislation to "permit negotiation of substantial tariff reductions in GATT, preferably on an across-the-board basis, but perhaps by broad categories of products." The proposal included domestic measures to cushion the effects of increased imports on American industry and labor.[14] Ball's Task Force Report likewise recommended "authority to reduce tariffs across the board by an average of 50 percent of the 1961 rates in five annual stages through 1966."[15]

The Bowie Report contained other key elements of what Joseph Kraft would later call Kennedy's "grand design." Support for the entry of the United Kingdom into the Common Market was one of them. This support was in turn tightly linked to American support for the European Communities. Bowie was very much in sync with the Eisenhower administration in favoring an expansion of the European Communities to include the rest of Western Europe because of their political implications. He remained rather cool toward a wider European trading zone, which threatened to water down or destroy the EEC while creating greater adjustment difficulties for non-members. He also dismissed an Atlantic grouping as politically impracticable; Kennedy would later do the same.

Both for practical and political reasons, the EEC approach was the preferred one. Rather than creating a European-wide free trade area, Bowie favored a more radical approach by which the United Kingdom would "accept the philosophy of the Common Market and directly negotiate its adherence on terms which did not sacrifice the political institutions or objectives of the Six. The UK should be encouraged to adopt this course."[16] Bowie's recommendation came at a time when Macmillan was seriously beginning to consider a bold move to enter the Common Market. The pronouncements of Jean Monnet's Action Committee reflected the same general atmosphere. About one month before Bowie handed in his report, the committee welcomed the acceptance to the three communities of not only the United Kingdom but other European countries as well.[17] A few months later, Acheson joined the chorus and recommended that "the U.S. should look with favor on any trend in British thinking which contemplates eventual membership in the six." No longer were the British to entertain any doubts that the United States did indeed support "the economic and political coalescence of the six." They were "not to be encouraged to stay apart from the six" either by hopes of weakening the European Communities or by hopes of a " 'special relation' between the Commonwealth and the U.S." Similarly, the Six would be expected not "to put the price of admission of Great Britain to their association too high (in political terms) for acceptance, provided that there [was] to be no weakening of the essential ties among the six." Not mincing words, Acheson concluded: "Over time, the U.K. might become convinced that its position apart from the continent did not constitute a promising base of power—particularly if the U.S. was dealing ever more closely with growing strength on the continent."[18]

The Bowie Report did not mention the "special relation," but it did insist that UK membership in the Communities was both an economic and political necessity for Britain and would greatly benefit the Communities while strengthening the Atlantic Alliance as a whole. Ball's Task Force Report was more circumspect. It recognized Britain's full membership in the Communities as a possible way of torpedoing British schemes for "discriminatory" free trade area arrangements, but predicted that such membership was unlikely. Although industrial circles appeared to favor such a move, British government and public opinion were "clearly not yet prepared" for it. At the very least, the government would "hold back even tentative gestures in this direction pending a disclosure of the policies of the Kennedy administration."[19] Despite these initial doubts, Ball later committed the United States to supporting British entry into the Common Market, even prior to securing Kennedy's approval on the matter.

Both the Bowie and the Ball reports agreed that the rift between the Six and the Seven must be healed in a manner that would not discriminate against the United States. They also agreed that EFTA did not have much to offer in terms of economic integration and even less in terms of "political objectives of a positive character." The Six, although they too could discriminate against outside countries, including the United States, once again appeared as the favorites. Trade discrimination on their part would be acceptable because of the anticipated advantages their economic and political unification could bring to the unity of the West. By contrast, Bowie warned that if Britain did not separate from EFTA and join the Communities, EFTA might well disrupt the cohesiveness of the Alliance.[20]

The importance of avoiding fragmentation in the Alliance helped focus Bowie's argument in favor of continued support for the European Communities. Compared to the immediate postwar period, when there existed a sense of common purpose for members of the alliance, who all faced the common tasks of rebuilding Europe and assuming a common defense effort against the Soviet Union, the late 1950s and early 1960s showed "less consensus on how to meet . . . a more complex set of issues." Consensus and the "will to divert resources from social welfare to defense and foreign affairs" were weakened both by "Soviet stress on detente and coexistence" and "the broader spectrum of necessary action," which tended to "widen the gap between the large and the small."[21] Reading between the lines, one sees the allusion to the Suez episode. In order to counteract the trend towards Atlantic fragmentation, which had been most visible during that incident, the West needed catalysts to focus the common political will of the Atlantic nations. European political and economic integration promised to be such a catalyst at the European level. Once united, Western Europe would better be able to coordinate its policies with those of the United States.

The evolution of the respective power positions of Western Europe and the United States could constitute a potentially divisive factor in the alliance unless an attempt was made to channel European energies to common endeavors among themselves and with the United States. Renewed economic vigor in Western Europe proved that the Marshall Plan had been largely successful. Not only could Europe forgo American economic assistance, but the European economic success story had also transformed Western Europe into a vigorous competitor of the United States. Economic strength marched hand in hand with European aspirations for more political influence in world councils. Yet the economic giant did not yet possess sufficient political cohesion to adopt a common foreign policy or to fine tune it to that of the United States. Hence efforts were loosely coordinated and clashes of interests occurred between the United States and its European allies and among European nations themselves. As a result of all this, the specter of European nationalism revived despite the best efforts of postwar American and European partisans of European integration to ban it. Providentially, European integration could kill two birds with one stone: it could help Europeans gain more influence in a world where great powers such as China, the USSR, and the United States increasingly stole the show, while it also offered one of the most effective means of uniting the divided councils of the Atlantic Alliance. Economic realities dictated political soundness. No European members could rival the United States "in terms of resources and GNP." In fact, "the largest European members represent[ed] only 10 to 12 percent as much as the United States. With such disparity, equal influence on common policy [was] out of the question, whatever the forms or fictions. The result [was] frequent friction and frustration, leading to unilateral national action." On the other hand, a "Europe able to act as an effective entity would deserve and could exercise comparable influence on common policy and action. Disposing resources much nearer to those of the United States, such a Europe could join in the genuine *partnership of equals*."[22]

In a similar way, Jean Monnet and some of his closest European collaborators had long advocated the participation of the United Kingdom in the European unification process. Monnet saw no point in pushing for an agreement between the Six and the Seven that would freeze the United Kingdom in its current allegiance to the Seven and make it more difficult for the British to join the Common Market at a later date. He much preferred British participation in the Common Market. British participation, he hoped, would lift the debate to a higher plane and allow the Common Market and its new participant to sit down at the discussion table with the United States and seek common solutions to monetary and trade problems on an equal basis. The claim for equality seemed to him all the more justified in the context of the American balance-of-payments deficit, which showed the increasing interdependence of the United States on the rest of the world.[23]

When Kennedy took office, Western Europe was already well on its way to becoming the economic equal of the United States. By the early sixties, the treatment of the economic anemia of European allies and potential customers had been remarkably successful. The result was a new relationship among the Atlantic nations, which, according to Ball, was "no longer a relationship of the weak to the strong, of the followers to the leader," but rather "something far healthier—the relationship of the strong to the stronger." During the immediate postwar period, the United States had been "a towering economic Mount Everest" largely independent of its European friends for its prosperity. The European nations seemed economic dwarfs, cowering in the mighty shadow of the United States. This was no longer true. The United States was no longer "the single giant among nations," but rather "the largest giant in a world of giants, the strongest among the strong, the first among equals."[24] Yet the largest economic giant of all showed signs of failing strength.

The diagnosis of the State of the Union in early 1961 yielded a disturbing picture. Addressing Congress only ten days after his inauguration, Kennedy summed it up in one short line : "the American economy is in trouble."[25] The trouble showed in numbers: "7 months of recession, 3 1/2 years of slack, 7 years of diminished economic growth, and 9 years of falling farm income."[26] Kennedy inherited economic growth at a stagnant, or even receding, average rate of 2.5 to 3 percent a year. Insufficient growth of the GNP failed to sustain the employment needs of a growing population. By the end of 1961, unemployment reached the unacceptably high figure of 6 percent. Just a few years after the 1954 and 1958 recessions, the American economy had entered yet another recession in the spring of 1960. The United States fared no better when one regarded the deficit of its balance of payments and its gold outflow. Contrary to the early 1950s, the country was no longer accumulating huge reserves. Talk of an incurable dollar gap, indefinitely widened by the inability of European countries to earn foreign exchange, was no longer possible. Instead, West European countries were now doing well—extremely well—holding more and more American dollars, while the gold outflow from American reserves intensified. Between 1950 and 1962, the gold outflow reached a total of $8 billion. By 1961, American gold reserves totaled about $17.8 billion, and by 1967 they had declined to $12.1 billion.[27] Although the United States continued to show a large balance-of-trade surplus, this surplus was offset by American military and economic aid expenditures abroad as well as by capital exports to acquire foreign companies, most of all in the increasingly attractive European economies. Over the period 1958-1961, the United States' balance of payments showed an average overall deficit of $3.4 billion.[28] Strongly influenced by his father, who considered the state of American gold stocks and the deficit as infallible barometers of American strength, the president was almost obsessed with finding a cure for the deficit, or at the very least a palliative. George Ball and others tried to minimize the importance of the deficit and pointed out that an obsession with the balance of payments "threatened to produce serious distortions of policy." Reflecting upon the Kennedy administration, Ball later wrote: "Compared with our later experience when, in 1977, for example, the deficit in our overall balance of accounts amounted to $20 billion, the deficits of $2 billion we were then running now seem almost de minimis. But at that time, Americans were not yet adjusted to the idea that America should be other than a surplus nation."[29]

The president, in attempting to "simultaneously increase . . . growth at home, reduce unemployment, and strengthen the dollar by eliminating the deficit in [American] international payments,"[30] relied heavily on American allies, and in particular on prosperous Western European countries such as Germany, to encourage their citizens to invest in the United States, to eliminate obstacles to the flow of American exports, and to foot the bill for a larger portion of foreign aid and military expenditures. The campaign in favor of the establishment of the OECD, which the administration continued through its ratification in 1961, hinged on providing a framework for distributing burdens more equally among increasingly economically equal and interdependent allies.

The American balance-of-payments deficit, argued American leaders, had a mirror image: the surplus of Germany and other countries. The old saw that "[w]hen the United States sneezes, all of Europe contracts influenza" no longer adequately depicted a world where the United States was now equally vulnerable to "the contagion of economic maladjustments."[31] In a world of increasing interdependence it was only fair to expect the surplus nations to relieve the burden of the United States. During discussions in Congress on the new Trade Expansion Act (TEA), which was mostly an attempt to deal with the mounting challenge of the Common Market and the EFTA countries, some voices claimed that the United States, in light of its past and present contributions to "the free world complex for trade, for aid to underdeveloped areas, for military defense," was in all "justice and fairness . . . entitled to something more than reciprocity."[32] Professor Jacob Viner of Princeton agreed that the Common Market "owed" the United States something. He added: "It is, I think, to be regretted that we did not make some effort in advance to see that the Common Market should be so fashioned that we would have advance claims to negotiate with them on means of lessening its potential adverse effects on us."[33] The United States had in a way given its Western European allies a blank check, and it was only fair to expect some tangible return on this act of faith to the United States from a prosperous Western Europe.

Ball's Task Force Report to Kennedy put the blame for the United States' balance-of-payments deficit on "other major industrialized powers" because of their failure "to pursue adequate policies of growth." Ball hoped that these "powers," which obviously included the European Communities and of course Germany, would be persuaded to contribute more to the common tasks of military defense and assistance to developing countries. Beyond that, the report looked forward to a general liberalization of trade, which would not only counter the rift between the Six and the Seven but also make it possible for industrialized countries to pursue expansionist policies. Growth and trade were inextricably intertwined. Unless the United States could persuade its partners to adopt domestic policies of growth, it would be forced to search for other ways to balance its international payments, notably by restricting foreign imports into the United States. On the other hand, "sustained economic growth" in the West would not be achieved unless trade were freed from "artificial restrictions and protectionist devices" that prevented it from expanding, diverted it, and generally fostered "inefficient production" while simultaneously restraining economic growth.[34] In an era of increasing economic interdependence, the industrial nations could hurt one another by adopting discriminatory and protective trade policies. Hence Ball developed one of the most basic tenets of the salesman's credo for both the new OECD and the new Trade Expansion Act: "we must see to it that trade serves as a cement to bind our political systems more closely together rather than as a source of discord between us."[35] Failing that, the Soviet Union would find a way to take advantage of the divided councils of the Western world.

The rift between EFTA and the Six was a potentially divisive economic and political factor for the West; a split between a protectionist Common Market and the United States would weaken the West even more. In order to avoid these bleak developments, Ball proposed to harness the energies of the interdependent complex of industrial nations and channel them toward the common tasks of military defense and assistance to the developing countries. In March 1961, he spoke of the positive aspects of interdependence : "the ability of the Western nations, acting in partnership, to multiply their strength for the achievement of common tasks."[36]

Even earlier that year, Douglas Dillon hailed a "new era of partnership." The partnership had in effect three dimensions: "intra-European cooperation," a "full partnership" between Western Europe and North America, and "a new partnership between the old nations in the north and the new nations to the South."[37] In a world where colonial empires were rapidly vanishing, the new nations of the southern hemisphere offered a tremendous potential for growth for the United States and for other industrial nations. Helping developing countries gain foreign exchange and achieve a high growth rate by opening the markets of industrial countries to their exports would in the long run decrease their need for economic assistance and make them good customers for American exports. The United States had already crossed several "new frontiers"; by proposing to adapt to developing nations the basic principles that had presided over the Marshall Plan, the United States now turned to another new frontier. In doing so, the Organization for European Economic Cooperation lost one of its E's and became the Organization for Economic Cooperation and Development (OECD), with an emphasis on development.

At the heart of the twin partnerships of Western Europe/United States and Western industrial nations/developing countries was the definition of minimum requirements for the preservation of freedom. The Acheson Report commissioned by Kennedy in early 1961 defined freedom thus: "By free societies we mean those in which the consent of the governed plays an important role. Other societies may live in this environment, also. It is ecumenical. But the environment becomes inimical to freedom if the coercion of some societies by others makes wide inroads in the acceptance of consent." Most significant was Acheson's emphasis that it was "essential to this environment that it be spacious." Hence United States efforts to counter the Soviet threat not only in Europe but also in developing nations. For the tremendous task of holding the free world together, the United States needed not only the cement of mutually beneficial trade but also a lot of help from its friends. Upon graduating into the world of giants, the continental nations were expected to contribute more resources and a sense of common purpose to their long-time association with the United States.

The older nations occupied a crucial position in the coalition for freedom. The more powerful and prosperous they became, the more could be expected of them. But, regardless of their new prosperity, these nations possessed certain characteristics that made them natural "partners" of the United States, although Acheson did not use that word. The "influence and power of the United States alone is not sufficient to maintain this spacious environment," said the Acheson Report. "The coalition of the peoples and nations of Western Europe and North America is indispensable to this end, because of: a) Their geographical position. b) Their power—the resultant of population, resources, technology, and will, equally indispensable to defense and development. c) The common civilization and broad purposes which they share with us." In a time of conflict with the Soviet Union over Berlin, Laos, and elsewhere, the perception of the Soviet threat played, as in the past, a key role in magnifying the importance of the European element in the Western coalition.

The Acheson Report defined the grand design of the Soviet Union as an attempt "to disrupt the coalition" of the West and "reduce its capacity for effective action by separating its members from each other and especially from the people of Asia, Africa and South America." It was therefore of paramount importance to "maintain and strengthen the coalition: both its cohesion and power within the Atlantic area and its capacity for effective action outside that area."[38] In an earlier assessment, Acheson evaluated the situation in these terms: together the Atlantic nations controlled "industrial productive power and manpower three times that of the Soviet Union," but "should the resources of Western Europe be disposable by the Soviet Union, it would exceed the United States in productive capacity and man power. Russian hegemony over the Eastern Hemisphere, perhaps even over South America, would be more than possible, and the problems confronting the United States would become unmanageable." Growth in production in the industrialized countries was crucial to bolster the "free world" against the Soviet threat. Only in this way could the West continue "to bear the burdens of defense, to improve living standards of growing populations, and to provide investment capital for economic growth and improved conditions of life in undeveloped areas of America, Asia, and Africa."[39]

Ball's task force reached a similar conclusion. Unless the industrialized nations of the West grew more rapidly they would not be able to help those developing countries that largely depended on Western markets and capital for their advancement. In turn, developing countries would not become good export outlets for American goods. The Soviet bloc would be only too glad to step in. The bloc would continue its current practice of concluding bilateral commercial treaties with developing countries that effectively increased their dependence on its funds, markets, and technical assistance, thus making them more sensitive to Soviet political pressure.[40]

In December 1961, William Clayton, one of the artisans of the Marshall Plan, testified along with Acheson before the Joint Economic Committee in Congress. Using cold war rhetoric he too stressed the importance of the Western coalition to preserve developing countries from falling under Soviet influence. In his view, economic cement was an essential ingredient in the American/Western European partnership, and this included an association of the United States and Canada with the "trade aspects of the Common Market movement." Instead of a divided alliance, the Soviets would then face "a united West, with political and economic aggregation so powerful that their cold war objectives could not be realized." Entering the key variable of American balance of payments into the equation for a viable strategy for the "free world," Clayton made it abundantly clear that in order to reduce its deficit and protect the dollar from devaluation the United States must have markets in which it could trade freely. In that sense, the overused cliché of "free world" took on an added, and yet still familiar dimension (reminiscent of Cordell Hull's program) of a world free from trade barriers. Reducing obstacles to trade among Western nations and developing countries and expanding American export markets became the cure-all to alleviate the first signs of American economic decline.[41]

Eisenhower believed in streamlining American expenses both at home and abroad. But such frugality was not the policy of the Democratic administration that succeeded him. The expansionist policies of the Kennedy administration, which counted many Keynesians in its ranks, sought to increase domestic growth in the United States, promote full employment, *and* reduce the level of the balance-of-payments deficit, while increasing defense spending and fostering expensive social domestic programs. This was an impossible task unless America's friends helped; the more numerous these were, the better. The more they believed their interests to converge with those of the United States, the better. It now remained necessary to design a strategy to help "the Atlantic Community rediscover the cohesion and sense of purpose which marked its creation."[42] The Trade Expansion Act was part of that strategy.

THE TRADE EXPANSION ACT

On 6 December 1961, in a "trial balloon"[43] speech before the Economic Club of Chicago, McGeorge Bundy hailed the "Common Market miracle" as a "major challenge and a major opportunity" for the United States. That same day, President Kennedy addressed the National Association of Manufacturers in New York. Kennedy presented an either/or proposition: either the United States and Western Europe worked "together on problems of trade, payments and monetary reserves" or their "mutual strength" would be "splintered by a network of tariff walls, exchange controls, and the pursuit of narrow self-interest, in unrelated if not outright hostile policies on aid, trade, procurement, interest rates and currency."[44] The president then dwelt at some length on his favorite obsession, the American balance-of-payments deficit, to which he proposed his favorite remedy, trade expansion, in conjunction with a host of other measures calculated to maintain the position of the United States as the "free world's leader." Progressively homing in on his true objective, Kennedy then spoke of the need to replace the old Reciprocal Trade Agreements Act due to expire in June of 1962 with a "new and bold instrument of American trade policy." What the president was selling was a new trade program tailored to meet the challenges and to exploit the opportunities of the Common Market.

The Ball Task Force Report, which Kennedy had commissioned the previous year, proposed focusing the new trade program on how to deal with the mounting challenge posed by the Common Market. The United States should, Ball insisted, "use the European Economic Community both as a justification for a major new round of trade negotiations and a precedent for reducing tariffs by percentage cuts across the board rather than the traditional item-by-item haggling."[45] "If United States production is not to be at a serious disadvantage in the rapidly growing Common Market," wrote Ball, "the President must be armed with weapons enabling him to bargain effectively for the generalization to the United States of the internal tariff cuts within these markets—or, at least, for the substantial reduction of their external tariff." The Common Market countries and the EFTA countries had reduced their internal tariffs by 30 percent and 20 percent, respectively, and had generalized the first 10 percent reduction to the rest of the world, including the United States. The two groups could probably also be persuaded, in light of the United States' previous record of "generosity" and its current balance-of-payments difficulties, to extend the second phase of reductions in their tariffs without requesting major concessions. Yet they would most likely not agree to further reductions in their tariffs unless Kennedy had the authority to offer a "substantial reduction" in American tariff levels. Five years down the road, the report warned, the Common Market and EFTA countries would have achieved internal tariff cuts of 70 or 80 percent. If the president were not armed with sufficient authority to entice these countries to generalize their tariffs to the rest of the world, the United States would soon find itself at "a formidable competitive disadvantage" in Europe. Similarly, the Acheson Report viewed the progress already being achieved in Europe with some concern. "The Europeans," the report maintained, "have already been moving, in the Common Market and the EFTA, away from the item-by-item approach to tariff reductions, and toward across the board percentage reductions. There is every indication that this new approach will be pushed further in the years ahead. If the European countries proceed alone on this course, they may discriminate against the U.S. and the less developed areas." If, however, Congress did pass a comprehensive bill endowing the president with far-reaching authority, this would demonstrate to the European nations America's commitment to solving its balance-of-payments problems by engaging in expansionist policies. Ball and his advisers anticipated that European nations might then be persuaded to follow the lead of the United States and lower their economic barriers while also disbursing more money for economic aid and military defense. Beyond that, they hoped that a general liberalization of trade would sap energy from renewed initiatives to bring about a European-wide free trade area that was largely discriminatory towards the United States.[46]

Having advanced to the key position of under secretary of state, Ball proceeded to sell his proposal to the highest circles of the administration, not least of all the president. In the course of 1961, he and his assistant, Robert Schaetzel, worked closely together in preparing versions of an entirely new trade expansion act.[47] Meanwhile, Kennedy appointed White House adviser Howard Petersen to join the effort to develop a new trade program. While Ball initially[48] wanted to wait and send a completely new bill to Congress in 1963, Petersen favored submitting a more conservative bill immediately. The reason for Ball's delaying tactic was the introduction of a key new variable in the Atlantic game: the recent application of the British to join the Common Market. By opening up the prospect of an ambitious round of trade negotiations in GATT, Ball reasoned, a new trade expansion act could lure away Macmillan's home support for U.K. membership in the Common Market. The Labour party, for example, had tentatively backed the prime minister mainly because previous free trade area schemes had floundered, and it could now be expected to withdraw its support when presented with a quite palatable alternative to Common Market membership. Kennedy, according to Ball, "wisely overruled" Ball's concerns.[49] Petersen ended up supporting the substance of Ball's proposal, while Ball eventually agreed to send the proposed bill to Congress early. Thus Kennedy retained the substance of Ball's proposal, while adopting Petersen's timing.[50]

Although at first afraid that the bill might be defeated by a protectionist Congress in an election year, events forced Kennedy's hand. By the fall, the Dillon Round was nearing an unspectacular conclusion. Because of the limitations of the American Reciprocal Trade Act, the American team was unable to accept a Common Market offer for a reciprocal across-the-board cut of 20 percent in industrial tariffs to the United States. Other decisive factors were the impending adoption of the Common Agricultural Policy (CAP) by the Six and the prospect of stepped-up competition from a Common Market enlarged by British membership. Key to the president's decision was the public reaction to two speeches. In early November, Ball addressed the National Foreign Trade Association in a trial-balloon speech. He suggested that the president's authority to negotiate trade agreements must be broadened "to meet the challenge of the European Economic Community," which meant that "at the minimum [the United States could] no longer afford to limit [American] negotiators to trading on an item-by-item basis and must authorize them to strike much broader and more ambitious bargains on behalf of United States industry."[51] On the same day that Ball delivered his speech, the Atlanticist team of William Clayton and Christian Herter made a plea before Congress requesting a "substantial broadening and reshaping of the act for another term of several years."[52] The public reaction to the two speeches was unexpectedly positive, which suggested that protectionism was not as prevalent as had been anticipated and that the bill would have a good chance of weathering Congressional attacks.[53] On 25 January, only a few days after the Six concluded an agreement on the CAP, Kennedy delivered a major address to Congress that presented the proposed Trade Expansion Act (TEA) in some detail. In its essentials, the act espoused Ball's approach. It was the result of intensive soul-searching within the administration over the consequences of an expanded and increasingly prosperous Common Market for the United States. Agriculture received particular attention.

Growth held a prominent place in American thinking on the matter. In the outline of the Trade Expansion Act that he sent to Congress, the president underscored the need to accelerate American economic growth. The emphasis on expansion was not only strongly reminiscent of the Bowie and Ball reports but also of the Acheson Report, in which growth appeared as a primary objective of the Atlantic countries. Sustained growth became a major weapon in the psychological and economic war against the Soviet Union. Growth would at the same time fuel the domestic needs of the Atlantic nations, allow for stepped-up military spending and more aid to developing countries, and demonstrate to the rest of the world, especially the Soviet Union, "the capacity of the Atlantic Community for dynamic economic growth." All three reports agreed that higher growth rates and a more efficient allocation of resources within the alliance required a better coordination of trade, aid, and fiscal policies of all the Atlantic nations—particularly the United States and Europe. The artisans of the Acheson Report, largely in tune with Monnet, placed their faith in the power of institutions and hoped that the OECD would play a key role in institutionalizing coordination among the Atlantic countries by developing organs that would "not only serve as forums for discussion" but would also be "capable of developing joint decisions and, in some cases, joint programs." Improved coordination would in turn promote high growth rates while avoiding balance-of-payments problems.[54]

Even though the Ball report chastised Europeans for not pursuing adequate policies of growth, European economies were in fact growing faster than the United States' economy. Kennedy and his staff were intent on discovering the secrets of the higher growth rates in Europe. In the spring of 1961, Kennedy asked the chairman of the Council of Economic Advisers to prepare a report on "Why Europe grows faster than the U.S.?" Walter Heller made a few suggestions in early May. He diagnosed persistently high levels of demand fueled by expansionary fiscal and monetary policies, an "aggressive development of export markets," "branching out into the Common Market," and the "development of the home markets." "It used to be," Heller noted, "when the U.S. economy sneezes, the rest of the world catches pneumonia. Now it's when the U.S. economy sneezes, the rest of the world says 'gesundheit!'" In addition, Heller highlighted a high degree of government investment, smaller defense expenditures, a tremendous increase in productivity, and easy access to American technology. "Apart from their own stepped-up technological efforts," said Heller, "the European countries have been drawing liberally on the backlog of technological and managerial advances scored in the U.S. In a sense, we built a nice stockpile of advanced technology and managerial and production techniques for them to draw on. No doubt, there is also some flow the other way, but so far, they are surely the net gainers on this score."[55]

While higher growth rates appeared to demonstrate that European economies had recovered well since the war, admittedly thanks in part to American help, some of Kennedy's advisers also expected that higher growth rates in the European Common Market would counteract its potential for trade diversion. On 19 June 1961, George Ball testified before the Subcommittee on International Exchange and Payments of the Congressional Joint Economic Committee. In assessing the impact of European growth on American trade, Ball suggested that even though the customs union would have trade diversionary effects, these effects would be more than offset by a significant increase in the Community's growth rate, which in turn would foster demand for foreign, and hence American, goods.[56] About two months later, Ball reiterated the same argument in a memorandum for the president on the inclusion of the United Kingdom in the European Common Market. He referred to a detailed State Department study completed about six months earlier. Its conclusions, he insisted, showed that "the net effect of European economic integration [would] be to expand rather than diminish United States industrial exports." The study evaluated the effects of the full achievement of both the Common Market and the European Free Trade Association. On the side of trade diversion, it estimated that the EEC would " have a *gross* effect on United States exports of about $390 million annually," while the EFTA would have "a *gross* effect of about $285 million annually." In accord with the Bowie Report, Ball selected 1970 (or sooner) as the time when the effects of such trade diversion would be felt. But trade diversion had a mirror image: trade creation. The State Department study was largely optimistic on this point and predicted that "an increase in the incremental growth rate of as little as 1/4 of 1% in the Common Market or the EFTA would enlarge the demand for [American] industrial goods so as to more than compensate for the diversionary effects resulting from the establishment of these two trading areas." There seemed to be excellent presumptions to expect economic integration "to increase the rate of economic growth considerably in excess of 1/4 of 1%. Certainly this ha[d] been the case so far in the Common Market."[57]

If the United Kingdom joined the Common Market, Ball suggested, "the *net* effect of British adherence to the Common Market" ought to favor American trade. Ball banked on the fact that the British growth rate lagged behind that of the Common Market as a whole. Hence, he thought that there was "every reason to believe that Britain's joining the EEC would have a stimulating effect in Britain as it so dramatically did in France," which was, of course, "the compelling motive for Macmillan's decision to apply for membership." The higher growth rate would, in turn, "compensate for whatever additional discrimination may result from Britain's joining the EEC."[58] Theodore Geiger, chief of international studies at the National Planning Association, and Robert Bowie pushed a similar point in a study paper[59] that they transmitted to the Joint Economic Committee at the end of November 1961. However, their study took the argument one step further than Ball's by suggesting that "the major uncertainty" was "not that the enlarged Common Market might fail to grow at an adequate rate, but that the United States would continue to be deficient in this basic respect." "In this sense," the report continued, "realization of potential opportunities for increased trade and investment between the two large entities depends more upon the United States than on the European Community."[60]

In May 1961, shortly after the approval of the Acheson Report by the president, the Joint Economic Committee of Congress established a Subcommittee on Foreign Economic Policy to explore new avenues of action to meet the combined challenges of the Common Market and the American balance-of-payments problem. Prominent experts from all walks of academic and business life, as well as members of current and past administrations, testified before the subcommittee. Among them were Christian Herter, William Clayton, Dean Acheson, Robert Bowie, Theodore Geiger, and George Ball. The subcommittee transmitted its conclusions to the Chairman of the Joint

Economic Committee on 17 January 1962. After having heard various testimonies on the need for a new trade act, including those of Ball and Bowie, the subcommittee underscored the desirability of increased growth in the United States to match that of the Common Market: "We cannot take advantage of the tremendous new trading opportunities which the rapid growth of the Common Market affords us, if our economy is loping along at only half their rate of growth; it is after all, the rate of growth even more than the level of tariffs which determines whether world trade expands or not."[61] One year later, shortly after de Gaulle's thundering press conference in January 1963 in which the French president rejected British membership in the Common Market, an obviously worried Kennedy told the National Security Council that the American "economic growth rate over the past ten years [had] been too slow, particularly in view of the great increase in [American] population." "We must avoid," continued the president, "another recession which would endanger our gold position and have a bad psychological effect on the American people. In comparison with the Russians who are making a major effort to improve their domestic economy, we must not give the impression of just drifting lest other states draw the conclusion that we cannot deal with our domestic economic problems." On a rather pathetic note, he added: "If we grow weaker economically, our influence abroad will be reduced. If this happens, the entire Free World position weakens. It is basic to our national security to have a strong domestic economy."[62]

In an age where large-scale military confrontation between East and West was becoming increasingly implausible (as the Cuban Missile Crisis would later demonstrate) the Kennedy team was gradually shifting the battleground for maintaining a spacious environment "in which free societies could flourish"[63] to the economic field (though this trend had already become apparent in previous administrations). Growth in both the United States and the European Common Market were key elements of this strategy for freedom; both received a prominent place in Kennedy's defense of the new Trade Expansion Act before Congress. Another essential element of economic defense was trade policy. In this, as in other matters, the United States looked after its own, albeit enlightened, self-interest.

The Acheson Report, as the Ball and Bowie reports had done earlier, recommended "a new initiative . . . looking to the accelerated across-the-board reduction of tariffs by major Atlantic nations or groups of nations—including the EEC, EFTA, and U.S.—with the benefits of these reductions being extended to the free world on a MFN basis." Expanding the horizon of the Atlantic Community somewhat, the report added that "Japan would, of course, have to be associated with such an effort." The "current method of negotiating tariff reductions item by item based on U.S. trade agreements legislation," said the report, "has reached a dead end."[64] By the time the Acheson Report was completed, in April 1961, the Dillon Round was about to enter its second phase. In November of that year, under growing frustration with the slow progress of the negotiations the GATT ministerial meeting at Geneva, espousing the American position, reached the conclusion that the item-by-item reductions that had been used "both in the past and during the present [Dillon Round] tariff conference . . . were no longer adequate to meet the changing conditions of world trade." Accordingly, attention was to be given "to the adoption of new techniques, in particular some form of linear tariff reduction."[65]

Two fears pushed Kennedy's advisers to advocate this method: the fear of discrimination by EEC and EFTA countries against the United States and the loss of United States leadership in liberal trade policy. About two months after Kennedy adopted the Acheson Report, George Ball told Congress of his concern that the "new dynamism in the Common Market" would snatch the leadership in liberal trade policies away from the United States.[66] The TEA presented nothing less than an attempt to rescue such leadership, and regain the initiative, while ensuring that the EEC and EFTA did not turn into an exclusionist club that would reduce tariffs among themselves while erecting high external tariffs against the United States and the rest of the "free world."

The rationale behind presenting the TEA to Congress seemed to be that an increase in the American export surplus would help expand the American economy, prevent inflation, correct the American balance of payments, and demonstrate the superiority of the capitalistic model over communism. Some of Kennedy's advisers cautioned him against establishing a direct link between the TEA and the reduction of the balance-of-payments deficit for both "substantive and tactical reasons." First, even though the United States had consistently maintained a high trade surplus, a mutual reduction of trade barriers in GATT would not necessarily translate *immediately* into a gain in the trade balance, and hence would not necessarily contribute to strengthening the balance of payments in the short-run.[67] Second, was it wise to give advance notice even to friendly allies that the United States was in fact launching the TEA as a way of solving its balance-of-payments deficit, and of raising American exports to Western Europe, which they hoped, according to Dillon, "would rise by a greater percentage than the exports of Western European countries to the United States"?[68] Yet Kennedy, encouraged by the Europeanists (and not least of all George Ball) made a strong plea to Congress on the benefits of increased trade for the U.S. balance of payments, insisting that "in recent years" American success in correcting the balance-of-payments deficit had "roughly" paralleled American success in maintaining an export surplus. By enlarging the $5 billion export surplus the United States currently enjoyed, the president told Congress that he hoped to be able to keep financing American security programs abroad and to restore equilibrium to the American balance of payments. In addition, if the United States succeeded in bringing down the external tariff of the Common Market, American manufacturing companies would perceive fewer benefits in locating their plants behind the tariff wall, exports of capital funds to Europe would be reduced and the American balance of payments would improve.[69]

The conclusions of the Subcommittee on Foreign Economic Policy also largely supported the recommendations that the Kennedy team had made during the previous months in preparation for its public presidential commitment. The report implicitly adopted the proposition that increased United States exports were needed to reduce the balance-of-payments deficit. It affirmed: "We must look principally to our exports to pay not only for the imported raw materials we need, but also to maintain our political and military position in the world. We either earn these things principally with our exports, or we will be forced to abandon positions we can ill afford to lose."[70]

THE TRADE EXPANSION ACT UNDER ATTACK

Such was not the position held by Republican Senator Prescott Bush from Connecticut, whose son later became president. He protested against "one-sided hearings" that had been "deliberately and hastily staged as a propaganda springboard for the administration's program."[71] Basing his observations on the testimony of professor of economics Henry C. Wallich of Yale University, Bush launched a direct attack on the most questionable part of the Kennedy package. Dr. Wallich, said Bush, had "advised the subcommittee that as the U.S. gross national product expands, imports increase at a faster rate than exports." Accordingly, the senator questioned whether Kennedy's advisers had fully grasped the effect an increase in GNP and a far-reaching reduction of American tariffs would have on the American balance of payments: "For tariff reductions, obviously, would increase imports even more rapidly than the normal expansion of imports to be anticipated from a rise in gross national product." Hence, the suggestion that one needed to address the root of the problem by asking Western Europe, Japan, and "other free nations" to shoulder more of the burdens of common defense.[72] Reflecting on the failure of his grand design in the wake of de Gaulle's January 1963 conference, a sobered Kennedy later proposed to not only "recognize the military interest of the Free World" but also to "consider very hard the narrower interests of the United States" and to ask European allies "to increase their defense forces."[73]

Before throwing his wholehearted support behind Kennedy's candidacy, George Ball had scrutinized his past to see whether he was free of his father's isolationism. Ball had found some comfort in the fact that young Kennedy had voted in 1949 to recommit the Trade Agreements Extension Act.[74] But Kennedy's economic liberalism was severely tested not only by the demands of his own constituency—the demands of the textile industry are a case in point—but also by de Gaulle's repeated assaults on his grand design and the reluctance of many European partners to engage in more burden-sharing exercises. In November 1963, two days before he was assassinated, Kennedy told Orville Freeman, then secretary of agriculture, "that he was coming to the opinion that the whole Kennedy Round had been oversold; that he was not at all sure that it was in the [United States] interest."[75]

Yet 1962 was not the time for doubts. The president needed all the support he could garner to push the new bill through Congress. Although Senator Bush expressed the minority position of the Subcommittee on Foreign Economic Policy on the Trade Expansion Act, his views were not to be taken lightly by a Democratic president. "Will mutual tariff reductions by the United States and the Common Market increase American industry's ability to compete in Western Europe?" asked Bush, thereby questioning another pillar of the administration's package. The senator's first line of attack was directed against the considerable wage differentials existing between the United States and European countries. Granted, economic theory cautioned against attributing too much importance to wage differentials and underscored instead the difference between unit labor costs. But what if that economic theory was outdated? What if modernized plants in Western Europe and Japan started producing as efficiently as those in the United States while at the same time holding wages lower than their American counterparts? Admittedly, wage rates in Europe would gradually rise, but Bush doubted whether they would elevate fast enough to allow American industries to compete. After all, said the senator, "U.S. wage rates will be rising also."[76] The recent imposition of quantitative restrictions on Japanese products by Western European countries brought up an obvious question: "If restrictive measures are necessary to protect labor in Western Europe against the lower wage rates in Japan, may they not also be necessary to protect American labor against the lower wage rates of Western Europe as well as of Japan?" Bush concluded that the tariff reductions contemplated by the administration would not increase the ability of the American industry to compete in world markets but might "have a seriously damaging effect upon American industry's ability to compete in domestic markets."

Criticizing the administration's "myopic concentration on the limited field of tariffs on industrial goods," Bush recommended that they seek "more fundamental solutions to the competitive problem," such as a "major reform in tax policy to enable American manufacturing industry, with its higher wage scales, to compete more effectively in world markets."[77] Bush also argued that the United States should attempt to organize a conference "to eliminate conflict in international economic policies" under article two of the NATO treaty. Claiming that trade barriers were not as serious an issue as, say, adopting a common attitude towards trade with the Sino-Soviet bloc or seeking to distribute the burdens of common defense more equitably between the United States and its allies, Bush in effect sought to bypass the limited framework of a partnership between equals. In his address to Congress, President Kennedy had spoken of "an integrated Western Europe, joined in trading partnership with the United States" that would "further shift the world balance of power to the side of freedom."[78] Bush preferred the broader councils of "a new alliance of free nations." To use Schaetzel's phrasing, Bush's tastes ran "to horse and rabbit stew—one oversized American horse and fourteen European rabbits."[79] Bush believed that the United States had every right to ask the European rabbits to behave; they did owe the United States something. "Would it not be reasonable," remarked the senator, "to say to the nations of Western Europe and particularly to those to whom we have given billions in Marshall Plan aid for the rebuilding of their industrial plants: Give us a breathing spell until you lower your tariffs to the level of ours?"[80]

At the end of the year, George Ball launched a vigorous counterattack against Bush and other like-minded protectionists. Restricting imports to improve the American balance of trade, Ball told Congress, was "both impractical and dangerous." First, the United States needed to import certain raw materials that it did not produce itself. Second, protectionism invited retaliation. Third, by curtailing imports from its allies, the United States would reduce its capacity to contribute to the military and economic strength of the free world. Fourth, if the United States were to retreat into protectionism, its leadership in economic liberalism would be lost. Worse still, if the United States went protectionist, so too would other nations of the free world. Evidently, Ball's nightmare was that a compartmentalized international economy would develop. In line with the "free traders" of earlier administrations, Ball's ideal vision was that of a global world economy with as few barriers to trade as possible. His world resembled an ever-expanding world pie rather than a restricted and fragmented pie. Hence he maintained his faith in America's ability to compete in world markets. He felt that the American balance-of-payments deficit could not be directly correlated to a significant long-range deterioration of America's competitive position in the world economy. "We are still the world's largest exporter and have been for many years," said Ball, ". . . those of little faith in our ability to increase exports seem . . . to misassess the soaring world demand for the products that the American economy produces best. This demand is expanding so rapidly that there should be plenty of room for all producers to grow. Rising demand is a phenomenon throughout the world. It is most dramatic in the European Common Market and Japan."[81] Ball did not deny the challenges presented by the Common Market, but he preferred to focus on the opportunities for United States export trade. Europe, he pointed out, was "presently at a far earlier stage of consumption than the United States. For every 1,000 inhabitants in the United States there are 340 automobiles; in the Common Market there are 78. In the United States, there are 1,030 radio sets for every 1000 inhabitants and 315 television sets; the corresponding figures in the Common Market are 244 and 60." He believed that the TEA was the perfect tool with which to pry open the expanding European consumer market, thus allowing American industrial and agricultural goods to flow in. These goods, he argued, would compete effectively with European products because the United States, having long had the experience of a "great mass market," possessed the clear lead in exploiting the techniques of mass production.[82]

Despite Ball's optimism, some high-ranking members of the Kennedy administration were not so confident that the Trade Expansion Act was such a good thing, especially in view of one of its most controversial features: an important part of the bill was contingent on British entry into the Common Market. Those who believed that the bill was being oversold felt that the strong campaign mounted by Ball and others for the adoption of the TEA was "a misdirection of the administration's limited political resources." "Getting America moving again," they thought, "required economic stimulus at home; the impact of foreign trade on employment and business activity was limited."[83] They objected most strongly to the 80 percent, or dominant supplier authority, clause. The TEA gave the president the general authority to make reciprocal 50 percent reductions across the board for most categories of products; exceptions were made for those few products previously qualifying for escape clause relief. In addition, the protection of national security could be invoked to "impose duties or suspend concessions" on some goods.[84] But the new act went much further than the 50 percent basic authority. It also authorized the president to reduce tariffs down to zero if he determined that "the United States and all countries of the European Economic Community together accounted for 80 percent or more of the aggregated world export value of all articles within such category."[85] The EEC was defined as encompassing those members it had at the time the authority was used, a clause that obviously left the door open for British entry. What the opponents of the 80 percent clause objected to was not the degree of the reduction sought but its underlying motivation: the intention of some members of the administration to employ it as a bargaining tool to force the British to join. The clause would indeed have been rendered almost meaningless if the British remained out of the Common Market. If one restricted the geographical scope of the 80 percent authority to the United States and the EEC without the United Kingdom then only two categories of products applied, margarine and aircraft. This was hardly the way to engage in significant negotiations. For Ball, it was a way of ensuring that the Labour party would not view the Trade Expansion Act as an alternative to British membership. For his critics, the 80 percent clause posed the danger of making itself contingent upon a foreign policy aim—getting the British to participate in the Common Market.

As a matter of fact, Monnet and Kohnstamm were also opposed to the 80 percent clause, which they considered as clear evidence that the TEA was designed to bring down the Common External Tariff, thereby robbing the emerging European Economic Community of one of its most distinctive features. In a "My dear George" letter, Monnet warned "against the dangers" posed by the part of the TEA that contemplated going beyond a 50 percent reduction of the external tariff. At "first statistical glance" such a reduction seemed to Monnet and his collaborators to "virtually amount to a policy of free trade for industrial products," which was "very much what the British [had] proposed in 1956." At this early stage in the history of the Common Market, Monnet contended, "the common tariff and the common commercial policy which follows from it is the field in which European policies have gone furthest. Accordingly, it is for the moment essential to the sense of union between the European people just as in the past the tariff was one of the formative elements of American unity. Free trade between Europe and America today would undermine the European institutions, the existence of which is the only hope of our obtaining a real Atlantic partnership between equals and a partnership will only be possible between equals."[86]

During the discussions on the Trade Expansion Act, a senator, frustrated with Ball's advocacy of what seemed to him a European position, felt compelled to remind him "that he was in the pay, not of M. Monnet, but of the United States."[87] Yet Ball did not see eye to eye with Monnet on everything. He did seek to protect United States' interests. He and Schaetzel attempted to convince Monnet and Kohnstamm that the 80 percent clause was needed "from the standpoint of political tactics." Congress, they argued, would never grant the president far-reaching authority for the TEA if the executive branch did not present a proposal that demonstrated their profound conviction that the Common Market represented an important challenge for the United States. If unimpressed with the sincerity of the administration's proposal, Congress would simply transform the new TEA into something that closely resembled the old Trade Agreements Act. Ball and Schaetzel saw the proposal for the 80 percent authority as a symbol of the administration's attempt to modify American attitudes towards the tariff. The Common Market challenge was the pretext, and the 80 percent authority the means, to magnify the importance of the Common Market and to win Congress over to the administration's proposal. Monnet and Kohnstamm remained unconvinced. In October 1962, Schaetzel pleaded with Kohnstamm and Monnet to break the silence of their Action Committee, whose position in general had been decidedly reserved on the trade expansion program.[88] Meanwhile, Representative Henry Reuss claimed that the goal of the Trade Expansion Act should be "to attempt to develop the widest possible trade among all free nations,"[89] as opposed to a restricted few.

On 22 August 1961, a few months before the president presented the outline of the TEA to Congress, Representative Reuss, along with twenty-one other Democratic congressmen, wrote a letter to the president, which was not made public at the time. Its signatories urged Kennedy to submit to Congress early in 1962 a completely new trade proposal that would replace existing legislation. They contemplated offering "the Six, the Seven and the other advanced countries of the free world a commitment for all to eliminate tariffs on industrial goods over the next ten years, with collateral efforts to liberalize quotas on such commodities as farm products and coal." The United States, they argued, would mostly benefit because American tariffs on industrial goods were generally lower than those of its partners, and the United States still enjoyed a comfortable trade surplus. Politically, by "generalizing the Common Market's particularism to the entire free world," the United States would "be keeping faith with the nations of Latin America and the rest of the world."[90] In early November 1962, Reuss wrote a personal letter to the president proposing an "action program for attaining a Free

World Community." "The President," he said, "should promptly call for a Free World Community of the leading western European countries, Canada, the United States, Australia, New Zealand and Japan, in order to bring about by, say, 1970, a free trade area as wide as the free world, a system of mutual support for international payments, and a widely and fairly shared assumption of the task of aiding developing areas." The central element common to both the joint statement of the Democratic congressmen and Reuss's letter was their insistence on facing up to economic challenges—the most pressing one being the Common Market—by addressing these problems within the scope of a "Free World Community," which somehow looked beyond the "particularism" of the Common Market and "would neither include nor exclude countries according to any preconceived design."[91] At the root of Reuss's opposition to the 80 percent clause was a world view different from that of the Europeanists. While Ball and others gave high priority to strengthening the European Community for political reasons, Reuss sought to break through the confines of the Atlantic partnership by diluting the Common Market in an internationalist soup.

During the discussions on the TEA, this position translated into the introduction of an amendment sponsored by Reuss and Senator Paul Douglas that, contrary to the administration's proposal, included EFTA within the scope of the 80 percent clause. The amendment, much to the Europeanists' chagrin, succeeded in making it through the Senate, but, much to their relief, was later dropped during a joint meeting of the Senate and the House. This was largely due to the consummate craftsmanship of the Kennedy administration in devising a strategy to get the TEA through the labyrinth of Congress, more or less in its original form. For a president who had the reputation of lacking rapport with Congress, Kennedy's tactics were quite effective in this particular fight.

Ball was the obvious candidate to conduct the negotiations, yet Luther Hodges, the secretary of commerce, was Kennedy's preferred choice to shepherd the bill through Congress. According to Ball's own testimony, the president had two reasons for selecting Hodges. First, Ball enjoyed "fencing" with senators and congressmen and his deep knowledge of the issues made him appear "too well-prepared." Kennedy once gave Ball some advice on this point: "A Senator told me the other day," said the president, "that some of his colleagues thought you had too many answers. They don't like a witness who seems to know more than they do." Yet the president's reservations about Ball's appearance before Congress played a secondary role in his selection of Hodges as pointman. Wilbur Mills, the chairman of the Ways and Means Committee, mainly determined this choice. He suggested that

Hodges, a former governor of North Carolina, "would reassure industrialists," who would think that he was "on their side, while the State Department, according to the perennial mythology, was more concerned with improving [American] foreign political relations than protecting American industry and agriculture."[92] Ball, who had "known Hodges ever since the days of the first Stevenson campaign," agreed with the president on this division of labor. Hodges would be the first to testify before Congress, leaving Ball "to pick up the pieces."[93] The strategy worked well. The bill passed easily, by a vote of 298 to 125 in the House on 28 June and 78 to 8 in the Senate on 19 September, and it was signed into law by Kennedy on 11 October 1962.

Besides the administration's salesmanship, the passage of the bill was also aided by mollifying some protectionist forces in the United States. Strong opposition to the bill was to be expected from the textile industry. When Kennedy's campaign commitments to help alleviate that industry's import problems came back to haunt him, in the form of insistent demands for protection against textiles imports, the president assigned Ball the unpleasant task of dealing with the problem. Despite Ball's strong aversion to knuckling under to the industry or its unions, the best he could do to avert the imposition of mandatory quotas was to negotiate an international agreement on cotton textiles. This agreement gave an importing nation the right to ask exporting countries to limit their exports in cases where these threatened to disrupt the importing nation's markets. Ball later deeply regretted having persuaded developing countries to go along with the agreement, for it ended up being applied "as to be almost as restrictive as mandatory quotas."[94] Yet results were positive at least in one instance: the international agreement in effect silenced opposition to the Trade Expansion Act from the textile industry, although the industry never openly backed the bill. Another move by the president helped curtail opposition to the bill from protectionist quarters. On 19 March 1962, Kennedy, heeding the recommendation of the Tariff Commission, announced substantial increases in tariffs on flat glass, carpets, and rugs. Belgium, the country besides Japan that had suffered most from the tariff hike, was strongly backed by its EEC partners in imposing retaliatory measures on a number of American products. Yet, once again, results proved positive on another front. The president's move became one of the most decisive factors in ensuring the success of the TEA.[95]

The responsibility for negotiating the trade legislation after the passage of the bill was left to Christian Herter, an old hand from the Eisenhower administration. One year before the president signed the Trade Expansion Act, Christian Herter and William Clayton, two Atlanticists, sent a report to the Subcommittee on Foreign Economic Policy in which they recommended that the United States promptly open negotiations to meet the growing challenge of the Common Market and work for "a trade partnership with a European Common Market, *at the same time stressing the absolute necessity of enlarging the area.*"[96] The fact that Herter was an Atlanticist did not seem to bother George Ball very much. Herter belonged to the moderates of the Atlantic Community movement and was a supporter of the Multilateral Force. Ball probably anticipated that he would be a good advocate for American economic interests. As was often the case, the distinctions between Atlanticists and Europeanists became blurred when two key elements were at stake: the interest of the United States in preventing nuclear proliferation and the importance of maintaining access to European markets. Ball himself suggested Herter's appointment. His choice was motivated in part by political reasons. The under secretary of state calculated that because Herter was a Republican his appointment would solidify the bipartisan support for the new negotiations.

In mid-January 1963, the Office of the Special Representative for Trade Negotiations was created by executive order as an agency of the Executive Office of the president. It possessed a broad mandate in the realm of negotiating trade agreements. As the head of the new agency, Herter was directly responsible to the president. In other words, the authority for conducting the negotiations was transferred from the State Department to the new agency, largely as a concession to Congress and the business community.[97] Herter was initially assigned William Gossett as deputy. Upon his resignation in June, Gossett was replaced by two deputies of the highest caliber, William Roth and Michael Blumenthal. Roth, a Democrat from California, assisted Herter in Washington, while Blumenthal did the actual bargaining in Geneva and fought with delegates from other countries to see to it that American interests received a fair hearing. Again, Ball was responsible for suggesting the appointment of this young, but exceptionally competent, economist and businessman.

At first Blumenthal worked in the State Department Economic Bureau, where Ball, each day more impressed with his work, assigned him increasingly challenging assignments. Among these were the negotiation of the International Coffee Agreement and a long-term arrangement regarding international trade in cotton textiles. When the time came to select a negotiator to conduct negotiations in Geneva, Ball "felt no qualms in overriding the sacred principles of seniority" and convincing Kennedy that Blumenthal was the man for the job. Not only was he competent but he was also fluent in French and German, an important public relations asset. Ball was impressed with the way that Blumenthal, an exile from Germany who had spent his youth in Shanghai and was interned by the Japanese for two years, had managed to make his way through Berkeley and Princeton and have "a brief but successful experience in business."[98] Michael Blumenthal was initially even more skeptical than Kennedy about the European Community. Ball, who soon became his friend, succeeded not so much in eliminating his skepticism as in tempering it. A "highly intelligent skeptic," Blumenthal quickly learned to make decisions that were consistent with the administration's policy on European unity.[99] Despite the administration's success in pushing the Trade Expansion Act through Congress, and initiating a major round of trade negotiations, plans for a partnership between the United States and the new Europe were far less successful in the political and military fields.

A PARTNERSHIP BETWEEN EQUALS
AND AMERICAN LEADERSHIP

The Bowie Report advocated the creation of a European entity that would be able to join in a "genuine partnership of equals with the United States." Kennedy later employed the phrase in his famous Independence Day speech of July 1962. Under Eisenhower, "partnership" had become a fashionable word to describe not only the relationship between the United States and its European allies but also relations between the United States and Latin American countries, for example. But Kennedy's partnership was a special kind; it was a partnership between equals. In 1963 Bowie wrote: "Europeans do not like the feeling of being wards of the United States."[100] How then could one ensure that European nations would reach both economic and political maturity while not deviating from a course congenial to the alliance? The Kennedy administration, building on the tradition evolved by its predecessors and incorporating the important variable of the American deficit, devised a two-part program. First, European energies should be concentrated on building a European political community solidly rooted in economic integration. This would give Europe greater influence in world councils and reduce the attraction of nationalism. Western Europe would thereby become the economic and political equal of the United States. Second, the potential of the European co-equal should be harnessed to that of the United States for two common enterprises—world economic development and military defense. Common institutions such as the OECD would help the European Community coordinate its economic policies with other members of the alliance while encouraging it to adopt a global orientation.

Several years later, the Nixon administration offended its European allies by referring to the regional concerns of Western Europe as opposed to the worldwide responsibilities of the United States. But by that time the partnership of equals had been subjected to the tests of time, European dissensions, economic developments, and the eccentricities of de Gaulle. From the beginning, however, the concept suffered from a major flaw—the assumption that the two partners could become equal in the economic, political, and military spheres. In his report, Acheson did not agree with Bowie on this specific point. Instead of a partnership of equals, the former secretary of state spoke of "an Atlantic commonwealth, in which common institutions would increasingly be developed to meet common problems."[101]

Bowie's concept was the one that the Kennedy administration retained. By opting for a partnership of equals, the Kennedy administration apparently imprisoned itself in a set of contradictions, or at least indulged in wishful thinking. The concept worked reasonably well on the economic level, where Western Europe was indeed approaching equality with the United States. But European political integration was still a long way off, and the United States had no intention of sharing its leadership in the military or nuclear field with a European political nonentity. Throughout the early sixties, administration spokesmen frequently stressed the important leadership role that the United States played in the alliance. Yet leadership did not dovetail neatly with partnership. Shortly after the rejection of the EDC by the French Assembly, Livingston Merchant, Eisenhower's assistant secretary for European affairs, had insisted that the new relationship of the United States relative to Western Europe could no longer be described accurately as leadership; partnership was a better word. Even though the United States would still have to assume the lead on many occasions, it could no longer "demand or dictate" but must rather "suggest and persuade."[102]

By the time Kennedy took office, Western Europe was well on its way to becoming the economic near equal of the United States and threatened to snatch American leadership in trade liberalization away from its powerful American ally. The Kennedy administration, while employing the rhetoric of partnership to describe the new state of transatlantic relations and insisting that the partnership should be equal, continued to speak of the indispensable leadership role of the United States. In so doing, the administration demonstrated the existence of a time lag between the concept and its applicability. It also revealed some inherent contradictions in the idea. Could a Europe speaking with many voices claim co-leadership or partnership with the United States? Of course the Bowie Report had planned for the long run, when Europe would be truly economically and politically united. But could any enterprise really function with two equal leaders?

The question was probably academic for President Kennedy. Europe did not yet speak with one voice, and how and when it would reach political integration was a matter of speculation. For the time being, the president and most of his advisers, while keeping in sight the final goals of European political integration and the partnership between equals, concentrated on establishing a concrete basis for this partnership: trade. Addressing Congress in January 1962, Kennedy evoked the picture of "two giant markets on either side of the ocean" that would "impart strength and vigor to each other, and . . . combine their resources and momentum to undertake the many enterprises which the security of free peoples demands." For the president, foreign trade was a key factor in the success of American foreign policy. In addition, a high degree of western economic unity *ipso facto* translated into more political unity. To the extent that a "trading partnership" between the United States and an integrated Europe contributed to western economic cohesion, it could "further shift the world balance of power to the side of freedom."[103]

To some members of the Kennedy administration a trading partnership between separate but equal entities seemed a distinct possibility. But political partnership seemed a more distant development, since it could be attained only when Europe was truly united. Whether a truly equal partnership in the field of defense would follow on the heels of economic and political partnership was a matter for debate, as the MLF saga would later demonstrate. For the time being, a more appropriate description of the concept favored by the Kennedy administration in the field of defense was integration, not partnership. European allies were encouraged to contribute more resources to the common defense effort, but their enhanced contribution was not to translate into effective control. European control of the nuclear deterrent was definitely off limits for the time being. Throughout the Kennedy administration, and in the beginning of the Johnson administration, American policymakers nevertheless wrestled with the need to satisfy the European thirst for greater control of their own defense, while at the same time maintaining an integrated deterrent to the Soviet threat. The MLF initiative was an attempt to reconcile these conflicting demands. Thus the concept of an Atlantic partnership of equals suffered both from a lag between theory and practice and from the reluctance of the United States to surrender its military leadership for strategic reasons. Speaking of burden sharing and partnership was one thing; renouncing or sharing leadership was another. Increased economic interdependence between the United States and Western Europe did not necessarily translate into a loss of hegemony for the United States. Despite the rise of the Common Market and the declining fortunes of the American economy, the United States, while recognizing that it had lost its position as solitary "Mount Everest" in the world economy, still claimed the role of first among equals in the political and military spheres. In those two areas, the partnership of equals most definitely included a senior partner.

Henry Kissinger, who worked as a part-time consultant under Kennedy for only a very short time,[104] later offered a pertinent analysis of the inherent contradictions of the Atlantic partnership of equals as envisaged by the American Europeanists. Kissinger believed that the assumption that Europe would adopt a common world view with the United States upon achieving European unity was inherently flawed. While George Ball argued that a united Europe could better mobilize European resources "in support of a common effort and a common view"[105] than a fragmented Europe, Kissinger contended that Europe did not possess the will to commit their resources to sharing the United States' burdens because American and European interests were not necessarily identical—particularly outside of the Atlantic area. The traumas of two world wars and decolonization, said Kissinger, had made Europeans reluctant to "run the risk of nuclear destruction on behalf of a distant area from which they [had] recently been ejected." They preferred instead to "shift the risks and the burdens" to the United States.[106] Having recently been forced to relinquish their global interests, Europeans now objected to assuming new worldwide responsibilities in a partnership where there existed "excessive concentration of decision-making in the hands of the senior partner." This was all the more true since the senior partner had exhibited the deplorable tendency to equate American interests with those of European nations. What was needed was a recognition by the United States that "the interests of Europe and the United States are not identical everywhere." It might then "be possible to agree on a permissible range of divergence," and each partner would "regain a measure of flexibility." Such flexibility, or autonomy, was essential in order to build a healthier relationship between Europe and the United States, in which a grown-up Europe could be granted control over its own resources. Kissinger advised less talk about sharing burdens and more about sharing responsibilities. This also meant sharing American leadership with European nations, even though that involved "a painful loss of some of [American] former pre-eminence."[107] Some loss of American hegemony was needed in order to revitalize the Alliance. This did not necessarily mean, however, that the Europeans needed to be an equal partner or that Europe had to be unified along federal lines.

Kissinger directly attacked the "twin pillars," or "dumbbell" concept, evolved by Europeanists (i.e., the partnership between equals) and questioned the "passionate commitment" of the United States to a "supranational structure in Europe." "Is it true that partnership is possible only among equals?" he asked. "What has been the real progress toward political integration? To what extent is it in the American interest to promote one form of European unity to the exclusion of other possible plans?" Assuming that a "strong and united Europe" was "on balance" in the interest of the United States, were there not "various roads to European unity?" Would it not be better to support the development of a "confederal Europe" that would "enable the United States to maintain an influence at many centers of decision rather than be forced to stake everything on affecting the views of a single, supranational body?"[108] Kissinger thus preferred to deal with a European partner at the level of the sovereign nation states, and in effect have many partners rather than one. But influencing "various centers of decision" could easily translate into playing one European nation against the other. Although Kissinger recommended that Europe recover its sense of identity and be allowed more autonomy and claimed that it was time to parcel out American leadership, he indirectly sought to maintain this leadership through an old method, often used by hegemons: divide and conquer. His agenda for the Atlantic Alliance was not to concentrate on encouraging European integration as a prerequisite to closer Atlantic relations but rather to devise "new forms of *Atlantic* cooperation" here and now. According to him, the time was "ripe to create a political body at the highest level for concerting the policies of the nations bordering the North Atlantic" as an integral part of the "constitution of an Atlantic Commonwealth."[109] Kissinger later reluctantly admitted that, for the time being, an Atlantic Community was impracticable.

Dean Acheson, while strongly favoring an integrated European Community, also considered that it "might be only a way station to still broader Atlantic unity." The "end goal" of the United States was to be "an Atlantic Commonwealth, in which common institutions would increasingly be developed to meet common problems."[110] The difference between Acheson's conception of an Atlantic Commonwealth and that of Kissinger lay not in their definitions of the end to be attained but in the timing and the means of reaching that end. Although Acheson did not subscribe to the concept of an equal partnership, he did favor European integration as a necessary milestone on the way to a more united Atlantic Community.

Therein lay all the difference between the "Atlanticists" and the "Europeanists." The "European integration first" option had long been privileged by the latter, while some Atlanticists had favored the "Atlantic Community now" approach. The "Union Now" approach, the concept cherished by Clarence Streit since 1938, was later revamped into an "Atlantic Unity Now" approach to accommodate the increasing, and soon predominant, number of moderates within the movement who preferred a form of Atlantic confederation and cooperation rather than federation. Among the moderates were such key American figures as Henry Kissinger, Christian Herter, Averell Harriman, Chester Bowles, Arthur Schlesinger, Eugene Rostow (Walt's brother), and even Monnet's close friend John McCloy; this was a clear indication that the views of some moderates converged with those of the Europeanists on key points and that some proponents of an Atlantic Community did not see any intrinsic contradictions between European integration and an Atlantic Community. For the sake of clarity we have somewhat overgeneralized the Atlantic movement; the term "Atlanticism" covered varying shades of commitment to the Atlantic Community.

Many "Atlanticists" were called upon to serve under Kennedy, some intermittently, some for the duration of the Kennedy administration. Kissinger, who served as a part-time consultant under Kennedy and then decided to act as an ad-hoc consultant only, was also a member of the Harvard University Center for International Affairs, which Robert Bowie directed. Thanks to the sympathy of the group of Europeanists, the views of Bowie and George Ball—though being tempered by full-time members of the Kennedy administration who remained decidedly cooler than the Europeanists towards Bowie's partnership idea—ultimately prevailed over those of Kissinger.

In his report, Bowie made clear that the idea of establishing an Atlantic confederation or community with common institutions at the present time was premature. Such a solution did not possess the necessary political base either in the United States or in Europe. In addition, the whole scheme threatened to jeopardize the European integration movement. It also "might divert attention and energies from the Soviet threat and the plight of the less developed countries in order to concentrate on political problems involving Western institutions, thus perpetuating the parochial viewpoint which prevailed during much of the last decade." Hence Bowie recommended thinking of an Atlantic confederation only as "an ultimate goal" instead of advancing unrealistic plans delegating "substantial powers for decision and action" to an Atlantic Confederation that would "risk instant failure" and "create new divisive forces within the Alliance."[111]

Monnet put it another way: "America and Europe will come together as fast as Europe unites and no faster." Monnet's American friend Eugene Rostow advocated strengthening Atlantic political cooperation to fend off the menace of a politically united Europe, which he thought might "veer into neutralism." He believed that it was all right to let Europe unite economically in "association with the United States" but that "politically, any structure must be capped by an Atlantic Institution." Monnet strongly disagreed with such a position. For Monnet, the Common Market would not make any progress if it were not envisioned as a "step towards ultimate political unity." Also, steady progress in economic union among the Six gradually strengthened their political cooperation. "No such foundation yet exists at the Atlantic level," he insisted. In fact, it was thanks to the development of European unity that it had "ceased to be considered utopian to speak of Atlantic partnership or even Atlantic union."[112]

The "European unity first" approach had prevailed since 1949, when Dean Acheson had opposed a resolution introduced in the American Senate and the House of Representatives by Estes Kefauver and twenty-six other senators that called for a convention to explore Atlantic union. Interestingly enough, John Foster Dulles, then a candidate for the Senate, had endorsed the resolution. Dulles then argued that a new agency was needed not only to "establish a genuine common defense" but also to consider economic and monetary problems "in accordance with the Federal principle that matters which are of common concern should be dealt with through an agency dedicated to the interests of all those concerned." In the introduction he wrote in January 1950 for the *New Federalist,* Dulles recommended carefully studying the federalist approach as a means of imparting added strength to the community of "free peoples." On a poignant note, he remarked that "most Americans have forgotten, and few Europeans have known, how light, but yet how strong, can be the bond of federation."[113]

Dulles altered his position during the Eisenhower administration, opposing the resolution several times, mainly on the grounds that it was premature. This apparent change of heart mainly reflected Eisenhower's position on the matter. Clarence Streit maintained a steady correspondence with Dulles, constantly pressing for the administration's support, or at least its tacit approval, of the resolution. A staunch advocate of European integration, the secretary nevertheless considered the option of creating a new Atlantic institution that would coordinate the policies of various organizations that addressed different aspects of Western unity. The issue sufficiently preoccupied him that he discussed the matter with Eisenhower in the spring of 1956. Dulles told his boss that he "was thinking vaguely of establishing a political body to which matters of common interest could come from any one of the many organizations now in being which reflected one or another aspect for Western unity. There was, for example, NATO, the Council of Europe, the OEEC, the EPU, the Brussels Treaty for European Union, the European Coal and Steel Community and the prospective EURATOM." Eisenhower's answer was diplomatic but quick and to the point and effectively put an end to Dulles's avowedly vague temptation to explore the issue further. This "was a sound approach," said Eisenhower, but only Western

European political integration was "adequate." "In this way, there could be created with 250,000,000 people with a great number of trained workers and with natural resources available from Africa, a genuine third force comparable to the United States or to the Soviet Union."[114] Rather than any kind of Atlantic federation or confederation, the president favored only better consultation within NATO.

Throughout most of the 1950s, the Eisenhower administration distanced itself from the Atlantic Resolution, first by insisting that the executive should in no way be associated with it, then by opposing it. Yet, in 1959, Secretary of State Herter, one of the moderates in the movement for Atlantic Unity, withdrew the State Department's opposition to the resolution. Moderates at this point clearly outweighed radical federalists. Herter's key position as secretary of state, and the moderate character of the resolution, perhaps succeeded in convincing the president to allow the Atlantic Resolution to be introduced. By the end of the Eisenhower administration, the resolution was passed by the House (288 to 103) and the Senate (51 to 44—Senators Kennedy and Johnson voted for it). Eisenhower signed it on 7 September 1960. By that time its contents had been considerably watered down and it contained no reference to federalism. The resolution set up an American Citizens Commission on NATO, composed of twenty representative private citizens who were to take part in an Atlantic convention in which other groups of private citizens from other NATO countries would participate. The convention was to "explore means by which greater cooperation and unity of purpose may be developed to the end that democratic freedom may be promoted by economic and political means." The administration's endorsement of the convention was careful and reserved. Long before the resolution was passed, the Department of State insisted that discussions be realistic and that "no governmental commitment [be] involved." The final bill stated that American delegates were "not in any way to speak for or represent the U.S. Government."[115]

A few months after Kennedy took office, the U.S. Citizens Committee was appointed. It elected Christian Herter and Will Clayton (President Truman's former under secretary of state) as co-chairmen.[116] Clayton was one of the main contributors to the Marshall Plan—many supporters of which later became Atlanticists. Two days before the committee first convened, Vice-President Johnson, who had appointed it, delivered an address in Paris on the tenth anniversary of SHAPE. Entitled "A True Atlantic Community," the address contained language that was strongly reminiscent of the Acheson Report, sometimes quoting from it verbatim. Johnson emphasized the importance of "an integrated European Community . . . to strengthen the

Atlantic Community." Like Acheson, he agreed that the "end goal" of the Atlantic nations should be "a true Atlantic Community in which common institutions will increasingly be developed to meet common problems." He also agreed that a "genuine political—as well as economic—community might appear increasingly feasible" as the "long-run goal"[117] of the United States. But the emphasis fell most definitely on "long-run."

While sympathetic to the need for better policy coordination in order to strengthen the Atlantic Community, the Kennedy administration did not support the creation of any far-reaching new Atlantic institutions for the time being. The drafters of the Acheson Report agreed that "some first steps" toward the ultimate goal of an Atlantic Commonwealth could "be conceived in the economic field," but they remained purposely vague on how and when political institutions might be created on the basis of an Atlantic Common-wealth joined by economic ties. The report had "no specific proposals to advance—only a general conviction that opportunities for action to this end [would] probably arise, if only under the impact of future crises, and that the U.S. and its allies [would] be in a better position to exploit those opportunities if they [were] clear beforehand that this is the general direction in which they want[ed] to move."[118] Similarly, the Bowie Report advocated "a pragmatic approach to Atlantic institutions." It proposed no new institutions but suggested that existing ones be revamped and bolstered. NATO and the OECD were to play complementary roles. The OECD posed a special problem because of the membership of neutral nations in the organization that prevented it from being used effectively as a channel for undertakings of a predominantly political character, least of all those with a burden-sharing component. Yet the very neutrality of the OECD's problem children could also become an asset in dealing with developing countries and in attracting Eastern European countries away from the Soviet Union.[119]

Deciding on the respective roles of NATO and the OECD in the economic field was not an easy task. As part of the discussion of the "Ten Years Plan" for the Atlantic alliance, as proposed by Herter at the NATO Council of Ministers in December 1959, Paul-Henri Spaak wanted to endow Article 2 of the Atlantic treaty with greater meaning. While "recognizing that NATO could not be an executive institution in the economic field," Spaak proposed turning it into "a forum for discussing, examining and possibly deciding principles of a common policy concerning relations with communist East European countries and underdeveloped countries."[120] Bowie partly rejoined Spaak on that point in conceding that the new OECD need not prevent NATO from involvement in some economic activities. Yet the activities he envis-aged for NATO were to be confined mainly to "strategic" issues, including the "Bloc economic activities and relations with the LDC's and NATO" and economic issues taken up by worldwide forums such as the United Nations, in which Western and Soviet bloc countries held membership.[121]

In order to improve the coordination of policies between the OECD and NATO, Bowie proposed that the United States, the United Kingdom, and "key EEC member states . . . maintain or establish a single national delegation to NATO and the OECD under the over-all direction of one man who would be the Permanent Representative of his Government to both organizations." Within NATO, Bowie proposed the creation of an "Atlantic Policy Group" composed of three or four people of "international repute" who would not represent national states and who would be charged with recommending "long-range plans and policies."[122] An important aspect of the Bowie Report, especially in the light of American balance-of-payments difficulties, was the way in which the roles of NATO and the OECD were described. They were to be "partial burden-sharing exercises, the one concentrated on the defense burden—the other on the aid burden." Perhaps "[t]he emphasis on political and defense considerations in NATO and on general economic and aid considerations in the OECD" could "never be fully reconciled." But it could "be minimized by establishing closest cooperation between the two Secretariats, by joint representation . . . and by efforts of the member states to follow compatible policies in both organizations."[123]

The Bowie Report thus envisaged some degree of political coordination and rationalization of decisionmaking at the Atlantic level but did not conceive of any new political institutions to ensure Atlantic Unity in the immediate future. Political unification was not precluded, but it appeared as a very distant development, which would evolve naturally from closer economic links among the Atlantic nations. By contrast, radical "Atlanticists" advocated the creation of political institutions immediately, without awaiting the creation of a trade partnership. Christian Herter, although an Atlanticist, disagreed with the radicals. He believed that military alliances and trade partnerships should precede the creation of Atlantic political institutions. Yet the moderates of the Atlantic Community movement had in mind a much clearer blueprint of these institutions than did the Europeanists. Herter proposed the creation of "a permanent High Council at the highest political level, to concert and plan, and in agreed cases to decide policy on matters of concern to the Community as a whole." He further imagined the establishment of an effective Atlantic consultative assembly as well as an Atlantic High Court of Justice.[124]

Some Atlanticists did not consider the creation of a truly united Europe as a prerequisite to closer Atlantic political ties. As we saw, George Ball and other Europeanists strongly dissented from this view. Ball did not believe that it made "sense to build more comprehensive institutions for European-American cooperation until the Europeans themselves progress toward unity." Europeans were willing to coordinate their trade and monetary policies with the United States and looked forward to the continuation of American nuclear protection in Europe. Yet they were not prepared to go beyond a certain level of intimacy. As Ball observed: "there is fear among Europeans that if they get too close to us we will absorb and smother them by the preponderance of our own size and weight and energy—and we may even get them into trouble through an excess of zeal."[125] The danger was that American hegemony might drown European integration in an Atlantic soup that would in effect reduce integration to its most simple component: the nation state. While insisting that European political and economic integration and Atlantic economic, political, and military unity proceed along parallel lines, some Atlanticists did not so much reveal their sympathy for the European integration movement as their desire to hold it in check or mitigate it through strong Atlantic institutions.

In this regard, Atlanticists in a way belonged to a tradition that first evolved during World War II or earlier. Since the very beginning of American planning for a united Europe, American architects had considered both the advantages and the disadvantages of European integration. They placed their hopes in a strong United Nations organization and in international security arrangements that would monitor the progress of a united Europe and ensure that it did not evolve into a protectionist area surrounded by high tariff barriers or a "third force" hostile to the United States. Once the East-West split became a reality, those who feared the development of an exclusive and neutral united Europe then turned their hopes towards the Atlantic Alliance as a means of guarding against too much independence on the part of Europeans. In this scenario, a regional Atlantic organization succeeded an international organization as the guardian of European regionalism. Both Atlanticists and Europeanists feared the development of an exclusive Europe to some degree. American Europeanists nevertheless remained hopeful that Europe would develop into a genuine economic and political partner of the United States, a positive "third force" that might occasionally disagree with the United States but "by and large . . . see things in the same general terms and react with the same humane impulses."[126] A trading partnership and a greater coordination in economic and political policies within the Alliance, they hoped, would help encourage the outward orientation of a united Europe and would ultimately lead to the creation of a true Atlantic Community with common institutions even in the political field—but only if such was the desire of Europeans and Americans alike.

Diehard Atlanticists wanted more guarantees, the creation of strong Atlantic political institutions as soon as possible, and, above all, Atlantic integration at all levels. Some did not hesitate to urge that the United States "join" the Common Market or take the lead in bringing together an Atlantic economic community. Such was not the view of the Kennedy administration. In testifying before Congress, George Ball and Robert Bowie made it clear that the trading partnership they wanted to develop with the Common Market did not in any way imply joining the Common Market. The president agreed. In an address to the National Association of Manufacturers on 6 December 1961 Kennedy explicitly declared :

> I am *not* proposing—nor is it either necessary or desirable, that we join the Common Market, alter our concepts of political sovereignty, establish a 'rich man's' trading community, abandon our traditional most-favored-nation policy, create an Atlantic free-trade area, or impair in any way our close economic ties with Canada, Japan, or the rest of the free world . . . We do not want Japan left out of this great market, or Latin America, which has depended so much on the European markets it may find it now increasingly difficult because of competition from Africa to sell in Europe—which could mean serious trouble for them and therefore for us in the long run, both political as well as economic.[127]

That same day, McGeorge Bundy rejected the idea of a "full-blown Atlantic union" in favor of a "partnership between the United States on the one hand and a great European power on the other."[128] All in all, the Atlantic union, or community, proposal, despite support in influential circles both inside and outside of government, eventually lost ground to the Atlantic partnership concept. This was partly the result of strong opposition from the Europeanists and partly the consequence of Kennedy's reluctance to enter into an exclusive economic and political arrangement with the Continent. The partnership between equals was after all only one of the partnerships in which the United States wanted to take part. Under Kennedy, administration spokesmen would often remind their audiences that the United States was a Pacific power and a member of the Western Hemisphere as well as an Atlantic nation.

Yet, in the short run, despite their aversion to the Atlantic union, or community, approach, most Europeanists agreed with Atlanticists in the field of defense, where Atlantic integration was still the preferred approach. By insisting that there could be "no truly easy and effective partnership between America and Europe until" there was "a Europe in the political sense,"[129] and by predicating increased European military control in the alliance upon greater European political integration, Europeanists perhaps unwittingly postponed the emergence of a truly equal European partner.

8

The MLF in Context

BEYOND THE NEW LOOK

During the last years of the Eisenhower presidency the New Look underwent some revision. Technical advances in Soviet nuclear weapons and their means of delivery encouraged a reassessment of the relative roles of NATO conventional, tactical, and strategic forces, while the growing desire of some Europeans to participate more in the control of their own defense encouraged American proposals for nuclear sharing. In August 1953, the Soviet Union detonated its first hydrogen bomb. The successful launching of the first Soviet satellite, Sputnik, in October 1957 now heralded the time when the Soviet Union would possess the capability of destroying American cities with intercontinental ballistic missiles. Some Europeans became increasingly doubtful that the United States would risk its cities for the defense of Europe, while the Eisenhower administration reappraised the emphasis it had placed until then on massive American retaliatory capability.

To be fair to the authors of NSC 162/2, the basic planning document of the New Look, they did foresee the implications of the Soviet's progress in nuclear capabilities, but they did not consider them relevant for the short term. Instead, they perceived a need for fiscal responsibility, which determined a policy that, according to Dulles, placed "more reliance on deterrent power and less dependence on local defensive power."[1] By the end of the Eisenhower administration, this policy was no longer satisfying, even to Dulles himself. United States superiority in nuclear missile capability, American leaders reasoned, was fast eroding. Soon the threat to unleash American nuclear power, regardless of the type of Soviet aggression, would lose its credibility. The proposal for early use of strategic and tactical nuclear weapons in the defense of Europe, even if the Soviet Union did not launch an all-out attack against Europe, was increasingly criticized within the administration.

The use of tactical nuclear weapons had originally been favored by Europeans and Americans alike as a means of offsetting the superiority of Soviet conventional forces in Europe, which the allied powers believed—wrongly as it later turned out—to be vastly superior to allied troops. At a 1956 NATO ministerial meeting, the decision was made to equip European tactical forces with nuclear warheads. Delivery vehicles were to be controlled by Allied troops, while the warheads remained under American control. The American president had the power to release the warheads, while SACEUR (the Supreme Allied Commander, Europe), an American, had the authority to fire them. Around the same time, the United States also made the decision to place the intermediate-range ballistic missiles (IRBMs) in Italy, Turkey, and Britain under shared control. This was done with a view towards compensating for an alleged American inadequacy in intercontinental ballistic missiles as well as with the intention of providing European allies with some degree of control over nuclear weapons. Yet tactical nuclear weapons and IRBMs were not the panacea for deficiencies in European defense. The Soviet Union also possessed tactical weapons, and *Opération carte blanche,* a war game organized by SHAPE, had amply demonstrated that the use of tactical nuclear weapons by both the Soviet Union and NATO would have devastating consequences for European populations, which would be virtually annihilated.[2] The Soviet Union was busy acquiring IRBMs, and those NATO countries that had agreed to the location of IRBMs on their territories would become primary targets for the Soviets. Within the Eisenhower administration, views differed on how best to adapt American strategy to changing circumstances.

On 2 May 1958, General Robert Cutler, the special assistant to the president for National Security Council affairs, briefed the National Security Council on the highlights of a new proposed statement of policy: NSC 5810. The discussion that ensued revealed differing viewpoints within the administration. One of the most important questions centered on how to respond to limited aggression in Europe in an age of approaching nuclear parity with the Soviet Union. As long as the United States still possessed nuclear superiority, the threat to retaliate, from the outset of hostilities, with nuclear weapons against a Soviet invasion seemed relatively credible. According to this strategy, conventional ground forces were to be used only to counter minor incursions or, more generally, to serve as a trip wire. They were not intended to defeat Soviet troops on the ground. Rather, their function was to "hold an attack until the total weight of the retaliatory power could be brought to bear."[3] Ground forces, armed with tactical nuclear weapons to compensate for their relative manpower inferiority, were expected to hold the line until full nuclear retaliation could be brought to bear on the aggressor. By the fall of 1957, SACEUR General Lauris Norstad himself began to openly question this policy. What if, he asked, war was started by accident, or by miscalculation? "A probing operation to achieve political advantage—a border incident, negligible in itself—might flare out of control."[4] To guard against this danger, Norstad recommended strengthening ground forces—both conventional and nuclear—to provide flexibility in dealing with limited aggressions in Europe. These forces would also serve to make allied defenses more credible to Soviet eyes. Allied defense on the ground, he hoped, would be of sufficient strength to force the Soviet Union to resort to considerable effort to break through it. This would give the Soviet policymakers time to "pause" and reconsider the consequences of pursuing the attack further, with the threat of full retaliation ever present in their minds. Norstad was not alone in his crusade for a better ground defense, yet some of his colleagues disagreed with his emphasis on the need to strengthen ground forces mainly by equipping them with small-yield nuclear weapons. Norstad's ground forces were not conventional forces.

Since 1953, Army Chief of Staff Matthew B. Ridgway had continually insisted on the need to give greater attention to limited conflicts and to ensure adequate conventional defense. His successor, General Maxwell Taylor, continued the tradition of his predecessor and argued forcefully against placing so much emphasis on the nuclear deterrent as to freeze conventional forces, which were indispensable in limited conflicts. Taylor also warned against using tactical nuclear weapons in limited conflicts because of the risk of escalation.[5] Both Ridgway and Taylor, however, encountered strong opposition from the president, who was firmly set against entangling American forces in small conventional wars and did not think tactical nuclear weapons would lead to escalation any more than "twenty ton blockbusters would."[6] The two chiefs of staff ultimately had to bow to the president's strategic preferences, but the debate did not end there. By the spring of 1958 Taylor's position had the support of both the Navy and the Marine Corps. More importantly, Secretary of State Dulles was beginning to argue along the same lines—he, too, now recommended placing greater emphasis on dealing with local conflicts. The Suez episode, he felt, had amply demonstrated the need for the expansion of both naval and conventional forces.[7] Robert Bowie later questioned the wisdom, in the approaching age of mutual deterrence, of relying on the threat to launch nuclear weapons right from the beginning. What if, he asked, the Soviets undertook "more limited probes or threats in order to reap political benefits," for example, by obstructing access to Berlin? NATO might then be faced with the agonizing choice of unleashing a large-scale nuclear war or of taking no action. If the latter, the Soviets would have called NATO's "bluff," and NATO would lose credibility among its members. The Soviet Union would only be too happy to "use threats and blackmail" to further weaken the alliance.[8]

The Eisenhower administration had so far expected that limited aggression would be largely confined to extra-European areas. American leaders reasoned that now that the Soviet Union was about to become capable of reaching American cities with nuclear bombs, it might be tempted to nibble away at Berlin or elsewhere in Europe, while calculating that the United States would be reluctant to launch a full-blown nuclear war to counter a limited threat against its allies. At the NSC meeting in May 1958, General Cutler echoed Bowie's concern about the inadequacy of the present strategy to deal with limited aggressions in Europe. In "this period of relative nuclear parity, limited aggression may not always be confined to less developed areas," he warned. Therefore, it was not necessarily "in the U.S. interest to deal with every limited aggression by applying whatever degree of military force [was] necessary to suppress it." The solution to this quandary was for the United States to "have a flexible capability so that it could determine the application of force best serving U.S. interests under the circumstances existing in each case of limited military aggression." The emphasis on a *flexible* capability prefigured the flexible-response strategy of the Kennedy years.

Although Secretary Dulles was generally singled out as the most ardent advocate of the massive retaliation option, he too was preoccupied with adding new elements to the basic military strategy in order to enable the United States to respond to limited wars as well as full-blown attacks. He therefore suggested that the basic security policy, when finally adopted by the administration, should not "compel us to allocate so much of our resources to maintenance of the nuclear deterrent that we will weaken our capability for limited war." He further recognized that the "massive nuclear deterrent was running its course as the principal element in our military arsenal" and insisted that "very great emphasis must be placed on the elements which in the next two or three years can replace the massive nuclear retaliatory capability." In other words, "the United States must be in a position to fight defensive wars which do not involve the total defeat of the enemy." His recommendation contained a caveat, however. Dulles did not believe that the United States "should permit a dangerous gap in or an increasing doubt as to the willingness of the United States to resort to massive nuclear retaliation until such time as we have something to take its place."[9] Maintaining appearances towards allies while at the same time preparing for the future was thus the preferred course of action. For Dulles, preparing for the future mostly meant improving tactical nuclear weapons while at the same time keeping conventional defense strong. He conceded that since present technology did not allow for the destructive power of "miniaturized" bombs to be targeted on a sufficiently limited area, more research was necessary to find a practical "limited bomb" that would not "kill all the Europeans or the Hungarians and the Poles" or, "if the wind shifted . . . risk killing the British or the French or the Dutch."[10] Dulles was fully aware of the budgetary implications of the policy he advocated. "We have got to do all this in the way of military programs and still remain solvent," he remarked. His concern for maintaining the solvency of the United States found a receptive ear in the president, who otherwise opposed the secretary's inclination to review the New Look in favor of a more flexible strategy.

Eisenhower was most reluctant to spend more American dollars to bolster the capability of the alliance to fight limited wars. The president stuck to his original policy in its essentials both because he did not believe in keeping limited wars under control, and also because he did not believe in depleting American resources to meet the requirements of a flexible strategy. To the president, "each small war [made] global war the more likely." He "could not believe that if the Soviets tried to seize Austria we could fight them in . . . a nice, sweet, World War II type of war." Strengthening ground forces, he also warned, would either weaken the nuclear deterrent by directing funds away from it to "mobile and tactical forces" or, if military spending were to be stepped up massively to meet the new goals, the result would be "a controlled economy" in the United States, which "would amount to a garrison state."[11] Eisenhower was not a Keynesian. By contrast, the Kennedy administration would claim that the United States *and* its allies did in fact possess sufficient means to adopt a more flexible response towards defense and that this did not involve any kind of controlled economy. On this, Eisenhower and the new administration dissented, but they found agreement on the necessity to ask allies to do more and spend more for the common defense. But this could not happen without some concessions to Europeans in the control of their own defense.

Still true to that which he thought before he became president, Eisenhower believed that Europeans must ultimately assume most of the costs and furnish most of the manpower for their own defense. By belaboring the point that the United States must withdraw most of its troops from Europe now that Europeans clearly possessed the financial means to care for themselves, the president was frequently at odds with John Foster Dulles. The secretary of state indeed believed that "European morale would never become high enough to permit [the United States] to withdraw [American] forces."[12] In times of American balance-of-payments difficulties, the renewed presidential emphasis on more self-reliance on the part of Europeans was hardly surprising. Eisenhower was sometimes quite vehement. During a meeting with Secretary Dulles in December 1958, the president recalled that "when he first went to SHAPE, there had been talk that the United States assistance to the NATO countries' defense efforts would be for a 'maximum' of five years. Since then the NATO countries [had] come to depend overly on the United States." It was now time to "wean" American allies from excessive dependence upon the United States "and to encourage them to make better efforts of their own."[13] About a year later the president spoke with Secretary of State Herter and General Norstad. Herter considered thinning out American forces in Europe and in effect reducing them to token forces. Eisenhower did not recommend withdrawing American forces at the present time since this might signal to the Germans that the United States was now less willing to defend the whole of Germany. Neither did he recommend reducing overall troop strength in Europe. But he did favor putting strong pressure on Europeans to assume more of their own defense, to rely more on their own forces, and to pay for the costs of American forces in Europe. Then the United States would be able to pull out most of its troops. The sooner this happened, the better.[14] European resources and the strong economic performance of their economies amply justified asking that Europeans take on more of the burden of common defense. After all, American forces had only been placed in Europe "on a stop-gap emergency basis." They were not meant to be a "permanent and definite commitment" as Europeans wanted to believe. The United States was doing more than its share in "carrying practically the whole weight of the strategic deterrent force, also conducting space activities, and atomic programs." It had "paid for most of the infrastructure, and maintain[ed] large air and naval forces as well as six divisions." Hardly pleased with this state of affairs, an angry president concluded that the Europeans were close to "making a sucker out of Uncle Sam."[15] Intent on saving American dollars, Eisenhower encouraged the Europeans to have more independence from the United States. He felt that this independence would bolster European morale and ultimately allow most American boys to go home. On this specific point, Eisenhower's thinking was quite close to that of one of his former comrades in arms: General Charles de Gaulle.

DE GAULLE, THE SPECIAL RELATIONSHIP,
AND EUROPEAN DEFENSE

While de Gaulle thought that French overdependence on the United States in the field of defense was unhealthy and that it destroyed the national morale and sense of responsibility, Eisenhower concurred "with De Gaulle that some action [was] necessary to bring up the sense of responsibility and the morale of the Europeans in behalf of their own defense."[16] The two men agreed that overdependence broke willpower and self-respect, but their agreement stopped there. Where they parted ways was on what level independence was to be exercised. While de Gaulle emphasized French national independence and the coordination of European national policies among themselves and with the United States, Eisenhower proposed increasing European self-reliance (manpower and financial) and *integration* of European military policy with American policy. Therein lay the very basis of a French-American disagreement that would continue to plague relations between the two countries throughout the Kennedy-Johnson period. The memorandum that de Gaulle addressed to Eisenhower and Macmillan in September 1958 and the lengthy reply from Eisenhower that followed one month later can best be understood in this context.

Following the Anglo-American military landing in Lebanon and Jordan in which there had been no coordination with French policy, the French president felt justified in pointing out that "Atlantic solidarity should not be confined to the NATO area but should also find its expression with regard to problems in other parts of the world."[17] He also felt justified in asking for high-level consultations between the United States, Britain, and France, for these were the countries that held both European and non-European responsibilities. But the idea of an Anglo-French-American directorate did not appeal to the American president. Eisenhower agreed that there was a need for greater consultation among NATO countries, but he objected to limiting high-level consultation to a chosen few who would then communicate their views on worldwide problems and nuclear issues to the rest of the NATO countries. At best, he felt, this sort of consultation must remain informal, and at any rate, the United Kingdom, the United States, and France could "not afford to adopt any system which would give to [their] other allies, or other free world countries, the impression that basic decisions affecting their own vital interests [were] being made without their participation."[18]

Prior to the often-quoted 17 September de Gaulle memorandum, Eisenhower had a discussion with the British on what topics should be discussed on a tripartite basis with the French in June 1958. The president declared that he was in no way favorable to establishing a sort of tripartite political standing group within NATO. He did, however, favor undertaking "a tripartite relationship with De Gaulle in those areas where there exist[ed] an historical basis for it, such as in the Summit preparations and the re-unification of Germany."[19] Otherwise he proposed to deal with the French on a bilateral basis. One year later, Eisenhower had slightly modified his position. Meeting de Gaulle halfway, he now felt that it might be useful to organize informal tripartite consultations not only on European problems but also on worldwide problems; "ad-hoc tripartite staff committees" could conceivably be organized to debate individual issues, with two important qualifications: these "arrangements" must not be formalized, as that would "cause trouble" with other allies; and they must "not affect NATO."[20] These views were expressed during a visit to Paris that the president made during his trip to Europe in September 1959. On 2 September, Eisenhower spoke with de Gaulle at the Palais de l'Elysée. The discussion revealed the full extent of the divergence between de Gaulle's and Eisenhower's views on the organization of the alliance and on European security. De Gaulle argued that the era of integration of NATO forces and of French forces within NATO had run its course, and he hailed the birth of a new era in which France would be responsible for its own defense and French forces would be coordinated, not *integrated*, with those of its allies, including the United States. Because of new technological advances in the nuclear field, it was necessary to change the situation in which the United States held ultimate responsibility for the defense of Europe. France wanted to have a say in NATO on par with the United States' to ensure that it would not be annihilated "without even having had the opportunity of expressing its views and without having any role." In addition, because of changing circumstances (such as the expansion of the threat to extra-European areas in the East and in Africa), NATO's activities were no longer to be confined to Europe and to the United States. Now was the time for consultation with France's privileged partners, the United Kingdom and the United States, who, unlike other European countries, possessed worldwide responsibilities as well as firsthand expertise in nuclear weapons. In making this request, de Gaulle revealed that he was shooting for yet another goal: a special relationship with the United States akin to the Anglo-American special relationship.[21]

After the Suez crisis, the United States had been anxious to renew its special relationship with the British. This desire translated into an agreement to resume cooperation in the most delicate and politically significant area of all: nuclear weapons. In May 1957, the United Kingdom demonstrated its willingness to have its own nuclear deterrent by exploding its first hydrogen bomb. One year later, Congress sanctioned the decision of President Eisenhower to amend the McMahon Act in order to permit "exchange of information on the design and production of warheads and the transfer of fissionable materials" with those countries that had made "substantial progress" on their own.[22] This effectively limited cooperation to Britain, as it was the only European country that had acquired an atomic bomb. De Gaulle now aspired to join the atomic club for the same reasons that had prompted the British to devote considerable resources to constructing the H-bomb—the political status that possession of the bomb would confer to middle-sized nations. Like the British, the French were spending billions of dollars to produce their own nuclear weapons. To de Gaulle, even though the French had not yet detonated their bomb (the first French bomb was tested on 13 February 1960), this warranted a level of cooperation and exchange of information between the United States and France comparable to that between the United States and Britain. But de Gaulle's hopes for building a three-way relationship, which would supplant the U.S.-U.K. "special relationship," were disappointed, although some American policymakers were in favor of helping the French with their nuclear program.

Eisenhower himself was not necessarily averse to helping the French develop their own atomic bomb, even though on the surface the special relationship of the "Anglo-Saxons" was enduring. In October 1957, Eisenhower wondered how best one could "maintain the closest possible contact with the British on matters of common concern" and how "it might be possible to meet and talk for just a few hours every now and then with Macmillan."[23] The special relationship was much more informal than had been the case during the war, which should have made it less exclusive.[24] In 1958, and then again in 1960, Eisenhower declared himself in favor of extending the same bilateral agreement on nuclear weapons to the French as to the British.[25] Why then did de Gaulle in fact not receive help from the United States? Part of the answer is that Congress did not favor such a move. Compared to their British colleagues, French generals and researchers lacked connections in Washington, particularly on the Hill, where "the mythology of secrecy" prevailed in the joint committee. Also, "officers with influence on the Hill, like Admiral Hyman Rickover, were strongly opposed to the sharing of their secrets with a France which they thought open to easy Communist penetration."[26]

On 9 June 1958, Secretary of State Dulles told Eisenhower that he anticipated great difficulty in convincing Congress to approve a bilateral agreement with France similar to that which the United States was concluding with the British.[27] Dulles met with de Gaulle in Paris one month later, on 5 July. Dulles's personal notes in preparation for his talk with the general revealed that the administration had decided against helping the French produce their own bomb. In essence, Dulles told de Gaulle that United States law prevented his government from assisting its allies, which obviously included France, in "acquiring a capacity to produce nuclear weapons of their own." As a consolation prize, Dulles offered to station nuclear weapons in France and to provide information so that the French planes and missiles could be tailored or built to deliver such weapons. Another consolation prize was the offer to help France with the construction of its nuclear submarine by way of exchanging "information on submarine propulsion reactors and supply of nuclear fuel and components." Dulles dealt a final blow to de Gaulle's hopes by implying that France's security and its influence in the Atlantic Alliance and other world organizations should not be "measured by its own nuclear weapons stockpile or production capacity."[28] Not surprisingly, the general told Dulles that France would go ahead with its nuclear program with or without American help.

Despite the president's willingness to assist the French, or perhaps because of his indecision in this matter, the balance eventually tilted in favor of those opposing a French nuclear program. As early as October 1957, the record shows that Eisenhower, giving in to his advisers, approved a policy statement on France (NSC 5721/1) that sought "to discourage production of nuclear weapons by a fourth country," and "persuade France not to undertake independent production of such weapons."[29] The president's decision indicated some ambivalence on his part towards helping the French. On the one hand, Eisenhower was not averse to extending nuclear cooperation with the British to the French; on the other, the president did not want the French to feel that American help and the subsequent production of a French bomb would give them a privileged political status in world councils or, more importantly, within NATO. What the president wanted was to strengthen NATO by making it more self-reliant, not to fragment it by giving one ally a favorable treatment.

De Gaulle's reaction came full force. Less than one year after being turned down by Dulles, de Gaulle wrote Eisenhower that he declined the American offer to station IRBMs with warheads under American control on French territory. He similarly refused to store American tactical nuclear weapons in France. Since "America intend[ed] to keep her secrets vis à vis France," thus compelling the French to rediscover them "at tremendous cost," de Gaulle felt justified in "adopting certain measures . . . as safeguards." As long as the United States maintained a monopoly on the control of nuclear weapons, France would not assume the risk of storing them on her territory.[30] About two weeks later, Eisenhower remarked that de Gaulle "merely want[ed] to make France the first nation of the world with himself the first Frenchman." His "primary concern" was that "other NATO nations [would] finally become weary with de Gaulle's attitude and lose enthusiasm for the organization."[31] When he met de Gaulle in the fall, Eisenhower insisted on the importance of all NATO countries being "united in the maximum support of NATO and European security." Answering de Gaulle's criticism on integrated forces, which according to him destroyed national morale, Eisenhower declared that the allies would not win the war without an integrated command. Therefore it "would be a mistake to have a series of national forces. Under this concept, where would United States forces fit into the picture? Would they not have to go home?"[32]

Thus, while de Gaulle favored coordination among independent national forces, Eisenhower spoke of integration of the same forces within NATO. While de Gaulle believed that the "defense of France must be French,"[33] Eisenhower thought that France should merely be consulted on matters of common concern within NATO. For Eisenhower, the ardent proponent of the EDC, *the defense of Europe should be European,* with this important caveat: the United States must retain the ultimate control of nuclear weapons. A European defense of Europe, yes, but under the guidance and control of an American leader in the nuclear field. Eisenhower's concept of a self-reliant third force Europe did not extend to the nuclear field. On this specific level, self-reliance and partnership gave way to integration, a word that de Gaulle abhorred.

NORSTAD'S MRBMs VERSUS BOWIE'S MLF

Yet the American president went considerably further than merely insisting that Europeans pay more for their own defense and provide more troops. He also suggested "making the Europeans furnish the Commander for the European NATO Command."[34] In a meeting at the White House in November 1959, the president told Paul-Henri Spaak that "in 1951, he had never thought that the United States command of NATO forces would last as long as it ha[d]. He had thought that in eight year's time an Englishman or a Frenchman would be in command, although he recognized that it would be difficult for Europe to agree on the choice of a commander."[35] Eisenhower assured Spaak that his plans for a more "self-dependent" Europe did not mean withdrawing all American forces from Europe; "token" forces would be maintained "throughout our lifetime."[36] At first glance, proposing a

European commander for the NATO Command entailed giving Europeans more control of their own defense. In fact, as de Gaulle and French Foreign Minister Couve de Murville later pointed out, this was an essentially symbolic and hollow proposal in the nuclear field, since no matter who was SACEUR the United States retained the ultimate control of nuclear weapons. During the Kennedy administration, when asked by C. L. Sulzberger "if France would be prepared to see an American general named as successor to Norstad at SHAPE," Couve de Murville bluntly retorted: "Who else but an American general if SACEUR is not to be just a figurehead? If a French general, for example, was named, he would have to have at his right hand an American general to do the atomic job under the situation as it now prevails. The only solution would be to have an American general."[37]

Making Europe more self-dependent required much more than a European SACEUR. It required giving Europeans better access to, and genuine control of, nuclear weapons, *strategic* as well as tactical. Reconciling the Europeans' desire for more control of their own destiny in the nuclear field with the Americans' insistence that European defense remain integrated, and not, as de Gaulle would have had it, merely coordinated, with that of the United States, was not an easy task. It implied reconciling two conflicting elements: European independence and Atlantic integration. Much thought was given to this problem in various quarters of the Eisenhower administration.

In a press conference on 16 July 1957, Secretary Dulles advanced the idea of establishing a NATO nuclear weapons stockpile to assure American allies that if they were attacked they would not have to beg Americans for "the use of atomic weapons." Such an "act of confidence" on the part of the United States, he felt, would have the desirable political consequence of reinvigorating the "fellowship of the North Atlantic community."[38] The proposal itself was initiated by General Norstad, the NATO Commander in Paris, and one of the closest confidants of President Eisenhower. Nuclear weapons were to be stockpiled in Europe under American custody and delivered to allies "in time of emergency."[39] The United States would also give its European allies delivery systems to fire nuclear weapons. A dual-key arrangement ensured that the United States would maintain a veto over the firing of these weapons. Thus, while allies were being given control of the missiles, they could not fire them without American approval. The "act of confidence" towards European allies in giving them more control over their own defense was a qualified one.

Around the same time, in 1957, Norstad advanced a second proposal. He proposed to develop a NATO medium-range ballistic missile force. It would have two main purposes: offsetting Soviet missile forces and giving the NATO commander, Norstad himself (and through him, Europeans), the control of *strategic* weapons based in Europe. This would have made NATO, in Norstad's terms, a "multilateral fourth nuclear power."[40] Norstad's first proposal was soon implemented. NATO agreed to establish American stocks of nuclear weapons in Europe, while the United States embarked on a campaign in European countries to place Thor and Jupiter IRBMs on their territory under a two-key system. Kennedy later had them removed. France declined the invitation for now well-known reasons. Germany did not want to take the risk of having the weapons on its territory because of its proximity to the Soviet Union. Finally, only the British, the Turks, and the Italians accepted the missiles. The British, however, refused to have them "integrated" by assigning them to SACEUR.

These missiles were liquid-fuel missiles of the first generation, "vulnerable to sabotage and direct attack"[41] and promising to become obsolete within a relatively short period. For Norstad, they were only a stopgap measure; something better was needed—Polaris missiles. These mobile, solid-propellant ballistic missiles would meet the requirements of Norstad's second proposal, unlike the Thor and Jupiter missiles. Norstad planned to keep the second-generation weapons (the Polarises) land-based and mobile by camouflaging them in trains and trucks.[42] A significant part of his proposal consisted of having the weapons produced by a sort of consortium of European nations according to American design specifications. This would have killed two birds with one stone: meeting American budgetary constraints by shifting more of the cost of manufacturing nuclear weapons to the allies while gaining control of the European production of nuclear weapons. In addition, a Polaris force produced, operated, targeted and perhaps fired by SACEUR, after authorization from the American president of course, would have signaled the beginning of a genuine European nuclear capability.

By the spring of 1960, all these proposals had been taken up with American allies and had generated considerable interest within Europe. Yet, although the first part of Norstad's proposal was implemented, the land-based MRBM force was never to see the light of day. Opposition from the powerful Congressional Joint Committee on Atomic Energy, lack of support from the Kennedy team, and opposition from de Gaulle combined to defeat it. Painting a grim picture of heavy Polaris missiles and launchers being transported all over European public roads, American and European critics viewed the idea as a political liability. American critics specifically worried that single European nations might use the land-based Polaris forces without prior authorization by NATO commanders.[43] In its most advanced form, Norstad's proposal envisaged that the three nuclear powers—France,

Britain, and the United States—would jointly decide by majority vote if an atomic strike should be launched. Norstad's strong advocacy of a more significant and independent role for SACEUR, which might eventually have implied that "a NATO commander who was not an American would be in a position to order [American] troops into a war,"[44] did not fit well with the strategy of the new Kennedy team. Having lost his campaign for land-based ballistic missiles and a more independent role for SACEUR, Norstad resigned in January 1963. His defeat coincided with the rise of another proposal, or, rather, concept: the Multilateral Force, which had been evolved by Bowie and his assistants in the course of 1960 and then revived during the Kennedy administration with strong backing from the Europeanists.

Like Norstad's proposal, the MLF was partly an attempt to grant European allies a higher degree of control over their nuclear defense. But the MLF proponents placed considerably more emphasis than Norstad on the integration of that control and on preventing discrimination between the European nuclear "haves" and "have-nots" of the alliance. For them, increased participation of Europeans in their own defense was intended to strengthen the alliance, not to weaken it by breeding resentment among the smaller European nations because of unequal treatment in the nuclear field.

In June 1960, Gerard Smith and Henry Owen of the Policy Planning Staff, accompanied by Robert Bowie and other Europeanists such as Assistant Secretary Foy Kohler (EUR) and Russ Fessenden (RA), attempted to sound out the views of NATO Secretary-General Paul-Henri Spaak on the idea of a "genuinely multi-national force, in which personnel of different nations would be intermingled so that no single country would have a national capability readily at hand—an EDC transplanted to the nuclear field." Spaak declared himself favorable to the idea, provided that the fateful term of EDC was not used.[45]

At the December 1959 meeting of the NATO Council, Herter had suggested that NATO ought to have a ten-year plan. That same month, the National Security Council agreed that "the Planning Board should undertake the immediate preparation of a Discussion Paper on the 'Implications of Sharing of Nuclear Weapons with Allies.'"[46] In February 1960, Bowie was asked on a consulting basis to prepare a report on the tasks facing the North Atlantic countries during the 1960s. Bowie and his aides completed their assignment in August 1960. The report explained the MLF concept and asked for an increase in conventional forces.[47] Continuing Taylor's line of argument, Bowie first advocated bolstering NATO's conventional forces to decrease "the likelihood of any limited hostilities in Europe spiralling into all-out conflict." Contrary to Norstad, Bowie insisted that the forces be non-nuclear. An "adequate" conventional defense, he hoped, would hold off a Soviet conventional attack for enough time to allow the Soviet

Union to consider the consequences of full-blown American strategic retaliation.[48] Bowie then advanced a second proposal as part of the defense "package"[49]
he advocated—the creation of a seaborne Polaris force. The main features of
what came to be known under the Kennedy administration as the MLF were
agreed upon by December 1960. For tactical reasons, the supporters of the MLF
planned to submit their proposal to NATO only after the American presidential
elections in November, "in order to avoid the possibility that they might become
involved in the political campaign."[50]

On 17 December 1960, President Eisenhower approved a statement of
policy by the National Security Council that recommended that the "United
States should present a *concept* [my emphasis] for a NATO MRBM force."[51]
The next day, at the December meeting of the NATO Council, Secretary of
State Herter briefed United States allies on the idea of a multilateral force of
MRBMs. The council greeted the proposal "with great interest" and referred
it to the permanent representatives for further study.[52] About one earlier,
Eisenhower and his secretaries of state, treasury, and defense had approved
the text of Herter's statement on the MRBMs. The statement proposed the
establishment of a multilateral force in two stages. Initially the United States
would commit to NATO "five Polaris submarines having a combined capability of firing eighty missiles" to be operational by the end of 1963. As a
second stage, the United States would contribute the five American Polaris
nuclear submarines to a multilateral force. An NSC document specified that
the United States "would consider the five Polaris submarines as a contribution to the NATO MRBM Force . . . and, in the event of its establishment,
would undertake not to withdraw them from NATO without NAC consent
during the life of the Treaty." The initial American contribution to the force
would later be relayed by the financial participation of allies who were
expected to "buy and contribute approximately 100 additional MRBMs in
order to help meet SACEUR's MRBM requirements through 1964." Under
no circumstances was the United States to finance the additional MRBMs.
For a permanent force to be created, the United States insisted that it must
be truly multilaterally owned and financed and effectively controlled, and
that "classified design data" for nuclear weapons and their delivery systems
be adequately protected. The United States would then be willing to "facilitate NATO procurement by sale of POLARIS missiles and of the required
equipment and vehicles for deployment." In addition, the United States
would also "be prepared to provide the warheads for these missiles and to
commit them to NATO, for the life of the Treaty." Yet these warheads would
remain under American custody. The initial Polaris missiles would be
deployed at sea.[53]

These specifications show that the MLF was designed to meet not only European desires for greater participation in their own defense but also American concerns for control over the development of European production of nuclear weapons and American hopes for increasing the financial contribution of their allies to nuclear defense. Contrary to Norstad's proposal, the MRBMs were not to be produced in Europe but to be purchased by the Europeans. There would be no joint decision of the United States, France, and the United Kingdom (the three first-rank nuclear powers in the alliance) in case a nuclear strike should be launched or in other matters. There would be no Franco-British nuclear "control group"[54] in which other European nations would take part as third-rank powers. As a matter of fact, the French and British nuclear programs were to be discouraged, not supported. One of the main concerns of successive American administrations during and since World War II had been to guard against German resentment by giving Germany a status equal to that of other European nations. A twin concern had been to counter divisive nationalistic trends on the Continent. Faithful to this tradition, the creators of the MLF calculated that the best way to reinforce European unity and Atlantic partnership while at the same time unifying the nuclear deterrent would be to create an MLF with submarines and missiles operated and controlled jointly by participants. Crews made up of various nationalities would man the submarines and control the missiles so that "no NATO member would predominate" and "no member could control the force or pull it apart."[55]

The MLF concept was undoubtedly directed against the spread, or the maintenance, of national nuclear forces in Europe. This was indeed the main concern that prompted Herter and Gerard Smith to commission the Bowie study. Herter's statement before the NATO Council was clearly antagonistic to the "creation of additional national nuclear weapons capabilities." Sounding a note very much akin to McNamara's Athens speech during the Kennedy administration, Herter criticized these forces as fostering divisions within the alliance, duplicating efforts, diverting resources, and increasing the likelihood of starting nuclear war "by miscalculation or accident." The Bowie Report had said much the same thing.[56] Some members of the executive branch and Congress worried most of all about a potential move on the part of the Germans to acquire an independent nuclear capability in the post-Adenauer era. Should the United States encourage the development of French and British nuclear capabilities, they reasoned, Germany, and perhaps Italy, would resent their inferior status within the alliance. Sooner or later they would embark on a national nuclear program to achieve equal status with France and the United Kingdom. The Kennedy administration pursued the same line of reasoning.

On 11 April 1961, Kennedy, speaking of Polaris missiles, declared that "the problem was to find an acceptable plan and at the same time discourage separate nuclear capabilities such as the French and the Germans."[57] A few days later, during a conversation with Paul Reynaud, the former prime minister of France, and Hervé Alphand, the French ambassador to the United States, the president was even more explicit. Kennedy told them that "it was not simply a question of France's having nuclear capability, but the next step would be for Germany to have this capability . . . this was dangerous in view of the fact that Adenauer might be leaving the scene some day."[58] Bowie and his "Cabal" voiced the same concerns. To them, a Franco-German control group in which other European nations would participate "would certainly leave intact the national forces under some façade." Therefore what was needed was a concept that would prevent a MRBM force from being "pulled apart into national components" and unify the alliance rather than fragment it.[59] Hence the recommendation for mixed-manning and joint control of the MLF. In a completely integrated force, no member nation could "withdraw any part of the ships." This was crucial for a number of reasons: "The full force could be counted on for performing a specified strategic function. In the absence of national units, no member could threaten or undertake withdrawal as a lever or pressure on the others. Moreover, no one nationality would have unimpeded access to missiles or equipment aboard ship. Beyond this, unlike divisive national forces, the joint force with mixed manning would be a striking symbol of the cohesion of the alliance and of the mutual dependence of its members for their security."[60] Bowie further calculated that the British and French nuclear forces might eventually be absorbed into the integrated force. The British, he reasoned, would probably not be able to sustain the costs of a nuclear force in the long run. Although nothing could be reasonably expected during de Gaulle's lifetime, the French, faced with prohibitive expenses and a long research process not facilitated in any way by the United States, might in the long run renounce a separate nuclear force.

The plan to provide for more cohesiveness within the alliance combined with yet another design that was intended to ensure that the political evolution of an integrated Europe was compatible with American interests. Encouraging European national forces, thought Bowie, would in fact be equivalent to supporting de Gaulle's conception of a European order subject to French hegemony and based on the preeminence of the nation-state. For Bowie, the French *force de frappe* was "mainly a means for political primacy: a symbol to distinguish [France] from Germany and Italy." The French force incarnated "de Gaulle's concept of Europe, based on nation-states, cooperating under French hegemony," which was in "essence . . . the opposite of European integration through the European Community. Hence, assistance to the French effort would endorse de Gaulle's concept of Europe and would jeopardize support for the genuine integration of the European Community."[61]

By contrast, the MLF would grant European allies a greater participation and control in nuclear deterrence, thereby satisfying their need for more "self-respect." Merely "sharing knowledge and planning" with European allies was not enough, since they aspired to joint control over nuclear weapons. For political reasons, it was essential to bring to an end the situation in which the Europeans felt that they remained "wards of the United States" because "the real power of decision rest[ed] indefinitely with the president of the United States."[62] "Self-respect" demanded that there should be "greater equality, at least for a unified Europe, in the matter of nuclear control." Although the MLF force was originally to be subject to American veto, Bowie envisaged that *if Europe united and if the Europeans wanted it* the United States might "be willing to reorganize the force . . . to permit its operation without the veto of the United States." The MLF might then evolve into either "(1) an integrated NATO force in which the United States, without a veto, would be one member, or (2) an integrated European force (without the United States as a member), closely coordinated with United States forces, but under ultimate European control." [63]

In the short run, the MLF would serve as a tool for tying Western Europe more solidly to the United States in the nuclear field. European defense efforts would be channeled towards a joint NATO force, over which the United States retained the ultimate control. It would be both an instrument of greater Atlantic and European cohesion. In the long-run, the MLF might even crown the achievement of European political unity by achieving real European control of a European force. Then and only then would there be a real European partner for the United States—an economic, political, and military partner. But by making European control over a European force or the creation of a NATO force without American veto conditional upon the unification of Europe, the artisans of the MLF postponed nuclear maturity for American allies to what seemed to be a distant future. More than a means of achieving European unity in the near future, the MLF was meant to be a confirmation of European economic and political unity and a means of cementing the alliance, providing a unified deterrent, and preventing the emergence of a German nuclear force. Before December 1962, few, even among the "Europeans," including Monnet and Kohnstamm themselves, thought that the MLF should top the list of priorities for achieving European unity. Only Walt Rostow believed in placing the Monnet sequence on its head.[64] Most of those who were sympathetic towards European integration considered the MLF as a possible contribution to European integration, but it was not their first order of priority. More than a means of giving Europeans genuine control of their own nuclear defense, the MLF was, above all, a means of discouraging European national ventures. It was also intended to serve as a carrot to encourage Europeans to unite politically.

EISENHOWER, KENNEDY, AND THE MLF

Eisenhower and the MLF

Since its inception under Eisenhower, the MLF had been much more a concept than a firm proposal. The NSC Statement of Policy on the NATO MRBM Force of December 1960 specified that the force should be "presented in terms which make it clear that the establishment of a permanent MRBM force will require study and consideration by NATO and that U.S. participation therein will require Congressional approval."[65] Yet Bowie's MLF proposal generated considerable interest on the part of Eisenhower; the president's successor in office would show much less enthusiasm. Twice Eisenhower called on Bowie to discuss the proposal.[66] The first meeting took place on 16 August, with only Bowie and the president present, and lasted for about an hour. There was a second meeting on 12 September 1960, this time with General Norstad and the president. Again, the president took a lively interest in discussing the MLF. Eisenhower emerged from the second meeting a convinced proponent of the MLF, but with one qualification: the United States must retain control of the force.[67] Eisenhower hoped that the MRBM force would extend nuclear cooperation "of political significance" to other members of the alliance besides England so that the alliance would remain "healthy" and "endure."[68] It could also placate the opposition for more nuclear sharing with allies from the Joint Committee on Atomic Energy. Should there be more nuclear sharing, the committee had indicated its preference for a multilateral arrangement over bilateral arrangements, for which it was "completely negative."[69] Accordingly, the president felt that if the executive "could conceive a well-safeguarded joint scheme, the Joint Committee would accept it." He was "sure that they would not agree to bilateral arrangements between the U.S. and selected allies." On the whole, the president's "primary area of concern"[70] was NATO. He favored the MLF idea because he wanted "to have some means of showing how necessary it is to work in close harmony with allies."[71]

During a meeting at the White House with Secretary General Paul-Henri Spaak, Acting Secretary Dillon, Merchant, Kohler, and Ambassador to NATO Burgess in early October, the president presented a strong case for the creation of a "foreign legion" type of force to be placed "under exclusive NATO control and financed by contributions of the member states." NATO control was necessary to discourage nationalism and to prevent the force from breaking apart into national components. The president anticipated "certain difficulties . . . before full integration could be obtained, due among other things to the lengthy training necessary."[72] Spaak concurred with the president that the proposed force would establish a closer bond between the United States and Europe. He also seemed to have indicated that every means should be used to encourage France to join the force. De Gaulle's plan to create a French nuclear strike force, he reasoned, was "meeting with considerable opposition in the French parliament. A proposal such as the one under discussion would undoubtedly receive strong support from the French public opinion and increase the opposition in France against an independent nuclear force and thus [put] pressure on de Gaulle." The president agreed that efforts should be made to gain French participation in the force, but he cautioned that if France declined, which was almost certain initially, and other allies went ahead with the force this "might well lead, step by step, to a withdrawal of France from the alliance."[73] This might explain the president's recommendation that the proposal be surrounded "with many 'ifs' including the necessity to take the matter with Congress"[74] when discussing it with allies. More "ifs" were later added during the Kennedy administration.

Kennedy and the MLF: Conflicting Advice

The Acheson Report, although endorsing the MLF concept in principle, was characteristically cool towards the idea of a permanent MLF force. While it gave priority to building NATO's non-nuclear forces, the first part of Bowie's proposal, the report also projected the establishment of a permanent MLF force—but made it conditional upon an agreement among Europeans for common control and a European buildup of non-nuclear forces. Since it was unlikely that European governments would find the financial means and the political support to improve non-nuclear as well as nuclear forces, and it was equally unlikely that they would agree on how to control nuclear forces in the short term, these requirements relegated the establishment of a Multilateral Force to the quite distant future. In addition, control of the MLF was to be centralized, which seemed to preclude the existence of a force without American veto. The Acheson Report accordingly contained many qualifying "ifs":

> *If* our NATO allies should wish, after completing the projected 1962-66 non-nuclear build-up, to expand further the NATO sea-borne missile forces projected above, this should be a matter for discussion with them at the time, including the possibility of some multilateral contribution by them *if* they should desire this and *if* its cost should become more manageable than the foregoing financial review would indicate. In any such future discussion, the US should be governed by the need to avoid (i) any diversion of required resources from non-nuclear tasks; (ii) any further foreign national ownership and control of MRBM forces; (iii) any weakening of centralized operational control over so important a part of the nuclear deterrent. The US should not facilitate European production of MRBM's or procurement of MRBM's for European national forces, whether or not these forces are committed to SACEUR.[75]

One might argue that the Norstad plan, including the proposal for European production of MRBMs, was defeated right there. Kennedy approved the Acheson Report on 21 April 1961. From then on, the MLF was put forward as a concept and became a carrot to entice Europeans to contribute more to common defense efforts, giving them some hope, albeit tenuous, that they would some day accede to military maturity and cease to be wards of the United States in the area of defense. Few in the administration believed that such military maturity would come soon. In the immediate future, the tentative presentation of the concept could be used to test European intentions regarding such a force, without committing the United States to any particular organization and control of the force. Bowie himself later affirmed that the issue of control was "manageable only if handled as an evolving factor" and that "in its initial form" the MLF was "no final or perfect solution."[76] Very much in keeping with Monnet, Hallstein, and other distinguished "Europeans," Bowie did not pretend to fix in advance the shape European integration would take. Rather, he considered progress towards European integration as an evolutionary process in which the United States had an important role to play, notably by initiating proposals such as the MLF. Yet the decision on whether to go along with American proposals or to find alternatives to them belonged to Europeans. The pace and shape of European integration was ultimately their responsibility.

President Kennedy held essentially the same view, although he was considerably less committed to the MLF proposal than were some of his advisers in the State Department. Kennedy's attitude of qualified support for the MLF reflected not only the lukewarm stance of the Acheson Report but also the conflicting views held by advisers in the Defense and State Departments, and certain members of the White House Staff, towards the desirability and feasibility of an MLF, and the eventual, although hypothetical, European—without American veto power—control of a European nuclear force. Most participants of the MLF saga now agree that the president was never quite "sold" on the MLF. Walt Rostow's testimony of the period paints the portrait of a president who "went through phases"[77] on the MLF. General Taylor speaks of a president who consistently "refused to say that he supported the MLF" and "didn't want the American flag to be put on top of it." "At no time," states Taylor, did the president say "he was for the MLF. Never did anyone in his administration say he was for the MLF."[78] George Ball recounts that "President Kennedy never made up his mind that the multilateral force was a good thing," and that he "never finally convinced himself that it might prevent the building up of conflicts and feelings of inequality and irresponsibility that flow from impotence among the Europeans."[79]

The noncommittal nature of the president's attitude towards the MLF can be attributed to a number of interrelated factors. First, Kennedy considered the MLF an interesting but exploratory idea, a device to test European intentions. According to George Ball, the president considered the MLF as "a Halloween apple" that the United States "dangled before the Europeans in case they wished to bite it."[80] Somewhat less critical of the president, Thomas Finletter, the ambassador to NATO, remembers that Kennedy had the feeling that the MLF was "something that was a very daring ideal" and "knew historically this was something which was a precedent-making enterprise and one which would be very difficult to achieve," and therefore the president "took it easy."[81] Second, the administration was divided over the issue. The main advocates of the proposal had their headquarters in the State Department, while the strongest opponents of the concept were located in the Pentagon. Not the least of these opponents was Paul Nitze, who was adamantly opposed to ever giving Europeans the authority to use the force without United States approval for fear they might get the United States in a war against its will.[82]

What is usually less well appreciated is that even the group of MLF proponents were divided over the issue. For some, like Walt Rostow, the MLF was to be number one on the list of American policy priorities—both as a significant device to progress towards the goal of a politically united Europe and as a means of strengthening the Atlantic Alliance. Most other MLF supporters, however, felt that the MLF was an important ingredient in American policy towards Europe but should preferably be added last to the policy mix. In the anticipated chain reaction that would lead to a fully united Europe, those whom Rostow called the members of the "Atlantic Establishment" viewed tariff negotiations and British entry in the Common Market as first-order catalysts for European integration. The nuclear question, though equally important, should preferably be tackled later. Probably mindful of the lessons of the EDC, Monnet, Ball, McGeorge Bundy, and the members of the European Bureau in the State Department deliberately placed the nuclear question last on the timetable of European integration. What they should have remembered from the EDC, however, was that one of the main causes of its defeat had been "the tentativeness and lack of conviction of the government that had originally proposed the idea."[83] Ironically, this last phrase belongs to George Ball, who, at least initially, was a partisan for maintaining a low profile for the MLF until other issues were successfully resolved. The tentativeness, or "cautiously passive"[84] attitude, of the American government towards the MLF did not solely rest with its opponents but also with the lack of cohesion among its advocates, not so much over the goals it was supposed to achieve as over how and when they should be achieved relative to other goals. The president, who was at first an "uncommitted thinker"[85] toward the MLF, let himself be swayed by the reluctance of his advisers to push it too strongly and too soon. For a while, namely until the time of the Nassau meeting in December 1962, Walt Rostow preached in the desert.

Rostow thought that it was nonsense to expect far-reaching political results for the unity of Europe from either the tariff negotiations of the Kennedy Round or the entry of Great Britain to the Common Market so long as Great Britain retained her national nuclear power.[86] There could be no politically united Europe if one or more of its members retained a privileged nuclear status (with its significant and much-coveted corollary—higher political standing in the European and Atlantic clubs) that was sanctioned by the United States. On this point, Rostow's argument did not differ much from that of the Bowie Report: there were to be no second- and third-rank powers in Western Europe. Both Rostow and Bowie heeded one of the most basic tenets of American policy since World War II—that inequality breeds resentment and encourages nationalism. Hence, they hoped to bring the British and the French down to the level of other European powers by emasculating these two nations of their national nuclear forces, which were their most significant claim to first-rank political status within Europe. This would eradicate a potentially divisive factor in Europe, and thus increase the likelihood of European political integration, by channeling French and British energies towards the construction of a new Europe.

Similarly to Rostow, George Ball opposed American assistance to European national nuclear forces on the grounds that "they were costly political baubles which wasted valuable British and French resources and had a potentially divisive and dangerous effect on the unity of Europe."[87] But unlike Rostow, Ball did not suggest moving towards European political unity on the simultaneous and parallel tracks of progress in the economic and nuclear fields. Most of the "Atlantic Establishment" preferred moving quickly on the economic track and much more slowly on the nuclear track. When de Gaulle rejected British entry in the Common Market during his January 1963 press conference, the "theologians" shifted gears on the MLF. Now that the French veto had blocked a British contribution to a united Europe in the economic field, the "theologians" and most of the Kennedy administration moved on the nuclear front. The MLF then became a political device for associating the British more closely with the Continent.

THE FRENCH *FORCE DE FRAPPE,* THE MLF, AND THE GERMAN QUESTION

In the meantime, the MLF was indeed a "Halloween apple" to be dangled mostly in front of the French to lure them away from a national independent venture in the nuclear field and to whet their appetite, according to Henry Owen, for an eventual participation "in the NATO nuclear deterrent . . . on a larger scale than would be represented by any national contribution they could make in the foreseeable future."[88] Henry Owen of the Policy Planning Staff in the State Department had participated in the preparation of both the Bowie and Acheson reports and played a key role in the bureaucratic politics of the MLF undertaking. On 21 April 1961, in preparation for the Kennedy-de Gaulle meeting on 31 May, Owen and Harry Rowan, deputy assistant secretary of defense, proposed a "New Approach to France."[89] In order to prevent the proliferation of nuclear weapons and to satisfy the desire of Europeans for more participation in their own defense, particularly in the nuclear field, Owen and Rowan proposed a number of interconnected steps; the MLF was one of them.

First on the list of priorities stood the elimination of the "privileged British status." Recognizing that "in matters nuclear, the road to Paris may well be through London," Rowan and Owen recommended that the "minimum objective" of the United States should be to convince Prime Minister Macmillan "to commit his warheads to the NATO Atomic Stockpile and his delivery weapons to NATO commanders, on the same basis as the U.S." A more far-reaching step was for the United States to "try to move him to cease the production of fissionable materials for weapons purposes if France [would] do the same." Adopting a now familiar line of thought, the two planners sought to bring the French and British nuclear forces down to the same level in order to thwart the national political and nuclear ambitions of both nations. Equality, they thought, would forestall the divisive forces of French and British nationalism and prevent the most divisive force of all from reemerging: German nationalism. In the nuclear field, German nationalism would be lethal to the North Atlantic Alliance. The road to Bonn seemed to be through London and, most of all, Paris. Hence the recommendation that the United States ask the French, like the British, to commit all of their nuclear forces to NATO and eventually "cease the production of fissionable materials for weapons purposes."

The reverse course of action—providing help to the French nuclear and missile program—was to be avoided at all costs, even though it was advocated by key players in the Defense Department. American help to the French would stimulate German aspirations for similar support from the United States, and "the mere prospect of a German MRBM and/or nuclear program would shake NATO to its foundations." Instead, in exchange for the promise of the destruction of French and British national nuclear forces, the United States would offer the French and British participation in a special nuclear committee that would "be provided with information about the number, type, and location of warheads committed to NATO, and about contingency plans for their use." German membership in the committee was "a must, sooner or later." The committee would determine guidelines on the use of nuclear weapons committed to NATO. Rowan and Owen envisioned that a War Council, with the same membership as the committee, would be charged with "reaching judgments about the application of the agreed guidelines to specific cases when they arise" and "making recommendations to the Council about other specific cases which arise and which are not covered by the guidelines." The president of the United States "would undertake to observe any guidelines or specific recommendations developed by the Nuclear Committee and approved by the Council in ordering the use of U.S. nuclear weapons committed to NATO. The British would make a similar undertaking." This last recommendation in effect opened the prospect for European joint control with the United States over American nuclear weapons assigned to NATO. The Owen-Rowan memorandum emphasized that the United States "must try to assure [their] European allies of effective participation in control both over U.S. tactical nuclear forces already committed to NATO and over the U.S. strategic forces (Polaris submarines and possibly B-47s in the U.K.) to be committed to NATO."[90]

But the president and his secretary of state hesitated on the degree of control that the United States should grant its allies. A personal cable from Secretary Rusk to American Ambassador to France General James Gavin in early May mentioned only the desirability of "greater allied and particularly French participation in planning and decision regarding [the] use [of] nuclear weapons committed to NATO."[91] The degree and nature of such participation were not specified. Meanwhile, the MLF received only lukewarm treatment, and there was every indication that real sharing of "control" over NATO's nuclear weapons with European allies loomed only in the distant future, if at all. To the authors of the 21 April memorandum, the MLF was a political device to give the French and other European allies the illusion, or rather the distant prospect, of some day possessing real control over their own defense. Although they were prepared to support Acheson's MLF proposal and to "suggest that French personnel—both military and scientific—could play a large role in the development of such a force," the authors were prepared to do so only after NATO had met its "non-nuclear goals." In fact, the practical details of the force itself did not preoccupy them much, for they thought it "highly doubtful if such a force would ever come into being, given the problems of command and control that would be involved; the long-term prospect and possibility of such a development would, however, strengthen the hand of those Frenchmen who oppos[ed] a national 'force de frappe,' even if it had little appeal to the General himself." Thus the main appeal of the MLF was not just to give Europeans the illusion of more control over nuclear strategic weapons but also to undermine the supporters of the *force de frappe,* or French strike force.

Rusk's letter to Gavin revealed, however, that Rusk was not so much preoccupied with the French *force de frappe* as with the effect this force would have on German aspirations for the control of nuclear weapons, especially if the United States chose to help the French. He thought that the financial burden of the French *force de frappe* would probably be too much for the French to bear. They might therefore be tempted to draw Germany into a joint venture. If the United States refrained from helping the French it was unlikely that the Germans would join such a venture. On the other hand, if the United States helped the *force de frappe,* the Germans might not only agree to cooperate with the French but also seek American help for their own nuclear program, even though Adenauer was strongly opposed to such a move. This, thought Rusk, "would shake NATO to its foundations."[92] This viewpoint was also that of the president. As for Jean Monnet, he very nearly espoused the same concerns as Kennedy. Always worried about German aspirations for equal status in the European club, he was also frankly opposed to a French *force de frappe*. All things considered, the main reason for the president's endorsement of the MLF concept on 25 April 1961 was the German question.

The next month, the president delivered an address before the Canadian Parliament in Ottawa that reaffirmed the intention of the United States to "commit to the NATO command five—and subsequently still more—Polaris atomic-missile submarines, which are defensive weapons, subject to any agreed NATO guidelines on their control and use, and responsive to the needs of all members but still credible in an emergency." "Beyond this," continued the president, "we look to the possibility of eventually establishing a NATO sea-borne force, which would be truly multilateral in ownership and control, if this should be desired and found feasible by our Allies, once NATO's non-nuclear goals have been achieved."[93]

This last sentence had been inserted by Henry Owen himself. Theodore Sorensen, who served as special counsel to the president, had sent a draft copy of the speech to Owen, who was then working in the White House to follow up on the Acheson Report. Henry Owen did not hesitate to seize the opportunity to modify the speech by incorporating a sentence that committed the president to supporting the MLF.[94] But the second part of the sentence reflected the same lack of enthusiasm as the Acheson Report to which Owen had contributed. Kennedy's support for the MLF was qualified by two important requirements: agreement among European powers, including agreement on how to finance the MLF, and a buildup of NATO's conventional forces. Despite these qualifications, Henry Owen nevertheless succeeded in giving the MLF official status in European and Atlantic councils. This was despite opposition to, or skepticism towards, the MLF and the assumptions behind it from various quarters of the Kennedy administration.

Douglas Dillon, the new secretary of the treasury, had been in favor of helping the French since the Eisenhower administration and maintained his convictions under the Kennedy administration. Paul Nitze, the assistant secretary of defense for international affairs, was a strong advocate for helping the French in order to secure their cooperation within NATO, and more subtly, to "smoke them out" on their intentions regarding NATO.[95] General Maxwell Taylor and Under Secretary of Defense Roswell Gilpatric shared his view. Less subtle was the position of Ambassador to France James Gavin, who was regarded within the Kennedy administration as a Gaullist ready to give de Gaulle all the help he wanted in exchange for harmonious relations with France.[96] Secretary Rusk and some of his colleagues in the State Department felt it necessary to regularly emphasize to him that helping the French nuclear force was not American policy, as Gavin regularly showered the president and the State Department with requests for assistance to France, including the provision of enriched uranium for military applications.[97] Eventually, Gavin resigned for "personal" reasons and was replaced by Charles Bohlen. As for the very influential Robert McNamara, he too initially favored helping the French, notably through some provision of uranium and exchange of technology.[98] The secretary of defense believed that close nuclear collaboration with the French might coax them into cooperating with the new American strategy, especially in strengthening NATO's conventional forces.[99] McNamara also intended to set up a sort of nuclear committee within NATO, in which the French would be given a prominent role. On this specific point, his proposal matched that of the Rowan-Owen memorandum. George Ball himself agreed with the idea of the nuclear committee inasmuch as it would have given Europeans "a sense of participation without actually having weapons of their own."[100] The Bowie Report had merely advocated the creation of a Steering Committee of the North Atlantic Council in which the stronger members of NATO (i.e., the United States, the United Kingdom, France, Germany, Italy, and perhaps Canada) would evolve proposals on European security issues and coordinate their policies "on extra-European matters." In order to safeguard the interests of smaller states, the Committee would report to the NAC, and representatives of smaller member states would attend as ad-hoc members when the Committee discussed issues which might affect their interests. "In time," the Committee might "consist of the US and the European Community when it could speak for its members."[101]

As far as the MLF was concerned, the Pentagon took the position that there was "no military requirement for European- and NATO-controlled nuclear weapons" and claimed that there was "no political demand in Europe along those lines."[102] This remained the Pentagon's position until the MLF became official policy in 1962.[103] McNamara felt that the MLF "had no military value."[104] And, until Nassau, he was not even convinced of its potential as a political device for cementing the alliance.[105] Only when the close cooperation with the French that he had envisaged proved impossible *in* NATO did McNamara turn toward the MLF as a means of integrating the deterrent and countering the divisive forces of separate national nuclear capabilities. At that juncture, McNamara joined forces with the "theologians," who favored the MLF, and became one of the most faithful supporters of the MLF. He still felt the MLF "didn't add any military strength" but nevertheless "thought it a worthwhile expenditure of money, *if* it had what was a clear need for a closer relationship in nuclear strategy."[106] For McNamara, the MLF was mostly valuable because of its potential to serve "as a channel of communication between the Western Europeans and the Americans."[107] He later made clear to the House Committee on Armed Services that integration of control was his main concern: "The essential point here is . . . that we must avoid the fragmentation and compartmentalization of NATO's nuclear power which could be dangerous to us all. If our European NATO partners wish to create a European strategic nuclear force, we certainly should have no objections. But we should insist that that force be closely integrated with our own so that it could be jointly targeted, and directed in a coordinated fashion."[108]

Turning the clock back a little, the MLF followed a nice, slow track after Kennedy's Ottawa speech and up until April/May 1962, when it started gathering momentum as an alternative to Norstad's proposal of providing NATO forces with MRBMs for national ownership and manning, which had whetted European appetites for more nuclear sharing. The "best way" to counter the divisive forces of European national nuclear programs, wrote Rusk to Gavin, was "through [the American] MRBM offer, and through possible other means to give Alliance a larger NATO nuclear role, if our allies so desire."[109] President Kennedy reviewed the message and approved it.

Yet Kennedy remained a practical man and was not averse to helping the French nuclear program, if only such help could translate into a strong French commitment to NATO. In the spring of 1962, Nitze, bypassing the State Department, went directly to the president to ask for permission to explore with the French possible ways of gaining access to American nuclear technologies. The president gave him his OK, and Nitze talked to French Ambassador to the United States Hervé Alphand, who suggested he get in touch with French General Gaston Lavaud, who was the key person involved in these matters. Nitze told Lavaud that the United States would be prepared both to help France master the nuclear reaction and to offer other scientific help if only France would make a strong commitment to NATO. Encouraged by his discussion with Nitze, Lavaud returned to Paris to try to convince de Gaulle to accept the American proposal. De Gaulle was highly resistant, the more so since Washington seemed to be of two minds on the matter and sent out conflicting signals. Also, the proposal had not been cleared with the State Department. When a French "shopping list" for purchase of equipment arrived in Washington, it was clear that the French were mainly interested in obtaining information that would considerably facilitate their efforts towards building an independent nuclear deterrent. The State Department "theologians," with Foy Kohler, the assistant secretary of state for European affairs, playing a prominent role, quickly mobilized to torpedo the Lavaud mission and succeeded in doing so. Kennedy rejected Lavaud's requests. Upon their arrival in the United States, the French, to their disappointment and anger, were only offered conventional weapons, which they didn't want to buy.[110]

Despite the skill of the bureaucrats in the State Department in backing the MLF and opposing support for national nuclear deterrents, the ambivalence of the American administration towards helping the French endured. In the fall of 1962, the United States approved the delivery to France of a number of formerly prohibited items on Lavaud's list; these included KC-jet tankers, which gave the French Mirage-IV bombers a wider range of action and thus increased the credibility of the *force de frappe*.[111] In December 1962, the Nassau meeting with Macmillan and the subsequent offer of Polaris to the French on terms similar to that granted the British once again demonstrated the administration's ambiguity towards helping the French, and for that matter, the British. Although the president now seemed to have committed himself to a line of policy that precluded help to independent national nuclear deterrents and supported the MLF, his latent indecision on the matter surfaced when pressing events compelled him to put the agreed line of policy into practice. As will later be shown, the Nassau Agreement between the United Kingdom and the United States was an intricate web of contradictions that attempted to reconcile not only U.S. and British views of the British deterrent but also embodied the parallel and contradictory lines of policy of both the advocates of the MLF and the partisans of help to the French and British deterrents.

Meanwhile, the agreed line of policy was expressed in a number of speeches by top-level American officials. By April 1962, Henry Owen had succeeded in gaining official presidential approval for a paper he wrote that opposed help to the French and reaffirmed the desirability of a multilateral NATO sea-based MRBM force of about two hundred missiles. The paper was subsequently issued as National Security Action Memorandum 147, which retained most of Owen's proposal. The force would be mixed-manned and multilaterally owned and controlled, and Europeans would bear a greater part of the costs. It would be seaborne to avoid some of the problems associated with Norstad's proposal for land-based missiles—mostly political problems associated with vulnerability, visibility on European roads, the dangers of collateral damage if the enemy decided to launch a nuclear attack to destroy the MRBMs, and the difficulty of adequate multilateral control. The force was not intended for "the separate defense of Europe" but was to be committed to the defense of the "entire alliance." The United States was prepared to furnish warheads for the missiles, but they were to remain under

U.S. custody. Under pressure from the Joint Chiefs of Staff, Kennedy refused to heed Owen's advice to grant European allies joint control of American Polaris submarines assigned to NATO. The president nevertheless agreed to leave open the possibility of some kind of control sharing with the allies, the main possibility being the targeting of the force.

By April 1962, the MLF was thus still very much a "Halloween apple" although it was now official policy. The MLF remained low on the list of Kennedy's and McNamara's priorities compared with a much more important agenda item: a new strategy for NATO. When the U.S. Mission to NATO and other European Organizations (USRO) received the authorization to present a number of thoughts on the MLF before the North Atlantic Council in mid-April, it was with the specific recommendation that these thoughts should not be presented as a U.S. blueprint to be blindly followed by Europeans. Mindful of the lessons of the EDC, the president and his advisers thought a misinterpretation of U.S. motives would not only ruin the chances of the MLF but more importantly prevent the United States from selling its views on flexible response to its allies.[112]

ATHENS AND THE MLF

McNamara's secret speech at the Athens NATO meeting in May and the subsequent declassified version of it that he delivered during the commencement exercises at the University of Michigan revealed the new American nuclear policy that had evolved over the past several months within the administration. The policy emphasized the need for central control of the Atlantic Alliance's forces, including those located in Europe, and strongly attacked small national nuclear forces, or most specifically, although it was not mentioned by name, the French *force de frappe,* which was not adequately coordinated or integrated with NATO strategy:

> In particular, relatively weak national nuclear forces with enemy cities as their targets are not likely to be sufficient to perform even the function of deterrence. If they are small, and perhaps vulnerable on the ground or in the air, or inaccurate, a major antagonist can take a variety of measures to counter them. Indeed, if a major antagonist came to believe there was a substantial likelihood of its being used independently, this force would be inviting a preemptive first strike against it. In the event of war, the use of such a force against the cities of a major nuclear power would be tantamount to suicide, whereas its employment against significant military targets would have a negligible effect on the outcome of the

conflict. Meanwhile the creation of a single additional national nuclear force encourages the proliferation of nuclear power with all of its attendant dangers.

In short, then, limited nuclear capabilities, operated independently, are dangerous, expensive, prone to obsolescence, and lacking in credibility as a deterrent.[113]

McGeorge Bundy remembers that "Kennedy approved these two paragraphs." The president had doubts about public debate with de Gaulle, but his high regard for McNamara overcame his reservations, though he did delete a sentence in which McNamara asserted that "in a world of threats, crises, and possibly even accidents 'a small force' appears more likely to deter its owner from standing firm under pressure than to inhibit a potential aggressor."[114] McNamara's desire for a centrally controlled deterrent, the preparatory work that had gone on during the Eisenhower administration and at the beginning of the Kennedy administration, and the strong stance of the "theologians" against helping national deterrents ultimately came together as an official statement of American policy at Athens. In press conferences following the Athens speech, Kennedy echoed the observations of his secretary of defense. Kennedy emphasized the importance of the NATO deterrent as opposed to national deterrents. On 27 June 1962, when asked if the United States had accepted "France's determination to build its own nuclear power," the president answered, "We have always accepted its determination to do so. What we have not agreed to is to participate in the development of a national deterrent. We believe that is inimical to the community interest of the Atlantic Alliance, that it encourages other countries to do the same." This remark was later much quoted and much misunderstood. Bundy notes that contrary to a widely held belief, "what Kennedy thought 'inimical' was not the French effort, but that Americans should participate in it."[115]

Meanwhile, the Athens speech reiterated American willingness to discuss the need for a MRBM force for NATO with its partners, as did later public speeches by other American policymakers in 1962. In August, Robert Schaetzel, the deputy assistant secretary for Atlantic affairs, gave a speech on "The United States and the Common Market" in New Brunswick, Canada. Schaetzel, who always wrote his own speeches,[116] reaffirmed the policy outlined by President Kennedy at Ottawa the previous year. Answering the desire of Europeans to play a greater role in nuclear defense, Schaetzel again indicated the willingness of the United States "to consider with the Europeans the question of whether and, if so, how a sea-based multilateral MRBM force such as the president spoke of in

Ottawa in May 1961 might be organized." But Schaetzel also insisted on specific criteria for American assistance to a multilateral approach to nuclear problems. In line with the policy outlined in the Bowie Report, Schaetzel emphasized that the joint venture "must not discriminate against, or be in favor of, individual countries" for "this would be politically divisive in the extreme." An MLF must also "be so integrated that no country could withdraw its contribution and reconstitute it as a national force." This meant that it "must be multilateral owned, controlled, and manned." In addition, the force "must be closely linked in military planning to other alliance nuclear force [*sic*]."[117]

The insistence on full coordination of the MLF with other deterrent forces of the alliance allayed McNamara's concerns for a centralized control of Atlantic Alliance forces, but it also signaled one of the main defects of the MLF proposal as presented by the United States, namely a fuzziness over what "full coordination of control" meant for the prospects of the MLF as a European endeavor. Charles Bohlen had several discussions with the president on this specific issue. He told him that he felt "the whole scheme was somewhat a fraudulent one" unless the United States was "prepared and to make it clear [they] were prepared . . . someday in the future if and when there was a European authority to be willing to reexamine the control mechanisms even up to and including the possible withdrawal of the United States." Bohlen, whom Kennedy held in high regard and appointed as ambassador to France later that year, apparently succeeded in convincing Kennedy of "the importance of creating the impression that [the United States] were not trying to delude the Europeans by any sort of gimmick or scheme but that [they] would be prepared to reexamine the whole situation" if and when a European authority was successfully organized.[118]

All in all, it was perhaps true that the United States, or at least part of the Kennedy administration, did intend to delude Europeans, but political necessity dictated a course of action that would give Europeans the "impression" that the MLF could someday, somehow lead to a genuine control of their own defense. It was equally important, again for political reasons, to show Europeans "that there was no truth in claims that the Americans would fear a strong Europe as a rival" and equally important to show continued American support for the European integration movement. Commenting on this period more than two decades after the fact, McGeorge Bundy wrote: "Our position in the summer and fall of 1962 was that our foreign policy in general, and our nuclear policy in particular, were consistent with our sympathetic support for what we still saw as the growing unity of Europe."[119]

The expression of Bohlen's concerns quickly translated into Bundy's Copenhagen speech on 27 September 1962, which, according to Bundy, was a very close presentation of the president's own views on the matter and an attempt "to show that [American] opposition to small national forces should not be read as proof of a general American determination to exclude even a new and united Europe from nuclear weapons."[120] Bundy first stressed the essential indivisibility of the nuclear defense of the Atlantic Community while denying assistance to "small, separate, national deterrents." He then assured the General Assembly of the Atlantic Treaty Association that the United States was not only attentive to "the common military needs of NATO" but also to the "special political and psychological forces" that were brought to bear on Europeans. Bundy's speech hardly disguised the fact that the MLF was designed to answer these political and psychological forces, and as such, remained a psychological and political bauble. True, Bundy exclaimed that it "would . . . be wrong to suppose that the reluctance which [the United States felt] with respect to individual, ineffective, and unintegrated forces would be extended automatically to a European force, genuinely unified and multilateral." Yet he also stated that this force must not only be "genuinely unified and multilateral" but also "effectively integrated with [the American] necessarily predominant strength in the whole nuclear defense of the alliance." Bundy then threw in a series of "ifs." All of the "appropriate agencies" of the American government would of course have to be fully consulted and give their approval to any "possible arrangements for assistance and cooperation." Then, Europe must decide how much it was prepared to disburse for the MLF. "Here, as elsewhere," said Bundy, "we run the risk of seeming to interfere whether we speak or keep silent." Bundy nevertheless specified that the United States did not "wish to press for a European answer" when in its "own honest judgment" NATO might "serve as well or better." Finally, Bundy could not agree more with the opinion American allies had expressed at the meeting—that the matter needed "time for careful thought and study" and that the current strength and forward planning of the alliance gave it plenty of time. If the MLF turned out to be more than a political bauble after all, if Europeans demonstrated a need and desire for "a genuinely multilateral European deterrent, integrated with [that of the United States] in NATO"; Bundy concluded that they would at least not find "a veto from the administration in the United States which stands in its way."[121]

Time was of the essence: by late 1961 a reassessment of Soviet missile strength relative to that of the United States had proved Democratic fears of a "missile-gap" a hoax and revealed a strategic superiority for the West. But most of Kennedy's advisers also recognized the necessity of maintaining this superiority. Hence an increase in military expenditures. In 1960, the Eisenhower defense budget had amounted to $43,685,000,000. By 1963, the Kennedy administration asked Congress to sanction a $51,640,000,000 defense budget.[122] Despite the president's initial preoccupation with balancing the budget, Keynesians such as Walter Heller, chairman of the Council of Economic Advisers, had by then succeeded in convincing Kennedy that a high growth rate sustained by stimuli such as tax cuts, which implied a "deliberate unbalancing of the budget," would in time produce enough revenue to maintain American solvency; growth would lead to solvency, not the other way around, as Eisenhower had argued.[123] Whereas Eisenhower had tried to constrain military spending, the Kennedy administration banked on a high growth rate to finance the new strategy of flexible response.

Old-new economics, the reassessment of Soviet capabilities, and the perceived necessity for centralization of control in turn persuaded the administration that the nuclear deterrent, in which the United States played a dominant role, was in no need of increased participation by Europeans for quite some time. By the end of 1962, the agreed line of policy of the administration was that the United States did "not believe [a] European role [in] nuclear defense urgent for military purposes since [the] present and programmed nuclear forces [were] adequate [for the] foreseeable future."[124] Hence McGeorge Bundy's repeated insistence at Copenhagen that a European force was no urgent matter, although the executive branch of the American government would not stand in the way of the organization of such a force *if* Europeans mustered sufficient resources and agreement among themselves to organize it and *if* Congress gave the necessary authorizations for the release of information that would help Europeans in such an endeavor. At the November 1962 NATO Parliamentarians Conference in Paris, George Ball rephrased some of the points made by Bundy at Copenhagen. "From a strictly military standpoint," he said, the United States did not view a European nuclear contribution to the alliance as "an urgent need." Yet, if Europeans indicated a desire to create a truly multilateral MRBM force "fully coordinated with the other deterrent forces" of NATO, the United States would give it "serious consideration." To maintain the spirit of the Atlantic partnership, the United States could not "dictate how such a force should be manned, financed, or organized." It could, however, make information available to its allies "with respect to the characteristics and capabilities" of the MLF. Yet to become the equal partner of the United States, Europe needed to progress further on the road to unity. NATO would then become the "military expression" of the Atlantic partnership. Working together, a united Europe and the United States would "achieve the indivisibility of response—the indivisibility of command and direction—that is the indispensable element of an effective defense in the nuclear age."[125] Both the Copenhagen and the Paris speeches had in common a lack of urgency for a European nuclear defense effort, a concern that such an effort should be fully integrated within NATO, and an insistence that the creation of a European force was something for Europeans to decide on their own. Once again the shadow of the EDC loomed behind this nonprescriptive attitude.[126] Throughout most of the Kennedy and Johnson administrations, unequivocal statements *à la Dulles,* urging Europeans to unite or else, were carefully avoided by most American policymakers: discretion and tact became the aspired virtues in addressing American policy towards Europe.

TRADING MONEY FOR BOMBS

On the issue of control of the MLF, the Ball and Bundy speeches sketched out the possibility of a European deterrent integrated with that of the United States. Bundy and Ball did not explicitly mention a European-controlled force, but their statements could be carried to their logical conclusion: a European-owned force, if it ever came into being, would have to be controlled solely by Europeans. Walt Rostow had no difficulty in saying this to representatives of the United Kingdom in a visit to Washington shortly before the Bundy speech.[127] As for the president, by July 1962, the month of the famous Interdependence Speech, he had apparently decided that he "would have no trouble transferring the special nuclear relationship from Britain to Europe" and that "it was perfectly viable in the Congress—if the British were to get out and the French were to get out—for [him] to make a special relationship with a Europe—if that unified Europe were really to share some of the economic, political, and military burdens around the world." This, noted the president, would be "a politically viable deal." But he couldn't "do it without [the Europeans] carrying more of the burden," and he couldn't "sell bombs to individual countries."[128]

On 2 July Rostow had a meeting with the president. He had previously sent him a memorandum that strongly argued the case for "enlarged responsibilities" on the part of Europeans to "ease [American] immediate balance of payments problems." Rostow proposed that Europeans do more "(a) with respect to aid to the underdeveloped areas; (b) to widen European capital markets to take some of the heat off the New York market; (c) to increase and systematize their foreign exchange contribution to compensate for U.S. military outlays undertaken in the common interest of the Atlantic alliance." All of these moves, indicated Rostow, "would fit naturally [into] an enlarged nuclear role for Europe."[129] While discussing Rostow's memo, the president agreed that this was indeed what the United States wanted its European partners to do, but how one could guide them in that direction was another question. Kennedy concluded that the "only leverage" the United States "really [had] was [its] nuclear knowledge and capability." "In the 1950s," said the president (still according to Walt Rostow's testimony), "they (the Europeans) spent their time making money: we spent our time making bombs. A partnership, in the end, is going to involve an exchange between their money and our bombs." But the president thought that such a partnership, namely the transfer of the special relationship from the United Kingdom to the new Europe, would not be possible before Europe united. "I am the president of the U.S.," said Kennedy, "but who is the president for Europe?"[130] Rostow pointed out that the partnership would only become a reality over time and "would gradually engage [Europeans] in the nuclear business; simultaneously some nuclear responsibility, the passage of time, and the use of their wealth could lead them to assume increased global responsibility; meanwhile, hopefully, they would move towards unity." In short, said Rostow, the job of the United States was to lead Europeans "in a process looking towards partnership rather than to strike a quick deal."[131] That same day, on 2 July, President Kennedy told Rostow he had to give a speech two days later, on a Wednesday. Since he didn't "want to talk about our Revolution much," would Rostow "draft up something" and "get it over to Ted Sorensen that same day along the lines [they'd] been talking?" Rostow later recalled:

> It was a morning to remember. He (the President) was cheerful about the Mexican trip (from which he had just returned). As we talked Caroline was going up and down the lawn on her pony. His engagements didn't seem tight. There was a leisurely quality to the talk—one of the best conversations I had with him as President. He was almost playful in sharpening up the links between bombs, widened European responsibility and European unity. And so I went back and got Henry Owen and we drafted something. Henry cleared it with EUR (the European Bureau in the State Department); and we got it over to Ted at the White House on Monday afternoon.

Here Rostow and Owen's role ended; Bundy and others at the White House and in the State Department then contributed their input. It is important to note that the president, if Rostow's testimony is correct, did play quite an active role in initiating and thinking up the main lines of the Interdependence Speech. By the summer and fall of 1962, the line of policy that the Europeanists had been advocating since the beginning of Kennedy's term in office and during the interregnum seemed to very nearly match the president's own thinking on the matter, although the president remained more of a pragmatist.

On 4 July 1962 the president delivered his famous Interdependence Speech at Independence Hall, Philadelphia. "We do not regard a strong and united Europe," said Kennedy, "as a rival but as a partner." There followed a description of the role the United States government had in mind for the new Europe:

> We believe that a united Europe will be capable of playing a greater role in the common defense, of responding more generously to the needs of poorer nations, of joining with the United States and others in lowering trade barriers, resolving problems of currency and commodities, and developing coordinated policies in all other economic, diplomatic, and political areas. We see in such a Europe a partner with whom we could deal on a basis of full equality in all the great and burdensome tasks of building and defending a community of free nations.
>
> It would be premature at this time to do more than to indicate the high regard with which we view the formation of this partnership. The first order of business is for our European friends to go forward in forming the more perfect union which will some day make this partnership possible.[132]

Kennedy was deliberately vague on the role Europeans would play in the "common defense" of the alliance, for he wanted to avoid giving the impression that the MLF was an urgent matter, and above all, that the United States was pressing it on its allies. In addition, like Robert McNamara, McGeorge Bundy, most of the American Europeanists, and Jean Monnet, the president did not believe in emphasizing the nuclear issue as an instrument of European unity at that specific point in time. He reasoned that such a course of action would have consequences detrimental to the negotiations for British entry into the Common Market. De Gaulle's recent pronouncements had amply demonstrated that there was every reason to be worried about linking the nuclear question to the Common Market negotiations and insisting on integration schemes, be it at the European or at the Atlantic level.

On 15 May 1962, de Gaulle had triggered the resignation of five of his Christian Democratic ministers by outlining his concept of Europe, which was antithetical to that of the Monnet group. Arguing the case for a *force de frappe,* de Gaulle also launched a nearly direct attack on the role of the United States as the "federator" of the new Europe. The next day de Gaulle had a conversation with American Ambassador Gavin. The general remarked that "he had been kind to [the United States] in his press conference." He then went on to say that the United States "should not be mixed up in Western European difficulties and should keep itself apart only bringing its weight to bear in case of necessity." To de Gaulle, "it would suffice for Western Europe to know that if war were to start it could rely on [the] US."[133] Kennedy's rebuttal was quick to come. On 17 May, the American president also gave a press conference. Aiming his comments at the general, Kennedy said the United States did "not believe in a series of national deterrents" but rather that "the NATO deterrent to which the United States has committed itself so heavily is—provides—very adequate protection." As for de Gaulle's observation that the United States should stay out of the affairs of Europe, Kennedy's answer was even more direct: "We cannot and do not take any European ally for granted and no one in Europe should take us for granted either . . . American public opinion has turned away from isolation but its faith must not be shattered."[134] The following day Kennedy had a top secret message cabled to Gavin in which he requested that he tell de Gaulle that the United States was quite unprepared "to accept the notion that we should stay out of all of Europe's affairs while remaining ready to defend her if war should come." "We cannot give this kind of blank check," he wrote. "In Berlin and Germany, in particular, all major questions of policy relate directly to the confrontations of the Soviet Union and therefore to questions of war and peace. General European policy in turn relates directly and sharply to the problem of Germany. We cannot and will not stand apart from these questions as long as our strength and will are committed to the defense of Europe against any Soviet attack." The president ended on a menacing note: "If Europe were ever to be organized so as to leave us outside, from these great issues of policy and defense, it would become most difficult for us to sustain our present guarantee against Soviet aggression." Directing all of his furor against de Gaulle's and Adenauer's efforts to organize Europe without the United States around a Franco-German rapprochement, Kennedy added: "We shall not hesitate to make this point to the Germans if they show signs of accepting any idea of a Bonn-Paris axis. General de Gaulle really cannot have both our military presence and our diplomatic absence, and you should make this point with emphasis."[135]

De Gaulle's 15 May conference, and the American reaction to it, fore-shadowed de Gaulle's veto of British entry into the Common Market and the French refusal in January 1963 to participate in any kind of "integrated" nuclear scheme with the United States on the same basis as the British. By that time, Kennedy had given priority to "strengthening the multilateral concept," not so much as a means of giving Europeans more control over their own defense but rather as a means of bolstering NATO and of increasing the dependence of Europeans on the United States. The MLF, he thought, would "strengthen [American] influence in Europe" and give the United States "the power to guide Europe and keep it strong."[136] Thus the president viewed the MLF as a possible political counterweight to the *force de frappe,* which he considered mainly as a French political device destined to give France first-rank status in world councils and a leading role in the new Europe. To him, the multilateral concept could serve as a palliative for British entry into the Common Market and as a vehicle for American influence in Western Europe. Rather than insisting on "interdependence," as he had publicly done in Philadelphia, behind the scenes Kennedy held quite a different discourse: here "dependence" and integration were the key words.

The MLF meant different things to different members of the Kennedy administration. To the president it became primarily a means of cementing Western unity and of maintaining American influence in Europe. To some Europeanists, it became a means of strengthening the Atlantic Alliance, reducing the pressures of proliferation by giving Germans and Italians alike some kind of participation in managing nuclear weapons, and an educational tool to coach those Europeans who did not possess a nuclear capability on the responsibilities of nuclear sharing, while also encouraging them to move towards unity. The Europeanists envisaged that the MLF might lead "by pragmatic stages to a European force directed by a single executive."[137] A 16 November 1962 document from the State Department made it clear, however, that if there was to be "European participation in nuclear defense," this participation "must be multilateral, sea borne in character and fully coordinated with other deterrent forces of the Alliance." Such a force "could be a European force (e.g., European Community) or a force including both European and non-European NATO members." Thus, instead of being "a strictly European nuclear force," it could also be "an evolving transatlantic" force.[138] This last possibility was the preference of George Ball, whose main concern was to suppress the proliferation of nuclear weapons. The fewer those who controlled them the better.[139]

To Ball, the MLF was more of a device to help Europeans progress towards unity than an end in itself and a possible step towards giving

Europeans real control over nuclear weapons. But Ball's aversion to nuclear proliferation conflicted with his commitment to European unification and the necessity to demonstrate to Europeans that the United States was in fact sincere in its desire to encourage Europe to become an equal partner. In the wake of de Gaulle's January 1963 press conference, and mainly intended to counter the general's disruptive action vis-à-vis both European unity and NATO, Ball recommended leaving "open—in the fields of nuclear policy and political consultation—the possibility of arrangements in which an effectively unified Europe would play a larger role than will be possible so long as these arrangements must run between the US and separate European nations." Significantly, he added: "In nuclear policy this means making more explicit our eventual willingness to consider allowing a united Europe to buy out the US share in the multilateral mixed manned force." Yet Ball also cautioned that the force must be "so integrated, through mixed manning and other means, as to preclude national withdrawal or any national use of elements of the force."[140] Mainly for political reasons, policymakers in the State Department and the White House generally adopted a similar attitude of tentatively holding out the possibility of transfer of control to Europeans—but at a very distant date and only if it should be found necessary to do so. The 16 November document indicated that if the Europeans decided that they wanted an MLF, the "United States administration would then take up [the] question [of] whether it should ask for Congressional action on [the] control of warheads (McMahon Act)." However, continued the document, "this question [is a] long way off. In first instance, [we] must know what the force would look like, whether the United States would be in or out, where the custody of weapons would lie etc."[141]

In November 1962, the MLF still remained a relatively low-key concept for the president and most of his advisers, including the Europeanists. By January 1963, the MLF had surfaced to the top of the list of presidential priorities. The concept was now needed to counteract de Gaulle's assaults against the Atlantic partnership among equals, maintain American influence in Europe, and strengthen the alliance. Also some believed that it could possibly serve as a means of progressing towards an integrated Europe linked in close partnership with the United States; a Europe that "would avoid the destructive national rivalries of the past." Contrary to de Gaulle's concept of a Europe based on the nation-state, the MLF was specifically directed against the nation-state. De Gaulle's Europe was not Kennedy's, nor, for that matter, was it Monnet's. The general would make this amply clear at his January 1963 press conference.

9

Conflicting World Views:
De Gaulle and the Americans

The Kennedy team had adopted the main features of its policy towards Europe by the end of 1961 and sought to put the Atlantic partnership of equals into practice. The administration, while advocating equality and partnership, simultaneously sought to maintain American leadership in Western Europe not only in the military field, where "interdependence" and "integration" dominated American thinking, but also in the economic and political spheres. It was one thing to ask European allies to share the economic and political burdens of the United States; it was quite another to renounce American hegemony and guidance in Europe—for at least the foreseeable future—until Europe became truly politically unified. While the United States sought to remain first among equals in the Atlantic Community, de Gaulle sought to become first among equals on the European continent. Kennedy much admired and respected the French general but was often puzzled "why so obviously a great man took such incomprehensible and petty positions."[1] Yet the positions that the general adopted, notably during his 15 May and 14 January conferences, were not so incomprehensible nor were they unpredictable. They originated in a conception of the relative roles of the United States, Europe, and France in world councils that clearly differed from the proposed Atlantic partnership among equals.

Well before Kennedy took office, de Gaulle had outlined the main tenets of his "grand design" for Europe and France in his memoirs and public statements. Yet few in the Kennedy administration, and more surprisingly, in the State Department, were thoroughly familiar with the general's writings;[2] those who were, including the president, did not believe he would act so soon upon his statements. Hence their surprise when the general did in fact do so. The consistent optimism of Monnet, Kohnstamm, and their collaborators about the prospects of British entry into the Common Market and the other elements of their grand design for Europe contributed to encouraging a similar mood among the American Europeanists. The discussions over the political organization of Europe proposed by the successive Fouchet plans and the negotiations for British entry into the Common Market, became battlegrounds for divergent approaches to European unity, and more generally, for the role of the United States relative to Europe. We shall not attempt here to review the intricacies of the negotiations for British entry or of the Fouchet plans; these have been discussed in great detail elsewhere.[3] Rather we shall focus on the world perceptions of some key participants, briefly review some of the concrete manifestations of these views, and analyze the reactions of the Kennedy team to specific moves, statements, or proposals which ran counter to, or were sympathetic to, the American blueprint for Europe.

Of all the challengers to the American design for Europe, de Gaulle was the most outspoken. His Europe was based on the nation-state and the primacy in Europe of what he considered the most important nation-state of all: France. Since World War II, one of the main reasons for United States support for European integration had been the desire to prevent the specter of nationalism from reemerging on the Continent. Very much a part of the tradition that had evolved since the war, the Europeanists in the Kennedy administration hailed the obsolescence of the nation-state as a positive development on the European scene. Some among them hoped it would facilitate the benevolent leadership of the United States in Europe, which would be made easier by the absence of contenders for European hegemony.[4] The Europeanists advocated the suppression of the British nuclear deterrent and a hands-off policy towards the French deterrent as a means of eradicating attempts by these two nations to gain first-rank political status on the European continent as well as in world councils. Not all of the members of the Kennedy team agreed with them—particularly those who sought to help the French build their own deterrent. Like Paul Nitze, Carl Kaysen, one of the most influential *éminences grises* of the White House, leaned towards helping the French and giving them equal status with the British.[5] President Kennedy, despite public pronouncements in which he favored a united Europe, felt that European nationalism would remain a reality to be reckoned with for some years to come. De Gaulle certainly brought this point home. Unlike Europeanists, and for that matter, Jean Monnet, the French general based his vision of Europe on the continued preeminence of the nation-state,

and vigorously combatted integrationist and federalist schemes that threatened to dilute its authority.

The French initiative for a political Europe, the Fouchet plans, while
sincerely directed towards the organization of political cooperation between the six EEC countries,[6] was also intended to limit the authority of
the European Community to only economic and technical activities,
thereby stripping it of any political ambitions. De Gaulle made this clear
to Adenauer during a meeting of the two men at Rambouillet at the end of
July 1960. The general "complained about the activities of the Commission
of the European Community" and pointed out that "he had indeed great
respect for Hallstein's qualifications, but that he could not accept that this
Commission accomplish political actions that belonged to the competence
of the nations that constituted the European Economic Community."
Deeply critical of the pretensions of the EEC to intervene in African affairs
and to allocate development aid without asking the individual governments
of the EEC, de Gaulle declared "he had long been opposed to supranational
organizations." For him there was only one such organization in Europe:
the Coal and Steel Community. The other organizations had "elected
themselves to this status (machten sich selbst dazu)." As he saw it, the
problem was that "these other organizations stood *de jure* under the
authority of the Council of Ministers, but *de facto* took decisions on their
own." He "did not in any way advocate that these organizations be
eliminated, especially the EEC, . . . but they were to be reformed so as to
be under the authority of the governments." As far as the EEC and Euratom
were concerned, it was "a pure question of organization." This was not the
case with the ECSC, where "the supranational element was anchored in the
treaty and would be hard to change." Adenauer let himself be swayed by
de Gaulle and agreed with him that the other Communities must not be
allowed "to develop into superstates," since they did not hold the ultimate
political responsibility. To counteract the transformation of the Communities into superstates, de Gaulle proposed the initiation of a "new phase of
the organization of Europe in the form of an organized cooperation of states
in the economic, political and cultural fields, as in the field of defense."
The heads of government would meet every three months or so, and their
meetings would be prepared by commissions to which employees and
experts would be appointed. A single European Assembly would complete
this "organized cooperation" at a later stage. Unlike Monnet, de Gaulle did
not favor direct elections to the assembly, rather, faithful to his predilection
for the preeminence of the nation-state, the general preferred to have the
assembly made out of "delegations from national parliaments," and he

further insisted that the assembly was to possess a "consultative character" only.[7]

On 5 September 1960, during one of his periodic press conferences, de Gaulle publicly outlined his blueprint for Europe. He emphasized that states must be the ultimate reality. Attempting to "build something that would efficiently encourage action and receive the approval of the people outside and beyond the nation states," was, he said, "nothing but a 'chimère.'" "It is true," continued the general, that "pending the time when the problem of Europe can be tackled as a whole, it has been possible to set up certain bodies of a more or less extra-national character. These bodies have their technical value, but do not, and cannot, exert authority and hence effective political influence."[8] Since authority rested with the nation-state, de Gaulle proposed to organize "the periodic cooperation of Western Europe . . . in the political, economic, cultural and defense fields." Very much after the pattern he had outlined to Adenauer, de Gaulle advocated periodic meetings of heads of states and the creation of preparatory commissions that would each be competent in a particular field and remain under the authority of governments. He also proposed the creation of an assembly and a "European referendum that would give this new start for Europe the characteristics of popular adhesion and intervention that were necessary to legitimize it."[9]

On the whole, reactions to the September press conference, both in France and abroad, were highly critical. Not only did de Gaulle seek to deprive the EEC of some of its authority but his proposal for organizing periodic European meetings on defense matters at the highest level, in effect outside of NATO, appeared to some to pose a threat to the cohesion of the Atlantic Alliance. On this last point, Adenauer and de Gaulle were at odds. During the Rambouillet conversations, de Gaulle had made no secret of his opinion of NATO, which he characterized as "a United States 'filiale' on the Continent." He even spoke of the possibility that France might some day leave NATO. Adenauer agreed with the general that some kind of reform of NATO was necessary but cautioned him against giving the impression that "Europe wanted to detach itself from the United States." This would, warned Adenauer, have the effect of strengthening American isolationism. He particularly worried about recent pronouncements by presidential candidate Kennedy that revealed a strong tendency towards adopting isolationist positions.[10]

In the aftermath of this conference, in October, Adenauer revealed the extent of his disagreement during a conversation with French Prime Minister Debré. After asking Debré to please "consider the following observation (sich doch einmal folgenden Gedanken durch den Kopf gehen . . . lassen)," he continued, "the closer the European states were linked with the United States, the stronger their political positions were at home. Even though one gave up some degree of military authority to integration, there was still much to be gained through integration since it reinforced authority at home." Adenauer further insisted that every West European was well aware of the fact that they could not survive "without the United States against an opponent such as the Soviet Union that was so well provided with nuclear weapons." "Should it be possible," continued Adenauer, "to find some kind of integration that would be acceptable for Europe," every European would "feel secure and be grateful to this government because of this." While agreeing with de Gaulle on the necessity of organizing political cooperation and of stripping the EEC of its possible political spillovers, Adenauer remained an integrationist in the field of defense. This was true, perhaps, more by necessity than by inclination. Some of Adenauer's earlier pronouncements, much before Rambouillet and before the Suez cease-fire, showed that Adenauer was also thinking of asserting Europe's independence from the United States in the field of defense. On 25 September 1956, he told his Brussels audience that European countries could not "fully develop their entire strength for their own benefit and that of mankind if they continue[d] to find their salvation and their security exclusively under the patronage of the United States." Dependency upon the United States must not become a "permanent condition . . . because it would cause the energies of Europe to wither and because surely the United States will not be inclined to give Europe an unreasonable amount of assistance permanently."[11] Yet then, as in 1960, Adenauer's desire for European maturity conflicted with the necessity, for security reasons, for Germany to strongly anchor the United States to Western Europe.

Not quite a month after his 5 September conference, de Gaulle regretted having discussed NATO "in such a frank way" with Adenauer. In a list of secret directives to Debré, he wrote that he had "thought [Adenauer] to be more truly European than he in fact was."[12] In the same list, the general, while deploring unfavorable reactions to his proposals by the Five, also showed confidence that, no matter what their criticisms were, "the Europe of cooperation was now launched." He felt that the best tactic to abate opposition to his proposals was to temporize and to avoid creating the impression that they "were directly aimed at [the Communities], or the treaties that instituted them." De Gaulle then further showed his hand: "If we succeed in bringing the Europe of cooperation among states into existence, the Communities will *ipso facto* be relegated to the place that belong to them." The general also stated that, "it is only if we do not succeed in bringing the political Europe into existence that we will directly attack the first fruits of integration."[13] The 14 January 1963 press conference, as well as later moves against both the EEC and NATO, demonstrated that the general had every intention of putting this threat into practice.

Charles de Gaulle's grand design for Europe rested on several premises, which he conveniently outlined in his memoirs. First of all came the primacy of the nation-state and of France. Second, two main fears: the fear of "the rise of a new Reich that might again threaten the safety"[14] of France; and the fear of being dominated by those whom de Gaulle called, quite to their surprise, the "Anglo-Saxons." To counter the first fear, de Gaulle sought to channel German energies into a Franco-German partnership, which he hoped to dominate and which he considered as the starting point for European-wide cooperation. In December 1961, commenting on the opposition that he had encountered (from Belgium and the Netherlands) to his proposals for a political Europe, de Gaulle told Adenauer that "once France and Germany were in agreement, the other [European nations] must then follow willy-nilly."[15] As for the second threat, de Gaulle intended to "persuade the states along the Rhine, the Alps, and the Pyrenees to form a political, economic, and strategic bloc; to establish this bloc as one of the three world powers and, should it become necessary, as the arbiter between the Soviet and American camps."[16] Inasmuch as the European Communities threatened to rob the nation-state of some of its authority and to become subject to the influence of the United States (the non-European federator) notably through the entry of an American Trojan Horse (Britain), the general could be expected to interfere in their development and to oppose British membership.

De Gaulle's reservations towards British entry into the Common Market—Macmillan officially applied for membership on 31 July 1961—were partly rooted in his fear of Anglo-Saxon domination. Memories from the war contributed to de Gaulle's phobia, which was perceptively analyzed by some members of the Kennedy team. White House Assistant Arthur Schlesinger called attention to Churchill's remark to the general in June 1944: "Here is something that you should know: whenever we have to choose between Europe and the open sea, we shall always choose the open sea. Whenever I have to choose between you and Roosevelt, I shall always choose Roosevelt."[17] In his 1961 memorandum proposing "A New Approach to France," Henry Owen of the Policy Planning Staff sought to illustrate de Gaulle's uneasiness towards "the Anglo-American combine" by referring to the general's memoirs, in which he spoke "bitterly of how this combination operated in 1944-45." One sentence particularly attracted Owen's attention: "America, Russia, and England," said de Gaulle, "were determining the great issues . . . Everything occurred as if our allies were intent on excluding France from their plans. We could not actually put an end to this banishment, but we could make it unendurable to those inflicting it on us." Owen drew the conclusion that this was still de Gaulle's grand design. "His boycott of NATO, his national nuclear program, his obstructive posture in non-NATO areas—all [were] designed to make unendurable the monopoly which he conceive[d] the U.S. and U.K. to have established over the resolution of issues of decisive moment to France."[18]

De Gaulle's and American Europeanists' grand design conflicted. Europeanists sought to emasculate the French and the British nuclear deterrents and bring all European nations down to the same level. Some conceived of an independent Europe but only so long as it was subject to the benevolent supervision of the United States within the wider framework of the Atlantic Alliance. Institutions such as the OECD and NATO were specifically designed to ensure that the partnership between equals would remain a partnership and to guard against the possibility that Europe might some day opt for an independent venture. De Gaulle's grand design was to break free from an overbearing mentor and assert French and European independence. In a brilliant analysis, Stanley Hoffmann has noted that the general intended to emancipate European nations in order to deprive the Superpowers of some of their power and thus allow other powers, such as, say, China, Japan, and a united Europe, to emerge, independent from American tutelage.[19] Such a distribution of power, thought de Gaulle, would ultimately give a better chance for détente with the Soviet Union and would better allow for German reunification. While "the Russians could never be expected to make concessions so long as they were faced with a monolithic bloc under American command," they "*could* be expected, some day, to accept the restoration of a European order liberated from both hegemonies so long as their loosened grip on their satellites was shown to be compatible with security from Germany and was compensated by a parallel loosening of America's grip."[20] De Gaulle also banked on the fact that in the near future Europe would grow "even more powerful than America"; her "industrial, political and cultural power would overcome American influence and Europe would then become the first element that the Russians needed." But, he added, "one must not allow the Russians to invade Europe prior to this development."[21] To put it another way, "Western Europe must come into existence" before any kind of settlement could be found with the Soviet Union, for how could there be any balance in Europe if "a poor France, a poor Germany, a poor Italy faced an enormous Russia?"[22] Accordingly, the Communities would fulfill a useful function so long as they contributed to the prosperity of France and that of

Western Europe, thereby enhancing the power of Western Europe vis-à-vis the Soviet Union and improving chances for an eventual peace settlement. But if the EEC threatened, by expanding its sphere of authority to the political realm, to become a superstate in effect controlled by the United States and to rob France of its political leadership on the Continent, its development was to be severely checked, and if necessary, stopped. While Europeanists claimed to be taking the long view, de Gaulle's historical perspective spanned decades, if not centuries. De Gaulle, however, failed to understand the importance and the nature of both political and economic factors in the eventual downfall of communism in the Soviet Union and its satellites. In December 1961, the general told Adenauer that he "actually did not believe that communism would last for ever. Even the communists would change, just as France would change. These were just historical moments, never eternity. The Soviets were first of all Russians. Some day, this large Russia would face an enormous Asia, especially China. There was no place in communism for two sovereigns. China was a candidate for the sovereignty. When the time came for the two sovereigns to compete, it would become necessary for Russia—that was in the natural order of things—to find an agreement with the West."[23] But, for these sweeping changes to come about, Western Europe must be allowed to exist independently from both the hegemony of the United States and the Soviet Union. Partly because of his war memories, de Gaulle was inclined to lump the British with the Americans and to be suspicious of their motives for wanting to buy a membership into the new Europe. If Britain did in fact act as an American "Trojan Horse" within the councils of the new Europe, this Europe would never wean itself from the United States or adopt its own policies in the economic and political, as well as defense, fields. And, as a result, long-term prospects for a real détente with the East would be ruined.

Such was not the line of thinking of the Kennedy administration. Kennedy's grand design for Europe rested on two important premises: the necessity for the West to form a common and cohesive front against communist expansion; and the imperative to maintain American leadership in Europe to ensure that European resources would be channelled towards meeting the "common tasks"[24] of the "free world." Kennedy preferred a Western bloc, encompassing an American senior partner and a European junior partner, to a third force Europe led by France. Only through Western cohesion, believed American leaders, could one negotiate with the Soviet Union. This was also the position of Jean Monnet and of many members of what Walt Rostow called the "Atlantic Establishment," although they preferred to think of the new Europe as an equal partner.

On 26 June 1962, more than one month after de Gaulle's press conference on 15 May and shortly before Kennedy delivered his famous 4 July speech, Monnet's Action Committee issued a common declaration that specifically sought to respond to one of de Gaulle's most preoccupying accusations. The integrationists, the general had said in thinly veiled terms, favored the creation of a politically amorphous Europe, which the United States would only be too happy to provide with the political guidance that it lacked. The Action Committee attempted to counter de Gaulle's accusation by emphasizing, very much like the American administration, the need for Western cohesion in order to negotiate peace with the East and the growing role for Europe in the partnership between equals: "The Action Committee for the United States of Europe . . . *considers that European economic and political unity including England and the establishment of a partnership between equals between Europe and the United States, are alone able to consolidate the West and to thereby create the conditions of peace between West and East.*"[25]

American support for European unity was qualified by the two premises of Western cohesion and American leadership. After de Gaulle's press conference of January 1963, in which he vetoed British entry, refused the offer of American help to the French deterrent on the same terms as the British, and generally rejected all of the basic tenets of Kennedy's grand design, the administration became engaged in a general reevaluation of the Atlantic partnership strategy. George Ball contributed a carefully worded and structured paper that held that the objectives of European unity and Atlantic partnership were still valid and proceeded to propose ways of defending them. European unity occupied a central position in Ball's grand design for Europe and the West. One of the key American objectives in Europe, he insisted, had "always been to deny Europe to Communist control." This objective had impelled the United States to propose the Marshall Plan and NATO. As Europe recovered its prosperity and grew in political stability under the military protection of Uncle Sam, the United States thought of a second objective: to ask Europe to combine its resources with those of the United States "to serve the whole free world." Yet this desirable objective could not be fulfilled unless Europe progressed further on the path towards unity, for "only a united Europe was likely to generate the confidence, the sense of responsibility, and the resources required to project its power outside of Europe." George Ball's design for Europe thus contained a strong burden-sharing element and was directed beyond the Atlantic partnership towards the larger community of the free world. Previous pronouncements by key members of the Kennedy team, including McGeorge

Bundy, likewise stressed the need for going beyond the confines of a Europe-first policy and showing interest in the problems of developing nations.[26] Yet—despite the avowed concern of the New Frontier for extra-European areas—the vision of the Europeanists, and much of the Kennedy administration, remained Eurocentric. This was Under Secretary Bowles's main complaint against the administration. Eurocentrism, though, and the unflagging support of most of the Kennedy team for European integration, did not imply blindness toward the possibility that a united Europe would not conform to the American grand design.

In principle, a united Europe could enhance Western security notably by providing resources for common concerns and by sidetracking West German aspirations for reunification through bilateral deals with the Soviet Union.[27] This had been a consistent line of argument in support of European integration since the outset of the Cold War. But George Ball harked back to an even earlier trend of thought that was strongly reminiscent of American consideration of the implications of a united Europe for American interests during World War II. The United States, he wrote, then "recognized that an integrated Europe would pose dangers, if it struck off on its own, seeking to play a role independent of the U.S."[28] The United States, continued Ball, had sought "to minimize the chances of such a split, and to ensure that the resources of a uniting Europe were used to best effect" by attempting to "strengthen the instruments of partnership between Europe and the US, e.g., NATO and OECD, at the same time as [the United States] promoted and encouraged the process of European integration."[29] In other words, the United States had sought to control the development of Europe by using "Atlantic" instruments. This was also consistent with the conclusions reached by American thinkers during World War II. European unity could be expected to make a great contribution to the world of free nations—whether this meant free from Nazism or communism—if it were controlled by a larger framework: the United Nations. When this failed within the context of the Cold War, American policymakers cast their hopes on NATO, which thus had the double function of strengthening the West and ensuring the development of a Western Europe compatible with American interests.

In the early 1960s the rhetoric changed, but the underlying objective remained the same. The United States needed what the Acheson Report called "a spacious environment for freedom."[30] This environment could not be maintained if Europe struck off on its own and started courting the Soviet Union. The Atlantic partnership idea was rooted in the perceived need to prevent a situation from developing in which the United States became isolated, a lonely giant in a hostile environment that did not share its outlook on the world economically, politically, and morally. Even after de Gaulle's bombshell, wrote Ball, the goal of a U.S.-European partnership was definitely still in the interest of the United States. The United States could not accept "the prospect of the US and Europe going their separate ways," for Europe might then fall prey to communism and no longer contribute to the sharing of common burdens with the United States. The advent of the nuclear age made it all the more essential for the United States to "have a voice and play a stabilizing role in European affairs."[31] Thus Ball, while promoting European unity, advocated Atlantic partnership with a view towards monitoring the development of the new Europe by keeping it solidly anchored to the United States. The United States had entered the war in order to have a voice in shaping the postwar peace, and American policymakers still had every intention of making this voice heard in Europe as well as in the rest of the world. The stakes were nothing less than the maintenance of "an environment in which free societies [could] survive and flourish."[32] For this the United States needed the resources and unconditional support of its Western European "cousins" with whom it shared common values. McGeorge Bundy said as much in a "trial balloon" speech before the Economic Club of Chicago in December 1961, in which he hailed the prospect of "a new Europe, with the economic strength, the military self-confidence, and the political unity of a true great power." Even though "great states" did not "usually rejoice in the emergence of other great states," the United States welcomed the emergence of a European power that would join forces with them against "Communist expansion." Beyond that, Americans needed their European "cousins" to defend a common civilization. Cousins "by history and culture, by language and religion" as well as by a sense "of human and social purpose," North Americans and Western Europeans were progressing hand in hand towards the El Dorado of the "age of everyman—the age in which a happy combination of work and leisure, of social activity and individual responsibility, [could] offer to all citizens what the greatest of past societies ha[d] achieved only for a few."[33]

The assumption of a common outlook on life and of shared moral and religious principles were determining factors in American support for the emergence of a new Europe. It is these values that the United States intended to spread to the rest of the world. Thinking in moral and religious terms, American policymakers sought to build a common front against the ungodly forces of communism and nondemocratic societies. Any rift in this common front was seen as a threat to the kind of peace the United States had sought to secure since World War II. In order to build this peace, the United States needed European moral support as well as European resources. As far as this last imperative was concerned, the Europeanists argued that "only a united Europe [was] likely to generate adequate resources."[34]

American backing for the European Common Market had economic as well as political motives. The Bundy speech emphasized that although "the Marshall Plan [had been] an economic undertaking" since "its immediate object was the economic recovery of the participating nations," its "larger purpose . . . was political—it was the maintenance of freedom in Western Europe against the combined threat of communism and chaos."[35] In the success of the Common Market (what Bundy did not hesitate to call the "Common Market miracle"), the United States saw both the confirmation that the "American system" worked outside of the United States and an opportunity for expanding American industrial and agricultural exports in Europe. Noting that an American export surplus was needed not only to provide jobs for Americans but also to pay for American security, Bundy almost went as far as saying that the United States must export or die. With a curious mixture of pragmatism and moralism, he spoke of the necessity of creating an "open market of freedom." The new Europe would contribute to the prosperity and moral health of the "free world" if it opened its markets to the United States and its friends, notably Japan and Latin America. The American design was indeed "clear and simple":[36] European resources and markets were needed to ensure American prosperity, and beyond that, the prosperity of "free nations" and "free nations-to-be."

A consistent trend in American thinking since the war had been to consider material prosperity as conducive to political and moral viability. The members of the Kennedy team were no different from their predecessors, even though their emphasis was perhaps less on moral rectitude and more on economic and political viability than during the Dulles years. In the context of growing concern for the American balance of payments, the United States needed European resources more than ever "to promote the defense, security, and trade of the free world."[37] To ensure that these resources would indeed be channeled towards common tasks and for common purposes, Kennedy's "wise men" sought not so much to create a "full-blown Atlantic Union," which they felt was "still constitutionally and psychologically out of range for the people of the United States," but rather to encourage the emergence of an Atlantic partnership in which European integration would play a key role and the United States retain a dominant voice.

It is specifically this dominant voice that de Gaulle hoped to silence. To this end, the general attempted to build a political Europe that would emancipate Europe from the United States. In so doing, de Gaulle challenged the Monnet scenario, which assumed that economic unity would gradually evolve toward political unity. Monnet, and for that matter, Spaak were briefly tempted to listen to the Gaullist sirens that called for a political-Europe-first policy. In the summer of 1960, Couve de Murville, the French foreign minister, a long-time acquaintance of Monnet's, briefly outlined to Monnet the main characteristics of de Gaulle's plans for a political Europe.[38] Monnet in turn discussed those plans with Paul-Henri Spaak of Belgium. Their first reaction was one of surprise; both knew how far apart their conception of a united Europe was from that of de Gaulle,[39] yet they decided to give him the benefit of the doubt. In July 1960, Jean Monnet even formulated a plan for a European confederation that included an executive branch where decisions would be taken by qualified majority and a directly elected legislative branch. The confederation was not to modify the Rome Treaties in any way.[40] As de Gaulle's projects unfolded, the full extent of the divergence between his and Monnet's concept of confederation came to light: de Gaulle wanted decisions to be made by unanimous agreement, which in effect secured the possibility of a French veto, and he did intend to modify, if not the letter, at least the substance of the Rome Treaties. Yet Monnet's pragmatism and optimism prompted him to seek a common ground with de Gaulle and to view confederation as a step leading towards a true federation, or something very close to it. Both Monnet and his American friend George Ball "had long gotten over any idea that you could take a very definite form by which you evolved into some kind of unified government, or that it would necessarily resemble anything that we had known before." To them it "was a matter of letting the thing evolve."[41]

In November 1960 this pragmatism led Monnet to outline far-reaching proposals for a European confederation for the members of his Action Committee in an attempt to secure their support for finding a common ground with de Gaulle. Monnet thought that part of de Gaulle's suggestions, "at this stage and under present circumstances," could help Europe progress toward federation by passing through some kind of "European confederation." A confederation might be needed during the interim stage of evolution of the new Europe, since no adequate framework existed in which the Six could jointly tackle political questions. It might also convince the European populace that European unification was not solely geared towards economic prosperity but also had a political dimension, and as such, was directed towards the rest of the world. Monnet proposed to set up "a Council of chiefs of state and government that would meet at fairly regular intervals," as well as councils of foreign, defense, and education ministers. The Council of Defense Ministers would be limited to developing "defense cooperation in its technical and logistic aspects." These councils would be "assisted by permanent organizations that would prepare their work." Two methods would then be at work: the integration method, and another method for political, educational, and defense questions. Monnet the pragmatist saw "great merit in letting these different organizations evolve together, within the context of a common European system: Council of the six heads of government, Councils of Foreign, Defense and Education Ministers, European Communities with their rules, their institutions and their responsibilities."[42]

Monnet and Spaak later found out that de Gaulle's grand design did not include anything more than a loose confederation—which seemed to preclude anything approaching real unity in the long run. Rather than letting the European Communities and the new confederal arrangements peacefully evolve side by side, de Gaulle intended to curtail the power of the European Communities through these new arrangements. The pragmatism of Monnet, Spaak, or George Ball had its limits; de Gaulle's proposals for a confederation could only be accepted as long as there was any hope that they could some day lead to some kind of unified European government. They could not be accepted if they contemplated setting up only a "debating society"[43] and were specifically targeted towards preventing a supranational Europe from emerging. Opposition to Monnet's overtures to de Gaulle by the members of his own committee, as well as the unfolding of the Fouchet negotiations, put an end to Monnet's plans for a rapprochement with de Gaulle.

Yet in 1961, at the first meetings of heads of states in Paris and Bad Godesberg, the French appeared to be willing to make concessions to their partners. The results of the July meeting in Bad Godesberg, near Bonn, seemed to warrant grounds for mild optimism, although the Dutch demand for British participation in the discussions for a political Europe was not heeded. The Dutch looked with considerable disfavor upon any European political arrangement that might weaken the Atlantic Alliance and ensure the domination of larger European states—in this case a Franco-German combine led by France—over smaller European states such as Holland. Accordingly, they were very insistent on British participation, with a view both towards maintaining an "Atlantic outlook" on the Continent, thereby keeping harmonious relations with the United States, and towards guarding against Franco-German hegemony on the Continent. De Gaulle and Adenauer opposed the Dutch at Bad Godesberg on this point, yet the French made a number of concessions. The final communiqué read in part: "Convinced that only a united Europe, allied with the United States and other free people, can face the perils that menace the free world . . . Looking forward to the adhesion to the European communities of other states ready to assume in all fields the same obligations and responsibilities, the heads of state and government are convinced that by organizing cooperation in this way, they will favor the execution of the Paris and Rome Treaties." On three counts—the Atlantic connection, the safeguard of the Treaties of Rome, and the potential entry of other participants in the European Communities—the objections of France's partners to the French initiatives appeared to have found satisfaction. Yet the Bad Godesberg declaration did not go much further than eliciting intentions and was the result of arduous negotiations among the Six. France's partners were particularly worried about de Gaulle's plans for European defense.[45] Had they known the full intent of the general's thinking on this point, they would have been even more concerned. Just one day prior to the conference, de Gaulle wrote the following note in one of his notebooks:

> European unity can exist only if Europe constitutes a political entity which is separate from other entities. A personality. But there can be no European political personality, if Europe does not have its own personality as far as defense is concerned. Politics always rest on defense. . . . This personality in the field of defense is needed, the more so since Europe constitutes a strategic whole. She is the ground of one and the same battle. America can loose the battle of Europe without disappearing. Europe cannot . . . What is NATO? It is the sum of Americans, Europe and a few minor participants (accessoires). But it is not the defense of Europe by Europe, it is the defense of Europe by Americans. We need another NATO. We first need a Europe that would possess its own defense. This Europe should be allied with America.[46]

The Berlin crisis was a crucial determinant of the general's thinking on this point. In view of Khrushchev's pressures to modify the status of Berlin, de Gaulle's mistrust of the Anglo-American combine surfaced again in the guise of a strong presumption that the Anglo-Saxons might be willing to make concessions to the Soviets on Berlin. Partly for this reason, the general intended to progress quickly on the track of the negotiations for the constitution of a political Europe. Hence the concessions at Bad Godesberg. The shock of the Berlin Wall occurred about one month after the conference, on 13 August. The lack of meaningful reaction by West German allies and the subsequent willingness of the United States to seek contacts with the Soviet Union to discuss the German question in terms that suggested the possibility of a *de facto* recognition of the East German regime weakened Adenauer's political position in his own country by undermining one of the most basic tenets of his policy, the idea that Western cohesion would be conducive to German reunification.[47] It also encouraged him to seek an even closer rapprochement with de Gaulle.

Meanwhile, the general encountered strong opposition to his proposals for a political Europe that would meddle in defense. The opposition came from Paul-Henri Spaak, who had so far supported the Fouchet negotiations.

While de Gaulle refused to enter into negotiations with the Soviet Union, Spaak favored such negotiations. Weary of the implications for NATO of a European Union that would take positions markedly different from the United States (notably on the issue of German reunification), Spaak now sought to secure some degree of Atlantic orientation for the new union by insisting on the participation of Great Britain in the union. Following the disagreement with de Gaulle over the defense issue, the announcement by the British on 31 July of their intention to negotiate their accession to the Common Market, only a few days after the conclusion of the Bad Godesberg conference, prompted Belgian Foreign Minister Spaak to join forces with Joseph Luns, his Dutch counterpart, in making their agreement to the Fouchet proposals conditional upon the entry of Great Britain into the Common Market. In November 1961, the Dutch and the Belgians favored the simultaneous participation of the British both in the political negotiations and in the negotiations for entry into the Common Market.[48] Such was not the position of de Gaulle, who wanted the political negotiations to remain an exclusive "6-only" affair until the constitution of the union in order to preserve an essentially French outlook for the union. Yet it might be argued that the British, like de Gaulle, were not too keen on supranational institutions and that their conception of a political union was in fact quite close to that of de Gaulle. This would, however, ignore a basic fact: if the British joined, there would be not one European leader, but two. The announcement of the British candidacy for the Common Market at a crucial stage of the political negotiations would later be remembered by de Gaulle as having played a major role in the defeat of the Fouchet plans in April 1962.

In December 1961, the Fouchet Committee proposed a plan for a European political union that contained sufficient concessions to France's partners to warrant hopes for its eventual acceptance by these partners; the concessions essentially espoused the declaration of intentions of the July conference.[49] Despite this auspicious beginning, de Gaulle presented a modified version of the plan in January 1962 that contained no references to the Atlantic Alliance or the entry of new members into the new organization. The new text also failed to address the demand of the Five for an explicit clause for a revision of the political treaty after three years, which would have at least left open the possibility for the union to evolve towards some kind of federation. Finally, the new de Gaulle version gave economic authority to the union, which would have interfered with the authority of the existing European Communities.

Not surprisingly, the reactions of France's partners were highly critical. Luns and Spaak were the most vocal. By April, positions were largely crystallized. Shortly before the ill-famed 17 April meeting in Paris, when the negotiations finally broke down, Lord Privy Seal Heath delivered a speech at the West European Union Assembly in which he clearly supported an intergovernmental approach towards European political cooperation, thereby apparently making a gesture of conciliation towards the French. However, Heath also insisted that the political and economic community that the United Kingdom favored should stand "shoulder to shoulder with the United States." "We quite accept," continued Heath, "that the European political union, if it is to be effective, will have a common concern for defense problems . . . What is essential, however, is that any European point of view or policy on defense should be directly related to the Atlantic Alliance." This did not please de Gaulle; nor did Heath's references to the intention of the United Kingdom to "retain [its] constitutional ties and arrangements for consultation with the Commonwealth." Last but not least, Heath wondered aloud if it would not be a good idea for the United Kingdom, as a soon-to-be member of the European Economic Community, "to join with you now in your discussions about the political framework of Europe."[50] While Spaak and Luns saw in this last sentence an encouragement to push for British adhesion to the political discussions, de Gaulle saw it as a threat to his grand design for Europe. The position of the Dutch and the Belgians was relatively simple: either Great Britain joined, in which case they would be willing to "buy her participation"[51] by accepting something less than supranational integration, or it was not allowed to join, in which case they were quite reluctant to forsake the guarantees that supranationalism offered small countries. The two countries showed themselves unwilling to compromise their position on this point; the French maintained theirs as well. We shall not engage in the futile exercise of distributing blame to the participants in the Paris discussion, but it is enough to note that de Gaulle viewed the British initiative as being one of the key factors in the failure of "his" political Europe. All along de Gaulle had been suspicious of British motives for wanting to enter the Common Market, and from now on his suspicion would be compounded by resentment.

Was Harold Macmillan sincere in wanting to join the new Europe as a full member, or was it just another scheme for dividing and reigning on the old continent? During de Gaulle's visit to Bonn on 20 May 1961, the general told Adenauer and German Foreign Minister von Brentano that he did not think "that England was cut out of the same wood as France and Germany. If then Britain joined, she would do it not in order to enter into a real cooperation, but rather to take on the role of arbiter, without fundamentally engaging herself." This, continued de Gaulle, "was quite natural since Britain was and remained an island, while France and Germany were on the Continent." The general nevertheless welcomed the recent change in the attitude of the United Kingdom towards the Common Market, but he added that "this did not mean in any way that Britain did not perhaps unconsciously wish to impede cooperation." Adenauer agreed with the general, while French Foreign Minister Couve de Murville said he was persuaded that "Great Britain would never agree to join as a full member. It would always make reservations, and perhaps the negotiations would then again be interrupted upon French initiative." Couve de Murville added that "one must always keep in mind that, if England joined the Common Market, Holland would join up on its side, as would Denmark and Norway. This would change the whole physiognomy of the Common Market."[52]

Thus, de Gaulle's veto of British entry into the Common Market was very much in the cards as early as 1961. Adenauer and Foreign Minister Couve de Murville both shared de Gaulle's reservations regarding British entry. George Ball's efforts earlier that year to convert Adenauer to his view that Britain was in fact sincere in wanting to join the European Community as a full member did not succeed in convincing the old man. Adenauer remained firm in his belief that "England did not want a political Community for the foreseeable future. It did perhaps want a commercial Community." Adenauer stood by his position even though Ball insisted that he and his colleagues had been very active in pointing out to the British that the United States was adamantly opposed to British entry if the British joined only for purely commercial reasons.[53]

The Kennedy administration had been bothered for some time by what a high-ranking member of the administration called "a love affair between two old men."[54] Adenauer's concern about American overtures to Moscow on the German question, as well as the breakdown of the Fouchet negotiations, worked to intensify this relationship. Since de Gaulle was not allowed to build a six-member European club, or failing that, a three-member European *directoire* (shortly before the Paris meeting he had approached the Italians and the Germans on this), the general turned towards the last possible alternative: a Franco-German special relationship, formalized in a Franco-German Treaty. His secret hope was, of course, that the other European nations would later join "willy-nilly." Two highly successful state visits contributed to strengthen Franco-German relations. In July Adenauer traveled to France, and the high point of his visit was a dramatic high mass in Rheims. Two months later, de Gaulle was welcomed by crowds of enthusiastic Germans. That same month, September, the two men started working on a Franco-German Treaty.[55]

Meanwhile, shortly after de Gaulle's 15 May 1962 press conference, which, as we saw, triggered the resignation of five of his ministers and occasioned a strong reaction on the part of President Kennedy, George Ball and Couve de Murville had an interesting conversation at the Quai d'Orsay in Paris. Ball began the discussion by enumerating the reasons for American support of European integration. This support, said Ball, "had been motivated primarily by political considerations." Tying Germany to the West was the main reason. This emphasis on political unity in turn explained American efforts to discourage "British efforts either to build a European Free Trade Area or to merge the Free Trade Association with Europe, since [the United States] had regarded these efforts as a step toward diluting the political content of Europe." Ball proceeded to insist on the sincerity of the British in asking to be considered for admission in the Common Market. The United States, he said, was persuaded that "the British were now on the verge of a major national decision." "While no British politician would dare to admit it," Ball continued, the Kennedy administration was "persuaded that the British were preparing to reverse four hundred years of policy towards the Continent. More and more Englishmen recognized that their destiny no longer lay in being the center of a world system—a posture they could no longer afford—and that their historic role should now be played out within a European framework." Accordingly, the United States was "of the view that if the United Kingdom became a full member of the European Community, the British would work toward progressively greater unity and would not drag their feet."[56]

Monnet's Action Committee, about a month later, echoed Ball's phrasing in projecting that British entry in the Common Market "would necessarily change the behavior of the United Kingdom as the behavior of each of our six countries changed."[57] Both Ball and Monnet had long held the view that the British would join the new European venture once they thought it in their interest to do so. With the Common Market now a going concern, the Europeanists believed that the United Kingdom would not only join but that the European outlook would progressively rub off on them. For the British, Europeanism would become an acquired taste.

At any rate, it was better to have the British in the new Europe than outside it. George Ball told Couve de Murville that "so long as Great Britain remained outside the Community, it would operate as a lodestone drawing with unequal degrees of force on different parts of the body of the Community. Thus Britain, outside the Community, would remain an element of disintegration but, inside the Community, Britain would ensure European cohesion." "The Britain of today," continued Ball, "was very different from the Britain they had known in the past." Specifically aiming at Gaullist objections on the matter—which Couve de Murville shared—Ball insisted that "a new class was coming into power which had not been oriented to the concept of Empire." It would, in his view, "readily adjust . . . to a major role within the European framework. It was a mistake to assume that Britain's adhesion to the Rome Treaty would mean a watering down of political progress." The United States, said Ball, "had always been interested in the idea of Europe as a full partner in [U.S.] endeavors." They "wanted very much, therefore, for Europe to move toward as much political integration as possible." Interestingly, Ball added that the United States "were not much concerned about the problems of a third force since [they] were persuaded that all of us were committed to the same general objectives."[58] Yet, as we saw earlier, the concern did exist, and it was one of the reasons for emphasizing the Atlantic partnership concept with a view to maintaining a common dedication to similar objectives within the Atlantic Community. It was also one of the main reasons for favoring British entry into the Common Market. The United Kingdom's entry into the Common Market was indeed one of the touchstones of the grand design.

The next chapter discusses specific American moves to implement the twin goals of European unity and Atlantic partnership in the context of the British application to the Common Market and related issues. No attempt is made to maintain a somewhat artificial division between the political, military, and economic spheres. All three converge in this specific issue to weave an intricate pattern of bureaucratic maneuvering, ties of friendship, and conflicting world views.

10

Implementing the Atlantic Partnership

GOING INTO EUROPE? SEEKING AMERICAN SUPPORT

During the last months of 1960 Harold Macmillan was slowly coming to accept the idea that Britain might have to join the Common Market instead of trying to water it down through broader "bridge-building" schemes. Monnet's expectations had proved right: as the Common Market became more and more of a reality, the *fait accompli* convinced the British that the time had come to participate fully in the European venture. In May 1960, the Six agreed to speed up the implementation of the Common Market. Instead of the originally planned period of twelve to fifteen years, they now aimed for a full customs union in eight years. Declining economic fortunes in the United Kingdom, stagnating British trade with the Commonwealth, and de Gaulle's initiatives for a political Europe increased Macmillan's fears that Britain would become more and more isolated from the economic fortunes and from the political councils of the new Europe. He was all the more concerned since the special relationship with the United States was showing signs of fatigue. During the latter part of the Eisenhower administration, the United States had been markedly cool toward British "European" initiatives, while it firmly endorsed the decisions of the Six favorites on most issues. The United States' propensity to side with the Common Market pointed to the forthcoming establishment of a new special relationship with the European Communities, which would be to the detriment of the special relationship with the United Kingdom.

Apparent encouragements to the United Kingdom from French quarters during the spring of 1961 further strengthened Macmillan's resolve. On 2 March 1962, Maurice Couve de Murville spoke to the Council of Europe's

Consultative Assembly and gave what was widely understood in Britain as a "beckoning signal"[1] to come in: "Our partners in the Common Market and we ourselves have always said that the Common Market was, and always remained open to any other European country which wished to join it. We persist in thinking that therein lies, for some at least, a valid possibility, and doubtless, the only really satisfactory solution. We persist in hoping, furthermore, that certain refusals, although repeated, will not be maintained."[2] In the same speech Couve de Murville also expressed his aversion to free-trade-area solutions, "which would have killed the germ of political union contained in the European Economic Community."[3] In June 1961 in Metz, de Gaulle himself said it was "necessary also that England come into the Common Market but without posing conditions."[4] The attitude of the new American administration toward the proposed British application for membership in the Common Market confirmed Macmillan's intentions.

Throughout July 1960, the British prime minister proceeded to place European-minded policymakers of the highest caliber in key positions in the British government. Duncan Sandys was moved to the Commonwealth Relations Office, Christopher Soames became minister of agriculture, Lord Home was moved to the Foreign Office, and Edward Heath, formerly minister of labor, was named Lord Privy Seal and given the responsibility of European affairs.[5] On 30 March 1961, shortly after the inauguration of President Kennedy, Sir Frank Lee, "an old wartime friend"[6] who now served as joint permanent secretary of the treasury, invited George Ball to meet with Heath and a number of other British civil servants. Ball, who was in London for a meeting of the Development Assistance Group, readily accepted. Like his friend Monnet, he was in favor of Britain becoming a full member in the Common Market as long as it did not impair the development of the European Communities. He intended to "encourage the British to take the plunge,"[7] but he had no idea how soon they would be ready for it. Hence Ball was surprised when, at the meeting, Edward Heath advised him of recent British conversations with the Six and then proceeded to outline the new British position toward European integration. "Provided an overall settlement could be found to take care of the Commonwealth, agriculture, and EFTA problems, the United Kingdom was," said Heath, "now ready to accept a common, or harmonized, tariff." The United Kingdom was further prepared to "accept any institutions that were 'consequent upon the establishment of a common, or harmonized, tariff.' " The United Kingdom was also "ready for the Six to negotiate with the Commonwealth countries regarding the reduction or elimination of British preferences, although arrangements would have to be made respecting the preferences now enjoyed by overseas territories in the United Kingdom and the Common Market."[8]

This represented considerable progress over previous British attempts to somehow water down the Common Market. Frank Lee asked Ball what the United States thought of the current split between the Six and the Seven. Ball replied by briefly outlining the reasons for American support of the EEC, including Franco-German rapprochement and the need to tie Germany firmly to the West to ensure against independent West German ventures in search of reunification. A European "structure" was all the more necessary since de Gaulle and Adenauer "were both old men." Like Monnet, Ball placed his faith in institutions as the guardians of accumulated wisdom: men died, while institutions persisted. He made clear that the reasons for American support of the EEC were mainly of a political nature. The United States, he said, was willing to sacrifice some of their trade interests to "facilitate the political promise of the EEC." Had the British joined the EEC sooner, their "political genius" would no doubt "have accelerated progress." The United States had been favorable to British membership, but now, particularly because of the American balance-of-payments deficit, they "would accept the added discrimination resulting from British entry only if it would reinforce the political character of the EEC." A specific concern was that British membership in the EEC might result in the "merger of two preferential systems for Africa—the British Commonwealth and the French system." Not only would such preferences foster uneconomical production and distort trade but also, if applied to the entire Common Market, could possibly hurt "outside producers, such as Latin America."[9]

Sir Frank Lee then put the question more directly: "Does the United States want Britain to join the Common Market? Might America perhaps even welcome some derogation in the agricultural field, since United States trade would benefit if the EEC did not adopt a common agricultural policy?" Robert Schaetzel "interjected that he thought a common agricultural policy essential to the development of the EEC, since there had to be a balance between industry and agriculture." In answering Lee's question, Ball insisted that the EEC's institutions must not "become mere technocratic bodies; they should continue to develop politically." If the United Kingdom was "prepared to recognize that the Rome Treaty [was] not a static document but a process that could eventually lead to an evolving European community—something in the nature of a European federation" and agreed to "join Europe on those terms", Ball was "confident" that his government would "regard this as a major contribution to Western solidarity and the stability of the free world." Indeed, as long as Britain did not join the EEC she was "a force for division rather than cohesion," "a giant lodestone drawing with unequal degrees of force on each member state."

However, if she joined she could "apply her unique political genius toward the creation of a unity that can transform the Western world."[10] Ball emerged from the meeting "exhilarated but feeling as though [he] had bailed out of an airplane without knowing the terrain underneath." He later recalled: "The President had given me no mandate to state American policy with such assurance; I had never reviewed the nuances of the subject with him, nor even asked his views on the critical questions Heath and I had covered. Thus, in describing the American position, I was not sure whether I was making American policy or interpreting it."[11]

Despite Ball's misgivings after the fact and the strong reservations of some of his colleagues, who viewed the British initiative as just another attempt to undermine the European movement, this time from inside, President Kennedy himself soon endorsed his statement. Ball's meeting with Heath and Lee had obviously been arranged in preparation for Macmillan's visit to the United States the following month. Ball therefore sought to provide the president with some advance background and advice. In a memorandum, Ball, now having second thoughts on the British initiative, cautioned Kennedy that Macmillan "probably still hoped to solve the problem" by a "traditional British-type compromise that would give the UK the best of both worlds—the full commercial advantages of a loose association with the Common Market without any economic or political involvement in the Continent." If, however, the president made it abundantly clear to Macmillan that the United States would favor only full membership, he would find senior British civil servants quite willing to support a full commitment of the United Kingdom to the European Communities. Once again reverting to the German question, Ball underscored the advantage that British membership could bind a post-Adenauer Germany more closely to the West. "If Britain remained aloof," he wrote, "such men as Erhard and Strauss, who did not share Adenauer's commitment to a Franco-German *rapprochement,* might exploit the 'division of Europe' as an excuse for breaking free from the Six, but if the British should wholeheartedly join the Six, the Community could furnish the glue to bind Germany irrevocably to the West."[12]

When the president and the prime minister met in Washington on 5 April, Macmillan asked Kennedy how the United States would react if the United Kingdom applied to join the European Community. The president almost immediately deferred to Ball, his number-one adviser in European affairs, who then basically repeated what he had told Heath and Lee in London: only full membership would be acceptable to the United States; the European Community was not a simple commercial arrangement but had political dimensions as well. Attentive to Monnet's concerns, Kennedy added that the United States would not favor an agreement between the Six and the Seven.[13] During a dinner at the British Embassy, an elated Macmillan "twice took [Ball] aside for private conversations":

> Despite his reputation for imperturbability, he seemed excited, speaking with enthusiasm about the new President and the people around him "who all seem to be full of ideas and drive." I mentioned the enormous help we had received from Sir Frank Lee and that I had had a long and searching talk with Heath and Lee on the Common Market. "But, of course, I know all about that," he replied. "Could you possibly think I would have spoken so freely if I had not known all you said to Lee and Heath?" Then, later in the evening he approached me again. "Yesterday was one of the greatest days in my life," he said with apparent emotion. "You know, don't you, that we can now do this thing and that we're going to do it. We're going into Europe. We'll need your help, since we'll have trouble with de Gaulle, but we're going to do it."[14]

Help from the United States was soon forthcoming in the form of private contacts. In mid-April, Kennedy told Italian ambassador Manlio Brosio that anchoring Germany to the West and "increasing its commitments to Western Europe" remained a key objective of American policy. He added that "Great Britain too had an important role to play and he hoped this could be a role even more closely allied with the European countries." When the ambassador inquired whether the United States "thought the British were prepared to join the Community of the Six," the president did not answer directly but indicated "there had been some indication that British relations with the continent were closer than they had been, and he personally thought that the closer they were the better."[15] A few days later, during a conversation with French Ambassador Hervé Alphand and Former Prime Minister Paul Reynaud in Washington, Kennedy, acting on Macmillan's express demand that the United States carry the British case to the French, was more explicit. The president, using the now-familiar line of argumentation that British membership was needed to tie Germany more closely to the West, told Alphand that "during the Macmillan visit [the United States] had expressed the great hope that Britain would join the European Community." Ambassador Alphand answered that "de Gaulle would accept Britain in the Community if Britain was prepared to accept the treaty."[16]

Yet General de Gaulle was much less encouraging during Kennedy's visit to France in early June. After voicing his usual grievances against NATO, the general agreed "to make no attack on NATO, now," but he indicated that he might want to act later after the Berlin crisis ended and he managed to get his army back from Algeria. De Gaulle also showed that he had no interest in the American offer of Polaris missiles, since they would have to be transferred to NATO and would thus not "reinforce French forces"; "he was for the alliance but against integration." Further rumblings of the general's discontent were heard when Kennedy touched on the issue of British membership in the Common Market. Once back in Washington, the president told Senator Fulbright that "in his judgment General De Gaulle [did] not really want the British in the Common Market. He appear[ed] to believe that they [would] not make the necessary political commitment, and in any case De Gaulle prefer[red] the present situation in which he [was] the dominant figure."[17]

Meanwhile, in late April, as de Gaulle struggled to restore order and unity in France after the failed insurrection of some French generals in Algeria, Monnet was busy conferring with David Bruce, who was in Paris for a few days, on the merits of taking the opportunity "presented by this dramatic instance of division in France" to immediately declare the British intention to enter the Common Market. This, they calculated, would be interpreted as a "generous lofty proceeding," showing confidence in the "future stability on [the] Continent" and "associating [the] British in time of dire difficulty with continental concerns." Writing to Ball at the State Department, they recommended that America not make any overt action on this point, which would "be resented and unproductive" in London, but "wondered whether [the] suggestion might not be made to [the] President of his considering an entirely confidential communication to Macmillan on this subject." Kennedy might "state his relief at the quelling of the rebellion" while at the same time implying that British participation in European affairs was much needed to improve cohesion in Western Europe. The president might then "speculate as to whether, in Britain's case, there were not some way, such as adhering to the Rome Treaty in which she might constructively, by taking early action, demonstrate intent to participate more actively in shaping European policies. This would at once be given strong American commendation and be hailed as an imaginative exercise of statesmanship." Bruce and Monnet were prompted to make these recommendations by recent indications in the London press that Macmillan might be contemplating the postponement of the British application to join the European Community because of the French disturbances. They hoped to transform Macmillan's pretext for procrastinating into a pretext for accelerating the United Kingdom's entry into the Common Market.[18]

Monnet had met with President Kennedy in March. He found him convinced that the United Kingdom must join the European Community.[19] Monnet soon informed Adenauer, who was about to leave for Washington to meet with Kennedy, that the United States would support British participation in the Common Market "as a participating member and not as an associate." The ultimate decision belonged to the British, of course. Recent contacts in London had convinced Monnet that a British decision on the matter was fast approaching. "They are beginning to realize that the 'special relationship' they had with the United States won't last," Monnet happily noted. "The time is that of common decisions and of 'grand ensembles' of which the European Community is an example."[20]

By a curious coincidence, on the same day that Monnet was writing to Adenauer and commenting on the "special relationship," McGeorge Bundy advised Kennedy on exactly the same issue. David Bruce, the American ambassador to the United Kingdom, had just told Bundy of a crucial conversation that he'd had with Ramsbotham of Macmillan's staff the previous night. Was George Ball speaking for the president, Ramsbotham asked, "when he said on Wednesday that relations between the United States and the United Kingdom would be strengthened, not weakened, if the UK moved toward membership in the Six"? Bundy wrote Kennedy Macmillan felt this was "a most important question" and needed "to know" if this was also Kennedy's "personal view." Could the president perhaps "make the same point directly and privately with Macmillan tomorrow?"[21] Kennedy obliged.[22]

THE MANY DIMENSIONS OF THE SPECIAL RELATIONSHIP

On 5 December 1962, Dean Acheson addressed a student conference at West Point Military Academy in New York. "Great Britain has lost an empire and has not yet found a role," he coolly noted. "The attempt to play a separate power role—that is, a role apart from Europe, a role based on a 'special relationship' with the United States, a role based on being the head of a 'common-wealth' which has no political structure, or unity, or strength and enjoys a fragile and precarious economic relationship by means of the sterling area and preferences in the British market—this role is about played out."[23] The speech caused an uproar in Britain. The State Department promptly cabled the American Embassy in London. The State Department, said the message, would not issue any public statements. In response to private inquiries, the Embassy should point out that, even though he frequently advised the president on policy, Acheson was not "at this moment an official of the Government" and had expressed only his views, not those of the American government. There was "certainly no need to apologize for or explain his intense interest in the Alliance of which he was one of the main architects." David Ormsby-Gore, the British Ambassador to the United States, who was a very close friend of Kennedy, was reported as saying that there was nothing in the Acheson speech that had not previously been said by British officials themselves. He further described Acheson as an "old and true friend of the United Kingdom."[24] Meanwhile Kennedy tried to cajole Macmillan into remaining silent on the matter. Yet, despite a personal call from the president, Macmillan bowed to the "cries of outrage and wounded dignity"[25] of his compatriots and publicly chided Acheson. "Insofar as he appeared to denigrate the resolution and will of Britain and the British people," wrote Macmillan," Mr. Acheson has fallen into an error which had been made by quite a lot of people in the course of the last four hundred years, including Philip of Spain, Louis the Fourteenth, Napoleon, the Kaiser and Hitler. He also seems wholly to misunderstand the role of the Commonwealth in world affairs."[26] Acheson was listed in curious company! Although the administration attempted to patch up matters with Macmillan after Acheson's speech, his statement corresponded not only to what some Britons had been saying themselves but also to the administration's thinking on the matter.

The 1961 Acheson Report, as will be recalled, did address the issue of the "special relationship" in somewhat direct terms. The coalescence of the Six must be the number-one priority of the United States, said the report. This meant that "Britain should not be encouraged by doubts of this attitude on our part to attempt to weaken that coalescence. Similarly, Great Britain should not be encouraged to stay apart from the six by hopes of a 'special relation' between the Commonwealth and the U.S." Consequently, the report recommended that the United States "look with favor on any trend in British thinking which contemplates eventual full membership in the six."[27]

The "special relation" was as curious a hybrid animal during the Kennedy administration as it had been under Eisenhower. Britain's financial misfortunes had forced her to considerably reduce her world commitments and to rely more and more on the United States. Suez was a mortifying episode for the British, as it demonstrated not only that the United Kingdom had lost much of its status as an independent power but also that the "special relationship" with the United States was waning. Yet, at the same time, Eisenhower had helped to perpetuate the illusion that the United Kingdom still maintained some of its status as a great power by supporting the amendment of the McMahon Act, which quite obviously favored the British. After the United Kingdom got in trouble for developing an intermediate-range ballistic missile known as "Blue Streak," Eisenhower made what Ball later considered as a second major blunder in American policymaking. By offering to provide the British with Skybolt missiles, with the agreement that the United States would pay for about 90 percent of the costs, Eisenhower once again helped the British retain their illusion of great power status by guaranteeing them access to American technology in the most politically appealing category of all—nuclear technology. As planned, Skybolt was to be an air-to-surface missile, and it had a limited range of 1,000 nautical miles. Yet it could extend the life of the British V-bomber force and hence maintain British inclusion in the nuclear club well into the 1970s.[28]

The advent of a new administration threatened to shatter the last pieces of the special relation, most of all in the nuclear field. The Europeanists on Kennedy's team were dead set against continuing to encourage Britain to remain in the nuclear club. Would it not be better, they argued, to help the British phase out their nuclear deterrent? Would this not help relieve them of a commitment they could barely afford and thus free their resources for a much more promising venture—participation in the European Community as a full member? If Britain was still to have a "special relationship" with the United States, it could only be within the wider framework of a partnership between the United States and the European Communities. As a member of the new Europe, Britain would not only contribute to harness Germany more solidly to the West but also dilute and direct what seemed to be an emerging coalition between the French and the Germans against American influence in Europe. Even though the Europeanists sought to eliminate Britain's privileged status and to make her the equal of its future European partners, they did see her role in Europe as a first among equals, able to assume the leadership of the new Europe. George Ball, writing at the time of the second British application to join the Common Market, gave a full description of the political role that he anticipated the United Kingdom would play by joining the Community instead of trying to build "peripheral alliances," such as the Seven, opposing it:

> Britain's application to accede to the Rome Treaty is epic in its implications. I have long been convinced that British initiative and leadership could spark a renascence of the European idea at a time when dark shadows of nationalism have begun to fall on the Continent, for Europe has sore need of British political maturity, just as Britain needs a dose of continental vitality. With the passing of the Fourth Republic and the temporary ineffectiveness of its "good Europeans,"

the Continent has been showing the cracks and fissures that warn of disunity. Italy is still too weak, the Benelux countries too small. Britain is the only state that could provide a third strong pillar for the European edifice along with Germany and France, because she has a special political heritage to offer. For three hundred years Britain has been a stranger to revolution, while France has endured absolutism, two empires, five republics, two constitutional monarchies and two dictatorships. In the ninety-five years since it became a nation, Germany has averaged one violent change of government every twenty-four years. The Weimar Republic and the Fourth Republic each saw twenty-two governments during their brief life spans, while, in contrast, during the last twenty-two years Britain has had only six governments. Intimate British participation in the affairs of the Continent could provide the necessary element of strength and solidity; it could moderate these latent instabilities and provide a permanent balance, securing democracy in Europe.[29]

The Europeanists hoped that the United Kingdom, besides exerting a stabilizing influence on the Continent, would prevent Europe from adopting a complacent regionalist or inward-looking attitude. Considering Britain's worldwide commercial interests, they calculated that its membership would inoculate the Community against bouts of protectionism. They also anticipated some gains from British leadership in securing more European monies to wage battle in the Third World not only to fight poverty but also to maintain a "spacious environment for freedom." To put it another way, the Kennedy administration expected the British to function as an advocate for American policies within Europe. While the European Communities were expected to tie Germany firmly to the West, the addition of the United Kingdom to the councils of the new Europe would ensure that the European Communities would remain firmly tied to the United States. In this way the "special relationship" was to be much more than a fiction.

The dimensions of the special relationship were many. It was based first of all on common language, institutions evolved from the same intellectual traditions, and a sense of complicity derived from common values. Yet traditional and cultural ties did not nearly exhaust the meaning of the special relationship. The more theoretical aspect of it, which was derived from historically based affinities, translated into special relationships between people, thus complementing the "special" relationship by "close" relationships. According to George Ball, "More often than not, British and American diplomats tend[ed] to like each other" (the "bitter Eden-Dulles relationship" was an exception).[30] These special relationships were in turn both of a personal and a practical nature. While friendships contributed to giving reality to the special relationship, working together on common problems gave it substance.

During the Kennedy administration events often threw British and American leaders "into the role of partners, and close partners." This point was strongly emphasized by Secretary of State Dean Rusk. By working together on "important matters,"[31] such as the Berlin Crisis, the Laos question, the Cuban Missile Crisis, the Trade Expansion Act, and the Nuclear Test-Ban Treaty, the "Anglo-Saxons" were cast into the role of associates, or partners, conducting common business. This was true even though one partner spoke with a dominant voice, while the other was cast in an advisory role. As Britain's pretensions to great power status diminished, its position as a second-rank power was reflected in the consultative character of its relation with the United States. And the United States much benefited from this British advice and support. During the Berlin crisis, the British strongly backed the American position of trying to reach an agreement with the Russians through negotiations, while de Gaulle was busy decrying any move towards accommodation. On the Laos question, Macmillan advised Kennedy to avoid military intervention, and Britain was later co-chairman with the United States at the Laos Peace Conference. During the Cuban Missile Crisis Macmillan was frequently consulted and his backing of the American president on the Cuban quarantine helped mobilize NATO's unanimity on the issue.[32]

By contrast, American relations with the French were marked by a distinctly uncooperative atmosphere. De Gaulle did not so much seek to counsel the United States as to assert French independence from the United States. This pattern showed in the most sensitive field of all: nuclear policy. There was no denying that the United States had strongly contributed to French resentment by flaunting the special relationship when giving the British access to classified information while denying it to the French; pragmatists such as McGeorge Bundy and Europeanists such as George Ball recognized this had been a major blunder of American policy. Yet French aims in acquiring access to nuclear technology were wholly different from that of the British. In a letter to French historian Raymond Aron, with whom he was in frequent touch, McGeorge Bundy gave a very apt description of how the special relationship manifested itself in the nuclear field: "in the nuclear field the particular object of British policy has been not so much to establish autonomy as to maintain a right of cautionary counsel to the United States. Thus British policy has aimed at intimacy with the United States, with an advisory relation to the safety-catch. Is it wholly unfair to say that French policy aims, by contrast, at increasing independence from the United States and immediate control of the trigger?"[33] Therein lay the basic difference between the special relationship and the French relationship—one was rooted in intimacy, and interdependence, while the other was characterized by distance and independence. As the Nassau Conference would later demonstrate, the special relationship did not exclude occasional and substantial misunderstandings. It would also demonstrate that although it did have its benefits for both parties there was a political price to be paid for it as well. It was the special relationship that was largely responsible for de Gaulle's veto of British membership. Personalities and idiosyncrasies played an important role in the increasing intimacy between the United Kingdom and the United States; de Gaulle aimed at anything but intimacy with the Anglo-Saxons.

The constellation of individuals holding the reigns of the Anglo-American relationship during the Kennedy administration was remarkable. The key figures were Macmillan, Ormsby-Gore, and Kennedy, with Ball, Bruce, Bundy, and others playing second fiddle (sometimes discordantly). On 13 December 1961, one year before Nassau, Ambassador Bruce sent a telegram to the Department of State giving his personal assessment of Macmillan, the man: "This is no mean man. He represents Edwardian and eighteenth century England in the grand tradition of the establishment, and also has an extensive appreciation of contemporary public opinion. He has charm, politeness, dry humor, self-assurance, a vivid sense of history, dignity, and character." As for Macmillan, the political animal, and the sincerity of his motives for wanting into the Common Market, Bruce continued: "I believe he sincerely desires UK entry into Common Market with concomitant assumption of political obligations. British economy is laggard, and should be improved by membership. Also, he must be conscious of possibility that after Adenauer and de Gaulle pass off scene, UK might well be political spokesman for bloc potentially as powerful as US or USSR." Commenting on the "special relationship," Bruce pointed out that although Macmillan had an American mother this "matter[ed] little." "Like Churchill," Macmillan had made "the maintenance of close ties with the US a cardinal point of policy," even though he had at times ventured on an independent and unsuccessful course in courting Moscow. Bruce's guess was that Macmillan—no longer able "to succeed as a middle man between the US and USSR, no longer on a basis of old friendship with the president of the United States, realizing that a revival of the classical balance of power in Europe with Great Britain weighing the scales [was] no longer possible"—would "go far to suit otherwise discordant notes to the US president's harmony." Bruce believed that Macmillan would "make all reasonable concessions to maintain at least public appearance of

US-UK concord on mutual problems, and sincerely h[old] to close US-UK special relationship." While by his own admission Bruce was "neither an intimate nor a friend" of Macmillan, Kennedy became just that.[34]

Macmillan had started out feeling worried about how the special relationship might fare under Kennedy. Now that Eisenhower, his old friend from the war years, had left the political scene, Macmillan wondered how an "ageing politician" like himself, "not yet old enough to be a statesman (which you are only called when you are dead)," might charm the "young, attractive, buoyant"[35] Kennedy. The Eisenhower/Macmillan relationship had had the advantage of a twenty-year-old "comradeship,"[36] and the two men could draw on common memories, but what would the Kennedy/Macmillan relationship be based upon?

Seventy-year-old Macmillan was the first to suit young Kennedy. In an attempt not to appear as a "stuffed shirt" or a "square," the prime minister decided to make contact with him "in the realm of ideas."[37] If, he thought, he could cast himself in the role of "a man who, although of advancing years," had "young and fresh thoughts,"[38] Kennedy would listen to him. On 19 December 1960 Macmillan proceeded to write a letter to the American president in which he couched, after much thought on his part, "one or two exciting ideas." He tried hard not to make his message "pompous, or lecturing or *too* radical!"[39] The letter touched upon various substantive issues, including the urgency of reaching an agreement on nuclear disarmament and the necessity of countering communism mainly through Western economic strength. Macmillan concluded his letter by offering to resume the special relationship, although he did not use the term. Believing that the fundamental interests of the United States and the United Kingdom were the same, Macmillan hoped for a rapprochement of policies that would also give them a "better chance of success." There was no denying it: "leadership in the Western World" now belonged mostly to the United States. But even though the "United Kingdom's power in the world" was comparatively "so much less" than the United States', it could still be of service to the free world through its "special ties with every continent," especially in the Commonwealth. Might Kennedy think that this was not enough? Macmillan then offered to put British courage and imagination to the test: "I can assure you that this country will not shrink from sacrifice, nor I believe have we lost our power to think and act imaginatively in the great crisis of our time."[40]

Kennedy and Macmillan first met at Key West, Florida in late March 1961. Kennedy had asked Macmillan to meet with him urgently as he was deeply worried about the turn of events in Laos. Although the American president seemed to be leaning toward intervention in Laos (albeit on a small scale and not without help from his allies) and Macmillan was decidedly cool towards taking any military action, the prime minister, almost from the beginning of his conversation with Kennedy, felt a "deep sense of relief."[41] Shortly after discussing Laos, Kennedy and Macmillan turned to the question of finding a successor to British Ambassador Caccia. Kennedy suggested David Ormsby-Gore in the most emphatic terms. "He is my brother's most intimate friend,"[42] said the president. Since the Kennedy brothers were very close and Kennedy greatly valued his brother's advice, this augured well for the future of the special relationship.

Jack Kennedy and David Ormsby-Gore were themselves friends. They had first become acquainted in London in the 1930s. Their two families were very close. When Ormsby-Gore began visiting the United States regularly, starting in 1954, he stayed with the Kennedys every year, either at Hyannisport or Palm Beach.[43] As the two friends grew older they both got involved in politics and kept track of each other's progress. Jack made it all the way from congressman to president, David from member of parliament, to minister of state at the Foreign Office.[44] Now, with Kennedy's strong backing, he was made British ambassador to the United States.

Only a few days after their first encounter at Key West, Kennedy and Macmillan met again, this time in Washington. This was an occasion not only to discuss British entry into the Common Market but also to meet the members of the new Kennedy administration. Macmillan was somewhat anxious, yet his fears were quickly dissipated—he liked the enthusiasm and apparent competence of the new team. He also liked Jacqueline Kennedy, with whom he soon formed a "warm friendship."[45] Later on, after the Bay of Pigs fiasco, Kennedy relied much on the enlightened advice of the prime minister, whom he privately referred to as "Uncle Harold." (Macmillan and Kennedy were related through the late Kathleen Kennedy's marriage to Macmillan's wife's nephew, Lord Hartington).[46] The two men became close and intimate friends and found they had a "considerable temperamental rapport." "It was the gay things that linked us together," Macmillan once told Schlesinger, "and made it possible for us to talk about the terrible things."[47]

If the Macmillan/Kennedy relationship was close, the David/Jack relationship was even closer. Kennedy felt free to discuss any matters with Ormsby-Gore, even the most secret. He also felt confident that nothing he said would be reported to Macmillan without his express permission. Hence Kennedy used his long conversations with Ormsby-Gore to sharpen his thoughts on foreign policy issues. But the two of them did not limit their talks to serious matters; they could also be totally frivolous.[48] Ormsby-Gore was, in more ways than one, Kennedy's soul companion. He was also an able and adroit ambassador. High-ranking members of the Kennedy team thoroughly enjoyed his company and respected his knowledge of foreign affairs. To many he became more than an ambassador; he became a member of the team.[49] Ormsby-Gore indeed possessed a knack for bypassing the traditional channels of decision-making of the American government and for reaching the key people in the administration, those whom Kennedy trusted and respected the most. As Dean Rusk was later to remark: "He understood that the formal processes of government do not always represent the way things actually work, and that in our government much depends upon the way in which confidence is delegated by the president of the United States; therefore there will always be individuals who are more important than others."[50] Through his acute perception of the American policymaking process, and his friendship with the president, Ormsby-Gore was able to wield considerable influence in the Department of State. He understood better than any foreign ambassador that the optimum time to advise the government of the United States was during the initial phases of discussion of any given issue, not later. Once the United States government had reached certain conclusions, often as the result of long and protracted internal negotiations, it was very hard to modify these conclusions.[51] The very complexity of the American constitutional system required such an elaborate procedure in reaching any foreign policy decision at all that the administration, once it had reached a conclusion, was understandably not very anxious to repeat that process, even to oblige a foreign government, no matter how friendly.

For the same reasons that launched Ormsby-Gore into the position of one of the *éminences grises* of the American administration, Jean Monnet also prevailed through the ins and outs of Washington. Monnet enjoyed a close and intimate relationship with the key figures of both the Eisenhower and the Kennedy administrations. The Dulles/Monnet and Ball/Monnet duos allowed Monnet to present his views to the highest levels of the American government at an early stage of decisionmaking, although he did not always have the privilege of doing so as directly or as frequently as did Ormsby-Gore. But then, Monnet's friends were many. Among them, George Ball, one of the main advocates of British membership in the European Communities, was not particularly liked in London. His attempts to safeguard the political integrity of the European Community venture, while at the same time trying to preserve American economic interests, made him a hard negotiator to deal with. In his memoirs, Ball recalled that his task, as he saw it, was "to stand like Horatio at the bridge and forestall any British deal that would either seriously dilute the political significance of the Community or discriminate against America."[52] Macmillan, in his memoirs, remembered that "President Kennedy was . . . helpful and sympathetic, . . ." but "there was always Mr. George Ball of the State Department who seemed determined to thwart our policy in Europe and the Common Market negotiations."[53] Ball and the British were at odds on two key issues: EFTA and the Commonwealth.

NO SLIDING SIDEWAYS INTO THE COMMUNITIES

In early May Macmillan put on his hat of adviser of the United States and proceeded to make further contact with the American president in the realm of ideas. Kennedy had requested that Macmillan write a memorandum summarizing the British position in preparation for his talks with General de Gaulle.[54] The memo was welcome, but also disappointing on one essential point. The prime minister seemed to have forgotten Ball's strong suggestion that the United Kingdom should join the EEC only if it were prepared to endorse the full political implications of the Rome Treaty and to ask for no favors. Macmillan's insistence on special arrangements for the United Kingdom (for agriculture and EFTA) blatantly conflicted with American recommendations. Ball soon brought this home to Macmillan. A memorandum explaining the American position on the relationship between the EEC and EFTA was quickly communicated to the British administration. Ball also wrote a long memorandum to help the president reply to Macmillan. "The effect of Macmillan's highly qualified approach," he pointed out, would be "disastrous to Western cohesion: it would loosen Germany's ties to the West, as well as encourage General De Gaulle to pursue his most nationalistic policies."[55]

The European Free Trade Association

British ambassador Harold Caccia (Ormsby-Gore had not yet replaced him) arranged for a meeting with Ball to discuss the American memorandum on EFTA. After an interesting exchange of views, touching upon most of the issues involved in the EEC/EFTA relationship, Kennedy's people, with Ball frequently acting as spokesman, often reiterated the American position not only to the British but also to the other EFTA countries. In doing so, Ball seemed to have forgotten one of the lessons of the failure of the EDC: high-pressure tactics by the United States were resented by its allies, and did not always serve the interests of those they were intended to help.

The British position was to try to negotiate Britain's entry into the Common Market while at the same time, with the Six, examining possible ways to accommodate the special economic and commercial problems of the EFTA neutrals that would result from that membership. Problems with EFTA would be discussed between the Six and, acting as a bloc, the Seven. Ball had no trouble showing his aversion to this scheme—it reminded him too much of previous British bridge-building efforts. His preferred course of action was to negotiate British entry in the Common Market first and to tackle EFTA problems later. At any rate the EFTA group was far from being a homogeneous whole, and EFTA itself appeared to be nothing more than a temporary agreement, since members could leave the association upon one year's notice, which was not the case with the Rome Treaty.

The United States, Ball told Caccia, would welcome the Norwegian and Danish applications for membership if they agreed to come in as full members of the EEC. The American administration would not, however, look with favor upon the conclusion of special arrangements with the EFTA neutrals. In his memoirs, Ball remarked that "Sweden and Switzerland defined 'neutrality' to suit their own purposes," and he had "no sympathy for such casuistry."[56] Austria was a special case, however, since the Soviet Union had agreed to the Austrian State Treaty, which guaranteed Austrian independence from the Soviet Union on the express condition that Austria remain neutral. Shortly after the United Kingdom applied for membership, the Soviet government, as was to be expected, strongly objected to Austrian membership in the European Economic Community on the grounds that its members were all members of NATO and that Austria would thus compromise its neutrality by joining the Community. Austria nevertheless was the first to apply for association with the EEC in December 1961, which Ball felt was greatly to its credit. But, although he was inclined to show some indulgence with the Austrians, he believed that any accommodation of the special problems of the Swedes and the Swiss by the EEC would allow them to have access to the trade benefits of participating in the Common Market without having to shoulder any of the political burdens of the Rome Treaty. This, he thought, would water down the political aspect of the Community.

George Ball thus largely espoused the position of previous administrations—both Democratic and Republican—that had supported European integration predominantly for political reasons, and he continued the trend, started under Eisenhower, of backing European integration *à la Six* rather than through EFTA-type agreements, which involved no political commitments. Ball also pursued another trend that had become increasingly prevalent during the last years of the Eisenhower administration. As the United

States became more and more preoccupied with its balance-of-payments situation, it began to look with suspicion at integrationist schemes on the Continent that only threatened to enlarge, without the redeeming features of political cohesion, a European trading bloc that already discriminated against the United States. During the Kennedy administration, economic considerations began to catch up with political considerations, although they still did not dominate American thinking towards European integration.

For both political and economic reasons, then, Ball argued the case against bringing EFTA and EEC countries together into a loose commercial arrangement. He made this amply clear to Ambassador Caccia. For Ball, the so-called split between the Six and the Seven, which Macmillan had frequently deplored during conversations with United States officials and which he felt could lead to a political split, was nothing but a hoax. The existence of two trading groups had in fact been largely beneficial to the Six and the Seven in terms of increased trade. Somewhat ironically, Ball remarked that "Europe had always been 'split.' Before the Six and the Seven were organized, there were 13 national states which were 'split' from one another. Now there were merely two trading groups . . . The case for lamentation over the existence of "the split of Europe was difficult to sustain in the face of the trade statistics: these show[ed] that U.K. trade with EEC had been expanding even while the so-called 'split' was deepening." At any rate, the United States had no intention of encouraging EFTA and the EEC to get together into a "single large trading bloc discriminatory against the United States."[57] Ambassador Caccia interjected, "Then you are not interested in European unity?" Ball answered "Not on the terms you have indicated." United States willingness to let the British, the Norwegians, and the Danes enter the EEC was proof enough that the United States supported European unity. Yet the United States "did not wish to see the Swiss and Swedes given the commercial advantages of the Common Market at no cost to themselves." When they decided to decline membership in NATO, Sweden and Switzerland had shown that they were not too keen on a close relationship with Europe. The United States "had never felt this was a major blow to European unity. On the other hand, the contribution which a major power such as the United Kingdom could make to Europe was a wholly different order than that of the smaller nations."[58] This last sentence summed up the case for American support of British entry into the Community, which, as will be remembered, the Eisenhower administration had not initially supported, mainly for fear that the British might squelch the political evolution of the European Communities.

What did in fact motivate this growing interest in (toward the end of the Eisenhower administration), and outright support for (under Kennedy), British membership in the European Communities? As the United States came to the realizations that the European Communities, which it had helped to create, might not be as economically outward-looking as it had hoped, and that they might not adopt a federalist, but a Gaullist, form of political unification, it quite naturally sought to protect its interests. By backing British membership in the Communities, the Kennedy team hoped not only to strengthen the Communities but also to contribute to their political stability and economic liberalism. In this context, EFTA caused a major headache for the new administration, and particularly the Europeanists (with Monnet speaking loudly from the prompter's box), not so much because it could intensify an economic and political split in Western Europe but because it threatened to keep the British out of the European Communities. But was British membership really a plus for the European Communities? Wouldn't it slow down the political evolution of a united Europe toward a community-type, or federal-type, of organization as it had in the past?

Despite Ball's vigorous intimations to the British that they consider the Rome Treaty as an evolving process and accept its political consequences, even Ball could not prevent the British from feeling more comfortable with a Gaullist-type of political organization for Europe. Paradoxically, British membership held the prospect of improving the chances for a confederated, as opposed to an integrated, Europe. Thus the United States, despite its strong commitment to European political integration, was willing to pay a price for British entry into the European Economic Community: a political price. For British membership would most likely delay the moment when a united Europe would speak with one voice. But for now the Kennedy team was more preoccupied with ensuring that the European Communities generally continued to speak in harmony with the United States. On this point the pragmatists and the Europeanists on the Kennedy team agreed: the first order of priority was to let the British in and to deal with the economic challenge of the EEC; there would be plenty of time later to deal with the consequences of British membership for the political outlook of the new Europe.

Optimism and pragmatism combined to prompt the Kennedy team to adopt a decidedly short-term outlook on British membership and the EFTA countries. Any obstacles that threatened to thwart the chances of British membership were to be cast aside. The special problems of EFTA countries, particularly of the neutrals, were such obstacles. As a matter of strategy, Ball sought to discourage the British from linking the negotiations for British entry into the Common Market with larger negotiations between EFTA and the Six. His main preoccupation, and that of Monnet, was that it would have assured the failure of the negotiations for British entry. Hence Ball's recommendation that the United Kingdom and the European Economic Community seek to accommodate the problems of the neutrals only after arrangements had been made for acceptance of the Rome Treaty by the United Kingdom and the other EFTA countries applying for membership.[59] Hence also his preference for making arrangements with the neutrals on an "individual nation basis."[60] Sound strategy dictated avoiding any resemblance to earlier attempts by the British to merge the Six and the Seven.

In practice these tactics had the effect of casting George Ball in the role of an unpopular negotiator. Not only did he frequently make his position known to representatives of EFTA countries privately but he also did so publicly, and Ball could be very direct. A public statement in London on 3 April 1962 was particularly offensive to the neutrals. Shortly afterwards, a Swiss newspaper, the *Neue Zürcher Zeitung,* wrote, no doubt referring to Ball: "When today in the United States, which is neither a member of the Common Market nor a European country, influential members of the government start up a veritable campaign against the association of Europe's neutrals with the Common Market, and when these circles already start issuing edicts that the neutrals shall be allowed no such association but merely an ordinary commercial treaty, this can only be regarded as one-sided interference in matters that are the real concern of the European countries."[61] But Ball was willing to incur the wrath of the neutrals. During the EFTA Ministerial Council held in London from 28 to 29 June 1961,[62] the British had, somewhat unwisely Ball thought, committed themselves to safeguarding the interests of the other EFTA members and had agreed that all EFTA members should remain united throughout the negotiations with the EEC. Ball saw it as his role to "disengage" the British "from a negotiating posture which would have assured the failure of the negotiations."[63] Ball in fact "assured the British negotiators—including Ted Heath—that America would run interference for them until we had pushed the neutrals into a forthcoming position; then, at the right time, [he] would soften [United States] objections so they could make some compromise arrangements that would not damage the Community."[64] Yet the British were not so grateful for Ball's high-pressure tactics. Both Macmillan and Opposition Leader Hugh Gaitskell agreed that it would be better for the United States to either soften its position or to stay out of the discussions altogether. The United States did in fact soften its opposition in the early summer of 1962. This accorded perfectly with Ball's strategy, which he had previously outlined to British negotiators.[65]

The Association of African States and the Commonwealth

On 28 February 1957, about one month before the signing of the European Common Market Treaty, President Eisenhower, in a joint statement with French Premier Mollet, indicated that he was in full agreement with the objective of the Six to associate the overseas territories with the Common Market.[66] Concurrently, Dulles mustered all of his powers of persuasion to convince German visitors to Washington that Germany, as a noncolonial power endowed with great economic strength, could play a significant role in furthering the development of a new relationship between Europe and Africa. Dulles specifically spoke of an "association of Europe and Africa out of which could come a whole new force in the world."[67] A simple look at a map made it plain that Africa was the "big hinterland of Europe."[68] "We tend to look at maps too much on the basis of an East-West projection," Dulles told German Foreign Minister von Brentano, "if we turned the map around, we would realize that Africa is the natural hinterland of Europe."[69] If Europe could successfully tap this great reservoir of resources and this great market, its prospects for the future would be considerably improved. They might actually be even greater than those of the Soviet Union or the United States. Rather than a "declining civilization,"[70] the so-called Old World might "develop into one of the greatest forces in the world."[71] To Dulles, when considering European challenges and opportunities in Africa, Europe was "not worn out, but on the threshold of great development in a manner which should inspire the imaginations of youth."[72]

Yet renewed vigor and rejuvenation for the Continent would not be forthcoming without decisive efforts on the part of Europeans. The Secretary of State deplored a relative sluggishness on the part of the colonial powers in granting more autonomy to colonies or overseas territories. If European colonial powers did not quicken their pace, he thought, change would occur not through peaceful evolution but through violent revolution. It would then be quite difficult to establish "proper relations"[73] with Africa, and the dream of "Eurafrica," cherished by some Europeans, would vanish. If, however, Europeans managed to guide African nations toward self-government through peaceful evolution, a "Young Europe" would then be able to engage in a fruitful association with a "Young Africa." Horace Greeley's old slogan, "Go West, young man," would accordingly be adapted for Europe into "Go South, young man."[74] Dulles was quite obviously thinking in terms of relatively recent American history. In a conversation with the German ambassador, the secretary of state did not hesitate to draw a parallel between circumstances in Europe and the situation of the United States in the not-too-distant past: "It was, of course," he said, "possible to have a unified Europe, but Europe needed the resources of Africa." In the United States, "the Eastern colonies had to federate but they could not have developed without the resources of the West and a sound relationship with the Western areas, . . . the same principles were applicable to Europe."[75]

While Dulles encouraged peaceful transition to self-government and believed that the association of a united Europe with Africa would greatly enhance the prospects for European unification, Kennedy was more wary of that association's implications. His concern was mainly for Latin America, a politically and economically vital "hinterland" for the United States. On 6 and 7 December 1961, the Six invited a great number of African countries to participate in a conference to negotiate the conditions of association of these countries with the new Europe. Negotiations continued throughout 1962 and 1963 and finally led to the signature of the Yaoundé convention on 20 July 1963 among the Community and seventeen African states and Madagascar. Anticipating these developments, Kennedy endeavored to insure that America's interests, as well as those of its friends, would not be harmed by the proposed associations.

In May 1961 Walter Hallstein, president of the Common Market Commission, paid a twelve-day visit to the United States. On 16 May, Hallstein met with Kennedy for about forty minutes. The first order of business that Kennedy brought up was the association of African States with the European Economic Community. Kennedy voiced his concern "about the possible adverse effects this Association might have on third countries, in particular Latin America."[76] Hallstein in turn retorted that the Commission had been considering the impact that "preferences accorded by the Community to African states would have on third countries, *and particularly Latin America.*"[77] He then pointed out that the preferences had a political role to play in orienting African countries toward Europe and the West. Moreover, in the interest of third countries, "the Commission had under active consideration a proposal to reduce these preferences, perhaps by as much as 50 percent, by lowering the common external tariff on certain key products but the economic situation in the Associated countries would require compensatory action." Hallstein's reassurances did not succeed in calming Kennedy's apprehensions. Twice during the meeting Kennedy again alluded to the possible detrimental effects that the association of African States could have for Latin America. Might the new Association not result in "discrimination in the case of a particular commodity . . . resulting in the loss of markets by Latin American countries?" asked the president. He particularly mentioned the case of coffee. At the end of the interview, Kennedy insisted that the joint communiqué of the Hallstein/Kennedy meeting include a "specific reference to their discussion of the Latin-American problem."[78] Hallstein agreed. The final communiqué, without directly linking the Association of African States with possible trade problems for Latin America, stated that "the President and Dr. Hallstein discussed in particular the effect of the coming of existence of the EEC upon trade with the Latin American countries."[79]

The State Department, while recognizing the "political and psychological importance" of ties between the EEC and African states,[80] was likewise preoccupied with the proposed associations. No doubt with a view to influencing and controlling the development of EEC arrangements with African States, or preventing them, the department recommended that the president propose to Hallstein a "joint US-UK-EEC discussion" on association "at an early date."[81] Rather than the establishment of special relations between the EEC countries and their former colonies, the State Department favored "a comprehensive and coordinated approach to the problems of Africa."[82] This was the initial position of George Ball, who advocated a comprehensive or universalist rather than fragmented approach to developing countries.

Ball distinguished between two systems of North-South relations: the "Open" and the "Closed." The United States had largely championed the first system, which was based on the assumption that "all industrial countries of the free world [would] accept responsibility for the economic, commercial and political well-being of all developing countries, without discrimination." The second system assumed "that specific industrial countries or groups of countries in the North [would] maintain special relations with specific developing countries or groups of countries in the South and [would] establish preferential and discriminatory arrangements to reinforce these relations."[83] The association of African states with the EEC fit the second description well. Ball disliked associate membership with the EEC not so much because of its direct potential for trade discrimination against the United States but because of its implications for outside countries, especially in Latin America. If the EEC accorded preferences to African countries, Ball thought, Latin American countries would increase their pressure on the United States for similar arrangements, especially since many Latin American products competed directly with African goods. And, if the United States gave in, it too would soon have to sustain the existence of its own "Closed" system, which might lead to other preferential systems around the world. Clearly such developments did not accord well with Ball's hopes for an "Open" system in which the most-favored-nation principle reigned supreme. The under secretary of state therefore set out to convince current and prospective members of the new Europe that their interests would best be served if they renounced their preferential arrangements. But Ball's crusade in 1962 and 1963 met only with "lukewarm response," be it with the French, the British, or the Common Market Commission.[84] As a result, Ball the pragmatist soon drew the conclusion that no matter how distasteful, the prospect of a series of special relationships between North and South was perhaps the only alternative, at least for the short term.

Ball firmly opposed arrangements for mere commercial preferences between the Common Market and the neutrals, because such arrangements avoided political responsibilities. He likewise opposed preferential arrangements between the EEC and African states unless they carried with them "the assumption of substantial obligations on the part of the industrialized partner."[85] By the end of the Johnson administration, Ball felt that if the EEC further extended its preferences to certain African countries, the United States would then feel justified in expecting the Community "to carry the burden of economic assistance and, where necessary, political tutelage for those African countries."[86] This meant that the United States would implicitly recognize special European interests and responsibilities in Africa, just as Europeans recognized the primacy of American responsibilities in Latin America. If Europeans alone were to benefit from preferential arrangements with African countries, so too would they alone have to carry the political and economic burdens previously shouldered jointly with the United States. The "economic assistance, education, health and defense of the African people"[87] would then appropriately become the primary responsibility of Europeans.

Both Kennedy and Ball had at first favored a universalist approach in which the developed nations of the "free world" would jointly support the economic, political, and strategic burdens in the Third World. The Acheson Report recommended that an "Atlantic Development Program" be established under the auspices of the OECD to provide assistance to developing countries.[88] In 1960 Kennedy wrote that Western nations should accept the end of colonialism and "must establish ... a full working partnership between the nations of the West and the nations of Africa."[89] Once elected Kennedy showed he took a great interest in Africa, largely because he considered it one of the most important levers in shifting the world political balance in favor of democracy. If Western nations could, under the benevolent leadership of the United States, coordinate their policies towards the developing world, thought Kennedy, African countries would not have to turn to Moscow for assistance. But by the end of the Johnson administration, Ball, one of Kennedy's closest and most trusted advisers on European and Third

World matters, evidently was in the process of modifying Kennedy's original vision. Ironically, Ball reverted to Dulles's inclination to consider Africa as the great hinterland of Europe.

George Ball did, after all, see some merit in the concept of Eurafrica, and in a division of the responsibilities of Western nations in the third world rather than a centralization of those responsibilities. First of all, the concept seemed to have gained some currency in Europe, especially in France. Also, American stakes in Africa were far less important than European interests and, "geographically and strategically, Africa mean[t] far more to Europe than to America."[90] Ball did not deny that there were "serious disadvantages to sectioning the world as one might an apple, cutting it into slices that define the special relationships between particular Northern and Southern areas." This was certainly "not the best way to allocate responsibilities for the poorer nations of the South." Indeed, it was "structurally reminiscent of colonialism," and, when compounded with commercial preferences, it prevented an efficient allocation of resources. Yet Ball was willing to envisage such an eventuality for the future, since it might "prove to be the only means of defining for Europeans a manageable area in which they [could] concentrate their foreign aid while looking after the education, health and defense of the African people."[91] In a nutshell, Ball was saying that a fragmented Europe did not possess the political maturity to shoulder world responsibilities. Until such time as Europe united, it would have to be content with regional responsibilities. The Nixon administration later scandalized Europeans by alluding to their regional interests as opposed to the worldwide responsibilities of the United States. Pragmatism pushed George Ball to adopt an essentially similar position.

If President Kennedy and George Ball were worried about the association of former French, Italian, and Belgian territories in Africa with the EEC, they were even more so about the prospects of extending EEC preferences to the Commonwealth, especially to Australia, New Zealand, and Canada. The United States had never really liked the Commonwealth. Cordell Hull had tried to destroy it, Dulles admitted to his difficulty in understanding it,[92] and Dean Acheson termed it an organization "which has no political structure, or unity, or strength, and enjoys a fragile and precarious economic relationship by means of the sterling area and preferences in the British market."[93] With the prospect of British entry into the Common Market, the Kennedy team now attempted to convince their British counterparts that the Commonwealth preference system was politically and economically unimportant to the United Kingdom. The British economy, argued American policymakers, stood to benefit much more from a new relationship with the new Europe than from economic and political entanglements with the Commonwealth. Yet Macmillan found it tremendously difficult to free himself from these very entanglements, which as we saw, he unskillfully presented as part of the United Kingdom's dowry for renewing its "special relationship" with the United States.

In late May 1961 the British Cabinet agreed to propose to Commonwealth members visits from various British ministers to inform them of the reasons why the United Kingdom intended to seek full membership in the Common Market. On 22 June the Cabinet approved a directive to be given to the ministers. The ministers were instructed to sketch out British reasons for joining the EEC. In order to cushion the blow, they were to insist that the United Kingdom would join only if it reached a common ground with the Community on "satisfactory arrangements . . . to safeguard the essential interests of the Commonwealth as well as those of the United Kingdom itself, and its EFTA partners."[94] This was a major blunder as far as Ball was concerned.

Of all the good "Europeans" whom Macmillan sent to tour the Commonwealth in early July, Duncan Sandys was given the hardest job. Visiting New Zealand, Australia, and Canada proved an unpleasant task. Communiqués following the talks were short and mostly expressed divergence of views rather than agreement. Mr. Keith Holyoake, the prime minister of New Zealand, made no secret that his government saw no possible compensation for "the loss of our existing contractual right of unrestricted and duty-free entry for our meat and dairy produce to the British market."[95] Australian Prime Minister Robert Menzies voiced his strong concern for the future of the Commonwealth if the British were to join Europe: "the Commonwealth," he said, "will not be quite the same."[96] While not specifically objecting to the United Kingdom entering into negotiations with the European Communities, his government was careful to avoid giving its approval.[97]

John George Diefenbaker of Canada proved even more intractable. This was no surprise to the British, since Diefenbaker had made amply clear on a number of previous occasions his aversion to the idea that the United Kingdom might join the Six. Satisfying Commonwealth members as well as British public opinion, which remained somewhat attached to the Commonwealth either as a symbol of past British glory or because it remembered the contributions of the white dominions during World War II, proved an arduous task for Macmillan. Hedging his bets on the Common Market, the prime minister attempted, according to Ball, "to slide sideways into the Common Market"[98] by publicly insisting on the need to find satisfactory arrangements for EFTA and the Commonwealth.

On 22 July the British Cabinet unanimously decided that the United Kingdom would apply to enter the Common Market.[99] Macmillan informed President Kennedy of this decision six days later. The American president offered his warm support and encouragement for this "bold decision" (especially "bold" because of the problems that Macmillan had courageously faced during the "preparatory discussions"). Not only could the British count on the "good will and firm support of the United States Government" for the "next stage of the negotiations," but Macmillan could personally count on Kennedy himself to help: "If at any time there are particular issues on which you think we might be helpful," wrote Kennedy, "I will count on you to let me know. In your relations with the great States of Europe and with the Commonwealth, the United States may not always be the best possible go-between, but in the ways in which we can be useful, within the framework of the discussions which our Governments have had in recent months, you can count on us absolutely. With warm personal wishes."[100]

Edward Heath also personally notified Jean Monnet of the British decision in a secret message received just one day before Macmillan made the announcement to the House of Commons. Thanking Monnet for his help thus far, the message openly indicated that the British government would gladly accept more help. Jean Monnet immediately answered Heath, assuring him of his support, and struck a responsive chord in emphasizing that British membership in the new Europe would lead to an "even closer association with the U.S." Yet for Monnet the basis of the new relationship was to be European unity "including G.B."[101] Monnet and the new Kennedy team agreed: British entry into the Common Market would provide the basis for a new special relationship with the United States. Yet it was still a long way to that new special relationship.

On 31 July, at the House of Commons, Macmillan announced the intention of the British government to make formal application under Article 237 of the Treaty of Rome. The prime minister's performance was delivered in an "uninspired way"[102] and included numerous references to the special interests of the United Kingdom and its friends, particularly the Commonwealth. Macmillan got off to a good start by evoking the political importance of the Treaty of Rome in promoting stability and unity in Europe and overall "strength in the struggle for freedom." The United Kingdom, he said, considered it its duty and interest to "contribute towards that strength by securing the closest possible unity within Europe." But the qualification Macmillan attached to his statement was of some magnitude. "At the same time," continued the prime minister, "if a closer relationship between the United Kingdom and the countries of the European Economic Community were to disrupt the long-standing and historic ties between the United Kingdom and the other nations of the Commonwealth, the loss would be greater than the gain."[103] Macmillan spoke from both sides of his mouth on the economic aspect of application as well. While conceding the importance of the EEC for expanding world trade and ultimately meeting the needs of developing countries, Macmillan added: "No British government could join the European Economic Community without prior negotiation with a view to meeting the needs of the Commonwealth countries, of our European Free Trade Association partners, and of British agriculture consistent with the broad principles and purposes which have inspired the concept of European unity and which are embodied in the Rome Treaty."[104] This last sentence did little to appease George Ball, who soon set out to write a memo to President Kennedy on the implications for American policy of Macmillan's statement on the EEC.

The Commonwealth figured prominently in Ball's report to the president. "Quite clearly," said Ball, "we cannot accept any form of association between the Commonwealth and the Community that even remotely follows the pattern of association now existing between the former French overseas territories and the Community." The consequences of such an association, warned Ball, would be detrimental to American trade, both in the agricultural and in the industrial fields. If Commonwealth countries gained "free or preferential access" to the Common Market, this would not only hurt American temperate agriculture but also "the tropical and temperate agriculture of Latin America." In addition, allowing Community members to gain "either free or preferential access to the market of the Commonwealth" would similarly be detrimental to American industry.[105] Aside from the impact on American trade, the association of the Commonwealth with the EEC would also have negative political consequences for it "would be a serious distortion of the whole concept of European unification."[106] Yet the failure of American efforts to convince the French to phase out their preferential arrangements and the determination of the EEC to negotiate associations with African countries, including former British colonies, left the American administration no choice but to acknowledge the political reality of the determination of the Community and to adapt its policy accordingly. Eventually, the United States halfheartedly accepted European preferences in Africa, yet this magnanimity did not extend to New Zealand, Australia, and Canada.

Secretary of State Rusk joined Ball in his efforts to convince Commonwealth countries that it was pointless to oppose British membership in the Common Market. The two men exploited every occasion to tell New

Zealand, Australian, and Canadian officials that the United States was strongly opposed to an extension of Commonwealth preferences to the Common Market. A meeting of the ANZUS (Australia, New Zealand, United States) Defense Pact allies in May 1962 was an occasion for Rusk to make these points to Australians and New Zealanders both publicly and privately. His remarks were not welcome. The Australian minister of trade was extremely direct: "I want all of our American friends to understand that our trading ties with Britain cannot be cut, either now or in a few years, without the most serious consequences to our export trade and the livelihood of our producers."[107] George Ball himself did not deny that the immediate suppression of Commonwealth preferences would indeed have serious consequences for Australia and especially for New Zealand, which earned more than half of its foreign exchange by selling its products to the United Kingdom, particularly dairy products.[108] In a memo to Kennedy in August 1961, Ball recognized that "while taking a firm position against the extension of Commonwealth preferences," the United States could not "reasonably expect the existing preferential system to be terminated over night." Ball recommended phasing out present arrangements "over a reasonable transition period." In practice this meant that the United States might "realistically have to face the possibility that the ultimate agreement between the United Kingdom and the Common Market [would] require some special cushioning arrangements for individual members of the Commonwealth."[109]

Despite "tense initial disagreements" with Australian Prime Minister Robert Menzies, Ball eventually succeeded in softening Menzies's opposition to British membership by promising American help to New Zealand and Australia during the transition period if the United Kingdom were to join the Common Market. A meeting of Menzies with top-level American policymakers in mid-June 1962 seems to have been the turning point in appeasing one of the most important opponents to British membership in the Common Market. George Ball was pleased with his achievement, not only because he had succeeded in removing one of the major obstacles to British membership but also because he genuinely liked and admired Menzies, "one of the most effective political figures of the postwar world. A colorful man of boundless energy and robust good humor" who "delighted" George Ball "by singing Australian country songs as [they] rode about together."[110] New Zealand's demands had been reasonable from the start, despite the fact that it stood to suffer much more from British membership in the Common Market than Australia or Canada. In light of New Zealand's vulnerability, Ball insisted on the need for special cushioning arrangements. European nations ultimately agreed that such arrangements would indeed be necessary. As for

Canada, American reassurances did not succeed in pacifying Diefenbaker, who continued his opposition campaign unabated. By the end of 1962, he was largely isolated in his crusade against British membership. Yet, even though Macmillan seemed to have been rather successful in pacifying Commonwealth and EFTA opposition to British membership, there remained some major roadblocks to British membership.

11

Roadblocks and Boundless Optimism: On the Road to Nassau

What were the real chances of the British entering the Common Market? On 15 May 1962, Michael Butler, first secretary at the British embassy in France, told François Duchêne, a close co-worker of Monnet's, that he was "90% sure De Gaulle want[ed] to stop British entry in the Common Market." During a recent meeting, de Gaulle had been reported as saying, among other things: "The British will never be able to accept integration within the Common Market, but we will be courteous enough not to tell them so."[1] That same day de Gaulle held a press conference in which he outlined his grand design for Europe, which clearly did not match that of the proponents of the Atlantic partnership. Yet Monnet and his collaborators continued to interpret events in a positive way, and hoped de Gaulle would refrain from torpedoing British entry into the Common Market, if only for fear that his European partners would then blame him for the failure of the talks, which would *ipso facto* doom the chances of his plans for a European political union.

By the end of the year, shortly before de Gaulle's resounding "no" to British entry, Monnet wrote to Dean Acheson: "I am following of course very closely the negotiations with the British. I have no doubt that they will succeed and that Great Britain will be a part of the European unity fairly soon."[2] Europeanists in Washington seemed similarly impervious to growing indications that de Gaulle might not let the British in. Were they guilty of distraction and wishful thinking? Were they not over-optimistic, given increasing evidence that the talks might fail? Did they evaluate this information correctly, ignore it, or misinterpret it? The roadblocks on the path to British entry were many, and de Gaulle was one of several.

For one thing, Macmillan had to face the strong opposition[3] of the Labour party. In October, the party unanimously voted against British membership in the Common Market. Europe, said Hugh Gaitskell, the head of the Labour party, might be a good idea *if* the United Kingdom succeeded in getting far better terms for its membership in the Common Market. But the conditions Gaitskell attached to British membership were so demanding as to preclude the chances for the success of the ongoing negotiations.[4] Given the declining popularity of the Macmillan government and the strong presumption that Gaitskell might succeed Macmillan, his opinions received special attention both in Great Britain and abroad. Gaitskell was an old friend of George Ball, but Ball did not succeed in convincing him of the economic and political merits of the Common Market. Despite Ball's and Kennedy's efforts to bring him around, Gaitskell persisted in considering the Common Market as nothing more than a purely commercial venture. In the *Discipline of Power,* Ball noted that his friend sent Kennedy a "carefully written brief, expounding the Labour party's reason for taking a negative view," which Kennedy received during the ill-fated Nassau meeting in December 1962. Kennedy asked Ball to draft a reply. Unfortunately, "the reply was never sent because Hugh died tragically in January a few days after de Gaulle's press conference."[5]

THE COMMON AGRICULTURAL POLICY

Agriculture was another major stumbling block. First, there were substantial differences between the British system of deficiency payments and the continental support system for domestic agriculture. Also, Commonwealth countries enjoyed preferential access to British markets for their agricultural produce, while the British in turn benefited from buying this produce at very low prices. The British demands for comparable outlets for temperate-zone Commonwealth agricultural products in the Common Market became one of the major bones of contention in the negotiations for British membership. De Gaulle commented on the overall situation during his famous January press conference. For him, the British system was clearly incompatible with the proposed community system. The United Kingdom imported her food supplies "at the lowest prices from the two Americas and the old Dominions" and heavily subsidized British farmers. By contrast, the EEC system consisted in "making a pool of the agricultural products of the entire Community, of strictly determining their prices, of forbidding subsidizing, of organizing their consumption between all the members and of making it obligatory for each of these members to pay to the Community any savings they might make by having foodstuffs brought in from outside instead of consuming those offered by the Common Market."[6]

Beside wide disparities between the continental and the British systems, the domestic stakes both in Britain and on the Continent were such as to greatly complicate negotiations by hardening the positions of the negotiators. On the British side, not only were members of the Labour party opposed to British membership but also some key members of the Conservative party, who urged firmness on the part of the government in dealing with the Common Market on agricultural issues. Sir Anthony Hurd, the chairman of the Conservative party's Agricultural Committee, was adamantly opposed to the current proposals of the Six and warned that the British electorate would not blindly acquiesce to higher food prices. The agricultural vote had traditionally been important to the Conservative party and disappointing results for its candidates in the November by-elections reinforced Hurd's misgivings.[7]

In Germany, high food prices were the norm for protecting inefficient, high-price producers. In October, German farmers rioted after receiving indications from Brussels that the new Common Agricultural Policy (CAP) would mean lower producer prices.[8] Badly in need of the farmers' vote, Adenauer and his party tried to appease this powerful force in German politics by showing a marked reluctance to extend the Common Market to agricultural products and to move towards the French position.

Unlike Germany, France was a large and relatively efficient agricultural producer, endowed with half of the Community's arable land. As farm surpluses piled up, farmers became increasingly dissatisfied with the current French agricultural policy. Understandably, the French government tried to defuse this explosive situation by seeking advantageous terms for its farmers during negotiations with its partners in the EEC. In order to extract concessions from its partners, the French did not hesitate to employ what resembled blackmail techniques. If the Five, particularly the Germans, wanted the British in, then there would be a price to be paid in the form of a further definition of the CAP, which would be tailored to French needs for larger markets and subsidized exports.[9] For the French it was essential that some of the most crucial details of the CAP be negotiated before the British became members of the Common Market. Increasingly suspicious of British motives, the French came to fear the creation of a coalition between the two major agricultural importers within the Community—Germany and the United Kingdom. The nightmare scenario envisaged that the British, once in the Common Market, would team up with the Germans to negotiate or renegotiate terms favorable to themselves, but detrimental to the major agricultural exporter in the EEC: France. The strong presumption that the British might serve as a channel for American interests not only for industrial goods but also for agricultural goods rendered British entry even less desirable.

American interests were essentially similar to those of the British, except for British demands for preferential access to the Common Market for Commonwealth agricultural goods.[10] Ball anticipated that since the United Kingdom had a tradition of low food prices for its consumers British adherence to the Common Market would tend to lower the level of protection for Common Market producers and thereby also reduce discrimination against the United States.[11] He said as much during a confidential conversation with French Ambassador Alphand in July 1962. With the avowed intention of making a few "helpful" points, since the ambassador had asked for American suggestions or proposals, Ball told Alphand that the British "were right in their emphasis on price, since otherwise marginal or inefficient producers would be brought into production leading to the creation of high-priced surpluses and disrupting world markets." The American interest, continued Ball, "was the same as the British in this regard."[12]

Beyond the issue of the impact of British membership on United States and other countries' agriculture, the whole problem of the development of the CAP needed to be addressed. George Ball and Robert Schaetzel were of two minds concerning the CAP. They considered it "essential to the development of the EEC, since there had to be a balance between industry and agriculture,"[13] and believed that it could help the EEC progress towards effective unity.[14] These considerations prompted them to launch a hard-sell campaign to persuade Orville Freeman that the CAP was not such a bad thing after all; after much effort, they succeeded in convincing this "Archetypical Secretary of Agriculture"[15] to support it. Although he initially backed the State Department's position, Freeman later had second thoughts on the matter. As for the two salesmen, they soon felt slightly ashamed to have put one of their colleagues and friends in what became an uncomfortable position in light of some of the later protectionist features of the CAP as it developed. While they continued to say they were not opposed to the CAP, they nevertheless cast themselves in the roles of Horatio at the bridge, watching for American interests.

The stakes were of sufficient magnitude to warrant such attention. In the early sixties, American agricultural exports made up about one-fourth of all American exports, and one out of every six harvested acres was exported. Of these exports, about 40 percent moved abroad to the Six Common Market countries. But not all agricultural exports were to be equally affected by the Common Agricultural Policy. Of the $1.2 billion in agricultural products sold to the Six, $400 million entered duty free because they were not produced in the Community. Another $400 million were subject to relatively low fixed duties. These products did not cause much concern to the United States. In fact, for some commodities, the Departments of State and Agriculture actually expected exports to the Community to increase as the EEC pursued its spectacular economic growth. Cotton, soybeans, and other oilseeds (perhaps also tobacco) belonged to that category.[16] The adoption by the Six of the variable levy system in January 1962, however, threatened to displace a third category of U.S. agricultural exports, which made up the other $400 million and competed with EEC production. The system of variable levies was designed to bring the prices of agricultural imports to the Community up to the level of Community prices by imposing a levy on them equal to the difference between the Common Market price and the import price. Not surprisingly, U.S. negotiators were keen to protect the $400 million in exports that would be subject to variable levies. These mostly consisted of wheat and feed grains;[17] another important item was poultry exports. The grains issue topped the list of American priorities for international commodity agreements. In the State Department, Robert Schaetzel and others proposed to freeze producer prices of grain at existing levels until the conclusion of a World Grains Agreement, which they planned to convene right after British entry into the Common Market. As a bargaining tool, the United States would have stated its agreement "to negotiate concerning its domestic price support."[18] Ambassador Butterworth in Brussels dissented. To him, freezing prices was a good idea as far as countries with low prices such as the Netherlands or France were concerned, but "such a US proposal would not promote and could even impede EEC action with respect to high grain prices such as those of Germany." He recommended that the United States ask for a "freezing of low prices and a reduction of high."[19] All agreed, however, on the necessity for the EEC to follow "reasonable price policies" so as to "permit further negotiations to be carried forward in a good atmosphere" with other countries' suppliers.[20] This was diplomatic language for possible retaliation if the Community opted for a "trade restrictive" policy in the agricultural field.[21]

THE CHICKEN WAR

By the time that the "Chicken War" commenced in November 1962, diplomatic language had given way to strong and direct recriminations against the CAP by the secretary of agriculture. There was a marked difference in tone between his cautiously optimistic pronouncements in support of Kennedy's Trade Expansion Act earlier in the year, in which he had emphasized the excellent sales potential of American agriculture in

Western European markets, and his menacing, indignant statements as 1962 drew to a close. In early 1962 the first effects of the CAP had not yet been felt, since the CAP had just been agreed to in January; by the end of 1962 the situation was different. Regulation Number 22, "on the progressive establishment of a common organization of the market in poultry meat" had been adopted in January 1962 along with other basic regulations that established the CAP. On 1 August 1962 levies on poultry went into effect. The powerful American poultry industry immediately began pressing the American government to protect its interests. These were indeed substantial. American poultry exports to the EEC had increased tremendously in recent years: from $2.3 million in 1958 to $35.5 million in 1961. Of these exports, 95 percent went to Germany alone. The American poultry industry not only hoped to maintain, but also to expand, this flourishing market, especially in Germany. EEC plans for developing its own poultry business seriously threatened the realization of these hopes. In August, the German duty on chicken rose from 4.3 to 9.6 cents per pound. By July 1963, duties had skyrocketed to 13.4 cents per pound.

Secretary Orville Freeman reacted quickly. His main concerns were, obviously, for the two items that stood to lose the most from the new levies, namely, poultry and grains. During a trip to Europe in November 1962 Freeman was very direct: "We don't like any part of the Common Market's new variable levy system for controlling imports of grains and poultry, and we are not going to stand by and allow our historical markets to be taken away."[22] Two days later, on 19 November, Freeman addressed the OECD, claiming that the United States had been "sharply troubled by the mounting evidence, such as the recent action on poultry, which suggests that the EEC, instead of moving toward a liberal trade policy for agriculture, actually is moving backward with regressive policies that could impair existing trade agreements." He sincerely hoped American negotiators would receive "adequate assurance" during forthcoming trade negotiations that export markets for American agricultural products would be maintained.[23]

The Chicken War epitomized the mounting concerns of American farmers and policymakers about the consequences of the CAP. Many Americans saw it as a sort of test case of EEC intentions. Ambassador John Tuthill made this amply clear during a press conference in August 1963. Referring to Herter's pronouncements the previous month, Tuthill reminded his audience: "Governor Herter told the officials with whom he met during his July visit to Europe just how vital the United States considered the poultry case. It was important not only because of the material and substantial damage already inflicted upon the United States but also because of the possibility that it might set a precedent for the way in which the variable levy system would work for other commodities."[24] Tuthill later became one of the main architects of a compromise between the EEC and the United States on the poultry issue. George Ball valued him greatly, and it is probably no mere coincidence that Tuthill replaced Butterworth as American ambassador to the European Communities in October 1962 just as the U.K. negotiations were marking time and the CAP was coming into effect. "Tuthill is our best man in Europe," George Ball told Herter just before sending Tuthill to Brussels, not only because of Tuthill's competence but also because of his valuable contacts in European circles, where he had many close friends, including Monnet, Hallstein, Marjolin, Rey, and Mansholt.[25] Sicco Mansholt was the main architect of the CAP. Jean Rey, the commissioner in charge of the Directorate-General for External Relations, later became the principal representative for the EEC in the negotiations on the poultry issue. He was also one of the single most important figures in ensuring the conclusion of the Kennedy Round. The Tuthill connection was important indeed.

By the time Tuthill came to Europe there was already much bad blood between the United States and the EEC, and the situation deteriorated further after de Gaulle's press conference in January. On the American side, Senator Fulbright, the chairman of the Foreign Relations Committee, proved particularly hard to deal with. By vocation an early defender of European political integration, in this particular instance Fulbright transformed into a staunch protectionist, defending the interests of his Arkansas constituents—as Arkansas was one of the major producers and exporters of chickens. Shortly after de Gaulle's press conference, Fulbright not only chastised the general for pursuing "a hopeless dream of French dominance in Europe divided from its friends and partners" but also launched a thinly veiled attack against the EEC. The United States, he said, would have "no other choice but to seek alternatives to its present foreign policy" if the EEC pursued protectionist policies.[26] The *New York Times* sounded an ominous note, pointing to the French veto and the Chicken War as evidence that European integration, which the United States had so long supported, might not turn out to be in the interest of the Atlantic Community after all: "The frozen chicken tariff may not be an earth-shaking event. Nor is the new French veto the end of European unification. But taken together, they again raise the whole question as to whether the European Economic Community is to be an inward-looking, high-tariff club or a liberal trade partner of the United States. On the answer to that question may depend the future shape and even the fate of the Atlantic Community."[27]

As the situation festered to the point where the Chicken War became the symbol of an Atlantic "malaise," and the United States threatened to take heavy retaliatory measures against EEC trade, Ambassador Tuthill took the initiative of phoning Herter from Antwerp, where he was visiting the American consul general. He suggested that the United States and the EEC submit the poultry issue to GATT arbitration. Tuthill said that Eric Wyndham White, director-general of GATT, would be prepared to set up some kind of ad-hoc committee. Herter followed Tuthill's advice.[28] There ensued a number of official and off-the-record meetings between Tuthill and EEC commission officials. Tuthill worked particularly closely with Jean Rey. The result was the conclusion of the Chicken War. While the United States had initially claimed that $46 million of its trade was affected by the poultry levies, the Commission calculated that trade damage to the United States would amount to no more than $19 million. The GATT committee settled for a compromise by estimating damage to the United States of $26 million and permitting the United States to retaliate on four products for a similar amount. On 22 November, Tuthill informed Jean Rey that the United States agreed to go along with the GATT decision.[29] Later that same day, John F. Kennedy was assassinated.

THE TRADE EXPANSION ACT AND FRENCH CONCERNS

Without entering into further details about the Chicken War, a few remarks are in order in connection with the negotiations for British entry. Beyond the levies affecting poultry and the whole system of variable levies, the CAP came under close American scrutiny in 1962 and 1963. The agreement by the Six on a Common Agricultural Policy in January 1962 had been an important factor in ensuring the passage of the Trade Expansion Act. The act itself, as presented to Congress in January 1962, contained provisions that allowed the American president to reduce tariffs to zero on agricultural products that did not meet the 80 percent dominant supplier clause, provided the president found that such a move would "tend to assure the maintenance or expansion of U.S. exports of such products."[30] In defending the TEA to Congress, George Ball emphasized that it was "designed expressly to provide bargaining powers that would enable the United States to maintain the position of U.S. farm products in the enormously important Western European market."[31] Senator Paul Douglas later introduced an amendment which evidently referred to the CAP: "Whenever a foreign country or instrumentality the products of which receive benefits of trade agreement concessions made by the United States . . . maintains non-tariff trade restrictions, including variable import fees, which substantially burden United States commerce . . . the President shall, to the extent that such action is consistent with the purposes of section 102 . . . suspend, withdraw, or prevent the application . . . or refrain from proclaiming benefits of trade agreement concession to . . . such country or instrumentality."[32] The amendment, the implementation of which was left to the president's discretion, was introduced not so much to restrict presidential authority as to pacify opposition from the Farm Bureau Federation and serve as a warning to the EEC.

Given the importance of the agricultural issue to the French government, such statements did not go unnoticed. Pressure from the United States to include agriculture in the future Kennedy Round and link future reductions of industrial tariffs to the EEC's willingness to lower its agricultural duties served to intensify French misgivings about Kennedy's agricultural grand design. Perhaps the American design was nothing else than an attempt to destroy the CAP, mused de Gaulle. If the Community members did not succeed in further consolidating the CAP before the Kennedy Round, the CAP, and perhaps the Common Market, might disappear for lack of a common position of the Six vis-à-vis the United States. Should the British join, such a common position would be harder to attain, since the British insisted on a host of exceptions for themselves and would be tempted to side with the United States on certain issues, thereby weakening the Community as a whole and the French bargaining position in particular. In fact, the TEA as a whole worried the French, and some of its features also worried Monnet.

On 30 March 1962, Valéry Giscard D'Estaing, who had just replaced Wilfrid Baumgarter as the French finance minister, frankly told Under Secretary George Ball that the French entertained severe reservations towards Kennedy's trade proposals.[33] On 31 October 1962, French Minister of Industry Maurice Bokanowski spoke of the "grave peril of diluting in a generalized free trade world the preference accorded to each other by members of the EEC" if the ambitions of the TEA were not limited.[34] Just prior to the 14 January press conference, and after the United States had agreed to give Polaris missiles to the British, distinguished members of the French press unveiled another French fear, namely the bastardization of the Community through British entry, which would promote American economic and political interests on the Continent from within the Common Market. On 10 January *Le Monde* carried one article by André Fontaine and another by Maurice Duverger. Both indicated in somewhat similar terms that "some people," or some people "in high places . . . were not far from seeing in England the Trojan Horse of the United States." While Fontaine feared the dissolution of the Common Market in a "vast free trade zone" if Britain joined, Duverger posed the question of British entry as a choice between a free trade area dominated by the United States and an autonomous Common Market free to design its own economic planning as it saw fit.

De Gaulle later echoed their pronouncements in his press conference, in which he demonstrated that he not only feared British entry but also the entry of the EFTA countries along with the United Kingdom. The Common Market that would emerge from the amalgamation of all these states and the Six would be quite different from that originally built by the Six, de Gaulle thought, especially since these states had "very important particularities." The result would be a loss of cohesion within the EEC, which would grow gradually weaker and then be absorbed by "a colossal Atlantic Community dependent upon and subject to the leadership of the United States."[35] All in all, then, what some French quarters objected to most strongly was American leadership on the Continent through the British and their followers. In fact, one of the most objectionable features of the Atlantic partnership proposal was the American pretension of maintaining this very leadership while at the same time speaking of a "partnership between equals." De Gaulle did not fail to see this contradiction in Kennedy's grand design and to denounce it. The Nassau Agreement provided him with a handy pretext with which to strike a fatal blow at one of the key components of the grand design: British membership. We shall return to this shortly.

BACKSTAGE WORK

The French, and some Europeans as well, objected not only to much of the substance of the grand design but also to the tactics used by Americans in their attempts to influence developments in Europe, and particularly the British application to join the Common Market. In this specific instance, the special relationship proved to be detrimental to the British, rather than helpful. The negotiations for British entry were somewhat complicated from the beginning by the fact that the Six negotiated with the British not as a single delegation but as six separate delegations. The Rome Treaty specified that "the admission of a new member in the Community must be unanimously accepted by the Council of Ministers." In other words, each member of the Six remained sovereign in its decision to accept a new member. This seemed to preclude having the interests of the Six represented by the

Commission, unless the Six unanimously charged the Commission to defend their interests. De Gaulle certainly had no intention of doing so. Under no circumstances did the general conceive of having French interests represented by the Commission, especially if the main negotiator was to be Paul-Henri Spaak; Hallstein fared little better in the eyes of the general. After entertaining the possibility of representation through the Commission for some time, Monnet, Hallstein, and friends found that other members of the Six were similarly reluctant to speak with the British through the Commission.[36] This greatly complicated American efforts to control the negotiations. Had Hallstein or Spaak been chosen as the spokesman for the Six, it would have been easy enough to monitor the negotiations for British entry from backstage; controlling six delegations was more complicated. George Ball, Robert Schaetzel, Assistant Secretary of State for European Affairs William Tyler, and others nevertheless attempted to communicate their views and gather information on the negotiations through privileged channels. Hallstein, Spaak, Monnet, Mansholt, Rey, Heath, Sir Frank Lee, and others were such channels; many of the contact persons belonged to Monnet's circle of friends. A few examples will serve to illustrate the point.

In early January 1962 Schaetzel and Ball cabled Brussels to ask Ambassador Douglas MacArthur II if he "would ask Hallstein if it would be possible for [Jean-François] Deniau to make a quick visit to Washington" sometime after the middle of the month. "Very useful conversations with Heath" had made them "more aware than before" of the crucial role Deniau played in the EEC/UK negotiations" and "particularly the detailed analytical work which he [was] supervising on the Common Market side and Eric Roll for the British."[37] The young Jean-François Deniau, who headed the EEC Delegation for Entry Negotiations, did come to Washington in early February for a short visit. Ball then cabled Bruce: "We have a feeling that U.K.-Six negotiations are marking time despite British insistence over the last six months that they must complete [the] process by the end of the summer." "Extensive conversations with Deniau" had given them the "distinct impression that sympathetic Europeans [were] sincerely baffled by the failure of British to get down to serious negotiation." Ball was "not alarmed about this situation" and mostly blamed "British internal and external politics." Nevertheless, he was sufficiently preoccupied to ask if there had "been a shift in British determination to proceed?" Did Bruce "give any credence to rumors that the British might stage a crisis, possibly in May, by breaking off the negotiations?"[38]

Throughout the negotiations, Europeanists in the State Department maintained contacts with some of the key figures in the negotiations for British entry. On the British side these were, among others, Ted Heath, in charge of conducting the actual negotiations, and Sir Frank Lee,[39] one of the main artisans of the British decision to enter the Common Market and the "linch-pin of the whole negotiating structure until his retirement from the Civil Service in the autumn of 1962."[40] Conversations with French Minister of Agriculture Pisani also proved useful on occasion. So, too, was the Italian connection. The United States banked on using Italian fears of being dominated by a Franco-German combine if the negotiations failed, to press distinguished Italian officials, notably Prime Minister Fanfani, to take positions that would again facilitate British entry.[41] The administration also attached some importance to the Spaak connection. Here it is important to note that the American ambassador to Belgium, Douglas MacArthur II, had become a close friend of Paul-Henri Spaak, whom he met several times during the week and sometimes several times a day.[42] Accordingly, he reported faithfully and at great length the conversations he had with the Belgian minister of foreign affairs. Besides the MacArthur connection, Spaak also met directly with President Kennedy; their discussions mostly pertained to the Congo, but they also touched upon European integration.[43]

During the opening battle of the Chicken War in November 1962, the administration made use of the MacArthur/Spaak connection to communicate "President Kennedy's deep concern over a number of protectionist devices that are being increasingly advocated by certain Common Market Countries with respect to American agricultural products, particularly poultry, grains, rice and certain other items." In a letter to Spaak, MacArthur emphasized in somewhat foreboding terms the importance of Western European markets for United States farm products and warned Spaak that EEC protectionism would invite retaliation from the United States, thereby posing a threat to Atlantic cohesion and "Free world cooperation." Protectionist policies in the agricultural field might also spill over to the industrial sector. It made no sense to "be internationalist and liberal-minded in trade policy relating to the industrial sector and at the same time nationalist and protectionist-minded in the agricultural sector." MacArthur ended on a friendly note: "The situation with respect to poultry is particularly pressing and we earnestly hope that with your broad and far-sighted vision you will be able to use your great influence in Belgium and with other members of the Common Market on this product and generally on behalf of liberal, understanding, and sympathetic trade policies . . ."[44] The letter was sent on 2 November. That same day the State Department insisted that Spaak meet with the president and the secretary of state not only to discuss the Congo but also "to talk about current problems between the United States and the

European Economic Community resulting from the latter's application of the Common Agriculture Policy."[45] During Spaak's visit to Washington later that month, he and Kennedy discussed a memorandum on agricultural protectionism in the EEC and worked out some of the substance for a telegram to the foreign ministers of the Six.[46] In late December, the State Department urged that the president meet with Ambassador MacArthur in light of his close contacts with Spaak and Spaak's "influence on the outcome of the British-EEC negotiations."[47]

Partly because of his friendship ties with Ambassador MacArthur, Spaak's influence was of some importance during the negotiations for British entry. Yet Spaak was not as well connected as Monnet in the United States. Monnet not only benefited from the close friendship of George Ball but also had one major advantage over Spaak—the ability to influence American decisions in their early stages as a "non-official actor." Monnet did not represent any government, while Spaak did. Monnet's task was also facilitated by the informal character of Kennedy's style of government, which contrasted with Eisenhower's highly structured administration. Spaak seems to have been closer to Eisenhower than to Kennedy, but even Eisenhower's organizational machinery proved no real obstacle to Monnet, who bypassed it through Dulles.

In December, when the negotiations for British entry were marking time, American Europeanists decided to appeal to the Hallstein connection. In an "Eyes Only" telegram to George Ball, William Tyler, and Robert Schaetzel, Ambassador Tuthill wrote that he felt that the "best hope for giving negotiations sense of direction would be for UK and Commission [specifically Heath and Hallstein] to form informal but intimate working alliance." He suggested approaching Hallstein first, and if he reacted favorably, proposing the same informal alliance to the British prime minister and Heath. The "indirect advantage of such an arrangement . . . would be to establish an effective point of contact" where the United States could voice its "own views when the chips are down." "At present," he noted, "proposals come from such a variety of sources that it is extremely difficult to know just where and when to intervene. In the future this will be increasingly important to us."[48] Four days later George Ball arranged to have Hallstein fly to Washington. On 8 December they had "a long and frank lunch." Ball warned that if the negotiations for British entry failed, it "would engender a deep bitterness on the part of a nation that would react with the chagrin of a rejected suitor . . . a Britain rejected, after making what it would necessarily regard as a fair and generous effort to join Europe, would be tempted to devote its energies toward dividing the Six and weakening the European structure."

The failure of the negotiations would also have a bad influence on the future shape of the Community, for it would strengthen those forces in the EEC that were "most inward-looking and restrictionist." It would also have adverse effects on American industrial and agricultural circles and American public opinion. The "logic of British accession to the EEC" had much contributed to American plans for an Atlantic partnership. In addition, Congress had voted on the TEA anticipating an enlarged EEC. "The Imagination of Americans had been caught by the vision of a united Europe implicit in the building of the Common Market, but American opinion had been only partially aware of the Common Market until the fact of the British application had given it a new reality." Should the negotiations fail, American business circles and the American public would blame the Six for their "lack of vision," and American fears of an inward-looking, protectionist EEC trading bloc would be heightened.

After this somewhat lengthy detour, in which he showed Hallstein the opening of Pandora's box if the negotiations for British entry failed, Ball adroitly proceeded to propose a means of remedying the present situation in which the Six and the British were not really working together as potential partners trying to resolve their differences. He suggested that the Commission begin serving "as a kind of bridge between the British and the Six." Concretely, this meant that Hallstein and Heath would meet "on a basis of confidence," with Hallstein acting "as a broker in bringing about solutions to the tough problems." The United States would continue to play a passive role in the negotiations, yet "consistent with the protection of [United States] interests," the United States "were prepared to be helpful in a discreet way." Ball then suggested to Hallstein that the United States might serve as a channel of communication between the Commission and the British. In diplomatic language, Ball indicated that Macmillan and Kennedy might discuss the negotiations at Nassau. While Ball "had no plans to see Heath in the future," the two of them "might have a talk some time within the next few months." Ball "therefore would appreciate any suggestions from Hallstein as to whether—and if so how—the United States could be a useful friend of the situation."[49]

What George Ball proposed was an informal triangular alliance between the Commission, the British, and the United States to overcome the opposition of the Six to some aspects of British entry. Hallstein accepted the offer. Two days after his conversation with Hallstein, an obviously satisfied George Ball wrote to the president that Hallstein had not only accepted his offer but had already made "one or two suggestions" that Ball "could pass to Heath as a starter." He ended on an optimistic note: "I think Hallstein was impressed with the seriousness that we attached to a quick conclusion of these negotiations and I feel we have paved the way for some work backstage that can give the negotiations a helpful shove. Meanwhile, you will be in a position to advise the prime minister at Nassau that we have struck a blow on his side."[50] Unfortunately, de Gaulle had a profound distaste for such backstage work, and instead of striking a blow for Macmillan's side, the American team probably unwittingly struck one against it.

Shortly after the Kennedy/Macmillan talks in April 1961, David Bruce, remembering the lessons of the EDC, had warned George Ball that "all possible precautions should be taken to avoid [his] being cast in [the] unpopular role of high pressure salesman or even 'honest broker.'"[51] Time and time again, the American ambassador to Britain repeated his warning. When in late July 1962 some State Department officials contemplated sending a memorandum to set forth the United States trading interests involved in the negotiations between the United Kingdom and the Six, Bruce immediately cabled that the "great merit" of the American method so far had been that the United States had avoided the center stage. As a result, the image of the United States was that of a "benevolent onlooker." "Personally," wrote David Bruce, "I think it is in both the US and UK interest to have us continue to speak from the prompter's box rather than from the middle of the stage."[52] Ball listened to Bruce's advice, and to that of Tuthill and Ormsby-Gore, all of whom were opposed to sending the memorandum. He killed the memo idea diplomatically, without antagonizing its supporters within the State Department, by putting his case to McGeorge Bundy in the form of a question. Did the benefits of sending the memorandum (mainly to satisfy the demands of agricultural lobbies) outweigh the risk of "throwing a spanner into the negotiations at a crucial moment?"[53] The memo was never sent. In this specific instance Ball and Bundy probably acted wisely. Yet Ball showed a tendency to forget Bruce's advice on occasion, and did appear as an "honest broker" in a number of situations. In addition, the new American strategy of speaking from the prompter's box did not always succeed. Even though the prompter avoided speaking from the middle of the stage, the voice was still too strong to go unnoticed.

Notwithstanding these reservations, the informal alliance between Europeanists in Washington, American ambassadors in Europe —particularly Tuthill, Bruce, and MacArthur—and, as Ball put it, "good European"[54] members of the European Commission, and otherwise "good Europeans," such as Monnet, proved useful in a number of instances. It was relatively successful in ending the Chicken War and in getting the Kennedy Round negotiations off the ground. It did not, however, succeed in overcoming the doubts de Gaulle entertained towards British entry. Yet it can be argued that the negotiations might have succeeded because de Gaulle was increasingly isolated among the Six during the spring of 1962 and was beginning to consider British entry as a displeasurable, but unavoidable, eventuality. It would be unreasonable to place the blame for the failure of the negotiations squarely on the shoulders of the Europeanists. As always, the picture that emerges is rather mixed. Not only did de Gaulle's grand design not agree with that of the Kennedy team, and not only did he feel that the British might serve as an American Trojan horse, but also the British themselves chose a style of negotiation that contributed to the failure of the negotiations.

BRITISH ENTRY? FOREBODING SIGNS

Despite indications by the British negotiators of the willingness of the United Kingdom to progressively phase out its own system of guarantees and to adopt the community system, British negotiating tactics weakened their own bargaining position. Attempts to seek safeguards for some of the British special interests, including agriculture, the Commonwealth, and the EFTA countries, condemned participants in the U.K./Common Market negotiations to protracted item-by-item discussions. In addition, the British team purposely reserved their major concessions for a package deal until near the end of the negotiations. This proved to be a significant tactical error—delaying tactics served only to gather support for French proposals and harden the position of the Six.[55] Had the British offered their proposals sooner, the momentum of the negotiations would probably have been maintained and de Gaulle would have had no choice but to go along with his partners.

Apart from this tactical error on the part of the British, their failure and that of the Six to present the negotiations as a major political event rather than as a series of commercial agreements also contributed significantly to slowing down the negotiations. At least that was the reading of the situation by most of those whom Walt Rostow called the members of the "Atlantic Establishment." As soon as the British applied for membership in the Common Market, Jean Monnet warned that the negotiations should be concluded as quickly as possible in order "to avoid confusion." "It is a mistake," he said, "to think that large-scale negotiations are necessary. Material problems should not impress us, they are not that hard to resolve.

What counts is the decision to consider issues within the perspective of a future reality, rather than the maintenance of the past."[56] In mid-December 1962, when the negotiations for British entry seemed in danger of failing, Monnet's Action Committee issued a joint declaration, asking that the negotiations be brought to a rapid conclusion. The declaration pinpointed one of the major defects of the talks: the failure of a common vision that could transcend national interests for both the Six and the new applicant and could prevent participants from getting entangled in "the discussion of the detailed implementing decisions."[57] Ball, Tuthill, and most of the Europeanists concurred with Monnet in his assessment of the absence of progress in the negotiations. Writing to the president on 10 December, George Ball not only distributed blame to de Gaulle and Adenauer and their evident distaste for British entry into Europe but also to the British and their "tendency to treat the negotiations as a commercial haggle rather than a major political undertaking."[58] Meanwhile, Tuthill directed some blame at the Six and their unwillingness "to tell domestic pressure groups that [the] political objective to helping [the] UK must be overriding." He also chastised the British for their inability to persuade "good Europeans" that British membership was so crucial to European integration as to warrant a "major concession on EEC principles, or to convince [the] Six governments that UK room for maneuver [was] so limited domestically [that the] Six must make some retreat on narrow national economic interests now."[59]

In seeking to understand the reasons for the slowdown of the United Kingdom/Common Market negotiations at the end of 1962 and to devise an appropriate strategy for reinvigorating the talks, Europeanists further diagnosed as one of the factors the declining domestic strength of the Macmillan government. Macmillan had indeed been defeated in several by-elections. And, while Macmillan went down, de Gaulle went up. His victory in the November legislative elections strengthened his hand enormously, and made him less willing to accept compromises on his own grand design for Europe. As Kennedy's Presidential Adviser David Klein phrased it, de Gaulle's victory meant that he would "be more of a man with a mission than before, more determined to rearrange France's internal political life, and probably less compromising on the international scene."[60] Macmillan's declining political fortunes and the likelihood that he might be succeeded by a Labour candidate, who would not be favorable to British entry, strengthened de Gaulle's resolve to defer British admission to the more distant future. Unfortunate moves on the part of the United States and the British at Nassau further strengthened this resolve, while at the same time providing a pretext for adjourning the negotiations.

FUMBLING OVER NASSAU AND THE MLF

On 27 May 1962 Macmillan wrote in his diary: "there seems an increasing impression that de Gaulle does *not,* repeat *not,* want us in Europe."[61] A few days later, the British prime minister met the French general at Château de Champs. Their meeting did not do much to reassure the prime minister. De Gaulle told his guest that British entry would change the political and economic character of the Community. He also objected to the United Kingdom's intimate ties with the United States. The general deemed the "American Alliance as essential," but feared that the American blueprint for Europe was "to make Europe into a number of satellite states." He, de Gaulle, clearly had a different plan in mind: he wanted Europe to be united so it could "look the Americans in the face." He wanted Europe to have a "European policy not only for Europe but all over the world." Most importantly, Europe was to have its own defense, "without which no government ha[d] any responsibility or authority," hence the importance of a nuclear deterrent force for France. Macmillan offered some help, but with a strong qualification— the United Kingdom might cooperate with France, but only inasmuch as this did not involve sharing secrets that the British had received from the United States "as heirs of the original founders of nuclear science in the war."[62] This, in effect, took most of the substance out of Macmillan's offer for help. The prime minister probably wanted to go much further than that in his offer of nuclear weapons cooperation with the French, but before the meeting Washington had made the point to him and his staff time and time again that the United States would not be favorable to Franco-British nuclear cooperation. Europeanists in Washington and in Europe fretted over the idea that Macmillan might be willing to trade nuclear know-how or weapons for French support in the Common Market negotiations. Reassurances from London that the prime minister had no such intention did not succeed in calming their apprehensions. In mid-May a British official told the American embassy in London that Macmillan might contemplate discussing with de Gaulle the "implications for common defense policy of UK becoming member of EEC and signatory of European political treaty in terms which will imply possibility of coordination of French and British defense policy in nuclear field."[63] This left room for concern on the American side.

   The worst scenario ran as follows: the British would join the EEC and the United Kingdom and France would then form an Anglo-French nuclear combine; British aid and association with France would then enhance "the stature and effectiveness of the French national nuclear force" and "would make it that much more difficult to hold the Germans in line."[64] The State

Department later made this point to George Brown, the deputy Labour leader, when he visited the president in early July 1962. In fact, the Kennedy team kept emphasizing to the British the crucial importance of separating nuclear issues from the Common Market negotiations. The United States had made up its mind not to give the French nuclear help. This basically gave Britain the lead in nuclear weapons in Europe, at least for the time being, thereby blatantly showing de Gaulle the advantages of the special U.S./U.K. relationship. American assistance to France in nuclear weapons, thought most Europeanists, would not buy de Gaulle's willingness to let the British into the Common Market and neither would a British offer of assistance to the French. At any rate, even if a British offer of assistance in nuclear weapons could weaken de Gaulle's resistance to British entry, the Europeanists, who mostly wanted to do away with both the French and British nuclear deterrents, strongly advised against it. Why focus de Gaulle's attention on a contentious issue? they reasoned. Would it not be wiser instead to simply "take the nuclear question out of the immediate forum of debate?"[65]

Macmillan partly obliged. He discussed nuclear matters with de Gaulle and agreed with him that the United States might hesitate to launch its nuclear weapons in case Europe were attacked and that "some European deterrent was perhaps necessary,"[66] but Macmillan's offer of cooperation was too limited to interest the general. Rather, it can be argued that the limits the United States indirectly placed on Macmillan's offer made it sufficiently meaningless as to make the general even more resentful towards the Americans, or to the "Anglo-Saxons," and British entry. In addition, the American team later did anything but keep the nuclear issue out of the immediate forum of debate. McNamara's speech and the American campaign for non-dissemination of nuclear weapons further angered de Gaulle and embarrassed the British. Finally, Nassau showed a tight interconnection between economic, political, and nuclear issues. The connection between nuclear matters and the Common Market negotiations that Kennedy and the Europeanists wanted to avoid proved to be unavoidable.

When Macmillan asked the Americans for Polaris missiles at Nassau in December, he refuted the Europeanists' argument that such an Anglo-American deal might complicate, if not condemn, negotiations for British entry. Macmillan had met with de Gaulle at Rambouillet on 15 and 16 December; the problem, said the prime minister, was not the special nuclear relationship but agriculture; the Community and the British had no disagreements on nuclear policy.[67] Macmillan apparently had not fully realized the extent of de Gaulle's aversion to the "special relationship"—political, economic, and, especially, nuclear. At Rambouillet, Macmillan told the general about the misfortunes of the Skybolt missile. If Skybolt were cancelled, he implied, he would ask Kennedy for Polaris missiles. De Gaulle later told Adenauer that Macmillan had completely neglected to mention Polaris to him.[68] In his memoirs, Macmillan insisted that he had indeed told de Gaulle of his intention to ask for Polaris missiles. The general himself, wrote Macmillan, "subsequently confirmed to various of my friends that I had told him at this meeting that if the United States administration cancelled Skybolt I would try to obtain Polaris in its place."[69] According to one scenario, de Gaulle showed no enthusiasm for an Anglo-American deal on Polaris and made the suggestion to Macmillan that they enter into a Franco-British joint venture, perhaps through reviving the Blue Streak missile. Macmillan misunderstood or perhaps failed to take up the offer, knowing full well the limits placed on British cooperation with France in nuclear matters due to the Anglo-American special nuclear relationship. Upon de Gaulle's insistence that Europe needed an independent nuclear force, Macmillan remarked, using somewhat unfortunate language, "that in the modern world independence was not an object in itself but a method of playing a worthy part in an alliance." To this, de Gaulle, so Macmillan remembers, "observed mournfully that in truth at the present time only the Soviet Union and the United States counted." The recent handling of the Cuban Missile Crisis had amply demonstrated this. In the wake of the 14 January conference, de Gaulle told Adenauer of Macmillan's failure to make any response to his proposal. His subsequent plea for Polaris at Nassau clearly demonstrated, he said, that England valued its special relationship with the United States to the point of sacrificing anything to it. Hence, "whenever the Americans would disagree with the Europeans, the English would think not like Europeans, but like Americans."[70] On Rambouillet, Macmillan wrote in his diary that he "thought the discussions about as bad as they could be from the European point of view."[71]

If Macmillan had seemingly failed to understand the importance that de Gaulle attached to an independent deterrent, he could have no doubts concerning de Gaulle's intentions towards British entry into the Common Market. De Gaulle had been very direct, to the point of shocking Foreign Minister Couve de Murville and Prime Minister Georges Pompidou. He objected to British entry, not just because of agriculture but also because the Five had rejected the Fouchet plan. Without the Fouchet plan, de Gaulle could not hope to maintain French supremacy on the Continent, especially since the British would be followed by other new members. France would have to share hegemony with Britain. On 12 January 1962, Christopher Soames, the British minister for agriculture, told Macmillan of a conversation with his French counterpart, who had explained de Gaulle's aversion to British entry thus: "My dear it is very simple. Now, with the Six, there are five hens and one rooster. If you join (with other countries), there will perhaps be seven or eight hens. But there will be *two* roosters. And it won't be as pleasurable."[72]

Equally displeasurable to de Gaulle was the thought that, since the Six had failed to agree on a common agenda for political matters, British membership would further intensify a tendency to side with the United States on key political and economic issues; Europe, as compared with de Gaulle's grand design for it, would then become little more than a shadow of the United States. At Rambouillet, Macmillan well understood that de Gaulle objected to British membership as a matter of principle. If Britain joined the Common Market would not be the same. Maybe someday the British would join but de Gaulle implied that the time had not yet come. Macmillan failed to inform the Americans at Nassau of any of this. Why remains a matter of conjecture. The result was that the Americans came away from Nassau believing that the Nassau Agreement was compatible with British admission to the Common Market if the United States offered Polaris to the French on similar terms as to the British.

NASSAU

Macmillan came to Nassau with the firm intention of obtaining Polaris. During the previous months, McNamara had been debating whether or not to cancel Skybolt. The story of the Skybolt cancellation has been told elsewhere in great detail, and here we shall review only its main features. Under Eisenhower, Macmillan had decided to scrap the British Blue Streak missile for a cheaper joint venture with the Americans. The Skybolt missile, calculated the British, could be launched from British strategic bombers and would accordingly prolong the life of the British independent deterrent. But by the time of the Nassau Conference, Skybolt was in trouble. Its development was proving too costly and too slow. To make matters worse, Skybolt had competitors: Polaris and Minuteman missiles. The development of the Minuteman missile was well beyond schedule, and, so the argument ran, it might make sense to save money by scrapping Skybolt and resolutely turning toward the future, in which manned bombers would increasingly look obsolete. By mid-October McNamara had decided that Skybolt ought to be cancelled. In early November, Kennedy, McGeorge Bundy, and Rusk approved his decision.[73] Soon the British were informed of American intentions. David Ormsby-Gore was not pleased, Minister of Defense Peter

Thorneycroft hinted that the British might be interested in Polaris, while Macmillan banked on his friendship with Kennedy to either restore Skybolt or obtain Polaris.

The Kennedy administration was divided over the issue of whether, and if so, how, to help prolong the life of the British deterrent. The Europeanists were firmly opposed to giving the British Polaris. George Ball, and, above all, Walt Rostow tried to convince Kennedy that the Skybolt cancellation offered a providential opportunity for excising Britain's deterrent. The conceptualists also pointed out that giving the British Polaris might upset the French and the Germans. In late November at a State Department meeting attended by Rowen of the Defense Department, Bowie, and others, Owen and Schaetzel declared that "Polaris risked the whole of European policy for nothing." Rusk then signed a State Department letter prepared by Owen and his peers and sent it along to McNamara. The letter recommended mentioning to the British only the possibilities: either continuing the Skybolt program, using Hound-Dog missiles, or participating in the MLF. Under no circumstances were the British to be encouraged to believe that the United States would help them "set up a nationally manned and owned MRBM force," for then "the difficulties of bringing EEC negotiations to a successful conclusion might be significantly enhanced." Also, "the political cost" of American persistence in denying "MRBM aid to France would be significantly increased."[74] During a conversation within the American delegation at Nassau, Assistant Secretary for European Affairs William Tyler told Kennedy that giving the British Polaris might confirm de Gaulle in his impression that the United States was "courting" the United Kingdom in order to gain a larger role in Europe through the United Kingdom. Such flaunting of the special relationship, said Tyler, would fortify de Gaulle's claim that the "United States was more interested in dominating Europe than in encouraging Europe to be really an independent and entirely self-reliant entity."[75] Walt Rostow put it another way: the Polaris alternative "would violate the prior American policy of not making available IRBMs or MRBMs on a bilateral basis and would strengthen de Gaulle's argument that Britain still looked to its bilateral ties across the Atlantic rather than to Europe for its future."[76] Tyler pointed out that such an exclusive Anglo-American deal might also breed German resentment, since it would publicly underscore the exclusion of Germany from the nuclear club.[77] Rostow concurred and amplified: "it would underline the third-class nuclear status of Germany and Italy, weaken their support for British entry into Europe, and upset the effort of previous years to encourage Europe to move toward collective rather than national solutions to its security and other problems."[78]

But if Skybolt was to be cancelled, and Polaris was out of bounds, what then could the United States offer the British? For the first time, George Ball was forced to look rather closely at the MLF proposal, which up until then had not received much of his attention. Faithful to the Monnet sequence, Ball had emphasized the Common Market negotiations, leaving the nuclear issue to be tackled at a later date; in fact, he was careful to avoid any connection between the Common Market negotiations and nuclear issues. He and other Europeanists now joined forces with Walt Rostow in viewing the MLF as a convenient means of "integrating" the British deterrent in a collective force. Meanwhile, McNamara and his assistant Paul Nitze leaned towards giving the British Polaris with the important proviso, however, that the British assign the Polaris force to NATO. They were also willing to extend the Polaris deal to the French, provided that they also assigned their force to NATO. After McNamara's disastrous visit to London in December 1962, he and Rusk agreed to offer the British Polaris to avoid a full-blown crisis in U.S.-U.K. relations. During a dinner organized by Ambassador Charles Bohlen, Rusk had to bear the combined assault of Schaetzel, Rostow, and other Europeanists for placing the British special relationship ahead of European unity. Somewhat irascibly, Rusk countered: "What do you want of me and the President? . . . we have to have somebody to talk to in the world . . . we can't talk to De Gaulle . . . or Adenauer; do you want to take Macmillan away and leave us nobody?"[79] It is true there was as yet no president of Europe for Kennedy to talk to; Europe was still a "nobody." Kennedy seemed undecided. All agreed on one point, however. It might be desirable, sooner or later, to phase out the United Kingdom's nuclear independence.[80] The agreement that emerged from the Nassau Conference—according to Ball "one of the worst prepared summit meetings in modern times"[81]—represented a compromise between British demands and conflicting positions within the American administration.

In the plane on the way to Nassau, Kennedy conferred with David Ormsby-Gore. The British ambassador tried and successfully managed to impress upon the president the importance, both for Macmillan and the United States, of maintaining the independent British nuclear deterrent. Ormsby-Gore painted a bleak picture of Macmillan's political situation, insisting that the prime minister had frequently referred in public to the importance of the special relationship for the United Kingdom. If Kennedy chose to cancel Skybolt, he might be responsible for the downfall of the Macmillan government. By depriving England of its nuclear deterrent, he would also inspire a wave of anti-Americanism in Britain, which the next British government, most likely a Labour government led by Hugh Gaitskell, might choose to exploit. Ill-prepared for the Nassau meeting and badly informed about the British political situation,[82] Kennedy was largely surprised by Ormsby-Gore's description of Macmillan's predicament. In the plane, the two friends developed a proposal that they thought was a generous offer to Macmillan. The Americans would abandon Skybolt for their own use but would generously contribute half of the forthcoming development costs for Skybolt to the British.

Yet, as they both discovered at Nassau, Macmillan had his heart set on Polaris. This was hardly surprising, given two major American blunders just prior to the Nassau meeting. On 11 December, McNamara, upon his arrival in London, with no regard whatsoever for the political consequences of his declaration, publicly announced that all five test flights of Skybolt had failed. Thorneycroft fulminated, while the British press stigmatized McNamara's declaration as the sign of a deep malaise within the alliance. Kennedy himself then made a declaration on American television on 17 December in which he argued the case for cancelling Skybolt, mainly for budgetary reasons. Macmillan learned of the president's declaration the next day, upon reaching Nassau. When Kennedy unwrapped the Skybolt deal, Macmillan told him that he was not interested—"The Lady has been violated in public."[83] The prime minister then made a passionate plea for Polaris. Macmillan was sentimental and eloquent. He was in trouble at home, he said, and if he came back to Britain empty-handed, British public opinion would crucify him and his government might fall. Placing the association of the United States and Britain in historical perspective, he made much of the "special relationship." Did President Kennedy want to be held responsible for the deterioration of relations between the United Kingdom and the United States? Did Kennedy want to be held responsible for the fall of the Macmillan government? He, Macmillan, had placed his trust in the United States when he chose to participate in the Skybolt venture. In exchange for American help, the United Kingdom had agreed to make Holy Loch in Scotland available to Polaris submarines. He, Macmillan, had had to withstand strong criticism at home for giving the Americans this base, not to mention the fact that this increased the likelihood that Britain might be targeted for nuclear annihilation. Would Kennedy now make a gesture on his behalf?

Kennedy was torn between his affection for his friend and fellow politician and his reluctance to offer him Polaris with no strings attached (that is, without committing the British to a multilateral force or to NATO). The president asked Ball, who was a last minute recruit to Nassau—Dean Rusk had decided to stay in Washington to host the annual diplomatic dinner at the State Department[84]—to state the case for the MLF. Macmillan was unmoved by Ball's arguments. The United Kingdom, he said, would keep its independent deterrent, and it had no interest in engaging in a multilateral venture. When Ball insisted that any Polaris offer would have to "be linked to a nuclear fleet manned by crews of mixed nationalities," Macmillan answered: "You don't expect our chaps to share their grog with Turks, do you?"[85] Ball then tried to impress upon him that a Polaris deal with Britain, without strings, would be offensive to the French, especially in light of the March 1962 American refusal to help the French with their enriched uranium plant. Kennedy came to his adviser's defense and spoke of the danger of nuclear proliferation and of the West's need for a coherent strategy, which clearly conflicted with the existence of separate deterrents.[86] Yet despite Kennedy's strong initial inclination to side with the Europeanists, the special relationship, or, one should say, the close personal relationship, that existed between him and Macmillan eventually took precedence over all other considerations. In a desire to help a friend and to keep the special relationship alive, Kennedy granted Macmillan Polaris. Besides a friend, Kennedy also needed a companion to help him share the heavy responsibility of controlling nuclear power. Even though, according to McGeorge Bundy, the president thought that the British nuclear deterrent was "a political necessity but a piece of military foolishness,"[87] and he was largely sympathetic with the viewpoint of the Europeanists, Kennedy opted for strengthening Macmillan's hand at home. Special ties, Kennedy's guilt over letting the cat out of the bag on Skybolt in public, previous commitments by the Eisenhower administration, a lack of information about the British political situation, and Macmillan's moving performance all combined to force the president's hand. Nassau thus became "a case in point where J.F.K. did overrule his subordinates in order to help Macmillan. It was a case of 'king to king,' and it infuriated the court."[88]

The agreement that resulted from the Nassau meeting was such a web of contradictions, and de Gaulle's reaction to it so negative, that Kennedy later commissioned Richard Neustadt to investigate the causes of what he considered a major blunder of his administration. In its essentials, the agreement, drafted jointly by McGeorge Bundy and, for the British, Philip de Zuleta, gave the British Polaris and left all the related issues sufficiently vague and ambiguous to allow each side to make its own interpretation. Article 6 specified that the United States would allocate some of its strategic forces, and the United Kingdom some of its bombers, to a NATO nuclear force. In Article 8 the United States agreed to make Polaris missiles without warheads available to the British. It was not clear whether the resulting British Polaris force would be included in a multinational or a multilateral nuclear force. *The Times* later wrote that the British got Polaris "at a knock-down price not much more than half the original estimate . . . a bargain that for most of its life has cost the Government less that 2% of its defence budget."[89] George Ball and the Europeanists found some grounds for contentment in Article 6, in which Kennedy and Macmillan "agreed that the purpose of their two governments with respect to the provision of the Polaris missiles must be the development of a multilateral NATO nuclear force in the closest consultation with other NATO allies." They agreed to "use their best endeavors to this end."[90] Yet "multilateral" meant different things to the different parties involved. To the Europeanists it meant a mixed-manned nuclear force. The British conveniently chose to interpret it as "multinational," by which they meant merely a cooperation among national nuclear forces.[91] Accordingly, the agreement did not commit them to contribute their Polaris submarines to the MLF, but only to NATO, and without mixed-manning. In addition, Macmillan had succeeded in adding a clause to the Nassau communiqué that the British forces to be included in the NATO multilateral force would "be used for the purposes of international defense of the Western Alliance in all circumstances . . . except where H.M.G. may decide that supreme national interests are at stake."[92] This, thought Macmillan, assured the continuation of the British *independent* deterrent. The Nassau Agreement, in all its ambiguities and all its allusions to a multilateral NATO nuclear force, had the incontrovertible result of giving the British Polaris without clearly committing them to a multilateral force. In this way, Nassau was a serious blow to the Europeanists' grand design. Not only had the United States entered into an exclusive deal with the British, but the MLF strings were not considered binding by the British.

ENTANGLING THE FRENCH

Mindful of de Gaulle's reaction to an exclusive Anglo-American deal, Kennedy, advised by William Tyler, decided to extend the Polaris offer to France on terms "similar"[93] to those offered the United Kingdom. On the last day of the conference, on 10 December, Kennedy and Macmillan each sent a letter to de Gaulle. Macmillan's letter emphasized the fact that he had succeeded in maintaining British nuclear independence under the terms of the Nassau Agreement. De Gaulle chose to interpret the agreement other-wise. In his January press conference, the general underscored not the fact that Britain had preserved its nuclear independence but lost it by committing its forces—present and future—to a multilateral force under the NATO American command. To Kennedy's offer of a similar agreement with the

French, de Gaulle said no thank you. Why buy Polaris missiles when France possessed neither warheads to arm them nor submarines to launch them? Yet de Gaulle's main objection was again one of principle: under no circumstances would the French agree to place their forces in a multilateral force under American control, for this would deprive them of their own independent deterrent. The more so because the MLF would naturally include "a web of connections, transmissions, interference and be subject to external controls to the extent that if it were suddenly deprived of one of its components, it might become paralyzed just at the time when it should act."[94] De Gaulle's language was highly perceptive on this point as McNamara, Nitze, and Ball had all looked upon the Polaris offer as a means of entangling him in one way or another.

McNamara and Nitze considered the Polaris offer a carrot to be dangled in front of the French in order to attract the *force de frappe* into NATO, gradually enmesh it in a complex network of connections, and eventually integrate it with the NATO deterrent. Their favorite means to achieve this end was not integration through the MLF but simply through Polaris assigned to NATO. Ball, on the other hand, thought it was perhaps acceptable to offer the British Polaris if "it made life bearable for Tories while they did their work of bringing Britain into the EEC. It was worth offering the French since a negotiation might *entangle* [italics added] them in such a way as to assure complaisance toward the British . . . on EEC." Once the British were admitted to the Common Market, thought Ball, the United States could quickly redefine the Nassau formula and safely return to "a truly multilateral solution"—the MLF. If this was not done, German demands for greater nuclear participation would intensify.[95] Ball thus planned to enmesh de Gaulle in a new negotiation on Polaris in order to soothe the general's aversion to British membership in the Common Market—one of the touchstones of Kennedy's grand design. Secretary Rusk and Ambassador to France Charles Bohlen concurred with their colleague; they both hoped that the general might "negotiate to see what did lie at the end and at what price . . . if the General did so he could not, at the same time, be beastly to the British."[96]

Despite an apparent initial interest in the American offer, the general was no dupe. Kennedy had offered de Gaulle an agreement "similar" to that offered the British. That seemed to imply more than just Polaris missiles, which would not have been very helpful to the French without additional support for their nuclear program. Unfortunately, a previous letter to Adenauer, which de Gaulle no doubt read, mentioned only an agreement on the "same" terms on Polaris.[97] Upon receiving Kennedy's message on 21 December, de Gaulle was reported as saying that he "was very impressed with the message" but wanted time "to reflect on it." He did not believe that the matter was "so urgent"[98] that Ambassador Bohlen need return immediately to France from Nassau; he would see him after the holidays, in early 1963. Meanwhile, Couve de Murville was carefully "non-committal" with respect to Kennedy's proposal. Lucet, director of the political office, and Grandville, an expert in nuclear matters at the Quai d'Orsay, showed more enthusiasm for Kennedy's proposal, but were equally noncommittal. Lucet "found it extremely interesting" and said "it was quite different from the Multilateral Force proposal outlined by Gerard Smith" in the fall. He added that the French did not, however, possess "proper warheads" for the missiles. Grandville thought the proposal a "fine step for NATO" and that it breathed life into it. Yet he pointed out that the proposal did not meet de Gaulle's current needs.

Time did not work in favor of Kennedy's grand design. De Gaulle soon found what he had expected, or chosen to believe, that not much lay at the end of the tunnel. In late December, Ambassador Alphand reported to Paris that Kennedy was "non-committal" about warheads.[99] On reporting to de Gaulle on 2 January, Ambassador Bohlen was rather vague in presenting Kennedy's offer. He said it would "open a wide field of cooperation between France and the United States," but did not specify whether this included nuclear information. He hoped that de Gaulle would nevertheless get the point.[100] In fact, the ambassador intended to hint that Kennedy was flexible on the issue. The president could not at this point in time make a definite offer to de Gaulle, largely because he had not covered bases within his own administration, particularly with the Joint Atomic Energy Committee. De Gaulle chose not to get the point.

To be fair to de Gaulle, despite Kennedy's sympathies for the French, his hands were partly tied by an internal debate within his own administration on whether or not to help the French. On 29 December, McGeorge Bundy reflected that there was an "evident tension between those, led by Bob McNamara, who want to make the Nassau pact lead on to prompt new arrangements with France and other NATO countries, and the convinced multilateralists of the Department of State who continued to believe that serious cooperation with France on the Nassau model" was "a mistake."[101] George Ball's talk with Couve de Murville on 10 January, in which he emphasized the multilateral aspect of the Nassau offer rather than Kennedy's willingness to help the French nuclear deterrent, confirmed the general in his impression that the American offer was just another trick to ensnare the French *force de frappe* within an Atlantic entanglement.

By that time, with or without Ball's comments to Couve de Murville, the general had decided to strike a fatal blow to Kennedy's grand design.

Nassau, or rather the interpretation de Gaulle chose to give to Nassau, provided him with a convenient excuse to bring the U.K. negotiations to an abrupt halt; it was not, however, the cause of de Gaulle's "*non*" to British entry. By December de Gaulle was largely engaged with Adenauer in laying the first bricks for his own grand design. In September he had submitted to Adenauer the draft of a Franco-German entente. In mid-November the German Cabinet had accepted the general's proposals, but not however, without insisting that any military cooperation between France and Germany must be related to the wider NATO context. Shortly after Rambouillet and just prior to Nassau, Couve de Murville and German Foreign Minister Gerhard Schroeder met to discuss a forthcoming Franco-German Treaty. The Americans were not informed of this at the time.[102] Meanwhile, Kennedy and Rusk planned to ask de Gaulle to come to Palm Beach to discuss the proposal and were trying to define what exactly they meant by offering de Gaulle "a similar arrangement." Dean Rusk advised the president that it might be better to schedule the visit after de Gaulle's meeting with Adenauer, scheduled for 21 January, for this would give both the French and the United States more time to work "on specifics."[103] Despite these good intentions, the timing was largely unfortunate. De Gaulle's conference preceded the Franco-German meeting, and Kennedy never got down to discussing specifics "en tête à tête" with de Gaulle.

BOUNDLESS OPTIMISM

Until 14 January, so it seems, Washington remained confident that an agreement could be reached with the French on Polaris and was hopeful that the British would join the Common Market. Yet clouds were, undeniably, gathering over the grand design. George Ball and others chose either to discount them or to hope that behind-the-scenes work would make them go away. Their boundless optimism was compounded by the fact that they had made no formal contingency plans in case the negotiations for British entry failed. George Ball forbade it, in part to avoid leaks. The only person that came close to doing any contingency planning was Walt Rostow, who wrote down his reflections for himself "without generating bureaucratic paper." If the Brussels negotiations broke down, he thought, the Monnet sequence would have to be reversed. This time one would have to "start with the nuclear affair," in which, unlike Brussels, the United States would participate.[104] Macmillan had made no contingency plans either. In July 1962, when asked by the journalist Sulzberger what he would do if Britain did not get into the Common Market, Macmillan answered, "I have always made it a rule in my life to avoid fall-back positions. When you have a fall-back position, you always fall back."[105] An added reason for the lack of a British fall-back position was, like the Americans, the need to avoid leaks.[106]

In mid-June 1962, Bruce told Schaetzel on the telephone that he thought the odds in favor of British entry into the Common Market remained about six to five in favor of success. Remembering the lessons of the EDC, Bruce strongly recommended, as he often did, that the United States remain on the sidelines, "avoid any sign of nervousness about the negotiations," and "refrain to the extent possible from discussing the matter publicly."[107] In early July, prospects for British entry looked reasonably good. Both de Gaulle and Adenauer, reported American Ambassador to France Gavin, had agreed that the movement toward European political unity "should not take such form as to hinder British negotiations with EEC in any way." On the down side, the two men also believed it necessary to move ahead on the political union without awaiting formal British entry into the Common Market.[108] De Gaulle's private conversations with Ambassador Alphand in late June seemed to indicate that the general no longer entirely rejected British entry into the Common Market and that he now thought it likely, although he was clearly not very enthusiastic at the prospect.[109] De Gaulle's change of heart was partly the result of the accelerated tempo of the negotiations in response to Heath's representations in the spring that the British internal situation made such a tempo necessary. A July deadline had been fixed in answer to his demands, but unfortunately the British had been unable to meet that deadline.

In mid-September, reports from key negotiators to the American Embassy in Paris still indicated that the success of the United Kingdom/EEC negotiations was now in sight and that Macmillan could now go only forward.[110] By the winter, though, momentum was lost again, and the negotiators were entangled in an intricate web of technical details, unable, so it seemed, to follow Monnet's advice to see the larger picture. By the end of November 1962, John Tuthill, the ambassador to the U.S. mission to the European Communities, painted a disturbing picture of the negotiations. Tuthill proceeded to list all of the various obstacles to British entry. First, there was agriculture. Then came the EFTA problem and the need to coordinate the United Kingdom's negotiations for entry into the three communities. The ECSC and Euratom negotiations were "at last well underway" he pointed out. Yet "informed sources in Brussels and Luxembourg" believed that the Six would hold back on British entry into both the ECSC and Euratom until the outcome of the United Kingdom/ EEC negotiations was "clearly predictable." British entry into Euratom offered particular problems in light of "certain delicate questions bearing on the US/UK military relationship." Tuthill concluded, somewhat somberly, that the negotiations might be completed by the end of 1963 and the treaties signed in early 1964. One would then have to ratify them. This was a far cry from earlier estimates by Monnet and others who had contemplated that the United Kingdom might be admitted by the end of 1962.[111]

In the early days of December, Tuthill became more alarmist. The negotiations were in a state of drift, he said. Some initiative was needed to give them "leadership and direction." Tuthill then proposed the triangular "informal but intimate working alliance" between the Commission, the British, and the United States[112] to somehow help the negotiations from behind the scenes. As we saw, Ball accepted Tuthill's proposal as sound, and Hallstein and Heath agreed to go along. On 4 December, President Kennedy himself told the Danish foreign minister that his recent talk with Adenauer had not left him with "a very optimistic impression of the prospects" for the negotiations for British entry. He then remarked that "there would be a very bad reaction in the UK if its application were rejected." "Within the limits of not seeming to involve [themselves] in a negotiation among Europeans, [the United States] were using [their] influence in favor of British admission."[113] Meeting Hallstein four days later, Ball painted a bleak picture of the Atlantic Alliance should the negotiations fail.[114] A few days later Secretary Rusk, accompanied by Ambassador Bohlen and William Tyler, called on Couve de Murville. They discussed the EEC's Common Agricultural Policy and touched upon the poultry problem.[115] Rusk later emphasized to Foreign Minister Schaus the "great importance" the United States attached to the negotiations for British entry and painted a vivid picture of the political and strategic value of European unity to the "North Atlantic Community." Schaus "was basically optimistic" and promised that "he would use to the best possible advantage his position as Chairman of [the] Council of Ministers of [the] Six beginning in January."[116]

Thus, behind the scenes, the American negotiators were contacting key figures in the U.K./EEC negotiations and thereby attempting to strengthen the British position. In doing so they perhaps refrained from discussing the matter too much in public, but did not follow David Bruce's advice to avoid displaying any sign of nervousness. Their backstage work pleased neither de Gaulle nor the other participants in the negotiations, including some of the British themselves. When Washington contemplated a major American intervention in late December, Tuthill warned that although it might be useful later, the time was "not yet." He then listed again some of the problems of the U.K./EEC negotiations—agriculture, the failure of the United Kingdom to present its case adequately in political terms—while also underscoring some of its achievements. The problems of the underdeveloped Commonwealth had mostly been solved, he said. Agreements were being reached on Canadian, Australian, and New Zealand problems, while the United Kingdom had accepted the entire "non-commercial" section of the Rome Treaty. He concluded his report by saying that the United States should continue to play the role of "sympathetic observer" and "to take a realistic but essentially hopeful and optimistic view of outlook, and so await developments of coming weeks."[117] By mid-December American ambassadorial reports from Europe were largely hopeful that the negotiations might still succeed, although not on the originally anticipated schedule.

After Nassau, reports from Paris began to get alarming. On 24 December, the American embassy in Paris telegraphed the State Department that Lyon, who had served during the interim between ambassadors Gavin and Bohlen, had played golf the previous day with Couve de Murville and Cyrus Sulzberger. The French foreign minister, said Lyon, had emphasized that the "U.S./U.K. Polaris Agreement rendered Britain's entry more difficult." Britain, Couve de Murville noted, had "not yet decided that she wanted to be really European." He singled out the British agricultural problem as the "outward manifestation of this attitude, seeking privileged situation [for] British farmers." Then came his most important accusation. Britain, he maintained, "still clung to her special ties with [the] Commonwealth and particularly [the] U.S." The fact that "Macmillan went to Nassau at this juncture prove[d] [that] Macmillan [had] not yet decided to be really European but [was] still holding on to Great Britain's special relationship with [the] United States." Couve de Murville then touched upon one of de Gaulle's most vivid fears: "Any arrangement which envisaged close linkage U.K.-Europe-U.S.," he said, "would result in all involved becoming Americanized." He was not opposed to the United States but wanted Europe to "maintain [its] own individuality." To make matters worse, Couve de Murville was "negatively non-committal" on the offer of Polaris to France. France, he pointed out, did not possess the submarines and would have problems in fabricating small warheads for the missiles. Furthermore, France was not in a position to fabricate uranium on her own.[118] Confirming Couve de Murville's comments, Ambassador Alphand reported in late December "a very sour view of Nassau from Paris—apparently not from de Gaulle personally but from Couve." The

French, he said, "regard this as merely a device for destroying their nuclear independence and increasing in an unacceptable way their expenditures on nuclear forces." Somewhat ironically, McGeorge Bundy told Kennedy: "Actually, as you know, the whole theory is that you can save them money if they'll let us."[119]

In early January 1963 George Ball took off for Europe, where he met with Adenauer on the MLF and also talked to Couve de Murville. Paying more attention to the report of a French friend of his, Charles Combault, who had briefly summarized for him the general's forthcoming conference, than to reports from the American embassy, Ball asked Couve de Murville if what he had just heard was true. If this was so, he warned, "it would create serious problems between Paris and Washington." Couve de Murville answered, "You are far too experienced to believe what you hear from press circles: you've been around too long for that, I can assure you there are no such ideas in this house." Couve de Murville had made similar assurances to Heath earlier that day; when Ball met him that evening Heath was in "ebullient good spirits" since Couve de Murville had given him "what he thought an unambiguous assurance that the way for British entry was still open." The next day Ball's confidence in Couve de Murville's assurances was shaken by the account of a reporter whom his friend Combault brought to see him. The reporter had attended a background meeting at the Elysée where he had been given an advance summary of the press conference; the report proved accurate, yet Ball chose to believe Couve de Murville. Writing his memoirs many years later, Ball was still trying to understand his incomprehensible behavior:

> Couve de Murville's unqualified assurance has haunted me ever since, and I have discussed it with Ted Heath, who feels equal mystification. Could de Gaulle have failed to take his own Foreign Minister into his confidence? The late Sir Pierson Dixon, who was at that time Britain's ambassador to Paris is reported to have believed that at that time Couve de Murville knew nothing of President de Gaulle's decision. I would like to believe that, but even though the General was famous for his secrecy, how could his Foreign Minister have been unaware of a matter on which the press had already been briefed?[120]

Yet Cecil Lyon's report of his conversation with Couve de Murville in late December was sufficiently clear on one point: Couve de Murville's viewpoint espoused that of de Gaulle's in its essentials. But then perhaps Ball had not read the ambassadorial cables that had come to Washington around Christmas.

"NO" TO KENNEDY'S GRAND DESIGN

On 14 January General de Gaulle said no to British entry into the Common Market, no to the Nassau offer, and yes to Franco-German cooperation. In essence, the general was saying no to Kennedy's grand design for Europe and firmly stating his intention to pursue his own vision for Europe. By an ironic stroke of fate, Adenauer accepted the MLF concept on the same day de Gaulle rejected it in his press conference. To add to the irony, Kennedy's State of the Union address coincided with de Gaulle's conference. The two statements symbolized in more ways than one the distance that separated Kennedy's grand design from that of de Gaulle. While the general spoke of independence and sought to guard Europe against American penetration, Kennedy reemphasized American support for European unity and hailed "a new era of interdependence and unity." While de Gaulle rejected the MLF and other integrative American schemes, Kennedy reaffirmed the Nassau offer while speaking of the necessity to "increase the role of our partners in planning, manning, and directing a truly multilateral nuclear force within an increasingly intimate NATO alliance."[121]

As a matter of strategy, McGeorge Bundy planned to emphasize to reporters "the difference in tone and temper between the president's State of the Union message and General de Gaulle's press conference." Ambassador Bohlen was "shocked"[122] by de Gaulle's rejection, as were most members of the Kennedy administration. Yet Europeanists and pragmatists alike continued to hope that the negotiations for British entry might still be successful. Bundy accordingly counseled the president to refrain from commenting on "General de Gaulle's attitude toward British entry in the Common market" so as not to interfere in the negotiations.[123] The American reaction was understandable given the decision by Great Britain and France's five partners to ignore the press conference and continue with the negotiations. Shortly after 14 January, both Monnet and Spaak made statements to the effect that the talks were approaching success and that the discussions for British entry should be continued. Spaak indicated that he did not believe that the "difficulties for British membership, both political and economic, in the European Community [were] as great as de Gaulle implie[d]."[124] Monnet expressed his belief that the "negotiations for British entry in the Common market might be rapidly concluded." He insisted that "it would be inconceivable that the negotiations should fail on matters that were in the end of secondary importance, compared to the objective of the union of the West." Echoing Kennedy's earlier pronouncements as well as his own, Monnet proceeded to paint his vision of Europe and the path to world peace he envisaged: "We have to realize that in order to attain world peace, the United Kingdom must unite with the Community and a relation of equal partners must be established between a united Europe, including England, and the United States. It is only by unifying the West that the conditions for a stable peace with the USSR can be created."[125] This short formula encapsulated the conception of Europe that de Gaulle had precisely rejected in his press conference. On 17 January, one day after Monnet delivered his speech, Couve de Murville asked that the negotiations be stopped. The Five initially refused, but finally gave in to the French request on 29 January.

12
##

After the Veto: The Grand Design on Trial

CONTINGENCY PLANNING AND THE
FRANCO-GERMAN HONEYMOON

As prospects for British entry dimmed, advice from American embassies
in Europe flowed into the State Department. Ambassador to France Bohlen
urged not to "debat[e] each point made by de Gaulle" at his press conference
but to make only an "objective and dispassionate comment . . . oriented
toward [a] general exposition" of American policies and their relation to the
Nassau proposals. This carefully restrained attitude would "strengthen respect for US motives," and signify both the importance and the "genu-
ineness" of American interest in Europe. As to the substance of de Gaulle's
press conference, Bohlen perceptively interpreted it as a "declaration of
independence of revitalized France and rejection of 'Anglo-Saxon' political,
economic, and military domination." De Gaulle's views, he continued, were
"calculated to appeal to latent anti-Americanism which [was the] product of
almost 20 years during which Europe ha[d] had to look to [the] US for
survival and protection."[1] From London, David Bruce suggested that in his
forthcoming press conference Kennedy might "reflect more in sorrow than
in anger on the parochial comments of the General" and "adopt the tone of
polite, unrecriminatory disbelief that the progress toward one of the most
hopeful experiments in Western European organization had run into difficulties over the terms and conditions for British entry into the Six."[2] From
Rome, Ambassador Reinhardt was largely in accord with the observations
of his colleagues. Calling for "quiet diplomacy," the ambassador recommended that the president's remarks should be "restrained and confident,
leaving image of mature constructive leadership in contrast with impression

of high-handed negativism created by de Gaulle in his press conference on January 14."[3] Other embassies made similar comments. Meanwhile key figures in Washington finally engaged in contingency planning.

By 18 January Walt Rostow and Paul Nitze had attempted to redefine American options and objectives should the negotiations fail; they did so partly in cooperation with the British. They first reached the conclusion that they should try to "keep the option open of Britain later joining the Common Market on full political terms." Therefore, "a break up of the Rome Treaty structure" was to be avoided, as were new Atlantic-oriented arrangements that might jeopardize British membership at a later date. Second, efforts were to be made through the Benelux countries, Italy, and Germany "to prevent de Gaulle from crystallizing the political structure within the Rome Treaty or a concerted European protectionist movement." For the immediate future, Nitze, Rostow, and Harold Caccia of the British Foreign Office agreed that Bonn needed some reassurance that the United States was still prepared to implement a forward strategy. To this effect the policy of strengthening conventional forces must be pursued. They further agreed to push for the MLF, while also pursuing the idea of a political committee within NATO to consult with American allies on nuclear planning. This was Nitze's brainchild, the software approach to European desire for more participation in nuclear planning, as opposed to the hardware approach of the MLF. Finally, the three men saw great merit in continuing to resolve trade problems within GATT and the OECD so as "to prevent a crystallization of protectionism on the Continent."[4] Ambassador Tuthill concurred with them on the necessity of pushing the MLF concept, which he saw as a means of unifying France's five partners around a common proposal and thereby strengthening their resolve to resist French demands and defend their own conception of Europe.[5] In addition, Tuthill proposed another initiative that could be pursued at a later date: the "design, development and manufacture of a nuclear weapon as a European Community enterprise."[6] The Kennedy team did not follow him on this point. On the same day that Tuthill sent his telegram to Washington, Kennedy spoke to the National Security Council in Washington.

For the most part, Kennedy supported Rostow's recommendation to push the multilateral concept so as to strengthen American influence in Europe and give the United States "the power to guide Europe and keep it strong."[7] This gave the signal for a heavy push on the MLF during the coming months. Obviously angered by developments in Europe, Kennedy also spoke of the need for the United States to look out primarily for its own interests, especially in the economic field, where he was much concerned about the

American balance of payments. I "do not think," said Kennedy, "that the Europeans will do anything for us even though we have done a lot for them. So we must have all our representatives looking out very strongly for the U.S. interests. We must be sure our economic house is in order and use our military, political power to protect our own interests." On an ominous note, Kennedy told the NSC: "We will be very tough about the actions that Europe takes. We maintain large forces in West Germany. If West Germany does not maintain sufficient forces but instead concentrates on agricultural production for instance to our detriment, we must take a strong position."[8]

While Kennedy made these points to the NSC, de Gaulle and Adenauer seemed to be on a honeymoon. On 22 January the two men announced the conclusion of the Franco-German Treaty of Cooperation. The reaction in Washington was one of shock. The United States had long been favorable to a Franco-German rapprochement, which they regarded as a *sine qua non* of greater European integration. Yet the United States also feared being confronted by a closed French-German system, which would engage in a policy independent from that of the alliance, notably by courting the Russians. In mid-January, before the administration even knew of the Franco-German Treaty, Walt Rostow expressed his concern for what was increasingly being viewed in Washington as a love affair between two old men. The question, as he saw it, "was whether politically [the United States]—who had fought two bloody wars over Germany—would abandon the Germans to de Gaulle politically."[9]

Earlier in the Kennedy administration, about a week after the erection of the Berlin wall, Carl Kaysen had contemplated giving some form of recognition to the GDR, accepting the Oder-Neisse line, leaving open possible discussions between the two German governments for a possible reunification, and discussing "mutual security guarantees for both Germanies by the Warsaw and NATO nations, including the creation of a nuclear-free zone in Germany." Kaysen anticipated that the "continuance of discussion between East and West German governments, and their elevation to an official level [would] make even more difficult the East German effort to seal completely the internal frontier." "The attractive power of West German success in contrast with East German failure," he thought, would "make itself felt in all these contacts, and, accordingly, [the United States was] to welcome, rather than fear them." His recommendation to leave the cold war stance was based on an important assumption. Since World War II, successive American administrations had been trying to tie West Germany firmly to the West, with the European unity movement, and later NATO, as the key instruments. Taking a long and perceptive view, Carl Kaysen now considered that "the rapid development of the EEC ha[d] so strongly tied the West German economy to that of its partners, that NATO [was] no longer the major political tie of Germany in Europe." The EEC, he admitted "has not yet directly tied Germany to the U.S. as do the political commitments [the United States] share with the present government on reunification, boundaries and Berlin," yet, he added, "it is not clear that a specific direct tie to the U.S. is more desirable than general ties to the Atlantic Community at large." Kaysen added a word of caution, however, by indicating that the situation had not yet progressed to the point where the United States could "view with indifference a change in Germany's relations with NATO at this moment." Yet it was "no longer the case that [the United States ran] a great risk of undercutting German participation by changing [its] views on the German question."[10] Kaysen's position contrasted sharply with that of Acheson and the hardliners, who advocated a cold war stance. By January 1963, Kaysen's views would be anathema in Washington.

Coming on the heels of de Gaulle's press conference, the Franco-German Treaty appeared to Washington pundits as a Franco-German conspiracy against NATO. In cooperation with the British, the American intelligence community conjured up the specter of a Paris-Bonn-Moscow axis that would reorganize the European arena, possibly leading "toward a Soviet withdrawal from East Germany to be followed by some form of confederation between the two parts of that severed country." Ball thought this would have meant "the end of NATO and the neutralization of Germany."[11] Badly shaken by the general's latest moves, the EEC no longer seemed to offer such a firm economic and political cement for tying Germany to the West, especially since de Gaulle and Adenauer now appeared to be looking East for solutions to European problems. The latent anti-Americanism of de Gaulle's press conference seemed to confirm such fears. As rumors amplified in Washington, the Kennedy team decided to confront the issue by asking the Germans themselves what the Franco-German Treaty meant.

In the first week of February, Karl Carstens, Ball's counterpart in the German Foreign Ministry, was urgently dispatched to Washington to respond to American demands for clarifications. George Ball and others gave him a hard time. Did the treaty mean that Germany approved of de Gaulle's rejection of British entry into the Common Market? What was the meaning of the military clauses of the treaty, and how could they possibly be compatible with NATO obligations, especially in light of de Gaulle's negative view of NATO? Was it wise to make overtures to the East without coordinating such overtures with the United States? Would not Khrushchev seize this opportunity to further divide the West? The fears proved unfounded. Carstens's visit showed that Adenauer and de Gaulle's romance was largely a private affair; German ministers and officials had not been much consulted and were angered by Adenauer's decision to go to France to sign the Franco-German Treaty. They soon took their revenge on the old man.

Out of that somewhat animated discussion in Washington emerged an agreement that a serious attempt would be made to water down the treaty.[12] Foreign Minister Schroeder and Heinrich von Brentano, the caucus chairman of the Bundestag after being ejected from his foreign minister post by Adenauer, were only too happy to draft a preamble to the treaty which in effect nullified most of its substance by reaffirming Germany's endorsement of some of the key elements of Kennedy's grand design. The preamble endeavored to preserve "a close partnership between Europe and the United States of America, . . . collective defense within the framework of the Atlantic Alliance, and the integration of the armed forces of the States bound together in that Alliance." It also gave its unqualified support to "the unification of Europe by following the course adopted by the establishment of the European Communities, with the inclusion of Great Britain and other States wishing to accede, and the further strengthening of those communities." Finally, it advocated "the elimination of trade barriers by nego-tiations between the European Economic Community, Great Britain and the United States of America within the framework of the General Agreement on Tariffs and Trade."[13]

On 16 May, the Bundestag ratified the Franco-German Treaty with the preamble. The treaty had become a sort of hybrid creature, in effect juxtaposing Kennedy's grand design with de Gaulle's own grand design. This of course did not escape de Gaulle, who subsequently acted as if the treaty had never existed. When he decided to withdraw from NATO, the general did not even consult the Germans. Meanwhile there was a sense of relief in Washington, as the menace of a closed Franco-German system retreated. Franco-German cooperation had safely been brought back from the edge of a bilateral agree-ment to cooperation within a wider European context. The fear that over the years the Franco-German partnership might become dominated by an increas-ingly powerful Germany, which might in turn be tempted to dominate other European nations, had been halted. Europeanists, remembering only too well lessons from the last World War, had sought to ensure that history would not be repeated. To them, any solution to the German problem would have to be found within the context of European integration.[14]

For the remainder of 1963, the Kennedy team actively courted the Germans in an effort to bring them back into the safe network of Atlantic connections. Kennedy's visit to Germany during his European trip was part of such an effort. Planning for the trip started around February 1963, after the Kennedy adminis-tration had carefully reviewed American policy towards Europe. In early March,

Jean Monnet expressed his enthusiasm for the prospect of a presidential visit to Germany. The effect of such a trip, he thought, would be "tremendous." He counseled the president to accept Mayor Willy Brandt's invitation to West Berlin and to make a stopover in Munich and Bonn as well. The topics, he said, might cover the themes of "peace, partnership and interdependence, somewhat along the lines of his 4 July speech in Philadelphia." Monnet added a bit of advice on the timing of the trip: "Since General de Gaulle is expected to be in Bonn in June, although no exact date has yet been fixed, presumably after ratification of the Franco-German Treaty, it might be well to forestall his plans by an early announcement of the president's proposed visit, which should preferably ante-date de Gaulle's."[15] David Bruce, with whom Monnet had spoken along these lines, strongly endorsed his friend's advice, as did John McCloy, whom Bruce later contacted. Ambassador Bruce soon reported this conversation to the president. Monnet's advice was followed. Kennedy's visit preceded de Gaulle's, which took place on 4 and 5 July 1963.

Monnet was in Washington in early June and helped the president formulate some of the themes for a major address on European integration and the United States, which Kennedy delivered at the Paulskirche in Frankfurt on 25 June, one day before his famous Berlin speech. Monnet was not, of course, the sole architect of this major address. McGeorge Bundy, Ted Sorensen, Arthur Schlesinger, Dean Rusk, William Tyler, and George Ball did most of the work of helping the president. The day before his arrival in Germany, Kennedy and his advisers were still frantically working on the Paulskirche and other presidential speeches. Much effort went into Kennedy's Paulskirche speech, which Sorensen called "one of the most carefully reworked speeches of his Presidency."[16] It was also one of his most inspired statements on the Atlantic partnership, perhaps even more so than the 4 July speech. More than a frantic, last minute attempt to give United States/European relations a helpful push, Paulskirche was a reassertion of the aims of the grand design in light of recent events, in which de Gaulle's *coup d'éclat* figured prominently.

RENEWED COMMITMENTS: EUROPEAN INTEGRATION WITHIN THE CONFINES OF THE ATLANTIC PARTNERSHIP

In February, Kennedy had recalled his ambassadors to Germany and Britain to Washington to participate in a thorough review of American policy towards Europe with Dean Rusk, George Ball, McGeorge Bundy, Schlesinger, and other officials. Dean Acheson, William Clayton, and Christian Herter were also asked to contribute their advice. David Bruce and George

Ball proved to be the most influential advisers, and they succeeded in convincing Kennedy that the United States should persist in its support of European integration and the Atlantic partnership.[17]

Prior to the review of American policy towards Europe, and one day after the announcement of the Franco-German Treaty, Jean Monnet was awarded, with Kennedy's backing, the Freedom Award Medal in New York City. George Ball served as a courier to deliver a letter from Kennedy praising Monnet while endorsing European unity and effective partnership between the United States and Europe. George Ball called Monnet an "incorrigible optimist." He also indirectly shot some arrows at the general in his praise of Monnet, whom he said had "never been tempted into the unhappy error—induced by a nostalgic longing for a world that never was—of seeking to recapture the past."[18] Monnet's journalist friend Walter Lippmann spoke of him as a man who could "induce and cajole men to work together for their own good." Meanwhile, Christian Herter called Monnet the "most authentic new frontiersman of our time," since the new frontier now lay not in North America but in the United States of Europe. Welcoming the idea of a new partnership between the United States and the new Europe, Herter, the Atlanticist, added, "Partnership, however, good as it is, can never remain the ultimate and final objective of Europe and America. The forces of history are working toward a broader and deeper relationship than that." Herter preferred to "talk about an Atlantic Community . . . toward which Jean Monnet's path [led]."[19] In the atmosphere of crisis that had followed de Gaulle's press conference and the announcement of the Franco-German Treaty, the differences between Atlanticists and Europeanists gave way to a convergence of views. On one thing, all agreed: Europe, united or not, must be somewhat monitored by the United States.

In early February, Kennedy instructed George Ball to draft a NSC document clearly stating the case for a broad strategy for pursuing the aims of the grand design. In doing so, Ball relied much on his own thoughts and much on the input of his colleagues, particularly David Bruce. The document embodied the main tenets of Kennedy's policy towards Europe for the remainder of his administration. The strategy George Ball outlined was designed "to frustrate de Gaulle's efforts to convince the Europeans that immediate Atlantic cooperation and progress towards European unity are mutually antithetical." This, he said, "is the heart of the case in Europe." In this brilliant report, Ball encapsulated the case for the continuation of basic American strategy towards Europe and European integration. American objectives, he said, remained essentially the same: denying Europe to communist control, mobilizing European resources "to serve the whole free world," containing Germany, and encouraging Europe to unite while discouraging it through such "instruments of partnership as NATO" and the OECD from playing "a role independent of the U.S." Ball could not have stated the case more clearly. European integration, yes, but controlled by Atlantic instruments; European unity within the confines of the Atlantic partnership.

As for the first part of the equation, Ball believed that only a united Europe could produce sufficient resources to help the United States carry its world-wide military and economic burdens. Although the European integration movement had suffered a severe setback, Ball, very much like Monnet, thought the process would continue because it had become and was becoming even more "solidly grounded in both European needs and European thinking." As for the second part of the equation, the U.S./European partnership, Ball still considered it to be both equally desirable and feasible—desirable because the United States still could not allow Europe to strike off on its own, for that would endanger the postwar American objectives of denying Europe to the Soviet Union and "mobilizing European resources for common tasks"; and feasible because anti-Americanism in Europe was counterbalanced by an even "deeper European feeling of shared values and interests with the United States." This was not to say, however, that America should maintain its way of approaching the joint issues of European unity and Atlantic partnership. The report did not recommend a change in objectives, but a shift in "emphasis and tactics." In order to overcome the obstacles thrown in the way of the grand design by de Gaulle, Ball planned to work on both the nuclear and the economic policy fronts to "dramatize" American willingness "to see a united Europe eventually act as an equal partner with the U.S." Like his colleague Rostow, Ball advocated developing the MLF concept and making "more explicit" America's "eventual willingness to consider allowing a united Europe to buy out the US share in the multilateral mixed manned force." He cautioned, however, that this "underlin[ed] the importance of setting up the force in a way that it [was] so integrated, through mixed manning and other means, as to preclude national withdrawal or any national use of elements of the force." In the field of political consultation—the software approach—Ball emphasized the importance of making clear American "willingness eventually to replace a five or six member NATO Executive Committee with a two member committee—the US and Europe."

In the way of specific steps, George Ball recommended first setting a target date for the completion of Ambassador Livingston Merchant's mission to Germany, with a view towards obtaining an executive agreement on the MLF by likely candidates (i.e, Belgium, Germany, Italy, and the United Kingdom) by that time. Second, he recommended speeding up the Trade Expansion Act negotiations. And third, showing American intentions to protect the freedom of West Berlin. In order to reassure the Germans of America's commitment to Germany, Ball, like Rostow, advocated emphasizing America's willingness to keep United States forces in Germany as long as a threat existed. No attempt was to be made to prevent the ratification of the Franco-German Treaty; instead, "discreet support" was to be given "for a Bundestag Resolution . . . to accompany the passage of the Treaty" that would "reaffirm the unambiguous commitment in words and deeds to 1. NATO; 2. the multilateral force—rather than to national or Franco-German nuclear programs; and 3. British accession to the Common market." With regard to France, Ball on the whole followed the advice of David Bruce. With the intention of keeping the door open for France to rejoin the mainstream of "legitimate ambitions of Europe" at a later date, the American attitude was to "be one of impeccable politeness without indulgence in recrimination or threats, while making clear the basic contrast between our goals and those of de Gaulle." This did not mean being naïve. "We should have well-informed contingency plans," continued Ball, "against a de Gaulle assault on NATO, our trade negotiations, or our balance of payments." As for the United Kingdom, while privately assuring the British of American support, nothing was to be done "publicly to reinforce the appearance of special ties." The British were to be encouraged to "stop being beastly to the Germans." Most importantly, they were to participate in the one venture that could still tie them more closely to the Continent—the MLF.[20]

By mid-February the review of American policy towards Europe had been completed. Ball was called upon to explain the administration's view on the post-14 January era to the Joint Economic Committee in a letter to Senator Paul Douglas. The letter matched the conclusions Ball had forwarded to the president on 9 February, although in somewhat less explicit terms.[21] Shortly after concluding the review of European policy, Kennedy wrote to Macmillan, whom he addressed as "Dear friend." His letter evidenced the privileged position Ambassador Ormsby-Gore enjoyed as a confidant of the most secret deliberations of the Kennedy team. It also underscored the special role that Ambassador Bruce had played in the review of American policy towards Europe. "As David Ormsby Gore will have told you," Kennedy wrote, "we have been doing a lot of hard work here in the last few weeks in an effort to sort out the problems we now have to deal with in the light of General de Gaulle's positions. David Bruce has been particularly helpful to us, and I hope you and he can have a talk when he gets back to London next week." The letter also confirmed the consummate craftsmanship of the Europeanists, who had persuaded Kennedy to take the long view after the shattering blows General de

Gaulle had dealt his grand design. Kennedy assured Macmillan that the "Atlantic connection" remained a top priority on the American agenda and left it to Bruce to explain to him the latest American "thinking on the NATO nuclear force" and to discuss Merchant's mission on the MLF. Stressing the need to meet "the legitimate interests of the non-nuclear members of NATO," Kennedy closely followed the recommendations of Ball's report and emphasized that only two main avenues for European integration and the Atlantic partnership remained: the MLF and the Kennedy Round. On this last issue Kennedy confided in Macmillan: "I must say my own great interest has increased, and also become more sensitive, since I found that the technicians have called all this 'the Kennedy Round.'" On a reassuring note, he added: "we quite understand that your people must examine the particular problem of your relations with the Continent, and I want you to know that the word 'association' does not in itself have any terrors for us."[22]

THE LAST AVENUES OF THE ATLANTIC PARTNERSHIP: THE KENNEDY ROUND AND THE MLF REVISITED

Christian Herter had already made known the basic American position on the Kennedy Round offensive at a meeting of the heads of delegations of the OECD. Briefly, Herter proposed cuts across the board to replace the unsatisfactory product-by-product approach, and he emphasized the need to eliminate or reduce nontariff barriers to trade and the need to include agriculture in the negotiations. Finally, the negotiations were to be conducted in such a way as to "establish a new and healthy trade relationship with the less-developed countries" by allowing them access to the markets of industrialized countries.[23] Yet the Kennedy Round seemed to run into difficulties. Rumors soon circulated in Washington, triggered in part by ambassadorial reports, that the French might veto the TEA as they had U.K. entry into the Common Market.[24] The rumors were not totally unfounded, given the preferences of certain French industrial groups, who claimed that French enterprises could not compete with the larger American firms. To counter the threat, Ambassador to France Bohlen advised the administration not to "put pressure on France through [the] Five" but rather "to rely on direct contacts, and, what is very important on our ability to carry commission with us."[25] As we saw, Tuthill's connections were to prove useful in this particular instance. The Hallstein connection was also soon put to good use during his visit to Washington on 4 March.

George Ball's recommendations to Kennedy for Hallstein's visit included a carefully worded threat that the Community should cooperate with the TEA or else. "Hallstein should carry away from Washington the knowledge that on economic questions we intend to defend the real interests we have at stake in our relations with the Common Market," Ball insisted, implying a distinction between American political and economic interests. *"Our consistent support for the European Community has been postulated on our assumption that the Community would be outward-looking and that the Common Market and the United States had a common interest in increased trade, lower barriers and economic cooperation. The continuance of our policy of support will depend—to a considerable extent—on a demonstration by the Community and its member countries that this assumption is still valid"*[emphasis in text].[26] Once again, George Ball assumed the role of Horatio at the bridge. American policymakers and negotiators increasingly followed suit as economic competition intensified between the United States and the EEC under subsequent administrations.

By May 1963 the Chicken War was raging, and the GATT ministers were trying to reach an agreement on ground rules for the Kennedy Round. The atmosphere of the conference, which the *Economist* said was "about as bitter as a meeting between allies could be,"[27] did not augur well for the Kennedy Round, which the United States thought would serve as a test case for European intentions. As for the MLF, the second main initiative open to the Kennedy and Johnson administrations, its fate was sealed by a combination of misunderstandings, bureaucratic maneuvering, and tentative commitments.

In late 1962, Gerard Smith and Admiral Lee, the leading advocates for the MLF, had been sent to Europe to provide European nations with more information on the force. The Smith-Lee mission was mainly a means of counteracting Norstad's proposal for land-based MRBM missiles for NATO. The MLF was put forward at that time as a way to avoid national ownership and manning of the missiles. The final confrontation on Norstad's proposal took place in early 1963. Norstad lost, resigned, and was replaced as SACEUR by General Lyman Lemnitzer, who supported neither the land-based MRBM nor the MLF.[28] Earlier on, with the Nassau meeting approaching, George Ball and other members of the Kennedy team took a closer look at the MLF, which had not much concerned them until that time, as a possible way of "integrating" the British deterrent. At Nassau, the Kennedy team had in effect granted the United Kingdom missiles for national ownership and manning. The MLF proposal then started on an ascending curve, gaining favor as a means of meeting German and Italian demands for greater participation in nuclear defense.[29] De Gaulle's conference gave it added significance as a political instrument. The MLF became the antidote to de Gaulle's vision of an independent Europe. Its advocates considered it a convenient channel for strengthening American influence in Europe and monitoring or encouraging European unification, as well as a tool for tying Germany firmly to the Atlantic network and for counteracting German bilateral arrangements with France.

On 30 January, Kennedy agreed to start negotiations on the MLF provided that the United States retained its veto on control arrangements and did not unduly engage its prestige in the MLF venture.[30] Livingston Merchant was appointed special ambassador and dispatched to Europe along with Gerard Smith and Admiral Lee to assess European interest and potential support on the matter. Merchant had held prominent positions in the Eisenhower administration, and as a former colleague of Robert Bowie's, he proved a faithful advocate of the MLF. So, too, did Ambassador to NATO Thomas Finletter. Ambassador Merchant became the head of a special office within the State Department that effectively coordinated negotiations with Finletter's office, while Walt Rostow, Henry Owen, and Robert Bowie backed the MLF through the Policy Planning Council. George Ball assured them a fair hearing at the highest levels of the administration. This organizational structure, coupled with informal inter-personal links, effectively succeeded in neutralizing the opposition to the MLF, which was led by Jeffrey Kitchen, who was the head of the State Department's Office of General Political and Military Affairs and was also in charge of the committee on the post-Nassau planning studies. Additional factors were the appointments of Robert Schaetzel as chairman of the subcommittee on the Multilateral Force and of his colleague, Henry Owen, as head of the subcommittee on France within Kitchen's committee.[31] Yet, as events would later demonstrate, this clever MLF machinery became gripped by the cautious pragmatism of the White House and the ineffective coordination of American actions (in the absence of clear channels for instruction, which was partly a result of Kennedy's dismantling of the NSC). The most important factor in the eventual downfall of the MLF, however, was the noncommittal attitude, or the downright opposition, to it in many European quarters.

Merchant, Smith, and Lee were in Europe from 22 February to 17 March. The Merchant mission was authorized to propose the negotiation of a preliminary agreement if two or more governments showed interest in the MLF. Guidelines included a proposal for establishing a committee that would fire MLF weapons only by unanimous vote; allies were encouraged to make alternative suggestions for control of the weapons. By that time the surface ship configuration seemed to be the preferred option, as compared to submarines in January.[32] In early March, Ambassador Merchant recommended that those nations who agreed to join in the preliminary agreement that would precede the creation of a preparatory commission on the MLF should also agree to certain key elements of the MLF concept as evolved by the United States. These included the acceptance of the unanimity rule for controlling the force, mixed-manning, surface ships, and a consensus that the MLF would not be built at the expense of NATO conventional forces. Merchant also wanted "a tacit agreement that the necessary resources were in fact in sight." Such preliminary clarifications, he thought, were necessary in order to avoid engaging American prestige in what "could develop into [a] fiasco" if participants entertained only vague views on the MLF. Despite these reservations, Ambassador Merchant was relatively optimistic that the preparatory commission would be ready to start its work in June, shortly after Kennedy's European trip, during which, he hoped, the president would initial the preliminary agreement.[33]

Yet European reactions to the Merchant mission hardly provided grounds for optimism. The French were antagonistic to the proposal. Although he declared himself favorable to the MLF in principle, Italian Prime Minister Fanfani indicated that no final decision regarding Italian participation could be taken before the Italian elections in May, and he expressed surprise at the American preference for surface ships as opposed to submarines. Spaak said he was personally in favor of the proposal but also remarked that the Belgian Senate and the Defense Ministry were strongly opposed to Belgian participation in the MLF.[34] To make matters worse, he showed much sympathy for the British decision to proceed with the establishment of multinational forces, even before exploring the multilateral concept. His American friend MacArthur II expressed strong reservations on this point.[35] Talks with the Germans in Bonn revealed skepticism over the choice of surface ships and doubts about the soundness of the unanimity rule as a mechanism of control. The Germans were worried not about the U.S. veto but about the veto that other European nations would be able to exercise. Accordingly, they proposed reviewing the whole issue of control once the force was ready.[36] The British generally showed skepticism about the MLF and expressed reservations about the financial burdens.

On 6 March, about a week before the end of Merchant's mission, McGeorge Bundy attempted to summarize the situation for the president. He prudently placed the mission within the wider perspective of other American efforts to give Europeans more responsibility for their own defense, like the Multinational Force, and insisted that the Merchant mission must not appear as if the United States were "trying to force a single solution on its friends." "If one answer does not work," thought Bundy, the United States should show its readiness "to help in finding others." By that time, Bundy was already showing himself to be a cautious advocate of the MLF. His job, as he saw it, was to preserve the president's options and not to commit his prestige to a single solution. Bundy the pragmatist took a careful look at European reactions regarding the MLF and concluded that it might be wise to explore not only the MLF but also other options. He further concluded that the MLF could "best be constructed on an *Atlantic* and *not* a strictly *European* basis." Recent soundings in Europe indicated that those European nations that had manifested interest in the MLF would prefer that it have "substantial American participation." The United States was "in favor of a more unified and powerful Europe," but if the Europeans themselves did not want a European nuclear force, thought Bundy, why bother? On the issue of submarines versus surface ships, Bundy, while indicating a preference for surface ships, recommended leaving the matter open. Taking once again a wider perspective, he emphasized that the real issue, submarines or no submarines, was that any attack on the MLF force would "engage the full strength of the U.S. as long as a large number of U.S. sailors [were] aboard." Meanwhile it was also important not to lose sight of the equally important goal of strengthening NATO's conventional forces.[37] McGeorge Bundy was not the only cautionary voice on the American side. Merchant himself recommended shying away from an "unsupportable optimism." Confusion, or "multibafflement," in the press as to the final result of the talks, he reasoned, was perhaps to the advantage of the United States, since the MLF venture was "by no means assured of success."[38]

Shortly after the Merchant team returned to Washington, the president, McNamara, and Rusk met on 22 March to review the MLF situation. The president agreed to write letters to Adenauer and Fanfani laying out the terms on which the United States was willing to make a firm commitment to the MLF. Admiral Lee and Ambassador Finletter suggested leaving open the possibility for reexamining both the composition of the force and its control once it came into being. Kennedy met them halfway. While he insisted that the force must be surface borne, he also agreed to make the offer more attractive by authorizing them to raise the possibility with the allies that submarines might be added to the force as it was modernized. On the control issue, Kennedy, Rusk, and McNamara concluded that the United States must retain its veto over the force, although the unanimity principle need not be respected should Europeans prefer other arrangements. While he agreed to write to Adenauer and Fanfani, the president was careful not to overcommit himself to the proposal. He firmly requested that there should be no consultation with Congress on the MLF until he had received a response from the Germans.[39]

It now remained to send a messenger to deliver both letters. William Tyler, the assistant secretary for European affairs, was given the job. The president's initial choice had been Gerard Smith, but Smith had caught the flu during his recent trip to Europe and was not available. Smith himself proposed that William Tyler replace him, to which the president readily agreed. Besides stating the case for the MLF, Tyler had another, perhaps even more important, mission. The assistant secretary also carried with him a message in the form of a letter explaining why Jacqueline Kennedy would not be able to go to Rome for a state visit that summer. The president wanted to keep the matter secret. Mrs. Kennedy was pregnant and would not be able to make the trip. Ironically, the MLF thus served as a cover-up for the primary reason of Tyler's trip to Italy. Tyler received his instructions while the president was having his hair cut. The assistant secretary first went to Bonn to talk to some German officials about the MLF and to attempt to justify the American preference for its surface fleet avatar. He registered only moderate success. Tyler then went to see Adenauer. The old man was taking a rest at his vacation home in Cadenabbia in the North of Italy. Kennedy's envoy and Adenauer spent the afternoon together discussing the MLF, among other things. Tyler's trip proved successful. About one month after his visit, the chancellor agreed to both of Kennedy's requirements for going ahead with the MLF: surface ships and the U.S. veto. He nevertheless indicated that he would expect both issues to be reexamined when the MLF became operational. The old man asked that a provisional agreement on the MLF be prepared for signature during the Kennedy visit to Germany in June. Tyler then left for Rome and talked to Fanfani about the MLF and Mrs. Kennedy.[40]

March and April thus registered some important progress for the MLF, especially on the German side. Since German agreement to the proposal had been Kennedy's major precondition for starting congressional consultations on the MLF, the defenders of the proposal gathered their forces to give a strong push to Bowie's brainchild, now severely crippled by Kennedy's preference for surface ships. They succeeded in obtaining the tepid support of the Joint Chiefs of Staff, who prepared a document stating that the MLF was desirable, feasible, and militarily useful. Most of the chiefs had never shown any real enthusiasm for the MLF, but they preferred it to Norstad's proposal for land-based missiles. Above all, the navy representatives, encouraged by admirals Lee and Ricketts, supported the proposal and eventually overcame the opposition of some of the chiefs.[41] Once again the MLF cabal showed itself to have the right men in the right places in the administration. Yet their efforts were hampered by Britain's reluctance to participate in the MLF and Kennedy's inclination to listen to Macmillan's pleas for postponing an agreement on the MLF.

Now that German support for the MLF had been secured, its proponents hoped to be given a green light by the president to give it a fair hearing on the Hill. Yet Kennedy, upon McNamara's advice,[42] threw a further obstacle in their path. The sole agreement of the Germans was not enough; he said, the British would have to get on board as well. This proved to be an impossible task. Despite Macmillan's apparent agreement at Nassau to support the MLF, the prime minister never really had any interest in going along with it. His successor, Alec Douglas-Home, was similarly uninterested, and Harold Wilson frankly opposed it and helped torpedo it with the British Atlantic Nuclear Force proposal. In early May, Ormsby-Gore, Ball, and Tyler had a meeting on the MLF. George Ball tried to convince David Ormsby-Gore that the United Kingdom should make a commitment to the MLF as soon as possible in order to form a common front with the United States and the Germans. He reminded the ambassador of previous commitments at Nassau. Ormsby-Gore hedged. He said that the United Kingdom had already made the financial commitment to buy Polaris missiles and to build submarines and warheads for them. And that the missiles would constitute a United Kingdom national force, which would then become part of the multilateral force. Ormsby-Gore obviously meant the multinational force. As for the MLF, the ambassador said the United Kingdom would "naturally give [it] a 'fair wind' and support it in general, but he doubted whether the UK would be prepared to assume a commitment to join a mixed-manned force and to accept a specific percentage of the costs of such force." George Ball tried to bring him around but did not succeed. Ormsby-Gore said he would report to Macmillan, but he did not make any promises.

With the realization that British views on the MLF sharply differed from American views, George Ball and William Tyler immediately set out to create a publicity campaign for the proposal. Tyler recommended that the president talk to David Ormsby-Gore and try to impress upon him the importance for the Atlantic partnership of reaching an agreement on the MLF. George Ball and Admiral Ricketts soon left for London to discuss the matter with the British. German contacts were encouraged to show the British their determination to push for the MLF. But German commitment to the MLF was not very deep. Apart from Adenauer, most members of the German government either did not fully grasp the details of the proposal or had a profound distaste for the idea of basing missiles on surface ships. Part of the publicity campaign had been aimed at softening Harold Wilson's opposition to the MLF, both through direct contacts with Washington officials and through German contacts. These tactics failed on both counts. Harold Wilson had talked to Kennedy in April. He remembered that the president had not been very keen on the MLF but thought that the Germans were in favor of it. As Harold Wilson later found out in May, the Germans were not really in favor of it but had thought that the United States wanted it. In effect, the Germans supported the MLF not because they wanted more participation in nuclear defense, but rather because it was an American proposal and had the potential to reinforce American presence in Europe and Germany.[43]

Notwithstanding these observations, the efforts of MLF backers to have the president initial a preliminary agreement on the MLF in June failed mostly because of Macmillan's precarious political situation at home. His government, recently tainted by the Profumo Scandal, which involved the British Defense Ministry, was in no position to spend what little political capital it had left for the elections on the MLF, especially since the proposal was opposed by both the British Navy and the Labour party.[44] In a letter to Kennedy, Macmillan asked that the MLF be put on the back burner for a while. Encouraged by George Ball and other MLF backers, Dean Rusk gave advice to Kennedy on how to answer Macmillan. He rejected the British plea for putting the MLF "in virtual cold storage," for he felt that it would then look in Europe as if the proposal were "losing momentum." This would give the advantage to de Gaulle and open the path to other, much less satisfactory solutions to the European nuclear problem, including German schemes for deploying MRBMs under national manning and ownership. Instead, Rusk counseled "modifying the form and procedure of talks and negotiations in such a way as to reduce visibility." If the British agreed to participate in the preliminary drafting process, which would "be carried on quietly in the NATO Headquarters in Paris, and to some extent, in capitals, . . . the formal convening of a multilateral group could be postponed until August or September."[45] This would have given the British and the Italians the opportunity to participate in the discussions of the MLF without being forced to make a political commitment to it.

Kennedy agreed to follow that suggestion, both in order to help his fellow politician and friend, Macmillan, and to remove the sense of deadline from the MLF, to which he did not want to overcommit himself. The president followed a middle course between the advice from the White House, where McGeorge Bundy sounded a rather negative note on the MLF, and the State

Department. Shortly before Kennedy set out for Europe, Bundy wrote him a long memo in which he recommended switching "from pressure to inquiry" on the MLF. Despite David Bruce's affirmations to the contrary, Bundy doubted whether the United States would be able to swing the British on board, given Macmillan's present difficulties at home. There was also a distinct lack of enthusiasm for the MLF in Italy; the same was true for Germany. "Only among the passionate pro-Europeans like Monnet," observed Bundy, was there "real support for the MLF, and this sentiment itself [was] conditional upon a clear offer to abandon the veto at an early stage if a genuinely European force [became] practicable." While he believed "in making this offer," he was also "more and more clear that it [was] a debating trick, for the present." With such limited support in Europe, why push a proposal that the Europeans themselves did not want? Also, how would the Soviet Union react? And then came an old fear, reminiscent of the EDC debate: wouldn't the Russians consider the United States to be the "nuclear rearmers of Germany"? Would this then not compromise Harriman's attempts to get their agreement on the test ban treaty? And how would the proposal fare in Congress? Bundy warned that pushing for the MLF would draw "directly upon the Presidential account since the State Department ha[d] no leverage and the Defense Department w[ould] not be able to make the case on straight military grounds." In fact, it would be "necessary to admit that on straight military grounds this force [was] not necessary." In all honesty, the administration had "said this too often—and it [was] too plainly the fact—"for it to "change [its] tune now." This was Bundy's most forceful argument: could Kennedy afford to squander part of his limited "Presidential account" on "amending the McMahon Act for the purpose of arming people who [were] themselves uncertain and divided on the need"? Would it not be wiser to spend it on the ratification of a test ban treaty, the defense of foreign aid, or the Kennedy Round? Having been elected by a very narrow margin and not particularly noted for his relationship with Congress, Kennedy was sensitive to this point. Bundy then speculated as to why the Kennedy team had gone as far as it had in pushing the MLF. The most important reason was, of course, that after Nassau the United States needed an initiative to meet the nuclear ambitions of Europe so as not to leave de Gaulle "a free field" to organize Europe according to his own grand design. Even though the MLF was faring badly, it was better to have put forward this proposal than none at all. Besides policy, there was another reason: senior members of the administration, such as Ball, Merchant, Rostow, Schaetzel, and Owen, had committed themselves to the MLF "as a means of blocking national deterrents, General de Gaulle, and all other obstacles to European unity."

Bundy accused them of having pressed the case of the MLF "more sharply and against a tighter timetable, at every stage" than either Kennedy or Rusk would have chosen. He conceded that he had let himself be persuaded by them more than once, "where he might have been more skeptical." Now was the time to redress the situation. As a matter of strategy, Bundy advised Kennedy not to "back away too sharply from the MLF," for this would be damaging to American prestige. Instead, the United States must go on showing its faith in the MLF as "a serious forward step toward NATO nuclear partnership" and "urge continuing study of the proposal, by an international planning staff in Paris." Also, the United States must not give up its "readiness to bear a full share if adequate European participation" did emerge. At the same time, Bundy advised Kennedy to "take off any sense of deadline" and "to widen the discussion to include other elements in the nuclear problem, such as consultation, control, alternative weapons systems, coordination of existing nuclear forces in the West, and non-proliferation." Finally, he recommended that the United States seek "a framework of discussion in which the French would be willing to participate" and "capitalize on one of the great facts which underlies European reluctance to pay for the MLF: namely serene confidence in [American] strategic superiority and will to use it in [the] defense of Europe."[46]

Bundy's memo did not circulate in the administration,[47] yet the president, who by many accounts was not so keen on the MLF, partly heeded his warnings and recommendations. The sense of deadline was removed. When Kennedy met Adenauer during his European trip in June, he let him know that it was not practical to proceed with the preliminary agreement at this stage, and he proposed widening the discussion to include other arrangements in case the MLF did not work. He did, however, express the hope that the MLF would eventually see the day. Kennedy's Paulskirche speech included a passage on the MLF. As we saw, Bundy, Schlesinger, and Sorensen from the White House, and Rusk, Ball, and Tyler from the State Department all worked on the speech. The result was a brilliant statement that strongly reaffirmed American support for the Atlantic partnership idea and European integration while at the same time lightly touching upon the MLF as a possibility to be explored, with an emphasis on the difficulties of the enterprise. There was no mention of a European force but rather of a new Atlantic force; neither was there any mention of relinquishing the U.S. veto at some later date. Yet the speech did refer to the possibility of giving Europeans more responsibility as Europe moved towards unity. But, to quote Bundy, was this anything more than a "debating trick"? Kennedy himself admitted that "developing a more closely unified Atlantic deterrent" might be "more difficult than to split the atom physically."[48]

The president was no doubt committed to European integration and the Atlantic partnership, as his Paulskirche speech amply demonstrated; the MLF was another story. Kennedy seemed to be going "through phases on it."[49] In June, he appeared ready to listen to Bundy's cautionary advice and to Macmillan's pleas for putting the MLF on the back burner. By mid-July, however, Kennedy asked Robert McNamara to investigate the possibility of conducting an experiment in mixed manning on an American ship. He thought his idea of a demonstration ship might buy time for the MLF until the British and the United States had their elections in 1964. By that time the president, who suspected the Germans of wanting to go ahead with the MLF for the sole reason of gaining the right to fire strategic weapons, began to perceive some of the real reasons for German support, namely the desire to tie the United States tighter to the defense of Germany and to reaffirm the Atlantic connection. Hence, perhaps, his renewed interest in the MLF. On 25 October, his idea for a demonstration ship was approved in principle.[50] The president mentioned it to Lord Home during his visit to Washington in the presence of William Tyler. Kennedy said it might well take a great deal of time before the mixed-manned demonstration experiment would be completed, perhaps more than a year. As William Tyler was later to recall "with a sense of poignancy," the president "laughed and said 'Of course, Bill Tyler will still be around then, but some of us may not be.' " Kennedy was speaking of his and Lord Home's political fortunes.[51]

Epilogue:
Johnson and the Atlantic Partnership

THE MLF AND EURATOM REVISITED

The U.S.S. *Biddle* was chosen to serve as the demonstration ship, and an international crew was assembled in the summer of 1964. The ship, later renamed the U.S.S. *Ricketts,* after the admiral who had backed the project, subsequently toured the ports of those nations taking part in the experiment: Germany, the United Kingdom, Italy, the Netherlands, Greece, Turkey, and the United States.[1] Yet by that time the MLF was on a downward path. When Lyndon Johnson took office, he was determined to pursue his predecessor's policies, notably by supporting the Kennedy Round and the MLF. He was, however, by no means familiar with the nuances of the MLF or the degree to which Kennedy had been committed to it. The MLF backers moved quickly to educate the new president. Shortly before his death, Kennedy had authorized the MLF supporters to brief Congress on their activities. They now proceeded to do just that. Merchant added a congressional liaison officer to his staff, and plans were made to have several officials brief Congress, particularly the Joint Committee on Atomic Energy. Yet the plans of the MLF cabal were short-circuited by the absence of any deadline, the lack of interest in Congress, and the limited amount of time that Rusk, McNamara, and others were able to devote to defending the proposal in Congress. What was clearly needed was a presidential initiative on the matter, and a new deadline.

The Johnson-Erhard[2] meeting of June 1964 provided the necessary impetus to breathe new life into the MLF. On 10 April 1964, while McNamara and McGeorge Bundy were out of Washington, Smith, Finletter, and Ball briefed the president on the MLF. Out of all the arguments in favor of the MLF, George Ball particularly underscored the need to meet German aspirations while tying Germany more closely to the United States. Although the president was far from grasping all of the complexities of the MLF case, he seemed to be impressed by that argument. "The Germans have gone off the reservation twice in our lifetime," he said, "and we've got to be sure that this doesn't happen again, that they don't go berserk." If the MLF gave Germany closer ties to the alliance, then the MLF would have to be supported and an agreement would have to be signed towards the end of the year, after the American presidential elections. Finletter, Smith, and Ball were elated.[3] They proceeded to cable all European embassies about the presidential decision. Ludwig Erhard agreed to go along with the proposed time schedule. The June communiqué of the Erhard visit to the United States stated in unequivocal terms that the president and the chancellor "were agreed that the proposed multilateral force would make a significant contribution to the military and political strength of NATO and that efforts should be continued to ready an agreement for signature by the end of the year."[4]

Supporters of the MLF now had to make sure that there would indeed be an agreement ready for signature by the end of the year. During the Kennedy administration, a working group with the task of preparing a draft treaty had been set up in the alliance headquarters in Paris. Despite the commitment to the MLF by the American ambassador to NATO, the task proved difficult. This was mainly because of Britain's reluctance to join the MLF. Erhard fretted over the possibility that the working group's lack of progress might prevent the treaty from being signed by the end of the year, which was especially crucial since German parliamentary elections were taking place in 1965, and the treaty would have to be ratified before then to ensure its success. Writing to Johnson, the German chancellor suggested that a German-American agreement be prepared, which other nations could join later as they saw fit. The American administration was quite cool towards the idea, especially since Erhard made the mistake of briefing the press about it. In a press conference on 8 October 1964, Secretary of State Rusk explicitly disavowed a German-American agreement.[5] This did not augur well for MLF. But the worst blow against the MLF once again came from the British.

Harold Wilson had won the British elections in October 1964, and Lyndon Johnson was elected to the presidency of the United States in his own right by a vast majority in November. There was no escaping this simple fact: the two men would have to meet before the end of the year, and their meeting would be decisive for the fate of the MLF. In order to prepare for it, McGeorge Bundy set up a special ad-hoc group in which Ball, McNamara,

Rusk, and Bundy himself participated. The group was given the mandate of preparing a coordinated position of the American administration on the MLF. Richard Neustadt was called in as a consultant to ensure not only that the MLF backers would not get carried away by their enthusiasm but also to avert misunderstandings between British and American negotiators. Clearly, the ghost of the Nassau Conference loomed over the Wilson/Johnson meeting. Just before Kennedy's death Neustadt had handed him a detailed report on the Nassau Conference. Kennedy planned to assimilate its conclusions to better prepare for later meetings. The lessons Neustadt had drawn from Nassau were now being brought to bear on the MLF. As a result, memos from the MLF proponents did not receive the attention they once did. The ad-hoc group set up by Bundy prevented the influence of MLF backers from being felt too strongly in the highest circles of government, while Neustadt acted as a moderating force in coordinating the staff work that contributed to the ad-hoc group.[6]

Besides the tempering influence of this new organizational structure within the United States government, outside forces were working effectively against the MLF. Wilson's opposition to the MLF was well known, as was de Gaulle's aversion to integrationist schemes, of which the MLF was a perfect example. Yet the French initially refrained from showing any categorical opposition to the MLF and told the Germans and the Americans that although they had no interest in the proposal, they would not lead any major offensive against it. Yet as the Wilson/Johnson meeting approached and the likelihood of an agreement on the MLF increased, French pressure to abandon the MLF suddenly came to bear heavily on the Germans. If the Germans did not follow suit, the French threatened to leave NATO—which they did anyway—and to create havoc in the Common Market. Erhard was in no position to ignore these warnings. Adenauer, who had been opposed to his candidacy and disliked him, remained as chairman of Erhard's party, the CDU. During a party caucus, the old man caused immense embarrassment to Erhard by reporting his own recent conversations with de Gaulle. The caucus ended with a resolution that called for putting the MLF in cold storage until it could be given a "more European character" and be less offensive to de Gaulle. Erhard's difficulties did not escape Johnson. Just prior to the Johnson visit, cables came in from Germany reporting that some key figures in Erhard's entourage were now in favor of postponing any agreement on the MLF in order to placate French opposition to it.[7] McGeorge Bundy reinforced Johnson's already growing doubts on the MLF.

As was often the case in the MLF saga, Bundy's role was pivotal. On 25 November, Neustadt went to London to prepare for the impending meeting.

Both he and Ambassador David Bruce told Wilson that a successful meeting would hinge on the acceptance of the MLF by the British. A similar message came through David Ormsby-Gore. That same day McGeorge Bundy wrote a memorandum to Rusk, McNamara, and Ball that strongly attacked the MLF, said that the United States should in fact "arrange to let [it] sink out of sight," and proposed to "ask the President for authority to work toward a future in which the MLF [did] not come into existence." Bundy's main argument was that the costs of its success now seemed "prohibitive." Britain was reluctant to join in the venture, Germany's governing party was divided over the issue, and the Italian government was weak and would not be able to withstand pressure from MLF opponents. In addition, the pursuit of the MLF venture could be detrimental to American efforts to reach an international agreement limiting the spread of nuclear weapons. It could also be damaging to Franco-German relations, given the French opposition to it. If the Germans felt forced to go along with Washington, they would blame the deterioration of relations with France on the United States. Finally, Bundy painted the bleak prospect of a heavy fight in Congress over the issue, which would draw heavily on the presidential account, especially since the Europeans themselves did not seem to want the MLF. He accordingly recommended an alternative course of action. His own conversations with the president had convinced him that Johnson was not really committed to the MLF. Why not then propose that he work jointly with Erhard to devise "a completely fresh look at the nuclear defenses of the Alliance, with an ostentatious inclusion of France in this process of discussion"? The really important issue in all this, he argued, was for Johnson to treat Erhard "with care and dignity"; and this could be done without clinging to the MLF.[8]

Bundy later discussed the matter with the select group of Ball, McNamara, and Rusk. They agreed with some of his observations but also pointed out that the president was bound by his previous commitment to the MLF. What would the Germans and other American allies think of American commitments if the United States reneged on the MLF? In conversations with the president, Ball and McNamara also seem to have argued that, although the congressional situation on the MLF was very weak, Congress could be brought to support the MLF if only the president would authorize a vigorous publicity campaign. In order to give a last push to the MLF before the Wilson/Johnson meeting, Ball went to London to emphasize to Wilson that the American government had no intention of going back on the MLF.[9] His efforts were short-circuited by McGeorge Bundy, who sent another memo on 6 December, this time not to his colleagues but to the president himself. The memo presented an "alternative view" on the MLF—most likely referring to the standard view defended by McNamara, Rusk, and Ball. Bundy presented it as an answer to the question that the president had asked the previous day, about Kennedy's reasons for being "tentative and careful about the MLF." Kennedy, he said, had "reacted very strongly and affirmatively" to a memo that he had sent him on 15 June 1963. Bundy adroitly seized on the opportunity to attach this memo to the Johnson memo. To the already lethal ingredients contained in the 15 June memo, Bundy now added more. If the United States pushed forward with the MLF, he said, the French would blame the United States for "dividing the Alliance and blocking the future of Europe and many who [did] not support de Gaulle [would] believe them." In addition, most of the professional military men were "cool at best, and many [were] openly opposed" to the MLF. Worse still, the Joint Committee and the Armed Services Committee were "very weary" of any treaty that involved an amendment to the McMahon Act. Contrary to Ball and McNamara, who argued that the president could convince Congress, Bundy noted that senatorial sentiment was strongly opposed to the MLF. Most senators were "skeptics and many outright opponents," while Bundy knew of "not one hardened supporter." Although Johnson had been elected by a very comfortable margin, this argument nevertheless carried some weight, for the president felt that his victory "had been a defeat of Goldwater extremism and not a solid liberal mandate." Johnson had no intention of confusing the Democrats and giving his enemies the opportunity to "catch him in a major defeat, as had happened to Wilson in 1919 or to Roosevelt in 1937."[10]

Although Ball and Bundy were on friendly terms, Ball later got "very angry" at McGeorge Bundy for not sending the memo to him prior to a meeting with the president in which Ball and McNamara had "made a fight" for the MLF.[11] Despite their efforts to reinvigorate it, the MLF was pretty much a dead letter prior to the Wilson/Johnson talks, which started on 7 December. A skillful negotiator, Wilson pointed out that the MLF would be "a fatal provocation" vis-à-vis the Russians, who claimed that it meant giving the Germans nuclear participation. He proposed an alternative to the MLF: a so-called Atlantic Nuclear Force (ANF), under which the British would commit their Polaris submarines, and the Americans a similar number, to NATO, placing them "under the unequivocal control of the Supreme Allied Commander, Europe." The next day Johnson had a heated discussion in the Oval Office with his advisers, but without the British. During this meeting Ball reportedly made his "last stand" on the MLF. Shortly afterwards, Johnson, while he did not accept the ANF proposal, nevertheless agreed to instruct the American delegation at NATO to study it. The communiqué of the Wilson/Johnson meeting was a carefully worded statement that neither reaffirmed American support for the MLF, nor showed American support for the ANF. The communiqué simply qualified the meeting as "an initial exchange of views as a preliminary to further discussions among interested members of the Alliance." Ball had clearly lost the day.

Johnson gave the last blow to the MLF with a leak to the press on Thanksgiving Day in 1965. James Reston of the *New York Times* served as a handy instrument to allow the MLF to "sink out of sight."[12] The journalist was slightly embarrassed about printing the news and asked the president whether this was really what he intended to do, for there had been no warning from the United States that it wanted to back away from the MLF. But such was the president's intention. The MLF was killed before Johnson consulted with the Germans. Foreign Minister Schroeder, who had been its leading defender, was caught by surprise and paid a political price as a result.[13] On the American side, there were limited casualties among the members of the MLF cabal. Gerard Smith, the leading supporter for the MLF, resigned. Under the circumstances, he did not feel very useful in his position of special adviser to the secretary for MLF negotiations. Yet Walt Rostow, one of the main preachers for the MLF, and Henry Owen, another backer, were promoted after its demise. Both enjoyed protection in high places, mainly by George Ball. Gerry Smith's resignation can be attributed in part to the under secretary's indication that the MLF might still get a chance if "there were not a special office dealing with the multi-lateral force with high visibility." The White House apparently did not specifically ask him for his resignation.[14]

After the demise of the Multilateral Force, Europeanists had no choice but to concentrate their energies on the peaceful uses of atomic energy both as a unifying factor in Western Europe and as a means of strengthening transatlantic ties. Even though Euratom did not seem to hold many of its promises, and the Kennedy administration had privately denounced U.S./Euratom American research cooperation as a drain on American resources, support for Euratom nevertheless continued under Johnson. After the official signing of the Euratom-U.S. Agreement in November 1958, three further agreements were signed by the two parties—in 1960, 1962, and 1963—which further expanded the supply of enriched uranium (200,000 kilograms) and plutonium (1500 kilograms) for Euratom while at the same time providing for intensive scientific cooperation. On 27 May 1964, the United States and Euratom agreed to undertake a new ten-year program for research collaboration on breeder, or fast neutron, reactors. More importantly, when bilateral agreements with the Six lapsed between 1965 and 1967 (with the exception of Italy, whose agreement did not expire until 1978), the United States decided to fold them into one single agreement with Euratom, thereby indicating American support for European integration. An additional move in this direction was the decision to make the Euratom supply agency the only channel for American supply of nuclear fuel, which had the advantage of eliminating the necessity for bilateral safeguards. Europeanists in the State Department and in American missions and embassies in Europe were in strong support of such a move as a way of strengthening European multilateralism. Dean Rusk himself wrote to the Atomic Energy Commission Chairman Glenn Seaborg to argue that this would be "a valuable contribution to the complementary objectives of European integration and Atlantic partnership which [had] been consistently supported by recent administrations."[15]

When problems arose during negotiations of the Non-Proliferation Treaty over the issue of preserving the system of Euratom safeguards, which existed concurrently with the universal safeguards system of the International Atomic Energy Agency, the State Department sided once again with Euratom and insisted that both systems should continue to exist in parallel.[16] While strengthening European multilateralism, the United States was also careful to protect its economic interests by assuring that Western Europe remained dependent on the American supply of enriched uranium. It largely succeeded in doing so: by 1967, the Europeans had not built any enrichment facilities for uranium, and the United States supplied about 99 percent of the total amount of enriched uranium distributed among the Six for peaceful use.

DO IT YOURSELF, MORE AND BETTER

In the non-nuclear field, the United States publicly adopted the position of benevolent onlooker. Shortly after taking office, President Johnson told the North Atlantic Council that the best way to honor Kennedy's memory was to continue to pursue the goal of Atlantic partnership while welcoming "the emergence of a Europe growing in unity and strength."[17] Despite this unchanged basic commitment to European integration, the manner and tone of American support changed. This was due in part to new economic circumstances, well-assimilated lessons of past American failures in encouraging European integration, and a relative impatience with the slow pace of progress towards European economic and political integration. A recurrent theme during the Johnson years was that the responsibility for building Europe rested primarily with Europeans themselves. Dean Rusk said as much in Brussels in May 1964 when he reaffirmed American support for European economic unity while insisting that this was "a European task and it must continued to be led and carried out by Europeans."[18]

Coupled with this hands-off attitude, the administration increasingly spoke of the necessity for Europe to assume world responsibilities in order to share economic, political, and military burdens more equitably with the United States. George Ball insisted that only large nations or entities had the resources and the power to endorse world responsibilities. He felt that there was "probably a direct correlation between the willingness of European nations to accept world responsibility and the speed with which they move[d] toward economic and political unity."[19] This had important consequences for the practice of Atlantic partnership. Unlike the Atlanticists, Ball did not believe in building an Atlantic political structure that would dilute efforts towards European unity. Yet in the absence of such unity, particularly political, the United States could not passively sit back and await the emergence of a united Europe. If there was no real equal interlocutor to talk to on an equal basis, the United States would have to turn towards Atlantic instruments of cooperation such as the OECD and NATO.[20] This also had far-reaching consequences for the equally important North/South partnership. If Europe did not unite, it would not be able to cast its relations with developing countries in terms of a truly international and generalized collective responsibility.[21] Instead of participating in "open" systems of North/South cooperation, Europeans would continue to have special and discriminatory ties with developing countries and thus encourage the development of "closed" systems, which in fact delimited spheres of influence. In the economic field the practice of the Atlantic partnership proved arduous.

During the preparation for the Kennedy Round, heated discussions and confrontations on the respective merits of the American proposal for equal linear tariff cuts versus EEC proposals for *écrêtement* or *double écart* lasted until March 1964 and led to no resolution of the disparities. With the beginning of the Kennedy Round scheduled for 4 May, the GATT ministers agreed to disagree and left it at that. Preliminary discussions in Geneva touched upon the issue of trade opportunities for developing countries, but there again not much was accomplished. A similar lack of progress characterized preliminary negotiations on agriculture, where participants could not agree on basic rules and procedures.[22] By May 1964, the objectives and basic strategy for the Kennedy Round negotiations, which Ball had outlined to President Kennedy in early March 1963,[23] were running into difficulties. Not only did it seem that the American president would not be able to make full use of the 50-percent authority provided by the Trade Expansion Act, but no agreement had been reached for guaranteeing access for American agricultural products to European markets, and no procedures had been agreed upon for dealing with developing countries.

A major crisis shook the Community to its foundations on 30 June 1965, when the French refused to take part in the activities of the Community—the so-called *politique de la chaise vide* [empty-chair policy]. Only after the resolution of the crisis, through the Luxembourg compromise of January 1966, did the EEC reach an agreement in July 1966 on the Common Agricultural Policy and subsequently decide to table its agricultural offers. Negotiations with developing countries were not fully engaged until the end of 1965. By March 1967, a grains arrangement, some agricultural concessions, the American selling price issue, and the disparities problems remained to be resolved with the EEC. Yet as pressure built up with the approaching expiration date of the TEA, both the EEC and the United States adopted more flexible positions.

The Kennedy Round was successfully concluded on 30 June 1967, on the day the TEA expired. The State Department and the American Mission to the European Communities concurred in their appraisal of the negotiations. Besides reinforcing the "world multilateral non-discriminatory trading system," the Kennedy Round had shown the ability of the EEC, through its Commission, to negotiate as a unit with the United States and other countries. Europeanists attributed the success of the EEC negotiators to the fact that "they had earned the confidence of the six member governments and were therefore able to negotiate, in effect, ad referendum"; they thought the Commission had been "strengthened immeasurably by this accomplishment."[24] Despite these laudatory remarks, the post-Kennedy Round period did not initiate an idyllic period of partnership for the United States and the EEC.

This was especially the case in the agricultural field. Despite constant efforts during the Kennedy Round to influence the Common Agricultural Policy to serve U.S. interests, American negotiators had failed to do so. In the months following the conclusion of the negotiations, countless problems arose on poultry, lard, feed grains, canned hams, canned tomatoes, and canned fruits among others.[25] Although good will was apparent from both the EEC and the United States, there were very few prospects for the resolution of the fundamental differences between American and EEC agricultural trade.

The Johnson years also revealed a profound disagreement between the EEC and the United States on the issue of tariff preferences to developing countries. The Americans maintained that selective preferences to developing countries tended to erode the sacrosanct most-favored-nation (MFN) principle while encouraging the establishment of spheres of influence and the "alignment of relations between developed and less developed countries into North-South blocs." Kennedy's concern that Latin American countries would seek special trade advantages from the United States to compensate for EEC discrimination against exports from developing countries not associated with the EEC persisted under the Johnson administration. Yet, despite a strong commitment to the gradual elimination of selective preferential trading arrangements, the Johnson administration eventually accepted the establishment of a special relationship between the EEC and the former dependent territories of Belgium, France, and Italy, and the signing of the 1 June Yaoundé Convention by eighteen independent African countries.

While still opposed to trade preferences in principle, in practice the Johnson administration decided to overlook exceptions to the MFN in light of the historical ties between certain African countries and Europe and "certain more liberal advantages, particularly in aid obtained through multi-lateralization of former bilateral ties."[26] This compromise position was largely the result of the combined efforts of the Bureau of European Affairs and the African Bureau of the State Department in convincing the rest of the administration that over the years the EEC would gradually inch towards the American position, and that preferences were needed for some developing countries, at least temporarily. Faced with the determination of the EEC and still committed to the twin goals of European integration and Atlantic partnership, the Johnson administration sanctioned the establishment of special spheres of influence in the Third World, or, to put it another way, a division of responsibilities between the United States and the EEC, which George Ball had ultimately, if halfheartedly, come to accept. The United States did not, however, condone the conclusion of agreements between the EEC and African countries that did not possess historical ties to EEC member countries. Hence there was strong American opposition to association arrangements with Nigeria and with the East African states of Tanzania, Kenya, and Uganda. The EEC did not comply with American wishes, however, and signed an agreement with Nigeria in July 1966, and another with East Africa in June 1968. All in all, Kennedy's Atlantic partnership encountered a number of difficulties on its economic flank, notably in putting the ambitions of the TEA into practice.

Europeanists became increasingly impatient with the slow progress of European unification in the wake of de Gaulle's veto to British entry and the demise of the MLF. They became even more impatient when de Gaulle threw another boulder in the path of European unification by boycotting Community institutions in June 1965. His action reflected in part his intention to maintain a formal veto power over Community decisions. Throughout the crisis, however, the United States carefully avoided making any public comments criticizing France and engaging in private contacts that might give de Gaulle reasons "for characterizing the defense of the Community by the Five as a defense of American interests rather than their own."[27] Yet the temptation to engage in such contacts was great. In October 1965, after a meeting during which the Five and the Commission "displayed a remarkable degree of collaboration," Ambassador John Tuthill, still serving as head of the American Mission to the European Communities, "urged the Department of State to depart from its guarded posture in order to informally tell the Ambassadors of the Five in Washington of [United States] pleasure with the progress made."[28] His recommendation was overruled by John Leddy, the assistant secretary for European affairs, who had just replaced William Tyler and had previously served as ambassador to the OECD. Leddy emphasized that it had been the express wish of the Five that the United States avoid "injecting" itself "publicly or privately into the issue thus ensuring that the burden of the crisis remain[ed] with the French."[29] His advice was followed, and the United States refrained as much as possible from private or public involvement until the end of the EEC crisis in January 1966.

This attitude also characterized the American position vis-à-vis renewed British efforts to join the Common Market in 1967. When the British started showing interest in reapplying for membership in early 1966, the American reaction was rather lukewarm. Assistant Secretary Leddy recommended that the secretary of state encourage British Foreign Secretary Stewart "if he found the latter seriously interested in EEC membership and willing to accept its political goals and institutional mechanisms." In a now familiar line of thought, Leddy insisted that the foreign secretary "should be reminded of [American] long-standing opposition to discriminatory European trading arrangements without compensating political benefits if he should be thinking of fundamentally new arrangements that would dilute the political content of the Treaty of Rome."[30] While Leddy was cautious, the Economic Bureau of the State Department was frankly opposed to early British application because it believed it could severely threaten the successful conclusion of the Kennedy Round.

Prior to Prime Minister Wilson's visit to Washington in late July 1966, State Department officials debated the possibility of recommending that President Johnson encourage Wilson to announce British candidacy to EEC membership. The Economic and European bureaus reached a compromise position. While they thought there were "advantages in reiterating at the highest level" the American position that the United Kingdom's future lay in Europe, they also agreed that a direct bid by the UK for EEC membership would just result in another French veto and that initiating any serious negotiations with the EEC before the Kennedy Round was concluded could "be the death knell of that enterprise."[31] Under Secretary George Ball followed their recommendation; he advised the president not to encourage early British entry but recommended that he reiterate American support for British entry into the Common Market in general terms. Heeding this advice, the president, in one of his major policy speeches, "Making Europe Whole: An Unfinished Task" in October of that year, told his audience in New York: "The outlines of a new Europe are clearly discernible. It is a stronger, increasingly united but open Europe—with Great Britain a part of it—and with close ties to America."[32] When Prime Minister Wilson announced on 10 November 1966 that the United Kingdom would seek membership in the EEC, the Department of State instructed American missions in Europe, if asked about the American position, to refer their interlocutors to Johnson's speech of 7 October.[33] Until de Gaulle's second veto of British membership on 27 November 1967, the American government treated British application for membership in a "low, unemotional key so as to attract minimum attention to the U.S. position."[34]

During the early years of the Johnson administration, the European Communities were actively engaged in a thorough institutional reform, which culminated in the signing of the Treaty of Brussels and established a single Commission and a single Council of Ministers of the European Communities on 8 April 1965. The Treaty of Brussels was ratified by June 1967 and went into effect in July 1967. The State Department was strongly in favor of merging the European Communities' executives. The result of having a single executive, calculated Europeanists, would be a single Community spokesman "having far greater authority and international prestige than even the present EEC Commission." "On balance, . . . this would be a positive rather than an adverse factor, for experience ha[d] shown the Executives to be in general more internationally minded and imbued with concern for the over-all Community interest than the Member States either singly or collectively." They also anticipated that this would simplify relations with the Communities, since the United States would only have to deal with one executive instead of three. Most importantly, they felt that merging the executives while at the same time strengthening the role of the European Parliament would boost the supranational outlook of the Communities, which was largely in accord with the goals of "a long-standing US support for the European integration movement."[35] Yet the goal of a supranational Europe was beginning to be increasingly questioned in influential circles.

IN SEARCH OF PEACE

Harold Van B. Cleveland, director of Atlantic Policy Studies for the COFR, cautioned against encouraging the creation of a "real European political-military union" that "would probably be created in a spirit of rivalry with the United States." He concluded that it seemed "unwise, therefore, for the United States to be as closely identified as it ha[d] been with the supranationalist strand of the European idea and with the classical European doctrine. The American attitude on political and military union ought to be more reserved and pragmatic."[36] Henry Kissinger later adopted a similarly "reserved and pragmatic" attitude towards Europe while serving under President Nixon. His views were already well defined in the mid-sixties. His testimony during the 1966 Hearings of the Senate Foreign Relations Committee on United States Policy Toward Europe was particularly revealing. When asked by Senator Frank Church whether the United States would "be better off" if a "federal union had been established in Europe," perhaps with de Gaulle as its president, Kissinger clearly voiced his preference for a confederal Europe over a federal Europe. Kissinger believed that a federal Europe would most likely adopt a "Gaullist policy, while a confederal Europe would permit [the United States] *to maintain an influence at many centers* [emphasis added] and it would probably be, in the long run, less likely to pursue such a policy." When you "destroy all existing political loyalties and tr[y] to form new ones, it [is] not inconceivable . . . that anti-Americanism might be one cohesive bond between Scotland and Sicily and Schleswig-Holstein and southern France." When Senator Church questioned him about the likelihood of the creation of an Atlantic union, in which "the United States and Canada and the countries of Western Europe [would] join under a common federal government with powers to conduct foreign policy, to establish a common currency, and to provide for the common defense," Kissinger answered that, although he had been "very attracted to the idea," he was now "becoming very worried about excessive concentrations of decision-making in too large units, and . . . would prefer now a certain pluralism in the world." His "instinct" was "in the direction . . . of Europe and the United States working together for common interests but not being so organically tied that they must do everything together, since that [was as] apt to lead to paralysis as to creativity." He concluded that the notion of "the global Atlantic commonwealth under one sovereignty" was not "in tune with the needs of our time."[37] On this the Europeanists and Kissinger now mostly agreed; but where they disagreed was on the desirability of European supranationalism for maintaining harmonious relations between the United States and Western Europe and American influence on the Continent.

The Europeanists' assumption that European integration and Atlantic partnership went hand in hand had profound implications for their conception of how the division of Europe between East and West might ultimately be ended and both Germanies reunified. During the last months of the Kennedy administration, the president, prompted by Ambassador to Yugoslavia George Kennan, was hard at work normalizing relations between the United States and Eastern Europe. Kennedy intended to use trade as a weapon to progressively detach the East European states from the Soviet

Union. Johnson continued the trend started by his predecessor by deciding to establish a special presidential committee to study increasing East-West trade, namely, the Miller Committee. European economic integration, if not political integration, was to serve as an additional weapon to lure East European states away from the Soviet Union and to ultimately bring about a European peace settlement in which Germany could be reunified. George Ball and the Europeanists, very much in line with Jean Monnet, saw indications in Eastern Europe that "the stability and prosperity that followed economic integration in Western Europe" had "created new aspirations" and had "stimulated new thinking in Eastern Europe." It was by capitalizing on these aspirations that they hoped to draw Western and Eastern Europe progressively closer together.

Testifying before the Senate Foreign Relations Committee in June 1966, George Ball explained the rationale behind American efforts to bridge-build with the East. The reunification of Germany, he thought, could best be attained by creating "a structure of unity in the West" that would function "as a very powerful magnet in which the German people" could eventually "be incorporated." Assuming that Europeans would achieve the specific kind of unity Ball envisioned, the framework could then "be gradually expanded to absorb more and more of the other peoples of Europe." Taking the long view, Ball prophesied: "This can come about simply because of the very strength and size of the unity itself . . . I think that Western Germany can belong to a system of Western unity, and that as détente proceeds and conditions are created for the German people to express themselves, there can ultimately be the adhesion of the East German people to some kind of system of Western unity."[38] Ball's formulation revealed a specific conception of a European peace settlement. Eastern European states, including East Germany, would adhere to, or be absorbed into, "some kind of *Western* unity," and this would be more likely to happen if the magnetic force of a united Western Europe remained closely joined with the United States. The same assumptions underlay President Johnson's speech, "Making Europe Whole: An Unfinished Task." While the speech paid ample tribute to Kennedy's partnership between equals, the president added ingredients more specific to his administration's policy mix. Johnson's Europe was expected "to move more confidently in peaceful initiatives toward the East" and to "provide a framework within which a unified Germany could be a full partner without arousing ancient fears." The new Europe would also be "a stronger, increasingly united but open Europe—with Great Britain a part of it—and *with close ties to America* [emphasis added]."[39]

This definition apparently did not allow for the existence of a positive "third-force" Europe, largely independent from both the Soviet Union and the United States. Despite their dismissal of Atlantic union schemes as impractical, Kennedy, Johnson, and the Europeanists were in fact talking of an "Atlantic," or an Atlantic-oriented, Europe. Ball's latent fear, which many of his American colleagues shared, was that a united Europe might strike off on its own, court the Soviet Union, and leave the United States as a lone, economic giant in a world hostile to its most cherished values of democracy and free trade. It was this fear, and the concomitant desire to ensure a "spacious living area for freedom," that motivated successive American administrations to couch the debate of an East-West settlement in terms of a struggle between a relatively homogeneous Atlantic Community and the Soviet Union and its satellites. A united Western Europe would play a positive role in the European peace settlement so long as it attracted Eastern European states towards the Western/American system with its political stability and economic prosperity. Yet European economic prosperity possessed the potential not only to attract Eastern European states but also to foster European independence.

As the Johnson administration drew to a close, U.S.–European relations became characterized more and more by increased competition rather than by Atlantic partnership. De Gaulle dealt violent blows to Atlantic partnership, by withdrawing France from integrated NATO military activities in 1966, and to European integration, by triggering the 1965 crisis and vetoing British membership for the second time. The United States, while reaffirming its support for European integration, looked increasingly to its own economic interests. Faced with the growing economic strength of the EEC and a notable lack of political cohesion among the member states of the new Europe, the American leadership sought to influence European economic policies to minimize the economic costs of its support for European integration. The Nixon administration did not so much favor European unity as fragmentation, for it allowed the president and his advisers, especially Kissinger, to influence European policies "at many centers of power." Divide and conquer was the rule.

Soon some posed the question, Why should the United States bear the economic costs of supporting the creation of a nonexistent political Europe? Additionally, the Europeans' lack of progress towards political unity resulted in a parallel lack of interest in European integration in the United States. To some, European economic integration appeared as a threat to western unity, rather than as an asset to western strength and cohesion. As the Vietnam war intensified, President Johnson and his advisers devoted most of their energies to the war and very little was left for European integration. Later, George Ball recounted: "The war was a vampire sucking dry the Administration's vitality and setting us at odds with other friendly governments."[40] Ball himself, strongly opposed to the administration's Vietnam policy, stayed on the Johnson team as long as there was any hope that he could help slow escalation in Vietnam. No longer able to do so, he left his post as under secretary of state on 30 September 1966.[41]

That same month, his colleague and friend Robert Schaetzel became ambassador to the European Communities in Brussels, thus replacing John Tuthill. Tuthill became American ambassador to Brazil, and was thus sent far away from his area of predilection and expertise—Europe and European integration. As the Johnson administration approached its end and was succeeded by other administrations, American Europeanists gradually vanished from the highest councils of government. With them also disappeared a crucial network of informal contacts between American Europeanists and "good" Europeans on the other side of the Atlantic. The wartime legacy of "personal relationships" that "lubricated Atlantic relations" and encouraged an atmosphere of "intimate cooperation"[42] among European and American politicians became a thing of the past, only to continue outside of the immediate circles of government. Whereas Monnet and other key European officials had had easy access to Eisenhower, Dulles, and Kennedy, they found it difficult to establish informal relations with their successors, particularly under the Nixon administration. Monnet's influence in Washington was based on informal contacts with key members of the American administration, who often were his friends. With their absence from the official Washington scene, his influence, and that of other "good" Europeans, declined in Washington. More generally, their passing from the governmental scene symbolized the arrival of a younger generation of American statesmen who felt less committed to building the kind of world that their predecessors had imagined in the wake of the atrocities and dislocations of World War II. Yet, in the late eighties and early nineties, as European integration regained momentum, U.S. policymakers in Washington did not hesitate to call upon their elders for advice on European matters. Although much less influential, the old guard was still at work behind the scenes. As a European peace settlement finally seemed in sight, their vision, and that of Monnet, acquired renewed relevance to the present. It was the vision of humanists searching not only for European political integration and economic prosperity per se but also for the prospect of peace on a worldwide scale.

NOTES

Notes to Introduction

1. John F. Kennedy, *The Strategy of Peace,* ed. Allan Nevins (New York: Harper and Brothers, 1960). Discussion with John Fisher, p. 227.
2. Jean Monnet, *Memoirs* (New York: Doubleday and Co, 1978), pp. 304-5.
3. Monnet, *Memoirs,* p. 465.
4. See Walter Lipgens, *A History of European Integration,* vol. 1 (Oxford: Clarendon Press, 1982).
5. Acheson Report, April 1961, Kennedy Library, Boston (hereafter cited as JFKL).
6. Some of the interviewees have requested confidentiality, in which case their names do not appear in the notes.
7. See Ernest May, "Writing Contemporary History," *Diplomatic History* (Spring 1984): 110.
8. This is not, however, to belittle the merits of such interpretations. On this specific point, see Graham Allison, "Conceptual Models and the Cuban Missile Crisis," *The American Political Science Review* (September 1969).
9. May, "Writing Contemporary History."
10. Defined as the executive branch of the American government. I do deal, however, with the attitudes of other parts of the government towards European integration as well, particularly Congress, and consider on occasion the attitudes of specific American interest groups, such as industrialists or farmers.
11. Defined as a set of guiding principles based on underlying beliefs, values, and motives designed to set the goals of a given administration and the ends to achieve these goals.
12. Defined as the reasons advanced to justify a given policy to the public and Congress in order to implement it. See Majone's distinction between motives and reasons, Giandomenico Majone, *Evidence, Argument, and Persuasion in the Policy Process* (New Haven: Yale University Press, 1989).
13. I purposely blur the somewhat artificial distinction between "policymakers" and "administrators."
14. See John Lewis Gaddis, *Strategies of Containment* (Oxford: Oxford University Press, 1982), p. ix.
15. This is called "consistency seeking," or the tendency of an individual to see what he expects to see and to assimilate incoming information to the images, hypotheses, and theories he already holds. The present discussion owes much to the work of Alexander George. See, for example, his *Presidential Decision Making in Foreign Policy: the Effective Use of Information and Advice* (Boulder, Co.: Westview Press, 1980), pp. 57-133.
16. Robert Schaetzel, *The Unhinged Alliance* (New York: Harper and Row, 1975), p. 46.
17. Walter Hallstein, recorded interview by Gordon Graig, 29 July 1964, Brussels, Belgium, The John Foster Dulles Oral History Project, Seeley Mudd Library, Princeton University (hereafter cited as PL).

Notes to Chapter 1: Setting the Stage

1. U.S. State Department, Division of Economic Studies, "How Would a European Full Customs Union Affect the Long-Run Economic Interests of the United States?" 17 September 1943, Record Group (RG) 59, The Records of Harley A. Notter, Box 84, National Archives (hereafter cited as NA).
2. Laurence H. Shoup and William Minter, *Imperial Brain Trust. The Council on Foreign Relations and United States Foreign Policy* (New York and London: Monthly Review Press, 1977). Dean Acheson, soon to be appointed as Truman's secretary of state, was a member of the Century Group, which had unofficial links with the Council on Foreign Relations; see Yves-Henri Nouailhat, "Les nouvelles élites américaines," *Relations Internationales* 47 (Fall 1986): 336.
3. President Roosevelt sent Hamilton Fish Armstrong to London in 1944 with the personal rank of Minister to work on the problems of the European Advisory Commission with Ambassador Winant. He was later appointed special adviser to the secretary of state and adviser to the American delegation at the San Francisco Conference in April-June 1945. John Foster Dulles was an adviser to the U.S. Delegation at San Francisco and took part in the Conference of Foreign Ministers in London in 1945. See War and Peace Studies Report, 1939–45, 18 December 1945, Hamilton Fish Armstrong Papers, Box 119, PL.
4. Henri Rieben, *Des guerres européennes à l'union de l'Europe* (Lausanne: Fondation Jean Monnet pour L'Europe [hereafter cited as FJM], 1987), note de réflexion de Jean Monnet, Algiers, 5 August 1943, p. 279.
5. In many cases, members of these organizations became high-level policymakers in the American government. For example, members of the Council on Foreign Relations held 42 percent of the top-level foreign policy jobs under Truman. Most of them came from law and business circles, with fewer than one-third being career diplomats. See Nouailhat, op. cit.
6. A case in point is Paul Hoffman. President of the Studebaker Corporation and an influential member of the BAC and the CED, he became the administrator of the Marshall Plan in Europe. In this capacity, he commissioned the COFR to report on American objectives in Europe and the means for attaining them. Another key figure for European affairs in the postwar years, Averell Harriman, the director of the Union Pacific Railroad, was a member of the BAC since 1933. See Philips H. Burch Jr., *Elites in American History*, vol. 3, *The New Deal to the Carter Administration* (New York: Holmes & Meier, 1980) p. 89.
7. Ibid., and Harley A. Notter, *Postwar Foreign Policy Preparation* (Washington, D.C.: Department of State, 1949).
8. William Tomlinson helped draft a report for the Advisory Committee, entitled "How Would Political Unification of Europe Affect the Interests of the United States?" See Subcommittee on Problems of European Organization of the Advisory Committee on Post-War Foreign Policy, 10 December 1943, RG 59, The Records of Harley A. Notter, Box 84, R63c, NA. Tomlinson subsequently worked very closely with Jean Monnet, the originator of the Schuman Plan for the European Coal and Steel Community, who is largely considered today as one of the "fathers" of the European Communities.
9. For more details, see Pascaline Winand, "American Policy Towards European Integration 1939-1945," M.A. thesis, Purdue University, 1985.
10. "Economic Trading Blocs and Their Importance for the United States," February 1941, COFR, War and Peace Studies, E. B27, p. 3.
11. William Diebold, Jr., "England's Interests in Continental Europe and the Mediterranean Basin," 29 August 1941, COFR, War and Peace Studies, E. B15.
12. Arthur D. Gayer, "United States Policy Toward International Cartels," 29 July 1941, COFR, War and Peace Studies, E. B74.
13. Herbert Feis, "On Our Economic Relations with Britain," *Foreign Affairs* (April 1943); Subcommittee on Economic Policy of the Advisory Committee on Post-War Foreign

Policy, "Factors in the Post-War International Payments Position of Great Britain," 11 September 1943, RG 59, The Records of Harley A. Notter, Box 82, E 174, NA.

14. Cordell Hull, *The Memoirs of Cordell Hull*, vol. 2 (New York: Macmillan, 1948), p. 1211.
15. Dean Acheson to Sir Frederick, 22 July 1941, RG 59, The Records of Assistant Secretary and Under Secretary of State Dean Acheson, Box 2, NA.
16. Subcommittee on Economic Policy, "Post-War Economic Unification of Europe," 19 November 1942, RG 59, The Records of Harley A. Notter, Box 81, E 36., NA; U.S. Department of State, Division of Economic Studies, "How Would a European Full Customs Union Affect the Long-Run Economic Interests of the United States?" 17 September 1943, RG 59, the Records of Harley A. Notter, Box 82, E 177, R 62, NA.
17. Leslie A. Wheeler, "Agricultural Surpluses in the Post-War World," *Foreign Affairs* (October 1941).
18. U.S. Department of State, Division of Economic Studies, "How Would a European Full Customs Union Affect the Long-Run Economic Interests of the United States?" op. cit.
19. Percy W. Bidwell, "Economic Aspects of the Post-War Treatment of Germany," 27 May 1944, COFR, War and Peace Studies, E. B 69.
20. Ronald Pruessen, *John Foster Dulles: The Road to Power* (The Free Press, 1982), p. 309; and ibid., Dulles to Frederick Stern, 20 November 1942, p. 312.
21. Pierre Mélandri, *Les Etats-Unis face à l'unification de l'Europe 1945-1954* (Paris: Pedone, 1980), p. 27.
22. Alvin H. Hansen and Jacob Viner, "American Interests in the Economic Unification of Europe with Respect to Trade Barriers," 14 September 1942, COFR, War and Peace Studies, R. B56.
23. Subcommittee on Problems of European Organization, "How Would the Political Unification of Europe Affect the Interests of the United States?" op. cit.
24. Subcommittee on Problems of European Organization, "How Would the Political Unification of Europe Affect the Interests of the United States?" op. cit.; and "How Would Closer Economic and Political Collaboration of Europe Affect the Interests of the United States?" 21 January 1944, RG 59, The Records of Harley A. Notter, Box 84, R63d, NA.
25. Harry S. Truman, *Memoirs, 1945. Year of Decisions* (New York: New American Library, 1965), p. 263.
26. Michael Hogan, *The Marshall Plan, America, Britain, and the Reconstruction of Western Europe, 1947-1952* (Cambridge: Cambridge University Press, 1987), p. 36.
27. See Melvyn P. Leffler, "The United States and the Strategic Dimensions of the Marshall Plan," *Diplomatic History* 12, no. 3 (Summer 1988): 279.
28. Quoted in Harry Bayard Price, *The Marshall Plan and Its Meaning* (Ithaca: Cornell University Press, 1955), p. 395.
29. John Foster Dulles, "Address on Foreign Policy to the National Publishers Association," *New York Herald Tribune*, 18 January 1947. A copy is in John Foster Dulles Speeches and Press Releases, Box 20, Dwight D. Eisenhower Library (hereafter cited as DDEL).
30. U.S. Department of State, *Germany, 1947-1949: The Story in Documents*, Washington, D.C., 1950, pp. 329–30, as quoted in Hogan, *Marshall Plan*, p. 38.
31. Kennan to Acheson, 23 May 1947, with attached recommendations of the Policy Planning Staff, *Foreign Relations of the United States* (hereafter cited as *FRUS*) *1947*, vol. 3: 223-30; and Kennan Memorandum, 16 May 1947, *FRUS, 1947*, vol. 3: 220-23, quoted in Hogan, *Marshall Plan*, p. 41. See also John Gillingham, *Coal, Steel and the Rebirth of Europe 1945-1955: the Germans and French from Ruhr Conflict to Economic Community* (Cambridge: Cambridge University Press, 1991), pp. 118-19.
32. Jones's memorandum to Acheson, 20 May 1947, with attached draft speech for Marshall, Joseph Jones Papers, Truman Library, Box 2, Folder: Marshall Plan Speech, quoted in Hogan, *Marshall Plan*, p. 42.
33. Charles E. Bohlen, *Witness to History 1929-1969* (New York: W. W. Norton and Company, 1973)

34. George Kennan, *Memoirs 1925-1950* (Boston: Little, Brown and Co., 1967), p. 341.
35. Quoted in Walter Isaacson and Evan Thomas, *The Wise Men* (New York: Simon and Schuster, 1986), p. 415.
36. Gillingham, *Coal, Steel and the Rebirth of Europe,* p. 118.
37. Harriman to Truman, 12 August 1947, in Harry S. Truman Library, PSF, Germany; Department of State Policy Statement, Germany, 16 August 1948, in *FRUS, 1948,* vol. 2: 1310, quoted in Hans-Jürgen Schröder, "Die Amerikanische Deutschlandpolitik und das Problem der Westeuropäischen Integration 1947/48-1950," in *Origins of the European Integration, March 1948-May 1950, Actes du colloque de Strasbourg 28–30 November 1984* (Brussels: Bruyland, 1986), pp. 78–79.
38. Kennan's answers to questions at the National War College, 10 April 1947, Box 17, Kennan Papers, quoted in: Melvyn P. Leffler, "The United States and the Strategic Dimensions of the Marshall Plan," *Diplomatic History* 12, no. 3 (Summer 1988): 282.
39. Leffler, "The United States and the Marshall Plan," p. 281.
40. Policy Planning Staff Meeting, 13.6, 1949, RG 59, Box 27, PPS, NA, quoted in Klaus Schwabe, "Der Marshall-Plan und Europa," *Origins of the European Integration,* op. cit., p. 69.
41. Hickerson Memorandum of Conversation with Lord Inverchapel, 21 January 1948, *FRUS, 1948,* vol. 3: 11.
42. Quoted in Isaacson and Thomas, *Wise Men,* p. 244.
43. Lovett to Harriman, 3 December 1948, *FRUS, 1948,* vol. 3: 301.
44. Bevin Dispatch to Hall Patch, 26 October 1949, FO 371, 78134, UR 10815, as quoted in Hogan, *Marshall Plan,* p. 284.
45. *FRUS, 1948,* vol. 3: 840.50 Recovery/3-348, Secretary of State to U.S. Political Adviser for Germany (Murphy), 5 March 1948, p. 389; *FRUS, 1948,* vol. 3: 840.50 Recovery/3-448, Memorandum, William T. Phillips to Assistant Secretary of State for Economic Affairs (Nitze), 4 March 1948, p. 387.
46. Hogan, *Marshall Plan,* pp. 283, 331.
47. "Summary of a Memorandum Representing Mr. Bevin's Views on the Formation of a Western Union," enclosed in Inverchapel to Marshall, 13 January 1948, *FRUS, 1948,* vol. 4: 4-6.
48. See Lawrence S. Kaplan, *NATO and the United States, The Enduring Alliance* (Boston: Twayne Publishers, 1988), p. 20.
49. Kennan, *Memoirs,* p. 400; as quoted in Isaacson and Thomas, *Wise Men,* p. 440.
50. The Brussels Pact, Article 1. For more details see Kaplan, *NATO.*
51. Hickerson to McWilliams, 27 November 1948, Policy Planning Staff Records, Box 27, "Europe 1947-1948," quoted in John Lewis Gaddis, *The Long Peace* (Oxford: Oxford University Press, 1987), p. 63.
52. North Atlantic Treaty Hearings, Senate Committee on Foreign Relations, 81st Cong., 1st sess. (Washington, D.C.: U.S. Government Printing Office [hereafter GPO], 1949), 2: 368-69, quoted in Kaplan, *NATO,* p. 26.
53. Kennan draft memorandum for Marshall and Lovett, 26 September 1948, Policy Planning Staff Records, Box 27, "Europe 1947-1948," quoted in Gaddis, *Long Peace,* p. 63.
54. 62 *Statutes* 137, Title I; U.S., Congress, House, Congressional Record, 80th Cong., 2nd sess., 1948, pp. 94, 3645-46.
55. For a full text of Hoffman's speech, see OEEC Document, C (49) p. 176.
56. English version in *Documents on American Foreign Relations,* vol. 12 (Princeton: Princeton University Press, 1951), p. 85.
57. Dulles to Monnet, 23 May 1950, Dulles Papers, Box 54, PL.
58. *FRUS, 1950,* vol. 3, 850.33/5-2050, U.S. Special Representative in Europe (Harriman) to Secretary of State, 21 May 1950, quoted in Gillingham, *Coal, Steel and the Rebirth of Europe,* p. 234.
59. Dulles to Monnet, 23 May 1950, Dulles Papers, Box 54, PL.

60. William Diebold, Jr., "Imponderables of the Schuman Plan," *Foreign Affairs* (October 1950): 120.
61. George Ball, *The Discipline of Power* (Boston: Little, Brown and Co., 1968).
62. Gillingham, *Coal, Steel and the Rebirth of Europe*, pp. 259–271. See also p. 42 of this book.
63. *Department of State Bulletin,* 25 August 1952, p. 284.

Notes to Chapter 2: The EDC, the EPC, and the ECSC Loan

1. Ball, *Discipline of Power*, p. 49.
2. Dean Acheson, *Present at the Creation* (New York: W. W. Norton and Co., 1969), p. 132.
3. Memorandum from the Secretary of State and the Acting Secretary of Defense (Lovett) to the President, 30 July 1951, *FRUS, 1951,* vol. 2, p. 838.
4. *FRUS, 1950,* vol. 3, Acheson's remarks to Bevin and Schuman, New York, 15 September 1950, p. 316.
5. Dean Acheson, *The Struggle for a Free Europe* (New York: W. W. Norton & Co., 1971), pp. 142–143; *FRUS, 1951,* vol. 3, part 1, 1981, Circular Telegram, The Secretary of State to Certain Diplomatic Offices, Washington, 29 January 1951, pp. 760–762.
6. Acheson Papers, Memorandums of Conversations, "The Position of Germany in the Defense of Western Europe," 31 July 1950, Harry S. Truman Library, quoted in Gillingham, *Coal, Steel and the Rebirth of Europe,* p. 253.
7. *FRUS, 1951,* vol. 3, part 1, 1981, Top Secret Telegram, The Secretary of State to the Embassy in France, Washington, 28 June 1951, p. 802.
8. Louis Galambos, ed., *The Papers of Dwight David Eisenhower. NATO and the Campaign of 1952: XII,* no. 304 (Baltimore and London: Johns Hopkins University Press, 1989).
9. Note from J.S.W. for Jean Monnet, Pre-Presidential Papers, no. 75, John McCloy (1), DDEL, and Jean Monnet's appointment books, 21 June 1951, FJM.
10. Monnet, *Memoirs,* p. 359.
11. *Department of State Bulletin,* 30 July 1951.
12. *FRUS, 1951,* vol. 3, part 1, Top Secret Telegram, The Ambassador in France (Bruce) to the Secretary of State, Paris, 3 July 1951, pp. 805–812.
13. Ibid., The Secretary of State to the Embassy in France, Washington, 16 July 1951, p. 835.
14. Ibid., Memorandum from the Secretary of State and the Acting Secretary of Defense (Lovett) to the President, Washington, 30 July 1951, pp. 849–852.
15. Galambos, *NATO and the Campaign of 1952,* no. 502.
16. Ibid., and *New York Times,* 27 November 1951.
17. Galambos, *NATO and the Campaign of 1952,* no. 578.
18. See, for example, *FRUS, 1952-54,* vol. 5, The Ambassador in France (Dunn) to the Department of State, 3 May 1952, Résumé of Adenauer-Eisenhower Conversation, p. 650.
19. Richard P. Stebbins, *The United States in World Affairs, 1953* (Published for the COFR, New York: Harper and Brothers, 1954), p. 154.
20. *Department of State Bulletin,* 9 June 1952, p. 895.
21. Quoted in Max Beloff, *The United States and the Unity of Europe* (Washington, D.C.: Brookings Institution, 1963), p. 67; the Act was approved on 20 June 1952.
22. *FRUS, 1952–54,* vol. 6, The Chargé to France to the Department of State, 20 March 1952, p. 28.
23. Ibid., The Ambassador to France (Dunn) to the Department of State, 13 July 1952, p. 123.
24. Roy Pryce, ed., *The Dynamics of European Union* (New York: Croom Helm, 1987), pp. 49-77; *FRUS, 1952-54,* vol. 6, The Ambassador to France to the Department of State, 13 July 1952, p. 120.

25. Pryce, *Dynamics of European Union*, pp. 49-77, and Robert Bowie's letter to Pascaline Winand, 30 June 1992. Robert Bowie to William Durkee, Executive Director, American Committee on United Europe (ACUE), May 1952, Report to the Director of the ACUE, ACUE, Walter Bedell Smith, Box 4, DDEL.

26. *FRUS, 1952–54,* vol. 6, The Secretary of State to the Office of the United States Representative to the European Coal and Steel Community at Paris, 21 November 1953, p. 329; and Memorandum by Rosalind Sawyer and Ruth H. Phillips of the Office of European Regional Affairs, 20 November 1953, p. 327.

27. *FRUS, 1952-54,* vol. 6, The Ambassador to France (Dunn) to the Department of State, 13 July 1952, p. 123.

28. Ibid., The Secretary of State to the Office of the United States Representative to the European Coal and Steel Community, at Paris, 21 November 1953, p. 329.

29. *FRUS, 1952–54,* vol. 5, The Secretary of State to the Embassy in France, Washington, 6 September 1952, p. 691.

30. *FRUS, 1952–54,* vol. 6, Memorandum of Conversation by the Secretary of State, 14 December 1952 and Memorandum of Conversation by the Special Assistant to the Secretary of State, 15 December 1952, pp. 249–257.

31. *FRUS, 1952-54,* vol. 5, editorial note, pp. 700-701.

32. Adenauer to McCloy, 1 December 1952, Ann Whitman File, Administrative Series, John McCloy, Box 25, DDEL; *FRUS, 1952–54,* vol. 5, editorial note, p. 702; *New York Times,* 7 January 1953, page 1, column 1.

33. For a text of Dulles's speech, see Beloff, *The United States and the Unity of Europe,* p. 80.

34. Dulles's speech to the American Association for the United Nations, New York, 29 December 1950, *Department of State Bulletin,* 15 January 1951, p. 88.

35. Eisenhower's radio address, 19 May 1953, *Public Papers of the Presidents of the U.S.: Dwight D. Eisenhower, 1953–1961* (Washington, D.C.: U.S. GPO, 1960-61), p. 307; Dwight D. Eisenhower, *The White House Years. Mandate for Change 1953-56* (New York: Doubleday & Co., 1963), p. 446.

36. Eisenhower, *White House Years. Mandate,* p. 446.

37. Dulles's speech to the COFR, 12 January 1954, *Department of State Bulletin,* 25 January 1954, p. 108.

38. Gaddis, *Long Peace,* p. 147.

39. Eisenhower, *The White House Years. Mandate,* p. 446.

40. NSC 162/2, 30 October 1953, p. 22, as quoted in Gaddis, *Long Peace,* p. 149.

41. Eisenhower, *White House Years. Mandate,* p. 127; Dulles's statement to the Senate Foreign Relations and House Foreign Affairs Committees, 4 May 1953, *Department of State Bulletin,* 25 May 1953, p. 737.

42. NSC 162/2, 30 October 1953, p. 8.

43. Eisenhower, *White House Years. Mandate,* pp. 446–447.

44. *Department of State Bulletin,* 9 February 1953, p. 208.

45. Galambos, *NATO and the Campaign of 1952,* pp. 171, 369.

46. Dulles to Eisenhower, 21 October 1953, Dulles White House Memos, Foreign Policy Subseries, Box 8, DDEL.

47. Galambos, *NATO and the Campaign of 1952.*

48. Ibid., p. 340.

49. Ibid., p. 767.

50. Ibid., p. 790.

51. *New York Times,* 18 January 1952.

52. Galambos, op. cit., note 1, p. 341 and diary, 11 June 1951, p. 214; Letter to Anthony Eden, 8 December 1951, p. 767; *New York Times,* 18 January 1952; Galambos, op. cit., DDE Diaries, 6 January 1953, pp. 1481–1482.

53. Dulles's 27 January 1953 speech, *Department of State Bulletin,* 9 February 1953, p. 214.

54. Eisenhower's letter to General Gruenther, in Eisenhower, *White House Years. Mandate,* p. 140.
55. Monnet to Dulles, 19 January 1953, AMH 46/5/1, FJM; Dulles to Monnet, 23 January 1953, AMH 46/5/2, FJM.
56. Allocution de Jean Monnet, 8 February 1953, AMH 46/5/5, FJM.
57. Adenauer to McCloy, 1 December 1952, Ann Whitman File, Administrative Series, Box 25, John McCloy, DDEL.
58. Gruenther to MacArthur II, 9 February 1953, Box 2, Douglas MacArthur II, NATO Series, DDEL.
59. Ibid.
60. See Douglas Brinkley, "Jean Monnet and the American Connection, 1953-63," Paper presented at the European Studies Associations' Conference, George Mason University, Fairfax, Virginia, 24 May 1989.
61. Eleanor Schoenebaum, ed., *Political Profiles: The Eisenhower Years* (New York: Columbia University Press, 1977).
62. Gruenther to MacArthur, op. cit.; and MacArthur II to Gruenther, 12 February 1953, Gruenther, Alfred, Box 2, Douglas MacArthur II, NATO Series, DDEL.
63. Dulles's Memorandum for the President, 18 February 1953, Dulles White House Memos, Box 1, "White House Correspondence:1953 (5)," DDEL.
64. *FRUS, 1952–54,* vol. 6, pp. 276–277.
65. Dulles to Jean Monnet, 19 February 1953, AMF 46/6/1, FJM; see also Monnet, *Memoirs,* p. 379.
66. See Monnet's appointment books, FJM.
67. Mélandri, Les Etats-Unis face à l'unification de l'Europe 1945-54 (Paris: Pedone, 1980), p.155.
68. *FRUS, 1952-54,* vol. 6, part 1, (Washington, D.C.: U.S. GPO, 1986), pp. xxii.
69. Monnet, *Memoirs,* pp. 271, 352; and Robert Bowie, interview for the FJM, 15 June 1981.
70. Schoenebaum, ed., *Political Profiles: The Eisenhower Years,* p. 564. Smith to Eisenhower, 17 August 1954, Walter Bedell Smith, Box 5, "Appointment as Under Secretary," DDEL; Eisenhower to Smith, Walter Bedell Smith, Box 5, Appointment as Under Secretary," DDEL; Smith to Donovan, 12 January 1953, Walter Bedell Smith, Box 4, "American Committee on United Europe (2)," DDEL.
71. Monnet to Dulles, 24 November 1952, Dulles Papers, Box 62, PL; Dulles to Monnet, 26 November 1952, Dulles Papers, Box 62, PL.
72. William Donovan to Walter Bedell Smith, 25 July 1951, American Committee on United Europe (1), Walter Bedell Smith, Box 4, DDEL.
73. Smith had been one of the directors of the American Committee on United Europe prior to his appointment as under secretary of state by Eisenhower.
74. Eisenhower to Monnet, Supreme Headquarters Allied Powers Europe, 28 December 1951, Pre-Presidential Papers, Box 78, Monn-(Misc), DDEL.
75. Monnet to Eisenhower, 8 November 1952, AM 46/8/15, FJM.
76. Eisenhower to Monnet, 19 November 1952, AM 46/8/16, FJM.
77. René Mayer, recorded interview by Loftus Becker, October 1964, JFD Oral History Project, PL; Walter Hallstein, recorded interview by Gordon Graig, July 1964, JFD Oral History Project, PL.
78. See, for example, *Reader's Digest,* April 1953, pp. 44–47.
79. *FRUS, 1952-54,* vol. 6, pp. 305–306, and John Foster Dulles, Memorandum for the President, 28 April 1953, Eisenhower Papers, Official Files 260-2, Box 919, "European Coal and Steel Community," DDEL.
80. Eighty-third Cong., 1st sess., U.S. Senate, Committee on Foreign Relations: Hearings, European Coal and Steel Community, 4–5 June 1953, pp. 15–17.
81. Ibid.
82. AMH 47/8/1, Lettre de Monsieur Etzel, Washington, 4 June 1953, FJM.

83. AMH 47/6, Monnet to Dulles, 8 June 1953, FJM.
84. *FRUS, 1952-54,* vol. 6, pp. 311-12; *Department of State Bulletin,* 29 June 1953, pp. 927-929; AMH 47/6/9, FJM.
85. *Department of State Bulletin,* 27 July 1953, pp. 107-108.
86. *FRUS, 1952-54,* vol. 6. See the summary of conversations held in Paris, 13-15 December, among Monnet, Dulles, Humphrey, Stassen, and their advisers, pp. 337–342.
87. Eisenhower to Adenauer, *New York Times,* 7 January 1953, p. 1.
88. George Ball to James Reston, 17 February 1953 ; James Reston to George Ball, 20 February 1953; George Ball to James Reston, 22 February 1953, in Adlai Stevenson Papers, Box 373, quoted in Mélandri, *Les Etats-Unis face à l'unification de l'Europe,* p. 395.
89. *Department of State Bulletin,* 23 February 1953.
90. February 3 letter to the President, in Eisenhower, *White House Years. Mandate,* p. 141.
91. Mélandri, op. cit., p. 405.
92. Eighty-third Cong., 1st sess., 1953, Conference Report, H. Report no. 770, 10 July 1953, p. 15; Mélandri, op. cit., pp. 407– 408; *FRUS, 1952-54,* vol. 5, part 1, Memorandum by the Assistant Secretary of State for European Affairs (Merchant) to the Secretary of State, 16 June 1953, with attachments, p. 794.
93. Eighty-third Cong., 1st sess., 1953, Conference Report, H. Report no. 770, 10 July 1953, 15; Mélandri, op. cit., pp. 407-408; *FRUS, 1952-54,* vol. 5, part 1, Memorandum by the Assistant Secretary of State for European Affairs (Merchant) to the Secretary of State, 16 June 1953, with attachments, p. 794; and ibid., editorial note, p. 795.
94. *FRUS, 1952-54,* vol. 5, part 1, The Secretary of State to the Embassy in France, 5 October 1953, and The United States Observer to the Interim Committee of the European Defense Community (Bruce) to the Department of State, 15 October 1953, pp. 815–819, 823–25.
95. Ibid., p. 827.
96. Ibid., editorial note, p. 693, and Memorandum of Discussion of State-Mutual Agency Joint Chiefs of Staff Meeting, held at the Pentagon, 28 January 1953, pp. 711-717.
97. Ibid., 159th meeting of the National Security Council, 13 August 1953, note 2, p. 799; ibid., Memorandum by Russell Fessenden of the Office of Regional Affairs to the Officer in Charge of Political-Military Affairs, Office of European Regional Affairs (Wolf), 21 July 1953, pp. 798-799; Townsend Hoopes, *The Devil and John Foster Dulles* (Boston: Little, Brown & Co., 1973), p. 164.
98. "Address before the National War College," 26 October 1953, in Dulles Papers, PL.; *FRUS, 1952-54,* vol. 5, part 1, The Ambassador in France (Dillon) to the Department of State, 23 October 1953, pp. 828-829.
99. See, for example, *FRUS, 1952-54,* vol. 5, part 1, The Secretary of State to the Embassy in France, 8 November 1953; The Secretary of State to the United States High Commissioner for Germany (Conant), at Bonn, 9 November 1953; The Secretary of State to the Chancellor of the Federal Republic of Germany (Adenauer), 20 November 1953, pp. 828-831 and pp. 854–855.
100. Ibid., editorial note, p. 859.; Eisenhower, *White House Years. Mandate,* pp. 244–246; Mélandri, op. cit., p. 425; and Joseph Laniel, *Jours de Gloire et Jours Cruels* (Paris: Presses de la Cité) p. 262. France and Germany finally agreed that, until the signing of the peace treaty, the Saar should remain autonomous and gain a European status under the Western European Union. The Saar population rejected this "Europeanization" in a plebiscite held 23 October 1955. The next year, France and Germany reached an agreement that the region should return to Germany.
101. Monnet met again with Dulles on the 15th. See Monnet's appointment books, FJM; see also Mélandri, op. cit., p. 428.
102. *FRUS, 1952-54,* vol. 6, pp. 337-346.
103. Bruce to Monnet, Personal and Confidential, 28 December 1953, AMH 46/8, FJM.
104. *FRUS, 1952-56,* vol. 6, p. 355.

105. Ibid., Dulles to Stassen, 9 January 1954, p. 351; and Tomlinson to Bruce, 26 January 1954, pp. 356-358.
106. Ibid., pp. 360, 368; Monnet to Dulles, 21 March 1954, AMH 51/5, FJM.
107. Monnet's appointment books, FJM; *FRUS, 1952-54,* vol. 6, pp. 377–385; Dulles to the President, 12 April 1954, O.F. 260-A-2, DDE Central Files, DDEL; Department of State Bulletin, 3 May 1954; "Dwight Eisenhower 1890-1969," Samuel Waugh, Box 1, 31 March 1969, "Mr. Waugh's experiences in D.C.," DDEL; Monnet, *Memoirs,* p. 390.
108. *FRUS, 1952-54,* vol. 5, Memorandum of Discussion held at the 187th Meeting of the National Security Council, 4 March 1954, p. 887.
109. Ibid., editorial note, p. 940.
110. Ibid., note 2, p. 877.
111. Ibid., p. 887.
112. Ibid., note 2, p. 932.
113. Ibid., The Secretary of State to the Embassy in the United Kingdom, Washington, 27 February 1954, p. 881.
114. Ibid., The United States Observer to the Interim Committee of the European Defense Community (Bruce) to the Department of State, Paris, 21 March 1954, pp. 903-904.
115. Ibid., Memorandum of Conversation, by the Counselor to the Department of State (MacArthur), Paris, 14 April 1954, pp. 932–935.
116. Ibid., Memorandum of Conversation, held at Prime Minister Laniel's Office in Paris, 14 April 1954, pp. 936–938.
117. Ibid., The Acting Secretary of State to the Embassy in France, Washington, 11 March 1954, p. 897.
118. Ibid., The Secretary of State to the Embassy in France, Washington, 20 May 1954, p. 963.
119. Ibid., p. 957.
120. Ibid., The Secretary of State to the President, Paris, 22 April 1954, p. 941.
121. Ibid., The Ambassador in France (Dillon) to the Department of State, Paris, 29 May 1954, p. 958.
122. Ibid., note 4, p. 969 and editorial note, p. 972.
123. Ibid., The Ambassador in France (Dillon) to the Department of State, Paris, 21 June 1954, pp. 978–979.
124. Ibid., Memorandum of Conversation, prepared in the Department of State, Washington, 27 June 1954, p. 986.
125. Ibid., The Ambassador in the United Kingdom (Aldrich) to the Embassy in France, London, 12 July 1954, pp. 1016-1017.
126. Ibid., and Memorandum by the Joint Chiefs of Staff to the Secretary of Defense (Wilson), Washington, 25 June 1954, p. 994.
127. Ibid., Memorandum of Conversation, by the Counselor of the Department of State (MacArthur), 13 July 1954, pp. 1018–1023.
128. Ibid.
129. Pierre Gerbet, *La Construction de l'Europe* (Paris: Notre Siecle, 1983), p. 179.
130. *FRUS, 1952-54,* vol. 5, The Ambassador to France (Dillon) to the Department of State, Paris, 15 August 1954, p. 1039, and The Secretary of State to the Embassy in Belgium, Washington, 17 August 1954, p. 1047.
131. Ibid., Prime Minister Churchill to the Secretary of State, London, 22 August 1954, pp. 170–171.
132. Ibid.
133. Note for Foreign Office (Kirkpatrick) and Minister of Defense (Earl Alexander of Tunis), 20 August 1954, and draft with numerous handwritten corrections by Churchill, 19 August 1954, both in PRO, PREM 11/618, quoted in Rolf Steininger, "John Foster Dulles, the European Defense Community and the German Question," in Richard H. Immerman, ed. *John Foster Dulles and the Diplomacy of the Cold War,* (Princeton: Princeton University Press, 1990), pp. 94–95.

134. *FRUS, 1952-54,* vol. 5, Prime Minister Churchill to the Secretary of State, London, 24 August 1954, p. 1077.
135. Ibid., The Acting Secretary of State to the Embassy in France, Washington, 26 August 1954, p. 1081.
136. Ibid., Memorandum of NSC meeting, 24 September 1954, pp. 1263-1266; ibid., Memorandum of Conversation, 27 September 1954, pp. 1277, 1286.
137. Ibid., Dulles to Embassy in France, 30 August 1954, pp. 1114, 1120; and Butterworth to the Assistant Secretary of State for European Affairs (Merchant), 1 September 1954, p. 1127; *Department of State Bulletin,* 13 September 1954, p. 363.
138. Bruce to Dulles, 16 September 1954, AMH 60/2/4, FJM; David Bruce Papers, 2 September 1954, quoted in Gillingham, "David K. E. Bruce and the European Defense Community Debacle," 23 September 1990, Paper presented at the Conference on Monnet and the Americans, Hyde Park, New York, October 1990.
139. Hoopes, *The Devil and Dulles,* p. 248.
140. *FRUS, 1952-1954,* vol. 5, Butterworth to the Assistant Secretary of State for European Affairs (Merchant), 1 September 1954, p. 1127 and Eisenhower to Smith, 3 September 1954, p. 1145.
141. See, for example, Transcript of Secretary Dulles's Press Conference, London, 2 October 1954, JFD, 81, PL. In this speech, Dulles also pointed out that although the Brussels organization would not be as supranational as the EDC, it would nevertheless have some supranational qualities and include the UK, which the EDC did not.
142. *FRUS, 1952-54,* vol. 5, editorial note, p. 973, and The Secretary of State to the Embassy in France, Washington, 17 June 1954, p. 974.
143. Eighty-third Cong., 2d sess., Committee Print, Report on European Mission, by Brigadier General Julius Klein, Special Consultant to Subcommittee on Armed Services (Washington, D.C.: U.S. GPO, 1955 [September-October 1954]). Final Recommendations, quoted in Pierre Mélandri, *Les Etats-Unis et le "défi" européen 1955-58* (Paris: Presses universitaires de France, 1975), p. 55.

Notes to Chapter 3: After the EDC

1. *FRUS, 1952-54,* vol. 6, Memorandum of Conversation, by Robert W. Barnett of the Office of European Regional Affairs, Washington, September 1954, p. 405, and The Secretary of State to the Office of the United States Representative to the European Coal and Steel Community, at Paris, Washington, 27 October 1954, p. 409; *FRUS, 1955-57,* vol. 4, Report By the Department of State to the Council on Foreign Economic Policy, Washington, 16 March 1955, p. 266.
2. *FRUS, 1952-54,* p. 409; The Deputy United States Representative to the European Coal and Steel Community (Tomlinson) to the Department of State, Luxembourg, 31 October 1954, p. 411; and note 4, p. 411. Negotiations among the British, representatives of the High Authority, and the governments of the six ECSC member states were successfully concluded by the end of the year, after overcoming the reservations of Mendès-France.
3. *FRUS, 1952-54,* vol. 6, Louis C. Boochever of the Office of European Regional Affairs to Robert Eisenberg of the Office of the United States Representative to the ECSC, at Luxembourg, Washington, 8 September 1954, p. 399; The increase in ECSC steel production, however, increased European demand for American coal. By January 1956, René Mayer announced the ECSC would import 25 million tons of American coal. *New York Times,* 23 February 1956; Mélandri, *"Défi" européen,* p. 93.
4. Complaints of small producers did, however, force the State Department to ask the High Authority to change its purchase policy. It took another two years for the High Authority to adopt new principles which allowed equal and nondiscriminatory access to all scrap

producers of good repute provided, however, that they were able to deliver at fixed dates and in great quantities. This last provision had the effect of making Luria Brothers the privileged partner of the ECSC. Mélandri, *"Défi" européen,* p. 95; *FRUS, 1955-57,* vol. 4, Report by the Department of State to the Council on Foreign Economic Policy, Washington, 16 March 1955, p. 271.

5. *FRUS, 1955-57,* vol. 4, Letter from the President of the High Authority of the ECSC (Monnet) to the Secretary of State, Luxembourg, 17 March 1955, pp. 275-276.

6. Ibid., pp. 283-286.

7. Ibid., editorial note, pp. 324-325.

8. My translation, quoted in Pascal Fontaine, *Le Comité d'Action pour les Etats-Unis d'Europe de Jean Monnet* (Lausanne: Centre de recherches européennes, 1974)

9. *FRUS, 1952-54,* vol. 6, The Secretary of State to the Office of the United States Representative to the European Coal and Steel Community, at Paris, Washington, 13 December 1954, p. 416, and The Secretary of State to the President of the High Authority of the ECSC (Monnet), Washington, 14 December 1954, p. 417.

10. Ibid., Monnet to Dulles, 1 December 1954; Dulles to Monnet, 13 December 1954; Dulles to Monnet, 14 December 1954, pp. 415-417; Dulles to Monnet, 27 October 1954, AMH 60/4/3, FJM.

11. During the following months, both Monnet and Spaak continued to advise the United States to "stay entirely in the background." *FRUS, 1955-57,* vol. 4, Memorandum from the Assistant Secretary of State for European Affairs (Merchant) to the Secretary of State, Washington, 12 April 1955, p. 279; and Memorandum from the Director of the Office of Political Affairs, U.S. Mission to the North Atlantic Treaty Organizations (Martin) to the Director of the Office of European Regional Affairs (Timmons), Paris, 10 November 1955.

12. Fontaine, *Comité d'Action,* p. 27.

13. Gerbet, *Construction de l'Europe,* p. 192.

14. Ibid.

15. Eisenhower, *White House Years. Mandate,* p. 223.

16. Gerbet, *Construction de l'Europe,* p. 193; Darryl A. Howlett, *Euratom and Nuclear Safeguards* (London: Macmillan, 1990), p. 40.

17. Gerbet, *Construction de l'Europe,* p. 194.

18. *FRUS, 1955-57,* vol. 4, Memorandum of Conversation, Department of State, 20 April 1955, p. 288.

19. Fontaine, *Comité d'Action,* pp. 29-39; Gerbet, *Construction de l'Europe,* p. 197.

20. Monnet, *Memoirs,* p. 403.

21. Gerbet, *Construction de l'Europe,* p. 198.

22. Ibid., p. 201; Pierre Uri, *Penser pour l'Action* (Paris: Odile Jacob, 1991), pp. 121-137.

23. *FRUS, 1955-57,* vol. 4, Memorandum of Conversation, Luxembourg, 11 June 1955, p. 296; Mélandri, *"Défi" européen,* p. 60.

24. *FRUS, 1955-57,* vol. 4, Memorandum from the Director of the Office of Political Affairs, U.S. Mission to the North Atlantic Treaty Organization and European Regional Organizations (Martin) to the Director of the Office of European Regional Affairs (Timmons), Paris, 10 November 1955.

25. Ibid., Letter from the Secretary of State to the President of the High Authority of the European Coal and Steel Community (Mayer), Washington, 8 June 1955, pp. 292-293.

26. Ibid., Memorandum of Conversation, Luxembourg, 11 June 1955, pp. 295-297; Samuel Waugh to Walter Bedell Smith, 7 July 1955, Walter Bedell Smith, 1955 Correspondence, Box 25, DDEL; and Department of State, Secretary's Memoranda of Conversation, Lot 64 D 199, editorial note, p. 297.

27. *Department of State Bulletin,* 24 October 1955, and Mélandri, *"Défi" européen,* p. 63.

28. Eisenhower to Monnet, 1 July 1955, White House Central Files, PPF 1-L "M," Box 171, DDEL.

29. *FRUS, 1955-57*, vol. 4, Telegram from the Secretary of State to the Embassy in France, Washington, 1 September 1955, pp. 330-331.
30. Ibid., Memorandum of Conversation, Paris, 25 October 1955, p. 337; and Memorandum of Conversation, Paris, 17 December 1955, pp. 367-368.
31. *New York Times,* 8 December 1955, p. 8.
32. *FRUS, 1955-57*, vol. 4, Memorandum prepared in the Office of European Regional Affairs, Washington, 6 December 1955, p. 358, and Telegram from the Acting Secretary of State to the Embassy in Italy, 30 May 1955, p. 290.
33. Ibid., Letter from the Acting Director of the Office of European Regional Affairs (Palmer) to the Counselor of the Embassy in Belgium (Sprouse) Washington, 8 July 1955, p. 312.
34. Ibid., Memorandum prepared in the Office of European Regional Affairs, "Peaceful Uses of Atomic Energy and European Integration," 6 December 1955, p. 356.
35. Ibid., p. 355.
36. Ibid., Letter from the Acting Director of the Office of European Regional Affairs (Palmer) to the Counselor of the Embassy in Belgium (Sprouse) Washington, 8 July 1955, p. 310.
37. Ibid., "Peaceful Uses of Atomic Energy and European Integration," p. 356.
38. Ibid., 267th meeting of the National Security Council, 21 November 1955, p. 349.
39. Ibid.
40. Ibid., Memorandum of a Conversation, Department of State, Washington, 15 July 1955, "Proposals for Six Nation European Atomic Energy Authority Patterned on the Schuman Plan," p. 314.
41. See ibid., Memorandum of Conversation, Washington, 22 November 1955, p. 350.
42. All above quotations ibid., Letter from the Secretary of State to Foreign Secretary Macmillan, Washington, 10 December 1955, pp. 362-364.

Notes to Chapter 4: Euratom and the U.S.-Euratom Agreement

1. *FRUS, 1955-57*, vol. 4, Memorandum of Conversation, Department of State, 20 April 1955, Words from Mr. Albert Coppé, p. 288; Monnet, *Memoirs,* pp. 417–430.
2. See, for example, *FRUS, 1955-57*, vol. 4, Memorandum of Conversation, Department of State, 14 May 1956, p. 441.
3. Ibid., Despatch from the Ambassador in the United Kingdom to the Department of State, London, 5 July 1955, p. 310.
4. Ibid., Memorandum from the Secretary of State to the President, Washington, 9 January 1956, pp. 388–389. Dulles had previously discussed the memo with Hoover, Merchant, and Gerard Smith.
5. *Department of State Bulletin,* 16 January 1956, p. 81.
6. *FRUS, 1955-57*, vol. 4, Memorandum of Conversation, Washington, 25 January 1956, pp. 390–399; Monnet to Dulles, 21 January 1956 and Monnet to Dulles, 24 January 1956, John Foster Dulles, Box 106, Dulles Papers, PL.
7. For a more detailed discussion, see Mélandri, *"Défi" européen,* p. 74 et seq.
8. Harold Macmillan, *Pointing the Way* (Melbourne: Macmillan, 1972), p. 44.
9. "OEEC Plan Favored by Britain," *The Times,* 14 February 1956 and "Atomic Plans for Europe: Britain Supports OEEC Scheme," *The Times,* 29 February 1956, reference in Howlett, *Euratom and Nuclear Safeguards.*
10. *FRUS, 1955-57*, vol. 4, note 4, p. 370.
11. Ibid., Memorandum from the Deputy Under Secretary of State (Murphy) to the Director of the International Cooperation Administration (Hollister), Washington, 16 February 1956. This memo provided guidance to Hollister prior to an OEEC meeting in late February.
12. *FRUS, 1955-57*, vol. 4, note 4, Robinson to Bowie.

13. Howlett, *Euratom and Nuclear Safeguards,* pp. 71–74.
14. See, for example, *FRUS, 1955-57,* vol. 4, note 4, Memorandum of Conversation, Paris, 28 April 1956, p. 443.
15. *FRUS, 1955-57,* vol. 4, Memorandum of Conversation, Department of State, Washington, 14 May 1956, pp. 438-444; Memorandum from the Assistant Secretary of State for European Affairs (Lebrick) and Philip. J. Farley of the Office of the Special Assistant to the Secretary of State for Atomic Energy Affairs to the Secretary of State, Washington, 26 September 1956, p. 466; Memorandum of Conversation, Paris, 17 December 1955, pp. 367-369; and Telegram from the Secretary of State to the Department of State, Paris, 17 December 1955, 6 p.m. and 9 p.m., pp. 369-373.
16. Ibid., Letter from the Special Assistant to the Ambassador in France (Robinson) to the Assistant Secretary of State for Policy Planning (Bowie), Paris, 27 December 1955, p. 379.
17. All above quotations, ibid., Telegram from the Ambassador in Germany (Conant) to the Department of State, Bonn, 9 February 1956, p. 414.
18. Ibid., Conant's letter to Merchant, 10 February, p. 415.
19. Ibid., Robinson to Bowie, 27 December 1955.
20. *FRUS, 1955-57,* vol. 4, Memorandum of Conversation, Washington, 25 January 1956, p. 397; and Telegram from the Secretary of State to the Embassy in Belgium, Washington, 24 May 1956, p. 443.
21. See for example, ibid., Smith to Merchant, 8 December 1955, and Bowie's remark during a conversation in Washington on 25 January 1956, pp. 360, 384.
22. Department of State Bulletin, 19 March 1956, pp. 269-270.
23. On 25 January 1956, Admiral Lewis Strauss, chairman of the AEC, made a proposal along those lines; see *FRUS, 1955-57,* vol. 4, Memorandum of Conversation, p. 396.
24. For the best account of United States interests in controlling the development of Euratom, and preventing the construction of an enrichment plant, see Mélandri, *"Défi" européen.* On the fear that the United Kingdom might be preferred to the United States as a source of material and assistance, see, for example *FRUS, 1955-57,* vol. 4, p. 395.
25. See, for example, *FRUS, 1955-57,* vol. 4, Memorandum of Conversation, Washington, 25 January 1956. (This was specifically the position of the secretary of state.)
26. Ibid., Memorandum of Conversation, Paris, 28 April 1956, p. 433.
27. Ibid., p. 501.
28. See ibid., Memorandum of Conversation, Department of State, Washington, 14 May 1956, pp. 435-444.
29. Ibid., p. 441.
30. *FRUS, 1955-57,* vol. 4, Telegram from the Ambassador in France (Dillon) to the Department of State, Paris, 3 February 1956, pp. 401–403.
31. Ibid., Memorandum of Conversation, Washington, 6 February 1956, pp. 406–407.
32. Ibid., Letter from the Deputy Under Secretary of State (Murphy) to the Chairman of the Atomic Energy Commission (Strauss), Washington, 7 August 1956, p. 456.
33. Gerbet, *Construction de l'Europe,* p. 214.
34. *FRUS, 1955-1957,* vol. 4, Telegram from the Ambassador in Belgium (Alger) to the Department of State, Brussels, 19 December 1956, pp. 497–498.
35. Monnet to General Alfred Gruenther, Paris, 28 September 1956, Gruenther Papers, Box 36, "Jean Monnet (2)," DDEL.
36. *FRUS, 1955-57,* vol. 4, Dillon to the Department of State, 19 November 1956, pp. 487–489.
37. Note sur la conversation avec M. Schaetzel, 12 November 1956, Max Kohnstamm's archives (hereafter cited as MKS); "A Target for Euratom," report submitted by Louis Armand, Franz Etzel, and Francesco Giordani at the requests of the governments of Belgium, France, German Federal Republic, Italy, Luxembourg, and the Netherlands, May 1957, MKS.

38. *FRUS, 1955-57,* vol. 4, Memorandum from the Assistant Secretary of State for European Affairs (Elbrick) and the Special Assistant to the Secretary of State for Atomic Energy Affairs (Smith) to the Secretary of State, Washington, 3 December 1956, pp. 491-495; invitation of Mr. John Foster Dulles and President Lewis Strauss for the Wise Men's visit to the United States, released to the press on 21 December 1956, MKS.

39. Monnet to Dulles, 26 November 1956, John Foster Dulles, Box 106, PL; *FRUS, 1955-57,* vol. 4, Memorandum of Conversation between the Secretary of State and Jean Monnet, Department of State, Washington, 10 January 1957, p. 501; Monnet to Eisenhower, 20 January 1957, DDE Central Files, PPF, 260-D Euratom, DDEL.

40. "Une association sur un pied d'égalité dans un intérêt mutuel."

41. Monnet to René Pleven, Paris, 24 January 1957, MKS.

42. Monnet to Meyer, Paris, 30 January 1957; Monnet to Smith, Paris, 30 January 1957; Monnet to McCloy, 30 January 1957; Monnet to Swatland, Paris, 30 January 1957; Monnet to Bowie, Paris, 30 January 1957; Monnet to Dulles, Paris, 30 January 1957; Monnet to Miss Barnaw, Paris, 30 January 1957, MKS.

43. Warren Unna, "Atoms for Europe," *Washington Post,* 2 February 1957; Dulles to Monnet, 4 February 1957, JFD, Box 120, PL.

44. *FRUS, 1955-57,* vol. 4, Memorandum of Conversation, Department of State, Washington, 4 February 1957, 11 a.m., pp. 512–515; Henri Tessier du Cros, *Louis Armand* (Paris: Editions Odile Jacob), p. 246; *FRUS, 1955-57,* vol. 4, Memorandum of Conference with the President, The White House, Washington, 6 February 1957, pp. 516–518; Short Note on the Meeting between the Wise Men and the Secretary of State, 4 February 1957 and Notes on Talks which took place on Wednesday, 6 February 1957, MKS; Joint Communiqué by the Department of State, the chairman of the AEC, and the Euratom Committee, 8 February 1957, Department of State for the Press, MKS.

45. The four American experts were Mr. Cook, Mr. Allen Vander Weyden, deputy director of the Division of International Affairs of the AEC, Mr. Fine, and Mr. Roddis.

46. Atomic Industrial Forum, Inc., Euratom Committee Meeting with U.S. Representatives, 13 February 1957, MKS; Kohnstamm to Monnet, 10 February 1957, MKS.

47. *FRUS, 1955-57,* vol. 4, Memorandum of a Conversation, Department of State, Washington, 8 February 1957, pp. 520-521; The appointment of Charles Ailleret was significant in this respect. See Mélandri, *"Défi" européen,* p. 127.

48. *FRUS, 1955-57,* vol. 4, Letter From the Secretary of State to Foreign Minister Spaak, Washington, 22 March 1957.

49. H. L. Nieburg, *Nuclear Secrecy and Foreign Policy* (Washington, D.C.: Public Affairs Press, 1963), pp. 137, 138, 142.

50. Schaetzel to Kohnstamm, 1 October 1957, K5, MKS.

51. Bob Schaetzel of the State Department, he warned Kohnstamm, was unpopular in the AEC: Kohnstamm Diary, European University Institute, 1991, pp. 4121–4122.

52. Even though Monnet was no longer head of the High Authority; Forum Memo, "Wanted a Program," November 1957, MKS; Discussion Meeting Report, Western European Integration, COFR, 23 October 1057, MKS; Kohnstamm to Allen Vander Weyden, 6 November 1957, K5, MKS; Schaetzel to Kohnstamm, 19 November 1957, K5, MKS; Itinerary of Mr. Kohnstamm's journey to the United States, 1957, K4, MKS; Schaetzel to Monnet, 6 November 1957, K5, MKS.

53. Allen Vander Weyden of AEC and Louis Boochever of the Office of European Regional Affairs in the State Department also attended the meeting. See *FRUS, 1955-57,* vol. 4, Memorandum by the Scientific Representative of the Atomic Energy Commission at the Embassy in France (Bishop), Paris, 27 November 1957, pp. 565–569.

54. This discussion is based on Charles-Lavauzelle, *Louis Armand,* (1986) and Tessier du Cros, *Louis Armand.*

55. Proposed Euratom Agreements, Hearings before the JCAE, Congress of the United States, 85th Cong., 2nd sess. on the proposed Euratom agreements and legislation to carry out

the proposed cooperative agreement, pp. 84-85; Schaetzel to Kohnstamm, 26 November 1957, Kohnstamm to Schaetzel, 5 December 1957, Schaetzel to Kohnstamm, 6 December 1957, K5, MKS.

56. Italics added.
57. Schaetzel to Kohnstamm, 17 December 1957, and Philip Farley, Memorandum for the File, 23 December 1957, MKS.
58. Kohnstamm to Schaetzel, 17 January 1958, MKS; Dulles, Memorandum for the President, 16 January 1958, DDE Central Files, Official Files of 260(2), Box 912, DDEL.
59. Memorandum for the Record, 1/7/58, White House Central File, Alpha File B 2137, O.F. 181, DDEL; Memorandum, "Meeting with Admiral Strauss," 27 January 1958, MKS; Memorandum, "Various Aspects of U.S.-Euratom Relationships," 27 January 1958, MKS; Schaetzel to Kohnstamm, 28 January 1958, MKS; Memorandum for the President, 28 January 1958, Whitman File, Dulles-Herter, Box 7, DDEL.
60. Kohnstamm met with Schaetzel, Vander Weyden, Cleveland, Mr. Cook (deputy general manager of AEC), Dillon, Shepard Stone, and Senator Pastore. See Schedule for Max Kohnstamm, MKS.
61. Doc. EUR/W.P. 11/58 E, United States Delegation, Joint U.S.-Euratom Working Party, MKS; Report of the Joint Euratom-United States Working Party, 3 April 1958, MKS.
62. "Brief Outline of Proposed Joint US-Euratom Program," 5/19/58, M 6, MKS; Phyllis D. Bernau to Jean Monnet, May 9 1958, JFD, Box 132, PL; Groupe de travail Etats-Unis Europe, Brussels, 30 May 1958, K6, MKS; *New York Times,* 9 June 1958.
63. Kohnstamm to Armand, 7 July 1958, MKS; Kohnstamm to Monnet, 1 July 1958, K6, MKS; Monnet to Dulles, 13 July 1958, JFD, Box 137, PL.
64. Ball to Kohnstamm, 18 July 1958, MKS 6; JCAE, Euratom Hearings. For a detailed discussion of the hearings, see Mélandri, *"Défi" européen,* pp. 174–179.
65. Kohnstamm to Pastore, 7 July 1958, MKS; Ball to Kohnstamm, 18 July 1958, K6, MKS; Schaetzel to Acheson, 29 August 1958, Acheson Papers, Manuscript and Archives, Yale University Library (hereafter cited as YL); Samuel Waugh to Kohnstamm, 15 August 1958, MKS.
66. *Department of State Bulletin* 60, 12 January 1959, pp. 69–74.
67. Ball to Kohnstamm, 20 November 1958, MKS.
68. Tessier du Cros, op. cit., pp. 256–266 and Charles-Lavauzelle, op. cit., pp. 119–125.

Notes to Chapter 5: Europe at Sixes and Sevens

1. *FRUS, 1955-57,* vol. 4, note 4, p. 370. The meeting took place on 15 December 1955.; ibid., Memorandum of Conversation, Department of State, Washington, 21 December 1955, p. 376, and Memorandum of Conversation (René Mayer and Eisenhower), The White House, Washington, 8 February 1956, p. 409.
2. Ibid., Telegram from the Secretary of State to the Embassy in Belgium, Washington, 24 May 1956, p. 444.
3. Gerbet, *Construction de l'Europe,* p. 213.
4. In 1954, upon the recommendation of Joseph Dodge, President Eisenhower established the Council on Foreign Economic Policy, which was charged with coordinating foreign economic policy. Its membership consisted in selected cabinet officers and the heads of other appropriate agencies. See Eisenhower, *White House Years. Mandate,* p. 294. The memo to Dodge was by Gabriel Hauge and was dated 9 February; see *FRUS, 1955-57,* vol. 4, note 2, p. 461, and CFEP Records, DDEL; *FRUS, 1955-57,* vol. 4, p. 461.
5. *FRUS, 1955-57,* vol. 4, Circular Airgram from the Secretary of State to Certain Diplomatic Missions, Washington, 13 July 1956, p. 450.
6. Ibid., Memorandum of Conversation, Department of State, Washington, 26 September 1956, pp. 464–65.

7. See, for example, ibid., Memorandum from the Director of the Office of British Commonwealth and Northern European Affairs to the Assistant Secretary of State for European Affairs, Washington, 9 October 1956, pp. 473–474. In his memoirs, Harold Macmillan describes a meeting he had with Paul-Henri Spaak in February 1956. According to him, Spaak, quite pessimistic about the chances of the Common Market, insisted that the United Kingdom "take the lead in the creation of a united Europe before it was too late." See Harold Macmillan, *Riding the Storm 1956-1959* (London: Harper and Row, 1971).

8. Randall to Dulles, 4 October 1956, CFEP Policy Papers, Box 7, Folder 4, DDEL; *Public Papers of the Presidents of the United States: Dwight D. Eisenhower, 1956*, pp. 1038–1045.

9. All above quotations from *FRUS, 1955-57*, vol. 4, Report by the Subcommittee on Regional Economic Integration of the Council on Foreign Economic Policy to the Council, Washington, 15 November 1956, pp. 482–486.

10. Ibid., p. 487.

11. *Department of State Bulletin,* 4 February 1957, p. 18.

12. See Ross B. Talbot, *The Chicken War* (Ames, Ia.: Iowa State University Press), 1978, p. 47.

13. *FRUS, 1955-57,* vol. 4, Telegram from the Secretary of State to the Embassy in Belgium, 26 January 1957, pp. 507–508.

14. Ibid., Memorandum From the Deputy Under Secretary of State for Economic Affairs (Dillon) to the Chairman of the Council on Foreign Economic Policy (Randall). Enclosure: Report to the CFEP regarding the European Common Market, 11 April 1957, pp. 549–553.

15. Ibid., and *FRUS, 1955-57,* vol. 4, Memorandum of Conversation Between the Secretary of State and the German Ambassador (Krekeler), Department of State, Washington, 11 February 1957; Memorandum of a Conversation, Department of State, Washington, 18 February 1957, pp. 523–526.

16. See, for example, *FRUS, 1955-57,* vol. 4, Memorandum of a Conversation, Department of State, Washington, 26 May 1957, p. 558.

17. Ibid., Circular Telegram from the Secretary of State to Certain Diplomatic Missions, 6 March 1957, pp. 534–536.

18. Macmillan, *Riding the Storm.*

19. Memorandum of Conversation, United States Delegation to the Ministerial Meeting of the North Atlantic Council, Bonn, Germany, 4 May 1957, Eisenhower Papers, Whitman File, Dulles/Herter, Box 9, "J. F. Dulles May '57," DDEL.

20. Macmillan, *Riding the Storm,* p. 437.

21. For more details about the Free Trade Area Negotiations, see Karl Kaiser, *EWG und Freihandelzone* (Leiden: Sijthof, 1963). See also Ernst Van der Beugel, *From Marshall Plan to Atlantic Partnership* (Amsterdam: Elsevier, 1965); Beloff, op. cit.; Gerbet, op. cit., pp. 232-234; Miriam Camps, *Britain and the European Community 1955-1963* (London: Oxford University Press, 1964).

22. *FRUS, 1955-57,* vol. 4, Telegram from the Acting Secretary of State to the Embassy in France, 10 October 1957, pp. 564–565.

23. For a more detailed discussion of this much-studied topic, see Thomas Lee Ilgen, "The Politics of Economics: United States-West European Monetary and Trade Relations, 1958-1971," Ph.D. diss., University of California, Santa Barbara, July 1976. See also Jean Marchal, *Le Système Monétaire International* (Paris: Editions Cujas, 1979).

24. *Documents on American Foreign Relations 1959* (Published for the COFR, New York: Harper and Brothers, 1960), p. 517.

25. United States Mission to the North Atlantic Treaty Organization and European Regional Organizations.

26. Randall to Dillon, 8 April 1958, DDE Central Files, O.F. 260 C, "European Community," DDEL.

27. "Macmillan Talks, Washington, 9-11 June 1958," White House Central Files, Confidential File, Subject Series, Box 76, State Department (June 58), Briefing Book Macmillan Visits (2), DDEL.

28. Van der Beugel, *From Marshall Plan to Atlantic Partnership*, p. 33.
29. Quoted in Fontaine, *Le Comité d'Action.*
30. Memorandum of Conversation, Jean Monnet and John Tuthill, Paris, 12 November 1958, Tuthill's Private Papers (hereafter cited as TP).
31. Mélandri, *"Défi" européen*, p. 196.
32. Memorandum of Conversation, Monnet and Tuthill, 9 June 1959, transmitted to the State Department, 11 June 1959, TP.
33. Letter to Randall, 2 September 1959, Eisenhower Papers, U.S. CFEP 1954-1961, Box 4, "Europe 1959 (1)," DDEL.
34. President's trip to Europe, 23 August 1959, Eisenhower Papers, U.S. CFEP Office of the Chairman Records 1954-61, Randall Series, Subject Subseries, DDEL.
35. Memorandum for Mr. Randall, 6 April 1960, Eisenhower Papers, Randall Series, Subject Subseries, Box 4, "Common Market," DDEL.
36. See *New York Times,* 20 March 1960.
37. Macmillan visit, 26 March 1960, Eisenhower Papers, White House Central Files, Confidential File, Subject Series, Box 80, State Department, March 60, "Macmillan Visit (1)," DDEL.
38. Memorandum of Conversation, 2 September 1959, Eisenhower Papers, Whitman File, International Meetings Series, Box 3, "Paris Visit, September 2-4, 1959(2)," DDEL.
39. Memorandum for Mr. Randall, 7 June 1960, Eisenhower Papers, Randall Series, Subject Subseries, Box 4, "Common Market (1)," DDEL.
40. Staff Notes, no. 281, 17 January 1958, Eisenhower Papers, Whitman File, DDE Diaries, Box 22, "Toner notes January 58," DDEL.
41. Dulles Memorandum, 16 January 1958, Eisenhower Papers, DDE Central Files, Box 919, "Official files of 260(2)," DDEL.
42. Schedule of the Visit of the Presidents of the European Community to the United States, 5 June 1958, MKS; The U.S. Visit, including press clippings, June 1959, MKS; Compte rendu de la visite des trois Présidents aux Etats-Unis, 26 June 1959, MKS.
43. Compte rendu, op. cit., MKS.
44. Department of State, Joint Communiqué, 12 June 1952, no. 419, MKS; Foreign Service Dispatch, U.S. Mission to the European Communities, Luxembourg, 23 June 1959, 850.33/6-2359, CAA, NA.
45. Memorandum of Conference with the President, 5 June 1959, Eisenhower Papers, Whitman File, DDE Diaries, Box 42, "Staff notes June 59 (2)," DDEL.
46. Briefing Memo from Herter, 19 April 1960, Eisenhower Papers, Whitman File, International Series, Box 12, "De Gaulle-Visit to the U.S." See also Chancellor Adenauer's Visit, Position Paper, 11 March 1960, Eisenhower Papers, White House Central Files, Confidential File, Subject Series, Box 80, "State Department March 1960-Briefing Book (2)," DDEL.
47. President's Trip to Europe, 23 August 1959, Eisenhower Papers, U.S. CFEP Office of the Chairman Records 1954-61, Randall Series, Subject Subseries, DDEL.
48. *FRUS, 1955-57,* vol. 4, Memorandum from the Deputy Under Secretary of State for Economic Affairs (Prochnow) to the Acting Secretary of State, Washington, 16 December 1955, pp. 366–367; ibid, Minutes of the 34th Meeting of the Council on Foreign Economic Policy, Washington, 20 December 1955, pp. 373–374; ibid, Memorandum of a Conversation, Department of State (with René Mayer), 10 February 1956, p. 404.
49. Ibid., Airgram from the Secretary of State to the Embassy in Luxembourg, Washington, 22 June 1956, pp. 448–450.
50. Ibid., Memorandum from the Chairman of the CFEP (Randall) to the Director of the Office of International Trade and Resources (Thibodeaux), Washington, 2 February 1957, p. 511.
51. Ibid., Telegram from the Acting United States Representative to the European Coal and Steel Community (Boochever) to the Department of State, Luxembourg, 21 February 1957, pp. 527–529.
52. Ibid., Memorandum of a Conversation, Department of State, 3-4 April 1957, pp. 344–349.

53. "La Crise Charbonnière," Centre de Documentation du Comité d'Action pour les Etats-Unis d'Europe, 10 April 1959, MKS; Raymond Aron, *Figaro,* 24 April 1959; John S. Hoghland to Senator Byrd, 2 April 1959 and enclosed memorandum dated 27 March 1959, 850. 33/3-1759, CS/W, NA.

54. Hoghland to Byrd, op. cit.

55. Department of State Telegram, 27 February 1959, Confidential File, 850.33/2-2759, NA.

56. Memorandum of Conversation, 13 March 1959, 850.33/3.1359, 2 462 a. 116, NA.

57. Telegram from Luxembourg, 23 May 1959, Classified File, 950.33/6-2359, NA.

58. "European Integration and Economic Cooperation," (in preparation for the Macmillan Talks, 9-11 June 1958), White House Central Files, Confidential File, Subject Series, Box 76, "State Department June 58," DDEL.

59. Statement by the Honorable John Foster Dulles Before the Senate Committee on Finance on Extension of the Trade Agreements Act, Department of State, For the Press, 20 June 1958, Dulles Papers, Box 134, PL.

60. Policy Statement by the CFEP on Scope of Public List for the 1960 Tariff Negotiations, 17 September 1959, Eisenhower Papers, U.S. CFEP Office of the Chairman Records 1954-61, Box 5, "CFEP 588," DDEL.

61. The new TAA authorized the President to raise tariffs on products threatened by foreign competition by 50 percent from their 1934 level; see Mélandri, *"Défi" européen,* pp. 197-198.

62. Ibid.

63. See Thomas L. Ilgen, *Autonomy and Interdependence. U.S.-Western European Monetary and Trade Relations, 1958-1984* (Totowa: Rowman and Allanheld, 1985).

64. Ibid., p. 26. The October 1959 "Buy American" policy was part of that scheme: recipients of American aid were to buy only United States products. "The intent of the . . . policy was," said Ilgen, "less to increase U.S. sales abroad than to encourage the Europeans to enlarge their own aid programs."

65. "The Future of NATO," 28 March 1956, drafted in S/P, EUR, OIR, Records of the Office of European Regional Affairs, Records of the Director 1955-60, Country Material RG 59, Lot File 61 D252, NA; "The Concept of the Atlantic Community," 27 April 1956 and attachments (shows Fuller and Owen worked on "The Future of NATO" study), RG 59, Europe Folder 1 of 2, Lot File 66 D 487, PPS Office F60, NA.

66. Wednesday, 1 April 1959, Executive Office Building, Clarence B. Randall Papers, vol. 11, Box 9, 1959, PL.

67. In April 1954, Clarence Randall held the opinion that "the Schuman Plan, quite apart from the cartel idea, made for Socialism because centralized control of funds would limit private initiative." Thursday, 3:00 p.m., Executive Offices. Clarence B. Randall Papers, Washington after the Commission, vol. 2, 8 April 1954, PL.

68. Clarence B. Randall Papers, Box 9, 1959, vol. 11, 27 April 1959, 3, PL

69. "A House Divided," OEEC, 27 August 1959, Randall Series, Subject Subseries, Box 4, DDEL.

70. Fontaine, *Comité d'Action,* p. 125.

71. Memorandum of Conversation, Paris, 9 June 1959, transmitted to the State Department on 11 June 1959, TP.

72. "A New Era of Atlantic Relations," 25 June 1959, TP; Fontaine, *Comité d'Action,* p. 125.

73. Tuthill to Dillon, Paris, 3 August 1959, TP.

74. Monnet to Eisenhower, 14 August 1959, Dwight D. Eisenhower Central Files, President's Personal File, Box 61, I-F-138, Europe August 1959, "France (3)," DDEL.

75. *Department of State Bulletin,* 29 June 1959, "Challenge of Economic Growth in the Free World," Address made before the Harvard University Alumni Association at Cambridge, Mass., on 11 June, pp. 955–957.

76. Telegram for the President from the Acting Secretary, 16 December 1959, Eisenhower Papers, Whitman File, Administrative Series, Box 11, "Dillon," DDEL.

77. Macmillan, *Pointing the Way.* In a memorandum to the President dated 28 February 1960, Herter referred to the recent British change in attitude: "While the UK still hopes for a

European-wide Free Trade Area as an eventual solution, they are now in agreement with us that it would not be advisable to press this concept now, but rather to concentrate on practical action to ease difficulties in trade between the two groupings and between both groupings and countries who are not members of either group. We are hopeful also that the British and ourselves will be able to restrain the more extreme elements in the EFTA, represented by the Swedes and the Swiss, whose natural desire is to press for perfect but impractical solutions as rapidly as possible." Memorandum for the President, European Economic Problems, 28 February 1960, Eisenhower Papers, Whitman File, Herter, Box 10, "Herter, Christian, February 1960," DDEL.

78. Fontaine, *Comité d'Action,* p. 125.
79. Telegram for the President, 16 December 1959, Eisenhower Papers, op. cit.
80. Fontaine, *Comité d'Action,* p. 127.
81. *Department of State Bulletin,* 1 February 1960.
82. Dillon's speech at the Austrian Foreign Affairs Society, 16 July 1960, United States Information Service, American Embassy.
83. Memorandum for the President by Secretary of State Christian Herter, 2 February 1960, Whitman File, Dulles-Herter, Box 10, "Herter, Christian Feb. 60," DDEL.
84. Fontaine, *Comité d'Action,* p. 127.
85. John Tuthill, letter to Pascaline Winand, 22 June 199
86. Chancellor Adenauer's Visit, Position Paper, 11 March 1960, White House Central Files, Confidential File, Subject Series, Box 80, State Department, March 60, Briefing Book (2), DDEL.
87. Ibid., and Macmillan Visit, Position Paper, 26 March 1960, White House Central Files, Confidential File, Subject Series, Box 80, State Department, March 60, Macmillan Visit (1), DDEL.
88. CFEP, The White House, 19 November 1959, U.S. CFEP, Office of the Chairman, Records 1954-61, CFEP Minutes 1959, 95th Meeting, DDEL.
89. Bürgenstock Conference, 28-29 May 1960, Jackson, C.D., Box 29, Time Inc. File, Bilderberg 1958-60-61 (1), DDE; Bürgenstock Conference, List of Participants, MKS.
90. Memorandum for the President, 27 September 1960, Clarence Randall, Box 10, 1960, vol. 16, Clarence B. Randall Papers, PL; Memorandum for the Honorable Clarence Randall, 21 September 1960, US CFEP Office of the Chairman, Records 1954-61, Box 1, CFEP Memos 1960, Karl Brandt to Clarence Randall, DDEL.

Notes to Chapter 6: The Kennedy Team

1. See, among others, Robert Schaetzel, John Tuthill, Henry Owen, recorded interviews by Pascaline Winand, January 1989.
2. Arthur Schlesinger, *A Thousand Days* (New York: Fawcett, 1965). On 1 January 1960 in Washington, John Kennedy declared: "Our democratic society must demonstrate that it can convert the North Atlantic ties, forged in the precarious war and postwar years, into a stable, creative partnership among equals." Kennedy, *Strategy of Peace.*
3. Schlesinger, *Thousand Days,* pp. 781-782.
4. George W. Ball, "The Period of Transition," in *Economic Unity in Europe: Programs and Problems* (New York: National Industrial Conference Board, January 21 1960), pp. 9–34, quoted in David L. Dileo, "Catch the Night Plane for Paris," presented at the Conference "Jean Monnet and the Americans," Hyde Park, New York, October 1990.
5. Schlesinger, *Thousand Days,* p. 143.
6. Ibid., p. 411.
7. William Mozdzierz, "Chester Bowles and the Sacrifice of the Politically Irrelevant," Research Seminar in American Diplomatic History for Professor Gaddis Smith, Yale University, May 1989.

8. See Bowles's letter to Adlai Stevenson, 23 July 1961, Chester Bowles Papers, YL.
9. For a more detailed discussion of the Chester Bowles story, see ibid.; Chester Bowles, *Promises to Keep* (New York: Harper and Row, 1971); Schlesinger, *Thousand Days*; and Schoenebaum, ed., *Political Profiles: The Kennedy Years.*
10. Bowles's letter to Adlai Stevenson, 23 July 1961, Chester Bowles Papers, YL, 12.
11. Bowles's letter to Eugene Rostow, 27 June 1961, Chester Bowles Papers, YL, 1.
12. Chester Bowles, recorded interview, 52, JFKL Oral History Program.
13. Bowles to President, 22 August 1961, NSF 82-91, Germany-Berlin 8/22/61, JFKL.
14. Memorandum to the President from the Under Secretary, 28 July 1961, Chester Bowles Papers, YL.
15. Foy Kohler played an important part in attempts to coordinate allied policy during the 1961-62 Berlin crisis. He was later appointed ambassador to the Soviet Union in July 1962.
16. Chester Bowles, 57, JFKL Oral History Program.
17. Letter to the President from Bowles, 21 August 1961, Chester Bowles Papers, YL.
18. Ibid.
19. Some Requirements of American Foreign Policy, by Chester Bowles, 1 July 1961, Chester Bowles Papers, YL.
20. All above quotations, ibid.
21. Monnet's speech at Dartmouth University, 11 June 1961.
22. See discussion about Christian Herter. Bowles was one of the signatories of the first Declaration of Atlantic Unity in October 1954.
23. Ambassador Tuthill, Robert Schaetzel, and Henry Owen, recorded interviews by Pascaline Winand. See also George McGhee, recorded interview by Minister Hillenbrand, August 1964, 22, JFKL Oral History Program.
24. George Ball, *The Past Has Another Pattern. Memoirs* (New York: W. W. Norton & Co., 1982).
25. All above quotations, Ball, *Memoirs,* p. 165.
26. Ball, *Memoirs,* p. 166; and Kennedy, *Strategy of Peace,* p. 67 et seq. (2 July 1957 speech).
27. Ball, *Memoirs,* p. 166.
28. Monnet, *Memoirs,* p. 327.
29. Monnet, *Memoirs,* p. 326; and Ball, *Memoirs,* p. 72.
30. Ball, *Memoirs,* pp. 72–73.
31. Monnet, *Memoirs,* p. 329.
32. Ball, *Memoirs,* p. 77. For more details on Ball's role in drafting the CEEC report, his trip to Washington (where he showed a pirated copy of the Committee draft to Charles Kindleberger and Paul Nitze of the State Department), and the subsequent American-European meeting on 30 August, see Ball, *Memoirs,* p. 77.
33. Ball, *Memoirs,* p. 89.
34. William Tomlinson suffered from a weak heart since his youth, and died in 1955 at the age of 37. For Monnet's recollections of his role and David Bruce's role in the Marshall plan, see Monnet, *Memoirs,* pp. 269–270.
35. Ball, *Memoirs,* p. 90.
36. Walter Hallstein, recorded interview by Gordon Graig, Brussels, Belgium, 29 July 1964, The John Foster Dulles Oral History Project, PL.
37. For an interesting analysis of the Monnet network of European and American friends, close acquaintances, allies, and sympathizers see Fontaine, *Comité d'Action,* pp. 54–60.
38. Robert Schaetzel and John Tuthill, recorded interviews by Pascaline Winand, January 1989, Washington, D.C.
39. Ball to Monnet, 1 September 1960, Ball Papers, Box 7, PL.
40. Schaetzel to Kohnstamm, 4 October 1960, Department of State, Washington, MKS; "Report to the Honorable John F. Kennedy from Adlai E. Stevenson, November, 1960," Personal Papers of J. Robert Schaetzel, Bethesda, Maryland, pp. PA 1-20. See Dileo, "Catch the Night Plane for Paris."
41. George Ball, Agendas, George Ball's Private Papers, Princeton.

42. Ibid., and George Ball, recorded interview by Pascaline Winand, August 1988, p. 2.
43. Monnet, *Memoirs,* pp. 464-465. See also original edition, Jean Monnet, *Mémoires,* vol. 2 (Paris: Fayard, 1976), pp. 698–699.
44. For Monnet's portrait of McCloy, see Monnet, *Memoirs,* p. 154.
45. Fondation Jean Monnet pour l'Europe, *Témoignages à la mémoire de Jean Monnet* (Lausanne: Centre de recherches européennes, 9 November 1989), p. 487.
46. Henry Owen, recorded interview by Pascaline Winand, Washington, D.C., 17 October 1990.
47. In his Memoirs, Monnet had this to say about Bruce: "David Bruce was already a friend of mine, and the mutual trust between us has helped solve many political problems. I should describe him as essentially a civilized man, because for me this general term has a very precise meaning. Bruce always takes account of others, and listens to them without trying to impose his point of view or insist that he is always right. He is always anxious to be fully convinced before attempting to convince others. He has fulfilled many important and difficult missions, and is free of political dogmatism—although himself a Democrat, he has served Republican administrations—and he never sees his country as a dominating force. Instead he looks for ways in which the United States can help other countries; and he is always trying to help others himself. That, to my mind, is what being civilized means." See Monnet, *Memoirs,* pp. 269–270; Robert Schaetzel, who knew David Bruce well, numbers him among the "theologians." See Robert Schaetzel, recorded interview by Pascaline Winand, 12 January 1989, Washington, D.C.
48. Dean Acheson, recorded interview by Lucius D. Battle, 27 April 1964, JFKL, pp. 9-10.
49. See Schlesinger, *Thousand Days,* p. 395.
50. See p. 314 et seq. of this book.
51. John Tuthill, recorded interview by Pascaline Winand, January 1989, Washington, D.C.
52. John Leddy was first appointed as assistant secretary of the treasury.
53. Dillon enjoyed considerable freedom of action as Dulles's under secretary for economic affairs. Dulles considered his particular field of expertise to be political affairs, and did not manifest an undue interest for economics. As a result, he would often delegate authority in this specific field to Dillon. This contrasted with Herter's position, who was working with Dulles on political affairs, and accordingly was left much less initiative.
54. John Tuthill, recorded interview by Pascaline Winand at his home, Washington, D. C., 18 October 1990.
55. Acheson Report, March 1961., N.S.F, Regional Security, pp. 211–220, JFKL.
56. Ibid.
57. Paul Nitze, recorded interview by Pascaline Winand, October 1990. Bowie came from Baltimore, as did Nitze's family. Bowie's roommate at Princeton was a Nitze cousin, although Bowie did not know Nitze then. (Robert Bowie, letter to Pascaline Winand, 30 June 1992.)
58. See Paul Nitze, *From Hiroshima to Glasnost, At the Center of Decision, A Memoir* (New York: Grove Weidenfeld, 1989), pp. 46–66.
59. Roswell Gilpatric was McNamara's deputy until 1963. James Perkins worked at the Carnegie Corporation and became president of Cornell University in 1963. See Nitze, *From Hiroshima to Glasnost,* pp. 177–178, 211–212; and Paul Nitze, recorded interview by Pascaline Winand, SAIS, Washington, D.C., October 1990.
60. George Ball, recorded interview by Pascaline Winand, August 1988, Princeton.
61. See David Halberstam,"The Very Expensive Education of McGeorge Bundy," *Harper's Magazine* (July 1969) p. 27. Bundy withdrew his support of the Republican party after its 1960 nomination of Nixon, and helped organize a committee in support of Senator Kennedy. See Schoenebaum, ed., *Political Profiles: The Kennedy Years.*
62. Walt Rostow and McGeorge Bundy made the recommendation to Kennedy to abandon the OCB and to let the secretary of state assume the coordinating function. Initially quite skeptical about the wisdom of following this specific course of action, Kennedy finally agreed to abolish the OCB. See Walt Rostow, recorded interview, 42, JFKL Oral History Program.
63. Ball, *Memoirs,* pp. 167–68.

64. Halberstam, op. cit., p. 33.
65. See George McGhee, recorded interview by Martin J. Hillenbrand, 13 August 1964, 22, JFKL Oral History Program.
66. See Schlesinger, *Thousand Days,* pp. 390, 398.
67. Personal interview of I. M. Destler, quoted in I. M. Destler, *Presidents, Bureaucrats and Foreign Policy* (Princeton: Princeton University Press, 1972).
68. Destler, *Presidents, Bureaucrats,* p. 100.
69. Richard M. Moose, *President and National Security,* Institute for Defense Analyses. Quoted in Destler, *Presidents, Bureaucrats,* p. 103.
70. Destler, *Presidents, Bureaucrats,* pp. 102, 104.
71. See Walt Rostow, *The Diffusion of Power* (New York: Macmillan, 1972), pp. 10–11. In the spring of 1946 Walt Rostow wrote a proposal which found support with Acheson and Clayton, and with Jean Monnet, who was in Washington at the time. The proposal "argued that the piecemeal negotiation of the peace treaties would simply consolidate the split of Europe, and that Byrnes should frame the treaty negotiations with proposals that would move the continent towards unity." See also Walt Rostow, recorded interview by Pascaline Winand, June 1986, Austin, Texas, p. 4.
72. See Schoenebaum, ed., *Political Profiles: The Kennedy Years.*
73. Walt Rostow's interview, JFKL, p. 43.
74. Ibid., p. 134. Also see introduction.
75. McGeorge Bundy, recorded interview by Pascaline Winand, New York, March 1989.
76. Schoenebaum, ed., *Political Profiles: The Kennedy Years.*
77. Author's interview with Carl Kaysen, Boston, MIT.
78. Ibid.
79. Robert Schaetzel, recorded interview by Pascaline Winand.
80. McGeorge Bundy, recorded interview by Pascaline Winand.
81. Christian Herter, *Toward an Atlantic Community* (Published for the COFR by Harper and Row, New York, 1963), p. 25.
82. Herter, *Atlantic Community,* pp. 30–31.
83. Ibid.
84. Ibid.
85. Ibid., p. 32.
86. Ibid., p. 42.
87. Ibid., p. 68.
88. *New York Times,* 11 January 1962.
89. Herter, *Atlantic Community,* p. 69.
90. In January 1962, ninety-two delegates from all members of NATO were officially appointed—but not authorized to speak for their government—to meet in Paris at "The Atlantic Convention of NATO Nations." They elected Christian Herter as chairman. See Istvan Szent-Miklosy, *The Atlantic Union Movement* (New York: Fountainhead Publishers, 1965), and *Freedom and Union,* February-March 1962.
91. See, for example, Irving Janis, *Groupthink,* 2d ed., (Boston: Houghton Mifflin, 1982).
92. Kennedy, *Strategy of Peace.* Discussion with John Fisher, p. 227.

Notes to Chapter 7: Kennedy's Inheritance

1. Deane Hinton, a foreign service officer, was on the staff of the American Mission to the European Communities in Brussels. Francis Williamson was a former director of the Office of Research and Analysis for Western Europe in the Department of State who had been recently assigned to the American Embassy in Bonn. Malcolm W. Hoag was a

member of the Rand Corporation, while Professor Knorr came from the Princeton Center for International Studies. Other members, such as General Twitchell, were from the Department of Defense.

2. Stevenson Report, part 1, p. 15.
3. Robert Bowie, "The North Atlantic Nations. Tasks for the 1960's. A Report to the Secretary of State" (hereafter cited as Bowie Report), August 1960. Published in the Nuclear History Program Occasional Paper Series, Center for International Security Studies, School of Public Affairs, University of Maryland, 1991, p. 76.
4. Acheson Report, p. 26.
5. Bowie Report, p. 75.
6. Ibid., p. 77.
7. Ibid.
8. Ibid., p. 78.
9. Ibid., p. 79.
10. Ibid., p. 80.
11. Ibid., p. 81.
12. Ibid.
13. Ibid., p. 82.
14. Ibid.
15. Report to the Honorable John F. Kennedy (hereafter cited as Report to JFK), Task Force on Foreign Economic Policy, 31 December 1960. Pre-Presidential Papers, Transition Files, Task Force Reports, Box 1073, JFKL, R-3.
16. Bowie Report, p. 82.
17. Quoted in Fontaine, *Comité d'Action,* p. 119.
18. Acheson Report, p. 25.
19. Report to JFK, p. 54.
20. Report to JFK, pp. 52–53; Bowie Report, p. 99.
21. Bowie Report, p. 96.
22. Italics added; Bowie Report, p. 98. Bowie uses the same term on p. 102 of his report.
23. See, for example, Monnet to C.P.M. Romme (president of the Dutch Catholic Parliamentary Group), 14 November 1959, MKS; Kohnstamm to Shepard Stone, 18 December 1959, MKS.
24. *Department of State Bulletin,* 27 March 1961, pp. 449-450, and 6 March 1961, p. 327.
25. *Department of State Bulletin,* 13 February 1961, p. 208.
26. Ibid., p. 207.
27. Source: *Federal Reserve Bulletin,* quoted in Ilgen's Ph.D. dissertation, op. cit., p. 193.
28. William S. Borden, "Defending Hegemony: American Foreign Economic Policy," in Thomas G. Patterson, ed., *Kennedy's Quest for Victory* (New York: Oxford University Press, 1989), pp. 59–60; and Walter Heller, Memorandum for the President, 26 June 1962, Box 16, Walter Heller Papers, JFKL.
29. Ball, *Memoirs,* p. 205. In attempting to deal with the balance-of-payments problem, the president adopted various measures including reducing duty free travel allowances for returning American tourists, tightening taxation on American foreign corporate subsidiaries, and stepping up "Buy American" provisions. The results were sometimes baffling. At the beginning of the administration, Kennedy commissioned Carl Kaysen to be in charge of the "gold budget." The operation of the "gold budget" entailed asking cabinet officers to estimate each month what part of their expenditure cost an outflow of dollars, in an attempt to reduce it. Saving foreign exchange unfortunately translated for the Defense Department in an overzealous search for economies. Shipping jeeps from Germany to the United States to have them repaired, which cost about half the price of the jeep, constituted an amusing example of the distortions thus created. See Carl Kaysen, recorded interview by Pascaline Winand, February 1989, MIT.
30. *New York Times,* 19 July 1963, pp. 30–31.

31. *Department of State Bulletin,* 6 March 1961, Dean Rusk, address made before the Government-Industry Conference sponsored by the National Industrial Conference Board, Inc., at Washington, D.C., on 13 February, p. 324.
32. Hearings before the Subcommittee on International Exchange and Payments of the Joint Economic Committee, Congress of the United States, 16 May, 19-21 June 1961 (Washington, D.C.: U.S. GPO, 1961).
33. Hearings before the Subcommittee on Foreign Economic Policy of the Joint Economic Committee, Congress of the United States, 4-14 December 1961 (Washington, D.C.: U.S. GPO, 1962).
34. Report to JFK, pp. 13–14.
35. *Trade Expansion Act of 1962,* hearings before the Committee on Ways and Means, House of Representatives, 87th Cong., 2d sess. on H.R. 9900, March-April 1962, part 1, p. 632.
36. *Department of State Bulletin,* 17 March 1961, p. 451.
37. Statement by Secretary of the Treasury Douglas Dillon before the Senate Committee on Foreign Relations on 14 February, "Administration urges ratification of the OECD convention," *Department of State Bulletin,* 6 March 1961, pp. 330–334.
38. Acheson Report, p. 2.
39. "A Critique of Current Foreign Policy," address by the Honorable Dean Acheson at the Colgate Foreign Policy Conference, Hamilton, New York, 30 June 1059, Lyndon B. Johnson Library (hereafter cited as LBJL), copy in the Dean Acheson Papers, YL, 4.
40. Report to JFK, 5, pp. 46–47. See also Stevenson Report, part 2.
41. Joint Economic Committee, op. cit.
42. Bowie Report.
43. Memorandum from Walter Stoessel to General Norstad, 14 December 1961, Norstad, Box 57, Eisenhower Papers, "B. Miscellaneous," DDEL.
44. *Department of State Bulletin,* 25 December 1961, p. 1040.
45. Ball, *Memoirs,* p. 197.
46. Report to JFK, pp. 22–29, 55; Acheson Report, p. 71; and Stevenson Report, part 2, p. 16 and PA 15-16.
47. Schlesinger, *Thousand Days,* p. 773.
48. By 23 August 1961 Ball recommended that "Congress adopt the most effective possible trade legislation next spring." See Memorandum for the President. George Ball, "U.K. adherence to the European Common Market," NSF Countries, United Kingdom, Box 170, "UK 8/21/61-," 9, JFKL.
49. Ball, *Memoirs,* p. 198. Kennedy did so all the more easily since Ball had first advised him to present an Omnibus Foreign Economic bill in the early spring, thereby taking advantage of the impetus of the new administration for a "hard congressional battle." Stevenson Report, part 1, pp. 12-13.
50. See Raymond A. Bauer, Ithiel de Sola Pool, and Lewis Anthony Dexter, *American Business and Public Policy: the Politics of Foreign Trade* (Cambridge: MIT Press, 1963), p. 74; and Ernest Preeg, *Traders and Diplomats* (Washington, D.C.: Brookings Institution, 1970), p. 44. Also Talbot, *Chicken War.*
51. *Department of State Bulletin,* 20 November 1961, p. 836.
52. *New York Times,* 2 November 1961.
53. George M. Taber, *John F. Kennedy and a Uniting Europe* (Bruges: College of Bruges, 1969), p. 65.
54. Acheson Report, pp. 65–66.
55. Memorandum to the President, 5 May 1961, CEA paper, NSF Departments and Agencies, Box 270A, "5/24/61," JFKL.
56. Hearings before the Subcommittee on International Exchange and Payments of the Joint Economic Committee, Congress of the United States, 16 May 16, 19-21 June 1961, (Washington, D.C.: U.S. GPO, 1961).
57. Ball, Memorandum for the President, 23 August 1961, op. cit., p. 3.

58. Ibid.
59. Miriam Camps, who later served as Henry Owen's deputy, contributed a valuable memorandum on British entry in the Common Market.
60. Robert Bowie and Theodore Geiger, *The European Economic Community and the United States.* 87th Cong., 1st sess., Report to the Subcommittee on Foreign Economic Policy of the Joint Economic Committee (Washington, D.C.: U.S. GPO, 1961).
61. *Trade Expansion Act of 1962,* Hearings before the Committee on Ways and Means. House of Representatives, 87th Cong., 2d sess., part 1. (Washington, D.C.: U.S. GPO, 1961), p. 113.
62. Remarks of the President to the NSC Meeting of 22 January 1963, NSC Meetings and Memos, Box 314, JFKL.
63. Acheson Report, p. 72.
64. Acheson Report, p. 71. Ball also pushed heavily for Japanese membership in the OECD; see Ball, *Memoirs,* p. 197.
65. Quoted in Preeg, *Traders and Diplomats,* p. 42.
66. Hearings Before the Subcommittee on International Exchange and Payments, p. 75. A similar statement by Ball is found on p. 70 of the same hearings.
67. Preeg, *Traders and Diplomats,* p. 50.
68. *Trade Expansion Act of 1962,* p. 818.
69. *Trade Expansion Act of 1962,* Hearings before the Committee on Ways and Means, House of Representatives, 87th Cong., 2d Sess., part 1, (Washington, D.C.: U.S. GPO, 1962), p. 4.
70. *Trade Expansion Act of 1962,* p. 114.
71. Ibid., p. 139.
72. Ibid., p. 143.
73. Remarks of President Kennedy to the NSC Meeting of 22 January 1963, op. cit.
74. Ball, *Memoirs,* p. 168.
75. Orville Freeman, recorded interview by Charles T. Morrissey, 22 July 1964, JFKL Oral History Project, p. 24.
76. *Trade Expansion Act of 1962,* p. 144.
77. Ibid., pp. 154, 145.
78. Ibid., p. 4.
79. Schaetzel, *Unhinged Alliance,* p. 40.
80. *Trade Expansion Act of 1962,* p. 141.
81. *Outlook for United States Balance of Payments,* Hearings before the Subcommittee on International Exchange and Payments of the Joint Economic Committee, 87th Cong., 2d Sess., 12-14 December 1962 (Washington, D.C.: U.S. GPO, 1963), p. 97 et seq.
82. Ibid. For a similar argument, see Petersen's letter to Mr. V. C. Royster, editor of the *Wall Street Journal,* 13 December 1961, Box 37, Petersen Memos, "Foreign Trade," JFKL.
83. Schlesinger, *Thousand Days,* p. 774.
84. *Trade Expansion Act of 1962,* p. 7.
85. *Congressional Quarterly,* 1962, fact sheet, p. 1063.
86. Monnet to Ball, 18 January 1961, MKS.
87. Grosser, *Western Alliance,* p. 104.
88. Kohnstamm to Monnet, 26 February 1962, MKS; Schaetzel to Kohnstamm, 25 October 1962, MKS.
89. *Congressional Quarterly,* op. cit., p. 1064.
90. Letter to the president by 22 Democratic congressmen, 22 August 1961, included with a letter to the president by Henry Reuss, 2 November 1961. Sorensen Subject Files, Box 29, "Balance of Payments- 11/2/61," JFKL.
91. *Congressional Quarterly,* op. cit., p. 1064.
92. Ball, *Memoirs,* p. 198.
93. Ibid.

94. Ibid., pp. 188-193.
95. See Taber, op. cit.; Talbot, op. cit; and Preeg, op. cit. Also, Parlement Européen, documents de séance 52, 26 Juin 1962. Rapporteur: M. Vredeling.
96. Emphasis added. *A New Look at Foreign Economic Policy in Light of the Cold War and the Extension of the Common Market of Europe*, Report to the Subcommittee on Foreign Economic Policy of the Joint Economic Committee, Congress of the United States, 87th Cong., 1st sess. (Washington, D.C.: U.S. GPO, 1961), p. 9.
97. Ibid.
98. Ball, *Memoirs*, p. 199.
99. Ambassador Tuthill, recorded interview by Pascaline Winand, 14 January 1989, Washington, D.C.
100. Robert Bowie, "Strategy and the Atlantic Alliance," *International Organization*, Volume 17, no. 3 (Summer 1963): 711.
101. Acheson Report, p. 25.
102. *Department of State Bulletin*, 22 November 1954, p. 761.
103. *Department of State Bulletin*, 12 February 1962, p. 233.
104. Kennedy had initially called upon Kissinger to serve as a full-time White House staff member for national security affairs. The president attached great importance to his appointment. (See Letter from McGeorge Bundy to Henry Kissinger, 28 January 1961, Kennedy Papers, NSF Meetings and Memos, Box 320, JFKL.) Because of other previous engagements, Kissinger decided to come in as a part-time consultant, and offered to "work practically full time" for Kennedy "between May 15th and September 1st." (See Letter from Kissinger to McGeorge Bundy, 5 June 1961, Kennedy Papers, NSF Meetings and Memos, Staff Memos, Box 314, "Kissinger 6/61-7/61," JFKL.) The president accordingly appointed him as part-time consultant to him on 17 February 1961. Despite his initial intention to increase his workload for the president in May, Kissinger later changed his mind and actually decreased it considerably. On 5 June 1961, he proposed to come in only as an ad-hoc consultant. The reason? Other staff members had been assigned responsibility in those areas in which he had developed the most expertise. Since Henry Owen—a Europeanist—worked on NATO and Berlin, and Carl Kaysen had been "charged with following military policy" (McGeorge Bundy explained to him that "only permanent staff members could work in the area of military policy"), he would "be coming to Washington almost for the sake of being there." (Ibid.) At the root of Kissinger's decision was perhaps yet another reason: the incompatibility of his views with those of the "Europeanists" in the State Department and key figures in the immediate surroundings of the president.
105. George W. Ball, "NATO and World Responsibility," *The Atlantic Community Quarterly*, vol. 2, (Summer 1964): 216.
106. Henry A. Kissinger, "What Kind of Atlantic Partnership?" *The Atlantic Community Quarterly*, vol. 7, 1 (Spring 1969): 22.
107. Ibid., pp. 24-25.
108. Ibid., pp. 27, 33.
109. Ibid., pp. 32-35.
110. Acheson Report, p. 25.
111. Bowie Report, pp. 100–101.
112. Monnet to Eugene Rostow, 18 January 1961, MKS.
113. Quoted in *Freedom and Union*, March 1955, p. 6.
114. Memorandum of Conversation with the President, 1 May 1956, Eisenhower Papers, DDE, J. F. Dulles, White House Memos, Box 4, DDEL, 2.
115. *Freedom and Union*, February 1960, p. 3, March 1960 and September 1960, p. 3.
116. *Freedom and Union*, April 1961.
117. *Freedom and Union*, May 1961, p. 9.
118. Acheson Report, p. 26.

119. Bowie Report, p. 103.
120. Paul-Henri Spaak, *Combats inachevés. De l'espoir aux déceptions* (Paris: Fayard, 1969), p. 213. *The Continuing Battle: Memoirs of a European, 1936-66,* translated from the French by Henry Fox (London: Weindenfeld, 1971).
121. Bowie Report, pp. 103–104.
122. Bowie Report, pp. 108, 107.
123. Bowie Report, p. 104.
124. Christian Herter, "Atlantica," in *Foreign Affairs,* vol. 41, no. 2 (January 1963).
125. Ball, *Discipline of Power,* p. 66. See also Schaetzel, *Unhinged Alliance,* p. 40.
126. Ball, *Discipline of Power,* p. 68.
127. *Department of State Bulletin,* 25 December 1961, p. 1046.
128. Beloff, *The United States and the Unity of Europe,* pp. 111–112.
129. Ball, *Discipline of Power,* p. 63.

Notes to Chapter 8: The MLF in Context

1. John Foster Dulles, "The Evolution of Foreign Policy," pp. 107-10, quoted in David N. Schwartz, *NATO's Nuclear Dilemmas* (Washington, D.C. : Brookings Institution, 1983), pp. 23–25.
2. John Steinbruner, *The Cybernetic Theory of Decision* (Princeton: Princeton University Press, 1974), p. 164; and Alfred Grosser, op. cit., p. 216.
3. Mutual Security Act of 1958, Senate Hearings, p. 187, quoted in Schwartz, *NATO's Nuclear Dilemmas,* p. 34.
4. "Text of General Norstad's Cincinnati Speech," p. 27, quoted in Schwartz, *NATO's Nuclear Dilemmas,* p. 58.
5. Dalan Alan Rosenberg, "The Origins of Overkill," *International Security* 7, no. 4 (Spring 1983): 41–42. See A. J. Goodpaster, MCP, May 1956-Goodpaster Folder, DDE Diaries, Box 15, ACWF-EPP, DDEL.
6. Rosenberg, "The Origins of Overkill," p. 42. See A. J. Goodpaster, May 1956-Goodpaster Folder, DDEL.
7. S. Everett Gleason, Memorandum, 2 May 1958, Subject: Discussion at the 364th Meeting of the NSC, Eisenhower Papers, NSC Folder, Box 10, NSC Series, ACWF-EPP, DDEL.
8. Robert Bowie, "Strategy and the Atlantic Alliance," *International Organization* 17, no. 3 (Summer 1963).
9. All above quotations from Top Secret Memo, 2 May 1958, Eisenhower Papers, Ann Whitman File, NSC Series, Box 10, "364th Meeting," DDEL.
10. John Foster Dulles, Western European Chiefs of Mission, 9 May 1958, John Foster Dulles Papers, pp. 29–30.
11. Top Secret Memo, 2 May 1958, Eisenhower Papers, Ann Whitman File, NSC Series, Box 10, "364th Meeting," DDEL.
12. Memorandum of Conversation with the President, 6 November 1959, Eisenhower Papers, Whitman File, DDE Diaries, Staff Notes, Box 45, p. 3, DDEL.
13. Memorandum for Smith, Merchant, and Reinhardt, 14 December 1958, Eisenhower Papers, John Foster Dulles, White House Memos, Box 8, "July-December Meetings with the President," DDEL.
14. Memorandum of Conversation with the President, 2 November 1959, Eisenhower Papers, Whitman File, DDE Diaries, Staff Notes, Box 45, "November 1958 (3)," DDEL.
15. Memorandum of Conversation with the President, 6 November 1959, Eisenhower Papers, Whitman File, DDE Diaries, Staff Notes, Box 45, 2, DDEL.
16. Memorandum of Conference with the President, 16 October 1959, Eisenhower Papers, Whitman File, DDE Diaries, Staff Notes, "October 1959(1)," 4, DDEL.

17. Charles de Gaulle, *Lettres, Notes et Carnets, Juin 1958-Décembre 1960* (Paris: Plon, 1985), p. 84.
18. Copy of Eisenhower's 20 October 1958 letter to de Gaulle in NSF, France, Kennedy Papers, Box 72, "3/1/63 - 3/9/63," JFKL.
19. Memorandum of Conversation, "Anglo-American Relations with General de Gaulle's Government," 9 June 1958, Eisenhower Papers, Ann Whitman Files, International Subseries, Box 21, 2, DDEL.
20. President's trip to Europe, August-September 1959, Palais de l'Elysée, 2 September 1959, Eisenhower Papers, Whitman File, International Meetings Series, Box 3, "Paris Visit, September 2-4, 1958(2)," pp. 4–5, DDEL.
21. Ibid.
22. See McGeorge Bundy, *Danger and Survival* (New York: Random House, 1988), p. 471.
23. Memorandum of Conversation with the President (Dulles/Eisenhower), 31 October 1957, Eisenhower Papers, Whitman File, DDE Diaries, Box 27, "October 57 Staff Notes (1)," DDEL.
24. For a lucid discussion of this specific point see Bundy, *Danger and Survival,* p. 481.
25. Memorandum of Conversation, "Anglo-American Relations with General de Gaulle's Government," 9 June 1958, Eisenhower Papers, Ann Whitman Files, International Subseries, Box 21, 1, DDEL; and Press Conference, 3 February 1960, *Public Papers of the Presidents: Eisenhower, 1960,* p. 152.
26. Bundy, *Danger and Survival,* p. 484.
27. Memorandum of Conversation, "Anglo-American Relations with General de Gaulle's Government," 9 June 1958, Eisenhower Papers, Ann Whitman Files, International Subseries, Box 21, 1, DDEL.
28. "Ideas used in talk with de Gaulle, not read," 5 July 1958, John Foster Dulles Papers, Box 127, PL.
29. NSC 5721/1 U.S. Policy on France, 19 October 1957, Eisenhower Papers, OSANSA, NSC Series, Policy Papers Subseries, Box 22, 13, DDEL.
30. De Gaulle, *Lettres, Notes et Carnets,* p. 227. English translation in Eisenhower Papers, International Series, Box 11, "De Gaulle—June 1958-30 October 1959," DDEL.
31. Memorandum of Conference with the President, 9 June 1959, Eisenhower Papers, Whitman File, DDE Diaries, Box 42, Staff Notes, "June 59 (2)," DDEL.
32. President's trip to Europe, August-September 1959, Palais de l'Elysée, 2 September 1959, Eisenhower Papers, Whitman File, International Meetings Series, Box 3, "Paris Visit, September 2-4, 1958 (2)," pp. 4–5, DDEL.
33. Charles de Gaulle, *Discours et messages,* vol. 3, p. 126.
34. Memorandum of Conversation with the President, 16 October 1959, Eisenhower Papers, Whitman File, DDE Diaries, Box 45, Staff Notes, "October 1959 (1)," DDEL.
35. Memorandum of Conversation, NATO problems, 24 November 1959, Eisenhower Papers, Whitman File, DDE Diaries, Box 46, Staff Notes, "December 59," DDEL.
36. Ibid.
37. C. L. Sulzberger, *The Last of the Giants* (New York: Macmillan, 1970), p. 882.
38. *Department of State Bulletin,* 5 August 1957, pp. 233–34.
39. Lauris Norstad, speech, *NATO Letter,* December 1956, p. 37.
40. *New York Times,* 11 March 1960, p. 1.
41. Steinbrunner, *Cybernetic Theory of Decision,* p. 184.
42. Ibid., p. 185.
43. For more details, see Schwartz, *NATO's Nuclear Dilemmas,* pp. 75-81; Bowie Report, pp. 37-38.
44. Sulzberger, *Last of the Giants,* p. 707. In his conversation with Sulzberger on 25 November 1960, Douglas Dillon revealed that he was very strongly opposed to this.
45. "NATO Long-Range Panning," Views of NATO Secretary-General Paul-Henri Spaak, 13 June 1960, Norstad Papers, Box 90, NATO General, 3, DDEL.

46. Chronology of project on the pros and cons of increased nuclear sharing with allies (including possible changes in legislation), 19 August 1960, Eisenhower Papers, OS-ANSA, NSC Series, Briefing Notes Subseries, Box 14, 1, DDEL.
47. Robert Bowie, recorded interview by Pascaline Winand, February 1989, Washington, D.C.
48. Bowie Report, pp. 16-17.
49. Ibid., p. 15.
50. "Spaak's Visit," 5 October 1960, Norstad Papers, Box 9, NATO General (4), DDEL.
51. Memorandum for the NSC Council, NATO MRBM Force, 22 December 1960, Eisenhower Papers, OSANSA, NSC Series, Briefing Notes Subseries, "NSC 6017," DDEL.
52. Quoted in Rostow, *Diffusion of Power,* p. 77.
53. NATO MRBM Force, op. cit.; Washington to USRO Paris, signed Herter, 10 December 1960, Norstad Papers, Box 85, "Atom—Nuclear Policy 60 (1)," DDEL.
54. Robert Bowie, "Strategy and the Atlantic Alliance," *International Organization* 17, no. 3 (Summer 63).
55. Ibid.
56. Washington to USRO Paris, 10 December 1960, op. cit.; Bowie Report, p. 29.
57. Department of State Memorandum of Conversation, 11 April 1961, NSF-120, "Italy General 1/20/61," 2, JFKL. The Stevenson Report recommended the creation of a European-based strategic nuclear deterrent in which French and British nuclear forces would be consolidated; see Stevenson Report, part 2, p. 29.
58. Department of State Memorandum of Conversation, 14 April 1961, Kennedy Papers, NSF Countries, France, Box 70, "5/1/61-," 2, JFKL.
59. Bowie, "Strategy and the Atlantic Alliance," p. 725.
60. Ibid., p. 727.
61. Ibid.
62. Ibid., p. 722.
63. Ibid., p. 728. The Bowie Report considered that the United States might allow the MLF "to be organized under the European Community or the WEU" (Western European Union), if these organizations undertook to put the force "at NATO disposal." In order to prevent the participating nations from having access to nuclear weapons design data, however, the U.S. would keep formal custody of nuclear warheads while "undertaking in advance" to release the Polaris warheads "whenever the force was ordered into action under the agreed procedures." Bowie hoped Europeans would readily accept this scheme since it "would not affect control for use." See Bowie Report, p. 34. In the report, the MLF was originally called Multinational Strategic Force or NATO Deterrent (NADET).
64. Rostow, interview, op. cit., p. 134.
65. NSC Memorandum, 22 December 1960 , op. cit., p. 2.
66. Robert Bowie, recorded interview, 10 August 1967, OH 102, Columbia University, pp. 44–5; Bowie Report, pp. v-vi.
67. Memorandum of Meeting with the President, 28 November 1960, Eisenhower papers, OSANSA 1952-61, Special Assistants Series, Presidential Subseries, Box 5, "1960 Meetings with President, Volume 2 (3)," 1, DDEL. The Bureau of the Budget advocated excluding the United States from the control of the force; see ibid., and Draft Record of Actions, 467th NSC Meeting, 17 November 1960, Eisenhower Papers, OSANSA, Special Assistants Series, Presidential Subseries, Box 5, "1960 Meetings with the President Volume 2(3)," Attachment B, 2, DDEL.
68. Memorandum of Conversation with the President, 12 September 1960, Eisenhower Papers, Whitman File, DDE Diaries, Box 53, "Staff Notes September 1960 (3)," DDEL.
69. Ibid., see also Letter from Clinton Anderson, chairman, JCAE, 16 May 1960, Eisenhower Papers, OSANSA, NSC Series, Briefing Notes Subseries, Box 15, and Draft Letter from the Assistant Secretary of Defense to Clinton Anderson, 31 August 1960, Eisenhower Papers, OSANSA, NSC Series, Briefing Notes Subseries, Box 14, DDEL.
70. Memorandum of Conversation with the President, 12 September 1960, op. cit., p. 2.

71. Memorandum of Conference with the President, 13 October 1960, Eisenhower Papers, Whitman File, Staff Notes, Box 53, "October 1960 (2)," 6, DDEL.
72. Memorandum of Conversation, NATO Atomic Force, 4 October 1960, Eisenhower Papers, Whitman File, DDE Diaries, Staff Notes, Box 53, "October 1960 (2)," DDEL.
73. NATO Atomic Force, op. cit., p. 2. Part of this document is still classified, hence caution should be exerted in attributing certain statements to Paul-Henri Spaak, but the presumption that Spaak did in fact make these statements is strong, given the list of participants provided in the document.
74. Memorandum of Conversation with the President, 13 October 1960, Eisenhower Papers, Whitman File, Staff Notes, Box 53, "October 1960 (2)," 5, DDEL.
75. Acheson Report, p. 62.
76. Bowie, "Strategy and the Atlantic Alliance," pp. 728-729.
77. Walt Rostow, recorded interview, 103, JFKL Oral History Program.
78. Maxwell D. Taylor, recorded interview, 16, JFKL Oral History Program.
79. Ball, *Discipline of Power,* pp. 207–208.
80. Ball, *Discipline of Power,* p. 208.
81. Thomas Finletter, recorded interview by Philip J. Farley, 7 May 1965, 6-7, JFKL Oral History Program.
82. Paul Nitze, recorded interview by Pascaline Winand, October 1990.
83. Ball, *Discipline of Power,* p. 209.
84. Ibid.
85. Steinbruner, *Cybernetic Theory of Decision,* p. 245. John Steinbruner's rendering of the MLF story is still the most detailed and reliable account on the MLF story, although McNamara's opposition towards the MLF was not as strong or enduring as he tends to portray it. On the MLF see also Bundy, *Danger and Survival,* p. 488 et seq.
86. Walt Rostow, interview, op. cit., pp. 133–34.
87. Ball, *Discipline of Power,* p. 205.
88. Henry Owen to Bundy, 21 April 1961, with enclosure, "A New Approach to France," NSF, Box 70-71, 4., JFKL. See also the second draft, 3 May 1961.
89. Ibid.
90. Ibid.
91. Personal Cable for Ambassador from Secretary, 5 May 1961, NSF Countries, Boxes 70-71, "5/1/61," 2, JFKL.
92. Ibid.
93. *Public Papers of the Presidents: Kennedy, 1961,* p. 385.
94. Henry Owen, recorded interview by Pascaline Winand, 12 January 1989,Washington, D.C.
95. See John Newhouse, *De Gaulle and the Anglo-Saxons* (New York: Viking Press, 1970), p. 155.
96. Interview material, source confidential.
97. See, for example, Letter from Gavin to the President, 13 November 1961, NSF Countries, France, Boxes 71-72, "11/1/61," and Cable from the Secretary to Ambassador Gavin, 5 May 1962, NSF Countries, France, Boxes 70-71, "3/5/62," JFKL.
98. George Ball, recorded interview by Pascaline Winand, August 1988, Princeton, p. 6.
99. Steinbruner, *Cybernetic Theory of Decision,* p. 217.
100. George Ball, interview, op. cit., p. 6.
101. Bowie Report, p. 105.
102. Memorandum to General Norstad from Walter J. Stoessel, Jr., 14 December 1961, Eisenhower Papers, Norstad, Box 57, "B. Miscellaneous," DDEL.
103. Maxwell D. Taylor, JFKL Oral History Project.
104. Robert McNamara, recorded interview, 26 February 1970, 2, JFKL Oral History Project.
105. George Ball, interview, op. cit., p. 5.
106. Ibid.

107. Ibid.
108. Hearings on Military Posture, Committee on Armed Services, House of Representatives, 88th Cong., 1st. sess., Washington, D.C., 1963, pp. 297–98, quoted in William Kaufmann, *The McNamara Strategy* (New York: Harper and Row, 1964).
109. Secretary to Ambassador Gavin, 5 May 1962, op cit. See also Henry Owen, recorded interview, 30 September 1974, Lyndon Baines Johnson Library (hereafter cited as LBJL), p. 7.
110. The intricacies of the Lavaud mission are still unclear, as testimonies differ; a word of caution is thus in order with this interpretation. See Paul Nitze, recorded interview by Pascaline Winand; and Nitze, *From Hiroshima to Glasnost.* See also Newhouse, op. cit., pp. 151–161; Steinbruner, op. cit., pp. 216–217; and Frank Costigliola, "The Failed Design," *Diplomatic History* 8, no. 3 (Summer 1984).
111. Newhouse, op. cit., p. 163, and Steinbruner, op. cit., pp. 218–219.
112. Rusk to Finletter, 9 March 1962, Norstad Papers, Box 91, U.S. Support for NATO 1962 (3), DDEL; and Rusk to USRO, 17 April 1962, Norstad Papers, Box 85, Nuclear Policy 1962 (2), DDEL. For more details see Steinbruner, op. cit., pp. 226-228; see also Rostow, *Diffusion of Power,* p. 239.
113. Address by McNamara at the University of Michigan, 16 June, *Department of State Bulletin,* 9 July 1962, pp. 67–68.
114. Bundy, *Danger and Survival,* p. 485. The Athens Speech was declassified on 17 August 1979; see "Remarks by Secretary McNamara, NATO Ministerial Meeting, 5 May 1962, Restricted Session."
115. Bundy, *Danger and Survival,* p. 486.
116. Robert Schaetzel, recorded interview by Pascaline Winand, January 1989, Washington, D.C.
117. *Department of State Bulletin,* 3 September 1962, p. 353.
118. Charles Bohlen, interview for the JFKL Oral History Program, 21 May 1961, p. 36.
119. Both quotations, Bundy, *Danger and Survival,* p. 497.
120. McGeorge Bundy, recorded interview by Pascaline Winand, New York, 1 March 1989, p. 3; and Bundy, *Danger and Survival,* p. 497.
121. *Department of State Bulletin,* 22 October 1962, pp. 604–605.
122. Kaufmann, *McNamara Strategy,* p. 77.
123. Gaddis, *Strategies of Containment,* p. 227.
124. Department of State Telegram, drafted by S. G. Freedman and approved by Schaetzel, 16 November 1962, Kennedy Papers, Regional Security, Boxes 211-220, "Multilateral Force Cables, 7/62," JFKL.
125. *Department of State Bulletin,* 3 December 1962, p. 835.
126. The Bowie Report specifically recommended that the "U.S. . . . need not and should not be a supplicant for creation of the multinational force." Since it would probably not come into existence for some time, the force would not "help to close any 'missile gap'"; also, should the MLF never be created, the interim program (INPRO) of U.S.-manned Polaris submarines under the control of SACEUR, "would remain as an acceptable alternative." Bowie Report, pp. 31-32.
127. Memorandum of Conversation, "European Strategy Discussion with Mr. Peter Thorneycroft," 13 September 1963, Kennedy Papers, NSF Countries, Box 170 A, "UK 9/6/62," JFKL.
128. This is according to Walt Rostow's testimony; Walt Rostow, recorded interview by the JFKL, 131–132.
129. Walt Rostow, interview, JFKL, p. 131.
130. Ibid.
131. Ibid.
132. *Department of State Bulletin,* 23 July 1962, p. 132.
133. Charles de Gaulle, *Discours et Messages. Avec le Renouveau Mai 1958-Juillet 1962* (Paris: Plon, 1970), pp. 402–427.
134. *Public Papers of the Presidents: Kennedy,* p. 400.

135. Memorandum for William H. Brubeck, executive secretary, Department of State, 18 May 1962, Kennedy Papers, NSF Countries, Boxes 70-71, "France 5/16/62," JFKL.
136. Carl Kaysen's notes on remarks by President Kennedy before the National Security Council, Tuesday, 22 January 1963, Kennedy Papers, NSF Meetings and Memos, Box 314, "NSF Meetings 1963," 3, JFKL.
137. See Ball, *Discipline of Power,* p. 206.
138. Ibid.
139. George Ball's support for the MLF, and the possibility for a united Europe to buy out the U.S. share has varied over the years. In a recent interview, George Ball denied he ever had such an idea. See George Ball, recorded interview by Pascaline Winand, August 1988, Princeton, p. 9.
140. Document dated 9 February 1963; no author mentioned, but reliable sources have confirmed that George Ball was the author of this memo. NSF Meetings and Memos, no. 510, Box 314, Kennedy Papers, "NSC Meetings and Memos 1963- 5/18/62 - 8/3/62," 5, JFKL.
141. Department of State Telegram, drafted by S. G. Freedman and approved by Schaetzel, 16 November 1962, Kennedy Papers, Regional Security, Boxes 211-220, "Multilateral Force Cables, 7/62," JFKL.

Notes to Chapter 9: Conflicting World Views

1. Schlesinger, *Thousand Days,* p. 795.
2. Ibid.
3. See, for example, the very detailed treatment of this topic by Robert Bloes, *Le "plan Fouchet" et le problème de l'Europe politique* (Bruges: College of Europe 1970). See also Alessandro Silj, *Europe's Political Puzzle, A Study of the Fouchet Negotiations* (Cambridge: Harvard University, 1967). For Spaak's testimony on the period see his *Combats Inachevés.*
4. On this point see Stanley Hoffmann, "The North Atlantic Area, as a Partial International System," *The Atlantic Community, Progress and Prospect,* F. O. Wilcox and H. F. Haviland, eds., (New York: Praeger, 1963), pp. 331.
5. Carl Kaysen, recorded interview by Pascaline Winand, MIT, August 1988. Carl Kaysen has noted that one of the most important American decisions that worked against the EEC was "the initial decision not to give the French some military assistance." According to him this was "less the president's decision than a congressional attitude which the president didn't want to fight."
6. Charles de Gaulle, *Lettres, Notes et Carnets, Juin 1958-Décembre 1960* (Paris: Plon, 1985), p. 401.
7. All above quotations from Konrad Adenauer, *Erinnerungen 1959-1963. Fragmente* (Stuttgart: Deutsche Verlags-Anstalt, 1968), pp. 61-67 (my translation).
8. De Gaulle, *Discours et Messages. Avec le Renouveau Mai 1958-Juillet 1962,* op. cit. (my translation).
9. Ibid.
10. Adenauer, *Erinnerungen.*
11. Quoted in James Richardson, *Germany and the Atlantic Alliance* (Cambridge, Mass.: Harvard University Press, 1966). Text of the address is in *Bulletin,* 26 September 1956, pp. 1726-1729; English translation quoted by Gerald Freund, *Germany between Two Worlds* (New York: Harcourt Brace, 1961), p. 115.
12. De Gaulle, *Lettres, Notes et Carnets, Juin 1958-Décembre 1960,* p. 399.
13. Ibid. This language is strongly reminiscent of a memo Alain Peyrefitte, the minister for information, sent to de Gaulle at the end of August 1969. For a summary of this very important document, see Bloes, op. cit., pp. 377-380.

14. Translated from "Le Salut," in Schlesinger, *Thousand Days,* p. 793.
15. Adenauer, *Erinnerungen,* p. 131.
16. Schlesinger, *Thousand Days.*
17. Ibid., p. 793.
18. Owen, "A New Approach to France," op. cit., p. 1.
19. Stanley Hoffmann, *Decline or Renewal. France Since the 1930s* (New York: Viking Press, 1974).
20. Ibid., p. 295.
21. Adenauer, *Erinnerungen,* p. 131.
22. Ibid., p. 132.
23. Ibid., p. 131.
24. Memorandum, 9 February 1963; reliable sources have indicated that George Ball was the author of this memo. NSF Meetings and Memos, Box 314, Kennedy Papers, "NSC Meetings 1963 5/18/62 - 8/3/62," 3, JFKL.
25. *Recueil des communiqués et déclarations du Comité d'Action pour les Etats-Unis d'Europe 1955-1965* (Lausanne: Centre de recherches européennes, 1965), p. 113.
26. McGeorge Bundy, address made before the Economic Club of Chicago, 6 December 1961, "Policy for the Western Alliance—Berlin and After," *Department of State Bulletin,* 12 March 1962, p. 419.
27. Memorandum, 9 February 1963, op. cit., p. 1.
28. Ibid., p. 2.
29. Ibid.
30. Acheson Report, p. 14.
31. Memorandum, 9 February 1963, op. cit., p. 3.
32. Acheson Report, p. 13.
33. McGeorge Bundy's speech, 6 December 1961, op. cit., p. 423.
34. Document, 9 February 1963, op. cit., p. 2.
35. Speech, 6 December, op. cit., p. 420.
36. All above quotations from 6 December Speech, op. cit.
37. Document, 9 February 1963, op. cit., p. 2.
38. Fontaine, *Comité d'Action,* p. 99.
39. Spaak, *Combats Inachevés,* p. 356.
40. Fontaine, *Comité d'Action,* p. 100.
41. George Ball, interview by Pascaline Winand, op. cit., p. 7. See also, for example, *Recueil des communiqués et déclarations du Comité d'Action pour les Etats-Unis d'Europe,* Déclaration commune du 11 juillet 1960, op. cit., p. 87.
42. Monnet's 22 November 1960 letter, quoted in Fontaine, *Comité d'Action,* pp. 101-102.
43. Interview with George Ball, op. cit., p. 7.
44. Quoted in Spaak, *Combats Inachevés,* p. 359.
45. Spaak, *Combats Inachevés,* pp. 360-361.
46. Charles de Gaulle, *Lettres, Notes et Carnets. Janvier 1961-Décembre 1963* (Paris: Plon, 1986), pp. 107-108.
47. Richardson, op. cit., p. 65. See also Taber, op. cit., pp. 112-113.
48. See, for example, Gerbet, *Construction de l'Europe.*
49. For a detailed discussion, see Spaak, op. cit.; Silj, op. cit.; and Bloes, op. cit.
50. Full text in Roy Price, *The Political Future of the European Community* (London: Marshbank, 1962), appendix 5, p. 105 et seq. For a good "summary" of the text, see Bloes, op. cit., pp. 355-356. See also Silj, op. cit., pp. 67-70.
51. Spaak, *Combats Inachevés,* p. 369.
52. Adenauer, *Erinnerungen,* pp. 109-110.
53. Ibid., p. 111.
54. Interview material.
55. Taber, *John F. Kennedy and a Uniting Europe,* p. 106.

56. Memorandum of Conversation. Participants: Maurice Couve de Murville, George Ball, Ambassador Gavin, 21 May 1962, Kennedy Papers, NSF Countries, Box 707, "France 6/1/62," JFKL.
57. *Recueil des communiqués et déclarations du Comité d'Action pour les Etats-Unis d'Europe 1955-1965,* op. cit., p. 115.
58. Memorandum of Conversation, 21 May 1962.

Notes to Chapter 10: Implementing the Atlantic Partnership

1. Nora Beloff, *The General Says No* (Middlesex: Penguin Books, 1963), p. 105.
2. Miriam Camps, *Britain and the European Community 1955-1963* (London: Oxford University Press, 1964), p. 344.
3. Beloff, *General Says No,* p. 105.
4. Robert Kleinman, *Atlantic Crisis,* (New York: W. W. Norton and Co., 1964), p. 66.
5. Camps, *Britain and the European Community,* p. 314.
6. Ball, *Memoirs,* p. 211.
7. Ibid., p. 210.
8. Ibid., p. 211.
9. Ibid.
10. Ball, *Discipline of Power,* p. 79.
11. Ball, *Memoirs,* p. 213.
12. Ibid., p. 214.
13. London, 13 April 1961, MKS.
14. Ibid.
15. Memorandum of Conversation, 1 April 1961, NSF, Box 120, "Italy General," 4, JFKL.
16. Memorandum of Conversation, 14 April 1961, NSF Countries, Boxes 70-71, "France 5/1/61-," 3, JFKL.
17. Memorandum of Conversation with the President and the Congressional Leadership, 6-7 June 1961, NSF Countries, Box 70-71, "France 6/1/61," JFKL.
18. All above quotations from Telegram for Under Secretary Ball, 26 April 1961, NSF Countries, Box 170, "UK 9/1/61-5/15/61," JFKL.
19. Monnet, *Memoirs,* p. 455.
20. Quoted 7 April 1961 in Fontaine, *Comité d'Action,* p. 119.
21. Memorandum for the President, 7 April 1961, NSF Countries, Box 170, "UK 5/1/61-5/15/61," JFKL.
22. London, 13 April 1961, MKS.
23. Quoted in David Nunnerley, *President Kennedy and Britain* (London: The Bodley Head, 1972).
24. Telegram from the State Department, 7 December 1962, NSF Countries, Box 170a, "UK 12/6/62," JFKL. Kennedy, although he did not make any public statement condemning the speech, nevertheless instructed McGeorge Bundy to ask the State Department to issue a press release invoking the "deep community of purpose and long practice of close cooperation between the UK and the USA . . . Special relationship may not be a perfect phrase, but sneers at Anglo-American reality would be equally foolish." McGeorge Bundy to Robert J. Manning, 7 December 1962, NSF Files n 170A/34, JFKL: quoted in Douglas Brinkley, "Dean Acheson and the Special Relationship: The West Point Speech of December 1962," *The Historical Journal* 33, 3 (1990) pp. 599-608.
25. Ball, *Discipline of Power,* p. 69.
26. Telegram from London to the Secretary of State, 8 December 1962, NSF Countries, Box 170 a, "UK 12/6/ 62," JFKL.
27. Acheson Report, p. 25.

28. Ball, *Discipline of Power,* pp. 98-100.

29. Ibid., p. 88.

30. Ibid., p. 91.

31. Dean Rusk, recorded interview by David Nunnerley, Monday, 9 February 1970.

32. Ibid.

33. Personal letter from McGeorge Bundy to Raymond Aron, 24 May 1962, NSF Countries, Box 70-71, "France 5/19/62," 3, JFKL.

34. Telegram from London to the Department of State, 13 December 1961, NSF countries, Box 170, "UK 12/1/61-12/10/61," JFKL.

35. Macmillan, *Pointing the Way,* p. 306.

36. Ibid., p. 307.

37. Ibid., p. 308.

38. Ibid.

39. Ibid., p. 309.

40. Ibid., p. 312.

41. Ibid., p. 356.

42. Ibid., p. 339.

43. Nunnerley, *President Kennedy and Britain,* p. 41.

44. Ibid.

45. Macmillan, *Pointing the Way,* p. 348.

46. Nunnerley, *President Kennedy and Britain,* op. cit., p. 35, and Macmillan, *Pointing the Way,* p. 306.

47. Arthur Schlesinger, quoted in Nunnerley, *President Kennedy and Britain,* p. 30.

48. Nunnerley, *President Kennedy and Britain,* p. 43.

49. Ibid., p. 42.

50. Dean Rusk, recorded interview by David Nunnerley, op. cit., p. 4.

51. Ibid.

52. Ball, *Memoirs,* p. 218.

53. Macmillan, *Pointing the Way,* p. 111.

54. Ibid., p. 354.

55. Ball, *Memoirs,* p. 215.

56. Ibid., p. 219.

57. "Possible UK Accession to the Treaty of Rome, " 12 May 1961, NSF Countries, Box 170, "UK 5/1/61-5/15/61," JFKL.

58. Ibid.

59. See "Great Britain and the Common Market," summary of Mr. Ball's Memorandum of 10 May 1961 Replying to Prime Minister Macmillan, NSF Department and Agencies, Box 284-285, "Department of State 5/1/61-5/19/61," and Memorandum for the President from Ball, 7 August 1961, NSF Countries, Box 170, "UK 8/1/61 - 8/20/61," JFKL.

60. Possible UK Accession to the Treaty of Rome, 12 May 1961, op. cit., p. 4.

61. *Neue Zürcher Zeitung,* 18 April 1962.

62. Camps, op. cit., pp. 355 et seq.

63. Memorandum for the President, 7 August 1961, op. cit., p. 3.

64. Ball, *Memoirs,* p. 219.

65. For more details on the attitude of the Department of State toward the EEC-EFTA question, see also State Department Telegram from Richard Vine, approved by Robert Schaetzel, 27 January 1962, NSF Countries, Box 170, "UK 1/62-," and Memorandum for Mr. Myer Rashish signed by Richard Vine, Office of European Regional affairs, 17 February 1962, Petersen Papers, Box 3, "EFTA," JFKL.

66. *Department of State Bulletin,* 18 March 1957, pp. 438-439.

67. *FRUS, 1955-57,* vol. 4, Memorandum of a Conversation, Department of State, Washington, D.C., 18 February 1957, Western European Security and Integration (Washington, D.C.: U.S. GPO, 1986), p. 525.

68. Ibid., Memorandum of Conversation between the Secretary of State and the German Ambassador (Krekeler), Department of State, Washington, D.C., 11 February 1957, p. 524.
69. Ibid., Memorandum of a Conversation, Department of State, Washington, D.C., 5 March 1957, p. 533.
70. Ibid.
71. Ibid., p. 524.
72. Ibid., p. 525.
73. Ibid., p. 524.
74. Ibid., p. 533.
75. Ibid., p. 524.
76. Memorandum for McGeorge Bundy, 2 June 1961, NSF Departments and Agencies, Box 284-285, "Department of State 6/1/61-6/16/61," JFKL.
77. Ibid.
78. Ibid.
79. *European Community* 47 (June 1961), p. 8.
80. "The African Problem," 10 May 1961, NSF Departments and Agencies, Boxes 284-285, "Department of State 5/1/61-5/19/61," JFKL.
81. Ibid.
82. Ibid.
83. Ball, *Discipline of Power*, p. 237.
84. Ibid., p. 239.
85. Ibid., p. 240.
86. Ibid.
87. Ibid.
88. Acheson Report, p. 11.
89. Kennedy, *Strategy of Peace*, introduction.
90. Ibid.
91. Ball, *Discipline of Power*, p. 242.
92. Drew Middleton, *The Supreme Choice—Britain and the European Community* (London: Secker and Warburg, 1963), p. 230.
93. Coral Bell, *Debatable Alliance* (London: Oxford University Press, 1964), p. 97. Quoted in Taber, op. cit., p. 52.
94. Harold Macmillan, *At the End of the Day 1961-1963* (London: Macmillan 1963), pp. 11-14.
95. *Guardian,* 1 July 1961, quoted in Camps, *Britain and the European Community,* p. 345.
96. *The Times,* 13 July 1961.
97. Camps, *Britain and the European Community,* p. 347.
98. George Ball, Memorandum for the President, 7 August 1961, NSF Countries, Box 170, "UK 8/1/61-8/20/61," JFKL.
99. Macmillan, *At the End the Day,* p. 16.
100. Ibid., p. 17.
101. Fontaine, *Comité d'Action,* p. 121.
102. Camps, *Britain and the European Community,* p. 357.
103. Quoted in *European Community* 49 (October 1961), pp. 1-2.
104. Ibid.
105. George Ball, Memorandum for the President, 7 August 1961, op. cit., p. 3. See also Ball, Memorandum for the President, 23 August 1961, NSF Countries, Box 170, "UK 8/21/61-," 5, JFKL.
106. Ball, Memorandum, 7 August 1961 , op. cit., p. 3.
107. *New York Times,* 14 May 1962, quoted in Taber, op. cit., p. 53.
108. Ball, *Memoirs,* p. 220.
109. George Ball, Memorandum for the President, 23 August 1961, op. cit., p. 6.
110. Ball, *Memoirs,* p. 220.

Notes to Chapter 11: Roadblocks and Boundless Optimism

1. My translation. The original sentence reads: "Les Anglais ne pourront jamais accepter l'intégration dans le Marché Commun mais nous serons trop courtois pour le leur dire." François Duchêne to Max Kohnstamm, 15 May 1962, MKS.
2. Monnet to Acheson, 23 November 1962, MKS.
3. See Beloff, *General Says No,* p. 135.
4. Macmillan, *At the End of the Day,* pp. 139–140.
5. Ball, *Discipline of Power,* p. 85.
6. Original text in Charles de Gaulle, *Discours et Messages. Pour l'effort, 1962-65* (Paris: Plon, 1970). Translation in Camps, *Britain and the European Community,* p. 474.
7. See Camps, *Britain and the European Community,* p. 462, and Sir Anthony Hurd's speech in Berkshire on 23 November 1962, *The Times,* 24 November 1962.
8. Ibid.
9. The issue of the financial regulations is a case in point. The EEC had agreed to create an agricultural fund for the stabilization of agricultural prices, to subsidize exports to third countries and facilitate structural readjustments. But while the Germans argued that the fund should be financed from the national budget on the same ratios that were used for the overall EEC budget, the French argued that the fund should be financed on the basis of import levy payments on foreign food stuff in proportion with the agricultural import ratio. Since France was the largest exporting country, the French proposal in effect meant that French exports would be subsidized in part by German and other importing countries.
10. See George Ball, Memorandum for the President, 23 August 1961, op. cit., p. 4.
11. Ibid.
12. State Department Telegram, 31 July 1962, NSF Countries, Box 71A, "France General 7/62-," 2, JFKL.
13. Ball, *Discipline of Power,* p. 79.
14. See, for example, Memorandum of Conversation on European Unity and Trade Problems. Participants: Ball, Bohlen, Tyler, and Schaetzel. On the French side: Couve de Murville, Ambassador Alphand, and Mr. Lucet. 8 October 1963, NSF Countries, Box 72A, "France General 10/12/63-10/17/63," JFKL.
15. Robert Schaetzel, recorded interview by Pascaline Winand, 12 January 1989, Washington, D.C., p. 3.
16. USDA, "Common Market Developments and U.S. Farm Exports," remarks by John P. Duncan, Jr., assistant secretary for marketing and foreign agriculture, at a meeting of the National Council of Farmer Cooperatives, San Francisco, 15 January 1962. Copy in Petersen Papers, Box 4, "Agriculture-Statements on Trade," JFKL. Also Ball's statement before the Subcommittee on International Exchange and Payments of the Joint Economic Committee, 13 December 1962, op. cit., p. 103.
17. For a detailed analysis of United States exports toward the Common Market, see *Les Etats-Unis face au marché commun agricole.* Avant-propos de L. Fauvel, 8 (Paris: Cujas, 1970). Marché et Structures agricoles.
18. State Department Telegram to Gavin, Bruce, Butterworth and Tuthill, 25 July 1962, NSF Countries, Box 170a, "UK 7/27/62," JFKL.
19. Telegram from Butterworth to the State Department, 26 July 1962, NSF Countries, Box 170a, "UK 7/27/62," JFKL.
20. Ibid.
21. John Duncan speech, op. cit.
22. *New York Times,* 17 November 1963.
23. Congressional Record, 88th Cong., 1st sess., 29 January 1963, pp. 1330-1333, quoted in Talbot, *Chicken War,* p. 75.

24. Press Release of the U.S. Mission to the European Communities, 9 August 1963, quoted in Taber, *John F. Kennedy and a Uniting Europe,* p. 144.

25. Ambassador John Tuthill, recorded interview by Pascaline Winand, 14 January 1989.

26. *Congressional Quarterly,* weekly report, 1 February 1963, pp. 114-115.

27. *New York Times,* 21 June 1963, quoted in Talbot, *Chicken War, p. 84.*

28. Interview with Ambassador Tuthill, op. cit.

29. For a detailed and extremely well informed treatment of the Chicken War, see Talbot, *Chicken War.* See also Taber, *John F. Kennedy and a Uniting Europe,* pp. 141-45. The present discussion owes much to both these accounts, as well as to personal interviews.

30. *The Trade Expansion Act of 1962,* p. 11.

31. Ibid., p. 641.

32. *Trade Expansion Act of 1962,* H.R. 11970, sec. 252. Quoted in Preeg, *Traders and Diplomats,* p. 48.

33. Telegram from Cecil Lyon to the Secretary of State, 22 December 1962, NSF Countries, Box 170 a, "UK 12/11/62 -12/31/62," JFKL. Document partly "sanitized."

34. *Le Monde,* 31 October 1962. Translation in Preeg, *Traders and Diplomats,* p. 54.

35. De Gaulle, *Discours et Messages. Pour L'effort,* p. 69.

36. Fontaine, *Comité d'Action,* p. 122.

37. Telegram from Ambassador to Ball, 10 January 1962, NSF Countries, Box 170, "UK 1/62-," JFKL.

38. State Department Telegram to Bruce from Ball, 16 February 1962, NSF Countries, Box 170 a, "UK General 2/1/62-2/21/62," JFKL.

39. See Telegram from Bruce to Ball, 10 May 1961, NSF Countries, Box 170, "UK 9/1/61-5/15/61," JFKL.

40. Camps, *Britain and the European Community,* p. 375.

41. See Gavin to Secretary of State, 24 March 1962, NSF Countries, Box 70-71, "France 3/11/62-." The Fanfani connection was also used on occasion. See Position Paper, 6 June 1961, NSF Countries, Box 21, "6/12/61-6/13/61" and 11 January 1963, NSF Countries, Box 21, Italy Subjects, "Fanfani Visit 1/6/63-1/17/63," JFKL.

42. See Spaak, *Combats Inachevés,* p. 253.

43. Most of the documents on Spaak at the JFKL are still unprocessed at the time of writing.

44. Letter from MacArthur II to Paul-Henri Spaak, 23 November 1962, Schlesinger Papers, Box 4, "Common Market," JFKL.

45. Memorandum for McGeorge Bundy, 23 November 1962, NSF Countries, Box 9-10, "Belgium 11/8/62-11/30/62," JFKL.

46. Memorandum for McGeorge Bundy, 5 December 1962, NSF Countries, Box 9-10, "12/1/62-1/10/63," JFKL.

47. Memorandum for McGeorge Bundy, 22 December 1962, NSF Countries, Box 9-10, "Belgium 12/1/62-1/10/63." See also Memorandum for McGeorge Bundy, 7 January 1963, NSF Countries, Box 9-10, "Belgium 1/62-3/62," JFKL.

48. Telegram from Brussels, 4 December 1962, NSF Countries, Box 170a, "UK 11/13/62-," JFKL.

49. Memorandum of George Ball, recorded conversation with Walter Hallstein, president of the European Economic Community, 8 December 1962, NSF Countries, Box 170a, "UK 12/16/62," JFKL.

50. Memorandum for the President, 10 December 1962, NSF Countries, Box 170a, "UK 12/16/62," JFKL.

51. Bruce to Ball, 10 May 1961, NSF Countries, Box 170, "9/1/61-5/15/61," JFKL.

52. Bruce to Ball, 27 July 1962, NSF Countries, Box 170a, "UK 7/27/62," JFKL.

53. Memorandum for McGeorge Bundy, 27 July 1962, NSF Countries, Box 170a, "7/27/62-," JFKL.

54. Memorandum for the President, 10 December 1962, NSF Countries, Box 170a,"UK 12/16/62," JFKL.

55. Beloff, *General Says No,* p. 122.
56. Monnet's declaration to the AFP, 1 August 1961, quoted in Fontaine. op. cit., p. 122.
57. *European Community* (January 1963), p. 8.
58. Memorandum for the President from Ball, 10 December 1962, op. cit.
59. Telegram from Tuthill to the Secretary of State, 17 December 1962, NSF Countries, Box 170a, "UK 12/11/62-12/31/62," JFKL.
60. David Klein to McGeorge Bundy, 27 November 1962, NSF Countries, Box 71A, "France 11/20/62," JFKL.
61. Macmillan, *At the End of the Day,* pp. 119–122.
62. Ibid.
63. Bruce to Secretary of State, 17 May 1962, NSF Countries, Box 170a, "UK General 3/62," JFKL.
64. Dean Rusk to the President, 7 July 1962, NSF Countries, Box 170 a, "UK 6/21/62-7/9/62," JFKL.
65. David Klein to McGeorge Bundy, 27 November 1962, NSF Countries, Box 71A, "France 11/20/62," JFKL.
66. Alistair Home, "The Macmillan Years and Afterwards," in *The "Special Relationship." Anglo-American relations since 1945,* Roger Louis and Hedley Bull, eds. (Oxford: Clarendon Press, 1986).
67. Nunnerley, *President Kennedy and Britain,* p. 156; and Ball, *Memoirs,* p. 266.
68. Adenauer, *Erinnerungen,* p. 202.
69. Macmillan, *At the End of the Day,* p. 348.
70. Adenauer, *Erinnerungen,* p. 202.
71. Macmillan, *At the End of the Day,* p. 34.
72. "Mon cher c'est très simple. Maintenant, avec les six, il y a cinq poules et un coq. Si vous joignez (avec des autres pays), il y aura peut-être sept ou huit poules. Mais il y aura *deux* coqs. Alors—ce n'est pas aussi agréable." Quoted in Macmillan, *At the End of the Day,* p. 365.
73. Richard Neustadt, *Alliance Politics* (New York: Columbia University Press, 1970), p. 40.
74. Richard Neustadt Report to Kennedy (hereafter cited as Neustadt Report), 15 November 1963, NSF, Box 319-324, "Skybolt and Nassau," JFKL, pp. 28, 31.
75. William Tyler, interview by the Kennedy Library, 7 March 1964, JFKL.
76. Rostow, *Diffusion of Power.*
77. Ball, *Memoirs,* p. 245.
78. Rostow, *Diffusion of Power,* p. 245.
79. Neustadt Report, pp. 70–71.
80. Neustadt Report, pp. 91–95.
81. Ball, *Memoirs,* p. 265.
82. Walt Rostow, interview by the Kennedy Library, JFKL, p. 102.
83. Nunnerley, *President Kennedy and Britain,* p. 155.
84. Bohlen, *Witness to History 1929-1969,* p. 499.
85. Ball, *Memoirs,* p. 267.
86. Ibid.
87. McGeorge Bundy, recorded interview by David Nunnerley, 30 January 1970, JFKL.
88. Neustadt Report, op. cit.
89. *The Times,* 27 January 1983, quoted in Home, *The Macmillan Years,* p. 98.
90. *Public Papers of the Presidents: John F. Kennedy, 1962,* p. 554.
91. Neustadt Report, pp. 94–101.
92. *Public Papers of the Presidents: John F. Kennedy, 1962,* p. 554.
93. Neustadt Report, pp. 97–98.
94. "...un enchevêtrement de liaisons, de transmissions, d'interférences à l'intérieur d'elle-même et un enveloppement de sujétions extérieures tels que, si on lui arrachait soudain une partie intégrante d'elle-même, on risquerait fort de la paralyser juste au moment où, elle devrait agir." De Gaulle, *Discours et Messages. Pour l'effort,* pp. 75–76.

95. Neustadt Report, p. 101.
96. Ibid., p. 105.
97. Ibid., p. 98.
98. Lyon to Secretary of State, 21 December 1962, NSF Countries, Box 71, "France 12/18/62," JFKL.
99. Neustadt Report, p. 103.
100. *Bohlen, Witness to History,* p. 501.
101. McGeorge Bundy to the President, 20 December 1969, NSF Countries, Box 71A, "12/27/62-," JFKL.
102. Ball, *Memoirs,* p. 265.
103. Dean Rusk to the President, 24 December 1962, NSF Countries, Box 71A, "France 12/18/62," JFKL.
104. Walt Rostow, recorded interview by Richard Neustadt, p. 137.
105. Sulzberger, *Last of the Giants.*
106. Meeting among Harold Caccia, W. W. Rostow, and Paul H. Nitze, 18 January 1963, NSF Countries, Box 171-173, "UK 1/11/63-1/29/63," JFKL.
107. Ambassador Bruce-Robert Schaetzel, 13 June 1962, NSF Countries, Box 170a, "UK General 6/1/62-6/20/62," JFKL.
108. Gavin to Secretary of State, 8 July 1962, NSF Countries, Box 71A, "France General 7/62," JFKL.
109. Alphand, *L'étonnement d'être.*
110. Lyon to Secretary of State, 15 September 1962, NSF Countries, Box 170a, "UK 9/16/62," JFKL.
111. Tuthill to the Department of State, 29 November 1962, NSF Countries, Box 170a, "UK 11/13/62," JFKL.
112. Tuthill to Ball, Tyler, and Schaetzel, 4 December 1962, NSF Countries, Box 170a, "UK 11/13/62," JFKL.
113. Memorandum of Conversation, "EEC," 4 December 1962, NSF Countries, Box 170a, "UK 12/62," JFKL.
114. Ball-Hallstein Conversation, 8 December 1962, op. cit.
115. Memorandum, 13 December 1962, NSF Countries, Box 71A, "France 12/1/62," JFKL.
116. Rusk to Department of State, 15 December 1962, NSF Countries, Box 170a, "UK 12/11/62-12/31/62," JFKL.
117. Tuthill to Secretary of State, 17 December 1962, NSF Countries, Box 170a, "UK 12/11/62-12/31/62," JFKL.
118. Lyon to Secretary of State, 24 December 1962, NSF Countries, Box 71A, "France 12/18/62," JFKL.
119. McGeorge Bundy to the President, 29 December 1962, op. cit.
120. Ball, *Memoirs,* p. 269.
121. *Public Papers of the Presidents of the United States: John F. Kennedy, 1963,* pp. 11-12.
122. Bohlen, *Witness to History,* p. 501.
123. McGeorge Bundy to President, 14 January 1963, NSF Countries, Box 73A-74, "France Subjects. De Gaulle Press Statement," JFKL.
124. Spaak's 15 January Press Conference. Translation in MacArthur to Secretary of State, 16 January 1963, NSF Countries, Box 73A-74, "France Subjects. De Gaulle Press Statement 11/14/63 Part 2," JFKL.
125. Bohlen to State Department, 17 January 1963, NSF Countries, Box 73A-74, "France Subjects. De Gaulle Press Statement Part 3," JFKL.

Notes to Chapter 12: After the Veto

1. Bohlen to Secretary of State, 21 January 1963, NSF Countries, Box 73A-74, "France Subjects 1/14/63 Part 3," JFKL.

2. Bruce to Secretary of State, 22 January 1963, Telegrams no. 13498 and 13499, NSF Countries, Box 73A-74, "France Subjects. De Gaulle Press Statement Part 3," JFKL.
3. Reinhardt to Secretary of State, 22 January 1963, NSF Countries, Box 73A-74, "France Subjects. De Gaulle Press Statement Part 3," JFKL.
4. Caccia, Rostow, and Nitze, 18 January 1963, op. cit.
5. Tuthill to Secretary of State, 22 January 1963, NSF Countries, Box 73A-74, "France Subjects. De Gaulle Press Statement Part 3," JFKL.
6. Ibid.
7. Remarks by President Kennedy before the NSC, Tuesday, 22 January 1963, NSF Meetings and Memos, Box 314, "NSC Meetings 1963 5/18/62-8/3/62," JFKL.
8. Ibid.
9. Dean Rusk to the President, 8 October 1962, NSF Countries, Box 170a, "UK 10/1/62"; Memorandum of Conversation between Michael Cary and Walt Rostow, 18 January 1963, NSC Countries, Box 171-173, "UK 1/11/63-1/29/63," JFKL.
10. "Thoughts on Berlin," Carl Kaysen, 22 August 1961, WH3, Schlesinger, White House, "Berlin General," JFKL.
11. Ball, *Memoirs,* p. 271.
12. Ibid., p. 272.
13. Full translation of text in *Freedom and Union* (July-August 1963), p. 19; text of Franco-German Treaty in *Freedom and Union* (March 1963), pp. 21-22.
14. On this point, see Ball, *Discipline of Power,* p. 161.
15. "Eyes Only" Telegram from Bruce to the President and the Secretary, 4 March 1963, NSC Countries, Box 171-173, "UK 2/12/63," JFKL.
16. Theodore Sorensen, *Kennedy* (New York: Harper & Row, 1965), p. 574.
17. Taber, *John F. Kennedy and a Uniting Europe,* p. 123.
18. *Freedom and Union* (February 1963), p. 17.
19. Ibid.
20. All above quotations from Secret Report, 9 February 1963; unsigned, personal interviews indicate George Ball as the author. NSF Meetings and Memos, Box 314, NSF Meetings 1963, no. 510, "5/18/62-8/3/62," JFKL.
21. *Department of State Bulletin,* 18 March 1963.
22. Kennedy to Macmillan, 21 February 1963, NSF Regional Security, Box 223-231, "NATO Pipe Embargo 2/63," JFKL.
23. OECD Restricted Document, 31 January 1963, Herter Box 16, "Trips Europe 1/24/63-2/14/63," JFKL.
24. Bohlen to Secretary of State, 21 February 1963, NSF France, Box 72, "1/1/63-1/23/63," JFKL.
25. Bohlen to Secretary of State, 25 February 1963, NSF France, Box 72, JFKL.
26. George Ball to the President, 1 March 1963, NSF Belgium, "Hallstein Visit," JFKL.
27. Quoted in Taber, *John F. Kennedy and a Uniting Europe,* p. 137.
28. Henry Owen, recorded interview by Paige Mulhollan, 18 December 1968, LBJL; Lyman Lemnitzer, recorded interview, 11 February 1970, JFKL.
29. Planning for Prime Minister Fanfani's visit to Washington on January 16-17 included a detailed discussion of the MLF proposal. Position Paper, 10 January 1963, NSF Countries, Box 21, "Italy Subjects. Fanfani Visit 1/6/63-1/17/63," JFKL.
30. Rostow, *Diffusion of Power,* p. 247.
31. Steinbruner, *Cybernetic Theory of Decision,* pp. 250–253.
32. Ibid., p. 270.
33. Merchant to Secretary, 4 March 1963, NSF Regional Security, Box 211-220, "MLF," JFKL.
34. Ibid., MacArthur to Merchant and Finletter, 6 March 1963, NSF Regional Security , Box 211-220, "MLF," JFKL.
35. MacArthur to Secretary of State, 7 March 1963, NSF Regional Security, Box 211-220, "MLF Cables 3/11/63-3/10/63," JFKL.

36. From Bonn to Secretary of State, 8 March 1963, NSF Regional Security, Box 211-220, "MLF Cables 3/11/63-3/20/63," JFKL; and Steinbruner, op. cit., p. 274.
37. Bundy to President, 6 March 1963, and Briefing Item "Initial West European Assessment of U.S. Multilateral Force Proposals," 7 March 1963, NSF Regional Security, Box 211-220, "MLF 3/6/63-3/28/63," JFKL.
38. Ibid., and Merchant to Secretary of State, 10 March 1963, NSF Regional Security, Box 211-220, "MLF Cables 3/1/63-3/10/63," JFKL.
39. Carl Kaysen, Memorandum for the Secretary of State and the Secretary of Defense, 23 March 1963, NSF Regional Security, Box 211-220, "MLF 3/9/63-3/28/63," JFKL.
40. Gerard Smith, recorded interview by Paige Mulhollan, 29 April 1969, JFKL, p. 4. William Tyler, recorded interview by the JFKL, 7 March 1964; Steinbruner, op. cit., p. 277.
41. Steinbruner, op. cit., pp. 277–278.
42. Gerard Smith, recorded interview by Paige Mulhollan, 29 April 1969, LBJL.
43. Luncheon conversation between Ambassador Ormsby-Gore, Secretary Ball, and Mr. William Tyler, 3 March 1963, NSC Countries, Box 171-173, "UK 4/19/63-5/14/63," JFKL; Steinbruner, op. cit., p. 279; Harold Wilson, *A Personal Record* (Boston: Atlantic Monthly Press, 1971), p. 41; and Bundy, *Danger and Survival,* p. 495.
44. Steinbruner, op. cit., p. 280.
45. Dean Rusk to the President, 27 May 1963, NSC Countries, Box 174-175, "UK Macmillan Correspondence. 5/29/63-Tab 15," JFKL.
46. Bundy's Memorandum to the President, "The MLF and the European Tour," 15 June 1963, NSF Memos to the President, Box 2, "McGeorge Bundy, vol. 7," LBJL.
47. See Steinbruner, op. cit., p. 83, but Steinbruner documents the existence of this memo after the president's trip to Europe.
48. *Department of State Bulletin,* 22 July 1963.
49. Rostow's interview, op. cit.; Neustadt speaking.
50. Rostow, *Diffusion of Power,* p. 247. Rostow's interview, op. cit., p. 104.
51. William Tyler interview, op. cit., p. 37.

Notes to Epilogue

1. Rostow, *Diffusion of Power,* p. 247; Steinbruner, op. cit., p. 284.
2. Ludwig Erhard succeeded Konrad Adenauer in October 1963. That same month, Macmillan resigned.
3. Gerard Smith, recorded interview, op. cit., p. 6; Steinbruner, op. cit., p. 288.
4. *New York Times,* 13 June 1964.
5. Steinbruner, op. cit., p. 291.
6. Steinbruner, op. cit., p. 305 et seq.
7. Ibid.
8. McGeorge Bundy, Memorandum to Rusk, McNamara, and Ball, 25 November 1964, NSF Memoirs to the President, Box 2, "McGeorge Bundy, vol. 7, 10/1/64 to 12/31/64," LBJL.
9. Steinbruner, op. cit., and Wilson, *A Personal Record,* pp. 45–51.
10. Ibid.
11. Interview material.
12. Ibid., and George Ball, recorded interview by Paige Mulhollan, 9 July 1971, LBJL.
13. Robert Schaetzel and Robert Bowie, recorded interview by Pascaline Winand, 12 January 1989, Washington, D.C.; George McGhee, recorded interview by Paige Mulhollan, 1 July 1969, LBJL.
14. Henry Owen, recorded interview by Paige Mulhollan, 18 December 1968, LBJL.
15. Department of State Telegram 607 to U.S. Mission Geneva, 7 September 1964; from Brussels, Airgram A-92, 4 August 1965; Department of State Circular Airgram CA-1483,

22 August 1966; from Paris, Telegram 7477, 19 November 1966; from Paris, Airgram A-1046, 5 January 1967; Department of State Circular Airgram CA-6384, 23 February 1967; Department of State Circular Airgram CA-8366, 28 April 1967; from Bonn, Airgram A-154, 31 July 1967; from The Hague, Telegram 547, 8 August 1967, Administrative History of the Department of State, vol. 1, "U.S.-Euratom Relations," 70, LBJL.

16. Statement before the U.S. Senate Committee on Foreign Relations, 10 July 1968, Hearing on the Non-Proliferation Treaty, Administrative History of the Department of State, vol. 1, "U.S.-Euratom Relations," 78, LBJL.

17. *Department of State Bulletin,* 6 January 1964, p. 29.

18. Department of State Press Release no. 219, 8 May 1964.

19. *Department of State Bulletin,* 27 April 1964, p. 657 et seq.

20. Ibid., 25 July 1966, pp. 145–146.

21. Ibid., 27 April 1964, p. 657 et seq.

22. For a full discussion of the Kennedy Round, see, among others, Preeg, *Traders and Diplomats*; and John W. Evans, *The Kennedy Round in American Policy* (Cambridge, Mass.: Harvard University Press, 1971).

23. Memorandum for the President from George Ball, "Objectives and Strategy for TEA Negotiations," 8 March 1963. Mentioned in Administrative History of the Department of State, vol. 1, LBJL.

24. From Brussels, Telegram 5261, 12 April 1967, confidential; from Brussels, Airgram ECBUS A-633, 24 June 1967; Report on United States Negotiations, vols. 1 and 2 , Office of the Special Representative for Trade Negotiations, Department of State Circular Telegram 195839, 16 May 1967, Administrative History of the State Department, vol. 1, LBJL.

25. See Report on United States Negotiations, Office of the Special Representative for Trade Negotiations, LBJL.

26. U.S. Position Paper on Preferences of LDCs in Markets of Developed Countries (UNCTAD D-3), 13 April 1964; Department of State Circular Telegram 2065, 5 May 1964; Department of State Circular Airgram CA-5638, 30 January 1967; Department of State Circular Airgram CA-11991, 18 May 1964; Department of State Circular Telegram 28, 2 July 1964; Circular Airgram CA-3556, 8 November 1966, "Trade Relations Between Developed and Developing Countries," Administrative History of the Department of State, LBJL.

27. Background Paper, "EEC Crisis," for the OECD Ministerial Meeting at Paris, 25-26 November 1965, "C. Political—Economic Relations: 2. The European Communities," Administrative History of the Department of State, LBJL.

28. Limdis Telegram ECBUS 324, 27 October 1965, from Brussels USEC to the Department, "2. The European Communities," Administrative History of the Department of State, LBJL.

29. Limdis Telegram 439, 28 October 1965, from Madrid to the Department, "2. The European Communities," Administrative History of the Department of State, LBJL.

30. Memorandum, Assistant Secretary Leddy to the Secretary, 26 January 1966, "Enlargement of the European Communities (1) United Kingdom," Administrative History of the Department of State, LBJL.

31. Memorandum to the Under Secretary from E-Assistant Secretary Solomon and EUR-Deputy Assistant Secretary Stoessel, 19 July 1966, "Enlargement of the European Communities (1) United Kingdom," Administrative History of the Department of State, LBJL.

32. *Department of State Bulletin,* 24 October 1966, p. 624.

33. Department of State Telegram 83313 to Bern et al, 10 November 1966, Administrative History of the Department of State, "Enlargement of the European Communities (1) United Kingdom," LBJL.

34. Department of State Telegram 186605, 2 May 1967, Administrative History of the Department of State, LBJL.

35. Information Memoranda, Assistant Secretary John M. Leddy to Secretary Rusk, 7 June 1967 and 7 July 1967; INR Research Memorandum REU-48, 29 June 1963, Administrative History of the Department of State, LBJL.
36. Harold B. Van Cleveland, *The Atlantic Idea and Its European Rivals* (New York: McGraw-Hill, 1966), p.160.
37. United States Policy Toward Europe, Hearings before the Committee on Foreign Relations, U.S. Senate, 89th Cong., 2d sess., 20 June-22 July 1966, pp. 175–177.
38. Ibid., pp. 147–149.
39. Address by President Johnson before the National Conference of Editorial Writers in New York, N.Y., 7 October, *Department of State Bulletin,* 24 October 1966, p. 624.
40. Ball, *Memoirs,* p. 433.
41. George Ball was subsequently appointed as United States Ambassador to the United Nations.
42. Schaetzel, *Unhinged Alliance,* p. 46.

BIBLIOGRAPHY

ARCHIVES AND MANUSCRIPT COLLECTIONS

Acheson, Dean. Papers. Manuscripts and Archives, Yale University Library (hereafter YL).

Ball, George. Diaries. Princeton.

Berle, Adolf A. Papers. Franklin Roosevelt Library.

Bowles, Chester. Papers. YL.

Dulles, John Foster. Papers. Seeley Mudd Library, Princeton University (hereafter PL).

Eisenhower, Dwight D. Ann Whitman File. Dwight D. Eisenhower Library (hereafter DDEL).

Eisenhower, Dwight D. DDE White House Central Files. DDEL.

Eisenhower, Dwight D. International Series. DDEL.

Eisenhower, Dwight D. NSC Series. DDEL.

Eisenhower, Dwight D. Official Files. DDEL.

Eisenhower, Dwight D. Randall Series. DDEL.

Eisenhower, Dwight D. U.S. CFEP, Office of the Chairman, Records 1954-1961. Randall Series. DDEL.

Eisenhower, Dwight D. White House Office, OSANSA 1952-61. DDEL.

Estabrook, Robert H. Papers. DDEL.

Herter, Christian. White House Staff Files. John F. Kennedy Library (hereafter JFKL).

Johnson, Lyndon B. Administrative History of the Department of Agriculture, vol. 1. Lyndon B. Johnson Library (hereafter LBJL).

Johnson, Lyndon B. Administrative History of the Department of State, vol 1. LBJL.

Johnson, Lyndon B. Cabinet Papers. LBJL.

Johnson, Lyndon B. Confidential Files. LBJL.

Johnson, Lyndon B. National Security Files. LBJL.

Johnson, Lyndon B. Vice Presidential Security File. LBJL.

Johnson, Lyndon B. White House Central Files. LBJL.

Kennan, George F. Papers. PL.

Kennedy, John F. National Security Files. JFKL.

Kennedy, John F. Pre-Presidential Files. JFKL.

Kennedy, John F. President's Office File. JFKL.

Kennedy, John F. White House Central Files. JFKL.

Kohnstamm, Max. Archives. European University Institute, Florence.

Lamont, Tom. Papers. Baker Library, Harvard University.

McPherson, H. The Office Files of H. McPherson. LBJL.

Monnet, Jean. Archives. Fondation Jean Monnet pour l'Europe (hereafter FJM), Lausanne.

Norstad, Lauris. Papers. DDEL.

Peterson, Howard. White House Staff Files. JFKL.

Randall, Clarence B. Papers. PL.

Roosevelt, Franklin D. Papers. Franklin D. Roosevelt Library.

Schlesinger, Arthur. Papers. JFKL.

Sorenson, Theodore. Papers. JFKL.

Stevenson, Adlai. Papers. PL.

Tuthill, John. Private Papers. Washington, D.C.

U.S. Department of State. The Records of Harley A. Notter. Record Group 59. Diplomatic branch, National Archives, Washington, D.C.

INTERVIEWS

Acheson, Dean. Recorded interview by Lucius D. Battle, 27 April 1964. JFKL Oral History Project.

Alsop, Joseph. Recorded interview OH 176, Columbia University.

Ball, George. Recorded interview by Leonard Tennyson, 15 July 1981. FJM.

Ball, George. Recorded interview by Paige Mulhollan, 8-9 July 1971. LBJL Oral History Project.

Ball, George. Recorded interviews by Pascaline Winand, August 1989 and 23 October 1990, Princeton.

Bohlen, Charles. Recorded interview by the Kennedy Library, 21 May 1964. JFKL Oral History Project.

Bohlen, Charles. Recorded interview by Paige Mulhollan, 20 November 1968. University of Texas (hereafter cited as U.T.) Oral History Project.

Bowie, Robert. Recorded interview OH 102, 1967. Columbia Oral History Project, DDEL.

Bowie, Robert. Recorded interviews by Pascaline Winand, 12 January 1989 and 18 October 1990, Washington, D.C.

Bowie, Robert. Recorded interview by Richard D. Chaneller, 10 August 1964. Dulles Oral History Project, PL.

Bowles, Chester. Recorded interview by the Kennedy Library. JFKL Oral History Project.

Bruce, David. Recorded interview by Thomas H. Baker, 9 December 1971. U.T. Oral History Project.

Bruce, David. Recorded interview by the Kennedy Library. JFKL Oral History Project.

Bruce, David. Recorded interview by Philip A. Crowl, 9 June 1964. Dulles Oral History Project, PL.

Brzezinski, Zbigniew. Recorded interview by Paige Mulhollan, 12 November 1971. LBJL.

Bundy, McGeorge. Recorded interview by David Nunnerley. JFKL.

Bundy, McGeorge. Recorded interview by Pascaline Winand, 1 March 1989, New York.

Butterworth, Walton. Recorded interview by Richard D. Challener, 8 September 1965. Dulles Oral History Project, PL.

Couve de Murville, Maurice. Recorded interview by Philip A. Crowl, June 19, 1964, Dulles Oral History Project, PL.

Dillon, Douglas. Recorded interview, 1972. Columbia Oral History Project.

Dillon, Douglas. Recorded interview by Paige Mulhollan, 6 June 1969. U.T. Oral History Project.

Dillon, Douglas. Recorded interview, 24 June 1965. Dulles Oral History Project, PL.

Dulles, Eleanor. Recorded interview by Douglas Brinkley, May 1987.

Eisenhower, Dwight D. Recorded interview by Philip Crowl, 28 July 1964. OH 14, Dulles Oral History Project, PL.

Finletter, Thomas. Recorded interview by Philip J. Farley, 7 May 1965. JFKL Oral History Project.

Finletter, Thomas. Recorded interview by Paige Mulhollan, 29 October 1968. U.T. Oral History Project.

Foch, René. Recorded interview by Pascaline Winand, 11 October 1990. Franklin D. Roosevelt Library.

Freeman, Orville. Recorded interview by Charles T. Morrissey, 22 July 1964. JFKL Oral History Project.

Goodpaster, Andrew. Recorded interview by Malcolm McDonald, 10 April 1982, DDEL.

Goodpaster, Andrew. Recorded interview by Richard Challener, 11 January 1966, Dulles Oral History Project, PL.

Goodpaster, Andrew. Recorded interview by Dr. Thomas Soapes, 16 January 1978, DDEL.

Graham, Philip. Recorded interview by Leonard Tennyson, 28 July 1981. FJM.

Hallstein, Walter. Recorded interview by Gordon A. Graig, 29 July 1964. Dulles Oral History Project, PL.

Harriman, Averell. Recorded interview by Philip A. Crowl, 16 July 1966. Dulles Oral History Project, PL.

Herter, Christian. Recorded interview by Richard D. Challener, 31 August 1964. Dulles Oral History Project, PL.

Hoffmann, Stanley. Letter to Pascaline Winand, 29 February 1988.

Katz, Milton. Recorded interview by Leonard Tennyson, 28 June 1988. FJM.

Kaysen, Carl. Recorded interview by Pascaline Winand, February 1989, MIT, Boston.

Leddy, John M. Recorded interview by Paige Mulhollan, 12 March 1969. U.T. Oral History Project.

Lemnitzer, Lyman. Recorded interview, 11 February 1970. JFKL Oral History Project.

Lemnitzer, Lyman. Recorded interview by Ted Gittinger, 3 March 1962. LBJL.

Lucet, Charles. Recorded interview by Philip A. Crowl, 18 July 1966. Dulles Oral History Project, PL.

Luns, Joseph M. A. Recorded interview by Murrey Marder, 18 January 1965. JFKL Oral History Project.

Mayer, Rene. Recorded interview by Loftus Becker, October 1964. Dulles Oral History Project, PL.

Mann, Thomas C. Recorded interview by Philip A. Crowl, 24 May 1966. Dulles Oral History Project, PL.

McGhee, George. Recorded interview by Minister Hillenbrand, August 1964. JFKL Oral History Project.

McGhee, George. Recorded interview by Paige Mulhollan, 1 July 1969, LBJL.

McNamara, Robert. Recorded interview, 26 February 1970, JFKL Oral History Program.

Merchant, Livingston. Numbers 1 and 2, 1967-68. Columbia University Oral History Project.

Merchant, Livingston T. 17 April 1965. Dulles Oral History Project, PL.

Nitze, Paul. Recorded interview by Pascaline Winand, October 1990.

Nixon, Richard. Recorded interview by Richard D. Challener, 5 March 1965, Dulles Oral History Project, PL.

Norstad, Lauris. OH 385, 11 November 1976. DDEL.

Owen, Henry. Recorded interview by Paige Mulhollan, 18 December 1969. LBJL.

Owen, Henry. Recorded interviews by Pascaline Winand, 12 January 1989 and 17 October 1990, Washington, D.C.

Pineau, Christian. Recorded interview by Philip A. Crowl, 16 June 1965. Dulles Oral History Project, PL.

Radford, Arthur. Recorded interview by Philip A. Crowl, 8 May 1965. Dulles Oral History Project, PL.

Rostow, Walt. Recorded interview by Pascaline Winand, July 1986, Austin, Texas.

Rostow, Walt. Recorded interview by Richard Neustadt. JFKL Oral History Project.

Rusk, Dean. Recorded interview by David Nunnerley, 9 February 1970. JFKL Oral History Project.

Rusk, Dean. Recorded interviews by Paige Mulhollan, 28 July 1969 and 2 January 1970. U.T. Oral History Project.

Schaetzel, Robert. Recorded interview by Pascaline Winand, January 1989.

Schaetzel, Robert, and Henry Owen. Recorded interview by Pascaline Winand, 12 January 1989. Washington, D.C.

Smith, Alexander. Recorded interview by Philip A. Crowl, 16 April 1964. Dulles Oral History Project, PL.

Smith, Gerard. Recorded interview by Paige Mulhollan, 29 April 1969. LBJL.

Spaak, Paul-Henri. Recorded interview by Richard D. Challener, 1 November 1966. Dulles Oral History Project, PL.

Taylor, Maxwell D. Recorded interview by the Kennedy Library. JFKL Oral History Project.

Thorneycroft, Peter, recorded interview by the Kennedy Library, JFKL Oral History Project.

Tobin, James. Recorded interview by Pascaline Winand, 15 October 1990, Yale University.

Tuthill, John. Recorded interviews by Pascaline Winand, 14 January 1989 and 18 October 1990, Washington, D.C.

Tyler, William R. Recorded interview by the Kennedy Library, 7 March 1964. JFKL Oral History Project.

Wheeler, Earle. Recorded interview by Chester Clifton, 1964. JFKL Oral History Project.

PUBLISHED DOCUMENTS, AND POLITICAL
AND ORGANIZATIONAL PROFILES

Agricultural proposals in the European Economic Community, Sept.-Oct. 1960. Senate Committee on Foreign Relations, 86th Cong., 1960.

A New Look at Foreign Economic Policy in Light of the Cold War and the Extension of the Common Market of Europe. Subcommittee on Foreign Economic Policy of the Joint Economic Committee. Congress. Washington, D.C.: U.S. GPO, 1961.

Congressional Record.

Documents on American Foreign Relations, 1954, 1955, 1956, 1958, 1959, 1961, 1962. New York: Published for the Council on Foreign Relations by Harper and Brothers, Washington, D.C.

For Strengthening International Financial Arrangements. Hearings before the Subcommittee on International Exchange and Payments of the Joint Economic Committee. Congress, 16 May-21 June 1961. Washington, D.C.: U.S. GPO, 1961.

Foreign Commerce Study, Senate Committee on Interstate and Foreign Commerce, 86th Cong., 1960.

Foreign Economic Policy. Hearings before the Subcommittee on Foreign Economic Policy of the Joint Economic Committee. Congress, December 1961. Washington, D.C.: U.S. GPO, 1962.

Foreign Economic Policy for the 1960's. Report of the Joint Economic Committee to the Congress of the United States with Minority and other Views, 87th Cong., 2d sess. Washington, D.C.: U.S. GPO, 1962.

Foreign Relations of the United States 1951. Vol. 3. European Security and the German Question. Washington, D.C.: U.S. GPO, 1981.

Foreign Relations of the United States 1952-54. Vol. 5. Western European Security, Part 1. Washington, D.C.: U.S. GPO, 1983.

Foreign Relations of the United States 1952-54. Vol. 6. Western Europe and Canada, Part 1. Washington: U.S. GPO, 1986.

Foreign Relations of the United States 1955-57. Vol 4. Western European Security and Integration. Department of State publication. Office of the Historian, Bureau of Public Affairs. Washington, D.C.: U.S. GPO, 1986.

Galambos, ed. *The Papers of Dwight David Eisenhower. NATO and the Campaign of 1952: XII.* Baltimore and London: Johns Hopkins University Press, 1989.

Hearings before the Subcommittee on Foreign Economic Policy of the Joint Economic Committee. Congress of the United States, 4-14 December 1961. Washington, D.C.: U.S. GPO, 1962.

Lichtenstein, Nelson, ed. *Political Profiles. The Johnson Years.* Facts on File. New York: Columbia University Press.

Lichtenstein, Nelson, ed. *Political Profiles. The Kennedy Years.* Facts on File, 1976. New York: Columbia University Press.

Notter, Harley A. *Postwar Foreign Policy Preparation.* Washington, D.C.: Department of State, 1949.

Outlook for United States Balance of Payments. Hearings before the Subcommittee on International Exchange and Payments of the Joint Economic Committee, 87th Cong., 2d sess., December 1962. Washington, D.C.: U.S. GPO, 1963.

Public Papers of the Presidents of the U.S.: Dwight D. Eisenhower, 1953-1961. Washington, D.C.: U.S. GPO, 1960-61.

Public Papers of the Presidents of the U.S.: Harry S. Truman, 1945-1953. Washington, D.C.: U.S. GPO, 1961-66.

Public Papers of the Presidents of the U.S.: John F. Kennedy, 1961-1963. Washington, D.C.: U.S. GPO, 1962-64.

Public Papers of the Presidents of the U.S. Lyndon B. Johnson, 1963-1969. Washington, D.C.: U.S. GPO, 1963-69.

Schoenebaum, Eleanora, ed. *Political Profiles. The Eisenhower Years.* Facts on File. New York: Columbia University Press, 1977.

The European Economic Community and the United States. Robert Bowie and Theodore Geiger, Subcommittee on Foreign Economic Policy of the Joint Economic Committee, 87th Cong., 1st sess., November 1961. Washington, D.C.: U.S. GPO, 1961.

Trade Expansion Act of 1962. House of Representatives. Hearings before the Committee on Ways and Means, 87th Cong., 2d sess., March-April 1962. Washington, D.C.: U.S. GPO, 1962.

U.S. Department of State. *Department of State Bulletin.*

U.S. Department of State. *Foreign Relations of the United States, 1952-54.* Vol 6. Washington, D.C.: U.S. GOP, 1986.

U.S. Government Organization Manual.

Renewal of Trade Agreements Act. Part 1. House Committee on Ways and Means, 85 Cong., 1958.

BOOKS

Acheson, Dean. *Power and Diplomacy.* Cambridge, Mass.: Harvard University Press, 1958.

Acheson, Dean. *Present at the Creation.* New York: W. W. Norton & Co., 1969.

Acheson, Dean. *Sketches from Life of Men I Have Known.* New York: Harper and Brothers, 1959.

Adenauer, Konrad. *Erinnerungen 1959-63. Fragmente.* Stuttgart: Deutsche Verlags-Anstalt, 1968.

Adenauer, Konrad. *Mémoires III, 1956-63.* Paris: Hachette, 1969.

Alphand, Hervé. *L'Etonnement d'être. Journal 1939-1973.* Paris: Fayard, 1977.

Alsop, Steward. *The Center: People and Power in Political Washington.* New York: Harper and Row, 1968.

Anderson, Patrick. *The President's Men.* New York: Doubleday & Co., 1968.

Andrews, Stanley. *Agriculture and the Common Market.* Ames, Ia.: Iowa State University Press, 1973.

Aron, Raymond. *République impériale. Les Etats-Unis dans le Monde 1945-72.* Paris: Colman-Lévy, 1973.

Aron, Raymond, et Daniel Lerner (sous la direction de). *La querelle de la CED.* A. Collin, 1956.

Atlantic Institute for International Affairs. *The Nine and NATO. The Alliance and the Community: An Uncertain Relationship.* Paris: The Atlantic Papers 2/1974, 1974.

Bailey, Richard. *The European Community in the World.* London: Hutchinson, 1973.

Bailey, Richard. *The European Connection.* Oxford: Pergamon Press, 1983.

Ball, George W. *Diplomacy for a Crowded World.* Boston: Little, Brown and Co., 1976.

Ball, George W. "Policy and Processes." In *Towards a Wiser Colossus.* The Louis Martin Sears Lectures, Purdue University, 1970-71. Stegenga, editor. Lafayette, Indiana, 1972.

Ball, George W. *The Discipline of Power.* Boston: Little, Brown and Co., 1969.

Ball, George W. *The Past Has Another Pattern. Memoirs.* New York: W. W. Norton & Co., 1982.

Bandulet, Bruno. *Adenauer zwischen West und Ost.* Munich, 1970.

Barnett, Richard J. *The Alliance: America-Europe-Japan—Makers of the Postwar World.* New York: Simon and Schuster, 1983.

Beloff, Max. *The United States and the Unity of Europe.* Washington, D.C.: Brookings Institution, 1963.

Beloff, Nora. *The General Says No.* Middlesex: Penguin Books, 1963.

Benoit, Emile. *Europe at Sixes and Sevens.* New York: Columbia University Press, 1961.

Berding, Andrew H. *The Making of Foreign Policy.* Washington, D.C.: Potomac Books, 1966.

Berle, Beatrice Bishop and Travis Beal Jacobs, eds. *Navigating the Rapids 1918-1971. From the Papers of Adolf A. Berle.* New York: Harcourt Brace Jovanovich, 1973.

Beugel, Ernst Van der. *From Marshall Aid to Atlantic Partnership.* Amsterdam: Elsevier, 1966.

Bloes, Robert. *Le "Plan Fouchet" et le Problème de l'Europe Politique.* Bruges: College of Europe, 1970.

Bohlen, Charles. *Witness to History 1929-1969.* New York: W. W. Norton & Co., 1973.

Bowie, Robert R. *Shaping the Future.* New York: Columbia University Press, 1964.

Brandt, Willy. *People and Politics 1960-1975.* Boston: Little, Brown and Co., 1976.

Bromberger, Merry, and Serge Bromberger. *Les Coulisses de l'Europe.* Paris: Presses de la Cité, 1968.

Buchan, Alastair. *Europe's Future, Europe's Choices.* New York: Columbia University Press, 1969.

Buchan, Alastair, and Philip Windsor. *Arms and Stability in Europe.* London: The Institute for Strategic Studies, 1963.

Buckton James, Dorothy. *The Contemporary Presidency.* New York: Bobbs-Merrill, 1973.

Bundy, McGeorge. *Danger and Survival.* New York: Random House, 1988.

Bundy, McGeorge. *The Pattern of Responsibility.* First published Boston: Houghton Mifflin, 1952.

Bundy, McGeorge. *The Strength of Government.* Cambridge, Mass.: Harvard University Press, 1968.

Bunkina, M. K. *USA versus Western Europe: New Trends.* Moscow: Progress Publishers, 1979.

Calleo, David. *The Atlantic Fantasy: The U.S., NATO, and Europe.* Baltimore: Johns Hopkins University Press, 1970.

Camps, Miriam. *Britain and the European Community 1955-1963.* London: Oxford University Press, 1964.

Camps, Miriam. *What Kind of Europe? The Community since de Gaulle's Veto.* London: Oxford University Press, 1965.

Caro, Robert A. *The Years of Lyndon Johnson. The Path to Power.* New York: Alfred A. Knopf, 1983.

Casadio, Gian Paolo. *Transatlantic Trade. USA-EEC Confrontation in the GATT Negotiations.* Institute of Economics, University of Bologna: Saxon House, Lexington Books, 1973.

Cerami, Charles. *Alliance Born of Danger.* New York: 1963.

Christian, George. *The President Steps Down.* New York: Macmillan, 1970.

Clark, Keith C., ed. *The President and the Management of National Security.* New York: Praeger, 1969.

Cleveland, Harlan. *NATO: The Transatlantic Bargain.* New York: Harper and Row, 1970.

Cleveland, Harold B. van. *The Atlantic Idea and Its European Rivals.* New York: McGraw-Hill, 1966.

Cohen, Warren I. *Dean Rusk.* Totowa, N.J.: Cooper Square Publishers, 1980.

Comité d'Action pour les Etats-Unis d'Europe 1955-1965. *Recueil des déclarations et communiqués.* Lausanne: Centre de recherches européennes, 1965.

Cooper, Richard N. *The Economics of Interdependence. Economic Policy in the Atlantic Community.* New York: McGraw-Hill, 1968.

Coppock, John. *Atlantic Agricultural Unity: Is It Possible?* Published for the Council on Foreign Relations. New York: McGraw-Hill, 1966.

Courtois, Bernard. *Les Etats-Unis face au marché commun agricole.* Paris: Cujas, 1970.

Couve de Murville, Maurice. *Une Politique Etrangère 1958-1969.* Paris: Plon, 1971.

Cromwell, William C., ed. *Political Problems of Atlantic Partnership.* Bruges: College of Europe, 1969.

Czempiel, Ernst Otto, ed. *The Euro-American System. Economic and Political Relations between North America and Western Europe.* Boulder, Co.: Westview Press, 1976.

Dahrendorf, Ralf, and Theodore C. Sorensen. *A Widening Atlantic?* New York: Council on Foreign Relations, 1986.

Dallek, Robert. *The American Style of Foreign Policy.* New York: Alfred A. Knopf, 1983.

Davids, Jules. *Documents on American Foreign Relations.* Published for the Council on Foreign Relations. New York, 1964.

Davids, Jules. *The U.S. in World Affairs 1964.* Published for the Council on Foreign Relations. New York: Harper and Row, 1965.

De Gaulle, Charles. *Discours et Messages. Avec le Renouveau 1958-1962.* Paris: Plon, 1970.

De Gaulle, Charles. *Discours et Messages. Pour l'Effort 1962-1965.* Paris: Plon, 1970.

De Gaulle, Charles. *Lettres, Notes et Carnets. 1958-1960.* Paris: Plon, 1985.

De Gaulle, Charles. *Lettres, Notes et Carnets. 1961-1963.* Paris: Plon, 1986.

De Gaulle, Charles. *Mémoires d'espoir.* Vols. 1 and 2, Paris: Plon, 1970, 1971.

Delmas, Claude. *L'OTAN.* Paris: Presses universitaires de france, 1981.

Deporte, A. W. *Europe between the Superpowers: The Enduring Balance.* New Haven: Council on Foreign Relations, 1979.

De Rivera, Joseph. *The Psychological Dimension of Foreign Policy.* Columbus: Charles E. Merrill, 1968.

Destler, I. M. *Presidents, Bureaucrats and Foreign Policy.* Princeton: Princeton University Press, 1972.

Deutsch, Harold, et al. *The Changing Structure of Europe.* Minneapolis: University of Minnesota Press, 1970.

Deutsch, Karl, et al. *France, Germany and the Western Alliance.* New York: Scribner, 1967.

Deutsch, Karl W. *Arms Control and the Atlantic Alliance.* New York: John Wiley & Sons, 1967.

Diebold, William. *The Schuman Plan: A Study in Economic Cooperation, 1950-1959.* New York: Praeger, 1959.

Divine, Robert. *Foreign Policy and U.S. Presidential Elections: 1952-1960.* New York: New Viewpoints, 1974.

Donovan, Hedley. *Roosevelt to Reagan.* New York: Harper and Row, 1985.

Dulles, John Foster. *War and Peace.* New York: Macmillan, 1950.

Duroselle, Jean-Baptiste. *France and the United States.* Chicago: University of Chicago Press, 1976.

Duroselle, Jean-Baptiste. *Histoire Diplomatique de 1919 à nos jours.* Paris: Dalloz, 1981.

Duroselle, Jean-Baptiste. *L'idée de l'Europe dans l'histoire.* Paris: Denoël, 1965

Eisenhower, Dwight D. *The White House Years. Mandate for Change 1953-1956.* New York: Doubleday & Co., 1963.

Eisenhower, Dwight D. *The White House Years. Waging Peace 1956-1961.* New York: Doubleday & Co., 1965.

Evans, John W. *The Kennedy Round in American Trade Policy.* Cambridge: Harvard University Press, 1971.

Evans, Rowland, and Robert Novak. *Lyndon B. Johnson: The Exercise of Power.* New York: New American Library, 1966.

Falkowski, Lawrence S. *Presidents, Secretaries of State, and Crises in U.S. Foreign Relations: A Model and Predictive Analysis.* Boulder, Co.: Westview Press, 1978.

Feld, Werner J. *The European Common Market and the World.* Englewood Cliffs, N.J.: Prentice-Hall, 1967.

Ferrell, Robert H., ed. *The Eisenhower Diaries.* New York: W. W. Norton and Co., 1981.

Ferro, Maurice. *De Gaulle et l'Amérique.* Paris: Plon, 1973.

Finletter, Thomas. *Interim Report.* New York: W. W. Norton, 1968.

Finletter, Thomas. *Foreign Policy: The Next Phase: The 1960s.* Published for the Council on Foreign Relations. New York: Harper, 1960.

Fitzsimons, Louise. *The Kennedy Doctrine.* New York: Random House, 1972.

Fontaine, Pascal. *Jean Monnet, L'inspirateur.* Paris: Jacques Grancher, 1988.

Fontaine, Pascal. *Le Comité d'Action pour les Etats-Unis d'Europe.* Lausanne: Centre de recherches européennes, 1974.

Fox, William T., and Annette B. Fox. *NATO and the Range of American Choice.* New York: Columbia University Press, 1967.

Frank, Isaiah. *The European Common Market.* New York: Praeger, 1961.

Frankel, Charles. *High on Foggy Bottom: An Outsider's Inside View of the Government.* New York: Harper and Row, 1968.

Fromont, Jacques. *La politique étrangère des Etats-Unis à l'égard de l'Europe Occidentale de 1945 à 1955.* Brussels: Editions Labor, 1967.

Fulbright, J. W. *Old Myths and New Realities.* London: Jonathan Cape, 1964.

Fulbright, J. William. *Prospects for the West.* Cambridge, Mass.: Harvard University Press, 1963.

Fulbright, J. William. *The Arrogance of Power.* Toronto: Random House, 1966.

Gaddis, John Lewis. *Strategies of Containment*. New York: Oxford University Press, 1982.

Gaddis, John Lewis. *The Long Peace*. New York: Oxford University Press, 1987.

Galbraith, John Kenneth. *A Life in Our Times*. Boston: Houghton Mifflin, 1981.

Gallup, George H. *The Gallup Poll*. Vol. 3, 1959-71. New York.

George, Alexander. *Managing U.S.-Soviet Rivalry*. Boulder, Co.: Westview Press, 1983.

George, Alexander. *Presidential Decision-making in Foreign Policy: the Effective Use of Information and Advice*. Boulder, Co.: Westview Press, 1980.

Gerbet, Pierre. *La Construction de l'Europe*. Paris: Notre Siècle, 1983.

Gillingham, John. *Coal, Steel and the Rebirth of Europe: The Germans and the French from Ruhr Conflict to Economic Community*. Cambridge: Cambridge University Press, 1991.

Grosser, Alfred. *Les Occidentaux. Les Pays d'Europe et les Etats-Unis depuis la guerre*. Munich: Hanser Verlag, 1978.

Haas, Ernst B. *The Uniting of Europe*. Stanford: Stanford University Press, 1958.

Halberstam, David. *The Best and the Brightest*. New York: Random House, 1969.

Hallstein, Walter. *Europe in the Making*. New York: W. W. Norton & Co., 1972.

Hallstein, Walter. *United Europe*. Cambridge, Mass.: Harvard University Press, 1962.

Harriman, Averell. *America and Russia in a Changing World. A Half Century of Personal Observation*. London: Allen and Unwin, 1971.

Harrison, Reginal J. *Europe in Question*. London, 1974.

Heath, Edward. *Old World, New Horizons*. Cambridge, Mass.: Harvard University Press, 1970.

Henderson, Philipp Gregory. *Organizing the White House for Effective Leadership: Lessons from the Eisenhower Years*. Ann Harbor, Mich.: University Microfilms, 1986.

Herter, Christian. *Toward an Atlantic Community*. New York: Harper and Row, 1963.

Hess, John L. *The Case for De Gaulle: An American Viewpoint*. New York: William Morrow, 1968.

Hilsman, Roger. *To Move a Nation*. New York: Garden City, 1977.

Hinshaw, Randall. *The European Community and American Trade*. New York: Praeger, 1964.

Hodges, Michael, ed. *European Integration*. Middlesex: Penguin Books, 1972.

Hoffmann, Stanley. *Decline or Renewal? France since the 1930s*. New York: Viking Press, 1974.

Hoffman, Stanley H. *Dead Ends: American Foreign Policy in the New Cold War*. Cambridge, Mass.: Ballinger, 1983.

Hoffman, Stanley H. *Gulliver's Troubles; or the Setting of American Policy*. Published for the Council on Foreign Relations. New York: McGraw-Hill, 1968.

Hogan, Michael. *The Marshall Plan, America, Britain, and the Reconstruction of Western Europe, 1947-1952*. Cambridge: Cambridge University Press, 1987.

Hoopes, Townsend. *The Devil and John Foster Dulles*. Boston: Little Brown, 1973.

Howlett, Darryl A. *Euratom and Nuclear Safeguards*. London: Macmillan, 1990.

Hughes, Emmet John. *The Living Presidency*. New York: McCann and Geoghegan, 1972.

Hull, Cordell. *The Memoirs of Cordell Hull*. New York: Macmillan, 1948.

Hunter, Robert. *Security in Europe*. London: Elek Books, 1969.

Ilgen, Thomas L. *Autonomy and Interdependence. U.S.-Western European Monetary and Trade Relations, 1958-1984*. Totowa, N.J.: Rowman and Allanheld, 1985.

Ilgen, Thomas Lee. "The Politics of Economics: United States-West European Monetary and Trade Relations, 1958-1971." Ph.D. diss., University of California, Santa Barbara, 1976.

Immerman, Richard H., ed. *John Foster Dulles and the Diplomacy of the Cold War*. Princeton: Princeton University Press, 1990.

Inderfurth, Karl F. *Decisions of the Highest Order*. Pacific Grove: Brooks & Cole, 1988.

Isaacson, Walter, and Evan Thomas. *The Wise Men.* New York: Simon & Schuster, 1986.

Jackson, Henry M. *The National Security Council: Jackson Subcommittee Papers on Policy-Making at the Presidential Level.* New York: Praeger, 1965.

Johnson, Lyndon B. *The Johnson Presidential Press Conferences.* New York: Coleman, 1978.

Johnson, Lyndon B. *The Vantage Point.* New York: Holt, Rinehart and Winston, 1971.

Johnson, Richard. *Managing the White House.* New York: Harper and Row, 1974.

Johnson, Richard A. *The Administration of United States Foreign Policy.* Austin: University of Texas Press, 1971.

Kaiser, Karl. *Die europäische Herausforderung und die U.S.A.* Munich: Piper, 1973.

Kaiser, Karl. *EWG und Freihandelszone.* Leiden: Sijthof, 1963.

Kaplan, Lawrence. *NATO and the United States. The Enduring Alliance.* Boston: Twayne Publishers, 1988.

Kaspi, André. *La Mission de Jean Monnet à Alger mars - octobre 1943.* Paris: éditions Richelieu, 1971.

Kaufmann, William W. *The McNamara Strategy.* New York: Harper and Row, 1964.

Kennan, George F. *Memoirs 1925-1950.* Boston: Little, Brown and Co., 1967.

Kennedy, Robert F. *Thirteen Days.* New York: New American Library, 1969.

Kennedy, John F. *The Strategy of Peace.* New York: Harper & Brothers, 1960.

Kennedy, Paul. *The Rise and Fall of the Great Powers.* New York: Random House, 1987.

Kirsanov, A. W. *Die USA und Westeuropa.* Berlin: Akademie-Verlag, 1968.

Kissinger, Henry A. *Nuclear Weapons and Foreign Policy.* New York: W. W. Norton & Co., 1969.

Kissinger, Henry A. *The Troubled Partnership: A Re-Appraisal of the Atlantic Alliance.* New York: Council on Foreign Relations, 1965.

Kitter, Audry. *The US and the EEC: American reaction to and involvement in the "Common market."* Los Angeles: Center for the Study of Armament and Disarmament, California State University, 1973.

Kitzinger, U. W. *The Challenge of the Common Market.* Oxford: Basil Blackwell, 1962.

Kleinman, Robert. *Atlantic Crisis. American Diplomacy Confronts a Resurgent Europe.* New York: W. W. Norton and Co., 1964.

Klunk, Brian Edward. "The Idea of America's Mission and Its Role in the Beliefs and Diplomacy of John Foster Dulles and Jimmy Carter." Ph.D. diss., University of Virginia, 1985.

Koenig, Louis W. *The Chief Executive.* New York: Harcourt Brace Jovanovich, 1964, 1968, 1975.

Kohnstamm, Max. *Jean Monnet: The Power of the Imagination.* Florence: European University Institute, 1981.

Kohnstamm, Max. *The European Community and Its Role in the World.* Columbia: University of Missouri Press, 1964.

Kraft, Joseph. *The Grand Design. From Common Market to Atlantic Partnership.* New York: Harper and Brothers, 1962.

Krause, Lawrence B. *European Economic Integration and the United States.* Washington, D.C.: Brookings Institution, 1968.

Li, Teh-Kie. *L'influence du Marché Commun sur le commerce extérieur américain.* Fribourg, Thèse, 1969.

Lipgens, Walter. *A History of European Integration.* Vol. 1, 1945-47, London, 1982.

Lippmann, Walter. *Western Unity and the Common Market.* Boston: Little, Brown and Co., 1962.

Louis, William Roger, and Hedley Bull, eds. *The "Special Relationship."* Oxford: Clarendon Press, 1986.

Majone, Giandomenico. *Evidence, Argument, and Persuasion in the Policy Process.* New Haven: Yale University Press, 1989.

Mally, Gerhard. *The New Europe, the United States and the World.* Toronto: Lexington Books, 1974.

Mann, Dean E. *The Assistant Secretaries.* Washington, D.C.: Brookings Institution, 1965.

Marchal, Jean. *Le système monétaire international.* Paris: Cujas, 1979.

Marjolin, Robert. *Le travail d'une vie. mémoires 1911-1986.* Paris: R. Laffont, 1986.

Mason, Edward S. *Foreign Aid and Foreign Policy.* Published for the Council on Foreign Relations. New York: Harper & Row, 1964.

Maudling, Reginald. *Memoirs.* London: Sidwick and Jackson, 1978.

Macmillan, Harold. *At the End of the Day 1961-1963.* London: Macmillan, 1973.

Macmillan, Harold. *Pointing the Way.* Melbourne: Macmillan, 1972.

Macmillan, Harold. *Riding the Storm 1956-59.* New York: Harper and Row, 1971.

Mayne, Richard. *The Community of Europe.* London: Weidenfeld & Nicolson, 1962.

Mayne, Richard. *The Recovery of Europe.* London: Weidenfeld & Nicolson, 1970.

McCloy, John J. *Amérique-Europe. Relations de partenaires nécessaires à la paix.* Lausanne: FJM, 1982.

McNamara, Robert S. *The Essence of Security.* New York: Harper & Row, 1968.

Mélandri, Pierre. *L'Alliance atlantique.* Paris: Gallimard, 1979.

Mélandri, Pierre. *Les Etats-Unis face à l'Unification de l'Europe 1945-54.* Paris: Pedone, 1980.

Mélandri, Pierre. *Les Etats-Unis et le "défi" européen 1955-1958.* Paris: Presses universitaires de France, 1975.

Middleton, Drew. *The Supreme Choice—Britain and the European Community.* London: Secker and Warburg, 1963.

Milward, Alan S. *The Reconstruction of Western Europe 1945-1951.* London: Methuen & Co., 1984.

Monnet, Jean. *Amérique-Europe. Relations de Partenaires Nécessaires à la Paix.* Lausanne: FJM, 1963.

Monnet, Jean. *Les Etats-Unis d'Europe ont Commencé.* Paris: R. Laffont, 1955.

Monnet, Jean. *Mémoires.* Paris: Fayard, 1976; and *Memoirs,* Richard Mayne, trans., New York: Doubleday, 1978.

Neustadt, Richard E. *Alliance Politics.* New York: Columbia University Press, 1970.

Neustadt, Richard. *Presidential Power.* Cambridge: Harvard University Press, 1960, 1976.

Newhouse, John. *Collision in Brussels. The Common Market Crisis of June 1965.* New York: W. W. Norton, 1967.

Newhouse, John. *De Gaulle and the Anglo-Saxons.* New York: Viking Press, 1970.

Newhouse, John. *U.S. Troops in Europe.* Washington, D.C.: Brookings Institution, 1971.

Nitze, Paul. *From Hiroshima to Glasnost, At the Center of Decision. A Memoir.* New York: Grove Weidenfeld, 1989.

Nunnerley, David. *President Kennedy and Britain.* London: The Bodley Head, 1972.

Nye, Joseph S. *International Regionalism.* Boston: Little, Brown and Co., 1968.

Osgood, Robert E. *NATO. The Entangling Alliance.* Chicago: University of Chicago Press, 1962.

Parmet, Herbert S. *JFK. The Presidency of John F. Kennedy.* New York: Dial, 1983.

Paterson, Thomas G., ed. *Kennedy's Quest for Victory, American Foreign Policy, 1961-1963.* New York: Oxford University Press, 1989.

Pleven, René. *L'Union européenne.* Lausanne: FJM, 1984.

Polach, J. G. *Euratom.* New York: Oceana Publications, 1964.

Pollard, Sidney. *European Economic Integration 1815-1970*. London: Thams and Hudson, 1974.

Preeg, Ernest H. *Traders and Diplomats*. Washington, D.C.: Brookings Institution, 1970.

Price, Harry Bayard. *The Marshall Plan and Its Meaning*. Ithaca: Cornell University Press, 1955.

Rappaport, Armin. *History of American Diplomacy*. New York: Macmillan, 1975.

Recueil des communiqués et déclarations du Comité d'Action pour les Etats-Unis d'Europe 1955-1965. Lausanne: Centre de recherches européennes, 1965.

Reuss, Henry S. *The Critical Decade*. New York: McGraw-Hill, 1964.

Richardson, James L. *Germany and the Atlantic Alliance*. Cambridge, Mass.: Harvard University Press, 1966.

Rieben, Henri. *Des Guerres européennes à l'Union de l'Europe*. Lausanne: FJM, 1987.

Roach, James R., ed. *The U.S. and the Atlantic Community*. Austin: University of Texas Press, 1967.

Roberts, Charles. *L.B.J.'s Inner Circle*. New York: Delacorte Press, 1965.

Rockefeller, Nelson A. *Unity, Freedom and Peace*. New York: Random House, 1968.

Rossiter, Clinton. *The American Presidency*. New York: Harvest, 1960.

Rostow. W. W. *The Diffusion of Power*. New York: Macmillan, 1972.

Rostow, W. W. *View from the Seventh Floor*. New York: Harper and Row, 1964.

Rubin, Barry M. *Secrets of State: the State Department and the Struggle Over U.S. Foreign Policy*. New York: Oxford University Press, 1985.

Rühl, Lothar. *The Nine and Nato. The Alliance and the Community: an Uncertain Relationship*. Paris, 1974.

Schaetzel, Robert J. *The Unhinged Alliance*. Published for the Council on Foreign Relations. New York: Harper & Row, 1975.

Schlesinger, Arthur M., Jr. *A Thousand Days*. New York: Fawcett Premier, 1965.

Schwartz, David N. *NATO's Nuclear Dilemmas*. Washington, D.C.: Brookings Institution, 1983.

Serfaty, Simon. *France, De Gaulle and Europe*. Baltimore: Johns Hopkins University Press, 1968.

Servan-Schreiber, Jean-Jacques. *The American Challenge*. London: Hamish Hamilton, 1968. Trans. of *Le Défi Américain*. Paris: Denoël, 1967.

Shonfield, Andrew, ed. *International Economic Relations of the Western World, 1959-71*. London: Oxford University Press, 1976.

Silj, Alessandro. *Europe's Political Puzzle*. Center for International Affairs, Cambridge, Mass.: Harvard University Press, 1967.

Skloot, Edward. *The Decision to Send East-West Trade Legislation to Congress, 1965-66*. Appendices: Commission on the Organization of the Government for Conduct on Foreign Policy, June 1975. Vol. 3. Washington, D.C.: U.S. GPO.

Smith, Gaddis. *American Diplomacy during the Second World War. 1941-45*. New York: John Wiley & Sons, 1965.

Smith, Michael. *Western Europe and the United States. The Uncertain Alliance*. London: George Allen & Unwin, 1984.

Solomon, Robert. *The International Monetary System, 1945-1976: An Insider's View*. New York: Harper and Row, 1977.

Sorensen, Theodore C. *Decision-Making in the White House*. New York: Columbia University Press, 1963.

Sorensen, Theodore C. *Kennedy. 25 Years*. New York: Harper and Row, 1965, 1988.

Spaak, Paul-Henri. *Combats Inachevés*. Paris: Fayard, 1969; trans., *The Continuing Battle: Memoirs of a European, 1936 - 66*, translated from the French by Henry Fox (London: Weidenfeld, 1971.

Spaak, Paul-Henri. *La Pensée européenne et atlantique de Paul-Henri Spaak.* Paul-F Smets, ed. Brussels: Goemaere, 1980.

Spinelli, Altiero. *The Eurocrats.* Baltimore: The Johns Hopkins Press, 1966.

Stanley, Timothy W. *NATO in Transition: the Future of the Atlantic Alliance.* New York: Praeger, 1965.

Stebbins, Richard P. *The U.S. in World Affairs 1960.* Published for the Council on Foreign Relations. New York: Harper & Row, 1961.

Stebbins, Richard P. *The U.S. in World Affairs 1961.* Published for the Council on Foreign Relations. New York: Harper & Row, 1962.

Stebbins, Richard P. *The U.S. in World Affairs 1962.* Published for the Council on Foreign Relations. New York: Harper & Row, 1963.

Stebbins, Richard P. *The U.S. In World Affairs 1963.* Published for the Council on Foreign Relations. New York: Harper & Row, 1964.

Stegenga, James A., ed. *Toward a Wiser Colossus.* West Lafayette, Ind.: Purdue University Press, 1972.

Steinbruner, John D. *The Cybernetic Theory of Decision.* Princeton: Princeton University Press, 1974.

Stikker, Dirk. *Men of Responsibility: A Memoir.* New York: Harper, 1966.

Strange, Susan. *International Economic Relations of the Western World 1959-71.* New York: Oxford University Press, 1976.

Sulzberger, Cyrus. *The Last of the Giants.* New York: Macmillan, 1970.

Sulzberger, Cyrus L. *Dans le Tourbillon de l'Histoire.* Paris: Albin Michel, 1971.

Szent-Miklosy, Istvan. *The Atlantic Union Movement. Its Significance in World Politics.* Introduction by Hans Kohn. New York: Fountainhead, 1965.

Taber, George. *John F. Kennedy and a Uniting Europe.* Bruges: College of Europe, 1969.

Talbot, Ross B. *The Chicken War.* Ames, Ia.: Iowa State University Press, 1978.

Taylor, Maxwell D. *Swords and Plowshares.* New York: W. W. Norton, 1972.

Tessier du Cros, Henri. *Louis Armand: Visionnaire de la Modernité.* Paris: Editions Odile Jacob, 1987.

Truman, Harry S. *Memoirs. Year of Decisions,* Vol. 1. *Years of Trial and Hope,* Vol. 2. New York: Doubleday, 1955, 1956.

Turner, Henry A. *The Two Germanys Since 1945.* New Haven: Yale University Press, 1987.

Tuthill, John W. *The Decisive Years Ahead.* Saxon House, 1973.

Uri, Pierre. *Partnership For Progress.* New York: Harper and Row, 1963.

Von der Groeben, Hans. *The European Community: The Formative Years.* Luxembourg: Office for Official Publications of the European Communities, 1987.

Willequet, Jacques. *Paul-Henri Spaak.* Brussels, 1975.

Wilson, Harold. *A Personal Record. The Labour Government 1964-1970.* Boston: Little, Brown and Co., 1971.

Zorgbibe, Charles. *La Construction politique de l'Europe 1946-76.* Paris: Presses universitaires de France, 1978.

Zurcher, Arnold. *The Struggle to Unite Europe.* New York: New York University Press, 1958.

ARTICLES, PAPERS, NEWSPAPERS

Allison, G. T. "Conceptual Models and the Cuban Missile Crisis." 3, *American Political Science Review* 63 (1969): 40-79.

Allison, G. T., and M. H. Halperin. "Bureaucratic Politics: A Paradigm and Some Policy Implications." *World Politics* 24 (1972).

Artaud, Denise. "Le grand dessein de J. F. Kennedy: Proposition mythique ou occasion manquée?" *Revue d'Histoire Moderne et Contemporaine,* 29 (April-June 1982): 235-266.

Ball, George. "NATO and World Responsibility." *The Atlantic Community Quarterly* 2 (Summer 1964): 216.

Benoit, Emile. "The United States and a United Europe." *Current History* 42, no. 247 (March 1962): 172-179.

Bonnet, Henri. "Les Perspectives de la politique des Etats-Unis à l'égard de l'Europe et de la France." *Revue de Défense Nationale,* 22e année (April 1966).

Bowie, Robert R. "Strategy and the Atlantic Alliance." *International Organization* 17, no. 3 (Summer 1963): 709-732.

Brandon, Henry. "Skybolt." *The Times* (London), 8 December 1963.

Brinkley, Douglas. "Dean Acheson and the 'Special Relationship': The West Point Speech of December 1962." In *The Historical Journal* 33, no. 3 (1990): 599-608.

Brinkley, Douglas. "Jean Monnet and the American Connection." Paper presented at the European Studies Association's Conference, George Mason University, Fairfax, Virginia, 24 May 1989.

Buchan, Alastair. "Les Etats-Unis et l'Europe." *Politique étrangère* 28e année, no. 3. Paris, 1963.

Buchan, Alastair. "Partners and Allies." *Foreign Affairs* (July 1963).

Buchan, Alastair. "The Multilateral Force." *International Affairs* 40, no. 4 (October 1962).

Camps, Miriam. "European Unification in the Seventies." *International Affairs* 47, no. 4 (October 1971).

Coker, Christopher. "The Western Alliance and Africa 1949-81." *African Affairs* 8, no. 24 (July 1982).

Congressional Quarterly.

Costigliola, Frank. "The Failed Design: Kennedy, de Gaulle, and the Struggle for Europe." *Diplomatic History* 8, no. 3 (Summer 1984).

Cromwell, William C. "The Marshall Non-Plan, Congress and the Soviet Union." *Western Political Quarterly* 32 (December 1979).

Economist.

European Community, 1958-1965.

Fish, Steven M. "After Stalin's Death: the Anglo-American Debate over a New Cold War." *Diplomatic History* 10, no. 4 (Fall 1986).

Foch, René. "An Example of Atlantic Partnership: Euratom." *Atlantic Community Quarterly* 2, no.1 (1964): 72-80.

Foreign Affairs.

Fortune.

Freedom and Union, 1954-1967.

Gallois, Pierre M. "La nouvelle politique extérieure des Etats-Unis et la sécurité de l'Europe." *Revue de Défense Nationale* 19e année (April 1963).

Halberstam, David. "The Very Expensive Education of McGeorge Bundy." Harper's Magazine (July 1969).

Hallstein, Walter. "The European Community and Atlantic Partnership." *International Organization* 17, no. 3 (Summer 1963).

Harlech, Lord. "Suez Snabu, Skybolt Sabu." *Foreign Policy* 2 (Spring 1971): 38-50.

Herter, Christian. "Atlantica." *Foreign Affairs* 41, no. 2 (January 1963).

Hoffmann, Stanley. "Discord in Community: The North Atlantic Area as a Partial International System." *International Organization* 17, no. 3 (Summer 1963).

Immerman, Richard. "Eisenhower and Dulles: Who Made the Decisions?" *Political Psychology* 1 (Autumn 1979): 3-20.

Kaplan, Lawrence D. "Western Europe in 'The American Century': A Retrospective View." *Diplomatic History* (Spring 1982): 111-123.

Kissinger, Henry. "What Kind of Atlantic Partnership?" *The Atlantic Community Quarterly* 7, no. 1 (Spring 1969).

Krause, Lawrence B. "The Impact of Economic Relations on the Atlantic Alliance." *Orbis* 13, no. 1 (Spring 1969).

Kubricht, A. Paul. "Politics and Foreign Policy: A Brief Look at the Kennedy Administration's Eastern European Diplomacy." *Diplomatic History* 11, no. 2 (Summer 1987).

Lafeber, Walter. "Kennedy, Johnson and the Revisionists." *Foreign Service Journal* (April 1973): 31-39.

Leffler, Melvyn P. "The United States and the Strategic Dimensions of the Marshall Plan." *Diplomatic History* 1, no. 3 (Summer 1988).

Lippmann, Walter. "Whither Germany?" *Newsweek,* 11 October 1965, 27.

May, Ernest. "Writing Contemporary History." *Diplomatic History* (Spring 1984).

Merchant, Livingston. "Evolving United States Relations with the Atlantic Community," *International Organization* 17, no. 3 (Summer 1963).

Mozdzierz, William, "Chester Bowles and the Sacrifice of the Politically Irrelevant." Research Seminar in American Diplomatic History, Professor Gaddis Smith, Yale University, 9 May 1988.

Nato Letter.

Nau, Henry R. "A Political Interpretation of the Technology Gap Dispute." *Orbis* 15, no. 2 (1971).

New York Times.

Parker, William. "The Schuman Plan—A Preliminary Prediction." *International Organization* 6, no. 3 (1952).

Paterson, Thomas G. "Bearing the Burden: A Critical Look at JFK's Foreign Policy." *The Virginia Quarterly Review* 54 (Spring 1978): 193-212.

Rappaport, Armin. "The United States and European Integration: The First Phase." *Diplomatic History* 5, no. 2 (Spring 1981).

Richardson, James. "The Concept of Atlantic Community." *Journal of Common Market Studies* 3, no. 1.

Rosenberg, Dalan Alan. "The Origins of Overkill." *International Security* 7, no. 4 (Spring 1983).

Schelling, T. C. "Nuclear Strategy in Europe." *World Politics* 14 (3). Princeton University Press, 1961.

Skloot, Edward. "The Decision to Send East-West Trade Legislation to Congress 1965-1966," Appendices: *Commission on the Organization of the Government for Conduct on Foreign Policy* 3 (June 1975). U.S. Government Printing Office.

Stupak, Ronald J. "Dean Rusk on International Relations." *Australian Outlook* 25 (1971): 13-27.

Van Miert, Karel. "Les Etats-Unis et les Communautés européennes," *Chronique de Politique Etrangère* 26 (March 1973): 129-205.

Walla, Michael. "Selling the Marshall Plan at Home: The Committee for the Marshall Plan to Aid European Recovery." *Diplomatic History* 10, no. 3 (Summer 1986).

Wallich, Henry C. "The United States and the European Economic Community." *International Organization* 22, no. 4 (Autumn 1968): 841-853.

Wiegele, Thomas C. "The Origins of the MLF Concept, 1957-1960." *Orbis* 12 (Summer 1968): 465-89.

Zeiler, Thomas W. "Free-Trade Politics and Diplomacy: John F. Kennedy and Textiles." *Diplomatic History* (Summer 1987).

INDEX